RSMeans®

Square Foot Costs

22nd Annual Edition

D1560582

2001

Senior Editor

Barbara Balboni

Contributing Editors

Robert A. Bastoni
Howard M. Chandler
John H. Chiang, PE
Paul C. Crosscup
Jennifer L. Curran
Stephen E. Donnelly
J. Robert Lang
Robert C. McNichols
Robert W. Mewis
Melville J. Mossman, PE
John J. Moylan
Jeannene D. Murphy
Peter T. Nightingale
Stephen C. Plotner
Michael J. Regan
Stephen J. Sechovicz
Phillip R. Waier, PE

Manager, Engineering Operations

John H. Ferguson, PE

Group Vice President

Durwood S. Snead

Vice President and General Manager

Roger J. Grant

Vice President, Sales and Marketing

John M. Shea

Production Manager

Michael Kokernak

Production Coordinator

Marion E. Schofield

Technical Support

Thomas J. Dion
Michael H. Donelan
Jonathan Forgit
Mary Lou Geary
Gary L. Hoitt
Paula Reale-Camelio
Robin Richardson
Kathryn S. Rodriguez
Sheryl A. Rose
Elizabeth A. Ryan
James N. Wills

Book & Cover Design

Norman R. Forgit

Second Printing

Foreword

R.S. Means Co., Inc. is a subsidiary of CMD Group (Construction Market Data), a leading provider of construction information, products, and services in North America and globally. CMD's flagship product line includes more than 100 regional editions, national construction project information, sales leads, and over 70 local plan room/libraries in major business centers. CMD also publishes ProFile, a directory of more than 20,000 architectural firms in the U.S. Architect's First Source (AFS) provides Publishers First Source for Products, CSI's SPEC-DATA® and CSI's MANU-SPEC® building product directories for the selection of nationally available building products. R.S. Means provides Construction cost data and training, and consulting services in print, CD-ROM and online. Associated Construction Publications (ACP) provides regional magazines covering the U.S. highways heavy construction, and heavy equipment trader. Manufacturers' Survey Associates (MSA) provides surveys, plans, and specifications. CMD Group is headquartered in Atlanta and has 1,400 employees worldwide. CMD Group is owned by Cahners Business Information (www.cahners.com), a member of the Reed Elsevier plc group (NYSE: RUK and ENL). Cahners is the leading U.S. provider of business information to 16 vertical markets, including building & construction, entertainment, manufacturing, and retail. Cahners' content portfolio encompasses 140 Web sites as well as *Variety, Publishers Weekly, Design News* and 127 other market-leading business-to-business magazines. Cahners developed the leading business-to-business Web portals e-inSITE in the electronics industry, Manufacturing.net in manufacturing as well as Buildingteam.com and HousingZone.com in construction, and maintains an active program of Internet and print launches.

Our Mission

Since 1942, R.S. Means Company, Inc. has been actively engaged in construction cost publishing and consulting throughout North America.

Today, over 50 years after the company began, our primary objective remains the same: to provide you, the construction and facilities professional, with the most current and comprehensive construction cost data possible.

Whether you are a contractor, an owner, an architect, an engineer, a facilities manager, or anyone else who needs a fast and reliable construction cost estimate, you'll find this publication to be a highly useful and necessary tool.

Today, with the constant flow of new construction methods and materials, it's difficult to find the time to look at and evaluate all the different construction cost possibilities. In addition, because labor and material costs keep changing, last year's cost information is not a reliable basis for today's estimate or budget.

That's why so many construction professionals turn to R.S. Means. We keep track of the costs for you, along with a wide range of other key information, from city cost indexes . . . to productivity rates . . . to crew composition . . . to contractor's overhead and profit rates.

R.S. Means performs these functions by collecting data from all facets of the industry, and organizing it in a format that is instantly accessible to you. From the preliminary budget to the detailed unit price estimate, you'll find the data in this book useful for all phases of construction cost determination.

The Staff, the Organization, and Our Services

When you purchase one of R.S. Means' publications, you are in effect hiring the services of a full-time staff of construction and engineering professionals.

Our thoroughly experienced and highly qualified staff works daily at collecting, analyzing, and disseminating comprehensive cost information for your needs. These staff members have years of practical construction experience and engineering training prior to joining the firm. As a result, you can count on them not only for the cost figures, but also for additional background reference information that will help you create a realistic estimate.

The Means organization is always prepared to help you solve construction problems through its five major divisions: Construction and Cost Data Publishing, Electronic Products and Services, Consulting Services, Insurance Division, and Educational Services.

Besides a full array of construction cost estimating books, Means also publishes a number of other reference works for the construction industry. Subjects include construction estimating and project and business management; special topics such as HVAC, roofing, plumbing, and hazardous waste remediation; and a library of facility management references.

In addition, you can access all of our construction cost data through your computer with Means CostWorks 2001 CD-ROM, an electronic tool that offers over 50,000 lines of Means detailed construction cost data, along with assembly and whole building cost data. You can also access Means cost information from our Web site at www.rsmeans.com

What's more, you can increase your knowledge and improve your construction estimating and management performance with a Means Construction Seminar or In-House Training Program. These two-day seminar programs offer unparalleled opportunities for everyone in your organization to get updated on a wide variety of construction-related issues.

Means also is a worldwide provider of construction cost management and analysis services for commercial and government owners and of claims and valuation services for insurers.

In short, R.S. Means can provide you with the tools and expertise for constructing accurate and dependable construction estimates and budgets in a variety of ways.

Robert Snow Means Established a Tradition of Quality That Continues Today

Robert Snow Means spent years building his company, making certain he always delivered a quality product.

Today, at R.S. Means, we do more than talk about the quality of our data and the usefulness of our books. We stand behind all of our data, from historical cost indexes... to construction materials and techniques... to current costs.

If you have any questions about our products or services, please call us toll-free at 1-800-334-3509. Our customer service representatives will be happy to assist you or visit our Web site at www.rsmeans.com

Table of Contents

RESIDENTIAL
- INTRODUCTION
- WORKSHEET
- ECONOMY
- AVERAGE
- CUSTOM
- LUXURY
- ADJUSTMENTS

COMM./INDUST./INSTIT.
- INTRODUCTION
- EXAMPLES
- BUILDING TYPES
- DEPRECIATION

ASSEMBLIES
- FOUNDATIONS   1
- SUBSTRUCTURES   2
- SUPERSTRUCTURES   3
- EXTERIOR CLOSURE   4
- ROOFING   5
- INTERIOR CONSTRUCTION   6
- CONVEYING SYSTEMS   7
- MECHANICAL   8
- ELECTRICAL   9
- SPECIAL CONSTRUCTION   11
- SITE WORK   12

REFERENCE INFORMATION
- GENERAL CONDITIONS
- LOCATION FACTORS
- COST INDEXES
- GLOSSARY

How the Book Is Built: An Overview

A Powerful Construction Tool

You have in your hands one of the most powerful construction tools available today. A successful project is built on the foundation of an accurate and dependable estimate. This book will enable you to construct just such an estimate.

For the casual user the book is designed to be:

- quickly and easily understood so you can get right to your estimate
- filled with valuable information so you can understand the necessary factors that go into the cost estimate

For the regular user, the book is designed to be:

- a handy desk reference that can be quickly referred to for key costs
- a comprehensive, fully reliable source of current construction costs for typical building structures when only minimum dimensions, specifications and technical data are available. It is specifically useful in the conceptual or planning stage for preparing preliminary estimates which can be supported and developed into complete engineering estimates for construction.
- a source book for rapid estimating of replacement costs and preparing capital expenditure budgets

To meet all of these requirements we have organized the book into the following clearly defined sections.

How To Use the Book: The Details

This section contains an in-depth explanation of how the book is arranged . . . and how you can use it to determine a reliable construction cost estimate. It includes information about how we develop our cost figures and how to completely prepare your estimate.

Residential Section

Model buildings for four classes of construction—economy, average, custom and luxury—are developed and shown with complete costs per square foot.

Commercial, Industrial, Institutional Section

This section contains complete costs for 70 typical model buildings expressed as costs per square foot.

Assemblies Section

The cost data in this section has been organized in an ''Assemblies'' format. These assemblies are the functional elements of a building and are arranged according to the 12 divisions of the UniFormat classification system. The costs in this section include standard mark-ups for the overhead and profit of the installing contractor. The assemblies costs are those used to calculate the total building costs in the Commercial, Industrial, Institutional section.

Reference Section

This section includes information on General Conditions, Location Factors, Historical Cost Indexes, a Glossary, and a listing of Abbreviations used in this book.

Location Factors: Costs vary depending upon regional economy. You can adjust the ''national average'' costs in this book to 930 locations throughout the U.S. and Canada by using the data in this section.

Historical Cost Indexes: These indexes provide you with data to adjust construction costs over time. If you know costs for a project completed in the past, you can use these indexes to calculate a rough estimate of what it would cost to construct the same project today.

Glossary: A listing of common terms related to construction and their definitions is included.

Abbreviations: A listing of the abbreviations used throughout this book, along with the terms they represent, is included.

The Scope of This Book

This book is designed to be as comprehensive and as easy to use as possible. To that end we have made certain assumptions and limited its scope in two key ways:

1. We have established material prices based on a ''national average.''
2. We have computed labor costs based on a 30-city ''national average'' of union wage rates.

All costs and adjustments in this manual were developed from the *Means Building Construction Cost Data, Means Assemblies Cost Data, Means Residential Cost Data*, and *Means Light Commercial Cost Data*. Costs include labor, material, overhead, and profit, and general conditions and architect's fees where specified. No allowance is made for sales tax, financing, premiums for material and labor, or unusual business and weather conditions.

What's Behind the Numbers? The Development of Cost Data

The staff at R.S. Means continuously monitors developments in the construction industry in order to ensure reliable, thorough and up-to-date cost information.

While *overall* construction costs may vary relative to general economic conditions, price fluctuations within the industry are dependent upon many factors. Individual price variations may, in fact, be opposite to overall economic trends. Therefore, costs are continually monitored and complete updates are published yearly. Also, new items are frequently added in response to changes in materials and methods.

Costs—$ (U.S.)

All costs represent U.S. national averages and are given in U.S. dollars. The Means Location Factors can be used to adjust costs to a particular location. The Location Factors for Canada can be used to adjust U.S. national averages to local costs in Canadian dollars.

Factors Affecting Costs

Due to the almost limitless variation of building designs and combinations of construction methods and materials, costs in this book must be used with discretion. The editors have made every effort to develop costs for "typical" building types. By definition, a square foot estimate, due to the short time and limited amount of detail required, involves a relatively lower degree of accuracy than a detailed unit cost estimate, for example. The accuracy of an estimate will increase as the project is defined in more detailed components. The user should examine closely and compare the specific requirements of the project being estimated with the components included in the models in this book. Any differences should be accounted for in the estimate.

In many building projects, there may be factors that increase or decrease the cost beyond the range shown in this manual. Some of these factors are:

- Substitution of building materials or systems for those used in the model.
- Custom designed finishes, fixtures and/or equipment.
- Special structural qualities (allowance for earthquake, future expansion, high winds, long spans, unusual shape).
- Special foundations and substructures to compensate for unusual soil conditions.
- Inclusion of typical "owner supplied" equipment in the building cost (special testing and monitoring equipment for hospitals, kitchen equipment for hotels, offices that have cafeteria accommodations for employees, etc.).
- An abnormal shortage of labor or materials.

- Isolated building site or rough terrain that would affect the transportation of personnel, material or equipment.
- Unusual climatic conditions during the construction process.

We strongly urge that, for maximum accuracy, these factors be considered each time a structure is being evaluated.

If users require greater accuracy than this manual can provide, the editors recommend that the *Means Building Construction Cost Data* or the *Means Assemblies Cost Data* be consulted.

Final Checklist

Estimating can be a straightforward process provided you remember the basics. Here's a checklist of some of the items you should remember to do before completing your estimate.

Did you remember to . . .

- include the Location Factor for your city
- mark up the entire estimate sufficiently for your purposes
- include all components of your project in the final estimate
- double check your figures to be sure of your accuracy
- call R.S. Means if you have any questions about your estimate or the data you've found in our publications

Remember, R.S. Means stands behind its publications. If you have any questions about your estimate . . . about the costs you've used from our books . . . or even about the technical aspects of the job that may affect your estimate, feel free to call the R.S. Means editors at 1-800-334-3509.

Residential Section

Table of Contents

Introduction to Residential Section

The residential section of this manual contains costs per square foot for four classes of construction in seven building types. Costs are listed for various exterior wall materials which are typical of the class and building type. There are cost tables for Wings and Ells with modification tables to adjust the base cost of each class of building. Non-standard items can easily be added to the standard structures.

Cost estimating for a residence is a three-step process:
(1) Identification
(2) Listing dimensions
(3) Calculations

Guidelines and a sample cost estimating procedure are shown on the following pages.

Identification

To properly identify a residential building, the class of construction, type, and exterior wall material must be determined. Page 6 has drawings and guidelines for determining the class of construction. There are also detailed specifications and additional drawings at the beginning of each set of tables to further aid in proper building class and type identification.

Sketches for eight types of residential buildings and their configurations are shown on pages 8 and 9. Definitions of living area are next to each sketch. Sketches and definitions of garage types are on page 10.

Living Area

Base cost tables are prepared as costs per square foot of living area. The living area of a residence is that area which is suitable and normally designed for full time living. It does not include basement recreation rooms or finished attics, although these areas are often considered full time living areas by the owners.

Living area is calculated from the exterior dimensions without the need to adjust for exterior wall thickness. When calculating the living area of a 1-1/2 story, two story, three story or tri-level residence, overhangs and other differences in size and shape between floors must be considered.

Only the floor area with a ceiling height of six feet or more in a 1-1/2 story residence is considered living area. In bi-levels and tri-levels, the areas that are below grade are considered living area, even when these areas may not be completely finished.

Base Tables and Modifications

Base cost tables show the base cost per square foot without a basement, with one full bath and one full kitchen for economy and average homes and an additional half bath for custom and luxury models. Adjustments for finished and unfinished basements are part of the base cost tables. Adjustments for multi family residences, additional bathrooms, townhouses, alternate roofs, and air conditioning and heating systems are listed in modification tables below the base cost tables.

Costs for other modifications, including garages, breezeways and site improvements, are in the modification tables on pages 58 to 61.

Listing of Dimensions

To use this section of the manual only the dimensions used to calculate the horizontal area of the building and additions and modifications are needed. The dimensions, normally the length and width, can come from drawings or field measurements. For ease in calculation, consider measuring in tenths of feet, i.e., 9 ft. 6 in. = 9.5 ft., 9 ft. 4 in. = 9.3 ft.

In all cases, make a sketch of the building. Any protrusions or other variations in shape should be noted on the sketch with dimensions.

Calculations

The calculations portion of the estimate is a two-step activity:
(1) The selection of appropriate costs from the tables
(2) Computations

Selection of Appropriate Costs

To select the appropriate cost from the base tables, the following information is needed:
(1) Class of construction
    (a) Economy
    (b) Average
    (c) Custom
    (d) Luxury
(2) Type of residence
    (a) One story
    (b) 1-1/2 story
    (c) 2 story
    (d) 3 story
    (e) Bi-level
    (f) Tri-level
(3) Occupancy
    (a) One family
    (b) Two family
    (c) Three family
(4) Building configuration
    (a) Detached
    (b) Town/Row house
    (c) Semi-detached
(5) Exterior wall construction
    (a) Wood frame
    (b) Brick veneer
    (c) Solid masonry
(6) Living areas

Modifications are classified by class, type and size.

Computations

The computation process should take the following sequence:
(1) Multiply the base cost by the area
(2) Add or subtract the modifications
(3) Apply the location modifier

When selecting costs, interpolate or use the cost that most nearly matches the structure under study. This applies to size, exterior wall construction and class.

How to Use the Residential Square Foot Cost Pages

The following is a detailed explanation of a sample entry in the Residential Square Foot Cost Section. Each bold number below corresponds to the item being described on the facing page with the appropriate component of the sample entry following in parenthesis.

Prices listed are costs that include overhead and profit of the installing contractor. Total model costs include an additional mark-up for General Contractors' overhead and profit, and fees specific to class of construction.

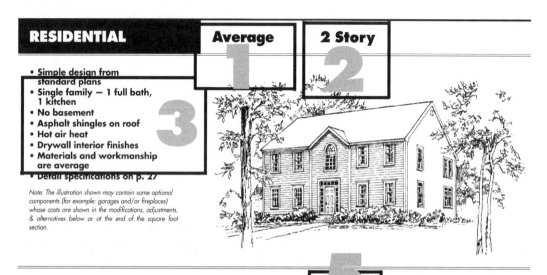

RESIDENTIAL — **Average** **1** — **2 Story** **2**

3
- Simple design from standard plans
- Single family — 1 full bath, 1 kitchen
- No basement
- Asphalt shingles on roof
- Hot air heat
- Drywall interior finishes
- Materials and workmanship are average
- Detail specifications on p. 27

Note: The illustration shown may contain some optional components (for example: garages and/or fireplaces) whose costs are shown in the modifications, adjustments, & alternatives below or at the end of the square foot section.

Base cost per square foot of living area

Exterior Wall	1000	1200	1400	1600	1800	2000	2200	2600	3000	3400	3800
Wood Siding - Wood Frame	95.75	86.05	82.40	79.95	76.55	73.80	.90	67.65	63.55	62.00	60.15
Brick Veneer - Wood Frame	103.15	92.90	88.85	86.05	82.35	79.4		72.45	68.00	66.20	64.15
Stucco on Wood Frame	96.00	86.25	82.65	80.15	76.75	74.0		67.80	63.70	62.15	60.25
Solid Masonry	113.85	102.85	98.10	94.95	90.70	87.45	84.00	79.35	74.35	72.25	69.90
Finished Basement, Add	13.55	13.05	12.60	12.30	12.00	11.80		11.10	10.80	10.60	10.45
Unfinished Basement, Add	5.55	5.20	4.90	4.70	4.50	4.40	4	3.95	3.75	3.65	3.50

Living Area change **5** **6** **7** **8** **4**

Modifications

Add to the total cost

Upgrade Kitchen Cabinets	$ + 2288
Solid Surface Countertops	+ 826
Full Bath - including plumbing, wall and floor finishes	+ 3599
Half Bath - including plumbing, wall and floor finishes	+ 2247
One Car Attached Garage	+ 8408
One Car Detached Garage	+ 11,015
Fireplace & Chimney	+ 4060

9

Adjustments

For multi family - add to total cost

Additional Kitchen	$ + 3924
Additional Bath	+ 3599
Additional Entry & Exit	+ 1085
Separate Heating	+ 1200
Separate Electric	+ 1363

For Townhouse/Rowhouse - Multiply cost per square foot by

Inner Unit	.90
End Unit	.95

10

Alternatives

Add to or deduct from the cost per square foot of living area

Cedar Shake Roof	+ 1.05
Clay Tile Roof	+ 2.25
Slate Roof	+ 3.85
Upgrade Walls to Skim Coat Plaster	+ .36
Upgrade Ceilings to Textured Finish	+ .44
Air Conditioning, in Heating Ductwork	+ 1.53
In Separate Ductwork	+ 3.91
Heating Systems, Hot Water	+ 1.32
Heat Pump	+ 2.05
Electric Heat	- .50
Not Heated	- 2.46

11

Additional upgrades or components

Kitchen Cabinets & Countertops	Page 58
Bathroom Vanities	59
Fireplaces & Chimneys	59
Windows, Skylights & Dormers	59
Appliances	60
Breezeways & Porches	60
Finished Attic	60
Garages	61
Site Improvements	61
Wings & Ells	37

12

1 Class of Construction (Average)

The class of construction depends upon the design and specifications of the plan. The four classes are economy, average, custom and luxury.

2 Type of Residence (2 Story)

The building type describes the number of stories or levels in the model. The seven building types are 1 story, 1-1/2 story, 2 story, 2-1/2 story, 3 story, bi-level and tri-level.

3 Specification Highlights (Hot Air Heat)

These specifications include information concerning the components of the model, including the number of baths, roofing types, HVAC systems, and materials and workmanship. If the components listed are not appropriate, modifications can be made by consulting the information shown lower on the page or the Assemblies Section.

4 Exterior Wall System (Wood Siding - Wood Frame)

This section includes the types of exterior wall systems and the structural frame used. The exterior wall systems shown are typical of the class of construction and the building type shown.

5 Living Areas (2000 SF)

The living area is that area of the residence which is suitable and normally designed for full time living. It does not include basement recreation rooms or finished attics. Living area is calculated from the exterior dimensions without the need to adjust for exterior wall thickness. When calculating the living area of a 1-1/2 story, 2 story, 3 story or tri-level residence, overhangs and other differences in size and shape between floors must be considered. Only the floor area with a ceiling height of six feet or more in a 1-1/2 story residence is considered living area. In bi-levels and tri-levels, the areas that are below grade are considered living area, even when these areas may not be completely finished. A range of various living areas for the residential model are shown to aid in selection of values from the matrix.

6 Base Costs per Square Foot of Living Area ($73.80)

Base cost tables show the cost per square foot of living area without a basement, with one full bath and one full kitchen for economy and average homes and an additional half bath for custom and luxury models. When selecting costs, interpolate or use the cost that most nearly matches the

residence under consideration for size, exterior wall system and class of construction. Prices listed are costs that include overhead and profit of the installing contractor, a general contractor markup and an allowance for plans that vary by class of construction. For additional information on contractor overhead and architectural fees, see the Reference Section.

7 Basement Types (Finished)

The two types of basements are finished or unfinished. The specifications and components for both are shown on the Building Classes page in the Introduction to this section.

8 Additional Costs for Basements ($11.80)

These values indicate the additional cost per square foot of living area for either a finished or an unfinished basement.

9 Modifications and Adjustments (Solid Surface Countertops $826)

Modifications and Adjustments are costs added to or subtracted from the total cost of the residence. The total cost of the residence is equal to the cost per square foot of living area times the living area. Typical modifications and adjustments include kitchens, baths, garages and fireplaces.

10 Multiplier for Townhouse/ Rowhouse (Inner Unit .90)

The multipliers shown adjust the base costs per square foot of living area for the common wall condition encountered in townhouses or rowhouses.

11 Alternatives (Skim Coat Plaster $.36)

Alternatives are costs added to or subtracted from the base cost per square foot of living area. Typical alternatives include variations in kitchens, baths, roofing, air conditioning and heating systems.

12 Additional Upgrades or Components (Wings & Ells page 37)

Costs for additional upgrades or components, including wings or ells, breezeways, porches, finished attics and site improvements, are shown in other locations in the Residential Square Foot Cost Section.

Building Classes

Economy Class

An economy class residence is usually built from stock plans. The materials and workmanship are sufficient to satisfy building codes. Low construction cost is more important than distinctive features. The overall shape of the foundation and structure is seldom other than square or rectangular.

An unfinished basement includes 7' high 8" thick foundation wall composed of either concrete block or cast-in-place concrete.

Included in the finished basement cost are inexpensive paneling or drywall as the interior finish on the foundation walls, a low cost sponge backed carpeting adhered to the concrete floor, a drywall ceiling, and overhead lighting.

Custom Class

A custom class residence is usually built from plans and specifications with enough features to give the building a distinction of design. Materials and workmanship are generally above average with obvious attention given to construction details. Construction normally exceeds building code requirements.

An unfinished basement includes a 7'-6" high 10" thick cast-in-place concrete foundation wall or a 7'-6" high 12" thick concrete block foundation wall.

A finished basement includes painted drywall on insulated 2" x 4" wood furring as the interior finish to the concrete walls, a suspended ceiling, carpeting adhered to the concrete floor, overhead lighting and heating.

Average Class

An average class residence is a simple design and built from standard plans. Materials and workmanship are average, but often exceed minimum building codes. There are frequently special features that give the residence some distinctive characteristics.

An unfinished basement includes 7'-6" high 8" thick foundation wall composed of either cast-in-place concrete or concrete block.

Included in the finished basement are plywood paneling or drywall on furring that is fastened to the foundation walls, sponge backed carpeting adhered to the concrete floor, a suspended ceiling, overhead lighting and heating.

Luxury Class

A luxury class residence is built from an architect's plan for a specific owner. It is unique both in design and workmanship. There are many special features, and construction usually exceeds all building codes. It is obvious that primary attention is placed on the owner's comfort and pleasure. Construction is supervised by an architect.

An unfinished basement includes 8' high 12" thick foundation wall that is composed of cast-in-place concrete or concrete block.

A finished basement includes painted drywall on 2" x 4" wood furring as the interior finish, suspended ceiling, tackless carpet on wood subfloor with sleepers, overhead lighting and heating.

Configurations

Detached House

This category of residence is a free-standing separate building with or without an attached garage. It has four complete walls.

Semi-Detached House

This category of residence has two living units side-by-side. The common wall is a fireproof wall. Semi-detached residences can be treated as a row house with two end units. Semi-detached residences can be any of the building types.

Town/Row House

This category of residence has a number of attached units made up of inner units and end units. The units are joined by common walls. The inner units have only two exterior walls. The common walls are fireproof. The end units have three walls and a common wall. Town houses/row houses can be any of the building types.

Building Types

One Story

This is an example of a one-story dwelling. The living area of this type of residence is confined to the ground floor. The headroom in the attic is usually too low for use as a living area.

One-and-a-half Story

The living area in the upper level of this type of residence is 50% to 90% of the ground floor. This is made possible by a combination of this design's high-peaked roof and/or dormers. Only the upper level area with a ceiling height of 6 feet or more is considered living area. The living area of this residence is the sum of the ground floor area plus the area on the second level with a ceiling height of 6 feet or more.

One Story with Finished Attic

The main living area in this type of residence is the ground floor. The upper level or attic area has sufficient headroom for comfortable use as a living area. This is made possible by a high peaked roof. The living area in the attic is less than 50% of the ground floor. The living area of this type of residence is the ground floor area only. The finished attic is considered an adjustment.

Two Story

This type of residence has a second floor or upper level area which is equal or nearly equal to the ground floor area. The upper level of this type of residence can range from 90% to 110% of the ground floor area, depending on setbacks or overhangs. The living area is the sum of the ground floor area and the upper level floor area.

Two-and-one-half Story

This type of residence has two levels of equal or nearly equal area and a third level which has a living area that is 50% to 90% of the ground floor. This is made possible by a high peaked roof, extended wall heights and/or dormers. Only the upper level area with a ceiling height of 6 feet or more is considered living area. The living area of this residence is the sum of the ground floor area, the second floor area and the area on the third level with a ceiling height of 6 feet or more.

Bi-level

This type of residence has two living areas, one above the other. One area is about 4 feet below grade and the second is about 4 feet above grade. Both areas are equal in size. The lower level in this type of residence is originally designed and built to serve as a living area and not as a basement. Both levels have full ceiling heights. The living area is the sum of the lower level area and the upper level area.

Three Story

This type of residence has three levels which are equal or nearly equal. As in the 2 story residence, the second and third floor areas may vary slightly depending on setbacks or overhangs. The living area is the sum of the ground floor area and the two upper level floor areas.

Tri-level

This type of residence has three levels of living area, one at grade level, one about 4 feet below grade and one about 4 feet above grade. All levels are originally designed to serve as living areas. All levels have full ceiling heights. The living area is a sum of the areas of each of the three levels.

Garage Types

Attached Garage

Shares a common wall with the dwelling. Access is typically through a door between dwelling and garage.

Basement Garage

Constructed under the roof of the dwelling but below the living area.

Built-In Garage

Constructed under the second floor living space and above basement level of dwelling. Reduces gross square feet of living area.

Detached Garage

Constructed apart from the main dwelling. Shares no common area or wall with the dwelling.

Building Components

1. Excavation	11. Collar Ties	21. Fascia	31. Backfill	41. Sub-floor
2. Sill Plate	12. Ridge Rafter	22. Downspout	32. Drainage Stone	42. Finish Floor
3. Basement Window	13. Roof Sheathing	23. Shutter	33. Drainage Tile	43. Attic Insulation
4. Floor Joist	14. Roof Felt	24. Window	34. Wall Footing	44. Soffit
5. Shoe Plate	15. Roof Shingles	25. Wall Shingles	35. Gravel	45. Ceiling Strapping
6. Studs	16. Flashing	26. Building Paper	36. Concrete Slab	46. Wall Insulation
7. Drywall	17. Flue Lining	27. Wall Sheathing	37. Column Footing	47. Cross Bridging
8. Plate	18. Chimney	28. Fire Stop	38. Pipe Column	48. Bulkhead Stairs
9. Ceiling Joists	19. Roof Shingles	29. Dampproofing	39. Expansion Joint	
10. Rafters	20. Gutter	30. Foundation Wall	40. Girder	

Exterior Wall Construction

Typical Frame Construction

Typical wood frame construction consists of wood studs with insulation between them. A typical exterior surface is made up of sheathing, building paper and exterior siding consisting of wood, vinyl, aluminum or stucco over the wood sheathing.

Brick Veneer

Typical brick veneer construction consists of wood studs with insulation between them. A typical exterior surface is sheathing, building paper and an exterior of brick tied to the sheathing, with metal strips.

Stone

Typical solid masonry construction consists of a stone or block wall covered on the exterior with brick, stone or other masonry.

Residential Cost Estimate Worksheets

Worksheet Instructions

The residential cost estimate worksheet can be used as an outline for developing a residential construction or replacement cost. It is also useful for insurance appraisals. The design of the worksheet helps eliminate errors and omissions. To use the worksheet, follow the example below.

1. Fill out the owner's name, residence address, the estimator or appraiser's name, some type of project identifying number or code, and the date.

2. Determine from the plans, specifications, owner's description, photographs or any other means possible the class of construction. The models in this book use economy, average, custom and luxury as classes. Fill in the appropriate box.

3. Fill in the appropriate box for the residence type, configuration, occupancy, and exterior wall. If you require clarification, the pages preceding this worksheet describe each of these.

4. Next, the living area of the residence must be established. The heated or air conditioned space of the residence, not including the basement, should be measured. It is easiest to break the structure up into separate components as shown in the example. The main house (A), a one-and-one-half story wing (B), and a one story wing (C). The breezeway (D), garage (E) and open covered porch (F) will be treated differently. Data entry blocks for the living area are included on the worksheet for your use. Keep each level of each component separate, and fill out the blocks as shown.

5. By using the information on the worksheet, find the model, wing or ell in the following square foot cost pages that best matches the class, type, exterior finish and size of the residence being estimated. Use the *modifications, adjustments, and alternatives* to determine the adjusted cost per square foot of living area for each component.

6. For each component, multiply the cost per square foot by the living area square footage. If the residence is a townhouse/rowhouse, a multiplier should be applied based upon the configuration.

7. The second page of the residential cost estimate worksheet has space for the additional components of a house. The cost for additional bathrooms, finished attic space, breezeways, porches, fireplaces, appliance or cabinet upgrades, and garages should be added on this page. The information for each of these components is found with the model being used, or in the *modifications, adjustments, and alternatives* pages.

8. Add the total from page one of the estimate worksheet and the items listed on page two. The sum is the adjusted total building cost.

9. Depending on the use of the final estimated cost, one of the remaining two boxes should be filled out. Any additional items or exclusions should be added or subtracted at this time. The data contained in this book is a national average. Construction costs are different throughout the country. To allow for this difference, a location factor based upon the first three digits of the residence's zip code must be applied. The location factor is a multiplier that increases or decreases the adjusted total building cost. Find the appropriate location factor and calculate the local cost. If depreciation is a concern, a dollar figure should be subtracted at this point.

10. No residence will match a model exactly. Many differences will be found. At this level of estimating, a variation of plus or minus 10% should be expected.

WORKSHEET

Adjustments Instructions

No residence matches a model exactly in shape, material, or specifications.

The common differences are:

1. Two or more exterior wall systems
   a. Partial basement
   b. Partly finished basement
2. Specifications or features that are between two classes
3. Crawl space instead of a basement

EXAMPLES

Below are quick examples. See pages 15-17 for complete examples of cost adjustments for these differences:

1. Residence "A" is an average one-story structure with 1,600 S.F. of living area and no basement. Three walls are wood siding on wood frame, and the fourth wall is brick veneer on wood frame. The brick veneer wall is 35% of the exterior wall area.

   Use page 28 to calculate the Base Cost per S.F. of Living Area.
   Wood Siding for 1,600 S.F. = $73.75 per S.F.
   Brick Veneer for 1,600 S.F. = $84.30 per S.F.
   .65 ($73.75) + .35 ($84.30) = $77.45 per S.F. of Living Area.

2. a. Residence "B" is the same as Residence "A"; However, it has an unfinished basement under 50% of the building. To adjust the $77.45 per S.F. of living area for this partial basement, use page 28.

   $77.45 + .50 ($7.15) = $81.03 per S.F. of Living Area.

   b. Residence "C" is the same as Residence "A"; However, it has a full basement under the entire building. 640 S.F. or 40% of the basement area is finished.

   Using Page 30:

   $77.45 + .40 ($18.70) + .60 ($7.15) = $89.22 per S.F. of Living Area.

3. When specifications or features of a building are between classes, estimate the percent deviation, and use two tables to calculate the cost per S.F.

   A two-story residence with wood siding and 1,800 S.F. of living area has features 30% better than Average, but 70% less than Custom.

   From pages 30 and 42:

   Custom 1,800 S.F. Base Cost = $94.80 per S.F.
   Average 1,800 S.F. Base Cost = $76.55 per S.F.
   DIFFERENCE = $18.25 per S.F.

   Cost is $76.55 + .30 ($18.25) = $82.03 per S.F. of Living Area.

4. To add the cost of a crawl space, use the cost of an unfinished basement as a maximum. For specific costs of components to be added or deducted, such as vapor barrier, underdrain, and floor, see the "Assemblies" section, pages 233 to 427.

14

Model Residence Example

First Floor Plan

Second Floor Plan

A = Main House
B = 1-1/2 Story Wing
C = 1 Story Wing
D = Breezeway
E = Garage
F = Open Covered Porch

15

RESIDENTIAL
COST ESTIMATE

OWNERS NAME:	**Albert Westenberg**	APPRAISER:	**Nicole Wojtowicz**
RESIDENCE ADDRESS:	**300 Sygiel Road**	PROJECT:	**# 55**
CITY, STATE, ZIP CODE:	**Three Rivers, MA 01080**	DATE:	**Jan. 2, 2001**

CLASS OF CONSTRUCTION	RESIDENCE TYPE	CONFIGURATION	EXTERIOR WALL SYSTEM
☐ ECONOMY	☐ 1 STORY	☑ DETACHED	☑ WOOD SIDING - WOOD FRAME
☑ AVERAGE	☐ 1½ STORY	☐ TOWN/ROW HOUSE	☐ BRICK VENEER - WOOD FRAME
☐ CUSTOM	☑ 2 STORY	☐ SEMI-DETACHED	☐ STUCCO ON WOOD FRAME
☐ LUXURY	☐ 2 1/2 STORY		☐ PAINTED CONCRETE BLOCK
	☐ 3 STORY	OCCUPANCY	☐ SOLID MASONRY (AVERAGE & CUSTOM)
	☐ BI-LEVEL	☑ ONE FAMILY	☐ STONE VENEER - WOOD FRAME
	☐ TRI-LEVEL	☐ TWO FAMILY	☐ SOLID BRICK (LUXURY)
		☐ THREE FAMILY	☐ SOLID STONE (LUXURY)
		☐ OTHER	

* LIVING AREA (Main Building)			* LIVING AREA (Wing or Ell) (B)			* LIVING AREA (Wing or Ell) (C)		
First Level	1288	S.F.	First Level	360	S.F.	First Level	192	S.F.
Second level	1288	S.F.	Second level	310	S.F.	Second level		S.F.
Third Level		S.F.	Third Level		S.F.	Third Level		S.F.
Total	2576	S.F.	Total	670	S.F.	Total	192	S.F.

* Basement Area is not part of living area.

MAIN BUILDING		COSTS PER S.F. LIVING AREA	
Cost per Square Foot of Living Area, from Page	30 #	$	67.65
Basement Addition: ____ % Finished, 100 % Unfinished		+	3.95
Roof Cover Adjustment: Cedar Shake Type, Page 30 (Add or Deduct)		( )	1.05
Central Air Conditioning: ☐ Separate Ducts ☑ Heating Ducts, Page 30		+	1.53
Heating System Adjustment: ____ Type, Page ____ (Add or Deduct)		( )	————
Main Building: Adjusted Cost per S.F. of Living Area		$	74.18

MAIN BUILDING TOTAL COST	$ 74.18 /S.F.	x	2,576 S.F.	x	————	=	$ 191,088
	Cost per S.F. Living Area		Living Area		Town/Row House Multiplier (Use 1 for Detached)		TOTAL COST

WING OR ELL (B) 1 - 1/2 STORY		COSTS PER S.F. LIVING AREA	
Cost per Square Foot of Living Area, from Page 37 #		$	60.35
Basement Addition: 100 % Finished, ____ % Unfinished		+	16.50
Roof Cover Adjustment: ____ Type, Page ____ (Add or Deduct)		( )	–
Central Air Conditioning: ☐ Separate Ducts ☑ Heating Ducts, Page 30 #		+	1.53
Heating System Adjustment: ____ Type, Page ____ (Add or Deduct)		( )	———
Wing or Ell (B): Adjusted Cost per S.F. of Living Area		$	78.38

WING OR ELL (B) TOTAL COST	$ 78.38 /S.F.	x	670 S.F.	=	$ 52,515
	Cost per S.F. Living Area		Living Area		TOTAL COST

WING OR ELL (C) 1 STORY		COSTS PER S.F. LIVING AREA	
Cost per Square Foot of Living Area, from Page 37 (WOOD SIDING)		$	90.45
Basement Addition: ____ % Finished, ____ % Unfinished		+	———
Roof Cover Adjustment: ____ Type, Page ____ (Add or Deduct)		( )	———
Central Air Conditioning: ☐ Separate Ducts ☐ Heating Ducts, Page ____		+	———
Heating System Adjustment: ____ Type, Page ____ (Add or Deduct)		( )	———
Wing or Ell (C) Adjusted Cost per S.F. of Living Area		$	90.45

WING OR ELL (C) TOTAL COST	$ 90.45 /S.F.	x	192 S.F.	=	$ 17,366
	Cost per S.F. Living Area		Living Area		TOTAL COST

	TOTAL THIS PAGE	260,969

Page 1 of 2

16

RESIDENTIAL
COST ESTIMATE

				QUANTITY	UNIT COST		$	260,969
Total Page 1								
Additional Bathrooms:	2 Full, 1 Half	2 @ 3599	1 @ 2247			+		9,445
Finished Attic:	N/A Ft. x ___ Ft.				S.F.			
Breezeway:	☑ Open ☐ Closed	12 Ft. x 12 Ft.		144	S.F.	15.80	+	2,275
Covered Porch:	☑ Open ☐ Enclosed	18 Ft. x 12 Ft.		216	S.F.	23.50	+	5,076
Fireplace:	☑ Interior Chimney	☐ Exterior Chimney						
	☑ No. of Flues (2)	☑ Additional Fireplaces	1 - 2nd Story			+		6850
Appliances:						+		—
Kitchen Cabinets Adjustments:			(±)					—
☑ Garage ☐ Carport	2 Car(s) Description	Wood, Attached	(±)					14,318
Miscellaneous:						+		

ADJUSTED TOTAL BUILDING COST | $ | 298,933

REPLACEMENT COST				INSURANCE COST		
ADJUSTED TOTAL BUILDING COST	$	298,933		ADJUSTED TOTAL BUILDING COST	$	
Site Improvements				Insurance Exclusions		
(A) Paving & Sidewalks	$			(A) Footings, sitework, Underground Piping	-$	
(B) Landscaping	$			(B) Architects Fees	-$	
(C) Fences	$			Total Building Cost Less Exclusion	$	
(D) Swimming Pools	$			Location Factor	x	
(E) Miscellaneous	$					
TOTAL	$	298,933		LOCAL INSURABLE REPLACEMENT COST	$	
Location Factor	x	1.05				
Location Replacement Cost	$	313,880				
Depreciation	-$	31,388				
LOCAL DEPRECIATED COST	$	282,492				

SKETCH AND ADDITIONAL CALCULATIONS

ECONOMY

1 Story

© Home Planners, Inc.

1-1/2 Story

2 Story

Bi-Level

Tri-Level

Components

1 Site Work

Site preparation for slab or excavation for lower level; 4' deep trench excavation for foundation wall.

2 Foundations

Continuous reinforced concrete footing, 8" deep x 18" wide; dampproofed and insulated 8" thick reinforced concrete block foundation wall, 4' deep; 4" concrete slab on 4" crushed stone base and polyethylene vapor barrier, trowel finish.

3 Framing

Exterior walls—2 x 4 wood studs, 16" O.C.; 1/2" insulation board sheathing; wood truss roof 24" O.C. or 2 x 6 rafters 16" O.C. with 1/2" plywood sheathing, 4 in 12 or 8 in 12 roof pitch.

4 Exterior Walls

Beveled wood siding and #15 felt building paper on insulated wood frame walls; sliding sash or double hung wood windows; 2 flush solid core wood exterior doors.
  Alternates:
  • Brick veneer on wood frame, has 4" veneer of common brick.
  • Stucco on wood frame has 1" thick colored stucco finish.
  • Painted concrete block has 8" concrete block sealed and painted on exterior and furring on the interior for the drywall.

5 Roofing

20 year asphalt shingles; #15 felt building paper; aluminum gutters, downspouts, drip edge and flashings.

6 Interiors

Walls and ceilings—1/2" taped and finished drywall, primed and painted with 2 coats; painted baseboard and trim; rubber backed carpeting 80%, asphalt tile 20%; hollow core wood interior doors.

7 Specialties

Economy grade kitchen cabinets—6 L.F. wall and base with plastic laminate counter top and kitchen sink; 30 gallon electric water heater.

8 Mechanical

1 lavatory, white, wall hung; 1 water closet, white; 1 bathtub, enameled steel, white; gas fired warm air heat.

9 Electrical

100 Amp. service; romex wiring; incandescent lighting fixtures, switches, receptacles.

10 Overhead and Profit

General Contractor overhead and profit.

Adjustments

Unfinished Basement:
7' high 8" concrete block or cast-in-place concrete walls.

Finished Basement:
Includes inexpensive paneling or drywall on foundation walls. Inexpensive sponge backed carpeting on concrete floor, drywall ceiling, and lighting.

ECONOMY

- **Mass produced from stock plans**
- **Single family — 1 full bath, 1 kitchen**
- **No basement**
- **Asphalt shingles on roof**
- **Hot air heat**
- **Drywall interior finishes**
- **Materials and workmanship are sufficient to meet codes**
- **Detail specifications on page 19**

Note: The illustration shown may contain some optional components (for example: garages and/or fireplaces) whose costs are shown in the modifications, adjustments, & alternatives below or at the end of the square foot section.

© Home Planners, Inc.

Base cost per square foot of living area

Exterior Wall	Living Area										
	600	800	1000	1200	1400	1600	1800	2000	2400	2800	3200
Wood Siding - Wood Frame	79.20	72.35	66.65	61.95	58.15	55.45	54.05	52.40	48.70	46.05	44.25
Brick Veneer - Wood Frame	85.45	77.95	71.70	66.55	62.30	59.35	57.85	55.95	51.90	49.00	47.00
Stucco on Wood Frame	77.50	70.85	65.30	60.70	57.05	54.40	53.05	51.45	47.80	45.25	43.50
Painted Concrete Block	80.20	73.25	67.50	62.70	58.80	56.10	54.70	52.95	49.20	46.55	44.65
Finished Basement, Add	18.25	17.15	16.40	15.70	15.15	14.75	14.55	14.25	13.85	13.50	13.25
Unfinished Basement, Add	9.20	8.25	7.55	6.95	6.50	6.15	6.00	5.75	5.35	5.10	4.85

Modifications

Add to the total cost

Upgrade Kitchen Cabinets	$ + 243
Solid Surface Countertops	+ 469
Full Bath - including plumbing, wall and floor finishes	+ 2868
Half Bath - including plumbing, wall and floor finishes	+ 1791
One Car Attached Garage	+ 7859
One Car Detached Garage	+ 10,137
Fireplace & Chimney	+ 3565

Adjustments

For multi family - add to total cost

Additional Kitchen	$ + 2077
Additional Bath	+ 2868
Additional Entry & Exit	+ 1085
Separate Heating	+ 1200
Separate Electric	+ 726

For Townhouse/Rowhouse - Multiply cost per square foot by

Inner Unit	.95
End Unit	.97

Alternatives

Add to or deduct from the cost per square foot of living area

Composition Roll Roofing	– .55
Cedar Shake Roof	+ 2.40
Upgrade Walls and Ceilings to Skim Coat Plaster	+ .46
Upgrade Ceilings to Textured Finish	+ .44
Air Conditioning, in Heating Ductwork	+ 2.49
In Separate Ductwork	+ 4.80
Heating Systems, Hot Water	+ 1.38
Heat Pump	+ 1.70
Electric Heat	– 1.20
Not Heated	– 3.16

Additional upgrades or components

Kitchen Cabinets & Countertops	Page 58
Bathroom Vanities	59
Fireplaces & Chimneys	59
Windows, Skylights & Dormers	59
Appliances	60
Breezeways & Porches	60
Finished Attic	60
Garages	61
Site Improvements	61
Wings & Ells	25

- **Mass produced from stock plans**
- **Single family — 1 full bath, 1 kitchen**
- **No basement**
- **Asphalt shingles on roof**
- **Hot air heat**
- **Drywall interior finishes**
- **Materials and workmanship are sufficient to meet codes**
- **Detail specifications on page 19**

Note: The illustration shown may contain some optional components (for example: garages and/or fireplaces) whose costs are shown in the modifications, adjustments, & alternatives below or at the end of the square foot section.

ECONOMY

Base cost per square foot of living area

Exterior Wall	Living Area										
	600	800	1000	1200	1400	1600	1800	2000	2400	2800	3200
Wood Siding - Wood Frame	90.95	76.35	67.80	64.40	62.00	57.70	55.80	53.45	49.00	47.50	45.55
Brick Veneer - Wood Frame	99.70	82.70	73.65	69.90	67.25	62.45	60.30	57.75	52.75	51.10	48.80
Stucco on Wood Frame	88.60	74.65	66.20	62.95	60.60	56.40	54.55	52.30	47.95	46.50	44.60
Painted Concrete Block	92.35	77.40	68.75	65.30	62.85	58.45	56.50	54.15	49.60	48.10	46.05
Finished Basement, Add	14.10	11.95	11.40	11.00	10.70	10.25	10.00	9.80	9.35	9.15	8.90
Unfinished Basement, Add	8.05	6.20	5.70	5.35	5.10	4.75	4.50	4.35	3.95	3.80	3.55

Modifications

Add to the total cost

Upgrade Kitchen Cabinets	$ + 243
Solid Surface Countertops	+ 469
Full Bath - including plumbing, wall and floor finishes	+ 2868
Half Bath - including plumbing, wall and floor finishes	+ 1791
One Car Attached Garage	+ 7859
One Car Detached Garage	+ 10,137
Fireplace & Chimney	+ 3565

Adjustments

For multi family - add to total cost

Additional Kitchen	$ + 2077
Additional Bath	+ 2868
Additional Entry & Exit	+ 1085
Separate Heating	+ 1200
Separate Electric	+ 726

For Townhouse/Rowhouse -
Multiply cost per square foot by

Inner Unit	.95
End Unit	.97

Alternatives

Add to or deduct from the cost per square foot of living area

Composition Roll Roofing	– .35
Cedar Shake Roof	+ 1.75
Upgrade Walls and Ceilings to Skim Coat Plaster	+ .46
Upgrade Ceilings to Textured Finish	+ .44
Air Conditioning, in Heating Ductwork	+ 1.87
In Separate Ductwork	+ 4.18
Heating Systems, Hot Water	+ 1.32
Heat Pump	+ 1.88
Electric Heat	– .95
Not Heated	– 2.91

Additional upgrades or components

Kitchen Cabinets & Countertops	Page 58
Bathroom Vanities	59
Fireplaces & Chimneys	59
Windows, Skylights & Dormers	59
Appliances	60
Breezeways & Porches	60
Finished Attic	60
Garages	61
Site Improvements	61
Wings & Ells	25

- **Mass produced from stock plans**
- **Single family — 1 full bath, 1 kitchen**
- **No basement**
- **Asphalt shingles on roof**
- **Hot air heat**
- **Drywall interior finishes**
- **Materials and workmanship are sufficient to meet codes**
- **Detail specifications on page 19**

Note: The illustration shown may contain some optional components (for example: garages and/or fireplaces) whose costs are shown in the modifications, adjustments, & alternatives below or at the end of the square foot section.

Base cost per square foot of living area

Exterior Wall	Living Area										
	1000	1200	1400	1600	1800	2000	2200	2600	3000	3400	3800
Wood Siding - Wood Frame	74.10	66.40	63.45	61.45	58.95	56.55	55.00	51.65	48.35	47.05	45.65
Brick Veneer - Wood Frame	80.85	72.65	69.30	67.05	64.20	61.60	59.80	56.00	52.35	50.90	49.30
Stucco on Wood Frame	72.25	64.70	61.90	59.95	57.55	55.15	53.65	50.45	47.25	46.05	44.70
Painted Concrete Block	75.15	67.40	64.40	62.35	59.80	57.35	55.75	52.35	49.00	47.70	46.25
Finished Basement, Add	9.60	9.20	8.85	8.65	8.40	8.25	8.05	7.75	7.50	7.35	7.25
Unfinished Basement, Add	5.00	4.65	4.35	4.15	3.95	3.80	3.65	3.40	3.20	3.05	2.95

Modifications

Add to the total cost

Upgrade Kitchen Cabinets	$ + 243
Solid Surface Countertops	+ 469
Full Bath - including plumbing, wall and floor finishes	+ 2868
Half Bath - including plumbing, wall and floor finishes	+ 1791
One Car Attached Garage	+ 7859
One Car Detached Garage	+ 10,137
Fireplace & Chimney	+ 3935

Adjustments

For multi family - add to total cost

Additional Kitchen	$ + 2077
Additional Bath	+ 2868
Additional Entry & Exit	+ 1085
Separate Heating	+ 1200
Separate Electric	+ 726

For Townhouse/Rowhouse -
Multiply cost per square foot by

Inner Unit	.93
End Unit	.96

Alternatives

Add to or deduct from the cost per square foot of living area

Composition Roll Roofing	– .30
Cedar Shake Roof	+ 1.20
Upgrade Walls and Ceilings to Skim Coat Plaster	+ .47
Upgrade Ceilings to Textured Finish	+ .44
Air Conditioning, in Heating Ductwork	+ 1.49
In Separate Ductwork	+ 3.80
Heating Systems, Hot Water	+ 1.28
Heat Pump	+ 1.99
Electric Heat	– .79
Not Heated	– 2.75

Additional upgrades or components

Kitchen Cabinets & Countertops	Page 58
Bathroom Vanities	59
Fireplaces & Chimneys	59
Windows, Skylights & Dormers	59
Appliances	60
Breezeways & Porches	60
Finished Attic	60
Garages	61
Site Improvements	61
Wings & Ells	25

Important: See the Reference Section for Location Factors (to adjust for your city) and Estimating Forms

- **Mass produced from stock plans**
- **Single family — 1 full bath, 1 kitchen**
- **No basement**
- **Asphalt shingles on roof**
- **Hot air heat**
- **Drywall interior finishes**
- **Materials and workmanship are sufficient to meet codes**
- **Detail specifications on page 19**

Note: The illustration shown may contain some optional components (for example: garages and/or fireplaces) whose costs are shown in the modifications, adjustments, & alternatives below or at the end of the square foot section.

Base cost per square foot of living area

Exterior Wall	Living Area										
	1000	1200	1400	1600	1800	2000	2200	2600	3000	3400	3800
Wood Siding - Wood Frame	68.55	61.25	58.70	56.90	54.70	52.40	51.05	48.10	45.05	43.95	42.70
Brick Veneer - Wood Frame	73.60	65.95	63.05	61.10	58.60	56.20	54.65	51.35	48.10	46.80	45.40
Stucco on Wood Frame	67.15	60.00	57.50	55.75	53.60	51.35	50.10	47.20	44.25	43.15	41.95
Painted Concrete Block	69.35	62.00	59.40	57.55	55.30	53.00	51.60	48.60	45.55	44.40	43.10
Finished Basement, Add	9.60	9.20	8.85	8.65	8.40	8.25	8.05	7.75	7.50	7.35	7.25
Unfinished Basement, Add	5.00	4.65	4.35	4.15	3.95	3.80	3.65	3.40	3.20	3.05	2.95

Modifications

Add to the total cost

Upgrade Kitchen Cabinets	$ + 243
Solid Surface Countertops	+ 469
Full Bath - including plumbing, wall and floor finishes	+ 2868
Half Bath - including plumbing, wall and floor finishes	+ 1791
One Car Attached Garage	+ 7859
One Car Detached Garage	+ 10,137
Fireplace & Chimney	+ 3935

Adjustments

For multi family - add to total cost

Additional Kitchen	$ + 2077
Additional Bath	+ 2868
Additional Entry & Exit	+ 1085
Separate Heating	+ 1200
Separate Electric	+ 726

For Townhouse/Rowhouse - Multiply cost per square foot by

Inner Unit	.94
End Unit	.97

Alternatives

Add to or deduct from the cost per square foot of living area

Composition Roll Roofing	– .30
Cedar Shake Roof	+ 1.20
Upgrade Walls and Ceilings to Skim Coat Plaster	+ .44
Upgrade Ceilings to Textured Finish	+ .44
Air Conditioning, in Heating Ductwork	+ 1.49
In Separate Ductwork	+ 3.80
Heating Systems, Hot Water	+ 1.28
Heat Pump	+ 1.99
Electric Heat	– .79
Not Heated	– 2.75

Additional upgrades or components

Kitchen Cabinets & Countertops	Page 58
Bathroom Vanities	59
Fireplaces & Chimneys	59
Windows, Skylights & Dormers	59
Appliances	60
Breezeways & Porches	60
Finished Attic	60
Garages	61
Site Improvements	61
Wings & Ells	25

ECONOMY

- **Mass produced from stock plans**
- **Single family — 1 full bath, 1 kitchen**
- **No basement**
- **Asphalt shingles on roof**
- **Hot air heat**
- **Drywall interior finishes**
- **Materials and workmanship are sufficient to meet codes**
- **Detail specifications on page 19**

Note: The illustration shown may contain some optional components (for example: garages and/or fireplaces) whose costs are shown in the modifications, adjustments, & alternatives below or at the end of the square foot section.

Design Basics, Inc.

Base cost per square foot of living area

Exterior Wall	Living Area										
	1200	1500	1800	2000	2200	2400	2800	3200	3600	4000	4400
Wood Siding - Wood Frame	62.45	57.40	53.55	52.15	50.05	48.05	46.60	44.55	42.25	41.55	39.70
Brick Veneer - Wood Frame	67.10	61.60	57.35	55.75	53.50	51.30	49.70	47.45	44.90	44.15	42.15
Stucco on Wood Frame	61.15	56.25	52.50	51.15	49.10	47.20	45.75	43.75	41.50	40.85	39.05
Solid Masonry	63.20	58.05	54.15	52.70	50.60	48.60	47.10	45.05	42.65	42.00	40.10
Finished Basement, Add*	11.45	10.90	10.45	10.25	10.05	9.85	9.65	9.45	9.25	9.10	8.95
Unfinished Basement, Add*	5.50	5.05	4.65	4.50	4.30	4.10	3.95	3.75	3.60	3.50	3.35

*Basement under middle level only.

Modifications

Add to the total cost

Upgrade Kitchen Cabinets	$ + 243
Solid Surface Countertops	+ 469
Full Bath - including plumbing, wall and floor finishes	+ 2868
Half Bath - including plumbing, wall and floor finishes	+ 1791
One Car Attached Garage	+ 7859
One Car Detached Garage	+ 10,137
Fireplace & Chimney	+ 3935

Adjustments

For multi family - add to total cost

Additional Kitchen	$ + 2077
Additional Bath	+ 2868
Additional Entry & Exit	+ 1085
Separate Heating	+ 1200
Separate Electric	+ 726

For Townhouse/Rowhouse - Multiply cost per square foot by

Inner Unit	.93
End Unit	.96

Alternatives

Add to or deduct from the cost per square foot of living area

Composition Roll Roofing	– .35
Cedar Shake Roof	+ 1.75
Upgrade Walls and Ceilings to Skim Coat Plaster	+ .40
Upgrade Ceilings to Textured Finish	+ .44
Air Conditioning, in Heating Ductwork	+ 1.24
In Separate Ductwork	+ 3.55
Heating Systems, Hot Water	+ 1.24
Heat Pump	+ 2.07
Electric Heat	– .70
Not Heated	– 2.66

Additional upgrades or components

Kitchen Cabinets & Countertops	Page 58
Bathroom Vanities	59
Fireplaces & Chimneys	59
Windows, Skylights & Dormers	59
Appliances	60
Breezeways & Porches	60
Finished Attic	60
Garages	61
Site Improvements	61
Wings & Ells	25

1 Story — Base cost per square foot of living area

Exterior Wall	Living Area							
	50	100	200	300	400	500	600	700
Wood Siding - Wood Frame	108.60	82.40	71.00	58.45	54.75	52.50	51.05	51.30
Brick Veneer - Wood Frame	124.40	93.65	80.40	64.70	60.35	57.75	56.05	56.15
Stucco on Wood Frame	104.35	79.35	68.45	56.75	53.20	51.10	49.70	50.00
Painted Concrete Block	111.20	84.20	72.55	59.45	55.65	53.35	51.85	52.10
Finished Basement, Add	27.60	22.55	20.45	16.90	16.20	15.80	15.50	15.30
Unfinished Basement, Add	16.95	12.65	10.90	7.95	7.35	7.00	6.75	6.55

1-1/2 Story — Base cost per square foot of living area

Exterior Wall	Living Area							
	100	200	300	400	500	600	700	800
Wood Siding - Wood Frame	86.10	69.10	58.55	51.90	48.80	47.20	45.25	44.70
Brick Veneer - Wood Frame	100.20	80.35	67.95	59.25	55.55	53.55	51.30	50.70
Stucco on Wood Frame	82.30	66.00	56.00	49.90	46.95	45.45	43.60	43.10
Painted Concrete Block	88.40	70.90	60.10	53.10	49.90	48.25	46.20	45.70
Finished Basement, Add	18.50	16.35	14.95	13.40	12.95	12.70	12.45	12.35
Unfinished Basement, Add	10.50	8.70	7.55	6.20	5.85	5.65	5.40	5.35

2 Story — Base cost per square foot of living area

Exterior Wall	Living Area							
	100	200	400	600	800	1000	1200	1400
Wood Siding - Wood Frame	88.65	65.55	55.50	45.10	41.85	39.85	38.60	39.00
Brick Veneer - Wood Frame	104.45	76.80	64.90	51.35	47.50	45.10	43.60	43.80
Stucco on Wood Frame	84.35	62.50	52.95	43.40	40.30	38.45	37.25	37.65
Painted Concrete Block	91.20	67.35	57.05	46.15	42.75	40.70	39.40	39.75
Finished Basement, Add	13.85	11.30	10.25	8.50	8.15	7.95	7.80	7.70
Unfinished Basement, Add	8.50	6.35	5.45	4.00	3.70	3.50	3.40	3.30

Base costs do not include bathroom or kitchen facilities. Use Modifications/Adjustments/Alternatives on pages 58-61 where appropriate.

1 Story

1-1/2 Story

2 Story

2-1/2 Story

Bi-Level

Tri-Level

	Components
1 Site Work	Site preparation for slab or excavation for lower level; 4' deep trench excavation for foundation wall.
2 Foundations	Continuous reinforced concrete footing, 8" deep x 18" wide; dampproofed and insulated 8" thick reinforced concrete foundation wall, 4' deep; 4" concrete slab on 4" crushed stone base and polyethylene vapor barrier, trowel finish.
3 Framing	Exterior walls—2 x 4 wood studs, 16" O.C.; 1/2" plywood sheathing; 2 x 6 rafters 16" O.C. with 1/2" plywood sheathing, 4 in 12 or 8 in 12 roof pitch, 2 x 6 ceiling joists; 1/2" plywood subfloor on 1 x 2 wood sleepers 16" O.C.; 2 x 8 floor joists with 5/8" plywood subfloor on models with more than one level.
4 Exterior Walls	Beveled wood siding and #15 felt building paper on insulated wood frame walls; double hung windows; 3 flush solid core wood exterior doors with storms. **Alternates:** • Brick veneer on wood frame, has 4" veneer of common brick. • Stucco on wood frame has 1" thick colored stucco finish. • Solid masonry has a 6" concrete block load bearing wall with insulation and a brick or stone exterior. Also solid brick or stone walls.
5 Roofing	25 year asphalt shingles; #15 felt building paper; aluminum gutters, downspouts, drip edge and flashings.
6 Interiors	Walls and ceilings—1/2" taped and finished drywall, primed and painted with 2 coats; painted baseboard and trim, finished hardwood floor 40%, carpet with 1/2" underlayment 40%, vinyl tile with 1/2" underlayment 15%, ceramic tile with 1/2" underlayment 5%; hollow core and louvered interior doors.
7 Specialties	Average grade kitchen cabinets—14 L.F. wall and base with plastic laminate counter top and kitchen sink; 40 gallon electric water heater.
8 Mechanical	1 lavatory, white, wall hung; 1 water closet, white; 1 bathtub, enameled steel, white; gas fired warm air heat.
9 Electrical	100 Amp. service; romex wiring; incandescent lighting fixtures, switches, receptacles.
10 Overhead and Profit	General Contractor overhead and profit.

Adjustments

Unfinished Basement:
7'-6" high cast-in-place concrete walls 8" thick or 8" concrete block.

Finished Basement:
Includes plywood paneling or drywall on furring on foundation walls, sponge backed carpeting on concrete floor, suspended ceiling, lighting and heating.

- Simple design from standard plans
- Single family — 1 full bath, 1 kitchen
- No basement
- Asphalt shingles on roof
- Hot air heat
- Drywall interior finishes
- Materials and workmanship are average
- Detail specifications on p. 27

Note: The illustration shown may contain some optional components (for example: garages and/or fireplaces) whose costs are shown in the modifications, adjustments, & alternatives below or at the end of the square foot section.

©Home Planners, Inc.

Base cost per square foot of living area

Exterior Wall	Living Area										
	600	800	1000	1200	1400	1600	1800	2000	2400	2800	3200
Wood Siding - Wood Frame	103.30	94.85	87.70	81.75	77.20	73.75	71.85	69.85	65.20	61.95	59.75
Brick Veneer - Wood Frame	116.50	107.30	99.50	93.05	88.05	84.30	82.25	80.05	75.00	71.50	69.05
Stucco on Wood Frame	109.80	101.35	94.15	88.20	83.65	80.15	78.25	76.25	71.60	68.35	66.10
Solid Masonry	125.55	115.40	106.90	99.70	94.10	90.00	87.70	85.15	79.70	75.85	73.05
Finished Basement, Add	23.35	21.95	20.90	19.95	19.20	18.70	18.45	18.05	17.45	17.05	16.65
Unfinished Basement, Add	10.20	9.20	8.55	7.95	7.45	7.15	6.95	6.70	6.35	6.05	5.85

Modifications

Add to the total cost

Upgrade Kitchen Cabinets	$ + 2288
Solid Surface Countertops	+ 826
Full Bath - including plumbing, wall and floor finishes	+ 3599
Half Bath - including plumbing, wall and floor finishes	+ 2247
One Car Attached Garage	+ 8408
One Car Detached Garage	+ 11,015
Fireplace & Chimney	+ 3640

Adjustments

For multi family - add to total cost

Additional Kitchen	$ + 3924
Additional Bath	+ 3599
Additional Entry & Exit	+ 1085
Separate Heating	+ 1200
Separate Electric	+ 1363

For Townhouse/Rowhouse - Multiply cost per square foot by

Inner Unit	.92
End Unit	.96

Alternatives

Add to or deduct from the cost per square foot of living area

Cedar Shake Roof	+ 2.10
Clay Tile Roof	+ 4.55
Slate Roof	+ 7.75
Upgrade Walls to Skim Coat Plaster	+ .30
Upgrade Ceilings to Textured Finish	+ .44
Air Conditioning, in Heating Ductwork	+ 2.56
In Separate Ductwork	+ 4.93
Heating Systems, Hot Water	+ 1.42
Heat Pump	+ 1.75
Electric Heat	− .67
Not Heated	− 2.63

Additional upgrades or components

Kitchen Cabinets & Countertops	Page 58
Bathroom Vanities	59
Fireplaces & Chimneys	59
Windows, Skylights & Dormers	59
Appliances	60
Breezeways & Porches	60
Finished Attic	60
Garages	61
Site Improvements	61
Wings & Ells	37

Important: See the Reference Section for Location Factors (to adjust for your city) and Estimating Forms

- **Simple design from standard plans**
- **Single family — 1 full bath, 1 kitchen**
- **No basement**
- **Asphalt shingles on roof**
- **Hot air heat**
- **Drywall interior finishes**
- **Materials and workmanship are average**
- **Detail specifications on p. 27**

Note: The illustration shown may contain some optional components (for example: garages and/or fireplaces) whose costs are shown in the modifications, adjustments, & alternatives below or at the end of the square foot section.

© By Designer

Base cost per square foot of living area

Exterior Wall	Living Area										
	600	800	1000	1200	1400	1600	1800	2000	2400	2800	3200
Wood Siding - Wood Frame	117.45	99.50	88.75	84.60	81.65	76.20	73.90	70.95	65.45	63.60	61.05
Brick Veneer - Wood Frame	127.05	106.45	95.20	90.65	87.40	81.45	78.85	75.65	69.60	67.55	64.70
Stucco on Wood Frame	117.75	99.70	88.95	84.80	81.85	76.35	74.10	71.10	65.55	63.70	61.20
Solid Masonry	139.70	115.65	103.70	98.60	95.00	88.35	85.40	81.85	75.10	72.70	69.50
Finished Basement, Add	19.15	16.25	15.55	15.00	14.60	14.05	13.70	13.45	12.85	12.60	12.25
Unfinished Basement, Add	8.70	6.90	6.40	6.05	5.80	5.40	5.20	5.00	4.65	4.45	4.25

Modifications

Add to the total cost

Upgrade Kitchen Cabinets	$ + 2288
Solid Surface Countertops	+ 826
Full Bath - including plumbing, wall and floor finishes	+ 3599
Half Bath - including plumbing, wall and floor finishes	+ 2247
One Car Attached Garage	+ 8408
One Car Detached Garage	+ 11,015
Fireplace & Chimney	+ 3640

Adjustments

For multi family - add to total cost

Additional Kitchen	$ + 3924
Additional Bath	+ 3599
Additional Entry & Exit	+ 1085
Separate Heating	+ 1200
Separate Electric	+ 1363

For Townhouse/Rowhouse -
Multiply cost per square foot by

Inner Unit	.92
End Unit	.96

Alternatives

Add to or deduct from the cost per square foot of living area

Cedar Shake Roof	+ 1.55
Clay Tile Roof	+ 3.25
Slate Roof	+ 5.60
Upgrade Walls to Skim Coat Plaster	+ .34
Upgrade Ceilings to Textured Finish	+ .44
Air Conditioning, in Heating Ductwork	+ 1.92
In Separate Ductwork	+ 4.29
Heating Systems, Hot Water	+ 1.35
Heat Pump	+ 1.94
Electric Heat	− .58
Not Heated	− 2.54

Additional upgrades or components

Kitchen Cabinets & Countertops	Page 58
Bathroom Vanities	59
Fireplaces & Chimneys	59
Windows, Skylights & Dormers	59
Appliances	60
Breezeways & Porches	60
Finished Attic	60
Garages	61
Site Improvements	61
Wings & Ells	37

- Simple design from standard plans
- Single family — 1 full bath, 1 kitchen
- No basement
- Asphalt shingles on roof
- Hot air heat
- Drywall interior finishes
- Materials and workmanship are average
- Detail specifications on p. 27

Note: The illustration shown may contain some optional components (for example: garages and/or fireplaces) whose costs are shown in the modifications, adjustments, & alternatives below or at the end of the square foot section.

Base cost per square foot of living area

Exterior Wall	Living Area										
	1000	1200	1400	1600	1800	2000	2200	2600	3000	3400	3800
Wood Siding - Wood Frame	95.75	86.05	82.40	79.95	76.55	73.80	71.90	67.65	63.55	62.00	60.15
Brick Veneer - Wood Frame	103.15	92.90	88.85	86.05	82.35	79.40	77.15	72.45	68.00	66.20	64.15
Stucco on Wood Frame	96.00	86.25	82.65	80.15	76.75	74.00	72.05	67.80	63.70	62.15	60.25
Solid Masonry	113.85	102.85	98.10	94.95	90.70	87.45	84.80	79.35	74.35	72.25	69.90
Finished Basement, Add	13.55	13.05	12.60	12.30	12.00	11.80	11.55	11.10	10.80	10.60	10.45
Unfinished Basement, Add	5.55	5.20	4.90	4.70	4.50	4.40	4.20	3.95	3.75	3.65	3.50

Modifications

Add to the total cost

Upgrade Kitchen Cabinets	$ + 2288
Solid Surface Countertops	+ 826
Full Bath - including plumbing, wall and floor finishes	+ 3599
Half Bath - including plumbing, wall and floor finishes	+ 2247
One Car Attached Garage	+ 8408
One Car Detached Garage	+ 11,015
Fireplace & Chimney	+ 4060

Adjustments

For multi family - add to total cost

Additional Kitchen	$ + 3924
Additional Bath	+ 3599
Additional Entry & Exit	+ 1085
Separate Heating	+ 1200
Separate Electric	+ 1363

For Townhouse/Rowhouse -
Multiply cost per square foot by

Inner Unit	.90
End Unit	.95

Alternatives

Add to or deduct from the cost per square foot of living area

Cedar Shake Roof	+ 1.05
Clay Tile Roof	+ 2.25
Slate Roof	+ 3.85
Upgrade Walls to Skim Coat Plaster	+ .36
Upgrade Ceilings to Textured Finish	+ .44
Air Conditioning, in Heating Ductwork	+ 1.53
In Separate Ductwork	+ 3.91
Heating Systems, Hot Water	+ 1.32
Heat Pump	+ 2.05
Electric Heat	– .50
Not Heated	– 2.46

Additional upgrades or components

Kitchen Cabinets & Countertops	Page 58
Bathroom Vanities	59
Fireplaces & Chimneys	59
Windows, Skylights & Dormers	59
Appliances	60
Breezeways & Porches	60
Finished Attic	60
Garages	61
Site Improvements	61
Wings & Ells	37

- **Simple design from standard plans**
- **Single family — 1 full bath, 1 kitchen**
- **No basement**
- **Asphalt shingles on roof**
- **Hot air heat**
- **Drywall interior finishes**
- **Materials and workmanship are average**
- **Detail specifications on p. 27**

Note: The illustration shown may contain some optional components (for example: garages and/or fireplaces) whose costs are shown in the modifications, adjustments, & alternatives below or at the end of the square foot section.

AVERAGE

Base cost per square foot of living area

Exterior Wall	Living Area										
	1200	1400	1600	1800	2000	2400	2800	3200	3600	4000	4400
Wood Siding - Wood Frame	95.35	90.20	81.35	80.30	77.75	72.95	69.80	65.85	64.15	60.60	59.70
Brick Veneer - Wood Frame	103.30	97.35	87.95	86.90	83.95	78.50	75.15	70.70	68.75	64.85	63.80
Stucco on Wood Frame	95.60	90.45	81.55	80.50	77.95	73.10	69.95	66.00	64.30	60.70	59.80
Solid Masonry	113.70	106.80	96.60	95.60	92.15	85.90	82.20	77.05	74.80	70.45	69.25
Finished Basement, Add	11.50	10.95	10.55	10.50	10.25	9.80	9.60	9.25	9.10	8.90	8.75
Unfinished Basement, Add	4.65	4.25	4.00	3.95	3.80	3.50	3.40	3.15	3.05	2.90	2.85

Modifications

Add to the total cost

Upgrade Kitchen Cabinets	$ + 2288
Solid Surface Countertops	+ 826
Full Bath - including plumbing, wall and floor finishes	+ 3599
Half Bath - including plumbing, wall and floor finishes	+ 2247
One Car Attached Garage	+ 8408
One Car Detached Garage	+ 11,015
Fireplace & Chimney	+ 4060

Adjustments

For multi family - add to total cost

Additional Kitchen	$ + 3924
Additional Bath	+ 3599
Additional Entry & Exit	+ 1085
Separate Heating	+ 1200
Separate Electric	+ 1363

For Townhouse/Rowhouse - Multiply cost per square foot by

Inner Unit	.90
End Unit	.95

Alternatives

Add to or deduct from the cost per square foot of living area

Cedar Shake Roof	+ .95
Clay Tile Roof	+ 1.95
Slate Roof	+ 3.35
Upgrade Walls to Skim Coat Plaster	+ .34
Upgrade Ceilings to Textured Finish	+ .44
Air Conditioning, in Heating Ductwork	+ 1.40
In Separate Ductwork	+ 3.77
Heating Systems, Hot Water	+ 1.19
Heat Pump	+ 2.10
Electric Heat	- .91
Not Heated	- 2.87

Additional upgrades or components

Kitchen Cabinets & Countertops	Page 58
Bathroom Vanities	59
Fireplaces & Chimneys	59
Windows, Skylights & Dormers	59
Appliances	60
Breezeways & Porches	60
Finished Attic	60
Garages	61
Site Improvements	61
Wings & Ells	37

- **Simple design from standard plans**
- **Single family — 1 full bath, 1 kitchen**
- **No basement**
- **Asphalt shingles on roof**
- **Hot air heat**
- **Drywall interior finishes**
- **Materials and workmanship are average**
- **Detail specifications on p. 27**

Note: The illustration shown may contain some optional components (for example: garages and/or fireplaces) whose costs are shown in the modifications, adjustments, & alternatives below or at the end of the square foot section.

AVERAGE

Base cost per square foot of living area

Exterior Wall	Living Area										
	1500	1800	2100	2500	3000	3500	4000	4500	5000	5500	6000
Wood Siding - Wood Frame	89.60	80.50	77.40	75.05	69.45	67.45	63.80	60.05	59.10	57.50	56.25
Brick Veneer - Wood Frame	97.00	87.40	83.85	81.15	75.05	72.70	68.60	64.50	63.35	61.65	60.10
Stucco on Wood Frame	89.85	80.75	77.65	75.20	69.65	67.60	63.95	60.20	59.20	57.65	56.35
Solid Masonry	106.85	96.50	92.35	89.25	82.40	79.65	74.95	70.35	69.05	67.05	65.25
Finished Basement, Add	9.85	9.50	9.25	9.05	8.70	8.50	8.25	8.05	7.95	7.85	7.75
Unfinished Basement, Add	3.75	3.50	3.35	3.20	2.95	2.85	2.65	2.55	2.50	2.45	2.35

Modifications

Add to the total cost

Upgrade Kitchen Cabinets	$ + 2288
Solid Surface Countertops	+ 826
Full Bath - including plumbing, wall and floor finishes	+ 3599
Half Bath - including plumbing, wall and floor finishes	+ 2247
One Car Attached Garage	+ 8408
One Car Detached Garage	+ 11,015
Fireplace & Chimney	+ 4615

Adjustments

For multi family - add to total cost

Additional Kitchen	$ + 3924
Additional Bath	+ 3599
Additional Entry & Exit	+ 1085
Separate Heating	+ 1200
Separate Electric	+ 1363

For Townhouse/Rowhouse - Multiply cost per square foot by

Inner Unit	.88
End Unit	.94

Alternatives

Add to or deduct from the cost per square foot of living area

Cedar Shake Roof	+ .70
Clay Tile Roof	+ 1.50
Slate Roof	+ 2.60
Upgrade Walls to Skim Coat Plaster	+ .32
Upgrade Ceilings to Textured Finish	+ .44
Air Conditioning, in Heating Ductwork	+ 1.40
In Separate Ductwork	+ 3.77
Heating Systems, Hot Water	+ 1.19
Heat Pump	+ 2.10
Electric Heat	– .71
Not Heated	– 2.67

Additional upgrades or components

Kitchen Cabinets & Countertops	Page 58
Bathroom Vanities	59
Fireplaces & Chimneys	59
Windows, Skylights & Dormers	59
Appliances	60
Breezeways & Porches	60
Finished Attic	60
Garages	61
Site Improvements	61
Wings & Ells	37

- **Simple design from standard plans**
- **Single family — 1 full bath, 1 kitchen**
- **No basement**
- **Asphalt shingles on roof**
- **Hot air heat**
- **Drywall interior finishes**
- **Materials and workmanship are average**
- **Detail specifications on p. 27**

Note: The illustration shown may contain some optional components (for example: garages and/or fireplaces) whose costs are shown in the modifications, adjustments, & alternatives below or at the end of the square foot section.

AVERAGE

Base cost per square foot of living area

Exterior Wall	Living Area										
	1000	1200	1400	1600	1800	2000	2200	2600	3000	3400	3800
Wood Siding - Wood Frame	88.65	79.50	76.30	74.05	71.10	68.50	66.90	63.05	59.35	58.00	56.35
Brick Veneer - Wood Frame	94.25	84.65	81.15	78.70	75.40	72.70	70.85	66.65	62.70	61.15	59.35
Stucco on Wood Frame	88.85	79.65	76.45	74.20	71.25	68.65	67.05	63.20	59.50	58.10	56.40
Solid Masonry	101.60	91.50	87.50	84.80	81.15	78.20	76.10	71.45	67.10	65.30	63.30
Finished Basement, Add	13.55	13.05	12.60	12.30	12.00	11.80	11.55	11.10	10.80	10.60	10.45
Unfinished Basement, Add	5.55	5.20	4.90	4.70	4.50	4.40	4.20	3.95	3.75	3.65	3.50

Modifications

Add to the total cost

Upgrade Kitchen Cabinets	$ + 2288
Solid Surface Countertops	+ 826
Full Bath - including plumbing, wall and floor finishes	+ 3599
Half Bath - including plumbing, wall and floor finishes	+ 2247
One Car Attached Garage	+ 8408
One Car Detached Garage	+ 11,015
Fireplace & Chimney	+ 3640

Adjustments

For multi family - add to total cost

Additional Kitchen	$ + 3924
Additional Bath	+ 3599
Additional Entry & Exit	+ 1085
Separate Heating	+ 1200
Separate Electric	+ 1363

For Townhouse/Rowhouse - Multiply cost per square foot by

Inner Unit	.91
End Unit	.96

Alternatives

Add to or deduct from the cost per square foot of living area

Cedar Shake Roof	+ 1.05
Clay Tile Roof	+ 2.25
Slate Roof	+ 3.85
Upgrade Walls to Skim Coat Plaster	+ .33
Upgrade Ceilings to Textured Finish	+ .44
Air Conditioning, in Heating Ductwork	+ 1.53
In Separate Ductwork	+ 3.91
Heating Systems, Hot Water	+ 1.32
Heat Pump	+ 2.05
Electric Heat	− .50
Not Heated	− 2.46

Additional upgrades or components

Kitchen Cabinets & Countertops	Page 58
Bathroom Vanities	59
Fireplaces & Chimneys	59
Windows, Skylights & Dormers	59
Appliances	60
Breezeways & Porches	60
Finished Attic	60
Garages	61
Site Improvements	61
Wings & Ells	37

- **Simple design from standard plans**
- **Single family — 1 full bath, 1 kitchen**
- **No basement**
- **Asphalt shingles on roof**
- **Hot air heat**
- **Drywall interior finishes**
- **Materials and workmanship are average**
- **Detail specifications on p. 27**

Note: The illustration shown may contain some optional components (for example: garages and/or fireplaces) whose costs are shown in the modifications, adjustments, & alternatives below or at the end of the square foot section.

©Design Basics, Inc.

Base cost per square foot of living area

Exterior Wall	Living Area										
	1200	1500	1800	2100	2400	2700	3000	3400	3800	4200	4600
Wood Siding - Wood Frame	82.80	76.50	71.70	67.90	65.00	63.35	61.70	59.95	57.25	55.00	53.80
Brick Veneer - Wood Frame	87.90	81.15	75.85	71.70	68.55	66.75	64.95	63.10	60.15	57.75	56.40
Stucco on Wood Frame	82.95	76.65	71.85	68.00	65.15	63.45	61.80	60.05	57.35	55.10	53.85
Solid Masonry	94.65	87.30	81.40	76.75	73.30	71.30	69.20	67.25	64.00	61.35	59.90
Finished Basement, Add*	15.50	14.80	14.20	13.65	13.35	13.15	12.90	12.70	12.45	12.20	12.10
Unfinished Basement, Add*	6.20	5.75	5.35	5.00	4.80	4.70	4.50	4.40	4.25	4.10	4.00

*Basement under middle level only.

Modifications

Add to the total cost

Upgrade Kitchen Cabinets	$ + 2288
Solid Surface Countertops	+ 826
Full Bath - including plumbing, wall and floor finishes	+ 3599
Half Bath - including plumbing, wall and floor finishes	+ 2247
One Car Attached Garage	+ 8408
One Car Detached Garage	+ 11,015
Fireplace & Chimney	+ 4060

Adjustments

For multi family - add to total cost

Additional Kitchen	$ + 3924
Additional Bath	+ 3599
Additional Entry & Exit	+ 1085
Separate Heating	+ 1200
Separate Electric	+ 1363

For Townhouse/Rowhouse - Multiply cost per square foot by

Inner Unit	.90
End Unit	.95

Alternatives

Add to or deduct from the cost per square foot of living area

Cedar Shake Roof	+ 1.55
Clay Tile Roof	+ 3.25
Slate Roof	+ 5.60
Upgrade Walls to Skim Coat Plaster	+ .29
Upgrade Ceilings to Textured Finish	+ .44
Air Conditioning, in Heating Ductwork	+ 1.28
In Separate Ductwork	+ 3.65
Heating Systems, Hot Water	+ 1.27
Heat Pump	+ 2.13
Electric Heat	– .41
Not Heated	– 2.37

Additional upgrades or components

Kitchen Cabinets & Countertops	Page 58
Bathroom Vanities	59
Fireplaces & Chimneys	59
Windows, Skylights & Dormers	59
Appliances	60
Breezeways & Porches	60
Finished Attic	60
Garages	61
Site Improvements	61
Wings & Ells	37

SOLID WALL

- **Post and beam frame**
- **Log exterior walls**
- **Simple design from standard plans**
- **Single family — 1 full bath, 1 kitchen**
- **No basement**
- **Asphalt shingles on roof**
- **Hot air heat**
- **Drywall interior finishes**
- **Materials and workmanship are average**
- **Detail specification on page 27**

Note: The illustration shown may contain some optional components (for example: garages and/or fireplaces) whose costs are shown in the modifications, adjustments, & alternatives below or at the end of the square foot section.

Base cost per square foot of living area

Exterior Wall	Living Area										
	600	800	1000	1200	1400	1600	1800	2000	2400	2800	3200
6" Log - Solid Wall	100.90	91.20	83.60	77.60	72.80	68.70	66.70	65.30	60.80	57.40	55.50
8" Log - Solid Wall	100.10	90.40	82.90	77.00	72.30	68.20	66.30	64.90	60.50	56.80	55.00
Finished Basement, Add	23.10	21.80	20.80	19.90	19.20	18.70	18.40	18.00	17.50	17.10	16.70
Unfinished Basement, Add	9.90	9.00	8.40	7.80	7.40	7.00	6.80	6.60	6.30	6.00	5.70

Modifications

Add to the total cost

Upgrade Kitchen Cabinets	$ + 2288
Solid Surface Countertops	+ 826
Full Bath - including plumbing, wall and floor finishes	+ 3599
Half Bath - including plumbing, wall and floor finishes	+ 2247
One Car Attached Garage	+ 8408
One Car Detached Garage	+ 11,015
Fireplace & Chimney	+ 3640

Adjustments

For multi family - add to total cost

Additional Kitchen	$ + 3924
Additional Bath	+ 3599
Additional Entry & Exit	+ 1085
Separate Heating	+ 1200
Separate Electric	+ 1363

For Townhouse/Rowhouse - Multiply cost per square foot by

Inner Unit	.92
End Unit	.96

Alternatives

Add to or deduct from the cost per square foot of living area

Cedar Shake Roof	+ 2.10
Air Conditioning, in Heating Ductwork	+ 2.56
In Separate Ductwork	+ 4.93
Heating Systems, Hot Water	+ 1.42
Heat Pump	+ 1.75
Electric Heat	– .67
Not Heated	– 2.63

Additional upgrades or components

Kitchen Cabinets & Countertops	Page 58
Bathroom Vanities	59
Fireplaces & Chimneys	59
Windows, Skylights & Dormers	59
Appliances	60
Breezeways & Porches	60
Finished Attic	60
Garages	61
Site Improvements	61
Wings & Ells	37

- **Post and beam frame**
- **Log exterior walls**
- **Simple design from standard plans**
- **Single family — 1 full bath, 1 kitchen**
- **No basement**
- **Asphalt shingles on roof**
- **Hot air heat**
- **Drywall interior finishes**
- **Materials and workmanship are average**
- **Detail specification on page 27**

Note: The illustration shown may contain some optional components (for example: garages and/or fireplaces) whose costs are shown in the modifications, adjustments, & alternatives below or at the end of the square foot section.

Base cost per square foot of living area

Exterior Wall	Living Area										
	1000	1200	1400	1600	1800	2000	2200	2600	3000	3400	3800
6" Log-Solid	101.00	83.20	79.50	76.60	73.50	70.60	68.50	64.50	59.70	58.20	56.60
8" Log-Solid	97.00	87.00	82.70	80.10	76.90	73.50	71.50	67.10	62.60	60.90	59.00
Finished Basement, Add	13.40	13.00	12.50	12.30	11.90	11.80	11.50	11.10	10.90	10.70	10.50
Unfinished Basement, Add	5.40	5.10	4.80	4.60	4.40	4.10	4.10	3.80	3.70	3.60	3.40

Modifications

Add to the total cost

Upgrade Kitchen Cabinets	$ + 2288
Solid Surface Countertops	+ 826
Full Bath - including plumbing, wall and floor finishes	+ 3599
Half Bath - including plumbing, wall and floor finishes	+ 2247
One Car Attached Garage	+ 8408
One Car Detached Garage	+ 11,015
Fireplace & Chimney	+ 4060

Adjustments

For multi family - add to total cost

Additional Kitchen	$ + 3924
Additional Bath	+ 3599
Additional Entry & Exit	+ 1085
Separate Heating	+ 1200
Separate Electric	+ 1363

For Townhouse/Rowhouse - Multiply cost per square foot by

Inner Unit	.92
End Unit	.96

Alternatives

Add to or deduct from the cost per square foot of living area

Cedar Shake Roof	+ 1.55
Air Conditioning, in Heating Ductwork	+ 1.53
In Separate Ductwork	+ 3.91
Heating Systems, Hot Water	+ 1.32
Heat Pump	+ 2.05
Electric Heat	– .50
Not Heated	– 2.46

Additional upgrades or components

Kitchen Cabinets & Countertops	Page 58
Bathroom Vanities	59
Fireplaces & Chimneys	59
Windows, Skylights & Dormers	59
Appliances	60
Breezeways & Porches	60
Finished Attic	60
Garages	61
Site Improvements	61
Wings & Ells	37

1 Story — Base cost per square foot of living area

Exterior Wall	Living Area							
	50	100	200	300	400	500	600	700
Wood Siding - Wood Frame	137.60	104.75	90.45	75.25	70.55	67.70	65.85	66.45
Brick Veneer - Wood Frame	148.65	110.85	94.50	75.85	70.45	67.20	65.10	65.50
Stucco on Wood Frame	138.00	105.00	90.65	75.30	70.60	67.80	65.90	66.50
Solid Masonry	177.85	133.45	114.40	91.20	84.90	81.15	79.65	79.65
Finished Basement, Add	37.10	29.95	26.95	21.95	20.95	20.35	19.95	19.65
Unfinished Basement, Add	17.90	13.65	11.85	8.90	8.30	7.95	7.70	7.55

1-1/2 Story — Base cost per square foot of living area

Exterior Wall	Living Area							
	100	200	300	400	500	600	700	800
Wood Siding - Wood Frame	113.70	91.00	77.35	69.00	64.90	62.90	60.35	59.60
Brick Veneer - Wood Frame	149.20	113.35	94.35	82.05	76.30	73.25	69.85	68.65
Stucco on Wood Frame	134.20	101.40	84.35	74.25	69.10	66.45	63.40	62.30
Solid Masonry	169.65	129.70	107.95	92.70	86.10	82.50	78.60	77.35
Finished Basement, Add	25.05	22.05	20.05	17.90	17.25	16.85	16.50	16.45
Unfinished Basement, Add	11.30	9.50	8.35	7.05	6.65	6.45	6.25	6.20

2 Story — Base cost per square foot of living area

Exterior Wall	Living Area							
	100	200	400	600	800	1000	1200	1400
Wood Siding - Wood Frame	114.60	85.05	72.15	59.20	55.00	52.40	50.75	51.50
Brick Veneer - Wood Frame	153.55	108.20	87.85	69.65	63.90	60.35	58.10	58.35
Stucco on Wood Frame	136.75	96.20	77.85	63.00	57.90	54.75	52.75	53.20
Solid Masonry	176.40	124.55	101.45	78.75	72.05	68.00	65.35	65.40
Finished Basement, Add	19.85	16.30	14.80	12.30	11.80	11.50	11.30	11.15
Unfinished Basement, Add	9.05	6.90	6.05	4.55	4.25	4.10	3.95	3.90

Base costs do not include bathroom or kitchen facilities. Use Modifications/Adjustments/Alternatives on pages 58-61 where appropriate.

Important: See the Reference Section for Location Factors (to adjust for your city) and Estimating Forms.

37

CUSTOM

1 Story

1-1/2 Story

2 Story

2-1/2 Story

Bi-Level

Tri-Level

CUSTOM

	Components
1 Site Work	Site preparation for slab or excavation for lower level; 4' deep trench excavation for foundation wall.
2 Foundations	Continuous reinforced concrete footing, 8" deep x 18" wide; dampproofed and insulated 8" thick reinforced concrete foundation wall, 4' deep; 4" concrete slab on 4" crushed stone base and polyethylene vapor barrier, trowel finish.
3 Framing	Exterior walls—2 x 6 wood studs, 16" O.C.; 1/2" plywood sheathing; 2 x 8 rafters 16" O.C. with 1/2" plywood sheathing, 4 in 12, 6 in 12 or 8 in 12 roof pitch, 2 x 6 or 2 x 8 ceiling joists; 1/2" plywood subfloor on 1 x 3 wood sleepers 16" O.C.; 2 x 10 floor joists with 5/8" plywood subfloor on models with more than one level.
4 Exterior Walls	Horizontal beveled wood siding and #15 felt building paper on insulated wood frame walls; double hung windows; 3 flush solid core wood exterior doors with storms. **Alternates:** • Brick veneer on wood frame, has 4" veneer high quality face brick or select common brick. • Stone veneer on wood frame has exterior veneer of field stone or 2" thick limestone. • Solid masonry has an 8" concrete block wall with insulation and a brick or stone facing. It may be a solid brick or stone structure.
5 Roofing	30 year asphalt shingles; #15 felt building paper; aluminum gutters, downspouts and drip edge; copper flashings.
6 Interiors	Walls and ceilings—5/8" drywall, skim coat plaster, primed and painted with 2 coats; hardwood baseboard and trim; sanded and finished, hardwood floor 70%, ceramic tile with 1/2" underlayment 20%, vinyl tile with 1/2" underlayment 10%; wood panel interior doors, primed and painted with 2 coats.
7 Specialties	Custom grade kitchen cabinets—20 L.F. wall and base with plastic laminate counter top and kitchen sink; 4 L.F. bathroom vanity; 75 gallon electric water heater; medicine cabinet.
8 Mechanical	Gas fired warm air heat/air conditioning; one full bath including bathtub, corner shower, built in lavatory and water closet; one 1/2 bath including built in lavatory and water closet.
9 Electrical	100 Amp. service; romex wiring; incandescent lighting fixtures, switches, receptacles.
10 Overhead and Profit	General Contractor overhead and profit.

Adjustments

Unfinished Basement:
7'-6" high cast-in-place concrete walls 10" thick or 12" concrete block.

Finished Basement:
Includes painted drywall on 2 x 4 wood furring with insulation, suspended ceiling, carpeting on concrete floor, heating and lighting.

- **A distinct residence from designer's plans**
- **Single family — 1 full bath, 1 half bath, 1 kitchen**
- **No basement**
- **Asphalt shingles on roof**
- **Forced hot air heat/air conditioning**
- **Drywall interior finishes**
- **Materials and workmanship are above average**
- **Detail specifications on page 39**

Note: The illustration shown may contain some optional components (for example: garages and/or fireplaces) whose costs are shown in the modifications, adjustments, & alternatives below or at the end of the square foot section.

©Design Basics, Inc.

Base cost per square foot of living area

Exterior Wall	Living Area										
	800	1000	1200	1400	1600	1800	2000	2400	2800	3200	3600
Wood Siding - Wood Frame	123.20	112.40	103.60	96.95	91.90	89.05	86.05	79.60	75.35	72.10	68.55
Brick Veneer - Wood Frame	134.05	122.85	113.65	106.70	101.45	98.45	95.30	88.65	84.20	80.80	77.10
Stone Veneer - Wood Frame	138.45	126.85	117.30	110.00	104.50	101.45	98.10	91.20	86.55	83.00	79.10
Solid Masonry	139.20	127.50	117.85	110.50	105.00	101.90	98.55	91.65	86.90	83.35	79.45
Finished Basement, Add	32.05	30.45	29.05	27.95	27.20	26.80	26.20	25.40	24.75	24.20	23.75
Unfinished Basement, Add	13.55	12.75	12.05	11.45	11.10	10.85	10.55	10.15	9.80	9.50	9.25

Modifications

Add to the total cost

Upgrade Kitchen Cabinets	$ + 634
Solid Surface Countertops	+ 1180
Full Bath - including plumbing, wall and floor finishes	+ 4265
Half Bath - including plumbing, wall and floor finishes	+ 2663
Two Car Attached Garage	+ 16,927
Two Car Detached Garage	+ 19,625
Fireplace & Chimney	+ 3830

Adjustments

For multi family - add to total cost

Additional Kitchen	$ + 8336
Additional Full Bath & Half Bath	+ 6886
Additional Entry & Exit	+ 1085
Separate Heating & Air Conditioning	+ 4017
Separate Electric	+ 1363

For Townhouse/Rowhouse -
Multiply cost per square foot by

Inner Unit	.90
End Unit	.95

Alternatives

Add to or deduct from the cost per square foot of living area

Cedar Shake Roof	+ 1.75
Clay Tile Roof	+ 4.20
Slate Roof	+ 7.45
Upgrade Ceilings to Textured Finish	+ .44
Air Conditioning, in Heating Ductwork	Base System
Heating Systems, Hot Water	+ 1.45
Heat Pump	+ 1.77
Electric Heat	− 1.98
Not Heated	− 3.30

Additional upgrades or components

Kitchen Cabinets & Countertops	Page 58
Bathroom Vanities	59
Fireplaces & Chimneys	59
Windows, Skylights & Dormers	59
Appliances	60
Breezeways & Porches	60
Finished Attic	60
Garages	61
Site Improvements	61
Wings & Ells	47

CUSTOM

- A distinct residence from designer's plans
- Single family — 1 full bath, 1 half bath, 1 kitchen
- No basement
- Asphalt shingles on roof
- Forced hot air heat/air conditioning
- Drywall interior finishes
- Materials and workmanship are above average
- Detail specifications on page 39

Note: The illustration shown may contain some optional components (for example: garages and/or fireplaces) whose costs are shown in the modifications, adjustments, & alternatives below or at the end of the square foot section.

©Donald A. Gardner Architects, Inc.

CUSTOM

Base cost per square foot of living area

Exterior Wall	Living Area										
	1000	1200	1400	1600	1800	2000	2400	2800	3200	3600	4000
Wood Siding - Wood Frame	113.35	106.75	102.15	95.15	91.80	87.70	80.50	77.70	74.30	71.85	68.40
Brick Veneer - Wood Frame	117.85	111.00	106.20	98.80	95.30	91.00	83.40	80.50	76.90	74.35	70.70
Stone Veneer - Wood Frame	122.45	115.35	110.30	102.55	98.85	94.40	86.40	83.30	79.50	76.85	73.05
Solid Masonry	123.25	116.05	111.00	103.15	99.40	94.95	86.85	83.75	79.95	77.30	73.40
Finished Basement, Add	21.30	20.45	19.90	19.05	18.55	18.15	17.25	16.85	16.40	16.15	15.80
Unfinished Basement, Add	9.10	8.70	8.40	7.95	7.70	7.50	7.05	6.85	6.60	6.50	6.30

Modifications

Add to the total cost

Upgrade Kitchen Cabinets	$ + 634
Solid Surface Countertops	+ 1180
Full Bath - including plumbing, wall and floor finishes	+ 4265
Half Bath - including plumbing, wall and floor finishes	+ 2663
Two Car Attached Garage	+ 16,927
Two Car Detached Garage	+ 19,625
Fireplace & Chimney	+ 3830

Adjustments

For multi family - add to total cost

Additional Kitchen	$ + 8336
Additional Full Bath & Half Bath	+ 6886
Additional Entry & Exit	+ 1085
Separate Heating & Air Conditioning	+ 4017
Separate Electric	+ 1363

For Townhouse/Rowhouse -
Multiply cost per square foot by

Inner Unit	.90
End Unit	.95

Alternatives

Add to or deduct from the cost per square foot of living area

Cedar Shake Roof	+ 1.30
Clay Tile Roof	+ 3.00
Slate Roof	+ 5.35
Upgrade Ceilings to Textured Finish	+ .44
Air Conditioning, in Heating Ductwork	Base System
Heating Systems, Hot Water	+ 1.38
Heat Pump	+ 1.87
Electric Heat	– 1.72
Not Heated	– 3.04

Additional upgrades or components

Kitchen Cabinets & Countertops	Page 58
Bathroom Vanities	59
Fireplaces & Chimneys	59
Windows, Skylights & Dormers	59
Appliances	60
Breezeways & Porches	60
Finished Attic	60
Garages	61
Site Improvements	61
Wings & Ells	47

CUSTOM

- A distinct residence from designer's plans
- Single family — 1 full bath, 1 half bath, 1 kitchen
- No basement
- Asphalt shingles on roof
- Forced hot air heat/air conditioning
- Drywall interior finishes
- Materials and workmanship are above average
- Detail specifications on page 39

Note: The illustration shown may contain some optional components (for example: garages and/or fireplaces) whose costs are shown in the modifications, adjustments, & alternatives below or at the end of the square foot section.

Base cost per square foot of living area

Exterior Wall	Living Area										
	1200	1400	1600	1800	2000	2400	2800	3200	3600	4000	4400
Wood Siding - Wood Frame	108.50	103.05	99.20	94.80	91.00	84.65	79.85	76.05	73.75	71.65	69.55
Brick Veneer - Wood Frame	113.30	107.60	103.55	98.85	94.95	88.20	83.05	79.10	76.65	74.40	72.20
Stone Veneer - Wood Frame	118.25	112.20	107.90	103.00	98.90	91.80	86.35	82.15	79.60	77.15	74.90
Solid Masonry	119.05	112.95	108.65	103.70	99.55	92.35	86.85	82.65	80.05	77.60	75.35
Finished Basement, Add	17.15	16.45	16.00	15.55	15.25	14.55	14.00	13.65	13.40	13.15	12.95
Unfinished Basement, Add	7.35	7.00	6.75	6.55	6.40	6.00	5.75	5.55	5.45	5.30	5.20

Modifications

Add to the total cost

Upgrade Kitchen Cabinets	$ + 634
Solid Surface Countertops	+ 1180
Full Bath - including plumbing, wall and floor finishes	+ 4265
Half Bath - including plumbing, wall and floor finishes	+ 2663
Two Car Attached Garage	+ 16,927
Two Car Detached Garage	+ 19,625
Fireplace & Chimney	+ 4320

Adjustments

For multi family - add to total cost

Additional Kitchen	$ + 8336
Additional Full Bath & Half Bath	+ 6886
Additional Entry & Exit	+ 1085
Separate Heating & Air Conditioning	+ 4017
Separate Electric	+ 1363

For Townhouse/Rowhouse -
Multiply cost per square foot by

Inner Unit	.87
End Unit	.93

Alternatives

Add to or deduct from the cost per square foot of living area

Cedar Shake Roof	+ .90
Clay Tile Roof	+ 2.10
Slate Roof	+ 3.70
Upgrade Ceilings to Textured Finish	+ .44
Air Conditioning, in Heating Ductwork	Base System
Heating Systems, Hot Water	+ 1.34
Heat Pump	+ 2.08
Electric Heat	– 1.72
Not Heated	– 2.88

Additional upgrades or components

- **A distinct residence from designer's plans**
- **Single family — 1 full bath, 1 half bath, 1 kitchen**
- **No basement**
- **Asphalt shingles on roof**
- **Forced hot air heat/air conditioning**
- **Drywall interior finishes**
- **Materials and workmanship are above average**
- **Detail specifications on page 39**

Note: The illustration shown may contain some optional components (for example: garages and/or fireplaces) whose costs are shown in the modifications, adjustments, & alternatives below or at the end of the square foot section.

Base cost per square foot of living area

Exterior Wall	Living Area										
	1500	1800	2100	2400	2800	3200	3600	4000	4500	5000	5500
Wood Siding - Wood Frame	110.40	98.70	92.95	88.80	84.60	79.55	77.25	72.85	70.85	68.60	66.40
Brick Veneer - Wood Frame	115.45	103.35	97.10	92.75	88.40	82.95	80.45	75.85	73.70	71.30	68.95
Stone Veneer - Wood Frame	120.60	108.05	101.30	96.75	92.25	86.40	83.75	78.90	76.60	74.10	71.55
Solid Masonry	121.40	108.85	102.00	97.40	92.85	86.95	84.30	79.40	77.10	74.50	72.00
Finished Basement, Add	13.65	13.00	12.30	11.95	11.65	11.20	10.90	10.60	10.35	10.20	10.00
Unfinished Basement, Add	5.90	5.55	5.20	5.00	4.90	4.65	4.50	4.35	4.20	4.10	4.00

Modifications

Add to the total cost

Upgrade Kitchen Cabinets	$ + 634
Solid Surface Countertops	+ 1180
Full Bath - including plumbing, wall and floor finishes	+ 4265
Half Bath - including plumbing, wall and floor finishes	+ 2663
Two Car Attached Garage	+ 16,927
Two Car Detached Garage	+ 19,625
Fireplace & Chimney	+ 4320

Adjustments

For multi family - add to total cost

Additional Kitchen	$ + 8336
Additional Full Bath & Half Bath	+ 6886
Additional Entry & Exit	+ 1085
Separate Heating & Air Conditioning	+ 4017
Separate Electric	+ 1363

For Townhouse/Rowhouse -
Multiply cost per square foot by

Inner Unit	.87
End Unit	.94

Alternatives

Add to or deduct from the cost per square foot of living area

Cedar Shake Roof	+ .75
Clay Tile Roof	+ 1.80
Slate Roof	+ 3.20
Upgrade Ceilings to Textured Finish	+ .44
Air Conditioning, in Heating Ductwork	Base System
Heating Systems, Hot Water	+ 1.22
Heat Pump	+ 2.14
Electric Heat	− 3.05
Not Heated	− 2.88

Additional upgrades or components

Kitchen Cabinets & Countertops	Page 58
Bathroom Vanities	59
Fireplaces & Chimneys	59
Windows, Skylights & Dormers	59
Appliances	60
Breezeways & Porches	60
Finished Attic	60
Garages	61
Site Improvements	61
Wings & Ells	47

- A distinct residence from designer's plans
- Single family — 1 full bath, 1 half bath, 1 kitchen
- No basement
- Asphalt shingles on roof
- Forced hot air heat/air conditioning
- Drywall interior finishes
- Materials and workmanship are above average
- Detail specifications on page 39

Note: The illustration shown may contain some optional components (for example: garages and/or fireplaces) whose costs are shown in the modifications, adjustments, & alternatives below or at the end of the square foot section.

Base cost per square foot of living area

Exterior Wall	Living Area										
	1500	1800	2100	2500	3000	3500	4000	4500	5000	5500	6000
Wood Siding - Wood Frame	110.35	98.80	94.35	90.75	83.85	81.00	76.40	71.80	70.50	68.50	66.75
Brick Veneer - Wood Frame	115.60	103.60	98.85	95.10	87.75	84.70	79.80	74.90	73.50	71.40	69.50
Stone Veneer - Wood Frame	120.90	108.55	103.50	99.50	91.75	88.50	83.25	78.10	76.60	74.35	72.30
Solid Masonry	121.80	109.35	104.25	100.20	92.40	89.10	83.80	78.60	77.10	74.80	72.75
Finished Basement, Add	12.00	11.40	11.00	10.65	10.15	9.85	9.50	9.20	9.05	8.90	8.75
Unfinished Basement, Add	5.15	4.90	4.65	4.50	4.25	4.10	3.90	3.75	3.70	3.60	3.50

Modifications

Add to the total cost

Upgrade Kitchen Cabinets	$ + 634
Solid Surface Countertops	+ 1180
Full Bath - including plumbing, wall and floor finishes	+ 4265
Half Bath - including plumbing, wall and floor finishes	+ 2663
Two Car Attached Garage	+ 16,927
Two Car Detached Garage	+ 19,625
Fireplace & Chimney	+ 4885

Adjustments

For multi family - add to total cost

Additional Kitchen	$ + 8336
Additional Full Bath & Half Bath	+ 6886
Additional Entry & Exit	+ 1085
Separate Heating & Air Conditioning	+ 4017
Separate Electric	+ 1363

For Townhouse/Rowhouse -
Multiply cost per square foot by

Inner Unit	.85
End Unit	.93

Alternatives

Add to or deduct from the cost per square foot of living area

Cedar Shake Roof	+ .60
Clay Tile Roof	+ 1.40
Slate Roof	+ 2.50
Upgrade Ceilings to Textured Finish	+ .44
Air Conditioning, in Heating Ductwork	Base System
Heating Systems, Hot Water	+ 1.22
Heat Pump	+ 2.14
Electric Heat	– 3.05
Not Heated	– 2.78

Additional upgrades or components

Kitchen Cabinets & Countertops	Page 58
Bathroom Vanities	59
Fireplaces & Chimneys	59
Windows, Skylights & Dormers	59
Appliances	60
Breezeways & Porches	60
Finished Attic	60
Garages	61
Site Improvements	61
Wings & Ells	47

Important: See the Reference Section for Location Factors (to adjust for your city) and Estimating Forms

- **A distinct residence from designer's plans**
- **Single family — 1 full bath, 1 half bath, 1 kitchen**
- **No basement**
- **Asphalt shingles on roof**
- **Forced hot air heat/air conditioning**
- **Drywall interior finishes**
- **Materials and workmanship are above average**
- **Detail specifications on page 39**

Note: The illustration shown may contain some optional components (for example: garages and/or fireplaces) whose costs are shown in the modifications, adjustments, & alternatives below or at the end of the square foot section.

CUSTOM

Base cost per square foot of living area

| Exterior Wall | Living Area | | | | | | | | | | |
---	1200	1400	1600	1800	2000	2400	2800	3200	3600	4000	4400
Wood Siding - Wood Frame	101.10	96.15	92.60	88.55	85.05	79.25	74.90	71.45	69.30	67.50	65.55
Brick Veneer - Wood Frame	104.75	99.55	95.85	91.60	88.00	81.90	77.35	73.70	71.45	69.55	67.55
Stone Veneer - Wood Frame	108.45	103.00	99.15	94.70	91.00	84.60	79.80	76.00	73.70	71.60	69.55
Solid Masonry	109.05	103.55	99.70	95.25	91.50	85.05	80.20	76.40	74.05	71.95	69.90
Finished Basement, Add	17.15	16.45	16.00	15.55	15.25	14.55	14.00	13.65	13.40	13.15	12.95
Unfinished Basement, Add	7.35	7.00	6.75	6.55	6.40	6.00	5.75	5.55	5.45	5.30	5.20

Modifications
Add to the total cost
Upgrade Kitchen Cabinets	$ + 634
Solid Surface Countertops	+ 1180
Full Bath - including plumbing, wall and floor finishes	+ 4265
Half Bath - including plumbing, wall and floor finishes	+ 2663
Two Car Attached Garage	+ 16,927
Two Car Detached Garage	+ 19,625
Fireplace & Chimney	+ 3830

Adjustments
For multi family - add to total cost
Additional Kitchen	$ + 8336
Additional Full Bath & Half Bath	+ 6886
Additional Entry & Exit	+ 1085
Separate Heating & Air Conditioning	+ 4017
Separate Electric	+ 1363

For Townhouse/Rowhouse - Multiply cost per square foot by
Inner Unit	.89
End Unit	.95

Alternatives
Add to or deduct from the cost per square foot of living area
Cedar Shake Roof	+ .90
Clay Tile Roof	+ 2.10
Slate Roof	+ 3.70
Upgrade Ceilings to Textured Finish	+ .44
Air Conditioning, in Heating Ductwork	Base System
Heating Systems, Hot Water	+ 1.34
Heat Pump	+ 2.08
Electric Heat	− 1.73
Not Heated	− 2.78

Additional upgrades or components
Kitchen Cabinets & Countertops	Page 58
Bathroom Vanities	59
Fireplaces & Chimneys	59
Windows, Skylights & Dormers	59
Appliances	60
Breezeways & Porches	60
Finished Attic	60
Garages	61
Site Improvements	61
Wings & Ells	47

- A distinct residence from designer's plans
- Single family — 1 full bath, 1 half bath, 1 kitchen
- No basement
- Asphalt shingles on roof
- Forced hot air heat/air conditioning
- Drywall interior finishes
- Materials and workmanship are above average
- Detail specifications on page 39

Note: The illustration shown may contain some optional components (for example: garages and/or fireplaces) whose costs are shown in the modifications, adjustments, & alternatives below or at the end of the square foot section.

©Design Basics, Inc.

Base cost per square foot of living area

Exterior Wall	Living Area										
	1200	1500	1800	2100	2400	2800	3200	3600	4000	4500	5000
Wood Siding - Wood Frame	103.70	94.85	87.95	82.75	78.70	75.85	72.30	68.65	67.40	63.55	61.60
Brick Veneer - Wood Frame	107.30	98.15	90.90	85.45	81.20	78.25	74.55	70.75	69.40	65.40	63.35
Stone Veneer - Wood Frame	111.00	101.45	93.90	88.15	83.75	80.70	76.80	72.90	71.45	67.30	65.15
Solid Masonry	111.55	102.00	94.40	88.60	84.15	81.15	77.20	73.20	71.80	67.60	65.45
Finished Basement, Add*	21.30	20.30	19.35	18.65	18.15	17.80	17.35	16.90	16.70	16.30	16.05
Unfinished Basement, Add*	9.00	8.50	8.00	7.65	7.40	7.20	6.95	6.75	6.65	6.45	6.30

*Basement under middle level only.

Modifications

Add to the total cost

Upgrade Kitchen Cabinets	$ + 634
Solid Surface Countertops	+ 1180
Full Bath - including plumbing, wall and floor finishes	+ 4265
Half Bath - including plumbing, wall and floor finishes	+ 2663
Two Car Attached Garage	+ 16,927
Two Car Detached Garage	+ 19,625
Fireplace & Chimney	+ 4320

Adjustments

For multi family - add to total cost

Additional Kitchen	$ + 8336
Additional Full Bath & Half Bath	+ 6886
Additional Entry & Exit	+ 1085
Separate Heating & Air Conditioning	+ 4017
Separate Electric	+ 1363

For Townhouse/Rowhouse -
Multiply cost per square foot by

Inner Unit	.87
End Unit	.94

Alternatives

Add to or deduct from the cost per square foot of living area

Cedar Shake Roof	+ 1.30
Clay Tile Roof	+ 3.00
Slate Roof	+ 5.35
Upgrade Ceilings to Textured Finish	+ .44
Air Conditioning, in Heating Ductwork	Base System
Heating Systems, Hot Water	+ 1.30
Heat Pump	+ 2.16
Electric Heat	− 1.54
Not Heated	− 2.78

Additional upgrades or components

Kitchen Cabinets & Countertops	Page 58
Bathroom Vanities	59
Fireplaces & Chimneys	59
Windows, Skylights & Dormers	59
Appliances	60
Breezeways & Porches	60
Finished Attic	60
Garages	61
Site Improvements	61
Wings & Ells	47

CUSTOM

1 Story Base cost per square foot of living area

Exterior Wall	Living Area							
	50	100	200	300	400	500	600	700
Wood Siding - Wood Frame	162.95	124.20	107.35	89.25	83.70	80.40	78.25	78.95
Brick Veneer - Wood Frame	175.15	132.90	114.60	94.05	88.05	84.45	82.10	82.70
Stone Veneer - Wood Frame	187.60	141.80	122.05	99.05	92.50	88.60	86.05	86.55
Solid Masonry	189.60	143.25	123.25	99.80	93.20	89.30	86.70	87.10
Finished Basement, Add	51.85	42.10	38.00	31.25	29.85	29.05	28.50	28.10
Unfinished Basement, Add	39.85	26.90	20.85	15.90	14.55	13.70	13.15	12.80

1-1/2 Story Base cost per square foot of living area

Exterior Wall	Living Area							
	100	200	300	400	500	600	700	800
Wood Siding - Wood Frame	133.95	108.35	92.70	83.05	78.25	76.05	73.10	72.25
Brick Veneer - Wood Frame	144.85	117.05	99.95	88.70	83.50	81.00	77.80	76.90
Stone Veneer - Wood Frame	156.00	125.95	107.35	94.50	88.80	86.05	82.55	81.65
Solid Masonry	157.75	127.35	108.55	95.40	89.70	86.85	83.30	82.40
Finished Basement, Add	34.45	30.45	27.70	24.70	23.90	23.35	22.85	22.80
Unfinished Basement, Add	23.50	17.45	14.70	12.45	11.65	11.10	10.65	10.45

2 Story Base cost per square foot of living area

Exterior Wall	Living Area							
	100	200	400	600	800	1000	1200	1400
Wood Siding - Wood Frame	136.10	101.75	86.75	71.70	66.75	63.80	61.90	62.80
Brick Veneer - Wood Frame	148.30	110.50	94.00	76.55	71.10	67.90	65.75	66.55
Stone Veneer - Wood Frame	160.75	119.40	101.40	81.50	75.55	72.00	69.70	70.35
Solid Masonry	162.80	120.80	102.65	82.25	76.25	72.70	70.35	70.95
Finished Basement, Add	25.95	21.05	19.00	15.65	14.95	14.55	14.30	14.10
Unfinished Basement, Add	19.95	13.45	10.45	7.95	7.30	6.85	6.60	6.40

Base costs do not include bathroom or kitchen facilities. Use Modifications/Adjustments/Alternatives on pages 58-61 where appropriate.

LUXURY

1 Story

1-1/2 Story

2 Story

2-1/2 Story

Bi-Level

Tri-Level

LUXURY

	Components
1 Site Work	Site preparation for slab or excavation for lower level; 4' deep trench excavation for foundation wall.
2 Foundations	Continuous reinforced concrete footing, 8" deep x 18" wide; dampproofed and insulated 12" thick reinforced concrete foundation wall, 4' deep; 4" concrete slab on 4" crushed stone base and polyethylene vapor barrier, trowel finish.
3 Framing	Exterior walls—2 x 6 wood studs, 16" O.C.; 1/2" plywood sheathing; 2 x 8 rafters 16" O.C. with 1/2" plywood sheathing, 4 in 12, 6 in 12 or 8 in 12 roof pitch, 2 x 6 or 2 x 8 ceiling joists; 1/2" plywood subfloor on 1 x 3 wood sleepers 16" O.C.; 2 x 10 floor joists with 5/8" plywood subfloor on models with more than one level.
4 Exterior Walls	Face brick veneer and #15 felt building paper on insulated wood frame walls; double hung windows; 3 flush solid core wood exterior doors with storms. **Alternates:** • Wood siding on wood frame, has top quality cedar or redwood siding or hand split cedar shingles or shakes. • Solid brick may have solid brick exterior wall or brick on concrete block. • Solid stone concrete block with selected fieldstone or limestone exterior.
5 Roofing	Red cedar shingles; #15 felt building paper; aluminum gutters, downspouts and drip edge; copper flashings.
6 Interiors	Walls and ceilings—5/8" drywall, skim coat plaster, primed and painted with 2 coats; hardwood baseboard and trim; sanded and finished, hardwood floor 70%, ceramic tile with 1/2" underlayment 20%, vinyl tile with 1/2" underlayment 10%; wood panel interior doors, primed and painted with 2 coats.
7 Specialties	Luxury grade kitchen cabinets—25 L.F. wall and base with plastic laminate counter top and kitchen sink; 6 L.F. bathroom vanity; 75 gallon electric water heater; medicine cabinet.
8 Mechanical	Gas fired warm air heat/air conditioning; one full bath including bathtub, corner shower, built in lavatory and water closet; one 1/2 bath including built in lavatory and water closet.
9 Electrical	100 Amp. service; romex wiring; incandescent lighting fixtures, switches, receptacles.
10 Overhead and Profit	General Contractor overhead and profit.

Adjustments

Unfinished Basement:
8" high cast-in-place concrete walls 12" thick or 12" concrete block.

Finished Basement:
Includes painted drywall on 2 x 4 wood furring with insulation, suspended ceiling, carpeting on subfloor with sleepers, heating and lighting.

- **Unique residence built from an architect's plan**
- **Single family — 1 full bath, 1 half bath, 1 kitchen**
- **No basement**
- **Cedar shakes on roof**
- **Forced hot air heat/air conditioning**
- **Double drywall interior**
- **Many special features**
- **Extraordinary materials and workmanship**
- **Detail specifications on page 49**

Note: The illustration shown may contain some optional components (for example: garages and/or fireplaces) whose costs are shown in the modifications, adjustments, & alternatives below or at the end of the square foot section.

eHome Planners, Inc.

Base cost per square foot of living area

Exterior Wall	Living Area										
	1000	1200	1400	1600	1800	2000	2400	2800	3200	3600	4000
Wood Siding - Wood Frame	140.85	130.50	122.70	116.75	113.30	109.85	102.35	97.35	93.65	89.55	86.10
Brick Veneer - Wood Frame	144.90	134.10	126.00	119.85	116.25	112.60	104.90	99.75	95.85	91.55	88.05
Solid Brick	154.10	142.45	133.55	126.95	123.10	119.05	110.80	105.15	100.85	96.25	92.45
Solid Stone	154.20	142.55	133.65	127.05	123.20	119.15	110.85	105.20	100.95	96.30	92.50
Finished Basement, Add	37.00	35.25	33.85	32.95	32.45	31.70	30.65	29.85	29.15	28.55	28.05
Unfinished Basement, Add	14.05	13.30	12.65	12.20	11.95	11.65	11.15	10.80	10.45	10.20	9.95

Modifications

Add to the total cost

Upgrade Kitchen Cabinets	$ + 837
Solid Surface Countertops	+ 1326
Full Bath - including plumbing, wall and floor finishes	+ 4948
Half Bath - including plumbing, wall and floor finishes	+ 3089
Two Car Attached Garage	+ 20,256
Two Car Detached Garage	+ 23,042
Fireplace & Chimney	+ 5410

Adjustments

For multi family - add to total cost

Additional Kitchen	$ + 10,706
Additional Full Bath & Half Bath	+ 7988
Additional Entry & Exit	+ 1629
Separate Heating & Air Conditioning	+ 4017
Separate Electric	+ 1363

For Townhouse/Rowhouse -
Multiply cost per square foot by

Inner Unit	.90
End Unit	.95

Alternatives

Add to or deduct from the cost per square foot of living area

Heavyweight Asphalt Shingles	– 1.75
Clay Tile Roof	+ 2.40
Slate Roof	+ 5.70
Upgrade Ceilings to Textured Finish	+ .44
Air Conditioning, in Heating Ductwork	Base System
Heating Systems, Hot Water	+ 1.56
Heat Pump	+ 1.92
Electric Heat	– 1.72
Not Heated	– 3.57

Additional upgrades or components

Kitchen Cabinets & Countertops	Page 58
Bathroom Vanities	59
Fireplaces & Chimneys	59
Windows, Skylights & Dormers	59
Appliances	60
Breezeways & Porches	60
Finished Attic	60
Garages	61
Site Improvements	61
Wings & Ells	57

- **Unique residence built from an architect's plan**
- **Single family — 1 full bath, 1 half bath, 1 kitchen**
- **No basement**
- **Cedar shakes on roof**
- **Forced hot air heat/air conditioning**
- **Double drywall interior**
- **Many special features**
- **Extraordinary materials and workmanship**
- **Detail specifications on page 49**

Note: The illustration shown may contain some optional components (for example: garages and/or fireplaces) whose costs are shown in the modifications, adjustments, & alternatives below or at the end of the square foot section.

©Larry E. Belk Designs

LUXURY

Base cost per square foot of living area

Exterior Wall	Living Area										
	1000	1200	1400	1600	1800	2000	2400	2800	3200	3600	4000
Wood Siding - Wood Frame	132.55	124.65	119.05	110.90	106.90	102.10	93.70	90.40	86.45	83.60	79.55
Brick Veneer - Wood Frame	137.15	129.00	123.20	114.65	110.45	105.50	96.70	93.25	89.10	86.15	81.95
Solid Brick	147.85	138.95	132.70	123.30	118.65	113.25	103.55	99.75	95.10	91.95	87.35
Solid Stone	148.00	139.15	132.85	123.40	118.75	113.35	103.65	99.85	95.20	92.05	87.40
Finished Basement, Add	25.95	24.90	24.20	23.10	22.50	22.00	20.90	20.40	19.80	19.55	19.05
Unfinished Basement, Add	10.05	9.60	9.30	8.80	8.55	8.30	7.75	7.55	7.25	7.15	6.90

Modifications

Add to the total cost

Upgrade Kitchen Cabinets	$ + 837
Solid Surface Countertops	+ 1326
Full Bath - including plumbing, wall and floor finishes	+ 4948
Half Bath - including plumbing, wall and floor finishes	+ 3089
Two Car Attached Garage	+ 20,256
Two Car Detached Garage	+ 23,042
Fireplace & Chimney	+ 5410

Adjustments

For multi family - add to total cost

Additional Kitchen	$ + 10,706
Additional Full Bath & Half Bath	+ 7988
Additional Entry & Exit	+ 1629
Separate Heating & Air Conditioning	+ 4017
Separate Electric	+ 1363

For Townhouse/Rowhouse -
Multiply cost per square foot by

Inner Unit	.90
End Unit	.95

Alternatives

Add to or deduct from the cost per square foot of living area

Heavyweight Asphalt Shingles	– 1.30
Clay Tile Roof	+ 1.75
Slate Roof	+ 4.15
Upgrade Ceilings to Textured Finish	+ .44
Air Conditioning, in Heating Ductwork	Base System
Heating Systems, Hot Water	+ 1.49
Heat Pump	+ 2.13
Electric Heat	– 1.72
Not Heated	– 3.29

Additional upgrades or components

Kitchen Cabinets & Countertops	Page 58
Bathroom Vanities	59
Fireplaces & Chimneys	59
Windows, Skylights & Dormers	59
Appliances	60
Breezeways & Porches	60
Finished Attic	60
Garages	61
Site Improvements	61
Wings & Ells	57

LUXURY

- **Unique residence built from an architect's plan**
- **Single family — 1 full bath, 1 half bath, 1 kitchen**
- **No basement**
- **Cedar shakes on roof**
- **Forced hot air heat/air conditioning**
- **Double drywall interior**
- **Many special features**
- **Extraordinary materials and workmanship**
- **Detail specifications on page 49**

Note: The illustration shown may contain some optional components (for example: garages and/or fireplaces) whose costs are shown in the modifications, adjustments, & alternatives below or at the end of the square foot section.

Base cost per square foot of living area

Exterior Wall	Living Area										
	1200	1400	1600	1800	2000	2400	2800	3200	3600	4000	4400
Wood Siding - Wood Frame	125.60	119.15	114.60	109.40	105.05	97.65	92.05	87.70	85.00	82.55	80.15
Brick Veneer - Wood Frame	130.55	123.80	119.05	113.55	109.05	101.25	95.35	90.80	87.95	85.35	82.85
Solid Brick	141.95	134.45	129.20	123.15	118.25	109.60	102.90	97.85	94.80	91.80	89.05
Solid Stone	142.15	134.60	129.35	123.25	118.40	109.70	103.05	97.95	94.90	91.85	89.15
Finished Basement, Add	20.90	20.05	19.50	18.90	18.55	17.65	17.00	16.50	16.25	15.85	15.70
Unfinished Basement, Add	8.10	7.75	7.50	7.20	7.05	6.65	6.35	6.10	6.00	5.80	5.75

Modifications

Add to the total cost

Upgrade Kitchen Cabinets	$ + 837
Solid Surface Countertops	+ 1326
Full Bath - including plumbing, wall and floor finishes	+ 4948
Half Bath - including plumbing, wall and floor finishes	+ 3089
Two Car Attached Garage	+ 20,256
Two Car Detached Garage	+ 23,042
Fireplace & Chimney	+ 5925

Adjustments

For multi family - add to total cost

Additional Kitchen	$ + 10,706
Additional Full Bath & Half Bath	+ 7988
Additional Entry & Exit	+ 1629
Separate Heating & Air Conditioning	+ 4017
Separate Electric	+ 1363

For Townhouse/Rowhouse -
Multiply cost per square foot by

Inner Unit	.86
End Unit	.93

Alternatives

Add to or deduct from the cost per square foot of living area

Heavyweight Asphalt Shingles	– .90
Clay Tile Roof	+ 1.20
Slate Roof	+ 2.85
Upgrade Ceilings to Textured Finish	+ .44
Air Conditioning, in Heating Ductwork	Base System
Heating Systems, Hot Water	+ 1.45
Heat Pump	+ 2.25
Electric Heat	– 1.54
Not Heated	– 3.11

Additional upgrades or components

Kitchen Cabinets & Countertops	Page 58
Bathroom Vanities	59
Fireplaces & Chimneys	59
Windows, Skylights & Dormers	59
Appliances	60
Breezeways & Porches	60
Finished Attic	60
Garages	61
Site Improvements	61
Wings & Ells	57

- **Unique residence built from an architect's plan**
- **Single family — 1 full bath, 1 half bath, 1 kitchen**
- **No basement**
- **Cedar shakes on roof**
- **Forced hot air heat/air conditioning**
- **Double drywall interior**
- **Many special features**
- **Extraordinary materials and workmanship**
- **Detail specifications on page 49**

Note: The illustration shown may contain some optional components (for example: garages and/or fireplaces) whose costs are shown in the modifications, adjustments, & alternatives below or at the end of the square foot section.

©Larry W. Garnett & Associates, Inc

Base cost per square foot of living area

Exterior Wall	Living Area										
	1500	1800	2100	2500	3000	3500	4000	4500	5000	5500	6000
Wood Siding - Wood Frame	126.70	113.25	106.60	101.05	94.35	88.70	83.35	81.05	78.45	75.90	73.70
Brick Veneer - Wood Frame	131.85	117.95	110.85	105.05	98.00	92.00	86.40	83.95	81.25	78.50	76.20
Solid Brick	143.75	128.90	120.60	114.25	106.35	99.65	93.45	90.65	87.60	84.60	82.00
Solid Stone	143.85	129.05	120.70	114.40	106.45	99.75	93.55	90.75	87.70	84.65	82.10
Finished Basement, Add	16.60	15.80	14.95	14.45	13.80	13.25	12.80	12.55	12.30	12.05	11.90
Unfinished Basement, Add	6.50	6.15	5.75	5.50	5.20	4.95	4.75	4.65	4.55	4.40	4.35

Modifications

Add to the total cost

Upgrade Kitchen Cabinets	$ + 837
Solid Surface Countertops	+ 1326
Full Bath - including plumbing, wall and floor finishes	+ 4948
Half Bath - including plumbing, wall and floor finishes	+ 3089
Two Car Attached Garage	+ 20,256
Two Car Detached Garage	+ 23,042
Fireplace & Chimney	+ 5925

Adjustments

For multi family - add to total cost

Additional Kitchen	$ + 10,706
Additional Full Bath & Half Bath	+ 7988
Additional Entry & Exit	+ 1629
Separate Heating & Air Conditioning	+ 4017
Separate Electric	+ 1363

For Townhouse/Rowhouse -
Multiply cost per square foot by

Inner Unit	.86
End Unit	.93

Alternatives

Add to or deduct from the cost per square foot of living area

Heavyweight Asphalt Shingles	– .75
Clay Tile Roof	+ 1.05
Slate Roof	+ 2.50
Upgrade Ceilings to Textured Finish	+ .44
Air Conditioning, in Heating Ductwork	Base System
Heating Systems, Hot Water	+ 1.31
Heat Pump	+ 2.32
Electric Heat	– 3.05
Not Heated	– 3.11

Additional upgrades or components

Kitchen Cabinets & Countertops	Page 58
Bathroom Vanities	59
Fireplaces & Chimneys	59
Windows, Skylights & Dormers	59
Appliances	60
Breezeways & Porches	60
Finished Attic	60
Garages	61
Site Improvements	61
Wings & Ells	57

Important: See the Reference Section for Location Factors (to adjust for your city) and Estimating Forms

- Unique residence built from an architect's plan
- Single family — 1 full bath, 1 half bath, 1 kitchen
- No basement
- Cedar shakes on roof
- Forced hot air heat/air conditioning
- Double drywall interior
- Many special features
- Extraordinary materials and workmanship
- Detail specifications on page 49

Note: The illustration shown may contain some optional components (for example: garages and/or fireplaces) whose costs are shown in the modifications, adjustments, & alternatives below or at the end of the square foot section.

Base cost per square foot of living area

	Living Area										
Exterior Wall	1500	1800	2100	2500	3000	3500	4000	4500	5000	5500	6000
Wood Siding - Wood Frame	126.35	113.00	107.85	103.60	95.65	92.35	87.05	81.75	80.30	77.95	76.00
Brick Veneer - Wood Frame	131.70	117.95	112.45	108.05	99.65	96.10	90.50	84.95	83.35	80.95	78.80
Solid Brick	144.05	129.35	123.10	118.20	108.90	104.85	98.45	92.30	90.45	87.75	85.25
Solid Stone	144.20	129.55	123.25	118.35	109.00	104.95	98.55	92.40	90.55	87.85	85.30
Finished Basement, Add	14.60	13.90	13.35	12.95	12.35	11.95	11.50	11.10	10.95	10.80	10.55
Unfinished Basement, Add	5.70	5.40	5.15	5.00	4.70	4.55	4.30	4.15	4.10	4.00	3.90

Modifications

Add to the total cost

Upgrade Kitchen Cabinets	$ + 837
Solid Surface Countertops	+ 1326
Full Bath - including plumbing, wall and floor finishes	+ 4948
Half Bath - including plumbing, wall and floor finishes	+ 3089
Two Car Attached Garage	+ 20,256
Two Car Detached Garage	+ 23,042
Fireplace & Chimney	+ 6485

Adjustments

For multi family - add to total cost

Additional Kitchen	$ + 10,706
Additional Full Bath & Half Bath	+ 7988
Additional Entry & Exit	+ 1629
Separate Heating & Air Conditioning	+ 4017
Separate Electric	+ 1363

For Townhouse/Rowhouse -
Multiply cost per square foot by

Inner Unit	.84
End Unit	.92

Alternatives

Add to or deduct from the cost per square foot of living area

Heavyweight Asphalt Shingles	– .60
Clay Tile Roof	+ .80
Slate Roof	+ 1.90
Upgrade Ceilings to Textured Finish	+ .44
Air Conditioning, in Heating Ductwork	Base System
Heating Systems, Hot Water	+ 1.31
Heat Pump	+ 2.32
Electric Heat	– 3.05
Not Heated	– 3.01

Additional upgrades or components

Important: See the Reference Section for Location Factors (to adjust for your city) and Estimating Forms

- **Unique residence built from an architect's plan**
- **Single family — 1 full bath, 1 half bath, 1 kitchen**
- **No basement**
- **Cedar shakes on roof**
- **Forced hot air heat/air conditioning**
- **Double drywall interior**
- **Many special features**
- **Extraordinary materials and workmanship**
- **Detail specifications on page 49**

Note: The illustration shown may contain some optional components (for example: garages and/or fireplaces) whose costs are shown in the modifications, adjustments, & alternatives below or at the end of the square foot section.

LUXURY

Base cost per square foot of living area

Exterior Wall	Living Area										
	1200	1400	1600	1800	2000	2400	2800	3200	3600	4000	4400
Wood Siding - Wood Frame	117.40	111.50	107.25	102.45	98.40	91.60	86.55	82.55	80.05	77.90	75.65
Brick Veneer - Wood Frame	121.10	114.95	110.55	105.60	101.40	94.30	89.05	84.85	82.25	80.00	77.70
Solid Brick	129.65	122.95	118.25	112.80	108.30	100.55	94.70	90.15	87.35	84.85	82.35
Solid Stone	129.75	123.05	118.30	112.85	108.40	100.65	94.80	90.25	87.45	84.90	82.40
Finished Basement, Add	20.90	20.05	19.50	18.90	18.55	17.65	17.00	16.50	16.25	15.85	15.70
Unfinished Basement, Add	8.10	7.75	7.50	7.20	7.05	6.65	6.35	6.10	6.00	5.80	5.75

Modifications

Add to the total cost

Upgrade Kitchen Cabinets	$ + 837
Solid Surface Countertops	+ 1326
Full Bath - including plumbing, wall and floor finishes	+ 4948
Half Bath - including plumbing, wall and floor finishes	+ 3089
Two Car Attached Garage	+ 20,256
Two Car Detached Garage	+ 23,042
Fireplace & Chimney	+ 5410

Adjustments

For multi family - add to total cost

Additional Kitchen	$ + 10,706
Additional Full Bath & Half Bath	+ 7988
Additional Entry & Exit	+ 1629
Separate Heating & Air Conditioning	+ 4017
Separate Electric	+ 1363

For Townhouse/Rowhouse - Multiply cost per square foot by

Inner Unit	.89
End Unit	.94

Alternatives

Add to or deduct from the cost per square foot of living area

Heavyweight Asphalt Shingles	– .90
Clay Tile Roof	+ 1.20
Slate Roof	+ 2.85
Upgrade Ceilings to Textured Finish	+ .44
Air Conditioning, in Heating Ductwork	Base System
Heating Systems, Hot Water	+ 1.45
Heat Pump	+ 2.25
Electric Heat	– 1.54
Not Heated	– 3.11

Additional upgrades or components

Kitchen Cabinets & Countertops	Page 58
Bathroom Vanities	59
Fireplaces & Chimneys	59
Windows, Skylights & Dormers	59
Appliances	60
Breezeways & Porches	60
Finished Attic	60
Garages	61
Site Improvements	61
Wings & Ells	57

Important: See the Reference Section for Location Factors (to adjust for your city) and Estimating Forms

LUXURY

- **Unique residence built from an architect's plan**
- **Single family — 1 full bath, 1 half bath, 1 kitchen**
- **No basement**
- **Cedar shakes on roof**
- **Forced hot air heat/air conditioning**
- **Double drywall interior**
- **Many special features**
- **Extraordinary materials and workmanship**
- **Detail specifications on page 49**

Note: The illustration shown may contain some optional components (for example: garages and/or fireplaces) whose costs are shown in the modifications, adjustments, & alternatives below or at the end of the square foot section.

Base cost per square foot of living area

Exterior Wall	Living Area										
	1500	1800	2100	2400	2800	3200	3600	4000	4500	5000	5500
Wood Siding - Wood Frame	110.60	102.50	96.50	91.70	88.35	84.25	80.10	78.55	74.15	71.95	69.45
Brick Veneer - Wood Frame	113.95	105.55	99.20	94.25	90.80	86.55	82.20	80.60	76.05	73.70	71.15
Solid Brick	121.65	112.45	105.50	100.20	96.50	91.85	87.10	85.35	80.45	77.85	75.05
Solid Stone	121.75	112.55	105.60	100.30	96.60	91.85	87.20	85.40	80.50	77.95	75.05
Finished Basement, Add*	24.70	23.55	22.60	22.00	21.60	21.00	20.45	20.20	19.65	19.35	19.00
Unfinished Basement, Add*	9.35	8.85	8.40	8.15	7.95	7.65	7.45	7.30	7.05	6.95	6.75

*Basement under middle level only.

Modifications

Add to the total cost

Upgrade Kitchen Cabinets	$ + 837
Solid Surface Countertops	+ 1326
Full Bath - including plumbing, wall and floor finishes	+ 4948
Half Bath - including plumbing, wall and floor finishes	+ 3089
Two Car Attached Garage	+ 20,256
Two Car Detached Garage	+ 23,042
Fireplace & Chimney	+ 5925

Adjustments

For multi family - add to total cost

Additional Kitchen	$ + 10,706
Additional Full Bath & Half Bath	+ 7988
Additional Entry & Exit	+ 1629
Separate Heating & Air Conditioning	+ 4017
Separate Electric	+ 1363

For Townhouse/Rowhouse -
Multiply cost per square foot by

Inner Unit	.86
End Unit	.93

Alternatives

Add to or deduct from the cost per square foot of living area

Heavyweight Asphalt Shingles	– 1.30
Clay Tile Roof	+ 1.75
Slate Roof	+ 4.15
Upgrade Ceilings to Textured Finish	+ .44
Air Conditioning, in Heating Ductwork	Base System
Heating Systems, Hot Water	+ 1.40
Heat Pump	+ 2.34
Electric Heat	– 1.37
Not Heated	– 3.01

Additional upgrades or components

Kitchen Cabinets & Countertops	Page 58
Bathroom Vanities	59
Fireplaces & Chimneys	59
Windows, Skylights & Dormers	59
Appliances	60
Breezeways & Porches	60
Finished Attic	60
Garages	61
Site Improvements	61
Wings & Ells	57

LUXURY

1 Story — Base cost per square foot of living area

Exterior Wall	Living Area							
	50	100	200	300	400	500	600	700
Wood Siding - Wood Frame	184.15	140.65	121.70	101.45	95.20	91.50	89.05	89.90
Brick Veneer - Wood Frame	196.65	149.55	129.15	106.35	99.70	95.65	93.05	93.75
Solid Brick	225.40	170.10	146.25	117.80	109.95	105.25	102.10	102.50
Solid Stone	225.75	170.35	146.50	117.95	110.10	105.35	102.25	102.65
Finished Basement, Add	64.90	52.30	47.05	38.30	36.55	35.50	34.80	34.30
Unfinished Basement, Add	27.55	21.55	19.05	14.90	14.05	13.55	13.20	13.00

1-1/2 Story — Base cost per square foot of living area

Exterior Wall	Living Area							
	100	200	300	400	500	600	700	800
Wood Siding - Wood Frame	150.00	121.15	103.60	92.80	87.45	85.00	81.70	80.75
Brick Veneer - Wood Frame	161.15	130.10	111.05	98.60	92.80	90.05	86.50	85.50
Solid Brick	186.80	150.65	128.15	111.95	105.10	101.70	97.50	96.35
Solid Stone	187.10	150.90	128.40	112.15	105.30	101.85	97.60	96.55
Finished Basement, Add	42.90	37.65	34.15	30.30	29.25	28.55	27.90	27.80
Unfinished Basement, Add	17.75	15.25	13.60	11.75	11.25	10.90	10.60	10.55

2 Story — Base cost per square foot of living area

Exterior Wall	Living Area							
	100	200	400	600	800	1000	1200	1400
Wood Siding - Wood Frame	150.90	112.35	95.50	78.65	73.10	69.80	67.70	68.75
Brick Veneer - Wood Frame	163.40	121.30	102.95	83.60	77.60	74.00	71.65	72.55
Solid Brick	192.10	141.85	120.00	95.05	87.85	83.60	80.75	81.35
Solid Stone	192.50	142.10	120.30	95.20	88.00	83.70	80.85	81.45
Finished Basement, Add	32.50	26.15	23.55	19.20	18.30	17.80	17.45	17.20
Unfinished Basement, Add	13.80	10.80	9.55	7.45	7.05	6.80	6.60	6.50

Base costs do not include bathroom or kitchen facilities. Use Modifications/Adjustments/Alternatives on pages 58-61 where appropriate.

Important: See the Reference Section for Location Factors (to adjust for your city) and Estimating Forms.

ADJUSTMENTS

Kitchen cabinets - Base units, hardwood *(Cost per Unit)*

	Economy	Average	Custom	Luxury
24″ deep, 35″ high,				
One top drawer,				
One door below				
12″ wide	$121	$161	$215	$280
15″ wide	161	215	285	375
18″ wide	171	228	305	400
21″ wide	179	239	320	420
24″ wide	200	267	355	465
Four drawers				
12″ wide	266	355	470	620
15″ wide	270	360	480	630
18″ wide	285	380	505	665
24″ wide	308	410	545	720
Two top drawers,				
Two doors below				
27″ wide	236	315	420	550
30″ wide	248	330	440	580
33″ wide	259	345	460	605
36″ wide	270	360	480	630
42″ wide	285	380	505	665
48″ wide	300	400	530	700
Range or sink base				
(Cost per unit)				
Two doors below				
30″ wide	200	267	355	465
33″ wide	215	286	380	500
36″ wide	224	299	400	525
42″ wide	240	320	425	560
48″ wide	251	335	445	585
Corner Base Cabinet				
(Cost per unit)				
36″ wide	182	242	320	425
Lazy Susan *(Cost per unit)*				
With revolving door	285	380	505	665

Kitchen cabinets - Wall cabinets, hardwood *(Cost per Unit)*

	Economy	Average	Custom	Luxury
12″ deep, 2 doors				
12″ high				
30″ wide	$117	$156	$205	$ 275
36″ wide	134	179	240	315
15″ high				
30″ wide	134	179	240	315
33″ wide	143	191	255	335
36″ wide	146	195	260	340
24″ high				
30″ wide	153	204	270	355
36″ wide	167	223	295	390
42″ wide	183	244	325	425
30″ high, 1 door				
12″ wide	107	142	190	250
15″ wide	122	162	215	285
18″ wide	134	178	235	310
24″ wide	145	193	255	340
30″ high, 2 doors				
27″ wide	161	214	285	375
30″ wide	172	229	305	400
36″ wide	194	259	345	455
42″ wide	211	281	375	490
48″ wide	236	315	420	550
Corner wall, 30″ high				
24″ wide	131	175	235	305
30″ wide	159	212	280	370
36″ wide	171	228	305	400
Broom Closet				
84″ high, 24″ deep				
18″ wide	330	440	585	770
Oven Cabinet				
84″ high, 24″ deep				
27″ wide	491	655	870	1145

Kitchen countertops *(Cost per L.F.)*

	Economy	Average	Custom	Luxury
Solid Surface				
24″ wide, no backsplash	82	109	145	190
with backsplash	89	118	155	205
Stock plastic laminate, 24″ wide				
with backsplash	11	15	20	25
Custom plastic laminate, no splash				
7/8″ thick, alum. molding	20	27	35	45
1-1/4″ thick, no splash	23	31	40	55
Marble				
1/2″ - 3/4″ thick w/splash	37	50	65	85
Maple, laminated				
1-1/2″ thick w/splash	36	49	65	85
Stainless steel				
(per S.F.)	69	92	120	160
Cutting blocks, recessed				
16″ x 20″ x 1″ (each)	60	81	105	140

Vanity bases *(Cost per Unit)*

2 door, 30" high, 21" deep	Economy	Average	Custom	Luxury
24" wide	123	164	220	285
30" wide	134	178	235	310
36" wide	152	202	270	355
48" wide	188	251	335	440

Solid surface vanity tops *(Cost Each)*

Center bowl	Economy	Average	Custom	Luxury
22" x 25"	$292	$394	$552	$596
22" x 31"	340	459	643	694
22" x 37"	390	527	738	797
22" x 49"	445	601	841	908

Fireplaces & chimneys *(Cost per Unit)*

	1-1/2 Story	2 Story	3 Story
Economy (prefab metal)			
Exterior chimney & 1 fireplace	$3565	$3935	$4310
Interior chimney & 1 fireplace	3410	3795	3975
Average (masonry)			
Exterior chimney & 1 fireplace	3640	4060	4615
Interior chimney & 1 fireplace	3410	3825	4165
For more than 1 flue, add	270	445	745
For more than 1 fireplace, add	2580	2580	2580
Custom (masonry)			
Exterior chimney & 1 fireplace	3830	4320	4885
Interior chimney & 1 fireplace	3595	4065	4380
For more than 1 flue, add	300	515	705
For more than 1 fireplace, add	2750	2750	2750
Luxury (masonry)			
Exterior chimney & 1 fireplace	5410	5925	6485
Interior chimney & 1 fireplace	5165	5650	5970
For more than 1 flue, add	445	745	1045
For more than 1 fireplace, add	4260	4260	4260

Windows & skylights *(Cost Each)*

	Economy	Average	Custom	Luxury
Fixed Picture Windows				
3'-6" x 4'-0"	$ 252	$ 315	$ 340	$ 506
4'-0" x 6'-0"	348	435	470	700
5'-0" x 6'-0"	385	482	520	900
6'-0" x 6'-0"	434	542	585	920
Bay/Bow Windows				
8'-0" x 5'-0"	1025	1275	1300	1350
10'-0" x 5'-0"	1375	1450	1475	1850
10'-0" x 6'-0"	1608	1696	1725	1950
12'-0" x 6'-0"	2167	2286	2325	2400
Palladian Windows				
3'-2" x 6'-4"		1328	1475	1718
4'-0" x 6'-0"		1373	1525	1777
5'-5" x 6'-10"		1733	1925	2243
8'-0" x 6'-0"		2115	2350	2738
Skylights				
46" x 21-1/2"	336	373	501	726
46" x 28"	440	489	624	905
57" x 44"	550	611	761	1103

Dormers *(Cost/S.F. of plan area)*

	Economy	Average	Custom	Luxury
Framing and Roofing Only				
Gable dormer, 2" x 6" roof frame	$18	$21	$24	$38
2" x 8" roof frame	19	22	25	40
Shed dormer, 2" x 6" roof frame	12	13	15	24
2" x 8" roof frame	13	14	16	26
2" x 10" roof frame	14	15	17	27

ADJUSTMENTS

ADJUSTMENTS

Appliances (Cost per Unit)

	Economy	Average	Custom	Luxury
Range				
30" free standing, 1 oven	$ 315	$ 870	$1148	$1425
2 oven	1475	1538	1569	1600
30" built-in, 1 oven	395	923	1186	1450
2 oven	1175	1563	1756	1950
21" free standing				
1 oven	350	483	549	615
Counter Top Ranges				
4 burner standard	258	417	496	575
As above with griddle	480	580	630	680
Microwave Oven	169	372	474	575
Combination Range, Refrigerator, Sink				
30" wide	960	1443	1684	1925
60" wide	2825	3249	3461	3673
72" wide	3200	3680	3920	4160
Comb. Range, Refrig., Sink, Microwave Oven & Ice Maker	4959	5703	6075	6447
Compactor				
4 to 1 compaction	440	478	496	515
Deep Freeze				
15 to 23 C.F.	495	580	623	665
30 C.F.	895	1010	1068	1125
Dehumidifier, portable, auto.				
15 pint	214	246	262	278
30 pint	249	287	305	324
Washing Machine, automatic	445	835	1030	1225
Water Heater				
Electric, glass lined				
30 gal.	320	393	429	465
80 gal.	650	838	931	1025
Water Heater, Gas, glass lined				
30 gal.	450	553	604	655
50 gal.	715	883	966	1050
Water Softener, automatic				
30 grains/gal.	580	667	711	754
100 grains/gal.	755	869	925	982
Dishwasher, built-in				
2 cycles	365	425	455	485
4 or more cycles	360	543	634	725
Dryer, automatic	440	648	751	855
Garage Door Opener	266	316	340	365
Garbage Disposal	79	157	195	234
Heater, Electric, built-in				
1250 watt ceiling type	150	186	204	222
1250 watt wall type	181	211	226	241
Wall type w/blower				
1500 watt	206	228	239	250
3000 watt	370	415	438	460
Hood For Range, 2 speed				
30" wide	110	360	485	610
42" wide	256	493	612	730
Humidifier, portable				
7 gal. per day	107	123	131	139
15 gal. per day	173	199	212	225
Ice Maker, automatic				
13 lb. per day	630	725	772	819
51 lb. per day	1025	1179	1256	1333
Refrigerator, no frost				
10-12 C.F.	505	655	730	805
14-16 C.F.	565	615	640	665
18-20 C.F.	595	740	813	885
21-29 C.F.	835	1955	2515	3075
Sump Pump, 1/3 H.P.	195	270	308	345

Breezeway (Cost per S.F.)

Class	Type	Area (S.F.)			
		50	100	150	200
Economy	Open	$ 16.20	$13.80	$11.55	$11.30
	Enclosed	77.70	60.05	49.85	43.65
Average	Open	20.60	18.10	15.80	14.40
	Enclosed	87.35	65.00	53.20	46.85
Custom	Open	29.65	26.05	22.70	20.80
	Enclosed	121.75	90.55	74.05	65.05
Luxury	Open	30.80	27.00	24.40	23.60
	Enclosed	124.15	92.05	74.45	66.70

Porches (Cost per S.F.)

Class	Type	Area (S.F.)				
		25	50	100	200	300
Economy	Open	$ 46.45	$ 31.10	$24.25	$20.60	$17.55
	Enclosed	92.85	64.70	48.95	38.15	32.70
Average	Open	57.80	36.85	28.25	23.50	23.50
	Enclosed	114.20	77.35	58.55	45.35	38.40
Custom	Open	75.65	50.20	37.85	33.00	29.60
	Enclosed	150.45	102.80	78.25	60.85	52.50
Luxury	Open	81.60	53.35	39.40	35.40	31.50
	Enclosed	159.75	112.20	83.30	64.65	55.70

Finished attic (Cost per S.F.)

Class	Area (S.F.)				
	400	500	600	800	1000
Economy	$12.45	$12.00	$11.45	$11.25	$10.95
Average	19.60	19.05	18.70	18.40	17.90
Custom	24.15	23.55	23.10	22.70	22.25
Luxury	30.60	29.95	29.20	28.55	28.05

Alarm system (Cost per System)

	Burglar Alarm	Smoke Detector
Economy	$ 350	$ 52
Average	400	64
Custom	676	131
Luxury	1025	162

Sauna, prefabricated
(Cost per unit, including heater and controls—7' high)

Size	Cost
6' x 4'	$3875
6' x 5'	3900
6' x 6'	4600
6' x 9'	5050
8' x 10'	6575
8' x 12'	8775
10' x 12'	8675

Garages *

(Costs include exterior wall systems comparable with the quality of the residence. Included in the cost is an allowance for one personnel door, manual overhead door(s) and electrical fixture.)

Class	Type									
	Detached			Attached			Built-in		Basement	
	One Car	Two Car	Three Car	One Car	Two Car	Three Car	One Car	Two Car	One Car	Two Car
Economy										
Wood	$10,137	$15,418	$20,700	$ 7859	$13,548	$18,829	$-1426	$-2852	$1093	$1375
Masonry	14,021	20,278	26,536	10,289	16,955	23,212	-1903	-3806		
Average										
Wood	11,015	16,516	22,018	8408	14,318	19,820	-1534	-3067	1242	1674
Masonry	14,149	20,439	26,729	10,369	17,067	23,357	-1919	-3345		
Custom										
Wood	12,720	19,265	25,811	9857	16,927	23,472	-3732	-4184	1742	2673
Masonry	15,582	22,847	30,113	11,648	19,438	26,703	-4084	-4887		
Luxury										
Wood	15,055	23,042	31,028	11,745	20,256	28,243	-3879	-4478	2441	3714
Masonry	18,600	27,478	36,356	13,963	23,365	32,243	-4314	-5349		

*See the Introduction to this section for definitions of garage types.

Swimming pools (Cost per S.F.)

Residential (includes equipment)	
In-ground	$ 18 - 45
Deck equipment	1.30
Paint pool, preparation & 3 coats (epoxy)	2.69
Rubber base paint	2.50
Pool Cover	.70
Swimming Pool Heaters *(Cost per unit)*	
(not including wiring, external piping, base or pad)	
Gas	
155 MBH	$ 2525
190 MBH	3400
500 MBH	8250
Electric	
15 KW 7200 gallon pool	1975
24 KW 9600 gallon pool	2600
54 KW 24,000 gallon pool	3900

Wood and coal stoves

Wood Only	
Free Standing (minimum)	$ 1225
Fireplace Insert (minimum)	1235
Coal Only	
Free Standing	$ 1395
Fireplace Insert	1528
Wood and Coal	
Free Standing	$ 2870
Fireplace Insert	2940

Sidewalks (Cost per S.F.)

Concrete, 3000 psi with wire mesh	4" thick	$ 2.42
	5" thick	2.93
	6" thick	3.29
Precast concrete patio blocks (natural)	2" thick	7.40
Precast concrete patio blocks (colors)	2" thick	7.75
Flagstone, bluestone	1" thick	10.50
Flagstone, bluestone	1-1/2" thick	13.85
Slate (natural, irregular)	3/4" thick	10.08
Slate (random rectangular)	1/2" thick	14.82
Seeding		
Fine grading & seeding includes lime, fertilizer & seed	per S.Y.	1.68
Lawn Sprinkler System	per S.F.	.67

Fencing (Cost per L.F.)

Chain Link, 4' high, galvanized	$ 10.30
Gate, 4' high (each)	113.00
Cedar Picket, 3' high, 2 rail	9.00
Gate (each)	114.00
3 Rail, 4' high	10.05
Gate (each)	123.00
Cedar Stockade, 3 Rail, 6' high	10.25
Gate (each)	122.00
Board & Battens, 2 sides 6' high, pine	14.80
6' high, cedar	21.00
No. 1 Cedar, basketweave, 6' high	11.75
Gate, 6' high (each)	136.00

Carport (Cost per S.F.)

Economy	$ 5.85
Average	9.08
Custom	13.69
Luxury	15.66

Insurance Exclusions

Insurance exclusions are a matter of policy coverage and are not standard or universal. When making an appraisal for insurance purposes, it is recommended that some time be taken in studying the insurance policy to determine the specific items to be excluded. Most homeowners insurance policies have, as part of their provisions, statements that read "the policy permits the insured to exclude from value, in determining whether the amount of the insurance equals or exceeds 80% of its replacement cost, such items as building excavation, basement footings, underground piping and wiring, piers and other supports which are below the undersurface of the lowest floor or where there is no basement below the ground." Loss to any of these items, however, is covered.

Costs for Excavation, Spread and Strip Footings and Underground Piping

This chart shows excluded items expressed as a percentage of total building cost.

Class	Number of Stories			
	1	1-1/2	2	3
Luxury	3.4%	2.7%	2.4%	1.9%
Custom	3.5%	2.7%	2.4%	1.9%
Average	5.0%	4.3%	3.8%	3.3%
Economy	5.0%	4.4%	4.1%	3.5%

Architect/Designer Fees

Architect/designer fees as presented in the following chart are typical ranges for 4 classes of residences. Factors affecting these ranges include economic conditions, size and scope of project, site selection, and standardization. Where superior quality and detail is required or where closer supervision is required, fees may run higher than listed. Lower quality or simplicity may dictate lower fees.

The editors have included architect/designers fees from the "mean" column in calculating costs.

Listed below are average costs expressed as a range and mean of total building cost for 4 classes of residences.

Class			Range	Mean
Luxury	—	Architecturally designed and supervised	5%–15%	10%
Custom	—	Architecturally modified designer plans	$2000–$3500	$2500
Average	—	Designer plans	$800–$1500	$1100
Economy	—	Stock plans	$100–$500	$300

Depreciation as generally defined is "the loss of value due to any cause." Specifically, depreciation can be broken down into three categories: **Physical Depreciation, Functional Obsolescence,** and **Economic Obsolescence.**

Physical Depreciation is the loss of value from the wearing out of the building's components. Such causes may be decay, dry rot, cracks, or structural defects.

Functional Obsolescence is the loss of value from features which render the residence less useful or desirable. Such features may be higher than normal ceilings, design and/or style changes, or outdated mechanical systems.

Economic Obsolescence is the loss of value from external features which render the residence less useful or desirable. These features may be changes in neighborhood socio-economic grouping, zoning changes, legislation, etc.

Depreciation as it applies to the residential portion of this manual deals with the observed physical condition of the residence being appraised. It is in essence *"the cost to cure."*

The ultimate method to arrive at *"the cost to cure"* is to analyze each component of the residence.

For example:

Component, Roof Covering − Cost = $2400
Average Life = 15 years
Actual Life = 5 years
Depreciation = 5 ÷ 15 = .33 or 33%

$2400 × 33% = $792 = Amount of Depreciation

The following table, however, can be used as a guide in estimating the % depreciation using the actual age and general condition of the residence.

Depreciation Table — Residential

Age in Years	Good	Average	Poor
2	2%	3%	10%
5	4	6	20
10	7	10	25
15	10	15	30
20	15	20	35
25	18	25	40
30	24	30	45
35	28	35	50
40	32	40	55
45	36	45	60
50	40	50	65

ADJUSTMENTS

Commercial/Industrial/Institutional Section

Table of Contents

Introduction to the Commercial/
Industrial/Institutional Section

General

The Commercial/Industrial/Institutional section of this manual contains base building costs per square foot of floor area for 70 model buildings. Each model has a table of square foot costs for combinations of exterior wall and framing systems. This table is supplemented by a list of common additives and their unit costs. A breakdown of the component costs used to develop the base cost for the model is on the opposite page. The total cost derived from the base cost and additives must be modified using the appropriate location factor from the Reference Section.

This section may be used directly to estimate the construction cost of most types of buildings knowing only the floor area, exterior wall construction and framing systems. To adjust the base cost for components which are different than the model, use the tables from the Assemblies Section.

Building Identification & Model Selection

The building models in this section represent structures by use. Occupancy, however, does not necessarily identify the building, i.e., a restaurant could be a converted warehouse. In all instances, the building should be described and identified by its own physical characteristics. The model selection should also be guided by comparing specifications with the model. In the case of converted use, data from one model may be used to supplement data from another.

Adjustments

The base cost tables represent the base cost per square foot of floor area for buildings without a basement and without unusual special features. Basement costs and other common additives are listed below the base cost table. Cost adjustments can also be made to the model by using the tables from the Assemblies Section. This table is for example only.

Dimensions

All base cost tables are developed so that measurement can be readily made during the inspection process. Areas are calculated from exterior dimensions and story heights are measured from the top surface of one floor to the top surface of the floor above. Roof areas are measured by horizontal area covered and costs related to inclines are converted with appropriate factors. The precision of measurement is a matter of the user's choice and discretion. For ease in calculation, consideration should be given to measuring in tenths of a foot, i.e., 9 ft. 6 in. = 9.5 ft., 9 ft. 4 in. = 9.3 ft.

Floor Area

The expression "Floor Area" as used in this section includes the sum of floor plate at grade level and above. This dimension is measured from the outside face of the foundation wall. Basement costs are calculated separately. The user must exercise his own judgment, where the lowest level floor is slightly below grade, whether to consider it at grade level or make the basement adjustment.

How to Use the Commercial/ Industrial/Institutional Section

The following is a detailed explanation of a sample entry in the Commercial/Industrial/Institutional Square Foot Cost Section. Each bold number below corresponds to the item being described on the following page with the appropriate component or cost of the sample entry following in parenthesis.

Prices listed are costs that include overhead and profit of the installing contractor and additional mark-ups for General Conditions and Architects' Fees.

COMMERCIAL/INDUSTRIAL/ INSTITUTIONAL   **M.010**   **Apartment, 1-3 Story**   **1**   **2**

Costs per square foot of floor area

Exterior Wall	S.F. Area	8000	12000	15000	19000	22500		29000	32000	36000
	L.F. Perimeter	213	280	330	350	400		442	480	520
Face Brick with Concrete Block Back-up	Wood Joists	128.40	115.40	110.15	103.05	100.45	98.95	95.4	94.40	93.00
	Steel Joists	127.40	115.15	110.20	103.85	101.45	1	96.9	96.00	94.75
Stucco on Concrete Block	Wood Joists	113.50	101.90	97.25	91.60	89.30	88.00	5.3	84.45	83.30
	Steel Joists	120.15	108.45	103.80	98.05	95.75		91.7	90.85	89.65
Wood Siding	Wood Frame	112.15	100.70	96.10	90.70	88.45		.5	83.70	82.55
Brick Veneer	Wood Frame	119.40	107.05	102.05	95.65	93.20	91.8	88.6	87.70	86.40
Perimeter Adj., Add or Deduct	Per 100 L.F.	14.05	9.35	7.50	5.95	5.00		3.85	3.50	3.10
Story Hgt. Adj., Add or Deduct	Per 1 Ft.	2.5	2.30	2.20	1.80	1.80	1.75	1.55	1.50	1.45

For Basement, add $20.90 per square foot of basement area

The above costs were calculated using the basic specifications shown on the facing page. These costs should be adjusted where necessary for design alternatives and owner's requirements. Reported completed project costs, for this type of structure, range from $35.40 to $132.25 per S.F.

3   **4**   **5**   **6**   **7**   **8**   **9**

Common additives

Description	Unit	$ Cost
Appliances		
Cooking range, 30" free standing		
1 oven	Each	330 - 1475
2 oven	Each	1475 - 1600
30" built-in		
1 oven	Each	415 - 1550
2 oven	Each	1200 - 2050
Counter top cook tops, 4 burner	Each	277 - 610
Microwave oven	Each	196 - 630
Combination range, refrig. & sink, 30" wide	Each	1175 - 2375
72" wide	Each	3575
Combination range, refrigerator, sink,		
microwave oven & icemaker	Each	5275
Compactor, residential, 4-1 compaction	Each	460 - 540
Dishwasher, built-in, 2 cycles	Each	475 - 715
4 cycles	Each	475 - 975
Garbage disposer, sink type	Each	124 - 279
Hood for range, 2 speed, vented, 30" wide	Each	194 - 750
42" wide	Each	340 - 1050
Refrigerator, no frost 10-12 C.F.	Each	520 - 830
18-20 C.F.	Each	615 - 930

10

Description	Unit	$ Cost
Closed Circuit Surveillance, One station		
Camera and monitor	Each	1375
For additional camera stations, add	Each	745
Elevators, Hydraulic passenger, 2 stops		
2000# capacity	Each	42,725
2500# capacity	Each	43,425
3500# capacity	Each	47,225
Additional stop, add	Each	3650
Emergency Lighting, 25 watt, battery operated		
Lead battery	Each	289
Nickel cadmium	Each	655
Laundry Equipment		
Dryer, gas, 16 lb. capacity	Each	710
30 lb. capacity	Each	2775
Washer, 4 cycle	Each	795
Commercial	Each	1200
Smoke Detectors		
Ceiling type	Each	149
Duct type	Each	405

1 Model Number (M.010)

"M" distinguishes this section of the book and stands for model. The number designation is a sequential number.

2 Type of Building (Apartment, 1-3 Story)

There are 43 different types of commercial/industrial/institutional buildings highlighted in this section.

3 Exterior Wall Construction and Building Framing Options (Face Brick with Concrete Block Back-up and Open Web Steel Bar Joists)

Three or more commonly used exterior walls, and in most cases, two typical building framing systems are presented for each type of building. The model selected should be based on the actual characteristics of the building being estimated.

4 Total Square Foot of Floor Area and Base Perimeter Used to Compute Base Costs (22,500 Square Feet and 400 Linear Feet)

Square foot of floor area is the total gross area of all floors at grade, and above, and does not include a basement. The perimeter in linear feet used for the base cost is for a generally rectangular economical building shape.

5 Cost per Square Foot of Floor Area ($101.45)

The highlighted cost is for a building of the selected exterior wall and framing system and floor area. Costs for buildings with floor areas other than those calculated may be interpolated between the costs shown.

6 Building Perimeter and Story Height Adjustments

Square foot costs for a building with a perimeter or floor to floor story height significantly different from the model used to calculate the base cost may be adjusted, add or deduct, to reflect the actual building geometry.

7 Cost per Square Foot of Floor Area for the Perimeter and/or Height Adjustment ($5.00 for Perimeter Difference and $1.80 for Story Height Difference)

Add (or deduct) $5.00 to the base square foot cost for each 100 feet of perimeter difference between the model and the actual building. Add (or deduct) $1.80 to the base square foot cost for each 1 foot of story height difference between the model and the actual building.

8 Optional Cost per Square Foot of Basement Floor Area ($20.90)

The cost of an unfinished basement for the building being estimated is $20.90 times the gross floor area of the basement.

9 Range of Cost per Square Foot of Floor Area for Similar Buildings ($35.40 to $132.25)

Many different buildings of the same type have been built using similar materials and systems. Means historical cost data of actual construction projects indicates a range of $35.40 to $132.25 for this type of building.

10 Common Additives

Common components and/or systems used in this type of building are listed. These costs should be added to the total building cost. Additional selections may be found in the Assemblies Section.

How to Use the Commercial/ Industrial/Institutional Section (Continued)

The following is a detailed explanation of a specification and costs for a model building in the Commercial/Industrial/Institutional Square Foot Cost Section. Each bold number below corresponds to the item being described on the following page with the appropriate component of the sample entry following in parenthesis.

Prices listed are costs that include overhead and profit of the installing contractor.

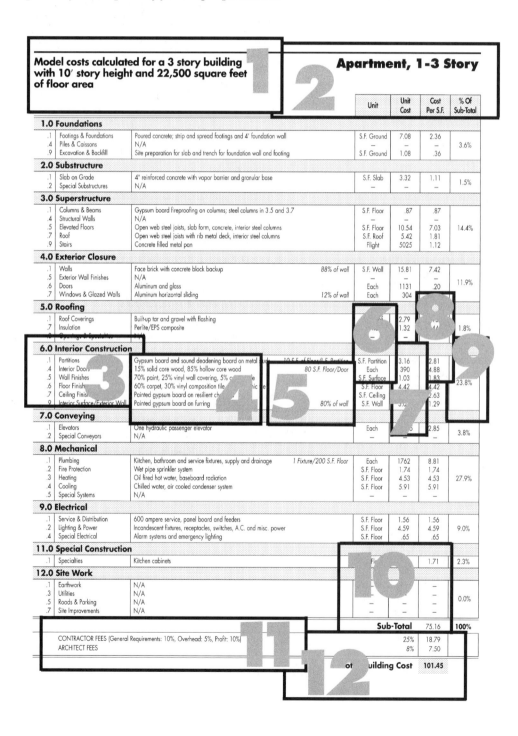

Model costs calculated for a 3 story building with 10' story height and 22,500 square feet of floor area **1** **2** **Apartment, 1-3 Story**

				Unit	Unit Cost	Cost Per S.F.	% Of Sub-Total
1.0 Foundations							
.1	Footings & Foundations	Poured concrete; strip and spread footings and 4' foundation wall		S.F. Ground	7.08	2.36	3.6%
.4	Piles & Caissons	N/A		–	–	–	
.9	Excavation & Backfill	Site preparation for slab and trench for foundation wall and footing		S.F. Ground	1.08	.36	
2.0 Substructure							
.1	Slab on Grade	4" reinforced concrete with vapor barrier and granular base		S.F. Slab	3.32	1.11	1.5%
.2	Special Substructures	N/A		–	–	–	
3.0 Superstructure							
.1	Columns & Beams	Gypsum board fireproofing on columns; steel columns in 3.5 and 3.7		S.F. Floor	.87	.87	
.4	Structural Walls	N/A		–	–	–	
.5	Elevated Floors	Open web steel joists, slab form, concrete, interior steel columns		S.F. Floor	10.54	7.03	14.4%
.7	Roof	Open web steel joists with rib metal deck, interior steel columns		S.F. Roof	5.42	1.81	
.9	Stairs	Concrete filled metal pan		Flight	5025	1.12	
4.0 Exterior Closure							
.1	Walls	Face brick with concrete block backup	88% of wall	S.F. Wall	15.81	7.42	
.5	Exterior Wall Finishes	N/A		–	–	–	11.9%
.6	Doors	Aluminum and glass		Each	1131	.20	
.7	Windows & Glazed Walls	Aluminum horizontal sliding	12% of wall	Each	304		
5.0 Roofing							
.1	Roof Coverings	Built-up tar and gravel with flashing			2.79		1.8%
.7	Insulation	Perlite/EPS composite			1.32		
	Openings & Specialties	N/A					
6.0 Interior Construction							
.1	Partitions	Gypsum board and sound deadening board on metal studs	10 S.F. of Floor/S.F. Partition	S.F. Partition	3.16	2.81	
.4	Interior Doors	15% solid core wood, 85% hollow core wood	80 S.F. Floor/Door	Each	390	4.88	
.5	Wall Finishes	70% paint, 25% vinyl wall covering, 5% ceramic tile		S.F. Surface	1.03	1.83	23.8%
.6	Floor Finish	60% carpet, 30% vinyl composition tile, 10% ceramic tile		S.F. Floor	4.42	4.42	
.7	Ceiling Finish	Painted gypsum board on resilient channels		S.F. Ceiling		2.63	
.9	Interior Surface/Exterior Wall	Painted gypsum board on furring	80% of wall	S.F. Wall		1.29	
7.0 Conveying							
.1	Elevators	One hydraulic passenger elevator		Each		2.85	3.8%
.2	Special Conveyors	N/A		–	–	–	
8.0 Mechanical							
.1	Plumbing	Kitchen, bathroom and service fixtures, supply and drainage	1 Fixture/200 S.F. Floor	Each	1762	8.81	
.2	Fire Protection	Wet pipe sprinkler system		S.F. Floor	1.74	1.74	
.3	Heating	Oil fired hot water, baseboard radiation		S.F. Floor	4.53	4.53	27.9%
.4	Cooling	Chilled water, air cooled condenser system		S.F. Floor	5.91	5.91	
.5	Special Systems	N/A		–	–	–	
9.0 Electrical							
.1	Service & Distribution	600 ampere service, panel board and feeders		S.F. Floor	1.56	1.56	
.2	Lighting & Power	Incandescent fixtures, receptacles, switches, A.C. and misc. power		S.F. Floor	4.59	4.59	9.0%
.4	Special Electrical	Alarm systems and emergency lighting		S.F. Floor	.65	.65	
11.0 Special Construction							
.1	Specialties	Kitchen cabinets		Floor		1.71	2.3%
12.0 Site Work							
.1	Earthwork	N/A		–	–	–	
.3	Utilities	N/A		–	–	–	0.0%
.5	Roads & Parking	N/A		–	–	–	
.7	Site Improvements	N/A		–	–	–	
					Sub-Total	75.16	100%
	CONTRACTOR FEES (General Requirements: 10%, Overhead: 5%, Profit: 10%)					25%	18.79
	ARCHITECT FEES					8%	7.50
					Total Building Cost	101.45	

6 **8** **9** **10** **11** **12** **3** **4** **5** **7**

70

1
Building Description
(Model costs are calculated for a three-story apartment building with 10' story height and 22,500 square feet of floor area)

The model highlighted is described in terms of building type, number of stories, typical story height and square footage.

2
Type of Building
(Apartment, 1-3 Story)

3
Division 6.0 Interior Construction
(6.4 Interior Doors)

System costs are presented in divisions according to the 12-division UniFormat classifications. Each of the component systems are listed.

4
Specification Highlights
(15% solid core wood; 85% hollow core wood)

All systems in each subdivision are described with the material and proportions used.

5
Quality Criteria
(80 S.F. Floor/Door)

The criteria used in determining quantities for the calculations are shown.

6
Unit (Each)

The unit of measure shown in this column is the unit of measure of the particular system shown that corresponds to the unit cost.

7
Unit Cost ($390)

The cost per unit of measure of each system subdivision.

8
Cost per Square Foot ($4.88)

The cost per square foot for each system is the unit cost of the system times the total number of units divided by the total square feet of building area.

9
% of Sub-Total (23.8%)

The percent of sub-total is the total cost per square foot of all systems in the division divided by the sub-total cost per square foot of the building.

10
Sub-Total ($75.16)

The sub-total is the total of all the system costs per square foot.

11
Project Fees
(Contractor Fees) (25%)
(Architect Fees) (8%)

Contractor Fees to cover the general requirements, overhead and profit of the General Contractor are added as a percentage of the sub-total. Architect Fees, also as a percentage of the sub-total, are also added. These values vary with the building type.

12
Total Building Cost ($101.45)

The total building cost per square foot of building area is the sum of the square foot costs of all the systems plus the General Contractor's general requirements, overhead and profit, and the Architect fees. The total building cost is the amount which appears shaded in the Cost per Square Foot of Floor Area table shown previously.

Examples

Example 1

This example illustrates the use of the base cost tables. The base cost is adjusted for different exterior wall systems, different story height and a partial basement.

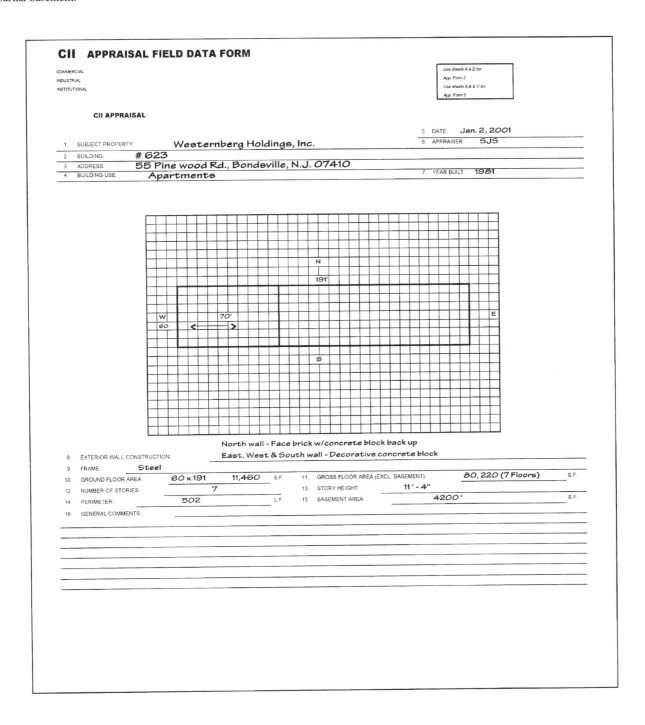

CII APPRAISAL FIELD DATA FORM

COMMERCIAL
INDUSTRIAL
INSTITUTIONAL

Use sheets A & D for App. Form 2
Use sheets A,B & C for App. Form 3

CII APPRAISAL

5. DATE: Jan. 2, 2001
6. APPRAISER: SJS

1. SUBJECT PROPERTY: Westernberg Holdings, Inc.
2. BUILDING: # 623
3. ADDRESS: 55 Pine wood Rd., Bondsville, N.J. 07410
4. BUILDING USE: Apartments
7. YEAR BUILT: 1981

North wall - Face brick w/concrete block back up
East, West & South wall - Decorative concrete block

8. EXTERIOR WALL CONSTRUCTION:
9. FRAME: Steel
10. GROUND FLOOR AREA: 60 x 191   11,460   S.F.
11. GROSS FLOOR AREA (EXCL. BASEMENT)   80,220 (7 Floors)   S.F.
12. NUMBER OF STORIES: 7
13. STORY HEIGHT: 11' - 4"
14. PERIMETER: 502   L.F.
15. BASEMENT AREA   4200'   S.F.
16. GENERAL COMMENTS:

Example 1 (continued)

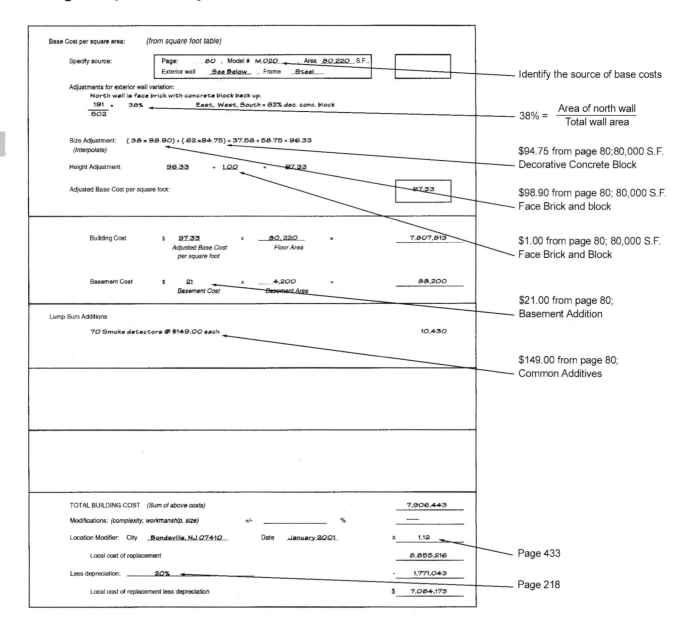

Base Cost per square area: *(from square foot table)*

Specify source:

| Page: | 80 | Model # | M.020 | , | Area | 80.220 | S.F., |
| Exterior wall | See Below | , | Frame | Steel | | | |

Identify the source of base costs

Adjustments for exterior wall variation:
  North wall is face brick with concrete block back up.

$$\frac{191}{502} = 38\%$$ East, West, South = 62% dec. conc. block

$$38\% = \frac{\text{Area of north wall}}{\text{Total wall area}}$$

Size Adjustment: (.38 × 98.90) + (.62 × 94.75) = 37.58 + 58.75 = 96.33
  (Interpolate)

$94.75 from page 80; 80,000 S.F.
Decorative Concrete Block

Height Adjustment: 96.33   +   1.00   =   97.33

Adjusted Base Cost per square foot: 97.33

$98.90 from page 80; 80,000 S.F.
Face Brick and block

Building Cost $ 97.33   x   80,220   =   7,807,813
                  Adjusted Base Cost   Floor Area
                  per square foot

$1.00 from page 80; 80,000 S.F.
Face Brick and Block

Basement Cost $ 21   x   4,200   =   88,200
                 Basement Cost   Basement Area

$21.00 from page 80;
Basement Addition

Lump Sum Additions

   70 Smoke detectors @ $149.00 each   10,430

$149.00 from page 80;
Common Additives

TOTAL BUILDING COST   *(Sum of above costs)*   7,906,443

Modifications: *(complexity, workmanship, size)*   +/- _____ %   —

Location Modifier: City   Bondsville, NJ 07410   Date   January 2001   x   1.12

   Local cost of replacement   8,855,216

Page 433

Less depreciation: 20%   - 1,771,043

   Local cost of replacement less depreciation $ 7,084,173

Page 218

Example 2

This example shows how to modify a model building.

Model #M.020, 4–7 Story Apartment, page 80, matches the example quite closely. The model specifies a 6-story building with a 10′ story height.

The following adjustments must be made:
- add stone ashlar wall
- adjust model to a 5-story building
- change partitions
- change floor finish
- change plumbing

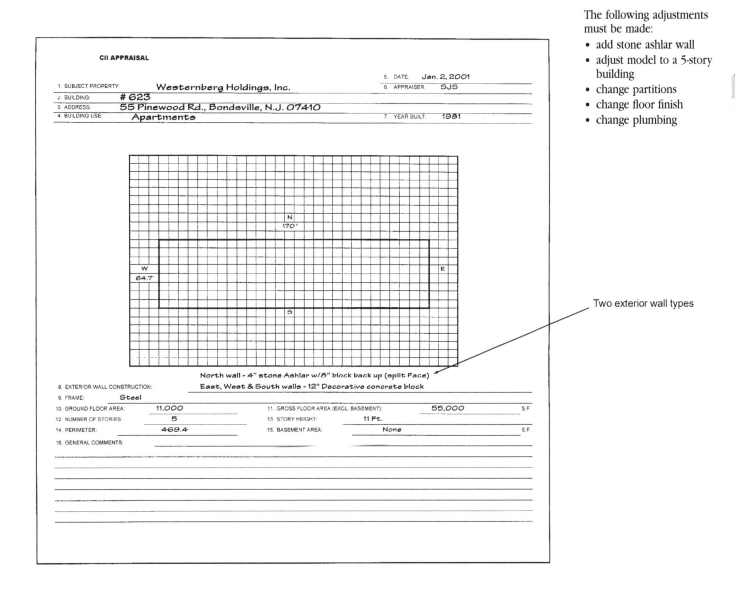

CII APPRAISAL

5. DATE:	Jan. 2, 2001
1. SUBJECT PROPERTY:	Westernberg Holdings, Inc.
6. APPRAISER:	SJS
2. BUILDING:	# 623
3. ADDRESS:	55 Pinewood Rd., Bondsville, N.J. 07410
4. BUILDING USE:	Apartments
7. YEAR BUILT:	1981

N
170′

W
64.7′

E

S

Two exterior wall types

North wall - 4" stone Ashlar w/8" block back up (split Face)

8. EXTERIOR WALL CONSTRUCTION: East, West & South walls - 12" Decorative concrete block

9. FRAME: Steel

10. GROUND FLOOR AREA:	11,000	11. GROSS FLOOR AREA (EXCL. BASEMENT):	55,000	S.F.
12. NUMBER OF STORIES:	5	13. STORY HEIGHT:	11 Ft.	
14. PERIMETER:	469.4	15. BASEMENT AREA:	None	S.F.

16. GENERAL COMMENTS:

Example 2 (continued)

Square foot area (excluding basement) from item 11 ___55,000___ S.F.
Perimeter from item 14 ___469.4___ Lin. Ft.
Item 17-Model square foot costs (from model sub-total) $ ___77.10___

> From page 81, Model #M.020 Sub-total

NO.	SYSTEM/COMPONENT	DESCRIPTION		UNIT	UNIT COST	NEW F COST	MODEL F COST	+/- CHANGE
1.0	FOUNDATION							
.1	Footings and Foundations L.F. Length	Bay Size Same as model		S.F. Gnd.	7.20	1.44	1.20	+ .24
.4	Piles & Caissons							
.9	Excavation & Backfill Depth	Area 11,000 S.F.		S.F. Gnd.	1.02	0.20	0.17	+ .03
2.0	SUBSTRUCTURE							
.1	Slab on grade Material	Thickness Same as model		S.F. Slab	3.32	0.66	.55	+ .11
.2	Special Substructures Type							
3.0	SUPERSTRUCTURE							
.1	Columns, Beams, & Joists Size Type	Length Fireproof only		S.F. Floor L.F.	1.61	1.61	1.61	—
	Size Type	Length		L.F.				
.4	Structure Walls			S.F.				
.5	Elevated Floors Same as model			S.F. Floor	12.49	9.99	10.41	- .42
.7	Roof			S.F. Roof	5.08	1.02	0.85	+ .17
.9	Stairs 13 Flights			Flight	4070	0.96	1.09	- .13
4.0	EXTERIOR CLOSURE							
.1	Walls North wall - 4" stone ashlar Material on 8" conc. block Thickness 36 % of Wall			S.F. Wall	17	6.86	6.80	+ .06
	East, West & South walls - 12" Material split ribbed block Thickness 64 % of Wall			S.F. Wall				
	Material Thickness % of Wall			S.F. Wall				
.5	ior Wall Finishes Type			S.F. Surf				
.6	Doors Type Same as model	Number 4		Each	2637	.19	.18	+ .01
	Type	Number		Each				
.7	Windows & Glazed Walls Type	% of Wall		S.F. Wind.				
	Type 14 % of Wall	Each		S.F. Wind	304	1.33	1.42	- .09
5.0	ROOFING							
.1	Roof Coverings Material Same as model			S.F. Roof	2.70	0.54	0.45	+ .09
.7	Insulation Material	Thickness		S.F. Insul.	1.32	.26	.22	+ .04
.8	Openings & Specialities			S.F. Opng.				
6.0	INTERIOR CONSTRUCTION							
.1	Partitions 9' High Material Gypsum board on metal stud	Densit 8 S.F. Floor/L.F. Part.		S.F. Part.	3.62	4.07	3.62	+ .45
	Material	Density		S.F. Part.				
.4	Interior Doors Type	Number		Each	467	5.84	5.84	—
.5	Wall Finishes Material Same as model	but % of Wall 9'-0" High		S.F. Wall	1.13	2.54	2.26	+ .28
	Material			S.F. Wall				
.6	Floor Finishes Material Hardwood Carpet	60 % of Floor 30 % of Floor		S.F. Floor	4.42	6.46	4.42	+ 2.04
	Material Tile 10 % of Floor			S.F. Floor				
.7	Ceiling Finishes Material Same as model			S.F. Ceil.	2.80	2.80	2.80	—

Right-side annotations:

$\dfrac{\$1.02/\text{S.F. ground area}}{5\ \text{stories}}$

$\dfrac{\$1.02/\text{S.F. ground area}}{6\ \text{stories}}$

(Page 81, Line 3.1)

$\dfrac{\text{Area of Elevated Floors}}{\text{Building Floor Area}}$ — $\$12.49/\text{S.F.} \times 4 \times \dfrac{11,000\ \text{S.F.}}{55,000}$

$\dfrac{\$5.08/\text{S.F. roof}}{5\ \text{stories}}$

Windows are 14% of wall area, 15 S.F./window

$\dfrac{304}{15} \times .14 \times 469.4 \times 11 \times 5 + 55,000 = 1.33$

From Table 6.1-510 page 327 and 6.1-580 page 329

$\dfrac{\$3.62/\text{S.F. partition} \times 9\ \text{ft. high}}{8\ \text{S.F. floor/L.F. partition}}$

From Table 6.6-100 pages 338 & 339

Oak Strip, Fin. (max. price) @$7.69/S.F.
Carpet (26 oz.) @$3.64/S.F.
Ceramic Tile @$7.58/S.F.

.60 x 7.69 = 4.61
.36 x 3.64 = 1.09
.10 x 7.58 = .76
6.46

Bottom annotations:

North wall is 36% of wall area, e.g., $\dfrac{170 \times 11}{469.4 \times 11}$
From Table 4.1-242-2350 page 289
Stone ashlar @ $23.50/S.F. wall
East, west and south walls are 64% of wall area
From Table 4.1-212-1530 page 284
Split ribbed block @ $13.35/S.F. wall

New wall cost
.36 x $23.50/S.F. + .64 x $13.35/S.F. = $17.00/S.F. wall

Convert cost per S.F. wall to cost per S.F. of floor
Windows are 14% of wall area

$6.86 S.F. floor = $\dfrac{\$17.00/\text{S.F. wall} \times .86 \times 469.4\ \text{L.F.} \times 11\ \text{ft high} \times 5\ \text{stories}}{55,000\ \text{S.F. of floor}}$

Example 2 (Continued)

NO.	SYSTEM/COMPONENET						Unit	Unit Cost	New S.F. Cost	Model S.F. Cost	+/- Change
6.0	INTERIOR CONSTRUCTION										
.9	Interior Surface/Exterior Wall		Material		86 % of Wall	Board on furring	S.F. Surf.	3.02	1.22	1.21	+.01
			Material		% of Wall		S.F. Surf.				
7.0	CONVEYING										
.1	Elevators 2	Type	Same as model	Capacity		Stops	Each	131,400	4.78	4.38	+.40
.2	Special Conveyors	Type					Each				
8.0	MECHANICAL										
.1	Plumbing Kitchen, bath + service fixtures 1 Fixture /200					S.F. Floor	Each	1728	8.64	8.04	+.60
.2	Fire Protection		Same as model				S.F.	1.69	1.69	1.69	—
.3	Heating	Type	Same as model				S.F.	3.91	3.91	3.91	—
.4	Cooling	Type	Same as model				S.F.	5.53	5.53	5.53	—
.5	Special Systems						Each				
9.0	ELECTRICAL										
.1	Service Distribution		Same as model				S.F.	1.47	1.47	1.47	—
.2	Lighting & Power						S.F.	4.56	4.56	4.56	—
.4	Special Electrical						S.F.	0.36	0.36	0.36	—
11.0	SPECIAL CONSTRUCTION										
.1	Specialties						S.F.	2.06	2.06	2.06	—
12.0	SITE WORK										
.1	Earthwork										
.3	Utilities										
.5	Roads & Parking										
.7	Site Improvement										

469.4 L.F. x 11 ft. high x 5 stories

Unit Cost   86%

$3.02/S.F. wall x total S.F. wall x .86
55,000

ITEM						Total Change	+3.89
18	Adjusted S.F. cost $ 80.99 item 17 +/- changes						
19	Building area - from item 11 55,000 S.F. x adjusted S.F. cost					$	4,454,450
20	Basement area - from item 15 S.F. x S.F. cost $					$	—
21	Base building sub-total - item 20 + item 19					$	4,454,450
22	Miscellaneous addition (quality, etc.)					$	—
23	Sub-total - item 22 + 21					$	4,454,450
24	General conditions -25 % of item 23					$	1,113,613
25	Sub-total - item 24 + item 23					$	5,568,063
26	Architects fees 5.5 % of item 25					$	306,243
27	Sub-total - item 26 + item 27					$	5,874,306
28	Location modifier zip code 07410					x	1.12
29	Local replacement cost - item 28 x item 27					$	6,579,223
30	Depreciation 20 % of item 29					$	1,315,845
31	Depreciated local replacement cost - item 29 less item 30					$	5,263,378
32	Exclusions					$	—
33	Net depreciated replacement cost - item 31 less item 32					$	5,263,378

Use table on page 218

EXAMPLES

Costs per square foot of floor area

Exterior Wall	S.F. Area	8000	12000	15000	19000	22500	25000	29000	32000	36000
	L.F. Perimeter	213	280	330	350	400	433	442	480	520
Face Brick with Concrete Block Back-up	Wood Joists	128.40	115.40	110.15	103.05	100.45	98.95	95.40	94.40	93.00
	Steel Joists	127.40	115.15	110.20	103.85	101.45	100.00	96.95	96.00	94.75
Stucco on Concrete Block	Wood Joists	113.50	101.90	97.25	91.60	89.30	88.00	85.35	84.45	83.30
	Steel Joists	120.15	108.45	103.80	98.05	95.75	94.45	91.75	90.85	89.65
Wood Siding	Wood Frame	112.15	100.70	96.10	90.70	88.45	87.15	84.55	83.70	82.55
Brick Veneer	Wood Frame	119.40	107.05	102.05	95.65	93.20	91.80	88.65	87.70	86.40
Perimeter Adj., Add or Deduct	Per 100 L.F.	14.05	9.35	7.50	5.95	5.00	4.50	3.85	3.50	3.10
Story Hgt. Adj., Add or Deduct	Per 1 Ft.	2.65	2.30	2.20	1.80	1.80	1.75	1.55	1.50	1.45

For Basement, add $20.90 per square foot of basement area

The above costs were calculated using the basic specifications shown on the facing page. These costs should be adjusted where necessary for design alternatives and owner's requirements. Reported completed project costs, for this type of structure, range from $35.40 to $132.25 per S.F.

Common additives

Description	Unit	$ Cost
Appliances		
Cooking range, 30" free standing		
1 oven	Each	330 - 1475
2 oven	Each	1475 - 1600
30" built-in		
1 oven	Each	415 - 1550
2 oven	Each	1200 - 2050
Counter top cook tops, 4 burner	Each	277 - 610
Microwave oven	Each	196 - 630
Combination range, refrig. & sink, 30" wide	Each	1175 - 2375
72" wide	Each	3575
Combination range, refrigerator, sink,		
microwave oven & icemaker	Each	5275
Compactor, residential, 4-1 compaction	Each	460 - 540
Dishwasher, built-in, 2 cycles	Each	475 - 715
4 cycles	Each	475 - 975
Garbage disposer, sink type	Each	124 - 279
Hood for range, 2 speed, vented, 30" wide	Each	194 - 750
42" wide	Each	340 - 1050
Refrigerator, no frost 10-12 C.F.	Each	520 - 830
18-20 C.F.	Each	615 - 930

Description	Unit	$ Cost
Closed Circuit Surveillance, One station		
Camera and monitor	Each	1375
For additional camera stations, add	Each	745
Elevators, Hydraulic passenger, 2 stops		
2000# capacity	Each	42,725
2500# capacity	Each	43,425
3500# capacity	Each	47,225
Additional stop, add	Each	3650
Emergency Lighting, 25 watt, battery operated		
Lead battery	Each	289
Nickel cadmium	Each	655
Laundry Equipment		
Dryer, gas, 16 lb. capacity	Each	710
30 lb. capacity	Each	2775
Washer, 4 cycle	Each	795
Commercial	Each	1200
Smoke Detectors		
Ceiling type	Each	149
Duct type	Each	405

Model costs calculated for a 3 story building with 10' story height and 22,500 square feet of floor area

				Unit	Unit Cost	Cost Per S.F.	% Of Sub-Total
1.0 Foundations							
	.1	Footings & Foundations	Poured concrete; strip and spread footings and 4' foundation wall	S.F. Ground	7.08	2.36	
	.4	Piles & Caissons	N/A	—	—	—	3.6%
	.9	Excavation & Backfill	Site preparation for slab and trench for foundation wall and footing	S.F. Ground	1.08	.36	
2.0 Substructure							
	.1	Slab on Grade	4" reinforced concrete with vapor barrier and granular base	S.F. Slab	3.32	1.11	1.5%
	.2	Special Substructures	N/A	—	—	—	
3.0 Superstructure							
	.1	Columns & Beams	Gypsum board fireproofing on columns; steel columns in 3.5 and 3.7	S.F. Floor	.87	.87	
	.4	Structural Walls	N/A	—	—	—	
	.5	Elevated Floors	Open web steel joists, slab form, concrete, interior steel columns	S.F. Floor	10.54	7.03	14.4%
	.7	Roof	Open web steel joists with rib metal deck, interior steel columns	S.F. Roof	5.42	1.81	
	.9	Stairs	Concrete filled metal pan	Flight	5025	1.12	
4.0 Exterior Closure							
	.1	Walls	Face brick with concrete block backup *88% of wall*	S.F. Wall	15.81	7.42	
	.5	Exterior Wall Finishes	N/A	—	—	—	
	.6	Doors	Aluminum and glass	Each	1131	.20	11.9%
	.7	Windows & Glazed Walls	Aluminum horizontal sliding *12% of wall*	Each	304	1.30	
5.0 Roofing							
	.1	Roof Coverings	Built-up tar and gravel with flashing	S.F. Roof	2.79	.93	
	.7	Insulation	Perlite/EPS composite	S.F. Roof	1.32	.44	1.8%
	.8	Openings & Specialties	N/A	—	—	—	
6.0 Interior Construction							
	.1	Partitions	Gypsum board and sound deadening board on metal studs *10 S.F. of Floor/L.F. Partition*	S.F. Partition	3.16	2.81	
	.4	Interior Doors	15% solid core wood, 85% hollow core wood *80 S.F. Floor/Door*	Each	390	4.88	
	.5	Wall Finishes	70% paint, 25% vinyl wall covering, 5% ceramic tile	S.F. Surface	1.03	1.83	
	.6	Floor Finishes	60% carpet, 30% vinyl composition tile, 10% ceramic tile	S.F. Floor	4.42	4.42	23.8%
	.7	Ceiling Finishes	Painted gypsum board on resilient channels	S.F. Ceiling	2.63	2.63	
	.9	Interior Surface/Exterior Wall	Painted gypsum board on furring *80% of wall*	S.F. Wall	3.02	1.29	
7.0 Conveying							
	.1	Elevators	One hydraulic passenger elevator	Each	64,125	2.85	3.8%
	.2	Special Conveyors	N/A	—	—	—	
8.0 Mechanical							
	.1	Plumbing	Kitchen, bathroom and service fixtures, supply and drainage *1 Fixture/200 S.F. Floor*	Each	1762	8.81	
	.2	Fire Protection	Wet pipe sprinkler system	S.F. Floor	1.74	1.74	
	.3	Heating	Oil fired hot water, baseboard radiation	S.F. Floor	4.53	4.53	27.9%
	.4	Cooling	Chilled water, air cooled condenser system	S.F. Floor	5.91	5.91	
	.5	Special Systems	N/A	—	—	—	
9.0 Electrical							
	.1	Service & Distribution	600 ampere service, panel board and feeders	S.F. Floor	1.56	1.56	
	.2	Lighting & Power	Incandescent fixtures, receptacles, switches, A.C. and misc. power	S.F. Floor	4.59	4.59	9.0%
	.4	Special Electrical	Alarm systems and emergency lighting	S.F. Floor	.65	.65	
11.0 Special Construction							
	.1	Specialties	Kitchen cabinets	S.F. Floor	1.71	1.71	2.3%
12.0 Site Work							
	.1	Earthwork	N/A	—	—	—	
	.3	Utilities	N/A	—	—	—	
	.5	Roads & Parking	N/A	—	—	—	0.0%
	.7	Site Improvements	N/A	—	—	—	
				Sub-Total		75.16	100%
		CONTRACTOR FEES (General Requirements: 10%, Overhead: 5%, Profit: 10%)			25%	18.79	
		ARCHITECT FEES			8%	7.50	
				Total Building Cost		101.45	

BUILDING TYPES

Costs per square foot of floor area

Exterior Wall	S.F. Area	40000	45000	50000	55000	60000	70000	80000	90000	100000
	L.F. Perimeter	366	400	433	466	500	566	505	550	594
Face Brick with Concrete Block Back-up	Steel Frame	105.90	104.90	104.20	103.60	103.15	102.30	98.90	98.40	97.90
	R/Conc. Frame	111.65	110.65	109.80	109.15	108.60	107.75	103.80	103.20	102.60
Decorative Concrete Block	Steel Frame	100.60	99.75	99.15	98.60	98.15	97.45	94.75	94.25	93.80
	R/Conc. Frame	102.80	101.95	101.30	100.75	100.30	99.60	96.85	96.35	95.90
Precast Concrete Panels	Steel Frame	102.70	101.80	101.10	100.55	100.05	99.30	96.15	95.65	95.20
	R/Conc. Frame	104.70	103.80	103.10	102.55	102.05	101.30	98.15	97.65	97.15
Perimeter Adj., Add or Deduct	Per 100 L.F.	4.35	3.90	3.50	3.20	2.90	2.50	2.20	1.95	1.75
Story Hgt. Adj., Add or Deduct	Per 1 Ft.	1.45	1.45	1.40	1.35	1.35	1.30	1.00	.95	.95
For Basement, add $21.00 per square foot of basement area										

The above costs were calculated using the basic specifications shown on the facing page. These costs should be adjusted where necessary for design alternatives and owner's requirements. Reported completed project costs, for this type of structure, range from $41.85 to $121.35 per S.F.

Common additives

Description	Unit	$ Cost
Appliances		
Cooking range, 30" free standing		
1 oven	Each	330 - 1475
2 oven	Each	1475 - 1600
30" built-in		
1 oven	Each	415 - 1550
2 oven	Each	1200 - 2050
Counter top cook tops, 4 burner	Each	277 - 610
Microwave oven	Each	196 - 630
Combination range, refrig. & sink, 30" wide	Each	1175 - 2375
72" wide	Each	3575
Combination range, refrigerator, sink,		
microwave oven & icemaker	Each	5275
Compactor, residential, 4-1 compaction	Each	460 - 540
Dishwasher, built-in, 2 cycles	Each	475 - 715
4 cycles	Each	475 - 975
Garbage disposer, sink type	Each	124 - 279
Hood for range, 2 speed, vented, 30" wide	Each	194 - 750
42" wide	Each	340 - 1050
Refrigerator, no frost 10-12 C.F.	Each	520 - 830
18-20 C.F.	Each	615 - 930

Description	Unit	$ Cost
Closed Circuit Surveillance, One station		
Camera and monitor	Each	1375
For additional camera stations, add	Each	745
Elevators, Electric passenger, 5 stops		
2000# capacity	Each	97,700
3500# capacity	Each	103,700
5000# capacity	Each	108,200
Additional stop, add	Each	5500
Emergency Lighting, 25 watt, battery operated		
Lead battery	Each	289
Nickel cadmium	Each	655
Laundry Equipment		
Dryer, gas, 16 lb. capacity	Each	710
30 lb. capacity	Each	2775
Washer, 4 cycle	Each	795
Commercial	Each	1200
Smoke Detectors		
Ceiling type	Each	149
Duct type	Each	405

Important: See the Reference Section for Location Factors

Model costs calculated for a 6 story building with 10'-4" story height and 60,000 square feet of floor area

				Unit	Unit Cost	Cost Per S.F.	% Of Sub-Total
1.0 Foundations							
	.1	Footings & Foundations	Poured concrete; strip and spread footings and 4' foundation wall	S.F. Ground	7.20	1.20	
	.4	Piles & Caissons	N/A	—	—	—	1.8%
	.9	Excavation & Backfill	Site preparation for slab and trench for foundation wall and footing	S.F. Ground	1.02	.17	
2.0 Substructure							
	.1	Slab on Grade	4" reinforced concrete with vapor barrier and granular base	S.F. Slab	3.32	.55	0.7%
	.2	Special Substructures	N/A	—	—	—	
3.0 Superstructure							
	.1	Columns & Beams	Gypsum board fireproofing on columns, steel columns in 3.5 and 3.7	S.F. Floor	1.61	1.61	
	.4	Structural Walls	N/A	—	—	—	
	.5	Elevated Floors	Open web steel joists, slab form, concrete, steel columns	S.F. Floor	12.49	10.41	18.1%
	.7	Roof	Open web steel joists with rib metal deck, steel columns	S.F. Roof	5.08	.85	
	.9	Stairs	Concrete filled metal pan	Flight	4070	1.09	
4.0 Exterior Closure							
	.1	Walls	Face brick with concrete block backup 86% of wall	S.F. Wall	15.30	6.80	
	.5	Exterior Wall Finishes	N/A	—	—	—	
	.6	Doors	Aluminum and glass	Each	2637	.18	10.9%
	.7	Windows & Glazed Walls	Aluminum horizontal sliding 14% of wall	Each	304	1.42	
5.0 Roofing							
	.1	Roof Coverings	Built-up tar and gravel with flashing	S.F. Roof	2.70	.45	
	.7	Insulation	Perlite/EPS composite	S.F. Roof	1.32	.22	0.9%
	.8	Openings & Specialties	N/A	—	—	—	
6.0 Interior Construction							
	.1	Partitions	Gypsum board and sound deadening board on metal studs 8 S.F. Floor/L.F. Partitions	S.F. Partition	3.62	3.62	
	.4	Interior Doors	15% solid core wood, 85% hollow core wood 80 S.F Floor/Door	Each	467	5.84	
	.5	Wall Finishes	70% paint, 25% vinyl wall covering, 5% ceramic tile	S.F. Surface	1.13	2.26	
	.6	Floor Finishes	60% carpet, 30% vinyl composition tile, 10% ceramic tile	S.F. Floor	4.42	4.42	26.1%
	.7	Ceiling Finishes	Painted gypsum board on resilient channels	S.F. Ceiling	2.80	2.80	
	.9	Interior Surface/Exterior Wall	Painted gypsum board on furring 80% of wall	S.F. Wall	3.02	1.21	
7.0 Conveying							
	.1	Elevators	Two geared passenger elevators	Each	131,400	4.38	5.7%
	.2	Special Conveyors	N/A	—	—	—	
8.0 Mechanical							
	.1	Plumbing	Kitchen, bathroom and service fixtures, supply and drainage 1 Fixture/215 S.F. Floor	Each	1728	8.04	
	.2	Fire Protection	Standpipe and wet pipe sprinkler system	S.F. Floor	1.69	1.69	
	.3	Heating	Oil fired hot water, baseboard radiation	S.F. Floor	3.91	3.91	24.8%
	.4	Cooling	Chilled water, air cooled condenser system	S.F. Floor	5.53	5.53	
	.5	Special Systems	N/A	—	—	—	
9.0 Electrical							
	.1	Service & Distribution	1600 ampere service, panel board and feeders	S.F. Floor	1.47	1.47	
	.2	Lighting & Power	Incandescent fixtures, receptacles, switches, A.C. and misc. power	S.F. Floor	4.56	4.56	8.3%
	.4	Special Electrical	Alarm systems, emergency lighting, and intercom	S.F. Floor	.36	.36	
11.0 Special Construction							
	.1	Specialties	Kitchen cabinets	S.F. Floor	2.06	2.06	2.7%
12.0 Site Work							
	.1	Earthwork	N/A	—	—	—	
	.3	Utilities	N/A	—	—	—	
	.5	Roads & Parking	N/A	—	—	—	0.0%
	.7	Site Improvements	N/A	—	—	—	
				Sub-Total		77.10	100%
		CONTRACTOR FEES (General Requirements: 10%, Overhead: 5%, Profit: 10%)			25%	19.28	
		ARCHITECT FEES			7%	6.77	
				Total Building Cost		103.15	

BUILDING TYPES

81

BUILDING TYPES

Costs per square foot of floor area

Exterior Wall	S.F. Area	95000	112000	129000	145000	170000	200000	275000	400000	600000
	L.F. Perimeter	345	386	406	442	480	510	530	570	630
Ribbed Precast Concrete Panel	Steel Frame	119.40	117.30	114.95	113.80	112.00	110.05	106.10	102.90	100.50
	R/Conc. Frame	113.35	111.30	109.10	108.00	106.25	104.40	100.70	97.70	95.45
Face Brick with Concrete Block Back-up	Steel Frame	112.65	110.50	108.05	106.90	105.00	102.95	98.80	95.45	92.95
	R/Conc. Frame	115.70	113.50	111.10	109.95	108.05	106.05	101.95	98.60	96.15
Stucco on Concrete Block	Steel Frame	106.00	104.15	102.25	101.25	99.80	98.25	95.25	92.85	91.00
	R/Conc. Frame	109.00	107.15	105.30	104.35	102.85	101.35	98.40	96.00	94.20
Perimeter Adj., Add or Deduct	Per 100 L.F.	4.80	4.05	3.55	3.15	2.65	2.25	1.65	1.15	.75
Story Hgt. Adj., Add or Deduct	Per 1 Ft.	1.60	1.55	1.40	1.40	1.25	1.10	.85	.65	.50

For Basement, add $21.50 per square foot of basement area

The above costs were calculated using the basic specifications shown on the facing page. These costs should be adjusted where necessary for design alternatives and owner's requirements. Reported completed project costs, for this type of structure, range from $54.45 to $125.60 per S.F.

Common additives

Description	Unit	$ Cost
Appliances		
Cooking range, 30" free standing		
1 oven	Each	330 - 1475
2 oven	Each	1475 - 1600
30" built-in		
1 oven	Each	415 - 1550
2 oven	Each	1200 - 2050
Counter top cook tops, 4 burner	Each	277 - 610
Microwave oven	Each	196 - 630
Combination range, refrig. & sink, 30" wide	Each	1175 - 2375
72" wide	Each	3575
Combination range, refrigerator, sink,		
microwave oven & icemaker	Each	5275
Compactor, residential, 4-1 compaction	Each	460 - 540
Dishwasher, built-in, 2 cycles	Each	475 - 715
4 cycles	Each	475 - 975
Garbage disposer, sink type	Each	124 - 279
Hood for range, 2 speed, vented, 30" wide	Each	194 - 750
42" wide	Each	340 - 1050
Refrigerator, no frost 10-12 C.F.	Each	520 - 830
18-20 C.F.	Each	615 - 930

Description	Unit	$ Cost
Closed Circuit Surveillance, One station		
Camera and monitor	Each	1375
For additional camera stations, add	Each	745
Elevators, Electric passenger, 10 stops		
3000# capacity	Each	210,500
4000# capacity	Each	212,500
5000# capacity	Each	216,500
Additional stop, add	Each	5500
Emergency Lighting, 25 watt, battery operated		
Lead battery	Each	289
Nickel cadmium	Each	655
Laundry Equipment		
Dryer, gas, 16 lb. capacity	Each	710
30 lb. capacity	Each	2775
Washer, 4 cycle	Each	795
Commercial	Each	1200
Smoke Detectors		
Ceiling type	Each	149
Duct type	Each	405

Important: See the Reference Section for Location Factors

Model costs calculated for a 15 story building with 10'-6" story height and 145,000 square feet of floor area

				Unit	Unit Cost	Cost Per S.F.	% Of Sub-Total
1.0 Foundations							
.1	Footings & Foundations	Poured concrete; strip and spread footings and 4' foundation wall		S.F. Ground	12.90	.86	
.4	Piles & Caissons	N/A		—	—	—	1.1%
.9	Excavation & Backfill	Site preparation for slab and trench for foundation wall and footing		S.F. Ground	1.02	.07	
2.0 Substructure							
.1	Slab on Grade	4" reinforced concrete with vapor barrier and granular base		S.F. Slab	3.32	.22	0.3%
.2	Special Substructures	N/A		—	—	—	
3.0 Superstructure							
.1	Columns & Beams	Gypsum board fireproofing on columns; steel columns in 3.5 and 3.7		S.F. Floor	3.03	3.03	
.4	Structural Walls	N/A		—	—	—	
.5	Elevated Floors	Open web steel joists, slab form, concrete, interior steel columns		S.F. Floor	9.44	8.81	15.5%
.7	Roof	Open web steel joists with rib metal deck, interior steel columns		S.F. Roof	3.83	.26	
.9	Stairs	Concrete filled metal pan		Flight	4070	1.21	
4.0 Exterior Closure							
.1	Walls	Ribbed precast concrete panel	87% of wall	S.F. Wall	16.21	6.77	
.5	Exterior Wall Finishes	N/A		—	—	—	
.6	Doors	Aluminum and glass		Each	1558	1.33	10.8%
.7	Windows & Glazed Walls	Aluminum horizontal sliding	13% of wall	Each	304	1.20	
5.0 Roofing							
.1	Roof Coverings	Built-up tar and gravel with flashing		S.F. Roof	2.55	.17	
.7	Insulation	Perlite/EPS composite		S.F. Roof	1.32	.09	0.3%
.8	Openings & Specialties	N/A		—	—	—	
6.0 Interior Construction							
.1	Partitions	Gypsum board on concrete block and metal studs	10 S.F. of Floor/L.F. Partition	S.F. Partition	8.23	8.23	
.4	Interior Doors	15% solid core wood, 85% hollow core wood	80 S.F. Floor/Door	Each	476	5.96	
.5	Wall Finishes	70% paint, 25% vinyl wall covering, 5% ceramic tile		S.F. Surface	1.12	2.23	
.6	Floor Finishes	60% carpet, 30% vinyl composition tile, 10% ceramic tile		S.F. Floor	4.42	4.42	28.8%
.7	Ceiling Finishes	Painted gypsum board on resilient channels		S.F. Ceiling	2.80	2.80	
.9	Interior Surface/Exterior Wall	Painted gypsum board on furring	80% of wall	S.F. Wall	3.02	1.10	
7.0 Conveying							
.1	Elevators	Four geared passenger elevators		Each	230,550	6.36	7.4%
.2	Special Conveyors	N/A		—	—	—	
8.0 Mechanical							
.1	Plumbing	Kitchen, bathroom and service fixtures, supply and drainage	1 Fixture/210 S.F. Floor	Each	1927	9.18	
.2	Fire Protection	Standpipe and wet pipe sprinkler systems		S.F. Floor	2.13	2.13	
.3	Heating	Oil fired hot water, baseboard radiation		S.F. Floor	3.91	3.91	24.1%
.4	Cooling	Chilled water, air cooled condenser system		S.F. Floor	5.53	5.53	
.5	Special Systems	N/A		—	—	—	
9.0 Electrical							
.1	Service & Distribution	4000 ampere service, panel board and feeders		S.F. Floor	1.32	1.32	
.2	Lighting & Power	Incandescent fixtures, receptacles, switches, A.C. and misc. power		S.F. Floor	4.93	4.93	9.2%
.4	Special Electrical	Alarm systems, emergency lighting, antenna, intercom and security television		S.F. Floor	1.64	1.64	
11.0 Special Construction							
.1	Specialties	Kitchen cabinets		S.F. Floor	2.13	2.13	2.5%
12.0 Site Work							
.1	Earthwork	N/A		—	—	—	
.3	Utilities	N/A		—	—	—	0.0%
.5	Roads & Parking	N/A		—	—	—	
.7	Site Improvements	N/A		—	—	—	
				Sub-Total		85.89	100%
	CONTRACTOR FEES (General Requirements: 10%, Overhead: 5%, Profit: 10%)				25%	21.47	
	ARCHITECT FEES				6%	6.44	
				Total Building Cost		113.80	

BUILDING TYPES

BUILDING TYPES

Costs per square foot of floor area

Exterior Wall	S.F. Area	12000	15000	18000	21000	24000	27000	30000	33000	36000
	L.F. Perimeter	440	500	540	590	640	665	700	732	770
Face Brick with Concrete Block Back-up	Steel Frame	124.80	120.85	117.10	114.90	113.25	111.00	109.55	108.25	107.40
	Bearing Wall	120.60	117.00	113.65	111.70	110.20	108.20	106.90	105.70	104.95
Precast Concrete	Steel Frame	116.60	113.45	110.50	108.75	107.45	105.65	104.55	103.50	102.80
Decorative Concrete Block	Bearing Wall	109.40	106.85	104.50	103.05	102.00	100.60	99.70	98.85	98.30
Concrete Block	Steel Frame	113.15	111.10	109.25	108.10	107.30	106.20	105.50	104.80	104.40
	Bearing Wall	106.00	103.75	101.70	100.45	99.55	98.30	97.50	96.80	96.35
Perimeter Adj., Add or Deduct	Per 100 L.F.	8.75	7.00	5.80	5.00	4.35	3.90	3.50	3.20	2.90
Story Hgt. Adj., Add or Deduct	Per 1 Ft.	1.35	1.25	1.10	1.05	1.00	.90	.90	.85	.80
For Basement, add $17.25 per square foot of basement area										

The above costs were calculated using the basic specifications shown on the facing page. These costs should be adjusted where necessary for design alternatives and owner's requirements. Reported completed project costs, for this type of structure, range from $52.25 to $138.50 per S.F.

Common additives

Description	Unit	$ Cost
Closed Circuit Surveillance, One station		
Camera and monitor	Each	1375
For additional camera stations, add	Each	745
Emergency Lighting, 25 watt, battery operated		
Lead battery	Each	289
Nickel cadmium	Each	655
Seating		
Auditorium chair, all veneer	Each	166
Veneer back, padded seat	Each	201
Upholstered, spring seat	Each	203
Classroom, movable chair & desk	Set	65 - 120
Lecture hall, pedestal type	Each	152 - 470
Smoke Detectors		
Ceiling type	Each	149
Duct type	Each	405
Sound System		
Amplifier, 250 watts	Each	1650
Speaker, ceiling or wall	Each	145
Trumpet	Each	271

Important: See the Reference Section for Location Factors

Model costs calculated for a 1 story building with 24' story height and 24,000 square feet of floor area

				Unit	Unit Cost	Cost Per S.F.	% Of Sub-Total
1.0 Foundations							
.1	Footings & Foundations	Poured concrete; strip and spread footings and 4' foundation wall		S.F. Ground	2.44	2.44	
.4	Piles & Caissons	N/A		—	—	—	4.4%
.9	Excavation & Backfill	Site preparation for slab and trench for foundation wall and footing		S.F. Ground	1.08	1.08	
2.0 Substructure							
.1	Slab on Grade	6" reinforced concrete with vapor barrier and granular base		S.F. Slab	3.96	3.96	4.9%
.2	Special Substructures	N/A		—	—	—	
3.0 Superstructure							
.1	Columns & Beams	Steel columns		S.F. Floor	.39	.39	
.4	Structural Walls	N/A		—	—	—	
.5	Elevated Floors	Open web steel joists, slab form, concrete	(balcony)	S.F. Floor	11.25	1.41	10.0%
.7	Roof	Metal deck on steel truss		S.F. Roof	5.46	5.46	
.9	Stairs	Concrete filled metal pan		Flight	5975	.75	
4.0 Exterior Closure							
.1	Walls	Precast concrete panel	80% of wall (adjusted for end walls)	S.F. Wall	16.39	8.39	
.5	Exterior Wall Finishes	N/A		—	—	—	16.7%
.6	Doors	Double aluminum and glass and hollow metal		Each	2527	1.27	
.7	Windows & Glazed Walls	Glass curtain wall	20% of wall	S.F. Window	29	3.73	
5.0 Roofing							
.1	Roof Coverings	Built-up tar and gravel with flashing		S.F. Roof	2.21	2.21	
.7	Insulation	Perlite/EPS composite		S.F. Roof	1.32	1.32	4.7%
.8	Openings & Specialties	Gravel stop and roof hatches		S.F. Roof	.27	.27	
6.0 Interior Construction							
.1	Partitions	Concrete Block and toilet partitions	40 S.F. Floor/L.F. Partition	S.F. Partition	5.90	2.36	
.4	Interior Doors	Single leaf hollow metal	400 S.F. Floor/Door	Each	534	1.34	
.5	Wall Finishes	70% paint, 30% epoxy coating		S.F. Surface	2.38	1.90	
.6	Floor Finishes	70% vinyl tile, 30% carpet		S.F. Floor	7.00	7.00	20.4%
.7	Ceiling Finishes	Fiberglass board, suspended		S.F. Floor	2.69	2.69	
.9	Interior Surface/Exterior Wall	Paint	80% of wall	S.F. Wall	2.12	1.09	
7.0 Conveying							
.1	Elevators	One hydraulic passenger elevator		Each	57,120	2.38	3.0%
.2	Special Conveyors	N/A		—	—	—	
8.0 Mechanical							
.1	Plumbing	Toilet and service fixtures, supply and drainage	1 Fixture/800 S.F. Floor	Each	2936	3.67	
.2	Fire Protection	Wet pipe sprinkler system		S.F. Floor	1.69	1.69	
.3	Heating	Included in 8.4		—	—	—	20.2%
.4	Cooling	Single zone rooftop unit, gas heating, electric cooling		S.F. Floor	10.95	10.95	
.5	Special Systems	N/A		—	—	—	
9.0 Electrical							
.1	Service & Distribution	800 ampere service, panel board and feeders		S.F. Floor	1.44	1.44	
.2	Lighting & Power	Fluorescent fixtures, receptacles, switches, A.C. and misc. power		S.F. Floor	7.86	7.86	15.7%
.4	Special Electrical	Alarm systems and emergency lighting, and public address system		S.F. Floor	3.28	3.28	
11.0 Special Construction							
.1	Specialties	N/A		—	—	—	0.0%
12.0 Site Work							
.1	Earthwork	N/A		—	—	—	
.3	Utilities	N/A		—	—	—	
.5	Roads & Parking	N/A		—	—	—	0.0%
.7	Site Improvements	N/A		—	—	—	
				Sub-Total		80.33	**100%**
	CONTRACTOR FEES (General Requirements: 10%, Overhead: 5%, Profit: 10%)				25%	20.08	
	ARCHITECT FEES				7%	7.04	
				Total Building Cost		**107.45**	

Costs per square foot of floor area

Exterior Wall	S.F. Area	2000	2700	3400	4100	4800	5500	6200	6900	7600
	L.F. Perimeter	180	208	236	256	280	303	317	337	357
Face Brick with Concrete Block Back-up	Steel Frame	167.10	156.85	150.80	145.55	142.35	139.90	137.05	135.35	133.95
	R/Conc. Frame	178.70	168.45	162.40	157.20	154.00	151.50	148.65	146.95	145.55
Precast Concrete Panel	Steel Frame	156.55	147.80	142.65	138.25	135.55	133.45	131.10	129.65	128.45
	R/Conc. Frame	168.15	159.45	154.25	149.85	147.15	145.05	142.70	141.25	140.05
Limestone with Concrete Block Back-up	Steel Frame	178.55	166.65	159.65	153.50	149.80	146.90	143.60	141.55	139.95
	R/Conc. Frame	190.20	178.25	171.25	165.15	161.45	158.55	155.20	153.20	151.55
Perimeter Adj., Add or Deduct	Per 100 L.F.	31.90	23.60	18.75	15.55	13.30	11.60	10.30	9.25	8.40
Story Hgt. Adj., Add or Deduct	Per 1 Ft.	3.05	2.60	2.35	2.10	2.00	1.85	1.75	1.70	1.60
For Basement, add $19.75 per square foot of basement area										

The above costs were calculated using the basic specifications shown on the facing page. These costs should be adjusted where necessary for design alternatives and owner's requirements. Reported completed project costs, for this type of structure, range from $81.85 to $201.25 per S.F.

Common additives

Description	Unit	$ Cost
Bulletproof Teller Window, 44" x 60"	Each	3175
60" x 48"	Each	4175
Closed Circuit Surveillance, One station		
Camera and monitor	Each	1375
For additional camera stations, add	Each	745
Counters, Complete	Station	4325
Door & Frame, 3' x 6'-8", bullet resistant steel		
with vision panel	Each	3675 - 4675
Drive-up Window, Drawer & micr., not incl. glass	Each	4975 - 9525
Emergency Lighting, 25 watt, battery operated		
Lead battery	Each	289
Nickel cadmium	Each	655
Night Depository	Each	7750 - 12,700
Package Receiver, painted	Each	1400
stainless steel	Each	2175
Partitions, Bullet resistant to 8' high	L.F.	233 - 380
Pneumatic Tube Systems, 2 station	Each	23,900
With TV viewer	Each	44,200

Description	Unit	$ Cost
Service Windows, Pass thru, steel		
24" x 36"	Each	2100
48" x 48"	Each	2950
72" x 40"	Each	3975
Smoke Detectors		
Ceiling type	Each	149
Duct type	Each	405
Twenty-four Hour Teller		
Automatic deposit cash & memo	Each	42,300
Vault Front, Door & frame		
1 hour test, 32"x 78"	Opening	3550
2 hour test, 32" door	Opening	4225
40" door	Opening	4625
4 hour test, 32" door	Opening	4325
40" door	Opening	5150
Time lock, two movement, add	Each	1650

Important: See the Reference Section for Location Factors

BUILDING TYPES

Model costs calculated for a 1 story building with 14' story height and 4,100 square feet of floor area

			Unit	Unit Cost	Cost Per S.F.	% Of Sub-Total
1.0 Foundations						
.1	Footings & Foundations	Poured concrete; strip and spread footings and 4' foundation wall	S.F. Ground	6.53	6.53	
.4	Piles & Caissons	N/A	—	—	—	6.8%
.9	Excavation & Backfill	Site preparation for slab and trench for foundation wall and footing	S.F. Ground	1.17	1.17	
2.0 Substructure						
.1	Slab on Grade	4" reinforced concrete with vapor barrier and granular base	S.F. Slab	3.32	3.32	2.9%
.2	Special Substructures	N/A	—	—	—	
3.0 Superstructure						
.1	Columns & Beams	Concrete columns	L.F. Columns	72	3.55	
.4	Structural Walls	N/A	—	—	—	
.5	Elevated Floors	N/A	—	—	—	12.2%
.7	Roof	Cast-in-place concrete slab	S.F. Roof	10.24	10.24	
.9	Stairs	N/A	—	—	—	
4.0 Exterior Closure						
.1	Walls	Face brick with concrete block backup 80% of wall	S.F. Wall	21	14.72	
.5	Exterior Wall Finishes	N/A	—	—	—	
.6	Doors	Double aluminum and glass and hollow metal	Each	2038	1.00	17.8%
.7	Windows & Glazed Walls	Horizontal aluminum sliding 20% of wall	Each	384	4.48	
5.0 Roofing						
.1	Roof Coverings	Built-up tar and gravel with flashing	S.F. Roof	2.94	2.94	
.7	Insulation	Perlite/EPS composite	S.F. Roof	1.32	1.32	4.1%
.8	Openings & Specialties	Gravel stop	L.F. Perimeter	6.40	.40	
6.0 Interior Construction						
.1	Partitions	Gypsum board on metal studs 20 S.F. of Floor/L.F. Partition	S.F. Partition	2.82	1.41	
.4	Interior Doors	Single leaf hollow metal 200 S.F. Floor/Door	Each	534	2.67	
.5	Wall Finishes	50% vinyl wall covering, 50% paint	S.F. Surface	1.00	1.00	
.6	Floor Finishes	50% carpet tile, 40% vinyl composition tile, 10% quarry tile	S.F. Floor	4.50	4.50	13.6%
.7	Ceiling Finishes	Mineral fiber tile on concealed zee bars	S.F. Ceiling	3.63	3.63	
.9	Interior Surface/Exterior Wall	Painted gypsum board on furring 80% of wall	S.F. Wall	3.08	2.15	
7.0 Conveying						
.1	Elevators	N/A	—	—	—	0.0%
.2	Special Conveyors	N/A	—	—	—	
8.0 Mechanical						
.1	Plumbing	Toilet and service fixtures, supply and drainage 1 Fixture/580 S.F. Floor	Each	3311	5.71	
.2	Fire Protection	Wet pipe sprinkler system	S.F. Floor	2.27	2.27	
.3	Heating	Included in 8.4	—	—	—	15.5%
.4	Cooling	Single zone rooftop unit, gas heating, electric cooling	S.F. Floor	9.62	9.62	
.5	Special Systems	N/A	—	—	—	
9.0 Electrical						
.1	Service & Distribution	200 ampere service, panel board and feeders	S.F. Floor	1.62	1.62	
.2	Lighting & Power	Fluorescent fixtures, receptacles, switches, A.C. and misc. power	S.F. Floor	6.98	6.98	9.2%
.4	Special Electrical	Alarm systems, emergency lighting, and security television	S.F. Floor	1.81	1.81	
11.0 Special Construction						
.1	Specialties	Vault door, automatic teller, drive up window, closed circuit T.V., night depository	S.F. Floor	20	20.24	17.9%
12.0 Site Work						
.1	Earthwork	N/A	—	—	—	
.3	Utilities	N/A	—	—	—	
.5	Roads & Parking	N/A	—	—	—	0.0%
.7	Site Improvements	N/A	—	—	—	

		Sub-Total	113.28	100%
CONTRACTOR FEES (General Requirements: 10%, Overhead: 5%, Profit: 10%)		25%	28.32	
ARCHITECT FEES		11%	15.60	

Total Building Cost   157.20

Costs per square foot of floor area

Exterior Wall	S.F. Area	12000	14000	16000	18000	20000	22000	24000	26000	28000
	L.F. Perimeter	460	491	520	540	566	593	620	645	670
Concrete Block	Steel Roof Deck	73.65	71.65	70.05	68.60	67.55	66.70	66.00	65.40	64.90
Decorative Concrete Block	Steel Roof Deck	77.15	74.85	73.00	71.35	70.15	69.20	68.35	67.65	67.10
Face Brick on Concrete Block	Steel Roof Deck	82.10	79.35	77.20	75.20	73.80	72.65	71.70	70.85	70.20
Jumbo Brick on Concrete Block	Steel Roof Deck	79.45	76.95	74.95	73.15	71.80	70.80	69.90	69.15	68.50
Stucco on Concrete Block	Steel Roof Deck	76.00	73.80	72.00	70.40	69.25	68.35	67.55	66.90	66.35
Precast Concrete Panel	Steel Roof Deck	74.80	72.70	71.05	69.50	68.40	67.50	66.80	66.15	65.60
Perimeter Adj., Add or Deduct	Per 100 L.F.	3.40	2.90	2.55	2.25	2.05	1.85	1.70	1.60	1.45
Story Hgt. Adj., Add or Deduct	Per 1 Ft.	.80	.70	.65	.60	.55	.55	.50	.50	.45
For Basement, add $19.55 per square foot of basement area										

The above costs were calculated using the basic specifications shown on the facing page. These costs should be adjusted where necessary for design alternatives and owner's requirements. Reported completed project costs, for this type of structure, range from $36.65 to $89.70 per S.F.

Common additives

Description	Unit	$ Cost
Bowling Alleys, Incl. alley, pinsetter, scorer, counter & misc. supplies, average	Lane	45,700
For automatic scorer, add (maximum)	Lane	7475
Emergency Lighting, 25 watt, battery operated		
Lead battery	Each	289
Nickel cadmium	Each	655
Lockers, Steel, Single tier, 60" or 72"	Opening	125 - 220
2 tier, 60" or 72" total	Opening	70 - 119
5 tier, box lockers	Opening	40 - 60
Locker bench, lam., maple top only	L.F.	18.05
Pedestals, steel pipe	Each	58
Seating		
Auditorium chair, all veneer	Each	166
Veneer back, padded seat	Each	201
Upholstered, spring seat	Each	203
Sound System		
Amplifier, 250 watts	Each	1650
Speaker, ceiling or wall	Each	145
Trumpet	Each	271

Model costs calculated for a 1 story building with 14' story height and 20,000 square feet of floor area

				Unit	Unit Cost	Cost Per S.F.	% Of Sub-Total
1.0 Foundations							
	.1	Footings & Foundations	Poured concrete; strip and spread footings and 4' foundation wall	S.F. Ground	2.22	2.22	
	.4	Piles & Caissons	N/A	—	—	—	6.9%
	.9	Excavation & Backfill	Site preparation for slab and trench for foundation wall and footing	S.F. Ground	1.28	1.28	
2.0 Substructure							
	.1	Slab on Grade	4" reinforced concrete with vapor barrier and granular base	S.F. Slab	3.32	3.32	6.6%
	.2	Special Substructures	N/A	—	—	—	
3.0 Superstructure							
	.1	Columns & Beams	Columns included in 3.7	—	—	—	
	.4	Structural Walls	N/A	—	—	—	
	.5	Elevated Floors	N/A	—	—	—	11.0%
	.7	Roof	Metal deck on open web steel joists with columns and beams	S.F. Roof	5.55	5.55	
	.9	Stairs	N/A	—	—	—	
4.0 Exterior Closure							
	.1	Walls	Concrete block _90% of wall_	S.F. Wall	7.99	2.85	
	.5	Exterior Wall Finishes	N/A	—	—	—	
	.6	Doors	Double aluminum and glass and hollow metal	Each	1445	.36	11.0%
	.7	Windows & Glazed Walls	Horizontal pivoted _10% of wall_	Each	1427	2.36	
5.0 Roofing							
	.1	Roof Coverings	Built-up tar and gravel with flashing	S.F. Roof	2.24	2.24	
	.7	Insulation	Perlite/EPS composite	S.F. Roof	1.32	1.32	7.2%
	.8	Openings & Specialties	Gravel stop and hatches	S.F. Roof	.09	.09	
6.0 Interior Construction							
	.1	Partitions	Concrete block _50 S.F. Floor/L.F. Partition_	S.F. Partition	6.55	1.31	
	.4	Interior Doors	Hollow metal single leaf _1000 S.F. Floor/Door_	Each	534	.53	
	.5	Wall Finishes	Paint and block filler	S.F. Surface	2.13	.85	
	.6	Floor Finishes	Vinyl tile _25% of floor_	S.F. Floor	2.16	.54	9.2%
	.7	Ceiling Finishes	Suspended fiberglass board _25% of area_	S.F. Ceiling	2.69	.67	
	.9	Interior Surface/Exterior Wall	Paint and block filler _90% of wall_	S.F. Wall	2.12	.76	
7.0 Conveying							
	.1	Elevators	N/A	—	—	—	0.0%
	.2	Special Conveyors	N/A	—	—	—	
8.0 Mechanical							
	.1	Plumbing	Toilet and service fixtures, supply and drainage _1 Fixture/2200 S.F. Floor_	Each	2794	1.27	
	.2	Fire Protection	Sprinklers, light hazard	S.F. Floor	1.44	1.44	
	.3	Heating	Included in 8.4	—	—	—	30.0%
	.4	Cooling	Single zone rooftop unit, gas heating, electric cooling	S.F. Floor	12.40	12.40	
	.5	Special Systems	N/A	—	—	—	
9.0 Electrical							
	.1	Service & Distribution	800 ampere service, panel board and feeders	S.F. Floor	1.73	1.73	
	.2	Lighting & Power	Fluorescent fixtures, receptacles, switches, A.C. and misc. power	S.F. Floor	7.13	7.13	18.1%
	.4	Special Electrical	Alarm systems and emergency lighting	S.F. Floor	.28	.28	
11.0 Special Construction							
	.1	Specialties	N/A	—	—	—	0.0%
12.0 Site Work							
	.1	Earthwork	N/A	—	—	—	
	.3	Utilities	N/A	—	—	—	
	.5	Roads & Parking	N/A	—	—	—	0.0%
	.7	Site Improvements	N/A	—	—	—	
				Sub-Total		50.50	**100%**
		CONTRACTOR FEES (General Requirements: 10%, Overhead: 5%, Profit: 10%)			25%	12.63	
		ARCHITECT FEES			7%	4.42	
				Total Building Cost		**67.55**	

BUILDING TYPES

89

BUILDING TYPES

Costs per square foot of floor area

Exterior Wall	S.F. Area	6000	8000	10000	12000	14000	16000	18000	20000	22000
	L.F. Perimeter	320	386	453	520	540	597	610	660	710
Face Brick with Concrete Block Back-up	Bearing Walls	101.45	97.45	95.10	93.55	90.65	89.70	87.65	87.00	86.45
	Steel Frame	103.00	99.05	96.75	95.20	92.30	91.40	89.40	88.70	88.20
Decorative Concrete Block	Bearing Walls	96.10	92.60	90.60	89.20	86.75	85.95	84.25	83.65	83.20
	Steel Frame	97.65	94.20	92.20	90.85	88.45	87.65	85.95	85.40	84.95
Precast Concrete Panels	Bearing Walls	94.80	91.45	89.50	88.15	85.85	85.05	83.45	82.90	82.45
	Steel Frame	96.35	93.05	91.10	89.80	87.55	86.75	85.15	84.65	84.20
Perimeter Adj., Add or Deduct	Per 100 L.F.	8.95	6.70	5.35	4.50	3.80	3.35	3.00	2.65	2.45
Story Hgt. Adj., Add or Deduct	Per 1 Ft.	1.45	1.35	1.25	1.20	1.05	1.05	.95	.90	.90
Basement—Not Applicable										

The above costs were calculated using the basic specifications shown on the facing page. These costs should be adjusted where necessary for design alternatives and owner's requirements. Reported completed project costs, for this type of structure, range from $44.00 to $106.10 per S.F.

Common additives

Description	Unit	$ Cost
Directory Boards, Plastic, glass covered		
30" x 20"	Each	565
36" x 48"	Each	1025
Aluminum, 24" x 18"	Each	425
36" x 24"	Each	535
48" x 32"	Each	745
48" x 60"	Each	1600
Emergency Lighting, 25 watt, battery operated		
Lead battery	Each	289
Nickel cadmium	Each	655
Benches, Hardwood	L.F.	82 - 153
Ticket Printer	Each	7000
Turnstiles, One way		
4 arm, 46" dia., manual	Each	425
Electric	Each	1550
High security, 3 arm		
65" dia., manual	Each	3150
Electric	Each	4375
Gate with horizontal bars		
65" dia., 7' high transit type	Each	4050

Important: See the Reference Section for Location Factors

Model costs calculated for a 1 story building with 14' story height and 12,000 square feet of floor area

Bus Terminal

				Unit	Unit Cost	Cost Per S.F.	% Of Sub-Total
1.0 Foundations							
	.1	Footings & Foundations	Poured concrete; strip and spread footings and 4' foundation wall	S.F. Ground	3.94	3.94	
	.4	Piles & Caissons	N/A	—	—	—	7.3%
	.9	Excavation & Backfill	Site preparation for slab and trench for foundation wall and footing	S.F. Ground	1.17	1.17	
2.0 Substructure							
	.1	Slab on Grade	6" reinforced concrete with vapor barrier and granular base	S.F. Slab	4.76	4.76	6.8%
	.2	Special Substructures	N/A	—	—	—	
3.0 Superstructure							
	.1	Columns & Beams	Columns included in 3.7	—	—	—	
	.4	Structural Walls	N/A	—	—	—	
	.5	Elevated Floors	N/A	—	—	—	5.4%
	.7	Roof	Metal deck on open web steel joists with columns and beams	S.F. Roof	3.76	3.76	
	.9	Stairs	N/A	—	—	—	
4.0 Exterior Closure							
	.1	Walls	Face brick with concrete block backup 70% of wall	S.F. Wall	21	8.94	
	.5	Exterior Wall Finishes	N/A	—	—	—	
	.6	Doors	Double aluminum and glass	Each	3275	1.09	19.2%
	.7	Windows & Glazed Walls	Store front 30% of wall	S.F. Window	18.75	3.41	
5.0 Roofing							
	.1	Roof Coverings	Built-up tar and gravel with flashing	S.F. Roof	2.55	2.55	
	.7	Insulation	Perlite/EPS composite	S.F. Roof	1.32	1.32	5.9%
	.8	Openings & Specialties	Gravel stop	L.F. Perimeter	6.40	.28	
6.0 Interior Construction							
	.1	Partitions	Lightweight concrete block 15 S.F. Floor/L.F. Partition	S.F. Partition	6.56	4.37	
	.4	Interior Doors	Hollow metal 150 S.F. Floor/Door	Each	534	3.56	
	.5	Wall Finishes	Glazed coating	S.F. Surface	.44	.59	
	.6	Floor Finishes	Quarry tile and vinyl composition tile	S.F. Floor	5.74	5.74	25.9%
	.7	Ceiling Finishes	Mineral fiber tile on concealed zee bars	S.F. Ceiling	3.63	3.63	
	.9	Interior Surface/Exterior Wall	Glazed coating 70% of wall	S.F. Wall	.45	.19	
7.0 Conveying							
	.1	Elevators	N/A	—	—	—	0.0%
	.2	Special Conveyors	N/A	—	—	—	
8.0 Mechanical							
	.1	Plumbing	Toilet and service fixtures, supply and drainage 1 Fixture/850 S.F. Floor	Each	2329	2.74	
	.2	Fire Protection	Wet pipe sprinkler system	S.F. Floor	2.21	2.21	
	.3	Heating	Included in 8.4	—	—	—	20.3%
	.4	Cooling	Single zone rooftop unit, gas heating, electric cooling	S.F. Floor	9.26	9.26	
	.5	Special Systems	N/A	—	—	—	
9.0 Electrical							
	.1	Service & Distribution	400 ampere service, panel board and feeders	S.F. Floor	1.11	1.11	
	.2	Lighting & Power	Fluorescent fixtures, receptacles, switches, A.C. and misc. power	S.F. Floor	4.81	4.81	9.2%
	.4	Special Electrical	Alarm systems and emergency lighting	S.F. Floor	.50	.50	
11.0 Special Construction							
	.1	Specialties	N/A	—	—	—	0.0%
12.0 Site Work							
	.1	Earthwork	N/A	—	—	—	
	.3	Utilities	N/A	—	—	—	
	.5	Roads & Parking	N/A	—	—	—	0.0%
	.7	Site Improvements	N/A	—	—	—	
				Sub-Total		69.93	100%
		CONTRACTOR FEES (General Requirements: 10%, Overhead: 5%, Profit: 10%)			25%	17.48	
		ARCHITECT FEES			7%	6.14	
				Total Building Cost		93.55	

BUILDING TYPES

91

Costs per square foot of floor area

Exterior Wall	S.F. Area	600	800	1000	1200	1600	2000	2400	3000	4000
	L.F. Perimeter	100	114	128	139	164	189	214	250	314
Brick with Concrete Block Back-up	Steel Frame	219.80	210.45	204.85	200.10	194.95	191.85	189.80	187.55	185.65
	Bearing Walls	216.75	207.40	201.75	197.05	191.90	188.80	186.70	184.45	182.60
Concrete Block	Steel Frame	192.25	186.90	183.65	180.95	178.00	176.25	175.05	173.75	172.70
	Bearing Walls	189.20	183.80	180.60	177.90	174.95	173.15	171.95	170.70	169.60
Galvanized Steel Siding	Steel Frame	192.40	187.75	184.95	182.60	180.05	178.50	177.45	176.35	175.45
Metal Sandwich Panel	Steel Frame	190.50	184.80	181.35	178.45	175.30	173.40	172.15	170.75	169.60
Perimeter Adj., Add or Deduct	Per 100 L.F.	64.55	48.40	38.75	32.30	24.25	19.35	16.10	12.90	9.70
Story Hgt. Adj., Add or Deduct	Per 1 Ft.	3.95	3.40	3.05	2.75	2.45	2.25	2.10	2.00	1.85
Basement—Not Applicable										

The above costs were calculated using the basic specifications shown on the facing page. These costs should be adjusted where necessary for design alternatives and owner's requirements. Reported completed project costs, for this type of structure, range from $78.90 to $224.10 per S.F.

Common additives

Description	Unit	$ Cost
Air Compressors, Electric		
1-1/2 H.P., standard controls	Each	1025
Dual controls	Each	1200
5 H.P., 115/230 volt, standard control	Each	2725
Dual controls	Each	2825
Emergency Lighting, 25 watt, battery operated		
Lead battery	Each	289
Nickel cadmium	Each	655
Fence, Chain link, 6' high		
9 ga. wire, galvanized	L.F.	15.90
6 ga. wire	L.F.	21
Gate	Each	287
Product Dispenser with vapor recovery		
for 6 nozzles	Each	16,500
Laundry Equipment		
Dryer, gas, 16 lb. capacity	Each	710
30 lb. capacity	Each	2775
Washer, 4 cycle	Each	795
Commercial	Each	1200

Description	Unit	$ Cost
Lockers, Steel, single tier, 60" or 72"	Opening	125 - 220
2 tier, 60" or 72" total	Opening	70 - 119
5 tier, box lockers	Opening	40 - 60
Locker bench, lam. maple top only	L.F.	18.05
Pedestals, steel pipe	Each	58
Paving, Bituminous		
Wearing course plus base course	Sq. Yard	5.60
Safe, Office type, 4 hour rating		
30" x 18" x 18"	Each	3125
62" x 33" x 20"	Each	6775
Sidewalks, Concrete 4" thick	S.F.	2.83
Yard Lighting,		
20' aluminum pole with 400 watt high pressure sodium fixture	Each	2165

Important: See the Reference Section for Location Factors

BUILDING TYPES

Model costs calculated for a 1 story building with 12' story height and 800 square feet of floor area

				Unit	Unit Cost	Cost Per S.F.	% Of Sub-Total
1.0 Foundations							
.1	Footings & Foundations	Poured concrete; strip and spread footings and 4' foundation wall		S.F. Ground	8.44	8.44	
.4	Piles & Caissons	N/A		—	—	—	6.4%
.9	Excavation & Backfill	Site preparation for slab and trench for foundation wall and footing		S.F. Ground	1.64	1.64	
2.0 Substructure							
.1	Slab on Grade	5" reinforced concrete with vapor barrier and granular base		S.F. Slab	4.18	4.18	2.7%
.2	Special Substructures	N/A		—	—	—	
3.0 Superstructure							
.1	Columns & Beams	Steel columns included in 3.7		—	—	—	
.4	Structural Walls	N/A		—	—	—	
.5	Elevated Floors	N/A		—	—	—	3.0%
.7	Roof	Metal deck, open web steel joists, beams, columns		S.F. Roof	4.75	4.75	
.9	Stairs	N/A		—	—	—	
4.0 Exterior Closure							
.1	Walls	Face brick with concrete block backup	70% of wall	S.F. Wall	21	25.20	
.5	Exterior Wall Finishes	N/A		—	—	—	
.6	Doors	Steel overhead hollow metal		Each	1873	9.37	25.3%
.7	Windows & Glazed Walls	Horizontal pivoted steel	5% of wall	Each	554	5.26	
5.0 Roofing							
.1	Roof Coverings	Built-up tar and gravel with flashing		S.F. Roof	4.04	4.04	
.7	Insulation	Perlite/EPS composite		S.F. Roof	1.32	1.32	3.4%
.8	Openings & Specialties	N/A		—	—	—	
6.0 Interior Construction							
.1	Partitions	Concrete block	20 S.F. Floor/S.F. Partition	S.F. Partition	6.34	3.17	
.4	Interior Doors	Hollow metal	600 S.F. Floor/Door	Each	534	.89	
.5	Wall Finishes	Paint		S.F. Surface	.84	.84	
.6	Floor Finishes	N/A		—	—	—	3.1%
.7	Ceiling Finishes	N/A		—	—	—	
.9	Interior Surface/Exterior Wall	N/A		—	—	—	
7.0 Conveying							
.1	Elevators	N/A		—	—	—	0.0%
.2	Special Conveyors	N/A		—	—	—	
8.0 Mechanical							
.1	Plumbing	Toilet and service fixtures, supply and drainage	1 Fixture/160 S.F. Floor	Each	4832	30.20	
.2	Fire Protection	N/A		—	—	—	
.3	Heating	Unit heaters		S.F. Floor	11.75	11.75	26.7%
.4	Cooling	N/A		—	—	—	
.5	Special Systems	N/A		—	—	—	
9.0 Electrical							
.1	Service & Distribution	400 ampere service, panel board and feeders		S.F. Floor	14.78	14.78	
.2	Lighting & Power	Fluorescent fixtures, receptacles, switches and misc. power		S.F. Floor	30	30.18	29.4%
.4	Special Electrical	Emergency power		S.F. Floor	1.34	1.34	
11.0 Special Construction							
.1	Specialties	N/A		—	—	—	0.0%
12.0 Site Work							
.1	Earthwork	N/A		—	—	—	
.3	Utilities	N/A		—	—	—	
.5	Roads & Parking	N/A		—	—	—	0.0%
.7	Site Improvements	N/A		—	—	—	

			Sub-Total	157.35	**100%**
	CONTRACTOR FEES (General Requirements: 10%, Overhead: 5%, Profit: 10%)		25%	39.34	
	ARCHITECT FEES		7%	13.76	

	Total Building Cost	**210.45**

BUILDING TYPES

Costs per square foot of floor area

Exterior Wall	S.F. Area	2000	7000	12000	17000	22000	27000	32000	37000	42000
	L.F. Perimeter	180	340	470	540	640	740	762	793	860
Decorative Concrete Brick	Wood Arch	166.55	125.25	116.15	109.40	106.85	105.25	102.05	99.95	99.00
	Steel Truss	162.65	121.30	112.25	105.45	102.95	101.30	98.10	96.00	95.10
Stone with Concrete Block Back-up	Wood Arch	192.05	139.00	127.25	118.40	115.10	113.00	108.80	106.00	104.85
	Steel Truss	183.70	130.60	118.90	110.05	106.75	104.60	100.45	97.60	96.45
Face Brick with Concrete Block Back-up	Wood Arch	185.05	135.25	124.25	115.95	112.85	110.85	106.95	104.35	103.25
	Steel Truss	176.70	126.85	115.85	107.55	104.50	102.50	98.60	95.95	94.90
Perimeter Adj., Add or Deduct	Per 100 L.F.	43.45	12.40	7.25	5.10	3.95	3.25	2.75	2.35	2.10
Story Hgt. Adj., Add or Deduct	Per 1 Ft.	2.55	1.40	1.10	.90	.85	.80	.70	.60	.60
For Basement, add $20.80 per square foot of basement area										

The above costs were calculated using the basic specifications shown on the facing page. These costs should be adjusted where necessary for design alternatives and owner's requirements. Reported completed project costs, for this type of structure, range from $50.35 to $202.35 per S.F.

Common additives

Description	Unit	$ Cost	Description	Unit	$ Cost
Altar, Wood, custom design, plain	Each	2075	Pews/Benches, Hardwood	L.F.	82 - 153
Deluxe	Each	10,700	Pulpits, Prefabricated, hardwood	Each	1350 - 7925
Granite or marble, average	Each	8575	Railing, Hardwood	L.F.	161
Deluxe	Each	26,900	Steeples, translucent fiberglass		
Ark, Prefabricated, plain	Each	7900	30" square, 15' high	Each	4700
Deluxe	Each	91,000	25' high	Each	5425
Baptistry, Fiberglass, incl. plumbing	Each	3625 - 6600	Painted fiberglass, 24" square, 14' high	Each	4125
Bells & Carillons, 48 bells	Each	550,000	28' high	Each	4750
24 bells	Each	220,000	Aluminum		
Confessional, Prefabricated wood			20' high, 3'- 6" base	Each	4650
Single, plain	Each	2925	35' high, 8'- 0" base	Each	17,600
Deluxe	Each	7325	60' high, 14'- 0" base	Each	39,700
Double, plain	Each	5575			
Deluxe	Each	16,400			
Emergency Lighting, 25 watt, battery operated					
Lead battery	Each	289			
Nickel cadmium	Each	655			
Lecterns, Wood, plain	Each	600			
Deluxe	Each	2925			

Model costs calculated for a 1 story building with 24' story height and 17,000 square feet of floor area

Church

				Unit	Unit Cost	Cost Per S.F.	% Of Sub-Total
1.0 Foundations							
.1	Footings & Foundations	Poured concrete; strip and spread footings and 4' foundation wall		S.F. Ground	5.03	5.03	
.4	Piles & Caissons	N/A		—	—	—	7.3%
.9	Excavation & Backfill	Site preparation for slab and trench for foundation wall and footing		S.F. Ground	1.08	1.08	
2.0 Substructure							
.1	Slab on Grade	4" reinforced concrete with vapor barrier and granular base		S.F. Slab	3.32	3.32	4.0%
.2	Special Substructures	N/A		—	—	—	
3.0 Superstructure							
.1	Columns & Beams	N/A		—	—	—	
.4	Structural Walls	N/A		—	—	—	
.5	Elevated Floors	N/A		—	—	—	17.4%
.7	Roof	Wood deck on laminated wood arches		S.F. Roof	13.65	14.56	
.9	Stairs	N/A		—	—	—	
4.0 Exterior Closure							
.1	Walls	Face brick with concrete block backup	80% of wall (adjusted for end walls)	S.F. Wall	25	15.25	
.5	Exterior Wall Finishes	N/A		—	—	—	22.3%
.6	Doors	Double hollow metal swinging, single hollow metal		Each	1078	.38	
.7	Windows & Glazed Walls	Aluminum, top hinged, in-swinging and curtain wall panels	20% of wall	S.F. Window	19.87	3.03	
5.0 Roofing							
.1	Roof Coverings	Asphalt shingles with flashing		S.F. Roof	1.58	1.58	
.7	Insulation	Polystyrene		S.F. Ground	1.18	1.42	3.9%
.8	Openings & Specialties	Gutters and downspouts		S.F. Ground	.30	.30	
6.0 Interior Construction							
.1	Partitions	Plaster on metal studs	40 S.F. Floor/L.F. Partitions	S.F. Partition	6.90	4.14	
.4	Interior Doors	Hollow metal	400 S.F. Floor/Door	Each	534	1.34	
.5	Wall Finishes	Paint		S.F. Surface	.80	.96	
.6	Floor Finishes	Carpet		S.F. Floor	5.47	5.47	16.8%
.7	Ceiling Finishes	N/A		—	—	—	
.9	Interior Surface/Exterior Wall	Painted plaster	80% of wall	S.F. Wall	3.47	2.12	
7.0 Conveying							
.1	Elevators	N/A		—	—	—	0.0%
.2	Special Conveyors	N/A		—	—	—	
8.0 Mechanical							
.1	Plumbing	Kitchen, toilet and service fixtures, supply and drainage	1 Fixture/2430 S.F. Floor	Each	2551	1.05	
.2	Fire Protection	Wet pipe sprinkler system		S.F. Floor	1.69	1.69	
.3	Heating	Oil fired hot water, wall fin radiation		S.F. Floor	5.81	5.81	18.4%
.4	Cooling	Split systems with air cooled condensing units		S.F. Floor	6.73	6.73	
.5	Special Systems	N/A		—	—	—	
9.0 Electrical							
.1	Service & Distribution	400 ampere service, panel board and feeders		S.F. Floor	.51	.51	
.2	Lighting & Power	Fluorescent fixtures, receptacles, switches, A.C. and misc. power		S.F. Floor	5.75	5.75	9.9%
.4	Special Electrical	Alarm systems, sound system and emergency lighting		S.F. Floor	2.04	2.04	
11.0 Special Construction							
.1	Specialties	N/A		—	—	—	0.0%
12.0 Site Work							
.1	Earthwork	N/A		—	—	—	
.3	Utilities	N/A		—	—	—	
.5	Roads & Parking	N/A		—	—	—	0.0%
.7	Site Improvements	N/A		—	—	—	
				Sub-Total		83.56	100%
	CONTRACTOR FEES (General Requirements: 10%, Overhead: 5%, Profit: 10%)				25%	20.89	
	ARCHITECT FEES				11%	11.50	
				Total Building Cost		115.95	

BUILDING TYPES

Costs per square foot of floor area

Exterior Wall	S.F. Area	2000	4000	6000	8000	12000	15000	18000	20000	22000
	L.F. Perimeter	180	280	340	386	460	535	560	600	640
Stone Ashlar Veneer On Concrete Block	Wood Truss	167.30	145.40	134.35	127.85	120.60	118.40	115.35	114.50	113.80
	Steel Joists	164.45	142.50	131.50	125.00	117.75	115.55	112.50	111.65	110.95
Stucco on Concrete Block	Wood Truss	153.65	134.75	125.75	120.55	114.75	113.00	110.65	109.95	109.40
	Steel Joists	151.00	132.15	123.15	117.95	112.15	110.35	108.05	107.35	106.75
Brick Veneer	Wood Frame	160.50	140.00	129.95	124.10	117.50	115.50	112.80	112.00	111.40
Wood Shingles	Wood Frame	152.40	133.70	124.85	119.75	114.05	112.25	110.00	109.30	108.75
Perimeter Adj., Add or Deduct	Per 100 L.F.	27.75	13.90	9.25	6.95	4.60	3.70	3.10	2.75	2.55
Story Hgt. Adj., Add or Deduct	Per 1 Ft.	3.05	2.35	1.90	1.65	1.30	1.20	1.05	1.00	1.00
For Basement, add $ 17.90 per square foot of basement area										

The above costs were calculated using the basic specifications shown on the facing page. These costs should be adjusted where necessary for design alternatives and owner's requirements. Reported completed project costs, for this type of structure, range from $ 49.75 to $ 162.80 per S.F.

Common additives

Description	Unit	$ Cost	Description	Unit	$ Cost
Bar, Front bar	L.F.	285	Sauna, Prefabricated, complete, 6' x 4'	Each	4075
Back bar	L.F.	227	6' x 9'	Each	5350
Booth, Upholstered, custom, straight	L.F.	144 - 265	8' x 8'	Each	6300
"L" or "U" shaped	L.F.	149 - 252	10' x 12'	Each	9125
Fireplaces, Brick not incl. chimney			Smoke Detectors		
or foundation, 30" x 24" opening	Each	2050	Ceiling type	Each	149
Chimney, standard brick			Duct type	Each	405
Single flue 16" x 20"	V.L.F.	62	Sound System		
20" x 20"	V.L.F.	69	Amplifier, 250 watts	Each	1650
2 flue, 20" x 32"	V.L.F.	102	Speaker, ceiling or wall	Each	145
Lockers, Steel, single tier, 60" or 72"	Opening	125 - 220	Trumpet	Each	271
2 tier, 60" or 72" total	Opening	70 - 119	Steam Bath, Complete, to 140 C.F.	Each	1275
5 tier, box lockers	Opening	40 - 60	To 300 C.F.	Each	1450
Locker bench, lam. maple top only	L.F.	18.05	To 800 C.F.	Each	4625
Pedestals, steel pipe	Each	58	To 2500 C.F.	Each	4925
Refrigerators, Prefabricated, walk-in			Swimming Pool Complete, gunite	S.F.	47 - 57
7'-6" High, 6' x 6'	S.F.	120	Tennis Court, Complete with fence		
10' x 10'	S.F.	95	Bituminous	Each	23,000 - 28,600
12' x 14'	S.F.	83	Clay	Each	25,600 - 31,600
12' x 20'	S.F.	73			

BUILDING TYPES

Important: See the Reference Section for Location Factors

Model costs calculated for a 1 story building with 12' story height and 6,000 square feet of floor area

			Unit	Unit Cost	Cost Per S.F.	% Of Sub-Total
1.0 Foundations						
.1	Footings & Foundations	Poured concrete; strip and spread footings and 4' foundation wall	S.F. Ground	5.58	5.58	7.0%
.4	Piles & Caissons	N/A	—	—	—	
.9	Excavation & Backfill	Site preparation for slab and trench for foundation wall and footing	S.F. Ground	1.17	1.17	
2.0 Substructure						
.1	Slab on Grade	4" reinforced concrete with vapor barrier and granular base	S.F. Slab	3.32	3.32	3.4%
.2	Special Substructures	N/A	—	—	—	
3.0 Superstructure						
.1	Columns & Beams	N/A	—	—	—	5.0%
.4	Structural Walls	Load bearing partition walls, see item 6.1	—	—	—	
.5	Elevated Floors	N/A	—	—	—	
.7	Roof	Wood truss with plywood sheathing	S.F. Ground	4.88	4.88	
.9	Stairs	N/A	—	—	—	
4.0 Exterior Closure						
.1	Walls	Stone ashlar veneer on concrete block 65% of wall	S.F. Wall	23	10.39	17.5%
.5	Exterior Wall Finishes	N/A	—	—	—	
.6	Doors	Double aluminum and glass, hollow metal	Each	1709	1.71	
.7	Windows & Glazed Walls	Aluminum horizontal sliding 35% of wall	Each	304	4.82	
5.0 Roofing						
.1	Roof Coverings	Asphalt shingles	S.F. Roof	1.06	1.30	1.9%
.7	Insulation	N/A	—	—	—	
.8	Openings & Specialties	Gutters and downspouts	S.F. Roof	.53	.53	
6.0 Interior Construction						
.1	Partitions	Gypsum board on metal studs, load bearing 14 S.F. Floor/L.F. Partition	S.F. Partition	3.44	2.46	19.1%
.4	Interior Doors	Single leaf wood 140 S.F. Floor/Door	Each	427	3.05	
.5	Wall Finishes	40% vinyl wall covering, 40% paint, 20% ceramic tile	S.F. Surface	1.89	2.70	
.6	Floor Finishes	50% carpet, 30% hardwood tile, 20% ceramic tile	S.F. Floor	5.98	5.98	
.7	Ceiling Finishes	Gypsum plaster on wood furring	S.F. Ceiling	2.92	2.92	
.9	Interior Surface/Exterior Wall	Painted gypsum board on furring 65% of wall	S.F. Wall	3.08	1.36	
7.0 Conveying						
.1	Elevators	N/A	—	—	—	0.0%
.2	Special Conveyors	N/A	—	—	—	
8.0 Mechanical						
.1	Plumbing	Kitchen, toilet and service fixtures, supply and drainage 1 Fixture/125 S.F. Floor	Each	1990	15.92	39.7%
.2	Fire Protection	Wet pipe sprinkler system	S.F. Floor	2.27	2.27	
.3	Heating	Included in 8.4	—	—	—	
.4	Cooling	Multizone rooftop unit, gas heating, electric cooling	S.F. Floor	20	20.25	
.5	Special Systems	N/A	—	—	—	
9.0 Electrical						
.1	Service & Distribution	400 ampere service, panel board and feeders	S.F. Floor	2.19	2.19	6.4%
.2	Lighting & Power	Fluorescent fixtures, receptacles, switches, A.C. and misc. power	S.F. Floor	3.60	3.60	
.4	Special Electrical	Alarm systems and emergency lighting	S.F. Floor	.43	.43	
11.0 Special Construction						
.1	Specialties	N/A	—	—	—	0.0%
12.0 Site Work						
.1	Earthwork	N/A	—	—	—	0.0%
.3	Utilities	N/A	—	—	—	
.5	Roads & Parking	N/A	—	—	—	
.7	Site Improvements	N/A	—	—	—	
			Sub-Total		96.83	**100%**

CONTRACTOR FEES (General Requirements: 10%, Overhead: 5%, Profit: 10%)		25%	24.21
ARCHITECT FEES		11%	13.31
	Total Building Cost		134.35

BUILDING TYPES

Costs per square foot of floor area

Exterior Wall	S.F. Area	4000	8000	12000	17000	22000	27000	32000	37000	42000
	L.F. Perimeter	280	386	520	585	640	740	840	940	940
Stone Ashlar on Concrete Block	Steel Joists	129.85	111.00	106.35	99.50	95.55	94.10	93.20	92.45	90.30
	Wood Joists	127.70	109.50	104.95	98.40	94.50	93.10	92.20	91.50	89.45
Face Brick on Concrete Block	Steel Joists	128.05	109.80	105.20	98.65	94.80	93.40	92.50	91.80	89.75
	Wood Joists	126.35	108.60	104.10	97.75	94.05	92.65	91.80	91.10	89.10
Decorative Concrete Block	Steel Joists	122.45	105.95	101.75	95.90	92.50	91.20	90.40	89.75	87.95
	Wood Joists	120.15	104.10	100.05	94.40	91.10	89.85	89.10	88.45	86.70
Perimeter Adj., Add or Deduct	Per 100 L.F.	16.60	8.30	5.55	3.95	3.00	2.45	2.05	1.80	1.60
Story Hgt. Adj., Add or Deduct	Per 1 Ft.	2.70	1.85	1.70	1.35	1.10	1.05	1.00	.95	.85

For Basement, add $18.60 per square foot of basement area

The above costs were calculated using the basic specifications shown on the facing page. These costs should be adjusted where necessary for design alternatives and owner's requirements. Reported completed project costs, for this type of structure, range from $50.00 to $143.70 per S.F.

Common additives

Description	Unit	$ Cost
Bar, Front bar	L.F.	285
Back bar	L.F.	227
Booth, Upholstered, custom, straight	L.F.	144 - 265
"L" or "U" shaped	L.F.	149 - 252
Emergency Lighting, 25 watt, battery operated		
Lead battery	Each	289
Nickel cadmium	Each	655
Flagpoles, Complete		
Aluminum, 20' high	Each	1075
40' High	Each	2675
70' High	Each	8250
Fiberglass, 23' High	Each	1400
39'-5" High	Each	2950
59' High	Each	7300
Kitchen Equipment		
Broiler	Each	4050
Coffee urn, twin 6 gallon	Each	6975
Cooler, 6 ft. long, reach-in	Each	3200
Dishwasher, 10-12 racks per hr.	Each	3050
Food warmer, counter 1.2 kw	Each	715

Description	Unit	$ Cost
Kitchen Equipment, cont.		
Freezer, 44 C.F., reach-in	Each	8325
Ice cube maker, 50 lb. per day	Each	1800
Lockers, Steel, single tier, 60" or 72"	Opening	125 - 220
2 tier, 60" or 72" total	Opening	70 - 119
5 tier, box lockers	Opening	40 - 60
Locker bench, lam. maple top only	L.F.	18.05
Pedestals, steel pipe	Each	58
Refrigerators, Prefabricated, walk-in		
7'-6" High, 6' x 6'	S.F.	120
10' x 10'	S.F.	95
12' x 14'	S.F.	83
12' x 20'	S.F.	73
Smoke Detectors		
Ceiling type	Each	149
Duct type	Each	405
Sound System		
Amplifier, 250 watts	Each	1650
Speaker, ceiling or wall	Each	145
Trumpet	Each	271

Important: See the Reference Section for Location Factors

Model costs calculated for a 1 story building with 12' story height and 22,000 square feet of floor area

Club, Social

				Unit	Unit Cost	Cost Per S.F.	% Of Sub-Total
1.0 Foundations							
.1	Footings & Foundations	Poured concrete; strip and spread footings and 4' foundation wall		S.F. Ground	3.53	3.53	6.5%
.4	Piles & Caissons	N/A		—	—	—	
.9	Excavation & Backfill	Site preparation for slab and trench for foundation wall and footing		S.F. Ground	1.08	1.08	
2.0 Substructure							
.1	Slab on Grade	4" reinforced concrete with vapor barrier and granular base		S.F. Slab	3.32	3.32	4.6%
.2	Special Substructures	N/A		—			
3.0 Superstructure							
.1	Columns & Beams	N/A		—	—	—	5.5%
.4	Structural Walls	Load bearing partition walls, see item 6.1		—	—	—	
.5	Elevated Floors	N/A		—	—	—	
.7	Roof	Metal deck on open web steel joists		S.F. Roof	3.93	3.93	
.9	Stairs	N/A		—	—	—	
4.0 Exterior Closure							
.1	Walls	Stone, ashlar veneer on concrete block	65% of wall	S.F. Wall	23	5.33	13.7%
.5	Exterior Wall Finishes	N/A			—		
.6	Doors	Double aluminum and glass doors		Each	1709	.47	
.7	Windows & Glazed Walls	Window wall	35% of wall	S.F. Window	32	4.02	
5.0 Roofing							
.1	Roof Coverings	Built-up tar and gravel with flashing		S.F. Roof	2.26	2.26	5.3%
.7	Insulation	Perlite/EPS composite		S.F. Roof	1.32	1.32	
.8	Openings & Specialties	Gravel stop		L.F. Perimeter	6.40	.19	
6.0 Interior Construction							
.1	Partitions	Lightweight concrete block	14 S.F. Floor/L.F. Partition	S.F. Partition	6.33	4.52	27.3%
.4	Interior Doors	Single leaf wood	140 S.F. Floor/Door	Each	427	3.05	
.5	Wall Finishes	65% paint, 25% vinyl wall covering, 10% ceramic tile		S.F. Surface	1.27	1.81	
.6	Floor Finishes	60% carpet, 35% hardwood, 15% ceramic tile		S.F. Floor	5.68	5.68	
.7	Ceiling Finishes	Mineral fiber tile on concealed zee bars		S.F. Ceiling	3.63	3.63	
.9	Interior Surface/Exterior Wall	Painted gypsum board on furring	65% of wall	S.F. Wall	3.47	.79	
7.0 Conveying							
.1	Elevators	N/A		—	—	—	0.0%
.2	Special Conveyors	N/A		—	—	—	
8.0 Mechanical							
.1	Plumbing	Kitchen, toilet and service fixtures, supply and drainage	1 Fixture/1050 S.F. Floor	Each	2310	2.20	30.6%
.2	Fire Protection	Wet pipe sprinkler system		S.F. Floor	1.69	1.69	
.3	Heating	Included in 8.4		—	—	—	
.4	Cooling	Multizone rooftop unit, gas heating, electric cooling		S.F. Floor	17.95	17.95	
.5	Special Systems	N/A		—	—	—	
9.0 Electrical							
.1	Service & Distribution	400 ampere service, panel board and feeders		S.F. Floor	.73	.73	6.5%
.2	Lighting & Power	Fluorescent fixtures, receptacles, switches, A.C. and misc. power		S.F. Floor	3.69	3.69	
.4	Special Electrical	Alarm systems and emergency lighting		S.F. Floor	.24	.24	
11.0 Special Construction							
.1	Specialties	N/A		—	—	—	0.0%
12.0 Site Work							
.1	Earthwork	N/A		—	—	—	0.0%
.3	Utilities	N/A		—	—	—	
.5	Roads & Parking	N/A		—	—	—	
.7	Site Improvements	N/A		—	—	—	
				Sub-Total		71.43	100%
	CONTRACTOR FEES (General Requirements: 10%, Overhead: 5%, Profit: 10%)				25%	17.86	
	ARCHITECT FEES				7%	6.26	
				Total Building Cost		95.55	

BUILDING TYPES

BUILDING TYPES

Costs per square foot of floor area

Exterior Wall	S.F. Area	15000	20000	28000	38000	50000	65000	85000	100000	150000
	L.F. Perimeter	350	400	480	550	630	660	750	825	1035
Face Brick with Concrete Block Back-up	Steel Frame	137.60	130.05	123.65	118.65	115.25	111.75	109.55	108.55	106.40
	Bearing Walls	138.40	130.05	122.90	117.30	113.40	109.35	106.80	105.65	103.20
Decorative Concrete Block	Steel Frame	132.60	125.75	120.00	115.55	112.55	109.60	107.65	106.80	104.90
	Bearing Walls	133.35	125.70	119.25	114.15	110.70	107.15	104.90	103.90	101.70
Stucco on Concrete Block	Steel Frame	130.40	123.70	117.95	113.65	110.65	107.75	105.85	105.00	103.20
	Bearing Walls	132.75	125.20	118.80	113.80	110.35	106.90	104.65	103.65	101.50
Perimeter Adj., Add or Deduct	Per 100 L.F.	6.25	4.70	3.35	2.45	1.85	1.45	1.05	.95	.65
Story Hgt. Adj., Add or Deduct	Per 1 Ft.	1.55	1.35	1.10	.95	.85	.65	.60	.55	.45

For Basement, add $21.80 per square foot of basement area

The above costs were calculated using the basic specifications shown on the facing page. These costs should be adjusted where necessary for design alternatives and owner's requirements. Reported completed project costs, for this type of structure, range from $70.40 to $174.20 per S.F.

Common additives

Description	Unit	$ Cost
Carrels Hardwood	Each	725 - 940
Clock System		
20 Room	Each	12,700
50 Room	Each	30,800
Elevators, Hydraulic passenger, 2 stops		
1500# capacity	Each	42,225
2500# capacity	Each	43,425
3500# capacity	Each	47,225
Additional stop, add	Each	3650
Emergency Lighting, 25 watt, battery operated		
Lead battery	Each	289
Nickel cadmium	Each	655
Flagpoles, Complete		
Aluminum, 20' high	Each	1075
40' High	Each	2675
70' High	Each	8250
Fiberglass, 23' High		1400
39'-5" High	Each	2950
59' High	Each	7300

Description	Unit	$ Cost
Lockers, Steel, single tier, 60" or 72"	Opening	125 - 220
2 tier, 60" or 72" total	Opening	70 - 119
5 tier, box lockers	Opening	40 - 60
Locker bench, lam. maple top only	L.F.	18.05
Pedestals, steel pipe	Each	58
Seating		
Auditorium chair, all veneer	Each	166
Veneer back, padded seat	Each	201
Upholstered, spring seat	Each	203
Classroom, movable chair & desk	Set	65 - 120
Lecture hall, pedestal type	Each	152 - 470
Smoke Detectors		
Ceiling type	Each	149
Duct type	Each	405
Sound System		
Amplifier, 250 watts	Each	1650
Speaker, ceiling or wall	Each	145
Trumpet	Each	271
TV Antenna, Master system, 12 outlet	Outlet	236
30 outlet	Outlet	151
100 outlet	Outlet	144

Important: See the Reference Section for Location Factors

Model costs calculated for a 2 story building with 12' story height and 50,000 square feet of floor area

				Unit	Unit Cost	Cost Per S.F.	% Of Sub-Total
1.0 Foundations							
.1	Footings & Foundations	Poured concrete; strip and spread footings and 4' foundation wall		S.F. Ground	2.80	1.40	
.4	Piles & Caissons	N/A		—	—	—	2.3%
.9	Excavation & Backfill	Site preparation for slab and trench for foundation wall and footing		S.F. Ground	1.02	.51	
2.0 Substructure							
.1	Slab on Grade	4" reinforced concrete with vapor barrier and granular base		S.F. Slab	3.32	1.66	2.0%
.2	Special Substructures	N/A		—	—	—	
3.0 Superstructure							
.1	Columns & Beams	Interior columns included in 3.7		—	—	—	
.4	Structural Walls	Concrete block bearing walls		S.F. Wall	6.17	1.87	
.5	Elevated Floors	Open web steel joists, slab form, concrete		S.F. Floor	10.05	5.03	13.1%
.7	Roof	Metal deck on open web steel joists, columns		S.F. Roof	5.54	2.77	
.9	Stairs	Concrete filled metal pan		Flight	5975	1.20	
4.0 Exterior Closure							
.1	Walls	Decorative concrete block	65% of wall	S.F. Wall	10.73	2.11	
.5	Exterior Wall Finishes	N/A		—	—	—	6.6%
.6	Doors	Double glass and aluminum with transom		Each	3275	.39	
.7	Windows & Glazed Walls	Window wall	35% of wall	S.F. Wall	28	2.98	
5.0 Roofing							
.1	Roof Coverings	Built-up tar and gravel with flashing		S.F. Roof	2.18	1.09	
.7	Insulation	Perlite/EPS composite		S.F. Roof	1.32	.66	2.2%
.8	Openings & Specialties	Gravel stop		L.F. Perimeter	6.40	.08	
6.0 Interior Construction							
.1	Partitions	Concrete block	20 S.F. Floor/L.F. Partition	S.F. Partition	5.90	2.95	
.4	Interior Doors	Single leaf hollow metal	200 S.F. Floor/Door	Each	534	2.67	
.5	Wall Finishes	95% paint, 5% ceramic tile		S.F. Surface	2.28	2.28	18.7%
.6	Floor Finishes	70% vinyl composition tile, 25% carpet, 5% ceramic tile		S.F. Floor	3.53	3.53	
.7	Ceiling Finishes	Mineral fiber tile on concealed zee bars		S.F. Ceiling	3.63	3.63	
.9	Interior Surface/Exterior Wall	Paint and block filler	65% of wall	S.F. Wall	2.12	.42	
7.0 Conveying							
.1	Elevators	Two hydraulic passenger elevators		Each	51,000	2.04	2.5%
.2	Special Conveyors	N/A		—	—	—	
8.0 Mechanical							
.1	Plumbing	Toilet and service fixtures, supply and drainage	1 Fixture/455 S.F. Floor	Each	4590	10.09	
.2	Fire Protection	Sprinklers, light hazard		S.F. Floor	1.28	1.28	
.3	Heating	Included in 8.4		—	—	—	30.5%
.4	Cooling	Multizone unit, gas heating, electric cooling		S.F. Floor	13.80	13.80	
.5	Special Systems	N/A		—	—	—	
9.0 Electrical							
.1	Service & Distribution	2000 ampere service, panel board and feeders		S.F. Floor	2.85	2.85	
.2	Lighting & Power	Fluorescent fixtures, receptacles, switches, A.C. and misc. power		S.F. Floor	8.27	8.27	18.1%
.4	Special Electrical	Alarm systems, communications systems and emergency lighting		S.F. Floor	3.88	3.88	
11.0 Special Construction							
.1	Specialties	Chalkboards, counters, cabinets		S.F. Floor	3.32	3.32	4.0%
12.0 Site Work							
.1	Earthwork	N/A		—	—	—	
.3	Utilities	N/A		—	—	—	0.0%
.5	Roads & Parking	N/A		—	—	—	
.7	Site Improvements	N/A		—	—	—	
				Sub-Total		82.76	100%
	CONTRACTOR FEES (General Requirements: 10%, Overhead: 5%, Profit: 10%)			25%		20.69	
	ARCHITECT FEES			7%		7.25	
				Total Building Cost		110.70	

BUILDING TYPES

Costs per square foot of floor area

Exterior Wall	S.F. Area	10000	15000	25000	40000	55000	70000	80000	90000	100000
	L.F. Perimeter	260	320	400	476	575	628	684	721	772
Face Brick with Concrete Block Back-up	R/Conc. Frame	137.85	127.50	117.30	110.20	107.45	105.05	104.30	103.45	102.95
	Steel Frame	142.55	132.25	122.00	114.90	112.20	109.80	109.05	108.20	107.70
Decorative Concrete Block	R/Conc. Frame	128.00	119.55	111.45	105.95	103.80	102.00	101.45	100.80	100.40
	Steel Frame	132.25	123.75	115.65	110.20	108.05	106.25	105.65	105.00	104.60
Precast Concrete Panels	R/Conc. Frame	131.65	122.45	113.55	107.45	105.05	103.05	102.40	101.65	101.20
	Steel Frame	136.30	127.05	118.15	112.05	109.65	107.65	107.00	106.25	105.80
Perimeter Adj., Add or Deduct	Per 100 L.F.	12.35	8.25	4.95	3.05	2.25	1.75	1.55	1.35	1.25
Story Hgt. Adj., Add or Deduct	Per 1 Ft.	2.40	1.95	1.50	1.10	.95	.80	.80	.70	.70
For Basement, add $21.00 per square foot of basement area										

The above costs were calculated using the basic specifications shown on the facing page. These costs should be adjusted where necessary for design alternatives and owner's requirements. Reported completed project costs, for this type of structure, range from $47.95 to $140.20 per S.F.

Common additives

Description	Unit	$ Cost
Carrels Hardwood	Each	725 - 940
Closed Circuit Surveillance, One station		
Camera and monitor	Each	1375
For additional camera stations, add	Each	745
Elevators, Hydraulic passenger, 2 stops		
2000# capacity	Each	42,725
2500# capacity	Each	43,425
3500# capacity	Each	47,225
Additional stop, add	Each	3650
Emergency Lighting, 25 watt, battery operated		
Lead battery	Each	289
Nickel cadmium	Each	655
Furniture	Student	1900 - 3600
Intercom System, 25 station capacity		
Master station	Each	2000
Intercom outlets	Each	126
Handset	Each	335

Description	Unit	$ Cost
Kitchen Equipment		
Broiler	Each	4050
Coffee urn, twin 6 gallon	Each	6975
Cooler, 6 ft. long	Each	3200
Dishwasher, 10-12 racks per hr.	Each	3050
Food warmer	Each	715
Freezer, 44 C.F., reach-in	Each	8325
Ice cube maker, 50 lb. per day	Each	1800
Range with 1 oven	Each	2400
Laundry Equipment		
Dryer, gas, 16 lb. capacity	Each	710
30 lb. capacity	Each	2775
Washer, 4 cycle	Each	795
Commercial	Each	1200
Smoke Detectors		
Ceiling type	Each	149
Duct type	Each	405
TV Antenna, Master system, 12 outlet	Outlet	236
30 outlet	Outlet	151
100 outlet	Outlet	144

Important: See the Reference Section for Location Factors

Model costs calculated for a 3 story building with 12′ story height and 25,000 square feet of floor area

				Unit	Unit Cost	Cost Per S.F.	% Of Sub-Total
1.0 Foundations							
.1	Footings & Foundations	Poured concrete; strip and spread footings and 4′ foundation wall		S.F. Ground	6.54	2.18	
.4	Piles & Caissons	N/A		—	—	—	2.9%
.9	Excavation & Backfill	Site preparation for slab and trench for foundation wall and footing		S.F. Ground	1.08	.36	
2.0 Substructure							
.1	Slab on Grade	4″ reinforced concrete with vapor barrier and granular base		S.F. Slab	3.32	1.11	1.3%
.2	Special Substructures	N/A		—	—	—	
3.0 Superstructure							
.1	Columns & Beams	Concrete columns		L.F. Column	63	4.40	
.4	Structural Walls	N/A		—	—	—	
.5	Elevated Floors	Concrete flat plate		S.F. Floor	9.24	6.16	17.4%
.7	Roof	Concrete flat plate		S.F. Roof	8.85	2.95	
.9	Stairs	Concrete		Flight	3325	1.73	
4.0 Exterior Closure							
.1	Walls	Face brick with concrete block backup	80% of wall	S.F. Wall	21	9.70	
.5	Exterior Wall Finishes	N/A		—	—	—	14.9%
.6	Doors	Double glass & aluminum doors		Each	3800	.91	
.7	Windows & Glazed Walls	Aluminum horizontal sliding	20% of wall	Each	493	2.47	
5.0 Roofing							
.1	Roof Coverings	Single ply membrane, loose laid and ballasted		S.F. Roof	2.19	.73	
.7	Insulation	Perlite/EPS composite		S.F. Roof	1.32	.44	1.4%
.8	Openings & Specialties	Gravel stop		L.F. Perimeter	6.40	.10	
6.0 Interior Construction							
.1	Partitions	Gypsum board on metal studs, concrete block	9 S.F. Floor/L.F. Partition	S.F. Partition	4.35	4.83	
.4	Interior Doors	Single leaf wood	90 S.F. Floor/Door	Each	427	4.74	
.5	Wall Finishes	95% paint, 5% ceramic tile		S.F. Surface	.85	1.88	
.6	Floor Finishes	80% carpet, 10% vinyl composition tile, 10% ceramic tile		S.F. Floor	5.90	5.90	21.7%
.7	Ceiling Finishes	90% paint, 10% suspended fiberglass board		S.F. Ceiling	.66	.66	
.9	Interior Surface/Exterior Wall	Paint	80% of wall	S.F. Wall	2.12	.98	
7.0 Conveying							
.1	Elevators	One hydraulic passenger elevator		Each	66,250	2.65	3.0%
.2	Special Conveyors	N/A		—	—	—	
8.0 Mechanical							
.1	Plumbing	Toilet and service fixtures, supply and drainage	1 Fixture/455 S.F. Floor	Each	3517	7.73	
.2	Fire Protection	Wet pipe sprinkler system		S.F. Floor	1.47	1.47	
.3	Heating	Included in 8.4		—	—	—	20.3%
.4	Cooling	Rooftop multizone unit system		S.F. Floor	8.65	8.65	
.5	Special Systems	N/A		—	—	—	
9.0 Electrical							
.1	Service & Distribution	800 ampere service, panel board and feeders		S.F. Floor	1.52	1.52	
.2	Lighting & Power	Fluorescent fixtures, receptacles, switches, A.C. and misc. power		S.F. Floor	6.36	6.36	11.8%
.4	Special Electrical	Alarm systems, communications systems and emergency lighting		S.F. Floor	2.47	2.47	
11.0 Special Construction							
.1	Specialties	Closet shelving, mirrors		S.F. Floor	4.61	4.61	5.3%
12.0 Site Work							
.1	Earthwork	N/A		—	—	—	
.3	Utilities	N/A		—	—	—	
.5	Roads & Parking	N/A		—	—	—	0.0%
.7	Site Improvements	N/A		—	—	—	
				Sub-Total		87.69	**100%**
	CONTRACTOR FEES (General Requirements: 10%, Overhead: 5%, Profit: 10%)				25%	21.92	
	ARCHITECT FEES				7%	7.69	
				Total Building Cost		**117.30**	

BUILDING TYPES

BUILDING TYPES

Costs per square foot of floor area

Exterior Wall		S.F. Area	20000	35000	45000	65000	85000	110000	135000	160000	200000
		L.F. Perimeter	260	340	400	440	500	540	560	590	640
Face Brick with Concrete Block Back-up	R/Conc. Frame		130.10	119.20	116.30	110.30	107.65	104.90	102.90	101.65	100.30
	Steel Frame		137.40	126.45	123.60	117.60	114.95	112.20	110.20	108.95	107.60
Decorative Concrete Block	R/Conc. Frame		120.80	112.20	109.90	105.40	103.40	101.35	99.90	98.95	97.95
	Steel Frame		128.20	119.60	117.30	112.80	110.80	108.75	107.30	106.35	105.35
Precast Concrete Panels With Exposed Aggregate	R/Conc. Frame		128.65	118.10	115.30	109.55	107.00	104.35	102.45	101.20	99.95
	Steel Frame		135.90	125.35	122.55	116.80	114.25	111.65	109.75	108.50	107.20
Perimeter Adj., Add or Deduct	Per 100 L.F.		11.75	6.70	5.20	3.55	2.75	2.15	1.75	1.50	1.20
Story Hgt. Adj., Add or Deduct	Per 1 Ft.		2.35	1.75	1.60	1.20	1.05	.90	.75	.65	.55
For Basement, add $20.75 per square foot of basement area											

The above costs were calculated using the basic specifications shown on the facing page. These costs should be adjusted where necessary for design alternatives and owner's requirements. Reported completed project costs, for this type of structure, range from $67.20 to $164.45 per S.F.

Common additives

Description	Unit	$ Cost		Description	Unit	$ Cost
Carrels Hardwood	Each	725 - 940		Kitchen Equipment		
Closed Circuit Surveillance, One station				Broiler	Each	4050
Camera and monitor	Each	1375		Coffee urn, twin, 6 gallon	Each	6975
For additional camera stations, add	Each	745		Cooler, 6 ft. long	Each	3200
Elevators, Electric passenger, 5 stops				Dishwasher, 10-12 racks per hr.	Each	3050
2000# capacity	Each	97,700		Food warmer	Each	715
2500# capacity	Each	100,700		Freezer, 44 C.F., reach-in	Each	8325
3500# capacity	Each	102,200		Ice cube maker, 50 lb. per day	Each	1800
Additional stop, add	Each	5500		Range with 1 oven	Each	2400
Emergency Lighting, 25 watt, battery operated				Laundry Equipment		
Lead battery	Each	289		Dryer, gas, 16 lb. capacity	Each	710
Nickel cadmium	Each	655		30 lb. capacity	Each	2775
Furniture	Student	1900 - 3600		Washer, 4 cycle	Each	795
Intercom System, 25 station capacity				Commercial	Each	1200
Master station	Each	2000		Smoke Detectors		
Intercom outlets	Each	126		Ceiling type	Each	149
Handset	Each	335		Duct type	Each	405
				TV Antenna, Master system, 12 outlet	Outlet	236
				30 outlet	Outlet	151
				100 outlet	Outlet	144

Important: See the Reference Section for Location Factors

Model costs calculated for a 6 story building with 12' story height and 85,000 square feet of floor area

				Unit	Unit Cost	Cost Per S.F.	% Of Sub-Total
1.0 Foundations							
.1	Footings & Foundations	Poured concrete; strip and spread footings and 4' foundation wall		S.F. Ground	8.52	1.42	
.4	Piles & Caissons	N/A		—	—	—	1.9%
.9	Excavation & Backfill	Site preparation for slab and trench for foundation wall and footing		S.F. Ground	1.02	.17	
2.0 Substructure							
.1	Slab on Grade	4" reinforced concrete with vapor barrier and granular base		S.F. Slab	3.32	.55	0.7%
.2	Special Substructures	N/A		—	—	—	
3.0 Superstructure							
.1	Columns & Beams	Steel columns with fireproofing		L.F. Column	130	2.45	
.4	Structural Walls	N/A		—	—	—	
.5	Elevated Floors	Concrete slab with metal deck and beams		S.F. Floor	12.84	10.70	19.8%
.7	Roof	Concrete slab with metal deck and beams		S.F. Roof	12.02	2.00	
.9	Stairs	Concrete filled metal pan		Flight	5975	1.27	
4.0 Exterior Closure							
.1	Walls	Decorative concrete block	80% of wall	S.F. Wall	11.86	4.02	
.5	Exterior Wall Finishes	N/A		—	—	—	7.2%
.6	Doors	Double glass & aluminum doors		Each	1978	.19	
.7	Windows & Glazed Walls	Aluminum horizontal sliding	20% of wall	Each	304	1.72	
5.0 Roofing							
.1	Roof Coverings	Single ply membrane, loose laid and ballasted		S.F. Roof	1.92	.32	
.7	Insulation	Perlite/EPS composite		S.F. Roof	1.32	.22	0.7%
.8	Openings & Specialties	Gravel stop		L.F. Perimeter	6.40	.04	
6.0 Interior Construction							
.1	Partitions	Concrete block	9 S.F. Floor/L.F. Partition	S.F. Partition	6.56	7.29	
.4	Interior Doors	Single leaf wood	90 S.F. Floor/Door	Each	427	4.74	
.5	Wall Finishes	95% paint, 5% ceramic tile		S.F. Surface	1.40	3.12	
.6	Floor Finishes	80% carpet, 10% vinyl composition tile, 10% ceramic tile		S.F. Floor	5.90	5.90	27.1%
.7	Ceiling Finishes	Mineral fiber tile on concealed zee bars, paint		S.F. Ceiling	.66	.66	
.9	Interior Surface/Exterior Wall	Paint and block filler	80% of wall	S.F. Wall	2.12	.72	
7.0 Conveying							
.1	Elevators	Four geared passenger elevator		Each	134,300	6.32	7.6%
.2	Special Conveyors	N/A		—	—	—	
8.0 Mechanical							
.1	Plumbing	Toilet and service fixtures, supply and drainage	1 Fixture/390 S.F. Floor	Each	2402	6.16	
.2	Fire Protection	Sprinklers, light hazard		S.F. Floor	1.42	1.42	
.3	Heating	Oil fired hot water, wall fin radiation		S.F. Floor	2.66	2.66	19.0%
.4	Cooling	Chilled water, air cooled condenser system		S.F. Floor	5.53	5.53	
.5	Special Systems	N/A		—	—	—	
9.0 Electrical							
.1	Service & Distribution	1200 ampere service, panel board and feeders		S.F. Floor	.70	.70	
.2	Lighting & Power	Fluorescent fixtures, receptacles, switches, A.C. and misc. power		S.F. Floor	6.22	6.22	11.4%
.4	Special Electrical	Alarm systems, communications systems and emergency lighting		S.F. Floor	2.54	2.54	
11.0 Special Construction							
.1	Specialties	Closet shelving, mirrors		S.F. Floor	3.78	3.78	4.6%
12.0 Site Work							
.1	Earthwork	N/A		—	—	—	
.3	Utilities	N/A		—	—	—	
.5	Roads & Parking	N/A		—	—	—	0.0%
.7	Site Improvements	N/A		—	—	—	
			Sub-Total			82.83	100%
	CONTRACTOR FEES (General Requirements: 10%, Overhead: 5%, Profit: 10%)				25%	20.71	
	ARCHITECT FEES				7%	7.26	
			Total Building Cost			110.80	

BUILDING TYPES

BUILDING TYPES

Costs per square foot of floor area

Exterior Wall	S.F. Area	12000	20000	28000	37000	45000	57000	68000	80000	92000
	L.F. Perimeter	470	600	698	793	900	1060	1127	1200	1320
Face Brick with Concrete Brick Back-up	Steel Frame	181.10	148.80	134.00	124.65	119.90	115.30	111.50	108.55	106.80
	Bearing Walls	178.50	146.25	131.45	122.10	117.35	112.75	108.95	105.95	104.20
Decorative Concrete Block	Steel Frame	176.60	145.40	131.15	122.20	117.60	113.15	109.60	106.80	105.15
	Bearing Walls	174.20	143.00	128.75	119.80	115.20	110.75	107.20	104.40	102.75
Stucco on Concrete Block	Steel Frame	175.50	144.55	130.45	121.60	117.05	112.65	109.15	106.45	104.75
	Bearing Walls	173.05	142.10	128.05	119.20	114.65	110.25	106.75	104.00	102.30
Perimeter Adj., Add or Deduct	Per 100 L.F.	7.10	4.25	3.05	2.30	1.90	1.55	1.25	1.05	.95
Story Hgt. Adj., Add or Deduct	Per 1 Ft.	1.30	1.00	.85	.70	.65	.65	.55	.50	.45
For Basement, add $20.20 per square foot of basement area										

The above costs were calculated using the basic specifications shown on the facing page. These costs should be adjusted where necessary for design alternatives and owner's requirements. Reported completed project costs, for this type of structure, range from $97.00 to $221.95 per S.F.

Common additives

Description	Unit	$ Cost
Cabinets, Base, door units, metal	L.F.	181
Drawer units	L.F.	345
Tall storage cabinets, open	L.F.	340
With doors	L.F.	420
Wall, metal 12-1/2" deep, open	L.F.	134
With doors	L.F.	239
Carrels Hardwood	Each	725 - 940
Countertops, not incl. base cabinets, acid proof	S.F.	31 - 46
Stainless steel	S.F.	81
Fume Hood, Not incl. ductwork	L.F.	690 - 1800
Ductwork	Hood	1750 - 6300
Glassware Washer, Distilled water rinse	Each	7275 - 9100
Seating		
Auditorium chair, all veneer	Each	166
Veneer back, padded seat	Each	201
Upholstered, spring seat	Each	203
Classroom, movable chair & desk	Set	65 - 120
Lecture hall, pedestal type	Each	152 - 470

Description	Unit	$ Cost
Safety Equipment, Eye wash, hand held	Each	231
Deluge shower	Each	550
Sink, One piece plastic		
Flask wash, freestanding	Each	1700
Tables, acid resist. top, drawers	L.F.	145
Titration Unit, Four 2000 ml reservoirs	Each	9200

Model costs calculated for a 1 story building with 12' story height and 45,000 square feet of floor area

College, Laboratory

BUILDING TYPES

				Unit	Unit Cost	Cost Per S.F.	% Of Sub-Total
1.0 Foundations							
	.1	Footings & Foundations	Poured concrete; strip and spread footings and 4' foundation wall	S.F. Ground	5.95	5.95	
	.4	Piles & Caissons	N/A	—	—	—	8.2%
	.9	Excavation & Backfill	Site preparation for slab and trench for foundation wall and footing	S.F. Ground	1.08	1.08	
2.0 Substructure							
	.1	Slab on Grade	4" reinforced concrete with vapor barrier and granular base	S.F. Slab	3.32	3.32	3.9%
	.2	Special Substructures	N/A	—	—	—	
3.0 Superstructure							
	.1	Columns & Beams	N/A	—	—	—	
	.4	Structural Walls	Grouted concrete block wall	S.F. Wall	2.63	2.63	
	.5	Elevated Floors	Metal deck on open web steel joists	S.F. Cover	10.05	1.31	7.9%
	.7	Roof	Metal deck on open web steel joists	S.F. Roof	2.78	2.78	
	.9	Stairs	N/A	—	—	—	
4.0 Exterior Closure							
	.1	Walls	Face brick with concrete block backup _75% of wall_	S.F. Wall	21	3.79	
	.5	Exterior Wall Finishes	N/A	—	—	—	7.8%
	.6	Doors	Glass and metal doors and entrances with transom	Each	2734	1.22	
	.7	Windows & Glazed Walls	Window wall _25% of wall_	S.F. Window	28	1.68	
5.0 Roofing							
	.1	Roof Coverings	Built-up tar and gravel with flashing	S.F. Roof	2.07	2.07	
	.7	Insulation	Perlite/EPS composite	S.F. Roof	1.32	1.32	4.4%
	.8	Openings & Specialties	Gravel stop and skylight	S.F. Roof	.33	.33	
6.0 Interior Construction							
	.1	Partitions	Concrete block _10 S.F. Floor/L.F. Partition_	S.F. Partition	4.98	4.98	
	.4	Interior Doors	Single leaf-kalamein fire doors _820 S.F. Floor/Door_	Each	659	.80	
	.5	Wall Finishes	60% paint, 40% epoxy coating	S.F. Surface	1.90	3.80	
	.6	Floor Finishes	60% epoxy, 20% carpet, 20% vinyl composition tile	S.F. Floor	4.58	4.58	21.3%
	.7	Ceiling Finishes	Mineral fiber tile on concealed zee runners	S.F. Ceiling	3.63	3.63	
	.9	Interior Surface/Exterior Wall	Paint and block filler _75% of wall_	S.F. Wall	2.12	.38	
7.0 Conveying							
	.1	Elevators	N/A	—	—	—	0.0%
	.2	Special Conveyors	N/A	—	—	—	
8.0 Mechanical							
	.1	Plumbing	Toilet and service fixtures, supply and drainage _1 Fixture/260 S.F. Floor_	Each	3785	14.56	
	.2	Fire Protection	Sprinklers, light hazard	S.F. Floor	1.44	1.44	
	.3	Heating	Included in 8.4	—	—	—	34.9%
	.4	Cooling	Multizone unit, gas heating, electric cooling	S.F. Floor	13.80	13.80	
	.5	Special Systems	N/A	—	—	—	
9.0 Electrical							
	.1	Service & Distribution	1000 ampere service, panel board and feeders	S.F. Floor	1.25	1.25	
	.2	Lighting & Power	Fluorescent fixtures, receptacles, switches, A.C. and misc. power	S.F. Floor	7.06	7.06	10.4%
	.4	Special Electrical	Alarm systems and emergency lighting	S.F. Floor	.57	.57	
11.0 Special Construction							
	.1	Specialties	Cabinets, fume hoods, lockers	S.F. Floor	1.00	1.00	1.2%
12.0 Site Work							
	.1	Earthwork	N/A	—	—	—	
	.3	Utilities	N/A	—	—	—	
	.5	Roads & Parking	N/A	—	—	—	0.0%
	.7	Site Improvements	N/A	—	—	—	
				Sub-Total		85.33	**100%**
	CONTRACTOR FEES (General Requirements: 10%, Overhead: 5%, Profit: 10%)				25%	21.33	
	ARCHITECT FEES				10%	10.69	
				Total Building Cost		**117.35**	

Costs per square foot of floor area

Exterior Wall	S.F. Area	15000	20000	25000	30000	35000	40000	45000	50000	55000
	L.F. Perimeter	354	425	457	513	568	583	629	644	683
Brick Face with Concrete Block Back-up	Steel Frame	114.80	111.40	107.85	106.25	105.10	103.25	102.50	101.30	100.75
	R/Conc. Frame	111.15	107.75	104.20	102.60	101.45	99.55	98.85	97.65	97.10
Precast Concrete Panel	Steel Frame	111.80	108.70	105.60	104.15	103.10	101.45	100.80	99.75	99.25
	R/Conc. Frame	108.45	105.30	102.10	100.60	99.55	97.90	97.20	96.15	95.65
Limestone Face Concrete Block Back-up	Steel Frame	119.50	115.60	111.50	109.65	108.30	106.15	105.25	103.85	103.20
	R/Conc. Frame	115.85	111.90	107.80	105.95	104.60	102.45	101.60	100.20	99.55
Perimeter Adj., Add or Deduct	Per 100 L.F.	6.25	4.70	3.70	3.15	2.70	2.35	2.05	1.90	1.70
Story Hgt. Adj., Add or Deduct	Per 1 Ft.	1.60	1.40	1.20	1.10	1.10	1.00	.95	.85	.80
For Basement, add $22.65 per square foot of basement area										

The above costs were calculated using the basic specifications shown on the facing page. These costs should be adjusted where necessary for design alternatives and owner's requirements. Reported completed project costs, for this type of structure, range from $78.30 to $160.40 per S.F.

Common additives

Description	Unit	$ Cost
Carrels Hardwood	Each	725 - 940
Elevators, Hydraulic passenger, 2 stops		
2000# capacity	Each	42,725
2500# capacity	Each	43,425
3500# capacity	Each	47,225
Emergency Lighting, 25 watt, battery operated		
Lead battery	Each	289
Nickel cadmium	Each	655
Escalators, Metal		
32" wide, 10' story height	Each	88,400
20' story height	Each	102,500
48" wide, 10' Story height	Each	92,900
20' story height	Each	107,000
Glass		
32" wide, 10' story height	Each	86,900
20' story height	Each	102,500
48" wide, 10' story height	Each	92,900
20' story height	Each	107,000

Description	Unit	$ Cost
Lockers, Steel, Single tier, 60" or 72"	Opening	125 - 220
2 tier, 60" or 72" total	Opening	70 - 119
5 tier, box lockers	Opening	40 - 60
Locker bench, lam. maple top only	L.F.	18.05
Pedestals, steel pipe	Each	58
Sound System		
Amplifier, 250 watts	Each	1650
Speaker, ceiling or wall	Each	145
Trumpet	Each	271

Important: See the Reference Section for Location Factors

BUILDING TYPES

Model costs calculated for a 2 story building with 12' story height and 25,000 square feet of floor area

				Unit	Unit Cost	Cost Per S.F.	% Of Sub-Total
1.0 Foundations							
	.1	Footings & Foundations	Poured concrete; strip and spread footings and 4' foundation wall	S.F. Ground	4.88	2.44	
	.4	Piles & Caissons	N/A	—	—	—	3.8%
	.9	Excavation & Backfill	Site preparation for slab and trench for foundation wall and footing	S.F. Ground	1.08	.54	
2.0 Substructure							
	.1	Slab on Grade	4" reinforced concrete with vapor barrier and granular base	S.F. Slab	3.32	1.66	2.1%
	.2	Special Substructures	N/A	—	—	—	
3.0 Superstructure							
	.1	Columns & Beams	Concrete columns	L.F. Column	118	3.40	
	.4	Structural Walls	N/A	—	—	—	
	.5	Elevated Floors	Concrete flat plate	S.F. Floor	10.68	5.34	18.6%
	.7	Roof	Concrete flat plate	S.F. Roof	9.85	4.93	
	.9	Stairs	Concrete	Flight	5125	.82	
4.0 Exterior Closure							
	.1	Walls	Face brick with concrete block backup 75% of wall	S.F. Wall	21	6.93	
	.5	Exterior Wall Finishes	N/A	—	—	—	13.2%
	.6	Doors	Double aluminum and glass	Each	1700	.27	
	.7	Windows & Glazed Walls	Window wall 25% of wall	S.F. Window	28	3.09	
5.0 Roofing							
	.1	Roof Coverings	Built-up tar and gravel with flashing	S.F. Roof	2.40	1.20	
	.7	Insulation	Perlite/EPS composite	S.F. Roof	1.32	.66	2.6%
	.8	Openings & Specialties	Gravel stop, hatches, gutters and downspouts	S.F. Roof	.32	.16	
6.0 Interior Construction							
	.1	Partitions	Gypsum board on metal studs 14 S.F. Floor/L.F. Partition	S.F. Partition	4.12	2.94	
	.4	Interior Doors	Single leaf hollow metal 140 S.F. Floor/Door	Each	534	3.81	
	.5	Wall Finishes	50% paint, 50% vinyl wall covering	S.F. Surface	.99	1.42	
	.6	Floor Finishes	50% carpet, 50% vinyl composition tile	S.F. Floor	4.69	4.69	21.2%
	.7	Ceiling Finishes	Suspended fiberglass board	S.F. Ceiling	2.69	2.69	
	.9	Interior Surface/Exterior Wall	Paint 75% of wall	S.F. Wall	2.12	.93	
7.0 Conveying							
	.1	Elevators	One hydraulic passenger elevator	Each	51,000	2.04	2.6%
	.2	Special Conveyors	N/A	—	—	—	
8.0 Mechanical							
	.1	Plumbing	Toilet and service fixtures, supply and drainage 1 Fixture/1040 S.F. Floor	Each	1872	1.80	
	.2	Fire Protection	Wet pipe sprinkler system	S.F. Floor	1.53	1.53	
	.3	Heating	Included in 8.4	—	—	—	22.0%
	.4	Cooling	Multizone unit, gas heating, electric cooling	S.F. Floor	13.80	13.80	
	.5	Special Systems	N/A	—	—	—	
9.0 Electrical							
	.1	Service & Distribution	600 ampere service, panel board and feeders	S.F. Floor	1.37	1.37	
	.2	Lighting & Power	Fluorescent fixtures, receptacles, switches, A.C. and misc. power	S.F. Floor	8.19	8.19	13.9%
	.4	Special Electrical	Alarm systems, communications systems and emergency lighting	S.F. Floor	1.26	1.26	
11.0 Special Construction							
	.1	Specialties	N/A	—	—	—	0.0%
12.0 Site Work							
	.1	Earthwork	N/A	—	—	—	
	.3	Utilities	N/A	—	—	—	
	.5	Roads & Parking	N/A	—	—	—	0.0%
	.7	Site Improvements	N/A	—	—	—	
				Sub-Total		77.91	**100%**

CONTRACTOR FEES (General Requirements: 10%, Overhead: 5%, Profit: 10%)		25%	19.48
ARCHITECT FEES		7%	6.81
	Total Building Cost		**104.20**

Costs per square foot of floor area

Exterior Wall	S.F. Area	4000	6000	8000	10000	12000	14000	16000	18000	20000
	L.F. Perimeter	260	340	420	453	460	510	560	610	600
Face Brick with Concrete Block Back-up	Bearing Walls	110.30	104.55	101.70	97.20	92.95	91.70	90.75	90.05	87.70
	Steel Frame	107.05	102.00	99.50	95.60	91.95	90.85	90.05	89.40	87.40
Decorative Concrete Block	Bearing Walls	97.10	92.55	90.30	86.80	83.50	82.50	81.80	81.25	79.45
	Steel Frame	98.25	94.35	92.40	89.50	86.75	85.95	85.30	84.85	83.35
Tilt Up Concrete Wall Panels	Bearing Walls	98.45	94.25	92.15	88.95	85.95	85.05	84.35	83.85	82.20
	Steel Frame	95.20	91.70	89.95	87.35	84.95	84.20	83.65	83.25	81.95
Perimeter Adj., Add or Deduct	Per 100 L.F.	14.80	9.90	7.40	5.95	4.90	4.20	3.70	3.25	2.95
Story Hgt. Adj., Add or Deduct	Per 1 Ft.	1.90	1.65	1.50	1.35	1.10	1.05	1.00	1.00	.85
For Basement, add $19.75 per square foot of basement area										

The above costs were calculated using the basic specifications shown on the facing page. These costs should be adjusted where necessary for design alternatives and owner's requirements. Reported completed project costs, for this type of structure, range from $47.90 to $152.75 per S.F.

Common additives

Description	Unit	$ Cost		Description	Unit	$ Cost
Bar, Front bar	L.F.	285		Movie Equipment		
Back bar	L.F.	227		Projector, 35mm	Each	9250 - 12,700
Booth, Upholstered, custom straight	L.F.	144 - 265		Screen, wall or ceiling hung	S.F.	6.30 - 9.65
"L" or "U" shaped	L.F.	149 - 252		Partitions, Folding leaf, wood		
Bowling Alleys, incl. alley, pinsetter				Acoustic type	S.F.	53 - 88
Scorer, counter & misc. supplies, average	Lane	45,700		Seating		
For automatic scorer, add	Lane	7475		Auditorium chair, all veneer	Each	166
Emergency Lighting, 25 watt, battery operated				Veneer back, padded seat	Each	201
Lead battery	Each	289		Upholstered, spring seat	Each	203
Nickel cadmium	Each	655		Classroom, movable chair & desk	Set	65 - 120
Kitchen Equipment				Lecture hall, pedestal type	Each	152 - 470
Broiler	Each	4050		Sound System		
Coffee urn, twin 6 gallon	Each	6975		Amplifier, 250 watts	Each	1650
Cooler, 6 ft. long	Each	3200		Speaker, ceiling or wall	Each	145
Dishwasher, 10-12 racks per hr.	Each	3050		Trumpet	Each	271
Food warmer	Each	715		Stage Curtains, Medium weight	S.F.	7.80 - 280
Freezer, 44 C.F., reach-in	Each	8325		Curtain Track, Light duty	L.F.	56
Ice cube maker, 50 lb. per day	Each	1800		Swimming Pools, Complete, gunite	S.F.	47 - 57
Range with 1 oven	Each	2400				

BUILDING TYPES

Important: See the Reference Section for Location Factors

Model costs calculated for a 1 story building with 12' story height and 10,000 square feet of floor area

				Unit	Unit Cost	Cost Per S.F.	% Of Sub-Total
1.0 Foundations							
.1	Footings & Foundations	Poured concrete; strip and spread footings and 4' foundation wall		S.F. Ground	6.52	6.52	
.4	Piles & Caissons	N/A		—	—	—	10.8%
.9	Excavation & Backfill	Site preparation for slab and trench for foundation wall and footing		S.F. Ground	1.17	1.17	
2.0 Substructure							
.1	Slab on Grade	4" reinforced concrete with vapor barrier and granular base		S.F. Slab	3.32	3.32	4.7%
.2	Special Substructures	N/A		—	—	—	
3.0 Superstructure							
.1	Columns & Beams	N/A		—	—	—	
.4	Structural Walls	Concrete block		S.F. Wall	6.17	1.01	
.5	Elevated Floors	N/A		—	—	—	6.9%
.7	Roof	Metal deck on open web steel joists		S.F. Roof	3.91	3.91	
.9	Stairs	N/A		—	—	—	
4.0 Exterior Closure							
.1	Walls	Face brick with concrete block backup	80% of wall	S.F. Wall	21	9.15	
.5	Exterior Wall Finishes	N/A		—	—	—	15.8%
.6	Doors	Double aluminum and glass and hollow metal		Each	1544	.62	
.7	Windows & Glazed Walls	Aluminum sliding	20% of wall	Each	445	1.51	
5.0 Roofing							
.1	Roof Coverings	Built-up tar and gravel with flashing		S.F. Roof	2.59	2.59	
.7	Insulation	Perlite/EPS composite		S.F. Roof	1.32	1.32	6.4%
.8	Openings & Specialties	Gravel stop and hatches		S.F. Roof	.69	.69	
6.0 Interior Construction							
.1	Partitions	Gypsum board on metal studs, toilet partitions	14 S.F. Floor/L.F. Partition	S.F. Partition	5.91	4.22	
.4	Interior Doors	Single leaf hollow metal	140 S.F. Floor/Door	Each	534	3.81	
.5	Wall Finishes	Paint		S.F. Surface	.57	.81	
.6	Floor Finishes	50% carpet, 50% vinyl tile		S.F. Floor	4.54	4.54	25.1%
.7	Ceiling Finishes	Mineral fiber tile on concealed zee bars		S.F. Ceiling	3.63	3.63	
.9	Interior Surface/Exterior Wall	Paint	80% of wall	S.F. Wall	2.12	.92	
7.0 Conveying							
.1	Elevators	N/A		—	—	—	0.0%
.2	Special Conveyors	N/A		—	—	—	
8.0 Mechanical							
.1	Plumbing	Kitchen, toilet and service fixtures, supply and drainage	1 Fixture/910 S.F. Floor	Each	4641	5.10	
.2	Fire Protection	Wet pipe sprinkler system		S.F. Floor	1.69	1.69	
.3	Heating	Included in 8.4		—	—	—	21.5%
.4	Cooling	Single zone rooftop unit, gas heating, electric cooling		S.F. Floor	8.51	8.51	
.5	Special Systems	N/A		—	—	—	
9.0 Electrical							
.1	Service & Distribution	200 ampere service, panel board and feeders		S.F. Floor	.66	.66	
.2	Lighting & Power	Incandescent fixtures, receptacles, switches, A.C. and misc. power		S.F. Floor	3.25	3.25	6.0%
.4	Special Electrical	Alarm systems and emergency lighting		S.F. Floor	.40	.40	
11.0 Special Construction							
.1	Specialties	Built-in coat racks, kitchen equipment, directory board, mailboxes		S.F. Floor	1.99	1.99	2.8%
12.0 Site Work							
.1	Earthwork	N/A		—	—	—	
.3	Utilities	N/A		—	—	—	
.5	Roads & Parking	N/A		—	—	—	0.0%
.7	Site Improvements	N/A		—	—	—	
				Sub-Total		71.34	100%
	CONTRACTOR FEES (General Requirements: 10%, Overhead: 5%, Profit: 10%)				25%	17.84	
	ARCHITECT FEES				9%	8.02	
				Total Building Cost		97.20	

BUILDING TYPES

Costs per square foot of floor area

Exterior Wall	S.F. Area	16000	23000	30000	37000	44000	51000	58000	65000	72000
	L.F. Perimeter	597	763	821	968	954	1066	1090	1132	1220
Limestone with Concrete Block Back-up	R/Conc. Frame	142.75	137.95	132.65	131.15	127.40	126.55	124.70	123.50	123.00
	Steel Frame	140.35	135.55	130.25	128.75	125.00	124.15	122.35	121.10	120.60
Face Brick with Concrete Block Back-up	R/Conc. Frame	135.75	131.70	127.50	126.25	123.35	122.60	121.20	120.25	119.85
	Steel Frame	133.35	129.30	125.15	123.85	120.95	120.20	118.80	117.85	117.45
Stone with Concrete Block Back-up	R/Conc. Frame	136.95	132.80	128.40	127.05	124.00	123.25	121.75	120.75	120.35
	Steel Frame	134.65	130.50	126.05	124.75	121.70	120.95	119.45	118.45	118.00
Perimeter Adj., Add or Deduct	Per 100 L.F.	4.80	3.30	2.55	2.10	1.75	1.50	1.35	1.15	1.05
Story Hgt. Adj., Add or Deduct	Per 1 Ft.	1.70	1.50	1.25	1.20	.95	.95	.85	.80	.75
For Basement, add $18.80 per square foot of basement area										

The above costs were calculated using the basic specifications shown on the facing page. These costs should be adjusted where necessary for design alternatives and owner's requirements. Reported completed project costs, for this type of structure, range from $84.35 to $157.20 per S.F.

Common additives

Description	Unit	$ Cost	Description	Unit	$ Cost
Benches, Hardwood	L.F.	82 - 153	Flagpoles, Complete		
Clock System			Aluminum, 20' high	Each	1075
20 room	Each	12,700	40' high	Each	2675
50 room	Each	30,800	70' high	Each	8250
Closed Circuit Surveillance, One station			Fiberglass, 23' high	Each	1400
Camera and monitor	Each	1375	39'-5" high	Each	2950
For additional camera stations, add	Each	745	59' high	Each	7300
Directory Boards, Plastic, glass covered			Intercom System, 25 station capacity		
30" x 20"	Each	565	Master station	Each	2000
36" x 48"	Each	1025	Intercom outlets	Each	126
Aluminum, 24" x 18"	Each	425	Handset	Each	335
36" x 24"	Each	535	Safe, Office type, 4 hour rating		
48" x 32"	Each	745	30" x 18" x 18"	Each	3125
48" x 60"	Each	1600	62" x 33" x 20"	Each	6775
Emergency Lighting, 25 watt, battery operated			Smoke Detectors		
Lead battery	Each	289	Ceiling type	Each	149
Nickel cadmium	Each	655	Duct type	Each	405

Important: See the Reference Section for Location Factors

BUILDING TYPES

Model costs calculated for a 1 story building with 14' story height and 30,000 square feet of floor area

				Unit	Unit Cost	Cost Per S.F.	% Of Sub-Total
1.0 Foundations							
.1	Footings & Foundations	Poured concrete; strip and spread footings and 4' foundation wall		S.F. Ground	2.61	2.61	
.4	Piles & Caissons	N/A		—	—	—	3.7%
.9	Excavation & Backfill	Site preparation for slab and trench for foundation wall and footing		S.F. Ground	1.08	1.08	
2.0 Substructure							
.1	Slab on Grade	4" reinforced concrete with vapor barrier and granular base		S.F. Slab	3.32	3.32	3.3%
.2	Special Substructures	N/A		—	—	—	
3.0 Superstructure							
.1	Columns & Beams	Concrete		L.F. Column	46	1.17	
.4	Structural Walls	N/A		—	—	—	
.5	Elevated Floors	N/A		—	—	—	14.5%
.7	Roof	Cast-in-place concrete waffle slab		S.F. Roof	13.20	13.20	
.9	Stairs	N/A		—	—	—	
4.0 Exterior Closure							
.1	Walls	Limestone panels with concrete block backup	75% of wall	S.F. Wall	34	9.90	
.5	Exterior Wall Finishes	N/A		—	—	—	12.4%
.6	Doors	Double wood		Each	1471	.34	
.7	Windows & Glazed Walls	Aluminum with insulated glass	25% of wall	Each	493	2.05	
5.0 Roofing							
.1	Roof Coverings	Built-up tar and gravel with flashing		S.F. Roof	2.23	2.23	
.7	Insulation	Perlite/EPS composite		S.F. Roof	1.32	1.32	3.6%
.8	Openings & Specialties	Gravel stop, hatches		S.F. Roof	.05	.05	
6.0 Interior Construction							
.1	Partitions	Plaster on metal studs, toilet partitions	10 S.F. Floor/L.F. Partition	S.F. Partition	8.51	10.21	
.4	Interior Doors	Single leaf wood	100 S.F. Floor/Door	Each	427	4.27	
.5	Wall Finishes	70% paint, 20% wood paneling, 10% vinyl wall covering		S.F. Surface	1.84	4.42	36.4%
.6	Floor Finishes	60% hardwood, 20% carpet, 20% terrazzo		S.F. Floor	9.29	9.29	
.7	Ceiling Finishes	Gypsum plaster on metal lath, suspended		S.F. Ceiling	6.90	6.90	
.9	Interior Surface/Exterior Wall	Painted plaster	75% of wall	S.F. Wall	3.47	1.00	
7.0 Conveying							
.1	Elevators	N/A		—	—	—	0.0%
.2	Special Conveyors	N/A		—	—	—	
8.0 Mechanical							
.1	Plumbing	Toilet and service fixtures, supply and drainage	1 Fixture/1110 S.F. Floor	Each	3507	3.16	
.2	Fire Protection	Wet pipe sprinkler system		S.F. Floor	1.44	1.44	
.3	Heating	Included in 8.4		—	—	—	18.6%
.4	Cooling	Multizone unit, gas heating, electric cooling		S.F. Floor	13.80	13.80	
.5	Special Systems	N/A		—	—	—	
9.0 Electrical							
.1	Service & Distribution	400 ampere service, panel board and feeders		S.F. Floor	.62	.62	
.2	Lighting & Power	Fluorescent fixtures, receptacles, switches, A.C. and misc. power		S.F. Floor	6.41	6.41	7.5%
.4	Special Electrical	Alarm systems and emergency lighting		S.F. Floor	.40	.40	
11.0 Special Construction							
.1	Specialties	N/A		—	—	—	0.0%
12.0 Site Work							
.1	Earthwork	N/A		—	—	—	
.3	Utilities	N/A		—	—	—	
.5	Roads & Parking	N/A		—	—	—	0.0%
.7	Site Improvements	N/A		—	—	—	
				Sub-Total		99.19	**100%**
	CONTRACTOR FEES (General Requirements: 10%, Overhead: 5%, Profit: 10%)				25%	24.80	
	ARCHITECT FEES				7%	8.66	
				Total Building Cost		**132.65**	

Costs per square foot of floor area

Exterior Wall	S.F. Area	30000	40000	45000	50000	60000	70000	80000	90000	100000
	L.F. Perimeter	410	493	535	533	600	666	733	800	795
Limestone with Concrete Block Back-up	R/Conc. Frame	151.15	145.45	143.65	140.15	137.65	135.75	134.40	133.35	130.90
	Steel Frame	149.45	143.75	141.90	138.45	135.90	134.05	132.70	131.60	129.20
Face Brick with Concrete Block Back-up	R/Conc. Frame	144.55	139.50	137.85	135.00	132.80	131.15	130.00	129.05	127.05
	Steel Frame	142.85	137.75	136.15	133.30	131.05	129.45	128.25	127.30	125.35
Stone with Concrete Block Back-up	R/Conc. Frame	145.75	140.60	138.90	135.95	133.70	132.00	130.80	129.80	127.75
	Steel Frame	144.05	138.90	137.20	134.20	131.95	130.25	129.05	128.10	126.05
Perimeter Adj., Add or Deduct	Per 100 L.F.	7.35	5.55	4.90	4.45	3.65	3.15	2.80	2.50	2.25
Story Hgt. Adj., Add or Deduct	Per 1 Ft.	2.35	2.15	2.05	1.85	1.70	1.65	1.60	1.55	1.40

For Basement, add $19.05 per square foot of basement area

The above costs were calculated using the basic specifications shown on the facing page. These costs should be adjusted where necessary for design alternatives and owner's requirements. Reported completed project costs, for this type of structure, range from $84.80 to $158.15 per S.F.

Common additives

Description	Unit	$ Cost
Benches, Hardwood	L.F.	82 - 153
Clock System		
20 room	Each	12,700
50 room	Each	30,800
Closed Circuit Surveillance, One station		
Camera and monitor	Each	1375
For additional camera stations, add	Each	745
Directory Boards, Plastic, glass covered		
30" x 20"	Each	565
36" x 48"	Each	1025
Aluminum, 24" x 18"	Each	425
36" x 24"	Each	535
48" x 32"	Each	745
48" x 60"	Each	1600
Elevators, Hydraulic passenger, 2 stops		
1500# capacity	Each	42,225
2500# capacity	Each	43,425
3500# capacity	Each	47,225
Additional stop, add	Each	3650

Description	Unit	$ Cost
Emergency Lighting, 25 watt, battery operated		
Lead battery	Each	289
Nickel cadmium	Each	655
Flagpoles, Complete		
Aluminum, 20' high	Each	1075
40' high	Each	2675
70' high	Each	8250
Fiberglass, 23' high	Each	1400
39'-5" high	Each	2950
59' high	Each	7300
Intercom System, 25 station capacity		
Master station	Each	2000
Intercom outlets	Each	126
Handset	Each	335
Safe, Office type, 4 hour rating		
30" x 18" x 18"	Each	3125
62" x 33" x 20"	Each	6775
Smoke Detectors		
Ceiling type	Each	149
Duct type	Each	405

Important: See the Reference Section for Location Factors

BUILDING TYPES

Model costs calculated for a 3 story building with 12' story height and 60,000 square feet of floor area

				Unit	Unit Cost	Cost Per S.F.	% Of Sub-Total
1.0 Foundations							
.1	Footings & Foundations	Poured concrete; strip and spread footings and 4' foundation wall		S.F. Ground	4.35	1.45	
.4	Piles & Caissons	N/A		—	—	—	1.8%
.9	Excavation & Backfill	Site preparation for slab and trench for foundation wall and footing		S.F. Ground	1.08	.36	
2.0 Substructure							
.1	Slab on Grade	4" reinforced concrete with vapor barrier and granular base		S.F. Slab	3.32	1.11	1.1%
.2	Special Substructures	N/A		—	—	—	
3.0 Superstructure							
.1	Columns & Beams	Steel columns		L.F. Column	46	1.39	
.4	Structural Walls	N/A		—	—	—	
.5	Elevated Floors	Concrete slab with metal deck and beams		S.F. Floor	14.25	9.50	16.1%
.7	Roof	Concrete slab with metal deck and beams		S.F. Roof	11.03	3.68	
.9	Stairs	Concrete filled metal pan		Flight	7000	1.17	
4.0 Exterior Closure							
.1	Walls	Face brick with concrete block backup	75% of wall	S.F. Wall	22	6.08	
.5	Exterior Wall Finishes	N/A		—	—	—	11.8%
.6	Doors	Double aluminum and glass and hollow metal		Each	1859	.19	
.7	Windows & Glazed Walls	Horizontal pivoted steel	25% of wall	Each	529	5.30	
5.0 Roofing							
.1	Roof Coverings	Built-up tar and gravel with flashing		S.F. Roof	2.31	.77	
.7	Insulation	Perlite/EPS composite		S.F. Roof	1.32	.44	1.3%
.8	Openings & Specialties	Gravel stop		L.F. Perimeter	6.40	.06	
6.0 Interior Construction							
.1	Partitions	Plaster on metal studs, toilet partitions	10 S.F. Floor/L.F. Partition	S.F. Partition	8.36	8.36	
.4	Interior Doors	Single leaf wood	100 S.F. Floor/Door	Each	427	4.27	
.5	Wall Finishes	70% paint, 20% wood paneling, 10% vinyl wall covering		S.F. Surface	1.84	3.68	34.1%
.6	Floor Finishes	60% hardwood, 20% terrazzo, 20% carpet		S.F. Floor	9.29	9.29	
.7	Ceiling Finishes	Gypsum plaster on metal lath, suspended		S.F. Ceiling	6.90	6.90	
.9	Interior Surface/Exterior Wall	Painted plaster	75% of wall	S.F. Wall	3.47	.94	
7.0 Conveying							
.1	Elevators	Five hydraulic passenger elevators		Each	76,560	6.38	6.5%
.2	Special Conveyors	N/A		—	—	—	
8.0 Mechanical							
.1	Plumbing	Toilet and service fixtures, supply and drainage	1 Fixture/665 S.F. Floor	Each	2473	3.72	
.2	Fire Protection	Wet pipe sprinkler system		S.F. Floor	1.47	1.47	
.3	Heating	Included in 8.4		—	—	—	19.5%
.4	Cooling	Multizone unit, gas heating, electric cooling		S.F. Floor	13.80	13.80	
.5	Special Systems	N/A		—	—	—	
9.0 Electrical							
.1	Service & Distribution	800 ampere service, panel board and feeders		S.F. Floor	.72	.72	
.2	Lighting & Power	Fluorescent fixtures, receptacles, switches, A.C. and misc. power		S.F. Floor	6.50	6.50	7.8%
.4	Special Electrical	Alarm systems and emergency lighting		S.F. Floor	.46	.46	
11.0 Special Construction							
.1	Specialties	N/A		—	—	—	0.0%
12.0 Site Work							
.1	Earthwork	N/A		—	—	—	
.3	Utilities	N/A		—	—	—	
.5	Roads & Parking	N/A		—	—	—	0.0%
.7	Site Improvements	N/A		—	—	—	
				Sub-Total		97.99	100%
	CONTRACTOR FEES (General Requirements: 10%, Overhead: 5%, Profit: 10%)				25%	24.50	
	ARCHITECT FEES				7%	8.56	
				Total Building Cost		131.05	

BUILDING TYPES

Costs per square foot of floor area

Exterior Wall	S.F. Area	12000	18000	24000	30000	36000	42000	48000	54000	60000
	L.F. Perimeter	460	580	713	730	826	880	965	1006	1045
Concrete Block	Steel Frame	78.20	73.95	72.05	69.25	68.35	67.25	66.65	65.90	65.25
	Bearing Walls	76.60	72.35	70.45	67.60	66.75	65.60	65.05	64.30	63.65
Precast Concrete Panels	Steel Frame	81.95	77.10	74.95	71.60	70.55	69.25	68.60	67.75	66.95
Insulated Metal Panels	Steel Frame	79.25	74.80	72.80	69.85	68.95	67.80	67.20	66.40	65.75
Face Brick on Common Brick	Steel Frame	91.25	84.90	82.15	77.50	76.15	74.35	73.50	72.25	71.15
Tilt-up Concrete Panel	Steel Frame	79.70	75.20	73.20	70.15	69.20	68.05	67.45	66.65	65.90
Perimeter Adj., Add or Deduct	Per 100 L.F.	3.55	2.40	1.85	1.45	1.20	1.05	.90	.80	.75
Story Hgt. Adj., Add or Deduct	Per 1 Ft.	.50	.45	.40	.35	.30	.30	.30	.25	.25
For Basement, add $18.95 per square foot of basement area										

The above costs were calculated using the basic specifications shown on the facing page. These costs should be adjusted where necessary for design alternatives and owner's requirements. Reported completed project costs, for this type of structure, range from $27.15 to $104.90 per S.F.

Common additives

Description	Unit	$ Cost	Description	Unit	$ Cost
Clock System			Dock Levelers, Hinged 10 ton cap.		
20 room	Each	12,700	6' x 8'	Each	4900
50 room	Each	30,800	7' x 8'	Each	4725
Dock Bumpers, Rubber blocks			Partitions, Woven wire, 10 ga., 1-1/2" mesh		
4-1/2" thick, 10" high, 14" long	Each	55	4' wide x 7' high	Each	130
24" long	Each	90	8' high	Each	140
36" long	Each	101	10' High	Each	165
12" high, 14" long	Each	93	Platform Lifter, Portable, 6' x 6'		
24" long	Each	105	3000# cap.	Each	7150
36" long	Each	121	4000# cap.	Each	8800
6" thick, 10" high, 14" long	Each	85	Fixed, 6' x 8', 5000# cap.	Each	9225
24" long	Each	116			
36" long	Each	140			
20" high, 11" long	Each	143			
Dock Boards, Heavy					
60" x 60" Aluminum, 5,000# cap.	Each	1150			
9000# cap.	Each	1175			
15,000# cap.	Each	1325			

BUILDING TYPES

Model costs calculated for a 1 story building with 20' story height and 30,000 square feet of floor area

			Unit	Unit Cost	Cost Per S.F.	% Of Sub-Total
1.0 Foundations						
.1	Footings & Foundations	Poured concrete; strip and spread footings and 4' foundation wall	S.F. Ground	2.41	2.41	
.4	Piles & Caissons	N/A	—	—	—	6.7%
.9	Excavation & Backfill	Site preparation for slab and trench for foundation wall and footing	S.F. Ground	1.08	1.08	
2.0 Substructure						
.1	Slab on Grade	4" reinforced concrete with vapor barrier and granular base	S.F. Slab	4.18	4.18	8.1%
.2	Special Substructures	N/A	—	—	—	
3.0 Superstructure						
.1	Columns & Beams	Steel columns included in 3.7	—	—	—	
.4	Structural Walls	N/A	—	—	—	
.5	Elevated Floors	N/A	—	—	—	10.5%
.7	Roof	Metal deck, open web steel joists, beams and columns	S.F. Roof	5.45	5.45	
.9	Stairs	N/A	—	—	—	
4.0 Exterior Closure						
.1	Walls	Concrete block 75% of wall	S.F. Wall	5.21	1.90	
.5	Exterior Wall Finishes	N/A	—	—	—	9.5%
.6	Doors	Double aluminum and glass, hollow metal, steel overhead	Each	1368	.68	
.7	Windows & Glazed Walls	Industrial horizontal pivoted steel 25% of wall	Each	619	2.35	
5.0 Roofing						
.1	Roof Coverings	Built-up tar and gravel with flashing	S.F. Roof	2.16	2.16	
.7	Insulation	Perlite/EPS composite	S.F. Roof	1.32	1.32	7.4%
.8	Openings & Specialties	Gravel stop, hatches	S.F. Roof	.36	.36	
6.0 Interior Construction						
.1	Partitions	Concrete block, toilet partitions 60 S.F. Floor/L.F. Partition	S.F. Partition	9.85	1.97	
.4	Interior Doors	Single leaf hollow metal and fire doors 600 S.F. Floor/Door	Each	534	.89	
.5	Wall Finishes	Paint	S.F. Surface	1.20	.48	
.6	Floor Finishes	Vinyl composition tile 10% of floor	S.F. Floor	2.90	.29	9.2%
.7	Ceiling Finishes	Fiberglass board on exposed grid system 10% of area	S.F. Ceiling	3.63	.36	
.9	Interior Surface/Exterior Wall	Paint and block filler 75% of wall	S.F. Wall	2.12	.77	
7.0 Conveying						
.1	Elevators	N/A	—	—	—	0.0%
.2	Special Conveyors	N/A	—	—	—	
8.0 Mechanical						
.1	Plumbing	Toilet and service fixtures, supply and drainage 1 Fixture/1000 S.F. Floor	Each	2900	2.90	
.2	Fire Protection	Sprinklers, ordinary hazard	S.F. Floor	2.14	2.14	
.3	Heating	Oil fired hot water, unit heaters	S.F. Floor	5.50	5.50	34.4%
.4	Cooling	Chilled water, air cooled condenser system	S.F. Floor	7.22	7.22	
.5	Special Systems	N/A	—	—	—	
9.0 Electrical						
.1	Service & Distribution	600 ampere service, panel board and feeders	S.F. Floor	.82	.82	
.2	Lighting & Power	High intensity discharge fixtures, receptacles, switches, A.C. and misc. power	S.F. Floor	6.23	6.23	14.2%
.4	Special Electrical	Alarm systems and emergency lighting	S.F. Floor	.30	.30	
11.0 Special Construction						
.1	Specialties	N/A	—	—	—	0.0%
12.0 Site Work						
.1	Earthwork	N/A	—	—	—	
.3	Utilities	N/A	—	—	—	
.5	Roads & Parking	N/A	—	—	—	0.0%
.7	Site Improvements	N/A	—	—	—	
			Sub-Total		51.76	100%
	CONTRACTOR FEES (General Requirements: 10%, Overhead: 5%, Profit: 10%)			25%	12.94	
	ARCHITECT FEES			7%	4.55	
			Total Building Cost		69.25	

BUILDING TYPES

BUILDING TYPES

Costs per square foot of floor area

Exterior Wall	S.F. Area	20000	30000	40000	50000	60000	70000	80000	90000	100000
	L.F. Perimeter	362	410	493	576	600	628	660	700	744
Face Brick Common Brick Back-up	Steel Frame	98.40	89.05	85.85	83.95	80.95	78.90	77.45	76.50	75.85
	Concrete Frame	98.30	88.95	85.75	83.85	80.85	78.80	77.35	76.40	75.75
Face Brick Concrete Block Back-up	Steel Frame	97.30	88.25	85.15	83.30	80.40	78.45	77.05	76.15	75.50
	Concrete Frame	97.00	87.95	84.85	83.00	80.10	78.15	76.80	75.85	75.20
Stucco on Concrete Block	Steel Frame	90.30	82.95	80.40	78.85	76.55	75.00	73.90	73.15	72.60
	Concrete Frame	90.00	82.65	80.05	78.55	76.25	74.70	73.55	72.85	72.30
Perimeter Adj., Add or Deduct	Per 100 L.F.	8.75	5.80	4.35	3.50	2.90	2.50	2.20	1.95	1.70
Story Hgt. Adj., Add or Deduct	Per 1 Ft.	2.45	1.85	1.65	1.55	1.35	1.20	1.15	1.05	1.00

For Basement, add $20.35 per square foot of basement area

The above costs were calculated using the basic specifications shown on the facing page. These costs should be adjusted where necessary for design alternatives and owner's requirements. Reported completed project costs, for this type of structure, range from $27.15 to $104.90 per S.F.

Common additives

Description	Unit	$ Cost
Clock System		
20 room	Each	12,700
50 room	Each	30,800
Dock Bumpers, Rubber blocks		
4-1/2" thick, 10" high, 14" long	Each	55
24" long	Each	90
36" long	Each	101
12" high, 14" long	Each	93
24" long	Each	105
36" long	Each	121
6" thick, 10" high, 14" long	Each	85
24" long	Each	116
36" long	Each	140
20" high, 11" long	Each	143
Dock Boards, Heavy		
60" x 60" Aluminum, 5,000# cap.	Each	1150
9000# cap.	Each	1175
15,000# cap.	Each	1325

Description	Unit	$ Cost
Dock Levelers, Hinged 10 ton cap.		
6'x 8'	Each	4900
7'x 8'	Each	4725
Elevator, Hydraulic freight, 2 stops		
3500# capacity	Each	62,700
4000# capacity	Each	65,200
Additional stop, add	Each	3675
Partitions, Woven wire, 10 ga., 1-1/2" mesh		
4' Wide x 7" high	Each	130
8' High	Each	140
10' High	Each	165
Platform Lifter, Portable, 6'x 6'		
3000# cap.	Each	7150
4000# cap.	Each	8800
Fixed, 6'x 8', 5000# cap.	Each	9225

Model costs calculated for a 3 story building with 12' story height and 90,000 square feet of floor area

Factory, 3 Story

BUILDING TYPES

				Unit	Unit Cost	Cost Per S.F.	% Of Sub-Total
1.0 Foundations							
	.1	Footings & Foundations	Poured concrete; strip and spread footings and 4' foundation wall	S.F. Ground	5.52	1.84	
	.4	Piles & Caissons	N/A	—	—	—	3.8%
	.9	Excavation & Backfill	Site preparation for slab and trench for foundation wall and footing	S.F. Ground	1.08	.36	
2.0 Substructure							
	.1	Slab on Grade	4" reinforced concrete with vapor barrier and granular base	S.F. Slab	5.56	1.85	3.2%
	.2	Special Substructures	N/A	—	—	—	
3.0 Superstructure							
	.1	Columns & Beams	Concrete columns	L.F. Column	105	2.66	
	.4	Structural Walls	N/A	—	—	—	
	.5	Elevated Floors	Concrete flat slab	S.F. Floor	11.80	7.87	25.1%
	.7	Roof	Concrete flat slab	S.F. Roof	10.49	3.50	
	.9	Stairs	Concrete	Flight	5125	.46	
4.0 Exterior Closure							
	.1	Walls	Face brick with common brick backup 70% of wall	S.F. Wall	23	4.56	
	.5	Exterior Wall Finishes	N/A	—	—	—	
	.6	Doors	Double aluminum & glass, hollow metal, overhead doors	Each	1316	.24	16.9%
	.7	Windows & Glazed Walls	Industrial, horizontal pivoted steel 30% of wall	Each	943	4.95	
5.0 Roofing							
	.1	Roof Coverings	Built-up tar and gravel with flashing	S.F. Roof	2.07	.69	
	.7	Insulation	Perlite/EPS composite	S.F. Roof	1.32	.44	2.2%
	.8	Openings & Specialties	Gravel stop, hatches	S.F. Roof	.36	.12	
6.0 Interior Construction							
	.1	Partitions	Gypsum board on metal studs, toilet partition 50 S.F. Floor/L.F. Partition	S.F. Partition	4.95	.99	
	.4	Interior Doors	Single leaf fire doors 500 S.F. Floor/Door	S.F. Door	659	1.32	
	.5	Wall Finishes	Paint	S.F. Surface	.57	.23	
	.6	Floor Finishes	90% metallic hardener, 10% vinyl composition tile	S.F. Floor	1.65	1.65	7.7%
	.7	Ceiling Finishes	Fiberglass board on exposed grid systems 10% of area	S.F. Ceiling	2.69	.27	
	.9	Interior Surface/Exterior Wall	N/A	—	—	—	
7.0 Conveying							
	.1	Elevators	Two hydraulic freight elevators	Each	91,800	2.04	3.5%
	.2	Special Conveyors	N/A	—	—	—	
8.0 Mechanical							
	.1	Plumbing	Toilet and service fixtures, supply and drainage 1 Fixture/1345 S.F. Floor	Each	2864	2.13	
	.2	Fire Protection	Wet pipe sprinkler system	S.F. Floor	1.93	1.93	
	.3	Heating	Oil fired hot water, unit heaters	S.F. Floor	2.82	2.82	24.5%
	.4	Cooling	Chilled water, air cooled condenser system	S.F. Floor	7.22	7.22	
	.5	Special Systems	N/A	—	—	—	
9.0 Electrical							
	.1	Service & Distribution	800 ampere service, panel board and feeders	S.F. Floor	.48	.48	
	.2	Lighting & Power	High intensity discharge fixtures, switches, A.C. and misc. power	S.F. Floor	6.60	6.60	13.1%
	.4	Special Electrical	Alarm systems and emergency lighting	S.F. Floor	.45	.45	
11.0 Special Construction							
	.1	Specialties	N/A	—	—	—	0.0%
12.0 Site Work							
	.1	Earthwork	N/A	—	—	—	
	.3	Utilities	N/A	—	—	—	
	.5	Roads & Parking	N/A	—	—	—	0.0%
	.7	Site Improvements	N/A	—	—	—	
				Sub-Total		57.67	100%
		CONTRACTOR FEES (General Requirements: 10%, Overhead: 5%, Profit: 10%)			25%	14.42	
		ARCHITECT FEES			6%	4.31	
				Total Building Cost		76.40	

119

Costs per square foot of floor area

Exterior Wall	S.F. Area	4000	4500	5000	5500	6000	6500	7000	7500	8000
	L.F. Perimeter	260	280	300	320	320	336	353	370	386
Face Brick Concrete Block Back-up	Steel Joists	110.20	108.15	106.50	105.20	102.25	101.10	100.25	99.45	98.70
	Bearing Walls	107.70	105.65	104.00	102.70	99.75	98.60	97.75	96.95	96.20
Decorative Concrete Block	Steel Joists	100.70	99.05	97.70	96.65	94.45	93.55	92.85	92.25	91.65
	Bearing Walls	98.40	96.70	95.40	94.35	92.10	91.25	90.55	89.90	89.35
Limestone with Concrete Block Back-up	Steel Joists	117.75	115.40	113.50	111.95	108.45	107.15	106.10	105.20	104.30
	Bearing Walls	115.45	113.10	111.20	109.65	106.15	104.80	103.80	102.90	102.00
Perimeter Adj., Add or Deduct	Per 100 L.F.	13.45	11.95	10.80	9.80	9.00	8.30	7.65	7.20	6.75
Story Hgt. Adj., Add or Deduct	Per 1 Ft.	1.75	1.70	1.65	1.60	1.45	1.40	1.35	1.35	1.30

For Basement, add $ 22.70 per square foot of basement area

The above costs were calculated using the basic specifications shown on the facing page. These costs should be adjusted where necessary for design alternatives and owner's requirements. Reported completed project costs, for this type of structure, range from $ 43.90 to $ 129.80 per S.F.

Common additives

Description	Unit	$ Cost
Appliances		
Cooking range, 30" free standing		
1 oven	Each	330 - 1475
2 oven	Each	1475 - 1600
30" built-in		
1 oven	Each	415 - 1550
2 oven	Each	1200 - 2050
Counter top cook tops, 4 burner	Each	277 - 610
Microwave oven	Each	196 - 630
Combination range, refrig. & sink, 30" wide	Each	1175 - 2375
60" wide	Each	3150
72" wide	Each	3575
Combination range refrigerator, sink		
microwave oven & icemaker	Each	5275
Compactor, residential, 4-1 compaction	Each	460 - 540
Dishwasher, built-in, 2 cycles	Each	475 - 715
4 cycles	Each	475 - 975
Garbage disposer, sink type	Each	124 - 279
Hood for range, 2 speed, vented, 30" wide	Each	194 - 750
42" wide	Each	340 - 1050

Description	Unit	$ Cost
Appliances, cont.		
Refrigerator, no frost 10-12 C.F.	Each	520 - 830
14-16 C.F.	Each	585 - 700
18-20 C.F.	Each	615 - 930
Lockers, Steel, single tier, 60" or 72"	Opening	125 - 220
2 tier, 60" or 72" total	Opening	70 - 119
5 tier, box lockers	Opening	40 - 60
Locker bench, lam. maple top only	L.F.	18.05
Pedestals, steel pipe	Each	58
Sound System		
Amplifier, 250 watts	Each	1650
Speaker, ceiling or wall	Each	145
Trumpet	Each	271

BUILDING TYPES

Model costs calculated for a 1 story building with 14' story height and 6,000 square feet of floor area

Fire Station, 1 Story

				Unit	Unit Cost	Cost Per S.F.	% Of Sub-Total
1.0 Foundations							
.1	Footings & Foundations	Poured concrete; strip and spread footings and 4' foundation wall		S.F. Ground	4.83	4.83	
.4	Piles & Caissons	N/A		—	—	—	8.1%
.9	Excavation & Backfill	Site preparation for slab and trench for foundation wall and footing		S.F. Ground	1.28	1.28	
2.0 Substructure							
.1	Slab on Grade	6" reinforced concrete with vapor barrier and granular base		S.F. Slab	4.18	4.18	5.5%
.2	Special Substructures	N/A		—	—	—	
3.0 Superstructure							
.1	Columns & Beams	Columns included in 3.7		—	—	—	
.4	Structural Walls	N/A		—	—	—	
.5	Elevated Floors	N/A		—	—	—	7.1%
.7	Roof	Metal deck, open web steel joists, beams on columns		S.F. Roof	5.41	5.41	
.9	Stairs	N/A		—	—	—	
4.0 Exterior Closure							
.1	Walls	Face brick with concrete block backup	75% of wall	S.F. Wall	21	11.79	
.5	Exterior Wall Finishes	N/A		—	—	—	
.6	Doors	Single aluminum and glass, overhead, hollow metal	15% of wall	S.F. Door	22	2.56	20.8%
.7	Windows & Glazed Walls	Aluminum insulated glass	10% of wall	Each	619	1.44	
5.0 Roofing							
.1	Roof Coverings	Built-up tar and gravel with flashing		S.F. Roof	2.76	2.76	
.7	Insulation	Perlite/EPS composite		S.F. Roof	1.32	1.32	6.0%
.8	Openings & Specialties	Gravel stop, skylights, roof hatches		S.F. Roof	.43	.43	
6.0 Interior Construction							
.1	Partitions	Concrete block, toilet partitions	17 S.F. Floor/L.F. Partition	S.F. Partition	6.63	3.90	
.4	Interior Doors	Single leaf hollow metal	500 S.F. Floor/Door	Each	534	1.07	
.5	Wall Finishes	Paint		S.F. Surface	1.19	1.40	
.6	Floor Finishes	50% vinyl tile, 50% paint		S.F. Floor	2.06	2.06	13.9%
.7	Ceiling Finishes	Fiberglass board on exposed grid, suspended	50% of area	S.F. Ceiling	3.63	1.82	
.9	Interior Surface/Exterior Wall	Acrylic glazed coating	75% of wall	S.F. Wall	.45	.25	
7.0 Conveying							
.1	Elevators	N/A		—	—	—	0.0%
.2	Special Conveyors	N/A		—	—	—	
8.0 Mechanical							
.1	Plumbing	Kitchen, toilet and service fixtures, supply and drainage	1 Fixture/375 S.F. Floor	Each	2576	6.87	
.2	Fire Protection	Wet pipe sprinkler system		S.F. Floor	2.27	2.27	
.3	Heating	Included in 8.4		—	—	—	31.2%
.4	Cooling	Rooftop multizone unit system		S.F. Floor	14.47	14.47	
.5	Special Systems	N/A		—	—	—	
9.0 Electrical							
.1	Service & Distribution	200 ampere service, panel board and feeders		S.F. Floor	.96	.96	
.2	Lighting & Power	Fluorescent fixtures, receptacles, switches, A.C. and misc. power		S.F. Floor	4.37	4.37	7.4%
.4	Special Electrical	Alarm systems		S.F. Floor	.30	.30	
11.0 Special Construction							
.1	Specialties	N/A		—	—	—	0.0%
12.0 Site Work							
.1	Earthwork	N/A		—	—	—	
.3	Utilities	N/A		—	—	—	
.5	Roads & Parking	N/A		—	—	—	0.0%
.7	Site Improvements	N/A		—	—	—	
				Sub-Total		75.74	100%
	CONTRACTOR FEES (General Requirements: 10%, Overhead: 5%, Profit: 10%)				25%	18.94	
	ARCHITECT FEES				8%	7.57	
				Total Building Cost		102.25	

Costs per square foot of floor area

Exterior Wall	S.F. Area	6000	7000	8000	9000	10000	11000	12000	13000	14000
	L.F. Perimeter	220	240	260	280	286	303	320	336	353
Face Brick with Concrete Block Back-up	Steel Joists	113.10	109.80	107.25	105.30	102.45	101.00	99.90	98.80	97.95
	Precast Conc.	120.20	116.90	114.45	112.50	109.70	108.25	107.15	106.05	105.25
Decorative Concrete Block	Steel Joists	105.15	102.35	100.20	98.55	96.25	95.05	94.10	93.20	92.50
	Precast Conc.	112.25	109.50	107.40	105.75	103.50	102.30	101.35	100.45	99.75
Limestone with Concrete Block Back-up	Steel Joists	121.60	117.75	114.80	112.55	109.10	107.40	106.05	104.80	103.80
	Precast Conc.	128.65	124.80	121.90	119.65	116.25	114.60	113.25	112.00	111.00
Perimeter Adj., Add or Deduct	Per 100 L.F.	15.45	13.20	11.60	10.30	9.25	8.45	7.70	7.10	6.60
Story Hgt. Adj., Add or Deduct	Per 1 Ft.	2.00	1.90	1.80	1.70	1.55	1.50	1.45	1.40	1.35

For Basement, add $21.65 per square foot of basement area

The above costs were calculated using the basic specifications shown on the facing page. These costs should be adjusted where necessary for design alternatives and owner's requirements. Reported completed project costs, for this type of structure, range from $43.90 to $129.80 per S.F.

Common additives

Description	Unit	$ Cost	Description	Unit	$ Cost
Appliances			Appliances, cont.		
Cooking range, 30" free standing			Refrigerator, no frost 10-12 C.F.	Each	520 - 830
1 oven	Each	330 - 1475	14-16 C.F.	Each	585 - 700
2 oven	Each	1475 - 1600	18-20 C.F.	Each	615 - 930
30" built-in			Elevators, Hydraulic passenger, 2 stops		
1 oven	Each	415 - 1550	1500# capacity	Each	42,225
2 oven	Each	1200 - 2050	2500# capacity	Each	43,425
Counter top cook tops, 4 burner	Each	277 - 610	3500# capacity	Each	47,225
Microwave oven	Each	196 - 630	Lockers, Steel, single tier, 60" or 72"	Opening	125 - 220
Combination range, refrig. & sink, 30" wide	Each	1175 - 2375	2 tier, 60" or 72" total	Opening	70 - 119
60" wide	Each	3150	5 tier, box lockers	Opening	40 - 60
72" wide	Each	3575	Locker bench, lam. maple top only	L.F.	18.05
Combination range, refrigerator, sink,			Pedestals, steel pipe	Each	58
microwave oven & icemaker	Each	5275	Sound System		
Compactor, residential, 4-1 compaction	Each	460 - 540	Amplifier, 250 watts	Each	1650
Dishwasher, built-in, 2 cycles	Each	475 - 715	Speaker, ceiling or wall	Each	145
4 cycles	Each	475 - 975	Trumpet	Each	271
Garbage diposer, sink type	Each	124 - 279			
Hood for range, 2 speed, vented, 30" wide	Each	194 - 750			
42" wide	Each	340 - 1050			

Important: See the Reference Section for Location Factors

Model costs calculated for a 2 story building with 14' story height and 10,000 square feet of floor area

BUILDING TYPES

				Unit	Unit Cost	Cost Per S.F.	% Of Sub-Total
1.0 Foundations							
.1	Footings & Foundations	Poured concrete; strip and spread footings and 4' foundation wall		S.F. Ground	5.24	2.62	
.4	Piles & Caissons	N/A		—	—	—	4.6%
.9	Excavation & Backfill	Site preparation for slab and trench for foundation wall and footing		S.F. Ground	1.28	.64	
2.0 Substructure							
.1	Slab on Grade	6" reinforced concrete with vapor barrier and granular base		S.F. Slab	4.18	2.09	2.9%
.2	Special Substructures	N/A		—	—	—	
3.0 Superstructure							
.1	Columns & Beams	N/A		—	—	—	
.4	Structural Walls	Included in 6.1		—	—	—	
.5	Elevated Floors	Open web steel joists, slab form, concrete		S.F. Floor	8.53	4.26	9.9%
.7	Roof	Metal deck on open web steel joists		S.F. Roof	2.78	1.39	
.9	Stairs	Concrete filled metal pan		Flight	7000	1.40	
4.0 Exterior Closure							
.1	Walls	Decorative concrete block	75% of wall	S.F. Wall	13.40	8.05	
.5	Exterior Wall Finishes	N/A		—	—	—	
.6	Doors	Single aluminum and glass, steel overhead, hollow metal	15% of wall	S.F. Door	17.15	2.06	16.6%
.7	Windows & Glazed Walls	Aluminum insulated glass	10% of wall	Each	493	1.72	
5.0 Roofing							
.1	Roof Coverings	Built-up tar and gravel with flashing		S.F. Roof	2.82	1.41	
.7	Insulation	Perlite/EPS composite		S.F. Roof	1.32	.66	3.2%
.8	Openings & Specialties	Gravel stop		L.F. Perimeter	6.40	.18	
6.0 Interior Construction							
.1	Partitions	Concrete block, toilet partitions	10 S.F. Floor/L.F. Partition	S.F. Partition	6.54	3.85	
.4	Interior Doors	Single leaf hollow metal	500 S.F. Floor/Door	Each	659	1.32	
.5	Wall Finishes	Paint		S.F. Surface	2.12	2.49	
.6	Floor Finishes	50% vinyl tile, 50% paint		S.F. Floor	2.06	2.06	15.9%
.7	Ceiling Finishes	Fiberglass board on exposed grid, suspended	50% of area	S.F. Ceiling	2.69	1.35	
.9	Interior Surface/Exterior Wall	Acrylic glazed coating	75% of wall	S.F. Wall	.45	.27	
7.0 Conveying							
.1	Elevators	One hydraulic passenger elevator		Each	51,100	5.11	7.2%
.2	Special Conveyors	N/A		—	—	—	
8.0 Mechanical							
.1	Plumbing	Kitchen toilet and service fixtures, supply and drainage	1 Fixture/400 S.F. Floor	Each	2392	5.98	
.2	Fire Protection	Wet pipe sprinkler system		S.F. Floor	1.88	1.88	
.3	Heating	Included in 8.4		—	—	—	31.2%
.4	Cooling	Rooftop multizone unit system		S.F. Floor	14.47	14.47	
.5	Special Systems	N/A		—	—	—	
9.0 Electrical							
.1	Service & Distribution	400 ampere service, panel board and feeders		S.F. Floor	1.04	1.04	
.2	Lighting & Power	Fluorescent fixtures, receptacles, switches, A.C. and misc. power		S.F. Floor	4.53	4.53	8.5%
.4	Special Electrical	Alarm systems and emergency lighting		S.F. Floor	.48	.48	
11.0 Special Construction							
.1	Specialties	N/A		—	—	—	0.0%
12.0 Site Work							
.1	Earthwork	N/A		—	—	—	
.3	Utilities	N/A		—	—	—	
.5	Roads & Parking	N/A		—	—	—	0.0%
.7	Site Improvements	N/A		—	—	—	
				Sub-Total		71.31	**100%**
	CONTRACTOR FEES (General Requirements: 10%, Overhead: 5%, Profit: 10%)				25%	17.83	
	ARCHITECT FEES				8%	7.11	
				Total Building Cost		96.25	

BUILDING TYPES

Costs per square foot of floor area

Exterior Wall	S.F. Area	4000	5000	6000	8000	10000	12000	14000	16000	18000
	L.F. Perimeter	180	205	230	260	300	340	353	386	420
Cedar Beveled Siding	Wood Frame	111.40	105.60	101.60	95.70	92.55	90.50	88.20	86.95	86.05
Aluminum Siding	Wood Frame	110.65	104.80	100.85	94.95	91.80	89.75	87.40	86.20	85.30
Board and Batten	Wood Frame	108.50	103.65	100.35	95.20	92.55	90.80	88.75	87.70	86.95
Face Brick on Block	Bearing Wall	130.40	123.45	118.70	111.10	107.25	104.70	101.50	99.95	98.85
Stucco on Block	Bearing Wall	118.30	112.35	108.30	102.20	98.95	96.85	94.40	93.15	92.25
Decorative Block	Wood Joists	115.25	109.10	104.90	98.50	95.15	92.90	90.35	89.00	88.05
Perimeter Adj., Add or Deduct	Per 100 L.F.	10.60	8.45	7.05	5.30	4.25	3.55	3.00	2.60	2.35
Story Hgt. Adj., Add or Deduct	Per 1 Ft.	1.35	1.25	1.15	1.00	.90	.85	.75	.75	.70
For Basement, add $14.00 per square foot of basement area										

The above costs were calculated using the basic specifications shown on the facing page. These costs should be adjusted where necessary for design alternatives and owner's requirements. Reported completed project costs, for this type of structure, range from $63.80 to $139.15 per S.F.

Common additives

Description	Unit	$ Cost
Appliances		
Cooking range, 30" free standing		
1 oven	Each	330 - 1475
2 oven	Each	1475 - 1600
30" built-in		
1 oven	Each	415 - 1550
2 oven	Each	1200 - 2050
Counter top cook tops, 4 burner	Each	277 - 610
Microwave oven	Each	196 - 630
Combination range, refrig. & sink, 30" wide	Each	1175 - 2375
60" wide	Each	3150
72" wide	Each	3575
Combination range, refrigerator, sink,		
microwave oven & icemaker	Each	5275
Compactor, residential, 4-1 compaction	Each	460 - 540
Dishwasher, built-in, 2 cycles	Each	475 - 715
4 cycles	Each	475 - 975
Garbage disposer, sink type	Each	124 - 279
Hood for range, 2 speed, vented, 30" wide	Each	194 - 750
42" wide	Each	340 - 1050

Description	Unit	$ Cost
Appliances, cont.		
Refrigerator, no frost 10-12 C.F.	Each	520 - 830
14-16 C.F.	Each	585 - 700
18-20 C.F.	Each	615 - 930
Elevators, Hydraulic passenger, 2 stops		
1500# capacity	Each	42,225
2500# capacity	Each	43,425
3500# capacity	Each	47,225
Laundry Equipment		
Dryer, gas, 16 lb. capacity	Each	710
30 lb. capacity	Each	2775
Washer, 4 cycle	Each	795
Commercial	Each	1200
Sound System		
Amplifier, 250 watts	Each	1650
Speaker, ceiling or wall	Each	145
Trumpet	Each	271

Important: See the Reference Section for Location Factors

Model costs calculated for a 2 story building with 10' story height and 10,000 square feet of floor area

Fraternity/Sorority House

		Description		Unit	Unit Cost	Cost Per S.F.	% Of Sub-Total
1.0 Foundations							
.1	Footings & Foundations	Poured concrete; strip and spread footings and 4' foundation wall		S.F. Ground	4.66	2.33	4.4%
.4	Piles & Caissons	N/A		—	—	—	
.9	Excavation & Backfill	Site preparation for slab and trench for foundation wall and footing		S.F. Ground	1.28	.64	
2.0 Substructure							
.1	Slab on Grade	4" reinforced concrete with vapor barrier and granular base		S.F. Slab	3.32	1.66	2.4%
.2	Special Substructures	N/A		—	—	—	
3.0 Superstructure							
.1	Columns & Beams	N/A		—	—	—	
.4	Structural Walls	Included in 6.1		—	—	—	
.5	Elevated Floors	Plywood on wood joists		S.F. Floor	3.10	1.55	5.2%
.7	Roof	Plywood on wood rafters (pitched)		S.F. Roof	2.66	1.49	
.9	Stairs	Wood		Flight	1189	.48	
4.0 Exterior Closure							
.1	Walls	Cedar bevel siding on wood studs, insulated	80% of wall	S.F. Wall	7.94	3.81	10.1%
.5	Exterior Wall Finishes	N/A		—	—	—	
.6	Doors	Solid core wood		Each	1429	1.00	
.7	Windows & Glazed Walls	Double hung wood	20% of wall	Each	428	2.05	
5.0 Roofing							
.1	Roof Coverings	Asphalt shingles with flashing (pitched)		S.F. Ground	1.40	.70	2.2%
.7	Insulation	Fiberglass sheets		S.F. Ground	1.12	.56	
.8	Openings & Specialties	Gutters and downspouts		S.F. Ground	.46	.23	
6.0 Interior Construction							
.1	Partitions	Gypsum board on wood studs	25 S.F. Floor/L.F. Partition	S.F. Partition	3.34	1.07	
.4	Interior Doors	Single leaf wood	200 S.F. Floor/Door	Each	427	2.14	
.5	Wall Finishes	Paint		S.F. Surface	.56	.36	
.6	Floor Finishes	10% hardwood, 70% carpet, 20% ceramic tile		S.F. Floor	6.62	6.62	20.5%
.7	Ceiling Finishes	Gypsum board on wood furring		S.F. Ceiling	2.92	2.92	
.9	Interior Surface/Exterior Wall	Painted gypsum board	80% of wall	S.F. Wall	1.32	.79	
7.0 Conveying							
.1	Elevators	One hydraulic passenger elevator		Each	51,100	5.11	7.5%
.2	Special Conveyors	N/A		—	—	—	
8.0 Mechanical							
.1	Plumbing	Kitchen toilet and service fixtures, supply and drainage	1 Fixture/150 S.F. Floor	Each	777	5.18	
.2	Fire Protection	Wet pipe sprinkler system		S.F. Floor	1.88	1.88	
.3	Heating	Oil fired hot water, baseboard radiation		S.F. Floor	4.02	4.02	24.5%
.4	Cooling	Split system with air cooled condensing unit		S.F. Floor	5.62	5.62	
.5	Special Systems	N/A		—	—	—	
9.0 Electrical							
.1	Service & Distribution	600 ampere service, panel board and feeders		S.F. Floor	2.99	2.99	
.2	Lighting & Power	Fluorescent fixtures, receptacles, switches, A.C. and misc. power		S.F. Floor	6.56	6.56	23.2%
.4	Special Electrical	Alarm, communication system and generator set		S.F. Floor	6.18	6.18	
11.0 Special Construction							
.1	Specialties	N/A		—	—	—	0.0%
12.0 Site Work							
.1	Earthwork	N/A		—	—	—	
.3	Utilities	N/A		—	—	—	0.0%
.5	Roads & Parking	N/A		—	—	—	
.7	Site Improvements	N/A		—	—	—	
			Sub-Total			67.94	100%
	CONTRACTOR FEES (General Requirements: 10%, Overhead: 5%, Profit: 10%)				25%	16.99	
	ARCHITECT FEES				9%	7.62	
			Total Building Cost			92.55	

BUILDING TYPES

125

Costs per square foot of floor area

Exterior Wall	S.F. Area	4000	6000	8000	10000	12000	14000	16000	18000	20000
	L.F. Perimeter	260	320	384	424	460	484	510	540	576
Vertical Redwood Siding	Wood Frame	105.80	95.85	91.05	87.45	84.90	82.85	81.35	80.25	79.45
Brick Veneer	Wood Frame	115.20	103.70	98.20	93.85	90.75	88.20	86.30	84.95	84.00
Aluminum Siding	Wood Frame	105.15	95.45	90.80	87.25	84.85	82.85	81.35	80.30	79.55
Brick on Block	Wood Truss	120.90	108.60	102.70	98.00	94.65	91.80	89.75	88.25	87.25
Limestone on Block	Wood Truss	132.50	118.10	111.25	105.50	101.40	97.90	95.35	93.50	92.25
Stucco on Block	Wood Truss	109.70	99.45	94.50	90.70	88.05	85.90	84.25	83.10	82.30
Perimeter Adj., Add or Deduct	Per 100 L.F.	7.75	5.15	3.85	3.10	2.60	2.20	1.90	1.70	1.55
Story Hgt. Adj., Add or Deduct	Per 1 Ft.	1.05	.85	.75	.70	.65	.55	.50	.50	.45

For Basement, add $18.70 per square foot of basement area

The above costs were calculated using the basic specifications shown on the facing page. These costs should be adjusted where necessary for design alternatives and owner's requirements. Reported completed project costs, for this type of structure, range from $62.25 to $191.40 per S.F.

Common additives

Description	Unit	$ Cost
Autopsy Table, Standard	Each	7575
Deluxe	Each	15,100
Directory Boards, Plastic, glass covered		
30" x 20"	Each	565
36" x 48"	Each	1025
Aluminum, 24" x 18"	Each	425
36" x 24"	Each	535
48" x 32"	Each	745
48" x 60"	Each	1600
Emergency Lighting, 25 watt, battery operated		
Lead battery	Each	289
Nickel cadmium	Each	655
Mortuary Refrigerator, End operated		
Two capacity	Each	11,400
Six capacity	Each	21,100

Description	Unit	$ Cost
Planters, Precast concrete		
48" diam., 24" high	Each	565
7" diam., 36" high	Each	1025
Fiberglass, 36" diam., 24" high	Each	460
60" diam., 24" high	Each	720
Smoke Detectors		
Ceiling type	Each	149
Duct type	Each	405

BUILDING TYPES

Important: See the Reference Section for Location Factors

Model costs calculated for a 1 story building with 12' story height and 10,000 square feet of floor area

				Unit	Unit Cost	Cost Per S.F.	% Of Sub-Total
1.0 Foundations							
.1	Footings & Foundations	Poured concrete; strip and spread footings and 4' foundation wall		S.F. Ground	3.27	3.27	
.4	Piles & Caissons	N/A		—	—	—	6.9%
.9	Excavation & Backfill	Site preparation for slab and trench for foundation wall and footing		S.F. Ground	1.17	1.17	
2.0 Substructure							
.1	Slab on Grade	4" reinforced concrete with vapor barrier and granular base		S.F. Slab	3.32	3.32	5.2%
.2	Special Substructures	N/A		—	—	—	
3.0 Superstructure							
.1	Columns & Beams	N/A		—	—	—	
.4	Structural Walls	N/A		—	—	—	
.5	Elevated Floors	N/A		—	—	—	5.9%
.7	Roof	Plywood on wood truss		S.F. Ground	3.76	3.76	
.9	Stairs	N/A		—	—	—	
4.0 Exterior Closure							
.1	Walls	1" x 4" vertical T & G redwood siding on wood studs	90% of wall	S.F. Wall	8.65	3.97	
.5	Exterior Wall Finishes	N/A		—	—	—	9.9%
.6	Doors	Wood swinging double doors, single leaf hollow metal		Each	1536	.92	
.7	Windows & Glazed Walls	Double hung wood	10% of wall	Each	344	1.46	
5.0 Roofing							
.1	Roof Coverings	Single ply membrane, fully adhered		S.F. Roof	1.59	1.59	
.7	Insulation	Polyisocyanurate sheets		S.F. Ground	1.14	1.14	4.8%
.8	Openings & Specialties	Gutters and downspouts		S.F. Ground	.33	.33	
6.0 Interior Construction							
.1	Partitions	Gypsum board on wood studs with sound deadening board	15 S.F. Floor/L.F. Partition	S.F. Partition	5.49	2.93	
.4	Interior Doors	Single leaf wood	150 S.F. Floor/Door	Each	427	2.85	
.5	Wall Finishes	50% wallpaper, 25% wood paneling, 25% paint		S.F. Surface	2.34	2.50	
.6	Floor Finishes	70% carpet, 30% ceramic tile		S.F. Floor	7.59	7.59	29.8%
.7	Ceiling Finishes	Fiberglass board on exposed grid, suspended		S.F. Ceiling	2.69	2.69	
.9	Interior Surface/Exterior Wall	Painted gypsum board on wood furring	90% of wall	S.F. Wall	1.65	.59	
7.0 Conveying							
.1	Elevators	N/A		—	—	—	0.0%
.2	Special Conveyors	N/A		—	—	—	
8.0 Mechanical							
.1	Plumbing	Toilet and service fixtures, supply and drainage	1 Fixture/770 S.F. Floor	Each	4689	6.09	
.2	Fire Protection	Wet pipe sprinkler system		S.F. Floor	1.69	1.69	
.3	Heating	Included in 8.4		—	—	—	29.7%
.4	Cooling	Multizone rooftop unit, gas heating, electric cooling		S.F. Floor	11.35	11.35	
.5	Special Systems	N/A		—	—	—	
9.0 Electrical							
.1	Service & Distribution	400 ampere service, panel board and feeders		S.F. Floor	1.16	1.16	
.2	Lighting & Power	Fluorescent fixtures, receptacles, switches, A.C. and misc. power		S.F. Floor	3.60	3.60	7.8%
.4	Special Electrical	Alarm systems and emergency lighting		S.F. Floor	.22	.22	
11.0 Special Construction							
.1	Specialties	N/A		—	—	—	0.0%
12.0 Site Work							
.1	Earthwork	N/A		—	—	—	
.3	Utilities	N/A		—	—	—	
.5	Roads & Parking	N/A		—	—	—	0.0%
.7	Site Improvements	N/A		—	—	—	
				Sub-Total		64.19	100%
	CONTRACTOR FEES (General Requirements: 10%, Overhead: 5%, Profit: 10%)				25%	16.05	
	ARCHITECT FEES				9%	7.21	
				Total Building Cost		87.45	

BUILDING TYPES

Costs per square foot of floor area

Exterior Wall	S.F. Area	12000	14000	16000	19000	21000	23000	26000	28000	30000
	L.F. Perimeter	440	474	510	556	583	607	648	670	695
E.I.F.S. on Concrete Block	Steel Frame	76.55	74.40	72.90	71.00	69.90	68.95	67.85	67.20	66.65
Tilt-up Concrete Wall	Steel Frame	73.30	71.40	70.05	68.40	67.40	66.60	65.65	65.05	64.60
Face Brick with Concrete Block Back-up	Bearing Walls	77.20	74.75	73.05	70.90	69.65	68.55	67.35	66.60	65.95
	Steel Frame	79.95	77.55	75.85	73.70	72.45	71.35	70.15	69.40	68.75
Stucco on Concrete Block	Bearing Walls	71.40	69.45	68.05	66.30	65.25	64.35	63.40	62.75	62.25
	Steel Frame	74.55	72.55	71.15	69.40	68.35	67.50	66.50	65.90	65.40
Perimeter Adj., Add or Deduct	Per 100 L.F.	4.85	4.15	3.65	3.05	2.80	2.50	2.25	2.10	1.95
Story Hgt. Adj., Add or Deduct	Per 1 Ft.	1.15	1.05	1.05	.90	.90	.85	.80	.75	.75
For Basement, add $21.20 per square foot of basement area										

The above costs were calculated using the basic specifications shown on the facing page. These costs should be adjusted where necessary for design alternatives and owner's requirements. Reported completed project costs, for this type of structure, range from $33.50 to $96.40 per S.F.

Common additives

Description	Unit	$ Cost
Emergency Lighting, 25 watt, battery operated		
Lead battery	Each	289
Nickel cadmium	Each	655
Smoke Detectors		
Ceiling type	Each	149
Duct type	Each	405
Sound System		
Amplifier, 250 watts	Each	1650
Speaker, ceiling or wall	Each	145
Trumpet	Each	271

Important: See the Reference Section for Location Factors

Model costs calculated for a 1 story building with 14' story height and 21,000 square feet of floor area

Garage, Auto Sales

				Unit	Unit Cost	Cost Per S.F.	% Of Sub-Total
1.0 Foundations							
	.1	Footings & Foundations	Poured concrete; strip and spread footings and 4' foundation wall	S.F. Ground	2.34	2.34	
	.4	Piles & Caissons	N/A	—	—	—	6.7%
	.9	Excavation & Backfill	Site preparation for slab and trench for foundation wall and footing	S.F. Ground	1.17	1.17	
2.0 Substructure							
	.1	Slab on Grade	4" reinforced concrete with vapor barrier and granular base	S.F. Slab	4.76	4.76	9.1%
	.2	Special Substructures	N/A	—	—	—	
3.0 Superstructure							
	.1	Columns & Beams	Steel columns included in 3.7	—	—	—	
	.4	Structural Walls	Metal siding support	S.F. Wall	4.96	1.35	
	.5	Elevated Floors	N/A	—	—	—	13.2%
	.7	Roof	Metal deck, open web steel joists, beams, columns	S.F. Floor	5.57	5.57	
	.9	Stairs	N/A	—	—	—	
4.0 Exterior Closure							
	.1	Walls	N/A 70% of wall	S.F. Wall	—	—	
	.5	Exterior Wall Finishes	E.I.F.S.	S.F. Wall	13.65	3.71	19.1%
	.6	Doors	Double aluminum and glass, hollow metal, steel overhead	Each	2423	2.08	
	.7	Windows & Glazed Walls	Window wall 30% of wall	S.F. Window	36	4.20	
5.0 Roofing							
	.1	Roof Coverings	Built-up tar and gravel with flashing	S.F. Roof	2.13	2.13	
	.7	Insulation	Perlite/EPS composite	S.F. Roof	1.32	1.32	6.9%
	.8	Openings & Specialties	Gravel stop and skylight	L.F. Perimeter	6.40	.18	
6.0 Interior Construction							
	.1	Partitions	Gypsum board on metal studs 28 S.F. Floor/L.F. Partition	S.F. Partition	3.10	1.33	
	.4	Interior Doors	Hollow metal 280 S.F. Floor/Door	Each	534	1.91	
	.5	Wall Finishes	Paint	S.F. Surface	.57	.49	13.7%
	.6	Floor Finishes	50% vinyl tile, 50% paint	S.F. Floor	2.06	2.06	
	.7	Ceiling Finishes	Fiberglass board on exposed grid, suspended 50% of area	S.F. Ceiling	2.69	1.35	
	.9	Interior Surface/Exterior Wall	N/A	—	—	—	
7.0 Conveying							
	.1	Elevators	N/A	—	—	—	0.0%
	.2	Special Conveyors	N/A	—	—	—	
8.0 Mechanical							
	.1	Plumbing	Toilet and service fixtures, supply and drainage 1 Fixture/1500 S.F. Floor	Each	3135	2.09	
	.2	Fire Protection	Wet pipe sprinkler system	S.F. Floor	2.21	2.21	
	.3	Heating	Gas fired hot water, unit heaters (service area)	S.F. Floor	2.50	2.50	20.3%
	.4	Cooling	Single zone rooftop unit, gas heating, electric (office and showroom)	S.F. Floor	3.56	3.56	
	.5	Special Systems	Underfloor garage exhaust system	S.F. Floor	.22	.22	
9.0 Electrical							
	.1	Service & Distribution	200 ampere service, panel board and feeders	S.F. Floor	.29	.29	
	.2	Lighting & Power	Fluorescent fixtures, receptacles, switches, A.C. and misc. power	S.F. Floor	4.35	4.35	9.3%
	.4	Special Electrical	Alarm systems and emergency lighting	S.F. Floor	.21	.21	
11.0 Special Construction							
	.1	Specialties	Hoists, compressor, fuel pump	S.F. Floor	.87	.87	1.7%
12.0 Site Work							
	.1	Earthwork	N/A	—	—	—	
	.3	Utilities	N/A	—	—	—	0.0%
	.5	Roads & Parking	N/A	—	—	—	
	.7	Site Improvements	N/A	—	—	—	
				Sub-Total		52.25	100%
		CONTRACTOR FEES (General Requirements: 10%, Overhead: 5%, Profit: 10%)			25%	13.06	
		ARCHITECT FEES			7%	4.59	
				Total Building Cost		69.90	

BUILDING TYPES

129

BUILDING TYPES

Costs per square foot of floor area

Exterior Wall	S.F. Area	85000	115000	145000	175000	205000	235000	265000	295000	325000
	L.F. Perimeter	529	638	723	823	923	951	1037	1057	1132
Face Brick with Concrete Block Back-up	Steel Frame	38.70	37.75	37.05	36.65	36.35	35.90	35.75	35.40	35.30
	R/Conc. Frame	32.45	31.50	30.75	30.40	30.10	29.65	29.45	29.15	29.00
Precast Concrete	Steel Frame	39.20	38.20	37.50	37.15	36.85	36.40	36.20	35.90	35.75
	R/Conc. Frame	32.45	31.45	30.75	30.40	30.10	29.65	29.45	29.15	29.00
Reinforced Concrete	Steel Frame	38.60	37.70	37.05	36.75	36.45	36.10	35.90	35.65	35.50
	R/Conc. Frame	31.60	30.75	30.05	29.75	29.50	29.10	28.95	28.65	28.55
Perimeter Adj., Add or Deduct	Per 100 L.F.	1.00	.75	.60	.50	.40	.35	.30	.30	.25
Story Hgt. Adj., Add or Deduct	Per 1 Ft.	.35	.30	.25	.25	.25	.25	.20	.20	.20
Basement—Not Applicable										

The above costs were calculated using the basic specifications shown on the facing page. These costs should be adjusted where necessary for design alternatives and owner's requirements. Reported completed project costs, for this type of structure, range from $19.00 to $78.70 per S.F.

Common additives

Description	Unit	$ Cost
Elevators, Electric passenger, 5 stops		
2000# capacity	Each	97,700
3500# capacity	Each	103,700
5000# capacity	Each	108,200
Barrier gate w/programmable controller	Each	3000
Booth for attendant, average	Each	11,700
Fee computer	Each	15,300
Ticket spitter with time/date stamp	Each	7000
Mag strip encoding	Each	18,600
Collection station, pay on foot	Each	111,500
Parking control software	Each	22,200 - 91,000
Painting, Parking stalls	Stall	8.00
Parking Barriers		
Timber with saddles, 4" x 4"	L.F.	5.80
Precast concrete, 6" x 10" x 6'	Each	43
Traffic Signs, directional, 12" x 18", high densit	Each	57

Important: See the Reference Section for Location Factors

Model costs calculated for a 5 story building with 10' story height and 145,000 square feet of floor area

				Unit	Unit Cost	Cost Per S.F.	% Of Sub-Total
1.0 Foundations							
	.1	Footings & Foundations	Poured concrete; strip and spread footings and 4' foundation wall	S.F. Ground	9.00	1.80	
	.4	Piles & Caissons	N/A	—	—	—	8.7%
	.9	Excavation & Backfill	Site preparation for slab and trench for foundation wall and footing	S.F. Ground	1.08	.22	
2.0 Substructure							
	.1	Slab on Grade	6" reinforced concrete with vapor barrier and granular base	S.F. Slab	4.11	.82	3.5%
	.2	Special Substructures	N/A	—	—	—	
3.0 Superstructure							
	.1	Columns & Beams	Precast concrete columns	S.F. Floor	5.25	5.25	
	.4	Structural Walls	Concrete block elevator shaft	S.F. Wall	10.44	.54	
	.5	Elevated Floors	Double tee precast concrete slab	S.F. Floor	8.30	6.64	54.4%
	.7	Roof	N/A	—	—	—	
	.9	Stairs	Concrete	Flight	2730	.19	
4.0 Exterior Closure							
	.1	Walls	Face brick with concrete block backup 40% of story height	S.F. Wall	21	2.10	
	.5	Exterior Wall Finishes	N/A	—	—	—	
	.6	Doors	N/A	—	—	—	9.0%
	.7	Windows & Glazed Walls	N/A	—	—	—	
5.0 Roofing							
	.1	Roof Coverings	N/A	—	—	—	
	.7	Insulation	N/A	—	—	—	0.0%
	.8	Openings & Specialties	N/A	—	—	—	
6.0 Interior Construction							
	.1	Partitions	Concrete block	S.F. Partition	6.50	.25	
	.4	Interior Doors	Hollow metal	Each	10,680	.07	
	.5	Wall Finishes	Paint	S.F. Surface	1.17	.09	
	.6	Floor Finishes	N/A	—	—	—	1.8%
	.7	Ceiling Finishes	N/A	—	—	—	
	.9	Interior Surface/Exterior Wall	N/A	—	—	—	
7.0 Conveying							
	.1	Elevators	Two hydraulic passenger elevators	Each	87,000	1.20	5.2%
	.2	Special Conveyors	N/A	—	—	—	
8.0 Mechanical							
	.1	Plumbing	Toilet and service fixtures, supply and drainage 1 Fixture/18,125 S.F. Floor	Each	14,500	.80	
	.2	Fire Protection	Standpipes and hose systems	S.F. Floor	.05	.05	
	.3	Heating	N/A	—	—	—	3.7%
	.4	Cooling	N/A	—	—	—	
	.5	Special Systems	N/A	—	—	—	
9.0 Electrical							
	.1	Service & Distribution	400 ampere service, panel board and feeders	S.F. Floor	.15	.15	
	.2	Lighting & Power	Fluorescent fixtures, receptacles, switches and misc. power	S.F. Floor	1.95	1.95	9.6%
	.4	Special Electrical	Alarm systems and emergency lighting	S.F. Floor	.13	.13	
11.0 Special Construction							
	.1	Specialties	Ticket dispensers, booths automatic gates	S.F. Floor	.96	.96	4.1%
12.0 Site Work							
	.1	Earthwork	N/A	—	—	—	
	.3	Utilities	N/A	—	—	—	
	.5	Roads & Parking	N/A	—	—	—	0.0%
	.7	Site Improvements	N/A	—	—	—	
				Sub-Total		23.21	100%
		CONTRACTOR FEES (General Requirements: 10%, Overhead: 5%, Profit: 10%)			25%	5.80	
		ARCHITECT FEES			6%	1.74	
				Total Building Cost		30.75	

Costs per square foot of floor area

Exterior Wall	S.F. Area	20000	30000	40000	50000	75000	100000	125000	150000	175000
	L.F. Perimeter	400	500	600	650	775	900	1000	1100	1185
Reinforced Concrete	R/Conc. Frame	60.25	55.90	53.70	51.65	48.85	**47.45**	46.45	45.80	45.25
Perimeter Adj., Add or Deduct	Per 100 L.F.	3.85	2.55	1.95	1.55	1.05	.75	.60	.50	.45
Story Hgt. Adj., Add or Deduct	Per 1 Ft.	1.50	1.20	1.10	.95	.75	.65	.60	.55	.50
Basement—Not Applicable										

The above costs were calculated using the basic specifications shown on the facing page. These costs should be adjusted where necessary for design alternatives and owner's requirements. Reported completed project costs, for this type of structure, range from $29.65 to $70.50 per S.F.

Common additives

Description	Unit	$ Cost
Elevators, Hydraulic passenger, 2 stops		
1500# capacity	Each	42,225
2500# capacity	Each	43,425
3500# capacity	Each	47,225
Barrier gate w/programmable controller	Each	3000
Booth for attendant, average	Each	11,700
Fee computer	Each	15,300
Ticket spitter with time/date stamp	Each	7000
Mag strip encoding	Each	18,600
Collection station, pay on foot	Each	111,500
Parking control software	Each	22,200 - 91,000
Painting, Parking stalls	Stall	8.00
Parking Barriers		
Timber with saddles, 4" x 4"	L.F.	5.80
Precast concrete, 6" x 10" x 6'	Each	43
Traffic Signs, directional, 12" x 18"	Each	57

BUILDING TYPES

Model costs calculated for a 2 story building with 10' story height and 100,000 square feet of floor area

			Unit	Unit Cost	Cost Per S.F.	% Of Sub-Total
1.0 Foundations						
.1	Footings & Foundations	Poured concrete; strip and spread footings and waterproofing	S.F. Ground	5.06	2.53	
.4	Piles & Caissons	N/A	—	—	—	17.2%
.9	Excavation & Backfill	Excavation 24' deep	S.F. Ground	7.05	3.53	
2.0 Substructure						
.1	Slab on Grade	5" reinforced concrete with vapor barrier and granular base	S.F. Slab	4.18	2.09	5.9%
.2	Special Substructures	N/A	—	—	—	
3.0 Superstructure						
.1	Columns & Beams	Concrete columns	L.F. Column	127	.64	
.4	Structural Walls	Concrete block elevator shaft	S.F. Wall	10.44	.39	
.5	Elevated Floors	Cast-in-place concrete beam and slab	S.F. Floor	20	8.26	50.4%
.7	Roof	Cast-in-place concrete beam and slab	S.F. Roof	16.45	8.23	
.9	Stairs	Concrete	Flight	4225	.21	
4.0 Exterior Closure						
.1	Walls	Cast-in place concrete	S.F. Wall	16.00	2.88	
.5	Exterior Wall Finishes	N/A	—	—	—	8.5%
.6	Doors	Steel overhead, hollow metal	Each	2975	.12	
.7	Windows & Glazed Walls	N/A	—	—	—	
5.0 Roofing						
.1	Roof Coverings	Neoprene membrane traffic deck	S.F. Roof	3.28	1.64	
.7	Insulation	N/A	—	—	—	4.7%
.8	Openings & Specialties	N/A	—	—	—	
6.0 Interior Construction						
.1	Partitions	Concrete block	S.F. Partition	6.76	.13	
.4	Interior Doors	Hollow metal	Each	4272	.04	
.5	Wall Finishes	Paint	S.F. Surface	1.82	.07	
.6	Floor Finishes	N/A	—	—	—	0.7%
.7	Ceiling Finishes	N/A	—	—	—	
.9	Interior Surface/Exterior Wall	N/A	—	—	—	
7.0 Conveying						
.1	Elevators	Two hydraulic passenger elevators	Each	51,000	1.02	2.9%
.2	Special Conveyors	N/A	—	—	—	
8.0 Mechanical						
.1	Plumbing	Drainage in parking areas, toilets, & service fixtures 1 Fixture/5000 S.F. Floor	Each	.82	.82	
.2	Fire Protection	Dry standpipe system, class 1	S.F. Floor	.08	.08	
.3	Heating	N/A	—	—	—	2.9%
.4	Cooling	Exhaust fans	S.F. Floor	.10	.10	
.5	Special Systems	N/A	—	—	—	
9.0 Electrical						
.1	Service & Distribution	200 ampere service, panel board and feeders	S.F. Floor	.08	.08	
.2	Lighting & Power	Fluorescent fixtures, receptacles, switches and misc. power	S.F. Floor	1.67	1.67	6.0%
.4	Special Electrical	Alarm systems and emergency lighting	S.F. Floor	.35	.35	
11.0 Special Construction						
.1	Specialties	Ticket dispensers, booths, automatic gates	S.F. Floor	.28	.28	0.8%
12.0 Site Work						
.1	Earthwork	N/A	—	—	—	
.3	Utilities	N/A	—	—	—	0.0%
.5	Roads & Parking	N/A	—	—	—	
.7	Site Improvements	N/A	—	—	—	
	Sub-Total				35.16	100%
	CONTRACTOR FEES (General Requirements: 10%, Overhead: 5%, Profit: 10%)			25%	8.79	
	ARCHITECT FEES			8%	3.50	
	Total Building Cost				47.45	

Costs per square foot of floor area

Exterior Wall	S.F. Area	2000	4000	6000	8000	10000	12000	14000	16000	18000
	L.F. Perimeter	180	260	340	420	500	580	586	600	610
Concrete Block	Wood Joists	104.10	89.35	84.40	81.95	80.50	79.50	77.00	75.30	73.90
	Steel Joists	103.85	89.50	84.70	82.35	80.95	79.95	77.50	75.80	74.45
Poured Concrete	Wood Joists	113.95	96.65	90.85	88.00	86.30	85.15	81.85	79.65	77.85
	Steel Joists	114.45	97.15	91.35	88.50	86.80	85.65	82.35	80.15	78.35
Stucco	Wood Frame	113.15	96.10	90.35	87.55	85.85	84.70	81.50	79.35	77.60
Insulated Metal Panels	Steel Frame	101.40	88.45	84.05	81.95	80.65	79.80	77.65	76.20	75.05
Perimeter Adj., Add or Deduct	Per 100 L.F.	16.75	8.40	5.60	4.20	3.35	2.80	2.40	2.10	1.85
Story Hgt. Adj., Add or Deduct	Per 1 Ft.	1.25	.90	.80	.75	.70	.70	.60	.55	.50
For Basement, add $ 20.00 per square foot of basement area										

The above costs were calculated using the basic specifications shown on the facing page. These costs should be adjusted where necessary for design alternatives and owner's requirements. Reported completed project costs, for this type of structure, range from $ 42.40 to $ 127.40 per S.F.

Common additives

Description	Unit	$ Cost
Air Compressors		
Electric 1-1/2 H.P., standard controls	Each	1025
Dual controls	Each	1200
5 H.P. 115/230 Volt, standard controls	Each	2725
Dual controls	Each	2825
Product Dispenser		
with vapor recovery for 6 nozzles	Each	16,500
Hoists, Single post		
8000# cap., swivel arm	Each	6425
Two post, adjustable frames, 11,000# cap.	Each	9050
24,000# cap.	Each	13,500
7500# Frame support	Each	7550
Four post, roll on ramp	Each	7000
Lockers, Steel, single tier, 60" or 72"	Opening	125 - 220
2 tier, 60" or 72" total	Opening	70 - 119
5 tier, box lockers	Opening	40 - 60
Locker bench, lam. maple top only	L.F.	18.05
Pedestals, steel pipe	Each	58
Lube Equipment		
3 reel type, with pumps, no piping	Each	8650
Spray Painting Booth, 26' long, complete	Each	15,800

BUILDING TYPES

Model costs calculated for a 1 story building with 14' story height and 10,000 square feet of floor area

				Unit	Unit Cost	Cost Per S.F.	% Of Sub-Total
1.0 Foundations							
	.1	Footings & Foundations	Poured concrete; strip and spread footings and 4' foundation wall	S.F. Ground	3.98	3.98	
	.4	Piles & Caissons	N/A	—	—	—	8.6%
	.9	Excavation & Backfill	Site preparation for slab and trench for foundation wall and footing	S.F. Ground	1.17	1.17	
2.0 Substructure							
	.1	Slab on Grade	6" reinforced concrete with vapor barrier and granular base	S.F. Slab	4.76	4.76	7.9%
	.2	Special Substructures	N/A	—	—	—	
3.0 Superstructure							
	.1	Columns & Beams	N/A	—	—	—	
	.4	Structural Walls	N/A	—	—	—	
	.5	Elevated Floors	N/A	—	—	—	5.2%
	.7	Roof	Metal deck on open web steel joists	S.F. Roof	3.12	3.12	
	.9	Stairs	N/A	—	—	—	
4.0 Exterior Closure							
	.1	Walls	Concrete block 80% of wall	L.F. Wall	7.98	4.47	
	.5	Exterior Wall Finishes	N/A	—	—	—	
	.6	Doors	Steel overhead and hollow metal 15% of wall	S.F. Door	11.81	1.24	10.7%
	.7	Windows & Glazed Walls	Hopper type commercial steel 5% of wall	Each	304	.71	
5.0 Roofing							
	.1	Roof Coverings	Built-up tar and gravel	S.F. Roof	2.50	2.50	
	.7	Insulation	Perlite/EPS composite	S.F. Roof	1.32	1.32	6.9%
	.8	Openings & Specialties	Gravel stop and skylight	S.F. Roof	.33	.33	
6.0 Interior Construction							
	.1	Partitions	Concrete block, toilet partitions 50 S.F. Floor/L.F. Partition	S.F. Partition	5.50	1.10	
	.4	Interior Doors	Single leaf hollow metal 3000 S.F. Floor/Door	Each	534	.18	
	.5	Wall Finishes	Paint	S.F. Surface	2.13	.85	
	.6	Floor Finishes	90% metallic floor hardener, 10% vinyl composition tile	S.F. Floor	.65	.65	7.0%
	.7	Ceiling Finishes	Gypsum board on wood joists in office and washrooms 10% of area	S.F. Ceiling	1.99	.20	
	.9	Interior Surface/Exterior Wall	Paint 80% of wall	S.F. Wall	2.12	1.19	
7.0 Conveying							
	.1	Elevators	N/A	—	—	—	0.0%
	.2	Special Conveyors	N/A	—	—	—	
8.0 Mechanical							
	.1	Plumbing	Toilet and service fixtures, supply and drainage 1 Fixture/500 S.F. Floor	Each	1235	2.47	
	.2	Fire Protection	Sprinklers, ordinary hazard	S.F. Floor	2.50	2.50	
	.3	Heating	Oil fired hot water, unit heaters	S.F. Floor	5.00	5.00	29.3%
	.4	Cooling	Split systems with air cooled condensing units	S.F. Floor	7.29	7.29	
	.5	Special Systems	Garage exhaust system	S.F. Floor	.33	.34	
9.0 Electrical							
	.1	Service & Distribution	200 ampere service, panel board and feeders	S.F. Floor	.32	.32	
	.2	Lighting & Power	Fluorescent fixtures, receptacles, switches, A.C. and misc. power	S.F. Floor	4.46	4.46	8.3%
	.4	Special Electrical	Alarm systems and emergency lighting	S.F. Floor	.17	.17	
11.0 Special Construction							
	.1	Specialties	Hoists	S.F. Floor	9.64	9.64	16.1%
12.0 Site Work							
	.1	Earthwork	N/A	—	—	—	
	.3	Utilities	N/A	—	—	—	
	.5	Roads & Parking	N/A	—	—	—	0.0%
	.7	Site Improvements	N/A	—	—	—	
				Sub-Total		59.96	**100%**
		CONTRACTOR FEES (General Requirements: 10%, Overhead: 5%, Profit: 10%)			25%	14.99	
		ARCHITECT FEES			8%	6.00	
				Total Building Cost		**80.95**	

Costs per square foot of floor area

Exterior Wall	S.F. Area	600	800	1000	1200	1400	1600	1800	2000	2200
	L.F. Perimeter	100	120	126	140	153	160	170	180	190
Face Brick with Concrete Block Back-up	Wood Truss	156.15	143.60	129.70	123.45	118.70	113.45	110.05	107.35	105.20
	Steel Joists	150.15	137.60	123.70	117.50	112.70	107.45	104.05	101.35	99.20
Enameled Sandwich Panel	Steel Frame	135.25	124.30	112.60	107.25	103.15	98.75	95.90	93.60	91.80
Tile on Concrete Block	Steel Joists	159.30	145.95	130.95	124.25	119.15	113.45	109.80	106.90	104.60
Aluminum Siding	Wood Frame	131.90	121.80	111.40	106.50	102.75	98.85	96.30	94.25	92.60
Wood Siding	Wood Frame	133.10	122.90	112.30	107.35	103.55	99.60	96.95	94.90	93.25
Perimeter Adj., Add or Deduct	Per 100 L.F.	75.90	56.90	45.55	37.95	32.55	28.45	25.30	22.80	20.65
Story Hgt. Adj., Add or Deduct	Per 1 Ft.	5.00	4.50	3.80	3.55	3.30	3.00	2.85	2.70	2.60
Basement—Not Applicable										

The above costs were calculated using the basic specifications shown on the facing page. These costs should be adjusted where necessary for design alternatives and owner's requirements. Reported completed project costs, for this type of structure, range from $30.50 to $154.00 per S.F.

Common additives

Description	Unit	$ Cost
Air Compressors		
Electric 1-1/2 H.P., standard controls	Each	1025
Dual controls	Each	1200
5 H.P. 115/230 volt, standard controls	Each	2725
Dual controls	Each	2825
Product Dispenser		
with vapor recovery for 6 nozzles	Each	16,500
Hoists, Single post		
8000# cap. swivel arm	Each	6425
Two post, adjustable frames, 11,000# cap.	Each	9050
24,000# cap.	Each	13,500
7500# cap.	Each	7550
Four post, roll on ramp	Each	7000
Lockers, Steel, single tier, 60" or 72"	Opening	125 - 220
2 tier, 60" or 72" total	Opening	70 - 119
5 tier, box lockers	Each	40 - 60
Locker bench, lam. maple top only	L.F.	18.05
Pedestals, steel pipe	Each	58
Lube Equipment		
3 reel type, with pumps, no piping	Each	8650

Important: See the Reference Section for Location Factors

Model costs calculated for a 1 story building with 12' story height and 1,400 square feet of floor area

				Unit	Unit Cost	Cost Per S.F.	% Of Sub-Total
1.0 Foundations							
	.1	Footings & Foundations	Poured concrete; strip and spread footings and 4' foundation wall	S.F. Ground	7.67	7.67	
	.4	Piles & Caissons	N/A	—	—	—	10.6%
	.9	Excavation & Backfill	Site preparation for slab and trench for foundation wall and footing	S.F. Ground	1.64	1.64	
2.0 Substructure							
	.1	Slab on Grade	6" reinforced concrete with vapor barrier and granular base	S.F. Slab	4.76	4.76	5.4%
	.2	Special Substructures	N/A	—	—	—	
3.0 Superstructure							
	.1	Columns & Beams	N/A	—	—	—	
	.4	Structural Walls	N/A	—	—	—	
	.5	Elevated Floors	N/A	—	—	—	5.6%
	.7	Roof	Plywood on wood trusses	S.F. Ground	4.88	4.88	
	.9	Stairs	N/A	—	—	—	
4.0 Exterior Closure							
	.1	Walls	Face brick with concrete block backup	60% of wall	S.F. Wall	21	16.56	
	.5	Exterior Wall Finishes	N/A		—	—	—	34.8%
	.6	Doors	Steel overhead, aluminum & glass and hollow metal	20% of wall	S.F. Door	25	6.61	
	.7	Windows & Glazed Walls	Store front and metal top hinged outswinging	20% of wall	S.F. Window	28	7.38	
5.0 Roofing							
	.1	Roof Coverings	Asphalt shingles with flashing	S.F. Ground	1.22	1.22	
	.7	Insulation	Perlite/EPS composite	S.F. Ground	1.00	1.00	2.5%
	.8	Openings & Specialties	N/A	—	—	—	
6.0 Interior Construction							
	.1	Partitions	Concrete block, toilet partitions	25 S.F. Floor/L.F. Partition	S.F. Partition	10.59	3.39	
	.4	Interior Doors	Single leaf hollow metal	700 S.F. Floor/Door	Each	534	.76	
	.5	Wall Finishes	Paint		S.F. Surface	1.19	.76	
	.6	Floor Finishes	Vinyl composition tile	35% of floor area	S.F. Floor	2.91	1.02	9.8%
	.7	Ceiling Finishes	Painted gypsum board on furring in sales area & washrooms	35% of floor area	S.F. Ceiling	2.92	1.02	
	.9	Interior Surface/Exterior Wall	Paint	60% of wall	S.F. Wall	2.12	1.67	
7.0 Conveying							
	.1	Elevators	N/A	—	—	—	0.0%
	.2	Special Conveyors	N/A	—	—	—	
8.0 Mechanical							
	.1	Plumbing	Toilet and service fixtures, supply and drainage	1 Fixture/235 S.F. Floor	Each	1760	7.49	
	.2	Fire Protection	N/A		—	—	—	
	.3	Heating	Oil fired hot water, wall fin radiation		S.F. Floor	5.00	5.00	21.4%
	.4	Cooling	Split systems with air cooled condensing units		S.F. Floor	6.42	6.42	
	.5	Special Systems	N/A		—	—	—	
9.0 Electrical							
	.1	Service & Distribution	200 ampere service, panel board and feeders	S.F. Floor	3.06	3.06	
	.2	Lighting & Power	Fluorescent fixtures, receptacles, switches, A.C. and misc. power	S.F. Floor	4.86	4.86	9.9%
	.4	Special Electrical	Alarm systems and emergency lighting	S.F. Floor	.74	.74	
11.0 Special Construction							
	.1	Specialties	N/A	—	—	—	0.0%
12.0 Site Work							
	.1	Earthwork	N/A	—	—	—	
	.3	Utilities	N/A	—	—	—	
	.5	Roads & Parking	N/A	—	—	—	0.0%
	.7	Site Improvements	N/A	—	—	—	

			Sub-Total	87.91	100%
CONTRACTOR FEES (General Requirements: 10%, Overhead: 5%, Profit: 10%)			25%	21.98	
ARCHITECT FEES			8%	8.81	

	Total Building Cost	**118.70**

BUILDING TYPES

BUILDING TYPES

Costs per square foot of floor area

Exterior Wall	S.F. Area	12000	16000	20000	25000	30000	35000	40000	45000	50000
	L.F. Perimeter	440	520	600	700	708	780	841	910	979
Reinforced Concrete Block	Lam. Wood Arches	105.20	101.20	98.80	96.90	93.95	92.85	91.85	91.20	90.65
	Rigid Steel Frame	103.85	99.85	97.40	95.55	92.60	91.50	90.50	89.85	89.30
Face Brick with Concrete Block Back-up	Lam. Wood Arches	122.55	116.60	113.00	110.15	105.15	103.40	101.80	100.75	99.95
	Rigid Steel Frame	121.20	115.20	111.60	108.75	103.75	102.05	100.45	99.40	98.55
Metal Sandwich Panels	Lam. Wood Arches	101.60	98.00	95.85	94.15	91.65	90.65	89.75	89.20	88.75
	Rigid Steel Frame	100.25	96.65	94.45	92.75	90.25	89.30	88.40	87.85	87.35
Perimeter Adj., Add or Deduct	Per 100 L.F.	4.45	3.35	2.65	2.15	1.80	1.50	1.35	1.20	1.05
Story Hgt. Adj., Add or Deduct	Per 1 Ft.	.65	.55	.50	.45	.40	.35	.35	.35	.35
Basement—Not Applicable										

The above costs were calculated using the basic specifications shown on the facing page. These costs should be adjusted where necessary for design alternatives and owner's requirements. Reported completed project costs, for this type of structure, range from $46.30 to $139.00 per S.F.

Common additives

Description	Unit	$ Cost
Bleachers, Telescoping, manual		
To 15 tier	Seat	79 - 109
16-20 tier	Seat	160 - 195
21-30 tier	Seat	170 - 205
For power operation, add	Seat	30 - 48
Gym Divider Curtain, Mesh top		
Manual roll-up	S.F.	9.25
Gym Mats		
2" naugahyde covered	S.F.	3.45
2" nylon	S.F.	5.10
1-1/2" wall pads	S.F.	6.70
1" wrestling mats	S.F.	4.62
Scoreboard		
Basketball, one side	Each	2750 - 17,300
Basketball Backstop		
Wall mtd., 6' extended, fixed	Each	1625 - 2125
Swing up, wall mtd.	Each	1825 - 2750

Description	Unit	$ Cost
Lockers, Steel, single tier, 60" or 72"	Opening	125 - 220
2 tier, 60" or 72" total	Opening	70 - 119
5 tier, box lockers	Opening	40 - 60
Locker bench, lam. maple top only	L.F.	18.05
Pedestals, steel pipe	Each	58
Sound System		
Amplifier, 250 watts	Each	1650
Speaker, ceiling or wall	Each	145
Trumpet	Each	271
Emergency Lighting, 25 watt, battery operated		
Lead battery	Each	289
Nickel cadmium	Each	655

Important: See the Reference Section for Location Factors

Model costs calculated for a 1 story building with 25' story height and 20,000 square feet of floor area

Gymnasium

				Unit	Unit Cost	Cost Per S.F.	% Of Sub-Total
1.0 Foundations							
	.1	Footings & Foundations	Poured concrete; strip and spread footings and 4' foundation wall	S.F. Ground	2.71	2.71	
	.4	Piles & Caissons	N/A	—	—	—	5.1%
	.9	Excavation & Backfill	Site preparation for slab and trench for foundation wall and footing	S.F. Ground	1.08	1.08	
2.0 Substructure							
	.1	Slab on Grade	4" reinforced concrete with vapor barrier and granular base	S.F. Slab	3.32	3.32	4.5%
	.2	Special Substructures	N/A	—	—	—	
3.0 Superstructure							
	.1	Columns & Beams	N/A	—	—	—	
	.4	Structural Walls	N/A	—	—	—	
	.5	Elevated Floors	N/A	—	—	—	18.3%
	.7	Roof	Wood deck on laminated wood arches	S.F. Ground	13.51	13.51	
	.9	Stairs	N/A	—	—	—	
4.0 Exterior Closure							
	.1	Walls	Reinforced concrete block (end walls included) 90% of wall	S.F. Wall	8.61	5.81	
	.5	Exterior Wall Finishes	N/A	—	—	—	11.4%
	.6	Doors	Aluminum and glass, hollow metal, steel overhead	Each	1061	.32	
	.7	Windows & Glazed Walls	Metal horizontal pivoted 10% of wall	Each	302	2.27	
5.0 Roofing							
	.1	Roof Coverings	EPDM, 60 mils, fully adhered	S.F. Ground	1.80	1.80	
	.7	Insulation	Polyisocyanurate	—	1.14	1.17	4.0%
	.8	Openings & Specialties	N/A	—	—	—	
6.0 Interior Construction							
	.1	Partitions	Concrete block, toilet partitions 50 S.F. Floor/L.F. Partition	S.F. Partition	7.20	1.44	
	.4	Interior Doors	Single leaf hollow metal 500 S.F. Floor/Door	Each	534	1.07	
	.5	Wall Finishes	50% paint, 50% ceramic tile	S.F. Surface	3.33	1.33	
	.6	Floor Finishes	90% hardwood, 10% ceramic tile	S.F. Floor	9.72	9.72	21.0%
	.7	Ceiling Finishes	Mineral fiber tile on concealed zee bars 15% of area	S.F. Ceiling	3.63	.54	
	.9	Interior Surface/Exterior Wall	Paint 90% of wall	S.F. Wall	2.12	1.43	
7.0 Conveying							
	.1	Elevators	N/A	—	—	—	0.0%
	.2	Special Conveyors	N/A	—	—	—	
8.0 Mechanical							
	.1	Plumbing	Toilet and service fixtures, supply and drainage 1 Fixture/515 S.F. Floor	Each	3182	6.18	
	.2	Fire Protection	Wet pipe sprinkler system	S.F. Floor	1.69	1.69	
	.3	Heating	Included in 8.4	—	—	—	23.2%
	.4	Cooling	Single zone rooftop unit, gas heating, electric cooling	S.F. Floor	9.26	9.26	
	.5	Special Systems	N/A	—	—	—	
9.0 Electrical							
	.1	Service & Distribution	400 ampere service, panel board and feeders	S.F. Floor	.66	.66	
	.2	Lighting & Power	Fluorescent fixtures, receptacles, switches, A.C. and misc. power	S.F. Floor	5.99	5.99	11.0%
	.4	Special Electrical	Alarm systems, sound system and emergency lighting	S.F. Floor	1.45	1.45	
11.0 Special Construction							
	.1	Specialties	Bleachers, sauna, weight room	S.F. Floor	1.11	1.11	1.5%
12.0 Site Work							
	.1	Earthwork	N/A	—	—	—	
	.3	Utilities	N/A	—	—	—	
	.5	Roads & Parking	N/A	—	—	—	0.0%
	.7	Site Improvements	N/A	—	—	—	
				Sub-Total		73.86	100%

CONTRACTOR FEES (General Requirements: 10%, Overhead: 5%, Profit: 10%)		25%	18.47
ARCHITECT FEES		7%	6.47
Total Building Cost			**98.80**

BUILDING TYPES

Costs per square foot of floor area

Exterior Wall	S.F. Area	5000	10000	15000	20000	30000	40000	50000	75000	100000
	L.F. Perimeter	300	410	500	580	710	830	930	1150	1300
Concrete Block Reinforced	Steel Frame	91.55	80.05	75.40	72.80	69.55	67.85	66.50	64.55	63.15
	Bearing Walls	95.10	83.50	78.80	76.15	72.90	71.10	69.80	67.80	66.35
Precast Concrete	Steel Frame	98.95	85.10	79.55	76.40	72.45	70.35	68.80	66.45	64.70
	Bearing Walls	102.20	88.35	82.75	79.60	75.70	73.60	72.05	69.65	67.95
Galv. Steel Siding	Steel Frame	90.95	79.65	75.05	72.50	69.35	67.60	66.30	64.35	63.00
Metal Sandwich Panel	Steel Frame	95.10	82.50	77.40	74.55	70.95	69.05	67.60	65.45	63.90
Perimeter Adj., Add or Deduct	Per 100 L.F.	12.10	6.05	4.05	3.00	2.00	1.50	1.20	.80	.60
Story Hgt. Adj., Add or Deduct	Per 1 Ft.	1.25	.85	.70	.60	.50	.40	.40	.30	.25
Basement—Not Applicable										

The above costs were calculated using the basic specifications shown on the facing page. These costs should be adjusted where necessary for design alternatives and owner's requirements. Reported completed project costs, for this type of structure, range from $26.55 to $121.20 per S.F.

Common additives

Description	Unit	$ Cost
Closed Circuit Surveillance, One station		
Camera and monitor	Each	1375
For additional camera stations, add	Each	745
Emergency Lighting, 25 watt, battery operated		
Lead battery	Each	289
Nickel cadmium	Each	655
Lockers, Steel, single tier, 60" or 72"	Opening	125 - 220
2 tier, 60" or 72" total	Opening	70 - 119
5 tier, box lockers	Opening	40 - 60
Locker bench, lam. maple top only	L.F.	18.05
Pedestals, steel pipe	Each	58
Safe, Office type, 4 hour rating		
30" x 18" x 18"	Each	3125
62" x 33" x 20"	Each	6775
Sound System		
Amplifier, 250 watts	Each	1650
Speaker, ceiling or wall	Each	145
Trumpet	Each	271

Model costs calculated for a 1 story building with 24' story height and 20,000 square feet of floor area

Hangar, Aircraft

				Unit	Unit Cost	Cost Per S.F.	% Of Sub-Total
1.0 Foundations							
.1	Footings & Foundations	Poured concrete; strip and spread footings and 4' foundation wall		S.F. Ground	2.73	2.73	
.4	Piles & Caissons	N/A		—	—	—	7.2%
.9	Excavation & Backfill	Site preparation for slab and trench for foundation wall and footing		S.F. Ground	1.17	1.17	
2.0 Substructure							
.1	Slab on Grade	6" reinforced concrete with vapor barrier and granular base		S.F. Slab	4.76	4.76	8.8%
.2	Special Substructures	N/A		—	—	—	
3.0 Superstructure							
.1	Columns & Beams	Steel columns included in 3.7		—	—	—	
.4	Structural Walls	Metal siding support		S.F. Floor	.30	.30	
.5	Elevated Floors	N/A		—	—	—	12.2%
.7	Roof	Metal deck, open web steel joists, beams, columns		S.F. Roof	6.29	6.29	
.9	Stairs	N/A		—	—	—	
4.0 Exterior Closure							
.1	Walls	Galvanized steel siding		S.F. Wall	5.57	1.94	
.5	Exterior Wall Finishes	N/A		—	—	—	30.3%
.6	Doors	Steel overhead and sliding	30% of wall	S.F. Door	29	6.23	
.7	Windows & Glazed Walls	Industrial horizontal pivoted steel	20% of wall	Each	1427	8.28	
5.0 Roofing							
.1	Roof Coverings	Elastomeric membrane		S.F. Roof	1.98	1.98	
.7	Insulation	Fiberboard		S.F. Roof	.98	.98	5.9%
.8	Openings & Specialties	Gravel stop and hatches		S.F. Roof	.23	.23	
6.0 Interior Construction							
.1	Partitions	Concrete block, toilet partitions	200 S.F. Floor/L.F. Partition	S.F. Partition	6.33	.53	
.4	Interior Doors	Single leaf hollow metal	5000 S.F. Floor/Door	Each	534	.11	
.5	Wall Finishes	Paint		S.F. Surface	.80	.08	
.6	Floor Finishes	N/A		—	—	—	1.3%
.7	Ceiling Finishes	N/A		—	—	—	
.9	Interior Surface/Exterior Wall	N/A		—	—	—	
7.0 Conveying							
.1	Elevators	N/A		—	—	—	0.0%
.2	Special Conveyors	N/A		—	—	—	
8.0 Mechanical							
.1	Plumbing	Toilet and service fixtures, supply and drainage	1 Fixture/1000 S.F. Floor	Each	2260	2.26	
.2	Fire Protection	Sprinklers, extra hazard		S.F. Floor	3.45	3.45	
.3	Heating	Unit heaters		S.F. Floor	4.62	4.62	19.3%
.4	Cooling	Exhaust fan		S.F. Floor	.16	.16	
.5	Special Systems	N/A		—	—	—	
9.0 Electrical							
.1	Service & Distribution	200 ampere service, panel board and feeders		S.F. Floor	.58	.58	
.2	Lighting & Power	High intensity discharge fixtures, receptacles, switches and misc. power		S.F. Floor	7.14	7.14	15.0%
.4	Special Electrical	Alarm systems and emergency lighting		S.F. Floor	.39	.39	
11.0 Special Construction							
.1	Specialties	N/A		—	—	—	0.0%
12.0 Site Work							
.1	Earthwork	N/A		—	—	—	
.3	Utilities	N/A		—	—	—	0.0%
.5	Roads & Parking	N/A		—	—	—	
.7	Site Improvements	N/A		—	—	—	
				Sub-Total		54.21	**100%**
	CONTRACTOR FEES (General Requirements: 10%, Overhead: 5%, Profit: 10%)				25%	13.55	
	ARCHITECT FEES				7%	4.74	
				Total Building Cost		72.50	

BUILDING TYPES

Costs per square foot of floor area

Exterior Wall	S.F. Area	25000	40000	55000	70000	85000	100000	115000	130000	145000
	L.F. Perimeter	388	520	566	666	766	866	878	962	1045
Face Brick with Structural Facing Tile	Steel Frame	157.10	147.50	140.85	138.20	136.45	135.20	133.20	132.50	131.90
	R/Conc. Frame	163.75	154.20	147.50	144.85	143.10	141.90	139.85	139.15	138.55
Face Brick with Concrete Block Back-up	Steel Frame	152.70	143.85	137.95	135.50	133.90	132.75	131.05	130.40	129.85
	R/Conc. Frame	159.40	150.50	144.60	142.20	140.55	139.45	137.70	137.10	136.50
Precast Concrete Panels	Steel Frame	152.15	143.35	137.55	135.15	133.55	132.45	130.75	130.15	129.60
	R/Conc. Frame	158.80	150.05	144.25	141.85	140.25	139.15	137.45	136.80	136.25
Perimeter Adj., Add or Deduct	Per 100 L.F.	5.90	3.70	2.70	2.15	1.75	1.50	1.25	1.15	1.00
Story Hgt. Adj., Add or Deduct	Per 1 Ft.	1.75	1.45	1.15	1.05	1.00	.95	.85	.80	.80
For Basement, add $20.90 per square foot of basement area										

The above costs were calculated using the basic specifications shown on the facing page. These costs should be adjusted where necessary for design alternatives and owner's requirements. Reported completed project costs, for this type of structure, range from $102.40 to $258.75 per S.F.

Common additives

Description	Unit	$ Cost
Cabinet, Base, door units, metal	L.F.	181
Drawer units	L.F.	345
Tall storage cabinets, 7' high, open	L.F.	340
With doors	L.F.	420
Wall, metal 12-1/2" deep, open	L.F.	134
With doors	L.F.	239
Closed Circuit TV (Patient monitoring)		
One station camera & monitor	Each	1375
For additional camera, add	Each	745
For automatic iris for low light, add	Each	1925
Doctors In-Out Register, 200 names	Each	13,000
Comb. control & recall, 200 names	Each	16,200
Recording register	Each	6125
Transformers	Each	280
Pocket pages	Each	920
Hubbard Tank, with accessories		
Stainless steel, 125 GPM 45 psi	Each	21,200
For electric hoist, add	Each	2325
Mortuary Refrigerator, End operated		
2 capacity	Each	11,400
6 capacity	Each	21,100

Description	Unit	$ Cost
Nurses Call Station		
Single bedside call station	Each	237
Ceiling speaker station	Each	105
Emergency call station	Each	143
Pillow speaker	Each	219
Double bedside call station	Each	385
Duty station	Each	243
Standard call button	Each	113
Master control station for 20 stations	Each	4550
Sound System		
Amplifier, 250 watts	Each	1650
Speaker, ceiling or wall	Each	145
Trumpet	Each	271
Station, Dietary with ice	Each	13,100
Sterilizers		
Single door, steam	Each	129,500
Double door, steam	Each	166,500
Portable, countertop, steam	Each	3100 - 4850
Gas	Each	32,100
Automatic washer/sterilizer	Each	44,200

Important: See the Reference Section for Location Factors

Model costs calculated for a 3 story building with 12' story height and 55,000 square feet of floor area

				Unit	Unit Cost	Cost Per S.F.	% Of Sub-Total
1.0 Foundations							
	.1	Footings & Foundations	Poured concrete; strip and spread footings and 4' foundation wall	S.F. Ground	5.19	1.73	
	.4	Piles & Caissons	N/A	—	—	—	1.9%
	.9	Excavation & Backfill	Site preparation for slab and trench for foundation wall and footing	S.F. Ground	1.08	.36	
2.0 Substructure							
	.1	Slab on Grade	4" reinforced concrete with vapor barrier and granular base	S.F. Slab	3.32	1.11	1.0%
	.2	Special Substructures	N/A	—	—	—	
3.0 Superstructure							
	.1	Columns & Beams	Concrete columns	L.F. Column	80	1.47	
	.4	Structural Walls	N/A	—	—	—	
	.5	Elevated Floors	Cast-in-place concrete beam and slab	S.F. Floor	13.02	8.68	14.1%
	.7	Roof	Cast-in-place concrete beam and slab	S.F. Roof	12.43	4.14	
	.9	Stairs	Concrete filled metal pan	Flight	4125	.98	
4.0 Exterior Closure							
	.1	Walls	Face brick and structural facing tile *85% of wall*	S.F. Wall	27	8.75	
	.5	Exterior Wall Finishes	N/A	—	—	—	
	.6	Doors	Double aluminum and glass and sliding doors	Each	1845	.20	9.4%
	.7	Windows & Glazed Walls	Aluminum sliding *15% of wall*	Each	493	1.19	
5.0 Roofing							
	.1	Roof Coverings	Built-up tar and gravel with flashing	S.F. Roof	2.31	.77	
	.7	Insulation	Perlite/EPS composite	S.F. Roof	1.32	.44	1.2%
	.8	Openings & Specialties	Gravel stop and hatches	S.F. Roof	.24	.08	
6.0 Interior Construction							
	.1	Partitions	Concrete block, gypsum board on metal studs *9 S.F. Floor/L.F. Partition*	S.F. Partition	4.54	5.04	
	.4	Interior Doors	Single leaf hollow metal *90 S.F. Floor/Door*	Each	534	5.93	
	.5	Wall Finishes	40% vinyl wall covering, 35% ceramic tile, 25% epoxy coating	S.F. Surface	2.62	5.82	25.3%
	.6	Floor Finishes	60% vinyl tile, 20% ceramic, 20% terrazzo	S.F. Floor	6.82	6.82	
	.7	Ceiling Finishes	Plaster on suspended metal lath	S.F. Ceiling	3.63	3.63	
	.9	Interior Surface/Exterior Wall	Glazed coating *85% of wall*	S.F. Wall	.45	.11	
7.0 Conveying							
	.1	Elevators	Two hydraulic hospital elevators	Each	73,425	2.67	2.5%
	.2	Special Conveyors	N/A	—	—	—	
8.0 Mechanical							
	.1	Plumbing	Kitchen, toilet and service fixtures, supply and drainage *1 Fixture/265 S.F. Floor*	Each	4441	16.76	
	.2	Fire Protection	Wet pipe sprinkler system	S.F. Floor	1.47	1.47	
	.3	Heating	Oil fired hot water, wall fin radiation	S.F. Floor	2.93	2.93	27.9%
	.4	Cooling	Chilled water, fan coil units	S.F. Floor	9.10	9.10	
	.5	Special Systems	N/A	—	—	—	
9.0 Electrical							
	.1	Service & Distribution	1200 ampere service, panel board and feeders	S.F. Floor	1.09	1.09	
	.2	Lighting & Power	Fluorescent fixtures, receptacles, switches, A.C. and misc. power	S.F. Floor	8.06	8.06	10.8%
	.4	Special Electrical	Alarm systems, communications systems and emergency lighting	S.F. Floor	2.55	2.55	
11.0 Special Construction							
	.1	Specialties	Conductive flooring, oxygen piping, curtain partitions	S.F. Floor	6.38	6.38	5.9%
12.0 Site Work							
	.1	Earthwork	N/A	—	—	—	
	.3	Utilities	N/A	—	—	—	
	.5	Roads & Parking	N/A	—	—	—	0.0%
	.7	Site Improvements	N/A	—	—	—	
				Sub-Total		108.26	**100%**
		CONTRACTOR FEES (General Requirements: 10%, Overhead: 5%, Profit: 10%)			25%	27.07	
		ARCHITECT FEES			9%	12.17	
				Total Building Cost		**147.50**	

BUILDING TYPES

Costs per square foot of floor area

Exterior Wall	S.F. Area	100000	125000	150000	175000	200000	225000	250000	275000	300000
	L.F. Perimeter	594	705	816	783	866	950	1033	1116	1200
Face Brick with Structural Facing Tile	Steel Frame	130.95	128.40	126.65	123.10	122.15	121.35	120.65	120.20	119.75
	R/Conc. Frame	138.00	135.45	133.75	130.20	129.20	128.40	127.75	127.25	126.85
Face Brick with Concrete Block Back-up	Steel Frame	128.20	125.80	124.15	121.05	120.15	119.40	118.75	118.30	117.95
	R/Conc. Frame	135.25	132.85	131.20	128.10	127.20	126.45	125.85	125.40	125.00
Precast Concrete Panels With Exposed Aggregate	Steel Frame	126.85	124.50	122.95	120.20	119.35	118.65	118.05	117.60	117.25
	R/Conc. Frame	133.20	130.85	129.30	126.55	125.65	124.95	124.40	123.95	123.60
Perimeter Adj., Add or Deduct	Per 100 L.F.	2.85	2.30	1.90	1.60	1.40	1.30	1.15	1.05	.95
Story Hgt. Adj., Add or Deduct	Per 1 Ft.	1.35	1.25	1.20	1.00	.95	.95	.95	.90	.90
For Basement, add $22.00 per square foot of basement area										

The above costs were calculated using the basic specifications shown on the facing page. These costs should be adjusted where necessary for design alternatives and owner's requirements. Reported completed project costs, for this type of structure, range from $103.70 to $255.50 per S.F.

Common additives

Description	Unit	$ Cost	Description	Unit	$ Cost
Cabinets, Base, door units, metal	L.F.	181	Nurses Call Station		
Drawer units	L.F.	345	Single bedside call station	Each	237
Tall storage cabinets, 7' high, open	L.F.	340	Ceiling speaker station	Each	105
With doors	L.F.	420	Emergency call station	Each	143
Wall, metal 12-1/2" deep, open	L.F.	134	Pillow speaker	Each	219
With doors	L.F.	239	Double bedside call station	Each	385
Closed Circuit TV (Patient monitoring)			Duty station	Each	243
One station camera & monitor	Each	1375	Standard call button	Each	113
For additional camera add	Each	745	Master control station for 20 stations	Each	4550
For automatic iris for low light add	Each	1925	Sound System		
Doctors In-Out Register, 200 names	Each	13,000	Amplifier, 250 watts	Each	1650
Comb. control & recall, 200 names	Each	16,200	Speaker, ceiling or wall	Each	145
Recording register	Each	6125	Trumpet	Each	271
Transformers	Each	280	Station, Dietary with ice	Each	13,100
Pocket pages	Each	920	Sterilizers		
Hubbard Tank, with accessories			Single door, steam	Each	129,500
Stainless steel, 125 GPM 45 psi	Each	21,200	Double door, steam	Each	166,500
For electric hoist, add	Each	2325	Portable, counter top, steam	Each	3100 - 4850
Mortuary Refrigerator, End operated			Gas	Each	32,100
2 capacity	Each	11,400	Automatic washer/sterilizer	Each	44,200
6 capacity	Each	21,100			

Model costs calculated for a 6 story building with 12' story height and 200,000 square feet of floor area

				Unit	Unit Cost	Cost Per S.F.	% Of Sub-Total
1.0 Foundations							
.1	Footings & Foundations	Poured concrete; strip and spread footings and 4' foundation wall		S.F. Ground	4.86	.81	
.4	Piles & Caissons	N/A		—	—	—	1.1%
.9	Excavation & Backfill	Site preparation for slab and trench for foundation wall and footing		S.F. Ground	1.08	.18	
2.0 Substructure							
.1	Slab on Grade	4" reinforced concrete with vapor barrier and granular base		S.F. Slab	3.32	.55	0.6%
.2	Special Substructures	N/A		—	—	—	
3.0 Superstructure							
.1	Columns & Beams	Fireproofed steel columns		L.F. Column	59	1.02	
.4	Structural Walls	N/A		—	—	—	
.5	Elevated Floors	Concrete slab with metal deck and beams		S.F. Floor	10.80	9.00	12.7%
.7	Roof	Metal deck, open web steel joists, beams, interior columns		S.F. Roof	4.87	.81	
.9	Stairs	Concrete filled metal pan		Flight	4070	.53	
4.0 Exterior Closure							
.1	Walls	Face brick and structural facing tile	70% of wall	S.F. Wall	27	6.07	
.5	Exterior Wall Finishes	N/A		—	—	—	9.9%
.6	Doors	Double aluminum and glass and sliding doors		Each	3011	.42	
.7	Windows & Glazed Walls	Aluminum sliding	30% of wall	Each	384	2.39	
5.0 Roofing							
.1	Roof Coverings	Built-up tar and gravel with flashing		S.F. Roof	2.28	.38	
.7	Insulation	Perlite/EPS composite		S.F. Roof	1.32	.22	0.7%
.8	Openings & Specialties	Gravel stop and hatches		S.F. Roof	.12	.02	
6.0 Interior Construction							
.1	Partitions	Gypsum board on metal studs with sound deadening board	9 S.F. Floor/L.F. Partition	S.F. Partition	4.08	4.53	
.4	Interior Doors	Single leaf hollow metal	90 S.F. Floor/Door	Each	534	5.93	
.5	Wall Finishes	40% vinyl wall covering, 35% ceramic tile, 25% epoxy coating		S.F. Surface	2.62	5.82	
.6	Floor Finishes	60% vinyl tile, 20% ceramic, 20% terrazzo		S.F. Floor	6.82	6.82	29.9%
.7	Ceiling Finishes	Plaster on suspended metal lath		S.F. Ceiling	3.63	3.63	
.9	Interior Surface/Exterior Wall	Glazed coating	70% of wall	S.F. Wall	.45	.10	
7.0 Conveying							
.1	Elevators	Six geared hospital elevators		Each	141,666	4.25	4.7%
.2	Special Conveyors	N/A		—	—	—	
8.0 Mechanical							
.1	Plumbing	Kitchen, toilet and service fixtures, supply and drainage	1 Fixture/275 S.F. Floor	Each	4067	14.79	
.2	Fire Protection	Standpipe and wet pipe sprinkler systems		S.F. Floor	1.27	1.27	
.3	Heating	Oil fired hot water, wall fin radiation		S.F. Floor	2.93	2.93	23.6%
.4	Cooling	Chilled water, fan coil units		S.F. Floor	2.07	2.07	
.5	Special Systems	N/A		—	—	—	
9.0 Electrical							
.1	Service & Distribution	4000 ampere service, panel board and feeders		S.F. Floor	1.13	1.13	
.2	Lighting & Power	Fluorescent fixtures, receptacles, switches, A.C. and misc. power		S.F. Floor	7.37	7.37	12.3%
.4	Special Electrical	Alarm systems, communications systems and emergency lighting		S.F. Floor	2.55	2.55	
11.0 Special Construction							
.1	Specialties	Conductive flooring, oxygen piping, curtain partitions		S.F. Floor	4.05	4.05	4.5%
12.0 Site Work							
.1	Earthwork	N/A		—	—	—	
.3	Utilities	N/A		—	—	—	
.5	Roads & Parking	N/A		—	—	—	0.0%
.7	Site Improvements	N/A		—	—	—	
				Sub-Total		89.64	100%
	CONTRACTOR FEES (General Requirements: 10%, Overhead: 5%, Profit: 10%)				25%	22.41	
	ARCHITECT FEES				9%	10.10	
				Total Building Cost		122.15	

BUILDING TYPES

BUILDING TYPES

Costs per square foot of floor area

Exterior Wall	S.F. Area	35000	55000	75000	95000	115000	135000	155000	175000	195000
	L.F. Perimeter	314	401	497	555	639	722	716	783	850
Face Brick with Concrete Block Back-up	Steel Frame	115.65	108.70	105.70	103.05	101.85	100.95	99.05	98.50	98.05
	R/Conc. Frame	118.75	111.80	108.85	106.20	105.00	104.10	102.20	101.65	101.15
Glass and Metal Curtain Walls	Steel Frame	110.30	104.35	101.75	99.60	98.55	97.75	96.30	95.80	95.45
	R/Conc. Frame	113.55	107.60	105.05	102.85	101.85	101.05	99.55	99.10	98.70
Precast Concrete Panels	Steel Frame	118.60	111.10	107.90	105.00	103.70	102.75	100.60	100.00	99.45
	R/Conc. Frame	122.65	115.00	111.75	108.75	107.45	106.50	104.25	103.65	103.10
Perimeter Adj., Add or Deduct	Per 100 L.F.	6.60	4.20	3.10	2.45	2.00	1.70	1.50	1.30	1.20
Story Hgt. Adj., Add or Deduct	Per 1 Ft.	1.85	1.50	1.40	1.25	1.15	1.10	.95	.95	.90
For Basement, add $ 20.90 per square foot of basement area										

The above costs were calculated using the basic specifications shown on the facing page. These costs should be adjusted where necessary for design alternatives and owner's requirements. Reported completed project costs, for this type of structure, range from $68.65 to $132.35 per S.F.

Common additives

Description	Unit	$ Cost	Description	Unit	$ Cost
Bar, Front bar	L.F.	285	Laundry Equipment		
Back bar	L.F.	227	Folders, blankets & sheets, king size	Each	52,500
Booth, Upholstered, custom, straight	L.F.	144 - 265	Ironers, 110" single roll	Each	28,700
"L" or "U" shaped	L.F.	149 - 252	Combination washer extractor 50#	Each	9975
Closed Circuit Surveillance, One station			125#	Each	26,500
Camera and monitor	Each	1375	Sauna, Prefabricated, complete		
For additional camera stations, add	Each	745	6' x 4'	Each	4075
Directory Boards, Plastic, glass covered			6' x 6'	Each	4850
30" x 20"	Each	565	6' x 9'	Each	5350
36" x 48"	Each	1025	8' x 8'	Each	6300
Aluminum, 24" x 18"	Each	425	10' x 12'	Each	9125
48" x 32"	Each	745	Smoke Detectors		
48" x 60"	Each	1600	Ceiling type	Each	149
Elevators, Electric passenger, 5 stops			Duct type	Each	405
3500# capacity	Each	103,700	Sound System		
5000# capacity	Each	108,200	Amplifier, 250 watts	Each	1650
Additional stop, add	Each	5500	Speaker, ceiling or wall	Each	145
Emergency Lighting, 25 watt, battery operated			Trumpet	Each	271
Lead battery	Each	289	TV Antenna, Master system, 12 outlet	Outlet	236
Nickel cadmium	Each	655	30 outlet	Outlet	151
			100 outlet	Outlet	144

Model costs calculated for a 6 story building with 10' story height and 135,000 square feet of floor area

				Unit	Unit Cost	Cost Per S.F.	% Of Sub-Total
1.0 Foundations							
.1	Footings & Foundations	Poured concrete; strip and spread footings and 4' foundation wall		S.F. Ground	7.32	1.22	
.4	Piles & Caissons	N/A		—	—	—	1.8%
.9	Excavation & Backfill	Site preparation for slab and trench for foundation wall and footing		S.F. Ground	1.08	.18	
2.0 Substructure							
.1	Slab on Grade	4" reinforced concrete with vapor barrier and granular base		S.F. Slab	3.32	.55	0.7%
.2	Special Substructures	N/A		—	—	—	
3.0 Superstructure							
.1	Columns & Beams	Included in 3.5 and 3.7		—	—	—	
.4	Structural Walls	N/A		—	—	—	
.5	Elevated Floors	Concrete slab with metal deck, beams, columns		S.F. Floor	11.73	9.78	14.8%
.7	Roof	Metal deck, open web steel joists, beams, columns		S.F. Roof	5.62	.94	
.9	Stairs	Concrete filled metal pan		Flight	5025	.52	
4.0 Exterior Closure							
.1	Walls	Face brick with concrete block backup	80% of wall	S.F. Wall	21	5.40	
.5	Exterior Wall Finishes	N/A		—	—	—	
.6	Doors	Glass amd metal doors and entrances		Each	2235	.16	10.2%
.7	Windows & Glazed Walls	Window wall	20% of wall	S.F. Window	34	2.21	
5.0 Roofing							
.1	Roof Coverings	Built-up tar and gravel with flashing		S.F. Roof	2.34	.39	
.7	Insulation	Perlite/EPS composite		S.F. Roof	1.32	.22	0.9%
.8	Openings & Specialties	Gravel stop and hatches		S.F. Roof	.24	.04	
6.0 Interior Construction							
.1	Partitions	Gypsum board and sound deadening board, steel studs	9 S.F. Floor/L.F. Partition	S.F. Partition	4.08	3.63	
.4	Interior Doors	Single leaf hollow metal	90 S.F. Floor/Door	Each	534	5.93	
.5	Wall Finishes	20% paint, 75% vinyl cover, 5% ceramic tile		S.F. Surface	1.46	2.59	
.6	Floor Finishes	80% carpet, 10% vinyl composition tile, 10% ceramic tile		S.F. Floor	4.62	4.62	25.1%
.7	Ceiling Finishes	Mineral fiber tile applied with adhesive		S.F. Ceiling	1.56	1.56	
.9	Interior Surface/Exterior Wall	Painted gypsum board on furring	80% of wall	S.F. Wall	3.08	.79	
7.0 Conveying							
.1	Elevators	Four geared passenger elevators		Each	131,287	3.89	5.1%
.2	Special Conveyors	N/A		—	—	—	
8.0 Mechanical							
.1	Plumbing	Kitchen, toilet and service fixtures, supply and drainage	1 Fixture/155 S.F. Floor	Each	1638	10.57	
.2	Fire Protection	Standpipes and hose systems and sprinklers, light hazard		S.F. Floor	1.48	1.48	
.3	Heating	Oil fired hot water, wall fin radiation		S.F. Floor	2.93	2.93	30.5%
.4	Cooling	Chilled water, fan coil units		S.F. Floor	8.27	8.27	
.5	Special Systems	N/A		—	—	—	
9.0 Electrical							
.1	Service & Distribution	2000 ampere service, panel board and feeders		S.F. Floor	.81	.81	
.2	Lighting & Power	Fluorescent fixtures, receptacles, switches, A.C. and misc. power		S.F. Floor	5.56	5.56	10.9%
.4	Special Electrical	Alarm systems, communications systems and emergency lighting		S.F. Floor	1.96	1.96	
11.0 Special Construction							
.1	Specialties	N/A		—	—	—	0.0%
12.0 Site Work							
.1	Earthwork	N/A		—	—	—	
.3	Utilities	N/A		—	—	—	
.5	Roads & Parking	N/A		—	—	—	0.0%
.7	Site Improvements	N/A		—	—	—	
				Sub-Total		76.20	**100%**
	CONTRACTOR FEES (General Requirements: 10%, Overhead: 5%, Profit: 10%)				25%	19.05	
	ARCHITECT FEES				6%	5.70	
				Total Building Cost		100.95	

BUILDING TYPES

Costs per square foot of floor area

Exterior Wall	S.F. Area	140000	243000	346000	450000	552000	655000	760000	860000	965000
	L.F. Perimeter	403	587	672	800	936	1073	1213	1195	1312
Face Brick with Concrete Block Back-up	Steel Frame	98.55	93.75	90.25	88.90	88.15	87.65	87.25	86.00	85.75
	R/Conc. Frame	99.75	94.95	91.45	90.10	89.35	88.85	88.45	87.20	86.95
Face Brick Veneer On Steel Studs	Steel Frame	96.60	92.10	88.90	87.70	87.00	86.55	86.15	85.05	84.80
	R/Conc. Frame	98.20	93.75	90.50	89.30	88.60	88.10	87.75	86.65	86.40
Glass and Metal Curtain Walls	Steel Frame	107.95	101.45	97.70	96.05	95.05	94.45	93.95	92.90	92.55
	R/Conc. Frame	109.55	103.05	99.30	97.65	96.65	96.05	95.55	94.50	94.15
Perimeter Adj., Add or Deduct	Per 100 L.F.	3.85	2.20	1.55	1.20	.95	.80	.70	.65	.55
Story Hgt. Adj., Add or Deduct	Per 1 Ft.	1.50	1.25	1.00	.90	.90	.85	.85	.70	.70
For Basement, add $21.65 per square foot of basement area										

The above costs were calculated using the basic specifications shown on the facing page. These costs should be adjusted where necessary for design alternatives and owner's requirements. Reported completed project costs, for this type of structure, range from $76.50 to $133.85 per S.F.

Common additives

Description	Unit	$ Cost	Description	Unit	$ Cost
Bar, Front bar	L.F.	285	Laundry Equipment		
Back bar	L.F.	227	Folders, blankets & sheets, king size	Each	52,500
Booth, Upholstered, custom, straight	L.F.	144 - 265	Ironers, 110" single roll	Each	28,700
"L" or "U" shaped	L.F.	149 - 252	Combination washer & extractor 50#	Each	9975
Closed Circuit Surveillance, One station			125#	Each	26,500
Camera and monitor	Each	1375	Sauna, Prefabricated, complete		
For additional camera stations, add	Each	745	6' x 4'	Each	4075
Directory Boards, Plastic, glass covered			6' x 6'	Each	4850
30" x 20"	Each	565	6' x 9'	Each	5350
36" x 48"	Each	1025	8' x 8'	Each	6300
Aluminum, 24" x 18"	Each	425	10' x 12'	Each	9125
48" x 32"	Each	745	Smoke Detectors		
48" x 60"	Each	1600	Ceiling type	Each	149
Elevators, Electric passenger, 10 stops			Duct type	Each	405
3500# capacity	Each	210,500	Sound System	Each	
5000# capacity	Each	216,500	Amplifier, 250 watts	Each	1650
Additional stop, add	Each	5500	Speaker, ceiling or wall	Each	145
Emergency Lighting, 25 watt, battery operated			Trumpet	Each	271
Lead battery	Each	289	TV Antenna, Master system, 12 outlet	Outlet	236
Nickel cadmium	Each	655	30 outlet	Outlet	151
			100 outlet	Outlet	144

Important: See the Reference Section for Location Factors

Model costs calculated for a 15 story building with 10' story height and 450,000 square feet of floor area

				Unit	Unit Cost	Cost Per S.F.	% Of Sub-Total
1.0 Foundations							
.1	Footings & Foundations	Poured concrete; strip and spread footings and 4' foundation wall		S.F. Ground	13.35	.89	
.4	Piles & Caissons	N/A		—	—	—	1.3%
.9	Excavation & Backfill	Site preparation for slab and trench for foundation wall and footing		S.F. Ground	1.08	.07	
2.0 Substructure							
.1	Slab on Grade	4" reinforced concrete with vapor barrier and granular base		S.F. Slab	3.32	.22	0.3%
.2	Special Substructures	N/A		—	—	—	
3.0 Superstructure							
.1	Columns & Beams	Steel columns included in 3.5 and 3.7		—	—	—	
.4	Structural Walls	N/A		—	—	—	
.5	Elevated Floors	Open web steel joists, slab form, concrete, columns		S.F. Floor	11.87	11.08	17.1%
.7	Roof	Metal deck, open web steel joists, beams, columns		S.F. Roof	4.95	.33	
.9	Stairs	Concrete filled metal pan		Flight	5025	1.02	
4.0 Exterior Closure							
.1	Walls	N/A		—	—	—	
.5	Exterior Wall Finishes	N/A		—	—	—	6.2%
.6	Doors	Glass and metal doors and entrances		Each	1998	.14	
.7	Windows & Glazed Walls	Glass and metal curtain walls	100% of wall	S.F. Wall	16.25	4.33	
5.0 Roofing							
.1	Roof Coverings	Built-up tar and gravel with flashing		S.F. Roof	2.25	.15	
.7	Insulation	Perlite/EPS composite		S.F. Roof	1.32	.09	0.3%
.8	Openings & Specialties	Gravel stop and hatches		S.F. Roof	.15	.01	
6.0 Interior Construction							
.1	Partitions	Gypsum board and sound deadening board, steel studs	9 S.F. Floor/L.F. Partition	S.F. Partition	4.08	3.63	
.4	Interior Doors	Single leaf hollow metal	90 S.F. Floor/Door	Each	534	5.93	
.5	Wall Finishes	20% paint, 75% vinyl cover, 5% ceramic tile		S.F. Surface	1.45	2.57	
.6	Floor Finishes	80% carpet tile, 10% vinyl composition tile, 10% ceramic tile		S.F. Floor	4.62	4.62	27.9%
.7	Ceiling Finishes	Gypsum board on resilient channel		S.F. Ceiling	2.80	2.80	
.9	Interior Surface/Exterior Wall	Painted gypsum board on furring	80% of wall	S.F. Wall	3.08	.66	
7.0 Conveying							
.1	Elevators	One geared freight, six geared passenger elevators		Each	235,500	3.14	4.3%
.2	Special Conveyors	N/A		—	—	—	
8.0 Mechanical							
.1	Plumbing	Kitchen, toilet and service fixtures, supply and drainage	1 Fixture/165 S.F. Floor	Each	1734	10.51	
.2	Fire Protection	Standpipes and hose systems and sprinklers, light hazard		S.F. Floor	2.28	2.28	
.3	Heating	Oil fired hot water, wall fin radiation		S.F. Floor	1.50	1.50	31.2%
.4	Cooling	Chilled water, fan coil units		S.F. Floor	8.27	8.27	
.5	Special Systems	N/A		—	—	—	
9.0 Electrical							
.1	Service & Distribution	6000 ampere service, panel board and feeders		S.F. Floor	.89	.89	
.2	Lighting & Power	Fluorescent fixtures, receptacles, switches, A.C. and misc. power		S.F. Floor	5.49	5.49	11.4%
.4	Special Electrical	Alarm systems, communications systems and emergency lighting		S.F. Floor	1.87	1.87	
11.0 Special Construction							
.1	Specialties	N/A		—	—	—	0.0%
12.0 Site Work							
.1	Earthwork	N/A		—	—	—	
.3	Utilities	N/A		—	—	—	
.5	Roads & Parking	N/A		—	—	—	0.0%
.7	Site Improvements	N/A		—	—	—	
				Sub-Total		72.49	**100%**
	CONTRACTOR FEES (General Requirements: 10%, Overhead: 5%, Profit: 10%)				25%	18.12	
	ARCHITECT FEES				6%	5.44	
				Total Building Cost		**96.05**	

BUILDING TYPES

Costs per square foot of floor area

Exterior Wall	S.F. Area	5500	12000	20000	30000	40000	60000	80000	100000	145000
	L.F. Perimeter	310	330	400	490	530	590	680	760	920
Face Brick with Concrete Block Back-up	Steel Frame	291.70	216.90	195.75	185.30	177.80	169.70	166.30	164.15	161.15
	R/Conc. Frame	296.45	221.60	200.45	189.95	182.45	174.35	170.95	168.80	165.80
Stucco on Concrete Block	Steel Frame	271.05	206.85	188.50	179.35	173.00	166.15	163.25	161.40	158.90
	R/Conc. Frame	275.65	211.40	193.05	183.90	177.55	170.70	167.80	165.95	163.45
Reinforced Concrete	Steel Frame	279.95	211.20	191.65	181.95	175.10	167.70	164.60	162.60	159.85
	R/Conc. Frame	284.50	215.75	196.20	186.50	179.65	172.25	169.15	167.15	164.45
Perimeter Adj., Add or Deduct	Per 100 L.F.	33.30	15.25	9.15	6.15	4.60	3.05	2.30	1.85	1.25
Story Hgt. Adj., Add or Deduct	Per 1 Ft.	7.95	3.90	2.85	2.30	1.90	1.40	1.20	1.05	.90
For Basement, add $29.45 per square foot of basement area										

The above costs were calculated using the basic specifications shown on the facing page. These costs should be adjusted where necessary for design alternatives and owner's requirements. Reported completed project costs, for this type of structure, range from $111.35 to $295.65 per S.F.

Common additives

Description	Unit	$ Cost	Description	Unit	$ Cost
Clock System			Emergency Lighting, 25 watt, battery operated		
20 room	Each	12,700	Nickel cadmium	Each	655
50 room	Each	30,800	Flagpoles, Complete		
Closed Circuit Surveillance, One station			Aluminum, 20' high	Each	1075
Camera and monitor	Each	1375	40' High	Each	2675
For additional camera stations, add	Each	745	70' High	Each	8250
Elevators, Hydraulic passenger, 2 stops			Fiberglass, 23' High	Each	1400
1500# capacity	Each	42,225	39'-5" High	Each	2950
2500# capacity	Each	43,425	59' High	Each	7300
3500# capacity	Each	47,225	Laundry Equipment	Each	
Additional stop, add	Each	3650	Folders, blankets, & sheets	Each	52,500
Emergency Generators, Complete system, gas			Ironers, 110" single roll	Each	28,700
15 KW	Each	12,800	Combination washer & extractor, 50#	Each	9975
70 KW	Each	25,500	125#	Each	26,500
85 KW	Each	28,400	Safe, Office type, 4 hour rating		
115 KW	Each	54,500	30" x 18" x 18"	Each	3125
170 KW	Each	71,500	62" x 33" x 20"	Each	6775
Diesel, 50 KW	Each	24,500	Sound System		
100 KW	Each	35,200	Amplifier, 250 watts	Each	1650
150 KW	Each	42,300	Speaker, ceiling or wall	Each	145
350 KW	Each	67,500	Trumpet	Each	271

Important: See the Reference Section for Location Factors

BUILDING TYPES

Model costs calculated for a 3 story building with 12' story height and 40,000 square feet of floor area

			Unit	Unit Cost	Cost Per S.F.	% Of Sub-Total
1.0 Foundations						
.1	Footings & Foundations	Poured concrete; strip and spread footings and 4' foundation wall	S.F. Ground	3.18	1.06	
.4	Piles & Caissons	N/A	—	—	—	1.1%
.9	Excavation & Backfill	Site preparation for slab and trench for foundation wall and footing	S.F. Ground	1.17	.39	
2.0 Substructure						
.1	Slab on Grade	4" reinforced concrete with vapor barrier and granular base	S.F. Slab	3.32	1.11	0.8%
.2	Special Substructures	N/A	—	—	—	
3.0 Superstructure						
.1	Columns & Beams	Steel columns	L.F. Column	43	1.17	
.4	Structural Walls	N/A	—	—	—	
.5	Elevated Floors	Concrete slab with metal deck and beams	S.F. Floor	15.05	10.03	12.4%
.7	Roof	Concrete slab with metal deck and beams	S.F. Roof	13.55	4.52	
.9	Stairs	Concrete filled metal pan	Flight	5975	.75	
4.0 Exterior Closure						
.1	Walls	Face brick with reinforced concrete block backup 85% of wall	S.F. Wall	21	8.53	
.5	Exterior Wall Finishes	N/A	—	—	—	12.1%
.6	Doors	Metal	Each	3675	.09	
.7	Windows & Glazed Walls	Bullet resisting and metal horizontal pivoted 15% of wall	S.F. Window	103	7.43	
5.0 Roofing						
.1	Roof Coverings	Built-up tar and gravel with flashing	S.F. Roof	2.34	.78	
.7	Insulation	Perlite/EPS composite	S.F. Roof	1.32	.44	1.0%
.8	Openings & Specialties	Gravel stop and hatches	S.F. Roof	.27	.09	
6.0 Interior Construction						
.1	Partitions	Concrete block 45 S.F. of Floor/L.F. Partition	S.F. Partition	6.56	1.75	
.4	Interior Doors	Hollow metal fire doors 930 S.F. Floor/Door	Each	534	.57	
.5	Wall Finishes	Paint	S.F. Surface	1.18	.63	5.6%
.6	Floor Finishes	70% vinyl composition tile, 20% carpet, 10% ceramic tile	S.F. Floor	2.56	2.56	
.7	Ceiling Finishes	Mineral tile on zee runners 30% of area	S.F. Ceiling	3.63	1.09	
.9	Interior Surface/Exterior Wall	Paint 85% of wall	S.F. Wall	2.12	.86	
7.0 Conveying						
.1	Elevators	One hydraulic passenger elevator	Each	98,800	2.47	1.9%
.2	Special Conveyors	N/A	—	—	—	
8.0 Mechanical						
.1	Plumbing	Toilet and service fixtures, supply and drainage 1 Fixture/78 S.F. Floor	Each	1721	22.07	
.2	Fire Protection	Standpipes and hose systems	S.F. Floor	.29	.29	
.3	Heating	Included in 8.4	—	—	—	24.9%
.4	Cooling	Rooftop multizone unit systems	S.F. Floor	10.81	10.81	
.5	Special Systems	N/A	—	—	—	
9.0 Electrical						
.1	Service & Distribution	600 ampere service, panel board and feeders	S.F. Floor	.75	.75	
.2	Lighting & Power	Fluorescent fixtures, receptacles, switches, A.C. and misc. power	S.F. Floor	6.51	6.51	7.8%
.4	Special Electrical	Alarm systems, intercom, and emergency lighting	S.F. Floor	3.07	3.07	
11.0 Special Construction						
.1	Specialties	Prefabricated cells, visitor cubicles	S.F. Floor	43	43.11	32.4%
12.0 Site Work						
.1	Earthwork	N/A	—	—	—	
.3	Utilities	N/A	—	—	—	
.5	Roads & Parking	N/A	—	—	—	0.0%
.7	Site Improvements	N/A	—	—	—	
			Sub-Total		132.93	**100%**

CONTRACTOR FEES (General Requirements: 10%, Overhead: 5%, Profit: 10%)		25%	33.23
ARCHITECT FEES		7%	11.64

Total Building Cost	**177.80**

BUILDING TYPES

Costs per square foot of floor area

Exterior Wall	S.F. Area	1000	2000	3000	4000	5000	10000	15000	20000	25000
	L.F. Perimeter	126	179	219	253	283	400	490	568	632
Decorative Concrete Block	Steel Frame	138.45	125.05	119.00	115.45	113.00	106.90	104.20	102.65	101.50
	Bearing Walls	139.50	125.80	119.65	115.95	113.45	107.25	104.50	102.90	101.75
Face Brick with Concrete Block Back-up	Steel Frame	159.20	140.35	131.85	126.80	123.35	114.80	111.00	108.80	107.20
	Bearing Walls	158.30	139.15	130.55	125.40	121.95	113.20	109.40	107.15	105.50
Metal Sandwich Panel	Steel Frame	138.45	125.75	120.00	116.60	114.30	108.50	105.95	104.45	103.35
Precast Concrete Panel	Bearing Walls	142.90	128.25	121.60	117.70	115.00	108.35	105.40	103.70	102.45
Perimeter Adj., Add or Deduct	Per 100 L.F.	36.70	18.35	12.25	9.15	7.35	3.70	2.45	1.80	1.50
Story Hgt. Adj., Add or Deduct	Per 1 Ft.	2.55	1.80	1.45	1.25	1.15	.80	.65	.55	.50
For Basement, add $19.50 per square foot of basement area										

The above costs were calculated using the basic specifications shown on the facing page. These costs should be adjusted where necessary for design alternatives and owner's requirements. Reported completed project costs, for this type of structure, range from $62.00 to $151.05 per S.F.

Common additives

Description	Unit	$ Cost
Closed Circuit Surveillance, One station		
Camera and monitor	Each	1375
For additional camera stations, add	Each	745
Emergency Lighting, 25 watt, battery operated		
Lead battery	Each	289
Nickel cadmium	Each	655
Laundry Equipment		
Dryers, coin operated 30 lb.	Each	2775
Double stacked	Each	5800
50 lb.	Each	3175
Dry cleaner 20 lb.	Each	34,800
30 lb.	Each	47,600
Washers, coin operated	Each	1200
Washer/extractor 20 lb.	Each	4175
30 lb.	Each	8025
50 lb.	Each	9975
75 lb.	Each	20,800
Smoke Detectors		
Ceiling type	Each	149
Duct type	Each	405

Important: See the Reference Section for Location Factors

Model costs calculated for a 1 story building with 12' story height and 3,000 square feet of floor area

				Unit	Unit Cost	Cost Per S.F.	% Of Sub-Total
1.0 Foundations							
.1	Footings & Foundations	Poured concrete; strip and spread footings and 4' foundation wall		S.F. Ground	5.44	5.44	
.4	Piles & Caissons	N/A		—	—	—	7.6%
.9	Excavation & Backfill	Site preparation for slab and trench for foundation wall and footing		S.F. Ground	1.28	1.28	
2.0 Substructure							
.1	Slab on Grade	5" reinforced concrete with vapor barrier and granular base		S.F. Slab	3.58	3.58	
.2	Special Substructures	N/A		—	—	—	4.0%
3.0 Superstructure							
.1	Columns & Beams	Fireproofing; steel columns included in 3.7		—	—	—	
.4	Structural Walls	N/A		—	—	—	
.5	Elevated Floors	N/A		—	—	—	6.1%
.7	Roof	Metal deck, open web steel joists, beams, columns		S.F. Roof	5.42	5.42	
.9	Stairs	N/A		—	—	—	
4.0 Exterior Closure							
.1	Walls	Decorative concrete block	90% of wall	S.F. Wall	10.43	8.22	
.5	Exterior Wall Finishes	N/A		—	—	—	
.6	Doors	Double aluminum and glass		Each	3025	1.01	13.3%
.7	Windows & Glazed Walls	Store front	10% of wall	S.F. Window	29	2.57	
5.0 Roofing							
.1	Roof Coverings	Built-up tar and gravel with flashing		S.F. Roof	3.32	3.32	
.7	Insulation	Perlite/EPS composite		S.F. Roof	1.32	1.32	6.7%
.8	Openings & Specialties	Gravel stop, gutters and downspouts		S.F. Roof	1.28	1.28	
6.0 Interior Construction							
.1	Partitions	Gypsum board on metal studs	60 S.F. Floor/L.F. Partition	S.F. Partition	3.12	.52	
.4	Interior Doors	Single leaf wood	750 S.F. Floor/Door	Each	427	.57	
.5	Wall Finishes	Paint		S.F. Surface	.57	.19	
.6	Floor Finishes	Vinyl composition tile		S.F. Floor	1.45	1.45	8.0%
.7	Ceiling Finishes	Fiberglass board on exposed grid system		S.F. Ceiling	1.99	1.99	
.9	Interior Surface/Exterior Wall	Painted gypsum board on furring	90% of wall	S.F. Wall	3.02	2.38	
7.0 Conveying							
.1	Elevators	N/A		—	—	—	0.0%
.2	Special Conveyors	N/A		—	—	—	
8.0 Mechanical							
.1	Plumbing	Toilet and service fixtures, supply and drainage	1 Fixture/600 S.F. Floor	Each	12,012	20.02	
.2	Fire Protection	Sprinkler, ordinary hazard		S.F. Floor	2.50	2.50	
.3	Heating	Included in 8.4		—	—	—	33.7%
.4	Cooling	Rooftop single zone unit systems		S.F. Floor	7.60	7.60	
.5	Special Systems	N/A		—	—	—	
9.0 Electrical							
.1	Service & Distribution	200 ampere service, panel board and feeders		S.F. Floor	2.40	2.40	
.2	Lighting & Power	Fluorescent fixtures, receptacles, switches, A.C. and misc. power		S.F. Floor	15.56	15.56	20.6%
.4	Special Electrical	Alarm systems and emergency lighting		S.F. Floor	.36	.36	
11.0 Special Construction							
.1	Specialties	N/A		—	—	—	0.0%
12.0 Site Work							
.1	Earthwork	N/A		—	—	—	
.3	Utilities	N/A		—	—	—	
.5	Roads & Parking	N/A		—	—	—	0.0%
.7	Site Improvements	N/A		—	—	—	
			Sub-Total			88.98	100%
	CONTRACTOR FEES (General Requirements: 10%, Overhead: 5%, Profit: 10%)				25%	22.25	
	ARCHITECT FEES				7%	7.77	
			Total Building Cost			119.00	

BUILDING TYPES

153

Costs per square foot of floor area

Exterior Wall	S.F. Area	7000	10000	13000	16000	19000	22000	25000	28000	31000
	L.F. Perimeter	240	300	336	386	411	435	472	510	524
Face Brick with Concrete Block Back-up	R/Conc. Frame	123.05	116.55	111.05	108.60	105.45	103.10	101.90	101.00	99.45
	Steel Frame	118.75	112.25	106.75	104.30	101.15	98.80	97.60	96.70	95.15
Limestone with Concrete Block	R/Conc. Frame	137.50	129.20	121.95	118.80	114.60	111.45	109.85	108.70	106.55
	Steel Frame	133.20	124.90	117.65	114.45	110.25	107.15	105.55	104.40	102.25
Precast Concrete Panels	R/Conc. Frame	115.60	110.05	105.45	103.35	100.75	98.80	97.80	97.05	95.75
	Steel Frame	111.30	105.75	101.15	99.05	96.45	94.50	93.50	92.75	91.45
Perimeter Adj., Add or Deduct	Per 100 L.F.	15.50	10.85	8.35	6.80	5.70	4.95	4.35	3.85	3.50
Story Hgt. Adj., Add or Deduct	Per 1 Ft.	2.35	2.05	1.75	1.65	1.45	1.35	1.30	1.25	1.15
For Basement, add $27.90 per square foot of basement area										

The above costs were calculated using the basic specifications shown on the facing page. These costs should be adjusted where necessary for design alternatives and owner's requirements. Reported completed project costs, for this type of structure, range from $59.40 to $152.40 per S.F.

Common additives

Description	Unit	$ Cost
Carrels Hardwood	Each	725 - 940
Closed Circuit Surveillance, One station		
Camera and monitor	Each	1375
For additional camera stations, add	Each	745
Elevators, Hydraulic passenger, 2 stops		
1500# capacity	Each	42,225
2500# capacity	Each	43,425
3500# capacity	Each	47,225
Emergency Lighting, 25 watt, battery operated		
Lead battery	Each	289
Nickel cadmium	Each	655
Flagpoles, Complete		
Aluminum, 20' high	Each	1075
40' high	Each	2675
70' high	Each	8250
Fiberglass, 23' high	Each	1400
39'-5" high	Each	2950
59' high	Each	7300

Description	Unit	$ Cost
Library Furnishings		
Bookshelf, 90" high, 10" shelf double face	L.F.	135
single face	L.F.	196
Charging desk, built-in with counter		
Plastic laminated top	L.F.	505
Reading table, laminated		
top 60" x 36"	Each	690

Model costs calculated for a 2 story building with 14' story height and 22,000 square feet of floor area

Library

				Unit	Unit Cost	Cost Per S.F.	% Of Sub-Total
1.0 Foundations							
.1	Footings & Foundations	Poured concrete; strip and spread footings and 4' foundation wall		S.F. Ground	4.54	2.27	
.4	Piles & Caissons	N/A		—	—	—	3.7%
.9	Excavation & Backfill	Site preparation for slab and trench for foundation wall and footing		S.F. Ground	1.17	.58	
2.0 Substructure							
.1	Slab on Grade	4" reinforced concrete with vapor barrier and granular base		S.F. Slab	3.32	1.66	2.2%
.2	Special Substructures	N/A		—	—	—	
3.0 Superstructure							
.1	Columns & Beams	Concrete columns		L.F. Column	60	1.85	
.4	Structural Walls	N/A		—	—	—	
.5	Elevated Floors	Concrete waffle slab		S.F. Floor	13.80	6.90	20.6%
.7	Roof	Concrete waffle slab		S.F. Roof	12.90	6.45	
.9	Stairs	Concrete filled metal pan		Flight	5975	.54	
4.0 Exterior Closure							
.1	Walls	Face brick with concrete block backup	90% of wall	S.F. Wall	21	10.54	
.5	Exterior Wall Finishes	N/A		—	—	—	
.6	Doors	Double aluminum and glass, single leaf hollow metal		Each	3275	.30	16.8%
.7	Windows & Glazed Walls	Window wall	10% of wall	S.F. Wall	35	1.98	
5.0 Roofing							
.1	Roof Coverings	Single ply membrane, EPDM, fully adhered		S.F. Roof	2.38	1.19	
.7	Insulation	Perlite/EPS composite		S.F. Roof	1.32	.66	2.4%
.8	Openings & Specialties	Gravel stop and hatches		L.F. Roof	.04	.02	
6.0 Interior Construction							
.1	Partitions	Gypsum board on metal studs	30 S.F. Floor/L.F. Partition	S.F. Partition	4.13	1.65	
.4	Interior Doors	Single leaf wood	300 S.F. Floor/Door	Each	427	1.42	
.5	Wall Finishes	Paint		S.F. Surface	.57	.46	
.6	Floor Finishes	50% carpet, 50% vinyl tile		S.F. Floor	3.69	3.69	16.2%
.7	Ceiling Finishes	Mineral fiber on concealed zee bars		S.F. Ceiling	3.63	3.63	
.9	Interior Surface/Exterior Wall	Painted gypsum board on furring	90% of wall	S.F. Wall	3.08	1.53	
7.0 Conveying							
.1	Elevators	One hydraulic passenger elevator		Each	53,680	2.44	3.2%
.2	Special Conveyors	N/A		—	—	—	
8.0 Mechanical							
.1	Plumbing	Toilet and service fixtures, supply and drainage	1 Fixture/1835 S.F. Floor	Each	2752	1.50	
.2	Fire Protection	Wet pipe sprinkler system		S.F. Floor	1.53	1.53	
.3	Heating	Included in 8.4		—	—	—	23.6%
.4	Cooling	Multizone unit, gas heating, electric cooling		S.F. Floor	14.95	14.95	
.5	Special Systems	N/A		—	—	—	
9.0 Electrical							
.1	Service & Distribution	400 ampere service, panel board and feeders		S.F. Floor	.70	.70	
.2	Lighting & Power	Fluorescent fixtures, receptacles, switches, A.C. and misc. power		S.F. Floor	7.36	7.36	11.3%
.4	Special Electrical	Alarm systems and emergency lighting		S.F. Floor	.57	.57	
11.0 Special Construction							
.1	Specialties	N/A		—	—	—	0.0%
12.0 Site Work							
.1	Earthwork	N/A		—	—	—	
.3	Utilities	N/A		—	—	—	
.5	Roads & Parking	N/A		—	—	—	0.0%
.7	Site Improvements	N/A		—	—	—	
				Sub-Total		76.37	100%
	CONTRACTOR FEES (General Requirements: 10%, Overhead: 5%, Profit: 10%)				25%	19.09	
	ARCHITECT FEES				8%	7.64	
				Total Building Cost		103.10	

BUILDING TYPES

155

BUILDING TYPES

Costs per square foot of floor area

Exterior Wall	S.F. Area	4000	5500	7000	8500	10000	11500	13000	14500	16000
	L.F. Perimeter	280	320	380	440	453	503	510	522	560
Face Brick with Concrete Block Back-up	Steel Joists	123.30	116.75	114.35	112.70	109.55	108.60	106.40	104.80	104.20
	Wood Truss	128.45	121.90	119.45	117.85	114.70	113.75	111.55	109.95	109.35
Stucco on Concrete Block	Steel Joists	115.50	110.25	108.30	106.95	104.50	103.70	102.00	100.80	100.30
	Wood Truss	120.65	115.40	113.45	112.10	109.65	108.85	107.20	105.95	105.45
Brick Veneer	Wood Truss	125.40	119.35	117.10	115.65	112.70	111.85	109.85	108.40	107.85
Wood Siding	Wood Frame	118.45	113.60	111.75	110.50	108.25	107.50	105.95	104.80	104.40
Perimeter Adj., Add or Deduct	Per 100 L.F.	11.30	8.25	6.45	5.35	4.50	3.95	3.45	3.10	2.85
Story Hgt. Adj., Add or Deduct	Per 1 Ft.	2.35	1.95	1.80	1.75	1.50	1.45	1.30	1.20	1.20
For Basement, add $18.15 per square foot of basement area										

The above costs were calculated using the basic specifications shown on the facing page. These costs should be adjusted where necessary for design alternatives and owner's requirements. Reported completed project costs, for this type of structure, range from $50.20 to $128.95 per S.F.

Common additives

Description	Unit	$ Cost	Description	Unit	$ Cost
Cabinets, Hospital, base			Directory Boards, Plastic, glass covered		
Laminated plastic	L.F.	281	30" x 20"	Each	565
Stainless steel	L.F.	335	36" x 48"	Each	1025
Counter top, laminated plastic	L.F.	54	Aluminum, 24" x 18"	Each	425
Stainless steel	L.F.	118	36" x 24"	Each	535
For drop-in sink, add	Each	505	48" x 32"	Each	745
Nurses station, door type			48" x 60"	Each	1600
Laminated plastic	L.F.	315	Heat Therapy Unit		
Enameled steel	L.F.	282	Humidified, 26" x 78" x 28"	Each	2725
Stainless steel	L.F.	350	Smoke Detectors		
Wall cabinets, laminated plastic	L.F.	205	Ceiling type	Each	149
Enameled steel	L.F.	223	Duct type	Each	405
Stainless steel	L.F.	320	Tables, Examining, vinyl top		
			with base cabinets	Each	1325 - 3525
			Utensil Washer, Sanitizer	Each	9125
			X-Ray, Mobile	Each	10,900 - 61,500

Important: See the Reference Section for Location Factors

Model costs calculated for a 1 story building with 10′ story height and 7,000 square feet of floor area

Medical Office, 1 Story

				Unit	Unit Cost	Cost Per S.F.	% Of Sub-Total
1.0 Foundations							
.1	Footings & Foundations	Poured concrete; strip and spread footings and 4′ foundation wall		S.F. Ground	4.11	4.11	
.4	Piles & Caissons	N/A		—	—	—	6.0%
.9	Excavation & Backfill	Site preparation for slab and trench for foundation wall and footing		S.F. Ground	1.17	1.17	
2.0 Substructure							
.1	Slab on Grade	4″ reinforced concrete with vapor barrier and granular base		S.F. Slab	3.32	3.32	3.8%
.2	Special Substructures	N/A		—	—	—	
3.0 Superstructure							
.1	Columns & Beams	N/A		—	—	—	
.4	Structural Walls	N/A		—	—	—	
.5	Elevated Floors	N/A		—	—	—	5.6%
.7	Roof	Plywood on wood trusses		S.F. Ground	4.88	4.88	
.9	Stairs	N/A		—	—	—	
4.0 Exterior Closure							
.1	Walls	Face brick with concrete block backup	70% of wall	S.F. Wall	21	8.04	
.5	Exterior Wall Finishes	N/A		—	—	—	16.0%
.6	Doors	Aluminum and glass doors and entrance with transoms		Each	1078	1.85	
.7	Windows & Glazed Walls	Wood double hung	30% of wall	Each	428	4.10	
5.0 Roofing							
.1	Roof Coverings	Asphalt shingles with flashing (Pitched)		S.F. Ground	1.32	1.32	
.7	Insulation	Fiber glass sheeets		S.F. Ground	1.00	1.00	3.1%
.8	Openings & Specialties	Gutters and downspouts		S.F. Ground	.41	.41	
6.0 Interior Construction							
.1	Partitions	Gypsum bd. & sound deadening bd. on wood studs w/insul.	6 S.F. Floor/L.F. Partition	S.F. Partition	5.49	7.32	
.4	Interior Doors	Single leaf wood	60 S.F. Floor/Door	Each	427	7.12	
.5	Wall Finishes	50% paint, 50% vinyl wall covering		S.F. Surface	.99	2.64	
.6	Floor Finishes	50% carpet, 50% vinyl composition tile		S.F. Floor	4.69	4.69	28.9%
.7	Ceiling Finishes	Mineral fiber tile on concealed zee bars		S.F. Ceiling	2.45	2.45	
.9	Interior Surface/Exterior Wall	Painted gypsum board on furring	70% of wall	S.F. Wall	3.02	1.15	
7.0 Conveying							
.1	Elevators	N/A		—	—	—	0.0%
.2	Special Conveyors	N/A		—	—	—	
8.0 Mechanical							
.1	Plumbing	Toilet and service fixtures, supply and drainage	1 Fixture/195 S.F. Floor	Each	2242	11.50	
.2	Fire Protection	Wet pipe sprinkler system		S.F. Floor	2.27	2.27	
.3	Heating	Included in 8.4		—	—	—	26.8%
.4	Cooling	Multizone unit, gas heating, electric cooling		S.F. Floor	9.79	9.79	
.5	Special Systems	N/A		—	—	—	
9.0 Electrical							
.1	Service & Distribution	200 ampere service, panel board and feeders		S.F. Floor	.97	.97	
.2	Lighting & Power	Fluorescent fixtures, receptacles, switches, A.C. and misc. power		S.F. Floor	4.91	4.91	9.8%
.4	Special Electrical	Alarm systems, intercom system, and emergency lighting		S.F. Floor	2.68	2.68	
11.0 Special Construction							
.1	Specialties	N/A		—	—	—	0.0%
12.0 Site Work							
.1	Earthwork	N/A		—	—	—	
.3	Utilities	N/A		—	—	—	
.5	Roads & Parking	N/A		—	—	—	0.0%
.7	Site Improvements	N/A		—	—	—	
				Sub-Total		87.69	**100%**
	CONTRACTOR FEES (General Requirements: 10%, Overhead: 5%, Profit: 10%)				25%	21.92	
	ARCHITECT FEES				9%	9.84	
				Total Building Cost		119.45	

BUILDING TYPES

157

Costs per square foot of floor area

Exterior Wall	S.F. Area	4000	5500	7000	8500	10000	11500	13000	14500	16000
	L.F. Perimeter	180	210	240	270	286	311	336	361	386
Face Brick with Concrete Block Back-up	Steel Joists	136.40	129.45	125.55	123.00	120.15	118.60	117.45	116.55	115.80
	Wood Joists	141.75	134.85	130.95	128.35	125.50	124.00	122.85	121.95	121.15
Stucco on Concrete Block	Steel Joists	128.95	123.10	119.85	117.65	115.35	114.05	113.10	112.35	111.75
	Wood Joists	134.05	128.30	125.05	122.90	120.60	119.35	118.40	117.65	117.00
Brick Veneer	Wood Frame	137.95	131.60	128.05	125.65	123.10	121.70	120.65	119.80	119.15
Wood Siding	Wood Frame	132.00	126.55	123.50	121.45	119.30	118.10	117.20	116.50	115.90
Perimeter Adj., Add or Deduct	Per 100 L.F.	19.15	13.95	10.95	9.00	7.65	6.70	5.90	5.30	4.80
Story Hgt. Adj., Add or Deduct	Per 1 Ft.	2.80	2.40	2.15	2.00	1.80	1.70	1.60	1.55	1.50

For Basement, add $20.15 per square foot of basement area

The above costs were calculated using the basic specifications shown on the facing page. These costs should be adjusted where necessary for design alternatives and owner's requirements. Reported completed project costs, for this type of structure, range from $51.50 to $175.90 per S.F.

Common additives

Description	Unit	$ Cost	Description	Unit	$ Cost
Cabinets, Hospital, base			Directory Boards, Plastic, glass covered		
Laminated plastic	L.F.	281	30" x 20"	Each	565
Stainless steel	L.F.	335	36" x 48"	Each	1025
Counter top, laminated plastic	L.F.	54	Aluminum, 24" x 18"	Each	425
Stainless steel	L.F.	118	36" x 24"	Each	535
For drop-in sink, add	Each	505	48" x 32"	Each	745
Nurses station, door type			48" x 60"	Each	1600
Laminated plastic	L.F.	315	Emergency Lighting, 25 watt, battery operated		
Enameled steel	L.F.	282	Lead battery	Each	289
Stainless steel	L.F.	350	Nickel cadmium	Each	655
Wall cabinets, laminated plastic	L.F.	205	Heat Therapy Unit		
Enameled steel	L.F.	223	Humidified, 26" x 78" x 28"	Each	2725
Stainless steel	L.F.	320	Smoke Detectors		
Elevators, Hydraulic passenger, 2 stops			Ceiling type	Each	149
1500# capacity	Each	42,225	Duct type	Each	405
2500# capacity	Each	43,425	Tables, Examining, vinyl top		
3500# capacity	Each	47,225	with base cabinets	Each	1325 - 3525
			Utensil Washer, Sanitizer	Each	9125
			X-Ray, Mobile	Each	10,900 - 61,500

Important: See the Reference Section for Location Factors

BUILDING TYPES

Model costs calculated for a 2 story building with 10′ story height and 7,000 square feet of floor area

					Unit	Unit Cost	Cost Per S.F.	% Of Sub-Total

1.0 Foundations

				Unit	Unit Cost	Cost Per S.F.	% Of Sub-Total
.1	Footings & Foundations	Poured concrete; strip and spread footings and 4′ foundation wall		S.F. Ground	5.66	2.83	
.4	Piles & Caissons	N/A		—	—	—	3.8%
.9	Excavation & Backfill	Site preparation for slab and trench for foundation wall and footing		S.F. Ground	1.08	.54	

2.0 Substructure

				Unit	Unit Cost	Cost Per S.F.	% Of Sub-Total
.1	Slab on Grade	4″ reinforced concrete with vapor barrier and granular base		S.F. Slab	3.32	1.66	1.9%
.2	Special Substructures	N/A		—	—	—	

3.0 Superstructure

				Unit	Unit Cost	Cost Per S.F.	% Of Sub-Total
.1	Columns & Beams	Included in 3.5 and 3.7		—	—	—	
.4	Structural Walls	N/A		—	—	—	
.5	Elevated Floors	Open web steel joists, slab form, concrete, columns		S.F. Floor	8.25	4.13	8.2%
.7	Roof	Metal deck, open web steel joists, beams, columns		S.F. Roof	3.26	1.63	
.9	Stairs	Concrete filled metal pan		Flight	5025	1.44	

4.0 Exterior Closure

				Unit	Unit Cost	Cost Per S.F.	% Of Sub-Total
.1	Walls	N/A		—	—	—	
.5	Exterior Wall Finishes	Stucco on concrete block	70% of wall	S.F. Wall	12.51	6.00	12.6%
.6	Doors	Aluminum and glass doors with transoms		Each	3275	.94	
.7	Windows & Glazed Walls	Outward projecting metal	30% of wall	Each	304	4.17	

5.0 Roofing

				Unit	Unit Cost	Cost Per S.F.	% Of Sub-Total
.1	Roof Coverings	Built-up tar and gravel with flashing		S.F. Roof	2.80	1.40	
.7	Insulation	Perlite/EPS composite		S.F. Roof	1.32	.66	2.7%
.8	Openings & Specialties	Gravel stop and hatches		S.F. Roof	.58	.29	

6.0 Interior Construction

				Unit	Unit Cost	Cost Per S.F.	% Of Sub-Total
.1	Partitions	Gypsum bd. & acous. insul. on metal studs	6 S.F. Floor/L.F. Partition	S.F. Partition	4.08	5.44	
.4	Interior Doors	Single leaf wood	60 S.F. Floor/Door	Each	427	7.12	
.5	Wall Finishes	45% paint, 50% vinyl wall coating, 5% ceramic tile		S.F. Surface	.99	2.64	27.0%
.6	Floor Finishes	50% carpet, 50% vinyl asbestos tile		S.F. Floor	4.69	4.69	
.7	Ceiling Finishes	Mineral fiber tile on concealed zee bars		S.F. Ceiling	2.45	2.45	
.9	Interior Surface/Exterior Wall	Painted gypsum board on furring	70% of wall	S.F. Wall	3.02	1.45	

7.0 Conveying

				Unit	Unit Cost	Cost Per S.F.	% Of Sub-Total
.1	Elevators	One hydraulic hospital elevator		Each	63,070	9.01	10.2%
.2	Special Conveyors	N/A		—	—	—	

8.0 Mechanical

				Unit	Unit Cost	Cost Per S.F.	% Of Sub-Total
.1	Plumbing	Toilet and service fixtures, supply and drainage	1 Fixture/160 S.F. Floor	Each	1390	8.69	
.2	Fire Protection	Wet pipe sprinkler system		S.F. Floor	1.88	1.88	
.3	Heating	Included in 8.4		—	—	—	23.2%
.4	Cooling	Multizone unit, gas heating, electric cooling		S.F. Floor	9.79	9.79	
.5	Special Systems	N/A		—	—	—	

9.0 Electrical

				Unit	Unit Cost	Cost Per S.F.	% Of Sub-Total
.1	Service & Distribution	400 ampere service, panel board and feeders		S.F. Floor	1.52	1.52	
.2	Lighting & Power	Fluorescent fixtures, receptacles, switches, A.C. and misc. power		S.F. Floor	4.91	4.91	10.4%
.4	Special Electrical	Alarm system, intercom system, and emergency lighting		S.F. Floor	2.68	2.68	

11.0 Special Construction

				Unit	Unit Cost	Cost Per S.F.	% Of Sub-Total
.1	Specialties	N/A		—	—	—	0.0%

12.0 Site Work

				Unit	Unit Cost	Cost Per S.F.	% Of Sub-Total
.1	Earthwork	N/A		—	—	—	
.3	Utilities	N/A		—	—	—	
.5	Roads & Parking	N/A		—	—	—	0.0%
.7	Site Improvements	N/A		—	—	—	

		Sub-Total			87.96	100%
	CONTRACTOR FEES (General Requirements: 10%, Overhead: 5%, Profit: 10%)			25%	21.99	
	ARCHITECT FEES			9%	9.90	
		Total Building Cost			119.85	

Costs per square foot of floor area

Exterior Wall	S.F. Area	2000	3000	4000	6000	8000	10000	12000	14000	16000
	L.F. Perimeter	240	260	280	380	480	560	580	660	740
Brick Veneer	Wood Frame	124.55	108.90	101.10	97.10	95.15	93.20	89.95	89.30	88.80
Aluminum Siding	Wood Frame	112.40	100.15	94.00	90.70	89.10	87.55	85.05	84.55	84.15
Wood Siding	Wood Frame	112.55	100.25	94.10	90.80	89.15	87.60	85.15	84.60	84.20
Wood Shingles	Wood Frame	114.90	101.95	95.50	92.05	90.35	88.70	86.10	85.55	85.10
Precast Concrete Block	Wood Truss	111.35	99.40	93.40	90.15	88.60	87.05	84.65	84.15	83.75
Brick on Concrete Block	Wood Truss	129.70	112.65	104.10	99.85	97.75	95.60	92.05	91.30	90.80
Perimeter Adj., Add or Deduct	Per 100 L.F.	19.40	12.90	9.65	6.50	4.85	3.90	3.20	2.75	2.40
Story Hgt. Adj., Add or Deduct	Per 1 Ft.	3.25	2.35	1.90	1.75	1.65	1.50	1.30	1.30	1.25
For Basement, add $13.90 per square foot of basement area										

The above costs were calculated using the basic specifications shown on the facing page. These costs should be adjusted where necessary for design alternatives and owner's requirements. Reported completed project costs, for this type of structure, range from $41.65 to $196.85 per S.F.

Common additives

Description	Unit	$ Cost
Closed Circuit Surveillance, One station		
Camera and monitor	Each	1375
For additional camera stations, add	Each	745
Emergency Lighting, 25 watt, battery operated		
Lead battery	Each	289
Nickel cadmium	Each	655
Laundry Equipment		
Dryer, gas, 16 lb. capacity	Each	710
30 lb. capacity	Each	2775
Washer, 4 cycle	Each	795
Commercial	Each	1200
Sauna, Prefabricated, complete		
6' x 4'	Each	4075
6' x 6'	Each	4850
6' x 9'	Each	5350
8' x 8'	Each	6300
8' x 10'	Each	6950
10' x 12'	Each	9125
Smoke Detectors		
Ceiling type	Each	149
Duct type	Each	405

Description	Unit	$ Cost
Swimming Pools, Complete, gunite	S.F.	47 - 57
TV Antenna, Master system, 12 outlet	Outlet	236
30 outlet	Outlet	151
100 outlet	Outlet	144

Model costs calculated for a 1 story building with 9' story height and 8,000 square feet of floor area

Motel, 1 Story

				Unit	Unit Cost	Cost Per S.F.	% Of Sub-Total
1.0 Foundations							
.1	Footings & Foundations	Poured concrete; strip and spread footings and 4' foundation wall		S.F. Ground	5.98	5.98	
.4	Piles & Caissons	N/A		—	—	—	10.0%
.9	Excavation & Backfill	Site preparation for slab and trench for foundation wall and footing		S.F. Ground	1.17	1.17	
2.0 Substructure							
.1	Slab on Grade	4" reinforced concrete with vapor barrier and granular base		S.F. Slab	3.32	3.32	4.7%
.2	Special Substructures	N/A		—	—	—	
3.0 Superstructure							
.1	Columns & Beams	N/A		—	—	—	
.4	Structural Walls	N/A		—	—	—	
.5	Elevated Floors	N/A		—	—	—	6.9%
.7	Roof	Plywood on wood trusses		S.F. Ground	4.88	4.88	
.9	Stairs	N/A		—	—	—	
4.0 Exterior Closure							
.1	Walls	Face brick on wood studs with sheathing, insulation and paper	80% of wall	S.F. Wall	16.60	7.17	
.5	Exterior Wall Finishes	N/A		—	—	—	18.0%
.6	Doors	Wood solid core		Each	1078	2.96	
.7	Windows & Glazed Walls	Wood double hung	20% of wall	Each	344	2.65	
5.0 Roofing							
.1	Roof Coverings	Asphalt shingles with flashing (pitched)		S.F. Ground	1.12	1.12	
.7	Insulation	Fiberglass sheets		S.F. Ground	1.00	1.00	3.6%
.8	Openings & Specialties	Gutters and downspouts		S.F. Ground	.46	.46	
6.0 Interior Construction							
.1	Partitions	Gypsum bd. and sound deadening bd. on wood studs	9 S.F. Floor/L.F. Partition	S.F. Partition	5.49	4.88	
.4	Interior Doors	Single leaf hollow core wood	300 S.F. Floor/Door	Each	384	1.28	
.5	Wall Finishes	90% paint, 10% ceramic tile		S.F. Surface	1.06	1.88	25.9%
.6	Floor Finishes	85% carpet, 15% ceramic tile		S.F. Floor	6.36	6.36	
.7	Ceiling Finishes	Painted gypsum board on furring		S.F. Ceiling	2.92	2.92	
.9	Interior Surface/Exterior Wall	Painted gypsum board on furring	80% of wall	S.F. Wall	3.02	1.14	
7.0 Conveying							
.1	Elevators	N/A		—	—	—	0.0%
.2	Special Conveyors	N/A		—	—	—	
8.0 Mechanical							
.1	Plumbing	Toilet and service fixtures, supply and drainage	1 Fixture/90 S.F. Floor	Each	972	10.80	
.2	Fire Protection	Wet pipe sprinkler system		S.F. Floor	2.27	2.27	
.3	Heating	Included in 8.4		—	—	—	22.9%
.4	Cooling	Through the wall electric heating and cooling units		S.F. Floor	3.24	3.24	
.5	Special Systems	N/A		—	—	—	
9.0 Electrical							
.1	Service & Distribution	200 ampere service, panel board and feeders		S.F. Floor	.83	.83	
.2	Lighting & Power	Fluorescent fixtures, receptacles, switches and misc. power		S.F. Floor	4.55	4.55	8.0%
.4	Special Electrical	Alarm systems		S.F. Floor	.29	.29	
11.0 Special Construction							
.1	Specialties	N/A		—	—	—	0.0%
12.0 Site Work							
.1	Earthwork	N/A		—	—	—	
.3	Utilities	N/A		—	—	—	
.5	Roads & Parking	N/A		—	—	—	0.0%
.7	Site Improvements	N/A		—	—	—	
				Sub-Total		71.15	**100%**
	CONTRACTOR FEES (General Requirements: 10%, Overhead: 5%, Profit: 10%)				25%	17.79	
	ARCHITECT FEES				7%	6.21	
				Total Building Cost		95.15	

BUILDING TYPES

161

Costs per square foot of floor area

Exterior Wall	S.F. Area	25000	37000	49000	61000	73000	81000	88000	96000	104000
	L.F. Perimeter	433	593	606	720	835	911	978	1054	1074
Decorative Concrete Block	Wood Joists	110.45	107.75	103.95	103.00	102.30	102.00	101.70	101.55	100.90
	Precast Conc.	117.60	114.90	111.15	110.15	109.45	109.15	108.90	108.70	108.10
Stucco on Concrete Block	Wood Joists	109.95	107.20	103.45	102.45	101.75	101.50	101.20	101.00	100.40
	Precast Conc.	117.70	114.95	111.20	110.20	109.55	109.25	108.95	108.75	108.15
Wood Siding	Wood Frame	108.65	106.00	102.50	101.55	100.90	100.65	100.35	100.15	99.60
Brick Veneer	Wood Frame	112.35	109.45	105.15	104.10	103.35	103.05	102.75	102.55	101.80
Perimeter Adj., Add or Deduct	Per 100 L.F.	3.20	2.15	1.60	1.30	1.10	1.00	.95	.85	.75
Story Hgt. Adj., Add or Deduct	Per 1 Ft.	1.15	1.05	.80	.80	.75	.75	.75	.70	.70

For Basement, add $18.20 per square foot of basement area

The above costs were calculated using the basic specifications shown on the facing page. These costs should be adjusted where necessary for design alternatives and owner's requirements. Reported completed project costs, for this type of structure, range from $41.65 to $196.85 per S.F.

Common additives

Description	Unit	$ Cost	Description	Unit	$ Cost
Closed Circuit Surveillance, One station			Sauna, Prefabricated, complete		
Camera and monitor	Each	1375	6' x 4'	Each	4075
For additional camera station, add	Each	745	6' x 6'	Each	4850
Elevators, Hydraulic passenger, 2 stops			6' x 9'	Each	5350
1500# capacity	Each	42,225	8' x 8'	Each	6300
2500# capacity	Each	43,425	8' x 10'	Each	6950
3500# capacity	Each	47,225	10' x 12'	Each	9125
Additional stop, add	Each	3650	Smoke Detectors		
Emergency Lighting, 25 watt, battery operated			Ceiling type	Each	149
Lead battery	Each	289	Duct type	Each	405
Nickel cadmium	Each	655	Swimming Pools, Complete, gunite	S.F.	47 - 57
Laundry Equipment			TV Antenna, Master system, 12 outlet	Outlet	236
Dryer, gas, 16 lb. capacity	Each	710	30 outlet	Outlet	151
30 lb. capacity	Each	2775	100 outlet	Outlet	144
Washer, 4 cycle	Each	795			
Commercial	Each	1200			

BUILDING TYPES

Model costs calculated for a 3 story building with 9' story height and 49,000 square feet of floor area

				Unit	Unit Cost	Cost Per S.F.	% Of Sub-Total
1.0 Foundations							
.1	Footings & Foundations	Poured concrete; strip and spread footings and 4' foundation wall		S.F. Ground	4.74	1.58	
.4	Piles & Caissons	N/A		—	—	—	2.3%
.9	Excavation & Backfill	Site preparation for slab and trench for foundation wall and footing		S.F. Ground	1.08	.36	
2.0 Substructure							
.1	Slab on Grade	4" reinforced concrete with vapor barrier and granular base		S.F. Slab	3.32	1.11	1.3%
.2	Special Substructures	N/A		—	—	—	
3.0 Superstructure							
.1	Columns & Beams	N/A		—	—	—	
.4	Structural Walls	Reinforced concrete block		S.F. Wall	10.44	2.56	
.5	Elevated Floors	Precast concrete plank		S.F. Floor	7.40	4.93	13.2%
.7	Roof	Precast concrete plank		S.F. Roof	7.03	2.34	
.9	Stairs	Concrete filled metal pan		Flight	5025	1.23	
4.0 Exterior Closure							
.1	Walls	Decorative concrete block	85% of wall	S.F. Wall	11.84	3.36	
.5	Exterior Wall Finishes	N/A		—	—	—	9.9%
.6	Doors	Aluminum and glass doors and entrance with transom		Each	1115	3.68	
.7	Windows & Glazed Walls	Aluminum sliding	15% of wall	Each	384	1.28	
5.0 Roofing							
.1	Roof Coverings	Built-up tar and gravel with flashing		S.F. Roof	2.31	.77	
.7	Insulation	Perlite/EPS composite		S.F. Roof	1.32	.44	1.7%
.8	Openings & Specialties	Gravel stop, hatches, gutters and downspouts		S.F. Roof	.60	.20	
6.0 Interior Construction							
.1	Partitions	Concrete block	7 S.F. Floor/L.F. Partition	S.F. Partition	9.54	10.90	
.4	Interior Doors	Wood hollow core	70 S.F. Floor/Door	Each	384	5.49	
.5	Wall Finishes	90% paint, 10% ceramic tile		S.F. Surface	1.06	2.42	
.6	Floor Finishes	85% carpet, 5% vinyl composition tile, 10% ceramic tile		S.F. Floor	6.36	6.36	34.3%
.7	Ceiling Finishes	Textured finish		S.F. Ceiling	2.70	2.70	
.9	Interior Surface/Exterior Wall	Painted gypsum board on furring	85% of wall	S.F. Wall	3.02	.86	
7.0 Conveying							
.1	Elevators	Two hydraulic passenger elevators		Each	64,190	2.62	3.1%
.2	Special Conveyors	N/A		—	—	—	
8.0 Mechanical							
.1	Plumbing	Toilet and service fixtures, supply and drainage	1 Fixture/180 S.F. Floor	Each	2833	15.74	
.2	Fire Protection	Sprinklers, light hazard		S.F. Floor	1.21	1.21	
.3	Heating	Included in 8.4		—	—	—	26.2%
.4	Cooling	Through the wall electric heating and cooling units		S.F. Floor	5.04	5.04	
.5	Special Systems	N/A		—	—	—	
9.0 Electrical							
.1	Service & Distribution	800 ampere service, panel board and feeders		S.F. Floor	1.14	1.14	
.2	Lighting & Power	Fluorescent fixtures, receptacles, switches and misc. power		S.F. Floor	5.01	5.01	8.0%
.4	Special Electrical	Alarm systems and emergency lighting		S.F. Floor	.54	.54	
11.0 Special Construction							
.1	Specialties	N/A		—	—	—	0.0%
12.0 Site Work							
.1	Earthwork	N/A		—	—	—	
.3	Utilities	N/A		—	—	—	
.5	Roads & Parking	N/A		—	—	—	0.0%
.7	Site Improvements	N/A		—	—	—	

	Sub-Total	83.87	**100%**
CONTRACTOR FEES (General Requirements: 10%, Overhead: 5%, Profit: 10%)		25%	20.97
ARCHITECT FEES		6%	6.31
	Total Building Cost	**111.15**	

Costs per square foot of floor area

Exterior Wall	S.F. Area	9000	10000	12000	13000	14000	15000	16000	18000	20000
	L.F. Perimeter	385	410	460	460	480	500	510	547	583
Decorative Concrete Block	Steel Joists	105.50	102.80	98.70	96.00	94.60	93.30	91.85	89.90	88.35
Painted Concrete Block	Steel Joists	99.30	96.85	93.15	90.90	89.60	88.45	87.20	85.50	84.10
Face Brick on Conc. Block	Steel Joists	114.25	111.20	106.55	103.25	101.60	100.10	98.35	96.10	94.30
Precast Concrete Panels	Steel Joists	108.40	105.55	101.30	98.40	96.90	95.55	94.00	91.95	90.30
Tilt-up Panels	Steel Joists	109.25	106.35	102.05	99.10	97.55	96.20	94.60	92.55	90.90
Metal Sandwich Panels	Steel Joists	100.85	98.35	94.50	92.20	90.85	89.65	88.40	86.60	85.15
Perimeter Adj., Add or Deduct	Per 100 L.F.	6.05	5.45	4.55	4.20	3.90	3.70	3.45	3.05	2.75
Story Hgt. Adj., Add or Deduct	Per 1 Ft.	.90	.85	.80	.75	.70	.70	.65	.65	.60

Basement—Not Applicable

The above costs were calculated using the basic specifications shown on the facing page. These costs should be adjusted where necessary for design alternatives and owner's requirements. Reported completed project costs, for this type of structure, range from $49.10 to $128.20 per S.F.

Common additives

Description	Unit	$ Cost
Emergency Lighting, 25 watt, battery operated		
Lead battery	Each	289
Nickel cadmium	Each	655
Seating		
Auditorium chair, all veneer	Each	166
Veneer back, padded seat	Each	201
Upholstered, spring seat	Each	203
Classroom, movable chair & desk	Set	65 - 120
Lecture hall, pedestal type	Each	152 - 470
Smoke Detectors		
Ceiling type	Each	149
Duct type	Each	405
Sound System		
Amplifier, 250 watts	Each	1650
Speaker, ceiling or wall	Each	145
Trumpet	Each	271

Important: See the Reference Section for Location Factors

Model costs calculated for a 1 story building with 20' story height and 12,000 square feet of floor area

Movie Theater

				Unit	Unit Cost	Cost Per S.F.	% Of Sub-Total
1.0 Foundations							
.1	Footings & Foundations	Poured concrete; strip and spread footings and 4' foundation wall		S.F. Ground	2.90	2.90	
.4	Piles & Caissons	N/A		—	—	—	7.3%
.9	Excavation & Backfill	Site preparation for slab and trench for foundation wall and footing		S.F. Ground	2.45	2.45	
2.0 Substructure							
.1	Slab on Grade	4" reinforced concrete with vapor barrier and granular base		S.F. Slab	3.32	3.32	4.5%
.2	Special Substructures	N/A		—	—	—	
3.0 Superstructure							
.1	Columns & Beams	N/A		—	—	—	
.4	Structural Walls	N/A		—	—	—	
.5	Elevated Floors	Open web steel joists, slab form, concrete	mezzanine 2250 S.F.	S.F. Mezz	6.68	1.25	12.0%
.7	Roof	Metal deck on open web steel joists		S.F. Roof	6.59	6.59	
.9	Stairs	Concrete filled metal pan		Flight	5975	1.00	
4.0 Exterior Closure							
.1	Walls	Decorative concrete block	100% of wall	S.F. Wall	13.40	10.27	
.5	Exterior Wall Finishes	N/A		—	—	—	14.9%
.6	Doors	Sliding mallfront aluminum and glass and hollow metal		Each	1421	.71	
.7	Windows & Glazed Walls	N/A		—	—	—	
5.0 Roofing							
.1	Roof Coverings	Built-up tar and gravel with flashing		S.F. Roof	2.31	2.31	
.7	Insulation	Perlite/EPS composite		S.F. Roof	1.32	1.32	5.3%
.8	Openings & Specialties	Gravel stop, hatches		S.F. Roof	.25	.25	
6.0 Interior Construction							
.1	Partitions	Concrete block, toilet partitions	40 S.F. Floor/L.F. Partition	S.F. Partition	6.97	2.79	
.4	Interior Doors	Single leaf hollow metal	705 S.F. Floor/Door	Each	534	.76	
.5	Wall Finishes	Paint		S.F. Surface	1.19	.95	
.6	Floor Finishes	Carpet 50%, ceramic tile 5%	50% of area	S.F. Floor	6.92	3.46	17.9%
.7	Ceiling Finishes	Mineral fiber tile on concealed zee runners suspended		S.F. Ceiling	3.63	3.63	
.9	Interior Surface/Exterior Wall	Paint	100% of wall	S.F. Wall	2.12	1.63	
7.0 Conveying							
.1	Elevators	N/A		—	—	—	0.0%
.2	Special Conveyors	N/A		—	—	—	
8.0 Mechanical							
.1	Plumbing	Toilet and service fixtures, supply and drainage	1 Fixture/500 S.F. Floor	Each	1405	2.81	
.2	Fire Protection	Wet pipe sprinkler system		S.F. Floor	2.06	2.06	
.3	Heating	Included in 8.4		—	—	—	18.0%
.4	Cooling	Single zone rooftop unit, gas heating, electric cooling		S.F. Floor	8.51	8.51	
.5	Special Systems	N/A		—	—	—	
9.0 Electrical							
.1	Service & Distribution	400 ampere service, panel board and feeders		S.F. Floor	1.10	1.10	
.2	Lighting & Power	Fluorescent fixtures, receptacles, switches, A.C. and misc. power		S.F. Floor	3.12	3.12	6.4%
.4	Special Electrical	Alarm systems, sound system and emergency lighting		S.F. Floor	.50	.50	
11.0 Special Construction							
.1	Specialties	Projection equipment, screen, seating		S.F. Floor	10.10	10.10	13.7%
12.0 Site Work							
.1	Earthwork	N/A		—	—	—	
.3	Utilities	N/A		—	—	—	
.5	Roads & Parking	N/A		—	—	—	0.0%
.7	Site Improvements	N/A		—	—	—	
				Sub-Total		73.79	**100%**
	CONTRACTOR FEES (General Requirements: 10%, Overhead: 5%, Profit: 10%)				25%	18.45	
	ARCHITECT FEES				7%	6.46	
				Total Building Cost		98.70	

BUILDING TYPES

165

Costs per square foot of floor area

Exterior Wall	S.F. Area	10000	15000	20000	25000	30000	35000	40000	45000	50000
	L.F. Perimeter	286	370	453	457	513	568	624	680	735
Precast Concrete Panels	Bearing Walls	112.40	107.40	104.90	101.10	99.75	98.80	98.15	97.65	97.15
	Steel Frame	115.15	110.20	107.65	103.85	102.50	101.60	100.95	100.40	99.95
Face Brick with Concrete Block Back-up	Bearing Walls	115.35	109.95	107.20	102.95	101.50	100.50	99.75	99.20	98.65
	Steel Joists	118.45	113.05	110.30	106.05	104.60	103.55	102.85	102.30	101.75
Stucco on Concrete Block	Bearing Walls	109.20	104.65	102.35	99.05	97.85	97.00	96.40	95.95	95.50
	Steel Joists	112.30	107.75	105.45	102.15	100.95	100.10	99.50	99.05	98.60
Perimeter Adj., Add or Deduct	Per 100 L.F.	7.35	4.90	3.70	2.90	2.45	2.10	1.80	1.60	1.50
Story Hgt. Adj., Add or Deduct	Per 1 Ft.	1.65	1.40	1.30	1.05	1.00	.95	.90	.85	.85

For Basement, add $18.85 per square foot of basement area

The above costs were calculated using the basic specifications shown on the facing page. These costs should be adjusted where necessary for design alternatives and owner's requirements. Reported completed project costs, for this type of structure, range from $53.05 to $131.75 per S.F.

Common additives

Description	Unit	$ Cost	Description	Unit	$ Cost
Beds, Manual	Each	910 - 1575	Kitchen Equipment, cont.		
Doctors In-Out Register, 200 names	Each	13,000	Ice cube maker, 50 lb. per day	Each	1800
Elevators, Hydraulic passenger, 2 stops			Range with 1 oven	Each	2400
1500# capacity	Each	42,225	Laundry Equipment		
2500# capacity	Each	43,425	Dryer, gas, 16 lb. capacity	Each	710
3500# capacity	Each	47,225	30 lb. capacity	Each	2775
Emergency Lighting, 25 watt, battery operated			Washer, 4 cycle	Each	795
Lead battery	Each	289	Commercial	Each	1200
Nickel cadmium	Each	655	Nurses Call System		
Intercom System, 25 station capacity			Single bedside call station	Each	237
Master station	Each	2000	Pillow speaker	Each	219
Intercom outlets	Each	126	Refrigerator, Prefabricated, walk-in		
Handset	Each	335	7'-6" high, 6' x 6'	S.F.	120
Kitchen Equipment			10' x 10'	S.F.	95
Broiler	Each	4050	12' x 14'	S.F.	83
Coffee urn, twin 6 gallon	Each	6975	12' x 20'	S.F.	73
Cooler, 6 ft. long	Each	3200	TV Antenna, Master system, 12 outlet	Outlet	236
Dishwasher, 10-12 racks per hr.	Each	3050	30 outlet	Outlet	151
Food warmer	Each	715	100 outlet	Outlet	144
Freezer, 44 C.F., reach-in	Each	8325	Whirlpool Bath, Mobile, 18" x 24" x 60"	Each	3850
			X-Ray, Mobile	Each	10,900 - 61,500

Important: See the Reference Section for Location Factors

Nursing Home

Model costs calculated for a 2 story building with 10' story height and 25,000 square feet of floor area

				Unit	Unit Cost	Cost Per S.F.	% Of Sub-Total
1.0 Foundations							
	.1	Footings & Foundations	Poured concrete; strip and spread footings and 4' foundation wall	S.F. Ground	3.08	1.54	
	.4	Piles & Caissons	N/A	—	—	—	2.9%
	.9	Excavation & Backfill	Site preparation for slab and trench for foundation wall and footing	S.F. Ground	1.17	.58	
2.0 Substructure							
	.1	Slab on Grade	4" reinforced concrete with vapor barrier and granular base	S.F. Slab	3.32	1.66	2.3%
	.2	Special Substructures	N/A	—	—	—	
3.0 Superstructure							
	.1	Columns & Beams	N/A	—	—	—	
	.4	Structural Walls	N/A	—	—	—	
	.5	Elevated Floors	Pre-cast double tees with concrete topping	S.F. Floor	8.17	4.09	11.5%
	.7	Roof	Pre-cast double tees	S.F. Roof	6.55	3.28	
	.9	Stairs	Concrete stair	Flight	4225	1.01	
4.0 Exterior Closure							
	.1	Walls	Vertical T & G redwood siding — 85% of wall	S.F. Wall	16.80	5.22	
	.5	Exterior Wall Finishes	N/A	—	—	—	9.5%
	.6	Doors	Double aluminum & glass doors, single leaf hollow metal	Each	1517	.30	
	.7	Windows & Glazed Walls	Wood double hung — 15% of wall	Each	384	1.40	
5.0 Roofing							
	.1	Roof Coverings	Built-up tar and gravel with flashing	S.F. Roof	2.26	1.13	
	.7	Insulation	Perlite/EPS composite	S.F. Roof	1.32	.66	2.8%
	.8	Openings & Specialties	Gravel stop, hatches, gutters and downspouts	S.F. Roof	.56	.28	
6.0 Interior Construction							
	.1	Partitions	Gypsum board on metal studs — 8 S.F. Floor/L.F. Partition	S.F. Partition	4.17	4.17	
	.4	Interior Doors	Single leaf wood — 80 S.F. Floor/Door	Each	427	5.34	
	.5	Wall Finishes	50% vinyl wall coverings, 45% paint, 5% ceramic tile	S.F. Surface	1.24	2.47	
	.6	Floor Finishes	95% vinyl tile, 5% ceramic tile	S.F. Floor	3.14	3.14	25.9%
	.7	Ceiling Finishes	Painted gypsum board	S.F. Ceiling	2.80	2.80	
	.9	Interior Surface/Exterior Wall	Painted gypsum board — 85% of wall	S.F. Wall	3.02	.94	
7.0 Conveying							
	.1	Elevators	One hydraulic hospital elevator	Each	63,000	2.52	3.5%
	.2	Special Conveyors	N/A	—	—	—	
8.0 Mechanical							
	.1	Plumbing	Kitchen, toilet and service fixtures, supply and drainage — 1 Fixture/230 S.F. Floor	Each	2166	9.42	
	.2	Fire Protection	Sprinkler, light hazard	S.F. Floor	3.05	3.05	
	.3	Heating	Oil fired hot water, wall fin radiation	S.F. Floor	4.33	4.33	30.1%
	.4	Cooling	Split systems with air cooled condensing units	S.F. Floor	5.18	5.18	
	.5	Special Systems	N/A	—	—	—	
9.0 Electrical							
	.1	Service & Distribution	800 ampere service, panel board and feeders	S.F. Floor	1.27	1.27	
	.2	Lighting & Power	Incandescent fixtures, receptacles, switches, A.C. and misc. power	S.F. Floor	6.19	6.19	11.5%
	.4	Special Electrical	Alarm systems and emergency lighting	S.F. Floor	.89	.89	
11.0 Special Construction							
	.1	Specialties	N/A	—	—	—	0.0%
12.0 Site Work							
	.1	Earthwork	N/A	—	—	—	
	.3	Utilities	N/A	—	—	—	
	.5	Roads & Parking	N/A	—	—	—	0.0%
	.7	Site Improvements	N/A	—	—	—	
				Sub-Total		72.86	**100%**
	CONTRACTOR FEES (General Requirements: 10%, Overhead: 5%, Profit: 10%)				25%	18.22	
	ARCHITECT FEES				11%	10.02	
				Total Building Cost		**101.10**	

Costs per square foot of floor area

Exterior Wall	S.F. Area	5000	8000	12000	16000	20000	35000	50000	65000	80000
	L.F. Perimeter	220	260	310	330	360	440	490	548	580
Face Brick with Concrete Block Back-up	Wood Joists	153.75	131.20	118.30	109.45	104.80	95.65	91.20	88.95	87.20
	Steel Joists	154.00	131.40	118.55	109.70	105.00	95.85	91.40	89.15	87.40
Glass and Metal Curtain Wall	Steel Frame	148.80	128.35	116.70	108.80	104.65	96.45	92.55	90.55	89.00
	R/Conc. Frame	152.35	131.90	120.25	112.35	108.15	100.00	96.10	94.10	92.55
Wood Siding	Wood Frame	126.10	108.60	98.65	92.10	88.60	81.80	78.60	76.95	75.70
Brick Veneer	Wood Frame	137.95	117.35	105.60	97.65	93.40	85.15	81.20	79.20	77.65
Perimeter Adj., Add or Deduct	Per 100 L.F.	25.45	15.90	10.60	8.00	6.35	3.65	2.55	2.00	1.55
Story Hgt. Adj., Add or Deduct	Per 1 Ft.	4.20	3.05	2.45	1.95	1.70	1.20	.95	.80	.65

For Basement, add $21.35 per square foot of basement area

The above costs were calculated using the basic specifications shown on the facing page. These costs should be adjusted where necessary for design alternatives and owner's requirements. Reported completed project costs, for this type of structure, range from $41.60 to $162.45 per S.F.

Common additives

Description	Unit	$ Cost
Clock System		
20 room	Each	12,700
50 room	Each	30,800
Closed Circuit Surveillance, One station		
Camera and monitor	Each	1375
For additional camera stations, add	Each	745
Directory Boards, Plastic, glass covered		
30" x 20"	Each	565
36" x 48"	Each	1025
Aluminum, 24" x 18"	Each	425
36" x 24"	Each	535
48" x 32"	Each	745
48" x 60"	Each	1600
Elevators, Hydraulic passenger, 2 stops		
1500# capacity	Each	42,225
2500# capacity	Each	43,425
3500# capacity	Each	47,225
Additional stop, add	Each	3650
Emergency Lighting, 25 watt, battery operated		
Lead battery	Each	289
Nickel cadmium	Each	655

Description	Unit	$ Cost
Smoke Detectors		
Ceiling type	Each	149
Duct type	Each	405
Sound System		
Amplifier, 250 watts	Each	1650
Speaker, ceiling or wall	Each	145
Trumpet	Each	271
TV Antenna, Master system, 12 outlet	Outlet	236
30 outlet	Outlet	151
100 outlet	Outlet	144

BUILDING TYPES

Important: See the Reference Section for Location Factors

Model costs calculated for a 3 story building with 12' story height and 20,000 square feet of floor area

				Unit	Unit Cost	Cost Per S.F.	% Of Sub-Total
1.0 Foundations							
	.1	Footings & Foundations	Poured concrete; strip and spread footings and 4' foundation wall	S.F. Ground	8.19	2.73	
	.4	Piles & Caissons	N/A	—	—	—	3.9%
	.9	Excavation & Backfill	Site preparation for slab and trench for foundation wall and footing	S.F. Ground	1.08	.36	
2.0 Substructure							
	.1	Slab on Grade	4" reinforced concrete with vapor barrier and granular base	S.F. Slab	3.32	1.11	1.4%
	.2	Special Substructures	N/A	—	—	—	
3.0 Superstructure							
	.1	Columns & Beams	Fireproofing; interior columns included in 3.5 and 3.7	L.F. Columns	23	1.83	
	.4	Structural Walls	N/A	—	—	—	
	.5	Elevated Floors	Open web steel joists, slab form, concrete, columns	S.F. Floor	8.41	5.61	13.4%
	.7	Roof	Metal deck, open web steel joists, columns	S.F. Roof	3.90	1.30	
	.9	Stairs	Concrete filled metal pan	Flight	5025	1.76	
4.0 Exterior Closure							
	.1	Walls	Face brick with concrete block backup _80% of wall_	S.F. Wall	21	10.91	
	.5	Exterior Wall Finishes	N/A	—	—	—	18.2%
	.6	Doors	Aluminum and glass, hollow metal	Each	2043	.62	
	.7	Windows & Glazed Walls	Aluminum outward projecting _20% of wall_	Each	493	2.78	
5.0 Roofing							
	.1	Roof Coverings	Built-up tar and gravel with flashing	S.F. Roof	2.79	.93	
	.7	Insulation	Perlite/EPS composite	S.F. Roof	1.32	.44	1.9%
	.8	Openings & Specialties	Gravel stop	S.F. Roof	6.92	.12	
6.0 Interior Construction							
	.1	Partitions	Gypsum board on metal studs, toilet partitions _20 S.F. Floor/L.F. Partition_	S.F. Partition	3.11	2.11	
	.4	Interior Doors	Single leaf hollow metal _200 S.F. Floor/Door_	Each	534	2.67	
	.5	Wall Finishes	60% vinyl wall covering, 40% paint	S.F. Surface	1.08	.86	
	.6	Floor Finishes	60% carpet, 30% vinyl composition tile, 10% ceramic tile	S.F. Floor	5.31	5.31	20.6%
	.7	Ceiling Finishes	Mineral fiber tile on concealed zee bars	S.F. Ceiling	3.63	3.63	
	.9	Interior Surface/Exterior Wall	Painted gypsum board on furring _80% of wall_	S.F. Wall	3.02	1.57	
7.0 Conveying							
	.1	Elevators	Two hydraulic passenger elevators	Each	67,000	6.70	8.5%
	.2	Special Conveyors	N/A	—	—	—	
8.0 Mechanical							
	.1	Plumbing	Toilet and service fixtures, supply and drainage _1 Fixture/1320 S.F. Floor_	Each	2125	1.61	
	.2	Fire Protection	Standpipes and hose systems	S.F. Floor	.60	.60	
	.3	Heating	Included in 8.4	—	—	—	17.8%
	.4	Cooling	Multizone unit gas heating, electric cooling	S.F. Floor	11.75	11.75	
	.5	Special Systems	N/A	—	—	—	
9.0 Electrical							
	.1	Service & Distribution	1000 ampere service, panel board and feeders	S.F. Floor	2.82	2.82	
	.2	Lighting & Power	Fluorescent fixtures, receptacles, switches, A.C. and misc. power	S.F. Floor	7.78	7.78	14.3%
	.4	Special Electrical	Alarm systems and emergency lighting	S.F. Floor	.61	.61	
11.0 Special Construction							
	.1	Specialties	N/A	—	—	—	0.0%
12.0 Site Work							
	.1	Earthwork	N/A	—	—	—	
	.3	Utilities	N/A	—	—	—	
	.5	Roads & Parking	N/A	—	—	—	0.0%
	.7	Site Improvements	N/A	—	—	—	
				Sub-Total		78.52	**100%**
		CONTRACTOR FEES (General Requirements: 10%, Overhead: 5%, Profit: 10%)			25%	19.63	
		ARCHITECT FEES			7%	6.85	
				Total Building Cost		**105.00**	

Costs per square foot of floor area

Exterior Wall	S.F. Area	20000	40000	60000	80000	100000	150000	200000	250000	300000
	L.F. Perimeter	260	360	400	420	460	520	600	640	700
Precast Concrete Panel	Steel Frame	121.50	105.70	97.50	92.75	90.40	86.55	84.95	83.50	82.70
	R/Conc. Frame	123.45	107.50	99.20	94.40	92.05	88.20	86.60	85.10	84.30
Face Brick with Concrete Block Back-up	Steel Frame	126.45	109.05	99.95	94.65	92.10	87.80	86.05	84.40	83.55
	R/Conc. Frame	128.05	110.65	101.55	96.25	93.70	89.40	87.60	86.00	85.10
Limestone Panel Concrete Block Back-up	Steel Frame	144.15	121.35	109.05	101.80	98.40	92.55	90.15	87.90	86.70
	R/Conc. Frame	145.75	122.90	110.65	103.40	99.95	94.10	91.70	89.45	88.30
Perimeter Adj., Add or Deduct	Per 100 L.F.	14.50	7.25	4.85	3.60	2.85	1.95	1.45	1.15	.95
Story Hgt. Adj., Add or Deduct	Per 1 Ft.	2.95	2.05	1.50	1.20	1.05	.80	.70	.60	.55
For Basement, add $ 23.05 per square foot of basement area										

The above costs were calculated using the basic specifications shown on the facing page. These costs should be adjusted where necessary for design alternatives and owner's requirements. Reported completed project costs, for this type of structure, range from $47.30 to $139.05 per S.F.

Common additives

Description	Unit	$ Cost
Clock System		
20 room	Each	12,700
50 room	Each	30,800
Closed Circuit Surveillance, One station		
Camera and monitor	Each	1375
For additional camera stations, add	Each	745
Directory Boards, Plastic, glass covered		
30" x 20"	Each	565
36" x 48"	Each	1025
Aluminum, 24" x 18"	Each	425
36" x 24"	Each	535
48" x 32"	Each	745
48" x 60"	Each	1600
Elevators, Electric passenger, 5 stops		
2000# capacity	Each	97,700
3500# capacity	Each	103,700
5000# capacity	Each	108,200
Additional stop, add	Each	5500
Emergency Lighting, 25 watt, battery operated		
Lead battery	Each	289
Nickel cadmium	Each	655

Description	Unit	$ Cost
Intercom System, 25 station capacity		
Master station	Each	2000
Intercom outlets	Each	126
Handset	Each	335
Smoke Detectors		
Ceiling type	Each	149
Duct type	Each	405
Sound System		
Amplifier, 250 watts	Each	1650
Speaker, ceiling or wall	Each	145
Trumpet	Each	271
TV Antenna, Master system, 12 oulet	Outlet	236
30 outlet	Outlet	151
100 outlet	Outlet	144

Important: See the Reference Section for Location Factors

Model costs calculated for an 8 story building with 12' story height and 80,000 square feet of floor area.

Office, 5-10 Story

			Unit	Unit Cost	Cost Per S.F.	% Of Sub-Total
1.0 Foundations						
.1	Footings & Foundations	Poured concrete; strip and spread footings and 4' foundation wall	S.F. Ground	10.72	1.34	
.4	Piles & Caissons	N/A	—	—	—	2.1%
.9	Excavation & Backfill	Site preparation for slab and trench for foundation wall and footing	S.F. Ground	1.17	.15	
2.0 Substructure						
.1	Slab on Grade	4" reinforced concrete with vapor barrier and granular base	S.F. Slab	3.32	.41	0.6%
.2	Special Substructures	N/A	—	—	—	
3.0 Superstructure						
.1	Columns & Beams	Steel columns w/ fireproofing	L.F. Columns	74	2.48	
.4	Structural Walls	N/A	—	—	—	
.5	Elevated Floors	Concrete slab with metal deck and beams	S.F. Floor	10.36	9.06	18.7%
.7	Roof	Metal deck, open web steel joists, interior columns	S.F. Roof	3.83	.48	
.9	Stairs	Concrete filled metal pan	Flight	5025	1.07	
4.0 Exterior Closure						
.1	Walls	Precast concrete panels _80% of wall_	S.F. Wall	17.61	7.10	
.5	Exterior Wall Finishes	N/A	—	—	—	
.6	Doors	Double aluminum and glass doors and entrance with transoms	Each	2385	.15	14.0%
.7	Windows & Glazed Walls	Vertical pivoted steel _20% of wall_	Each	384	2.58	
5.0 Roofing						
.1	Roof Coverings	Built-up tar and gravel with flashing	S.F. Roof	2.56	.32	
.7	Insulation	Perlite/EPS composite	S.F. Roof	1.32	.17	0.7%
.8	Openings & Specialties	N/A	—	—	—	
6.0 Interior Construction						
.1	Partitions	Gypsum board on metal studs, toilet partitions _30 S.F. Floor/L.F. Partition_	S.F. Partition	3.11	1.62	
.4	Interior Doors	Single leaf hollow metal _400 S.F. Floor/Door_	Each	534	1.34	
.5	Wall Finishes	60% vinyl wall covering, 40% paint	S.F. Surface	1.06	.71	
.6	Floor Finishes	60% carpet, 30% vinyl composition tile, 10% ceramic tile	S.F. Floor	5.31	5.31	19.8%
.7	Ceiling Finishes	Mineral fiber tile on concealed zee bars	S.F. Ceiling	3.63	3.63	
.9	Interior Surface/Exterior Wall	Painted gypsum board on furring _80% of wall_	S.F. Wall	3.02	1.22	
7.0 Conveying						
.1	Elevators	Four geared passenger elevators	Each	155,800	7.79	11.1%
.2	Special Conveyors	N/A	—	—	—	
8.0 Mechanical						
.1	Plumbing	Toilet and service fixtures, supply and drainage _1 Fixture/1370 S.F. Floor_	Each	2000	1.46	
.2	Fire Protection	Standpipes and hose systems	S.F. Floor	.17	.17	
.3	Heating	Included in 8.4	—	—	—	19.2%
.4	Cooling	Multizone unit gas heating, electric cooling	S.F. Floor	11.75	11.75	
.5	Special Systems	N/A	—	—	—	
9.0 Electrical						
.1	Service & Distribution	1600 ampere service, panel board and feeders	S.F. Floor	1.05	1.05	
.2	Lighting & Power	Fluorescent fixtures, receptacles, switches, A.C. and misc. power	S.F. Floor	7.71	7.71	13.8%
.4	Special Electrical	Alarm systems and emergency lighting	S.F. Floor	.91	.91	
11.0 Special Construction						
.1	Specialties	N/A	—	—	—	0.0%
12.0 Site Work						
.1	Earthwork	N/A	—	—	—	
.3	Utilities	N/A	—	—	—	
.5	Roads & Parking	N/A	—	—	—	0.0%
.7	Site Improvements	N/A	—	—	—	
			Sub-Total		69.98	100%
	CONTRACTOR FEES (General Requirements: 10%, Overhead: 5%, Profit: 10%)			25%	17.50	
	ARCHITECT FEES			6%	5.27	
			Total Building Cost		92.75	

BUILDING TYPES

BUILDING TYPES

Costs per square foot of floor area

Exterior Wall	S.F. Area	120000	145000	170000	200000	230000	260000	400000	600000	800000
	L.F. Perimeter	420	450	470	490	510	530	600	730	820
Double Glazed Heat Absorbing Tinted Plate Glass Panels	Steel Frame	102.50	98.75	95.65	92.85	90.75	**89.15**	84.35	81.80	80.20
	R/Conc. Frame	103.40	98.80	95.10	91.75	89.30	87.40	81.85	78.75	76.90
Face Brick with Concrete Block Back-up	Steel Frame	102.05	98.05	94.85	92.00	89.85	88.25	83.50	80.85	79.30
	R/Conc. Frame	97.45	93.45	90.35	87.50	85.40	83.85	79.15	76.50	75.00
Precast Concrete Panel With Exposed Aggregate	Steel Frame	99.45	95.70	92.80	90.15	88.20	86.70	82.35	79.95	78.55
	R/Conc. Frame	95.05	91.40	88.50	85.90	84.00	82.55	78.25	75.85	74.45
Perimeter Adj., Add or Deduct	Per 100 L.F.	6.05	4.95	4.25	3.60	3.10	2.80	1.80	1.20	.85
Story Hgt. Adj., Add or Deduct	Per 1 Ft.	2.45	2.15	1.90	1.70	1.50	1.40	1.05	.85	.70

For Basement, add $22.55 per square foot of basement area

The above costs were calculated using the basic specifications shown on the facing page. These costs should be adjusted where necessary for design alternatives and owner's requirements. Reported completed project costs, for this type of structure, range from $59.60 to $145.30 per S.F.

Common additives

Description	Unit	$ Cost	Description	Unit	$ Cost
Clock System			Escalators, Metal		
20 room	Each	12,700	32" wide, 10' story height	Each	88,400
50 room	Each	30,800	20' story height	Each	102,500
Directory Boards, Plastic, glass covered			48" wide, 10' story height	Each	92,900
30" x 20"	Each	565	20' story height	Each	107,000
36" x 48"	Each	1025	Glass		
Aluminum, 24" x 18"	Each	425	32" wide, 10' story height	Each	86,900
36" x 24"	Each	535	20' story height	Each	102,500
48" x 32"	Each	745	48" wide, 10' story height	Each	92,900
48" x 60"	Each	1600	20' story height	Each	107,000
Elevators, Electric passenger, 10 stops			Smoke Detectors		
3000# capacity	Each	210,500	Ceiling type	Each	149
4000# capacity	Each	212,500	Duct type	Each	405
5000# capacity	Each	216,500	Sound System		
Additional stop, add	Each	5500	Amplifier, 250 watts	Each	1650
Emergency Lighting, 25 watt, battery operated			Speaker, ceiling or wall	Each	145
Lead battery	Each	289	Trumpet	Each	271
Nickel cadmium	Each	655	TV Antenna, Master system, 12 oulet	Outlet	236
			30 oulet	Outlet	151
			100 outlet	Outlet	144

Important: See the Reference Section for Location Factors

Model costs calculated for a 16 story building with 10' story height and 260,000 square feet of floor area

				Unit	Unit Cost	Cost Per S.F.	% Of Sub-Total
1.0 Foundations							
.1	Footings & Foundations	Poured concrete; strip and spread footings and 4' foundation wall		S.F. Ground	13.44	.84	1.4%
.4	Piles & Caissons	N/A		—	—	—	
.9	Excavation & Backfill	Site preparation for slab and trench for foundation wall and footing		S.F. Ground	1.17	.07	
2.0 Substructure							
.1	Slab on Grade	4" reinforced concrete with vapor barrier and granular base		S.F. Slab	3.32	.21	0.3%
.2	Special Substructures	N/A		—	—	—	
3.0 Superstructure							
.1	Columns & Beams	Steel columns with fireproofing		L.F. Column	112	1.59	23.9%
.4	Structural Walls	N/A		—	—	—	
.5	Elevated Floors	Concrete slab, metal deck, beams		S.F. Floor	14.30	13.41	
.7	Roof	Metal deck, open web steel joists, beams, columns		S.F. Roof	4.52	.28	
.9	Stairs	Concrete filled metal pan		Flight	5975	.80	
4.0 Exterior Closure							
.1	Walls	N/A		—	—	—	15.3%
.5	Exterior Wall Finishes	N/A		—	—	—	
.6	Doors	Double aluminum & glass doors		Each	3660	.39	
.7	Windows & Glazed Walls	Double glazed heat absorbing, tinted plate glass wall panels	100% of wall	S.F. Wall	30	9.92	
5.0 Roofing							
.1	Roof Coverings	Single ply membrane, fully adhered		S.F. Roof	2.56	.16	0.4%
.7	Insulation	Perlite/EPS composite		S.F. Roof	1.32	.08	
.8	Openings & Specialties	N/A		—	—	—	
6.0 Interior Construction							
.1	Partitions	Gypsum board on metal studs, toilet partitions	30 S.F. Floor/L.F. Partition	S.F. Partition	3.11	1.17	17.6%
.4	Interior Doors	Single leaf hollow metal	400 S.F. Floor/Door	Each	534	1.34	
.5	Wall Finishes	60% vinyl wall covering, 40% paint		S.F. Surface	1.07	.57	
.6	Floor Finishes	60% carpet tile, 30% vinyl composition tile, 10% ceramic tile		S.F. Floor	4.31	4.31	
.7	Ceiling Finishes	Mineral fiber tile on concealed zee bars		S.F. Ceiling	3.63	3.63	
.9	Interior Surface/Exterior Wall	Painted drywall on metal furring	80% of wall	S.F. Wall	3.02	.79	
7.0 Conveying							
.1	Elevators	Four geared passenger elevators		Each	230,750	3.55	5.3%
.2	Special Conveyors	N/A		—	—	—	
8.0 Mechanical							
.1	Plumbing	Toilet and service fixtures, supply and drainage	1 Fixture/1345 S.F. Floor	Each	1116	.83	22.9%
.2	Fire Protection	Standpipes and hose systems and sprinklers, light hazard		S.F. Floor	2.70	2.70	
.3	Heating	Oil fired hot water		S.F. Floor	2.93	2.93	
.4	Cooling	Chilled water, fan coil units		S.F. Floor	9.02	9.02	
.5	Special Systems	N/A		—	—	—	
9.0 Electrical							
.1	Service & Distribution	2400 ampere service, panel board and feeders		S.F. Floor	.65	.65	12.9%
.2	Lighting & Power	Fluorescent fixtures, receptacles, switches, A.C. and misc. power		S.F. Floor	7.64	7.64	
.4	Special Electrical	Alarm systems and emergency lighting		S.F. Floor	.39	.39	
11.0 Special Construction							
.1	Specialties	N/A		—	—	—	0.0%
12.0 Site Work							
.1	Earthwork	N/A		—	—	—	0.0%
.3	Utilities	N/A		—	—	—	
.5	Roads & Parking	N/A		—	—	—	
.7	Site Improvements	N/A		—	—	—	
				Sub-Total		67.27	100%
	CONTRACTOR FEES (General Requirements: 10%, Overhead: 5%, Profit: 10%)				25%	16.82	
	ARCHITECT FEES				6%	5.06	
				Total Building Cost		89.15	

BUILDING TYPES

173

BUILDING TYPES

Costs per square foot of floor area

Exterior Wall	S.F. Area	7000	9000	11000	13000	15000	17000	19000	21000	23000
	L.F. Perimeter	240	280	303	325	354	372	397	422	447
Limestone with Concrete Block Back-up	Bearing Walls	156.40	146.15	137.30	131.15	127.25	123.30	120.80	118.75	117.00
	R/Conc. Frame	164.50	154.75	146.55	140.80	137.20	133.55	131.20	129.25	127.70
Face Brick with Concrete Block Back-up	Bearing Walls	137.90	129.25	122.30	117.45	114.35	111.30	109.25	107.65	106.30
	R/Conc. Frame	152.50	143.85	136.90	132.05	128.95	125.90	123.85	122.20	120.85
Decorative Concrete Block	Bearing Walls	131.05	123.00	116.80	112.45	109.60	106.90	105.10	103.60	102.40
	R/Conc. Frame	145.65	137.60	131.40	127.05	124.20	121.50	119.70	118.20	117.00
Perimeter Adj., Add or Deduct	Per 100 L.F.	20.80	16.15	13.25	11.20	9.70	8.60	7.70	6.95	6.35
Story Hgt. Adj., Add or Deduct	Per 1 Ft.	3.65	3.30	2.95	2.65	2.55	2.35	2.25	2.15	2.10
For Basement, add $16.85 per square foot of basement area										

The above costs were calculated using the basic specifications shown on the facing page. These costs should be adjusted where necessary for design alternatives and owner's requirements. Reported completed project costs, for this type of structure, range from $69.45 to $178.40 per S.F.

Common additives

Description	Unit	$ Cost		Description	Unit	$ Cost
Cells Prefabricated, 5'-6' wide,				Lockers, Steel, Single tier, 60" to 72"	Opening	125 - 220
7'-8" high, 7'-8" deep	Each	9500		2 tier, 60" or 72" total	Opening	70 - 119
Elevators, Hydraulic passenger, 2 stops				5 tier, box lockers	Opening	40 - 60
1500# capacity	Each	42,225		Locker bench, lam. maple top only	L.F.	18.05
2500# capacity	Each	43,425		Pedestals, steel pipe	Each	58
3500# capacity	Each	47,225		Safe, Office type, 4 hour rating		
Emergency Lighting, 25 watt, battery operated				30" x 18" x 18"	Each	3125
Lead battery	Each	289		62" x 33" x 20"	Each	6775
Nickel cadmium	Each	655		Shooting Range, Incl. bullet traps,		
Flagpoles, Complete				target provisions, and contols,		
Aluminum, 20' high	Each	1075		not incl. structural shell	Each	23,800
40' high	Each	2675		Smoke Detectors		
70' high	Each	8250		Ceiling type	Each	149
Fiberglass, 23' high	Each	1400		Duct type	Each	405
39'-5" high	Each	2950		Sound System		
59' high	Each	7300		Amplifier, 250 watts	Each	1650
				Speaker, ceiling or wall	Each	145
				Trumpet	Each	271

Important: See the Reference Section for Location Factors

Model costs calculated for a 2 story building with 12' story height and 11,000 square feet of floor area

				Unit	Unit Cost	Cost Per S.F.	% Of Sub-Total
1.0 Foundations							
.1	Footings & Foundations	Poured concrete; strip and spread footings and 4' foundation wall		S.F. Ground	5.54	2.77	
.4	Piles & Caissons	N/A		—	—	—	3.3%
.9	Excavation & Backfill	Site preparation for slab and trench for foundation wall and footing		S.F. Ground	1.17	.58	
2.0 Substructure							
.1	Slab on Grade	4" reinforced concrete with vapor barrier and granular base		S.F. Slab	3.32	1.66	1.6%
.2	Special Substructures	N/A		—	—	—	
3.0 Superstructure							
.1	Columns & Beams	N/A		—	—	—	
.4	Structural Walls	N/A		—	—	—	
.5	Elevated Floors	Open web steel joists, slab form, concrete		S.F. Floor	7.02	3.51	5.9%
.7	Roof	Metal deck on open web steel joists		S.F. Roof	2.71	1.36	
.9	Stairs	Concrete filled metal pan		Flight	5975	1.09	
4.0 Exterior Closure							
.1	Walls	Limestone with concrete block backup	80% of wall	S.F. Wall	34	18.22	
.5	Exterior Wall Finishes	N/A		—	—	—	25.7%
.6	Doors	Hollow metal		Each	1489	1.08	
.7	Windows & Glazed Walls	Metal horizontal sliding	20% of wall	Each	750	6.61	
5.0 Roofing							
.1	Roof Coverings	Built-up tar and gravel with flashing		S.F. Roof	2.78	1.39	
.7	Insulation	Perlite/EPS composite		S.F. Roof	1.32	.66	2.2%
.8	Openings & Specialties	Gravel stop		L.F. Perimeter	6.40	.18	
6.0 Interior Construction							
.1	Partitions	Concrete block, toilet partitions	20 S.F. Floor/L.F. Partition	S.F. Partition	5.90	3.42	
.4	Interior Doors	Single leaf kalamein fire door	200 S.F. Floor/Door	Each	534	2.67	
.5	Wall Finishes	90% paint, 10% ceramic tile		S.F. Surface	1.45	1.45	15.9%
.6	Floor Finishes	70% vinyl composition tile, 20% carpet tile, 10% ceramic tile		S.F. Floor	3.69	3.69	
.7	Ceiling Finishes	Mineral fiber tile on concealed zee bars		S.F. Ceiling	3.63	3.63	
.9	Interior Surface/Exterior Wall	Paint	80% of wall	S.F. Wall	2.12	1.12	
7.0 Conveying							
.1	Elevators	One hydraulic passenger elevator		Each	51,150	4.65	4.6%
.2	Special Conveyors	N/A		—	—	—	
8.0 Mechanical							
.1	Plumbing	Toilet and service fixtures, supply and drainage	1 Fixture/580 S.F. Floor	Each	2459	4.24	
.2	Fire Protection	Wet pipe sprinkler system		S.F. Floor	1.88	1.88	
.3	Heating	Oil fired hot water, wall fin radiation		S.F. Floor	6.39	6.39	20.0%
.4	Cooling	Split systems with air cooled condensing units		S.F. Floor	7.62	7.62	
.5	Special Systems	N/A		—	—	—	
9.0 Electrical							
.1	Service & Distribution	400 ampere service, panel board and feeders		S.F. Floor	1.20	1.20	
.2	Lighting & Power	Fluorescent fixtures, receptacles, switches, A.C. and misc. power		S.F. Floor	7.18	7.18	9.0%
.4	Special Electrical	Alarm systems and emergency lighting		S.F. Floor	.67	.67	
11.0 Special Construction							
.1	Specialties	Lockers, detention rooms, cells		S.F. Floor	11.85	11.85	11.8%
12.0 Site Work							
.1	Earthwork	N/A		—	—	—	
.3	Utilities	N/A		—	—	—	0.0%
.5	Roads & Parking	N/A		—	—	—	
.7	Site Improvements	N/A		—	—	—	
				Sub-Total		100.77	**100%**
	CONTRACTOR FEES (General Requirements: 10%, Overhead: 5%, Profit: 10%)			25%		25.19	
	ARCHITECT FEES			9%		11.34	
				Total Building Cost		137.30	

Costs per square foot of floor area

Exterior Wall	S.F. Area	5000	7000	9000	11000	13000	15000	17000	19000	21000
	L.F. Perimeter	300	380	420	486	468	513	540	580	620
Face Brick with Concrete Block Back-up	Steel Frame	104.50	98.45	92.50	90.10	84.55	83.05	81.20	80.20	79.40
	Bearing Walls	102.95	96.95	90.95	88.55	83.00	81.50	79.70	78.65	77.85
Limestone with Concrete Block Back-up	Steel Frame	116.75	109.60	102.00	99.10	91.90	90.05	87.70	86.45	85.40
	Bearing Walls	114.65	107.45	99.95	97.00	89.80	87.95	85.60	84.35	83.30
Decorative Concrete Block	Steel Frame	97.45	92.15	87.05	84.90	80.35	79.05	77.50	76.65	75.95
	Bearing Walls	95.90	90.60	85.50	83.35	78.80	77.50	75.95	75.10	74.40
Perimeter Adj., Add or Deduct	Per 100 L.F.	11.90	8.55	6.60	5.45	4.60	3.95	3.50	3.15	2.85
Story Hgt. Adj., Add or Deduct	Per 1 Ft.	1.90	1.65	1.45	1.35	1.10	1.05	1.00	.95	.95

For Basement, add $17.65 per square foot of basement area

The above costs were calculated using the basic specifications shown on the facing page. These costs should be adjusted where necessary for design alternatives and owner's requirements. Reported completed project costs, for this type of structure, range from $56.80 to $146.70 per S.F.

Common additives

Description	Unit	$ Cost
Closed Circuit Surveillance, One station		
Camera and monitor	Each	1375
For additional camera stations, add	Each	745
Emergency Lighting, 25 watt, battery operated		
Lead battery	Each	289
Nickel cadmium	Each	655
Flagpoles, Complete		
Aluminum, 20' high	Each	1075
40' high	Each	2675
70' high	Each	8250
Fiberglass, 23' high	Each	1400
39'-5" high	Each	2950
59' high	Each	7300

Description	Unit	$ Cost
Mail Boxes, Horizontal, key lock, 15" x 6" x 5"	Each	44
Double 15" x 12" x 5"	Each	78
Quadruple 15" x 12" x 10"	Each	137
Vertical, 6" x 5" x 15", aluminum	Each	36
Bronze	Each	58
Steel, enameled	Each	39
Scales, Dial type, 5 ton cap.		
8' x 6' platform	Each	8225
9' x 7' platform	Each	11,200
Smoke Detectors		
Ceiling type	Each	149
Duct type	Each	405

Important: See the Reference Section for Location Factors

Model costs calculated for a 1 story building with 14' story height and 13,000 square feet of floor area

				Unit	Unit Cost	Cost Per S.F.	% Of Sub-Total
1.0 Foundations							
.1	Footings & Foundations	Poured concrete; strip and spread footings and 4' foundation wall		S.F. Ground	3.65	3.65	
.4	Piles & Caissons	N/A		—	—	—	7.8%
.9	Excavation & Backfill	Site preparation for slab and trench for foundation wall and footing		S.F. Ground	1.17	1.17	
2.0 Substructure							
.1	Slab on Grade	4" reinforced concrete with vapor barrier and granular base		S.F. Slab	3.32	3.32	5.3%
.2	Special Substructures	N/A		—	—	—	
3.0 Superstructure							
.1	Columns & Beams	Fireproofing, steel columns included in 3.7		L.F. Column	22	.07	
.4	Structural Walls	N/A		—	—	—	
.5	Elevated Floors	N/A		—	—	—	8.6%
.7	Roof	Metal deck, open web steel joists, columns		S.F. Roof	5.27	5.27	
.9	Stairs	N/A		—	—	—	
4.0 Exterior Closure							
.1	Walls	Face brick with concrete block backup	80% of wall	S.F. Wall	21	8.49	
.5	Exterior Wall Finishes	N/A		—	—	—	18.3%
.6	Doors	Double aluminum & glass, single aluminum, hollow metal, steel overhead		Each	1547	.71	
.7	Windows & Glazed Walls	Double strength window glass	20% of wall	Each	493	2.16	
5.0 Roofing							
.1	Roof Coverings	Built-up tar and gravel with flashing		S.F. Roof	2.40	2.40	
.7	Insulation	Perlite/EPS composite		S.F. Roof	1.32	1.32	6.4%
.8	Openings & Specialties	Gravel stop		L.F. Perimeter	6.40	.23	
6.0 Interior Construction							
.1	Partitions	Concrete block, toilet partitions	15 S.F. Floor/L.F. Partition	S.F. Partition	5.90	5.11	
.4	Interior Doors	Single leaf hollow metal	150 S.F. Floor/Door	Each	534	3.56	
.5	Wall Finishes	Paint		S.F. Surface	1.00	1.60	
.6	Floor Finishes	50% vinyl tile, 50% paint		S.F. Floor	2.06	2.06	22.7%
.7	Ceiling Finishes	Mineral fiber tile on concealed zee bars	25% of area	S.F. Ceiling	3.63	.91	
.9	Interior Surface/Exterior Wall	Paint	80% of wall	S.F. Wall	2.12	.85	
7.0 Conveying							
.1	Elevators	N/A		—	—	—	0.0%
.2	Special Conveyors	N/A		—	—	—	
8.0 Mechanical							
.1	Plumbing	Toilet and service fixtures, supply and drainage	1 Fixture/1180 S.F. Floor	Each	2017	1.71	
.2	Fire Protection	Wet pipe sprinkler system		S.F. Floor	1.69	1.69	
.3	Heating	Included in 8.4		—	—	—	16.9%
.4	Cooling	Single zone, gas heating, electric cooling		S.F. Floor	7.11	7.11	
.5	Special Systems	N/A		—	—	—	
9.0 Electrical							
.1	Service & Distribution	600 ampere service, panel board and feeders		S.F. Floor	1.90	1.90	
.2	Lighting & Power	Fluorescent fixtures, receptacles, switches, A.C. and misc. power		S.F. Floor	5.83	5.83	13.1%
.4	Special Electrical	Alarm systems and emergency lighting		S.F. Floor	.39	.39	
11.0 Special Construction							
.1	Specialties	Cabinets, lockers, shelving		S.F. Floor	.55	.55	0.9%
12.0 Site Work							
.1	Earthwork	N/A		—	—	—	
.3	Utilities	N/A		—	—	—	
.5	Roads & Parking	N/A		—	—	—	0.0%
.7	Site Improvements	N/A		—	—	—	
				Sub-Total		62.06	**100%**
	CONTRACTOR FEES (General Requirements: 10%, Overhead: 5%, Profit: 10%)				25%	15.52	
	ARCHITECT FEES				9%	6.97	
				Total Building Cost		**84.55**	

BUILDING TYPES

177

Costs per square foot of floor area

Exterior Wall	S.F. Area	5000	10000	15000	21000	25000	30000	40000	50000	60000
	L.F. Perimeter	287	400	500	600	700	700	834	900	1000
Face Brick with Concrete Block Back-up	Steel Frame	162.95	137.45	128.05	121.70	120.55	115.30	112.15	108.90	107.30
	Bearing Walls	158.80	134.55	125.60	119.50	118.45	113.30	110.20	107.05	105.45
Concrete Block	Steel Frame	141.25	122.00	115.05	110.50	109.50	106.10	103.90	101.75	100.65
Brick Veneer	Steel Frame	157.75	133.50	124.65	118.70	117.55	112.80	109.90	106.90	105.45
Galvanized Steel Siding	Steel Frame	133.30	116.30	110.20	106.30	105.40	102.60	100.70	98.90	97.95
Metal Sandwich Panel	Steel Frame	135.30	117.85	111.55	107.50	106.60	103.70	101.75	99.90	98.95
Perimeter Adj., Add or Deduct	Per 100 L.F.	20.10	10.05	6.75	4.80	4.00	3.35	2.50	2.00	1.65
Story Hgt. Adj., Add or Deduct	Per 1 Ft.	4.10	2.85	2.40	2.05	2.00	1.70	1.50	1.25	1.20
For Basement, add $17.05 per square foot of basement area										

The above costs were calculated using the basic specifications shown on the facing page. These costs should be adjusted where necessary for design alternatives and owner's requirements. Reported completed project costs, for this type of structure, range from $53.60 to $167.10 per S.F.

Common additives

Description	Unit	$ Cost	Description	Unit	$ Cost
Bar, Front Bar	L.F.	285	Lockers, Steel, single tier, 60" or 72"	Opening	125 - 220
Back Bar	L.F.	227	2 tier, 60" or 72" total	Opening	70 - 119
Booth, Upholstered, custom straight	L.F.	144 - 265	5 tier, box lockers	Opening	40 - 60
"L" or "U" shaped	L.F.	149 - 252	Locker bench, lam. maple top only	L.F.	18.05
Bleachers, Telescoping, manual			Pedestals, steel pipe	Each	58
To 15 tier	Seat	79 - 109	Sauna, Prefabricated, complete		
21-30 tier	Seat	170 - 205	6' x 4'	Each	4075
Courts			6' x 9'	Each	5350
Ceiling	Court	5525	8' x 8'	Each	6300
Floor	Court	9650	8' x 10'	Each	6950
Walls	Court	19,200	10' x 12'	Each	9125
Emergency Lighting, 25 watt, battery operated			Sound System		
Lead battery	Each	289	Amplifier, 250 watts	Each	1650
Nickel cadmium	Each	655	Speaker, ceiling or wall	Each	145
Kitchen Equipment			Trumpet	Each	271
Broiler	Each	4050	Steam Bath, Complete, to 140 C.F.	Each	1275
Cooler, 6 ft. long, reach-in	Each	3200	To 300 C.F.	Each	1450
Dishwasher, 10-12 racks per hr.	Each	3050	To 800 C.F.	Each	4625
Food warmer, counter 1.2 KW	Each	715	To 2500 C.F.	Each	4925
Freezer, reach-in, 44 C.F.	Each	8325			
Ice cube maker, 50 lb. per day	Each	1800			

Important: See the Reference Section for Location Factors

Model costs calculated for a 2 story building with 12' story height and 30,000 square feet of floor area

Racquetball Court

				Unit	Unit Cost	Cost Per S.F.	% Of Sub-Total
1.0 Foundations							
.1	Footings & Foundations	Poured concrete; strip and spread footings and 4' foundation wall		S.F. Ground	4.62	2.31	
.4	Piles & Caissons	N/A		—	—	—	3.6%
.9	Excavation & Backfill	Site preparation for slab and trench for foundation wall and footing		S.F. Ground	1.17	.76	
2.0 Substructure							
.1	Slab on Grade	5" reinforced concrete with vapor barrier and granular base		S.F. Slab	4.18	2.72	3.2%
.2	Special Substructures	N/A		—	—	—	
3.0 Superstructure							
.1	Columns & Beams	Steel columns included in 3.5 and 3.7		—	—	—	
.4	Structural Walls	N/A		—	—	—	
.5	Elevated Floors	Open web steel joists, slab form, concrete, columns	50% of area	S.F. Floor	14.81	5.18	9.9%
.7	Roof	Metal deck on open web steel joists, columns		S.F. Roof	5.54	2.77	
.9	Stairs	Concrete filled metal pan		Flight	5025	.50	
4.0 Exterior Closure							
.1	Walls	Face brick with concrete block backup	95% of wall	S.F. Wall	21	11.25	
.5	Exterior Wall Finishes	N/A		—	—	—	15.7%
.6	Doors	Aluminum and glass and hollow metal		Each	1963	.27	
.7	Windows & Glazed Walls	Storefront	5% of wall	S.F. Window	67	1.90	
5.0 Roofing							
.1	Roof Coverings	Built-up tar and gravel with flashing		S.F. Roof	2.96	1.48	
.7	Insulation	Perlite/EPS composite		S.F. Roof	1.32	.86	3.0%
.8	Openings & Specialties	Gravel stop and hatches		S.F. Roof	.38	.19	
6.0 Interior Construction							
.1	Partitions	Concrete block, gypsum board on metal studs	25 S.F. Floor/L.F. Partition	S.F. Partition	5.90	2.42	
.4	Interior Doors	Single leaf hollow metal	810 S.F. Floor/Door	Each	534	.66	
.5	Wall Finishes	Paint		S.F. Surface	.94	.75	
.6	Floor Finishes	80% carpet tile, 20% ceramic tile	50% of floor area	S.F. Floor	5.08	2.54	12.0%
.7	Ceiling Finishes	Mineral fiber tile on concealed zee bars	60% of area	S.F. Ceiling	3.63	2.18	
.9	Interior Surface/Exterior Wall	Painted gypsum board on furring	95% of wall	S.F. Wall	3.02	1.69	
7.0 Conveying							
.1	Elevators	N/A		—	—	—	0.0%
.2	Special Conveyors	N/A		—	—	—	
8.0 Mechanical							
.1	Plumbing	Kitchen, bathroom and service fixtures, supply and drainage	1 Fixture/1000 S.F. Floor	Each	3610	3.61	
.2	Fire Protection	Sprinklers, light hazard		S.F. Floor	.25	.25	
.3	Heating	Included in 8.4		—	—	—	28.3%
.4	Cooling	Multizone unit, gas heating, electric cooling		S.F. Floor	20	20.30	
.5	Special Systems	N/A		—	—	—	
9.0 Electrical							
.1	Service & Distribution	400 ampere service, panel board and feeders		S.F. Floor	.54	.54	
.2	Lighting & Power	Fluorescent and high intensity discharge fixtures, receptacles, switches, A.C. and misc. power		S.F. Floor	8.89	8.89	11.3%
.4	Special Electrical	Alarm systems and emergency lighting		S.F. Floor	.25	.25	
11.0 Special Construction							
.1	Specialties	Courts, sauna baths		S.F. Floor	11.14	11.14	13.0%
12.0 Site Work							
.1	Earthwork	N/A		—	—	—	
.3	Utilities	N/A		—	—	—	
.5	Roads & Parking	N/A		—	—	—	0.0%
.7	Site Improvements	N/A		—	—	—	
				Sub-Total		85.41	100%
	CONTRACTOR FEES (General Requirements: 10%, Overhead: 5%, Profit: 10%)				25%	21.35	
	ARCHITECT FEES				8%	8.54	
				Total Building Cost		**115.30**	

BUILDING TYPES

Costs per square foot of floor area

Exterior Wall	S.F. Area	5000	6000	7000	8000	9000	10000	11000	12000	13000
	L.F. Perimeter	286	320	353	386	397	425	454	460	486
Face Brick with Concrete Block Back-up	Steel Joists	118.80	116.00	113.90	112.30	109.75	108.60	107.75	106.00	105.30
	Wood Joists	116.15	113.20	111.05	109.35	106.70	105.55	104.65	102.80	102.10
Stucco on Concrete Block	Steel Joists	114.50	111.95	110.10	108.65	106.40	105.40	104.65	103.10	102.45
	Wood Joists	109.00	106.55	104.70	103.30	101.20	100.20	99.45	98.00	97.40
Limestone with Concrete Block Back-up	Steel Joists	132.35	128.60	125.80	123.65	120.15	118.65	117.50	115.05	114.10
	Wood Joists	126.80	123.15	120.40	118.35	114.95	113.45	112.35	109.95	109.05
Perimeter Adj., Add or Deduct	Per 100 L.F.	10.95	9.15	7.80	6.85	6.10	5.50	4.95	4.55	4.20
Story Hgt. Adj., Add or Deduct	Per 1 Ft.	1.90	1.80	1.70	1.65	1.50	1.45	1.40	1.30	1.25
For Basement, add $17.90 per square foot of basement area										

The above costs were calculated using the basic specifications shown on the facing page. These costs should be adjusted where necessary for design alternatives and owner's requirements. Reported completed project costs, for this type of structure, range from $46.80 to $144.80 per S.F.

Common additives

Description	Unit	$ Cost	Description	Unit	$ Cost
Carrels Hardwood	Each	725 - 940	Lockers, Steel, single tier, 60" to 72"	Opening	125 - 220
Emergency Lighting, 25 watt, battery operated			2 tier, 60" to 72" total	Opening	70 - 119
Lead battery	Each	289	5 tier, box lockers	Opening	40 - 60
Nickel cadmium	Each	655	Locker bench, lam. maple top only	L.F.	18.05
Flagpoles, Complete			Pedestals, steel pipe	Each	58
Aluminum, 20' high	Each	1075	Seating		
40' high	Each	2675	Auditorium chair, all veneer	Each	166
70' high	Each	8250	Veneer back, padded seat	Each	201
Fiberglass, 23' high	Each	1400	Upholstered, spring seat	Each	203
39'-5" high	Each	2950	Classroom, movable chair & desk	Set	65 - 120
59' high	Each	7300	Lecture hall, pedestal type	Each	152 - 470
Gym Floor, Incl. sleepers and finish, maple	S.F.	9.75	Smoke Detectors		
Intercom System, 25 Station capacity			Ceiling type	Each	149
Master station	Each	2000	Duct type	Each	405
Intercom outlets	Each	126	Sound System		
Handset	Each	335	Amplifier, 250 watts	Each	1650
			Speaker, ceiling or wall	Each	145
			Trumpet	Each	271
			Swimming Pools, Complete, gunite	S.F.	47 - 57

BUILDING TYPES

Important: See the Reference Section for Location Factors

Model costs calculated for a 1 story building with 12' story height and 10,000 square feet of floor area

				Unit	Unit Cost	Cost Per S.F.	% Of Sub-Total
1.0 Foundations							
.1	Footings & Foundations	Poured concrete; strip and spread footings and 4' foundation wall		S.F. Ground	3.71	3.71	6.1%
.4	Piles & Caissons	N/A		—	—	—	
.9	Excavation & Backfill	Site preparation for slab and trench for foundation wall and footing		S.F. Ground	1.17	1.17	
2.0 Substructure							
.1	Slab on Grade	4" reinforced concrete with vapor barrier and granular base		S.F. Slab	3.32	3.32	4.2%
.2	Special Substructures	N/A		—	—	—	
3.0 Superstructure							
.1	Columns & Beams	Interior columns included in 3.7		—	—	—	6.2%
.4	Structural Walls	N/A		—	—	—	
.5	Elevated Floors	N/A		—	—	—	
.7	Roof	Metal deck, open web steel joists, beams, interior columns		S.F. Roof	4.95	4.95	
.9	Stairs	N/A		—	—	—	
4.0 Exterior Closure							
.1	Walls	Face brick with concrete block backup	85% of wall	S.F. Wall	21	9.13	16.4%
.5	Exterior Wall Finishes	N/A		—	—	—	
.6	Doors	Double aluminum and glass		Each	3637	1.46	
.7	Windows & Glazed Walls	Window wall	15% of wall	S.F. Window	32	2.51	
5.0 Roofing							
.1	Roof Coverings	Built-up tar and gravel with flashing		S.F. Roof	2.38	2.38	5.0%
.7	Insulation	Perlite/EPS composite		S.F. Roof	1.32	1.32	
.8	Openings & Specialties	Gravel stop		L.F. Perimeter	6.40	.27	
6.0 Interior Construction							
.1	Partitions	Concrete block, toilet partitions	8 S.F. Floor/S.F. Partition	S.F. Partition	5.90	8.41	26.6%
.4	Interior Doors	Single leaf hollow metal	700 S.F. Floor/Door	Each	534	.76	
.5	Wall Finishes	Paint		S.F. Surface	1.19	2.98	
.6	Floor Finishes	50% vinyl tile, 50% carpet		S.F. Floor	4.54	4.54	
.7	Ceiling Finishes	Mineral fiber tile on concealed zee bars		S.F. Ceiling	3.63	3.63	
.9	Interior Surface/Exterior Wall	Paint	85% of wall	S.F. Wall	2.12	.92	
7.0 Conveying							
.1	Elevators	N/A		—	—	—	0.0%
.2	Special Conveyors	N/A		—	—	—	
8.0 Mechanical							
.1	Plumbing	Toilet and service fixtures, supply and drainage	1 Fixture/455 S.F. Floor	Each	1856	4.08	26.5%
.2	Fire Protection	Sprinkler, light hazard		S.F. Floor	1.69	1.69	
.3	Heating	Oil fired hot water, wall fin radiation		S.F. Floor	6.39	6.39	
.4	Cooling	Split systems with air cooled condensing units		S.F. Floor	8.90	8.90	
.5	Special Systems	N/A		—	—	—	
9.0 Electrical							
.1	Service & Distribution	200 ampere service, panel board and feeders		S.F. Floor	.66	.66	9.0%
.2	Lighting & Power	Fluorescent fixtures, receptacles, switches, A.C. and misc. power		S.F. Floor	6.19	6.19	
.4	Special Electrical	Alarm systems and emergency lighting		S.F. Floor	.35	.35	
11.0 Special Construction							
.1	Specialties	N/A		—	—	—	0.0%
12.0 Site Work							
.1	Earthwork	N/A		—	—	—	0.0%
.3	Utilities	N/A		—	—	—	
.5	Roads & Parking	N/A		—	—	—	
.7	Site Improvements	N/A		—	—	—	
				Sub-Total		79.72	100%
	CONTRACTOR FEES (General Requirements: 10%, Overhead: 5%, Profit: 10%)				25%	19.93	
	ARCHITECT FEES				9%	8.95	
				Total Building Cost		108.60	

BUILDING TYPES

181

Costs per square foot of floor area

Exterior Wall	S.F. Area	2000	2800	3500	4200	5000	5800	6500	7200	8000
	L.F. Perimeter	180	212	240	268	300	314	336	344	368
Wood Siding	Wood Frame	149.65	139.15	133.90	130.40	127.60	124.45	122.85	120.85	119.70
Brick Veneer	Wood Frame	158.35	146.45	140.50	136.50	133.30	129.60	127.75	125.35	124.00
Face Brick with Concrete Block Back-up	Wood Joists	163.05	150.40	144.10	139.90	136.50	132.50	130.55	127.95	126.50
	Steel Joists	160.80	146.95	140.05	135.45	131.75	127.20	125.05	122.15	120.60
Stucco on Concrete Block	Wood Joists	153.90	142.75	137.15	133.45	130.45	127.00	125.30	123.10	121.85
	Steel Joists	144.10	132.95	127.35	123.65	120.65	117.20	115.50	113.30	112.05
Perimeter Adj., Add or Deduct	Per 100 L.F.	18.75	13.35	10.65	8.90	7.50	6.45	5.75	5.20	4.65
Story Hgt. Adj., Add or Deduct	Per 1 Ft.	1.95	1.65	1.50	1.40	1.30	1.20	1.10	1.05	1.00
For Basement, add $20.65 per square foot of basement area										

The above costs were calculated using the basic specifications shown on the facing page. These costs should be adjusted where necessary for design alternatives and owner's requirements. Reported completed project costs, for this type of structure, range from $72.40 to $169.00 per S.F.

Common additives

Description	Unit	$ Cost
Bar, Front Bar	L.F.	285
Back bar	L.F.	227
Booth, Upholstered, custom straight	L.F.	144 - 265
"L" or "U" shaped	L.F.	149 - 252
Cupola, Stock unit, redwood		
30" square, 37" high, aluminum roof	Each	490
Copper roof	Each	251
Fiberglass, 5'-0" base, 63" high	Each	2950 - 3575
6'-0" base, 63" high	Each	4450 - 4900
Decorative Wood Beams, Non load bearing		
Rough sawn, 4" x 6"	L.F.	7.05
4" x 8"	L.F.	8.10
4" x 10"	L.F.	9.75
4" x 12"	L.F.	11.15
8" x 8"	L.F.	13.90
Emergency Lighting, 25 watt, battery operated		
Lead battery	Each	289
Nickel cadmium	Each	655

Description	Unit	$ Cost
Fireplace, Brick, not incl. chimney or foundation		
30" x 29" opening	Each	2050
Chimney, standard brick		
Single flue, 16" x 20"	V.L.F.	62
20" x 20"	V.L.F.	69
2 Flue, 20" x 24"	V.L.F.	89
20" x 32"	V.L.F.	102
Kitchen Equipment		
Broiler	Each	4050
Coffee urn, twin 6 gallon	Each	6975
Cooler, 6 ft. long	Each	3200
Dishwasher, 10-12 racks per hr.	Each	3050
Food warmer, counter, 1.2 KW	Each	715
Freezer, 44 C.F., reach-in	Each	8325
Ice cube maker, 50 lb. per day	Each	1800
Range with 1 oven	Each	2400
Refrigerators, Prefabricated, walk-in		
7'-6" high, 6' x 6'	S.F.	120
10' x 10'	S.F.	95
12' x 14'	S.F.	83
12' x 20'	S.F.	73

Important: See the Reference Section for Location Factors

Model costs calculated for a 1 story building with 12' story height and 5,000 square feet of floor area

Restaurant

				Unit	Unit Cost	Cost Per S.F.	% Of Sub-Total
1.0 Foundations							
.1	Footings & Foundations	Poured concrete; strip and spread footings and 4' foundation wall		S.F. Ground	4.73	4.73	
.4	Piles & Caissons	N/A		—	—	—	6.3%
.9	Excavation & Backfill	Site preparation for slab and trench for foundation wall and footing		S.F. Ground	1.28	1.28	
2.0 Substructure							
.1	Slab on Grade	4" reinforced concrete with vapor barrier and granular base		S.F. Slab	3.32	3.32	3.5%
.2	Special Substructures	N/A		—	—	—	
3.0 Superstructure							
.1	Columns & Beams	Wood columns		S.F. Ground	.34	.85	
.4	Structural Walls	N/A		—	—	—	
.5	Elevated Floors	N/A		—	—	—	6.6%
.7	Roof	Plywood on wood truss (pitched)		S.F. Roof	4.88	5.46	
.9	Stairs	N/A		—	—	—	
4.0 Exterior Closure							
.1	Walls	Cedar siding on wood studs with insulation	70% of wall	S.F. Wall	7.82	3.94	
.5	Exterior Wall Finishes	N/A		—	—	—	
.6	Doors	Aluminum and glass doors and entrance with transom		Each	3185	3.19	14.1%
.7	Windows & Glazed Walls	Storefront windows	30% of wall	S.F. Window	29	6.29	
5.0 Roofing							
.1	Roof Coverings	Cedar shingles with flashing (pitched)		S.F. Roof	3.28	3.67	
.7	Insulation	Fiberglass sheets		S.F. Roof	1.00	1.12	5.6%
.8	Openings & Specialties	Gutters and downspouts and skylight		S.F. Roof	.52	.52	
6.0 Interior Construction							
.1	Partitions	Gypsum board on wood studs, toilet partition	25 S.F. Floor/L.F. Partition	S.F. Partition	730	1.92	
.4	Interior Doors	Hollow core wood	250 S.F. Floor/Door	Each	384	1.54	
.5	Wall Finishes	75% paint, 25% ceramic tile		S.F. Surface	1.79	1.43	
.6	Floor Finishes	65% carpet, 35% quarry tile		S.F. Floor	6.15	6.15	17.0%
.7	Ceiling Finishes	Mineral fiber tile on concealed zee bars		S.F. Ceiling	3.63	3.63	
.9	Interior Surface/Exterior Wall	Painted gypsum board on furring	70% of wall	S.F. Wall	3.08	1.55	
7.0 Conveying							
.1	Elevators	N/A		—	—	—	0.0%
.2	Special Conveyors	N/A		—	—	—	
8.0 Mechanical							
.1	Plumbing	Kitchen, bathroom and service fixtures, supply and drainage	1 Fixture/355 S.F. Floor	Each	2825	7.96	
.2	Fire Protection	Sprinklers, light hazard		S.F. Floor	1.69	1.69	
.3	Heating	Included in 8.4		—	—	—	36.4%
.4	Cooling	Multizone unit, gas heating, electric cooling		S.F. Floor	25	25.10	
.5	Special Systems	N/A		—	—	—	
9.0 Electrical							
.1	Service & Distribution	400 ampere service, panel board and feeders		S.F. Floor	2.76	2.76	
.2	Lighting & Power	Fluorescent fixtures, receptacles, switches, A.C. and misc. power		S.F. Floor	6.64	6.64	10.5%
.4	Special Electrical	Alarm systems and emergency lighting		S.F. Floor	.66	.66	
11.0 Special Construction							
.1	Specialties	N/A		—	—	—	0.0%
12.0 Site Work							
.1	Earthwork	N/A		—	—	—	
.3	Utilities	N/A		—	—	—	
.5	Roads & Parking	N/A		—	—	—	0.0%
.7	Site Improvements	N/A		—	—	—	
				Sub-Total		95.40	100%
	CONTRACTOR FEES (General Requirements: 10%, Overhead: 5%, Profit: 10%)				25%	23.85	
	ARCHITECT FEES				7%	8.35	
				Total Building Cost		127.60	

BUILDING TYPES

Costs per square foot of floor area

Exterior Wall	S.F. Area	2000	2800	3500	4000	5000	5800	6500	7200	8000
	L.F. Perimeter	180	212	240	260	300	314	336	344	368
Face Brick with Concrete Block Back-up	Bearing Walls	137.45	127.95	123.15	120.80	117.45	114.15	112.60	110.45	109.30
	Steel Frame	140.30	130.80	126.00	123.60	120.25	116.95	115.40	113.25	112.10
Concrete Block With Stucco	Bearing Walls	130.20	121.85	117.65	115.55	112.60	109.75	108.40	106.55	105.60
	Steel Frame	132.35	124.10	119.95	117.85	114.95	112.15	110.85	109.05	108.05
Wood Siding	Wood Frame	127.70	119.90	115.95	114.00	111.25	108.65	107.40	105.70	104.80
Brick Veneer	Steel Frame	136.10	127.25	122.80	120.60	117.45	114.40	113.00	111.00	110.00
Perimeter Adj., Add or Deduct	Per 100 L.F.	24.10	17.20	13.75	12.00	9.65	8.25	7.40	6.70	6.00
Story Hgt. Adj., Add or Deduct	Per 1 Ft.	3.15	2.65	2.40	2.30	2.10	1.90	1.80	1.65	1.60
Basement—Not Applicable										

The above costs were calculated using the basic specifications shown on the facing page. These costs should be adjusted where necessary for design alternatives and owner's requirements. Reported completed project costs, for this type of structure, range from $72.30 to $140.65 per S.F.

Common additives

Description	Unit	$ Cost	Description	Unit	$ Cost
Bar, Front Bar	L.F.	285	Refrigerators, Prefabricated, walk-in		
Back bar	L.F.	227	7'-6" High, 6' x 6'	S.F.	120
Booth, Upholstered, custom straight	L.F.	144 - 265	10' x 10'	S.F.	95
"L" or "U" shaped	L.F.	149 - 252	12' x 14'	S.F.	83
Drive-up Window	Each	4975 - 9525	12' x 20'	S.F.	73
Emergency Lighting, 25 watt, battery operated			Serving		
Lead battery	Each	289	Counter top (Stainless steel)	L.F.	118
Nickel cadmium	Each	655	Base cabinets	L.F.	281 - 335
Kitchen Equipment			Sound System		
Broiler	Each	4050	Amplifier, 250 watts	Each	1650
Coffee urn, twin 6 gallon	Each	6975	Speaker, ceiling or wall	Each	145
Cooler, 6 ft. long	Each	3200	Trumpet	Each	271
Dishwasher, 10-12 racks per hr.	Each	3050	Storage		
Food warmer, counter, 1.2 KW	Each	715	Shelving	S.F.	8.65
Freezer, 44 C.F., reach-in	Each	8325	Washing		
Ice cube maker, 50 lb. per day	Each	1800	Stainless steel counter	L.F.	118
Range with 1 oven	Each	2400			

Important: See the Reference Section for Location Factors

Model costs calculated for a 1 story building with 10' story height and 4,000 square feet of floor area

Restaurant, Fast Food

				Unit	Unit Cost	Cost Per S.F.	% Of Sub-Total
1.0 Foundations							
	.1	Footings & Foundations	Poured concrete; strip and spread footings and 4' foundation wall	S.F. Ground	4.93	4.93	
	.4	Piles & Caissons	N/A	—	—	—	6.9%
	.9	Excavation & Backfill	Site preparation for slab and trench for foundation wall and footing	S.F. Ground	1.28	1.28	
2.0 Substructure							
	.1	Slab on Grade	4" reinforced concrete with vapor barrier and granular base	S.F. Slab	3.32	3.32	3.7%
	.2	Special Substructures	N/A	—	—	—	
3.0 Superstructure							
	.1	Columns & Beams	N/A	—	—	—	
	.4	Structural Walls	N/A	—	—	—	
	.5	Elevated Floors	N/A	—	—	—	4.6%
	.7	Roof	Metal deck on open web steel joists	S.F. Roof	4.11	4.11	
	.9	Stairs	N/A	—	—	—	
4.0 Exterior Closure							
	.1	Walls	Face brick with concrete block backup 70% of wall	S.F. Wall	17.77	9.58	
	.5	Exterior Wall Finishes	N/A	—	—	—	23.5%
	.6	Doors	Aluminum and glass	Each	2525	5.05	
	.7	Windows & Glazed Walls	Window wall 30% of wall	S.F Window	32	6.40	
5.0 Roofing							
	.1	Roof Coverings	Built-up tar and gravel with flashing	S.F. Roof	2.99	2.99	
	.7	Insulation	Perlite/EPS composite	S.F. Roof	1.32	1.32	5.1%
	.8	Openings & Specialties	Gravel stop and hatches	S.F. Roof	.29	.29	
6.0 Interior Construction							
	.1	Partitions	Gypsum board on metal studs 25 S.F. Floor/L.F. Partition	S.F. Partition	4.11	1.48	
	.4	Interior Doors	Hollow core wood 1000 S.F. Floor/Door	Each	384	.38	
	.5	Wall Finishes	Paint	S.F. Surface	.57	.41	
	.6	Floor Finishes	Quarry tile	S.F. Floor	9.28	9.28	18.0%
	.7	Ceiling Finishes	Mineral fiber tile on concealed zee bars	S.F. Floor	3.63	3.63	
	.9	Interior Surface/Exterior Wall	Paint 70% of wall	S.F. Wall	2.12	.96	
7.0 Conveying							
	.1	Elevators	N/A	—	—	—	0.0%
	.2	Special Conveyors	N/A	—	—	—	
8.0 Mechanical							
	.1	Plumbing	Kitchen, bathroom and service fixtures, supply and drainage 1 Fixture/400 S.F. Floor	Each	2796	6.99	
	.2	Fire Protection	Sprinklers, light hazard	S.F. Floor	2.27	2.27	
	.3	Heating	Included in 8.4	—	—	—	21.3%
	.4	Cooling	Multizone unit, gas heating, electric cooling	S.F. Floor	9.62	9.62	
	.5	Special Systems	N/A	—	—	—	
9.0 Electrical							
	.1	Service & Distribution	400 ampere service, panel board and feeders	S.F. Floor	2.89	2.89	
	.2	Lighting & Power	Fluorescent fixtures, receptacles, switches, A.C. and misc. power	S.F. Floor	7.25	7.25	12.0%
	.4	Special Electrical	Alarm systems and emergency lighting	S.F. Floor	.63	.63	
11.0 Special Construction							
	.1	Specialties	Walk-in refrigerator	Each	17,676	4.42	4.9%
12.0 Site Work							
	.1	Earthwork	N/A	—	—	—	
	.3	Utilities	N/A	—	—	—	
	.5	Roads & Parking	N/A	—	—	—	0.0%
	.7	Site Improvements	N/A	—	—	—	
				Sub-Total		89.48	**100%**
		CONTRACTOR FEES (General Requirements: 10%, Overhead: 5%, Profit: 10%)			25%	22.37	
		ARCHITECT FEES			8%	8.95	
				Total Building Cost		**120.80**	

BUILDING TYPES

185

BUILDING TYPES

Costs per square foot of floor area

Exterior Wall	S.F. Area	10000	15000	20000	25000	30000	35000	40000	45000	50000
	L.F. Perimeter	450	500	600	700	740	822	890	920	966
Face Brick with Concrete Block Back-up	Steel Frame	132.10	120.00	116.25	114.00	110.70	109.40	108.10	106.35	105.20
	Lam. Wood Truss	134.75	123.15	119.55	117.40	114.20	113.00	111.75	110.10	109.00
Concrete Block	Steel Frame	122.15	115.15	112.90	111.55	109.65	108.90	108.15	107.15	106.50
	Lam. Wood Truss	118.75	111.75	109.45	108.10	106.25	105.50	104.75	103.75	103.10
Galvanized Steel Siding	Steel Frame	113.85	106.85	104.55	103.20	101.30	100.55	99.80	98.85	98.20
Metal Sandwich Panel	Steel Joists	119.55	111.05	108.35	106.70	104.40	103.50	102.65	101.45	100.60
Perimeter Adj., Add or Deduct	Per 100 L.F.	9.15	6.10	4.55	3.70	3.05	2.60	2.30	2.05	1.85
Story Hgt. Adj., Add or Deduct	Per 1 Ft.	1.40	1.05	.95	.90	.75	.75	.70	.65	.60
Basement—Not Applicable										

The above costs were calculated using the basic specifications shown on the facing page. These costs should be adjusted where necessary for design alternatives and owner's requirements. Reported completed project costs, for this type of structure, range from $42.70 to $133.10 per S.F.

Common additives

Description	Unit	$ Cost
Bar, Front Bar	L.F.	285
Back bar	L.F.	227
Booth, Upholstered, custom straight	L.F.	144 - 265
"L" or "U" shaped	L.F.	149 - 252
Bleachers, Telescoping, manual		
To 15 tier	Seat	79 - 109
16-20 tier	Seat	160 - 195
21-30 tier	Seat	170 - 205
For power operation, add	Seat	30 - 48
Emergency Lighting, 25 watt, battery operated		
Lead battery	Each	289
Nickel cadmium	Each	655
Lockers, Steel, single tier, 60" or 72"	Opening	125 - 220
2 tier, 60" or 72" total	Opening	70 - 119
5 tier, box lockers	Opening	40 - 60
Locker bench, lam. maple top only	L.F.	18.05
Pedestals, steel pipe	Each	58

Description	Unit	$ Cost
Rink		
Dasher boards & top guard	Each	151,000
Mats, rubber	S.F.	16.45
Score Board	Each	10,800 - 31,800

Important: See the Reference Section for Location Factors

Model costs calculated for a 1 story building with 24' story height and 30,000 square feet of floor area

Rink, Hockey/Indoor Soccer

BUILDING TYPES

				Unit	Unit Cost	Cost Per S.F.	% Of Sub-Total
1.0 Foundations							
.1	Footings & Foundations	Poured concrete; strip and spread footings and 4' foundation wall		S.F. Ground	2.78	2.78	
.4	Piles & Caissons	N/A		—	—	—	4.7%
.9	Excavation & Backfill	Site preparation for slab and trench for foundation wall and footing		S.F. Ground	1.08	1.08	
2.0 Substructure							
.1	Slab on Grade	6" reinforced concrete with vapor barrier and granular base		S.F. Slab	3.96	3.96	4.8%
.2	Special Substructures	N/A		—	—	—	
3.0 Superstructure							
.1	Columns & Beams	Wide flange beams and columns		S.F. Ground	8.71	8.71	
.4	Structural Walls	N/A		—	—	—	
.5	Elevated Floors	N/A		—	—	—	21.4%
.7	Roof	Metal deck on steel joist		S.F. Roof	8.84	8.84	
.9	Stairs	N/A		—	—	—	
4.0 Exterior Closure							
.1	Walls	Concrete block	95% of wall	S.F. Wall	8.13	4.57	
.5	Exterior Wall Finishes	N/A		—	—	—	
.6	Doors	Aluminum and glass, hollow metal, overhead		Each	1946	.52	7.4%
.7	Windows & Glazed Walls	Store front	5% of wall	S.F. Window	32	.96	
5.0 Roofing							
.1	Roof Coverings	Elastomeric neoprene membrane with flashing		S.F. Roof	2.07	2.07	
.7	Insulation	Perlite/EPS composite		S.F. Roof	1.32	1.32	4.3%
.8	Openings & Specialties	Hatches		S.F. Roof	.13	.13	
6.0 Interior Construction							
.1	Partitions	Concrete block	140 S.F. Floor/L.F. Partition	S.F. Partition	5.95	.51	
.4	Interior Doors	Hollow metal	2500 S.F. Floor/Door	Each	534	.21	
.5	Wall Finishes	Paint		S.F. Surface	1.17	.20	
.6	Floor Finishes	80% rubber mat, 20% paint	50% of floor area	S.F. Floor	4.72	2.36	5.9%
.7	Ceiling Finishes	Mineral fiber tile on concealed zee bar	10% of area	S.F. Ceiling	3.63	.36	
.9	Interior Surface/Exterior Wall	Paint	95% of wall	S.F. Wall	2.12	1.19	
7.0 Conveying							
.1	Elevators	N/A		—	—	—	0.0%
.2	Special Conveyors	N/A		—	—	—	
8.0 Mechanical							
.1	Plumbing	Toilet and service fixtures, supply and drainage	1 Fixture/1070 S.F. Floor	Each	3359	3.14	
.2	Fire Protection	Standpipes and hose systems		—	—	—	
.3	Heating	Oil fired hot water, unit heaters	10% of area	S.F. Floor	.50	.50	18.1%
.4	Cooling	Single zone, electric cooling	90% of area	S.F. Floor	11.16	11.16	
.5	Special Systems	N/A		—	—	—	
9.0 Electrical							
.1	Service & Distribution	600 ampere service, panel board and feeders		S.F. Floor	1.14	1.14	
.2	Lighting & Power	High intensity discharge and fluorescent fixtures, receptacles, switches, A.C. and misc. power		S.F. Floor	5.30	5.30	8.9%
.4	Special Electrical	Alarm systems, emergency lighting and public address		S.F. Floor	.89	.89	
11.0 Special Construction							
.1	Specialties	Dasher boards and rink (including ice making system)		S.F. Floor	20	20.07	24.5%
12.0 Site Work							
.1	Earthwork	N/A		—	—	—	
.3	Utilities	N/A		—	—	—	
.5	Roads & Parking	N/A		—	—	—	0.0%
.7	Site Improvements	N/A		—	—	—	
				Sub-Total		81.97	**100%**
	CONTRACTOR FEES (General Requirements: 10%, Overhead: 5%, Profit: 10%)				25%	20.49	
	ARCHITECT FEES				7%	7.19	
				Total Building Cost		**109.65**	

187

BUILDING TYPES

Costs per square foot of floor area

Exterior Wall	S.F. Area	25000	30000	35000	40000	45000	50000	55000	60000	65000
	L.F. Perimeter	700	740	823	906	922	994	1033	1100	1166
Face Brick with Concrete Block Back-up	Steel Frame	96.60	93.95	92.85	92.00	90.40	89.85	89.00	88.55	88.20
	Bearing Walls	92.95	90.25	89.15	88.30	86.70	86.15	85.30	84.90	84.55
Stucco on Concrete Block	Steel Frame	93.80	91.45	90.50	89.70	88.35	87.85	87.10	86.70	86.40
	Bearing Walls	90.10	87.75	86.80	86.00	84.65	84.10	83.40	83.00	82.70
Decorative Concrete Block	Steel Frame	94.20	91.85	90.85	90.05	88.65	88.15	87.40	87.00	86.70
	Bearing Walls	90.50	88.15	87.15	86.35	84.95	84.40	83.65	83.30	83.00
Perimeter Adj., Add or Deduct	Per 100 L.F.	2.60	2.15	1.85	1.65	1.45	1.30	1.15	1.05	1.00
Story Hgt. Adj., Add or Deduct	Per 1 Ft.	.85	.75	.70	.70	.65	.60	.60	.55	.55
For Basement, add $15.30 per square foot of basement area										

The above costs were calculated using the basic specifications shown on the facing page. These costs should be adjusted where necessary for design alternatives and owner's requirements. Reported completed project costs, for this type of structure, range from $48.30 to $128.90 per S.F.

Common additives

Description	Unit	$ Cost
Bleachers, Telescoping, manual		
To 15 tier	Seat	79 - 109
16-20 tier	Seat	160 - 195
21-30 tier	Seat	170 - 205
For power operation, add	Seat	30 - 48
Carrels Hardwood	Each	725 - 940
Clock System		
20 room	Each	12,700
50 room	Each	30,800
Emergency Lighting, 25 watt, battery operated		
Lead battery	Each	289
Nickel cadmium	Each	655
Flagpoles, Complete		
Aluminum, 20' high	Each	1075
40' high	Each	2675
Fiberglass, 23' high	Each	1400
39'-5" high	Each	2950
Kitchen Equipment		
Broiler	Each	4050
Cooler, 6 ft. long, reach-in	Each	3200

Description	Unit	$ Cost
Kitchen Equipment, cont.		
Dishwasher, 10-12 racks per hr.	Each	3050
Food warmer, counter, 1.2 KW	Each	715
Freezer, 44 C.F., reach-in	Each	8325
Ice cube maker, 50 lb. per day	Each	1800
Range with 1 oven	Each	2400
Lockers, Steel, single tier, 60" to 72"	Opening	125 - 220
2 tier, 60" to 72" total	Opening	70 - 119
5 tier, box lockers	Opening	40 - 60
Locker bench, lam. maple top only	L.F.	18.05
Pedestals, steel pipe	Each	58
Seating		
Auditorium chair, all veneer	Each	166
Veneer back, padded seat	Each	201
Upholstered, spring seat	Each	203
Classroom, movable chair & desk	Set	65 - 120
Lecture hall, pedestal type	Each	152 - 470
Sound System		
Amplifier, 250 watts	Each	1650
Speaker, ceiling or wall	Each	145
Trumpet	Each	271

Important: See the Reference Section for Location Factors

Model costs calculated for a 1 story building with 12' story height and 45,000 square feet of floor area

			Unit	Unit Cost	Cost Per S.F.	% Of Sub-Total
1.0 Foundations						
.1	Footings & Foundations	Poured concrete; strip and spread footings and 4' foundation wall	S.F. Ground	3.71	3.71	
.4	Piles & Caissons	N/A	—	—	—	7.4%
.9	Excavation & Backfill	Site preparation for slab and trench for foundation wall and footing	S.F. Ground	1.08	1.08	
2.0 Substructure						
.1	Slab on Grade	4" reinforced concrete with vapor barrier and granular base	S.F. Slab	3.32	3.32	5.1%
.2	Special Substructures	N/A	—	—	—	
3.0 Superstructure						
.1	Columns & Beams	N/A	—	—	—	
.4	Structural Walls	N/A	—	—	—	
.5	Elevated Floors	N/A	—	—	—	3.8%
.7	Roof	Metal deck on open web steel joists	S.F. Roof	2.45	2.45	
.9	Stairs	N/A	—	—	—	
4.0 Exterior Closure						
.1	Walls	Face brick with concrete block backup 70% of wall	S.F. Wall	21	3.62	
.5	Exterior Wall Finishes	N/A	—	—	—	8.6%
.6	Doors	Metal and glass 5% of wall	Each	2163	.38	
.7	Windows & Glazed Walls	Steel outward projecting 25% of wall	Each	493	1.58	
5.0 Roofing						
.1	Roof Coverings	Built-up tar and gravel with flashing	S.F. Roof	2.09	2.09	
.7	Insulation	Perlite/EPS composite	S.F. Roof	1.32	1.32	5.5%
.8	Openings & Specialties	Gravel stop	L.F. Perimeter	6.40	.13	
6.0 Interior Construction						
.1	Partitions	Concrete block, toilet partitions 20 S.F. Floor/L.F. Partition	S.F. Partition	1288	3.85	
.4	Interior Doors	Single leaf kalamein fire doors 700 S.F. Floor/Door	Each	534	.76	
.5	Wall Finishes	75% paint, 15% glazed coating, 10% ceramic tile	S.F. Surface	2.27	2.27	24.8%
.6	Floor Finishes	65% vinyl composition tile, 25% carpet, 10% terrazzo	S.F. Floor	5.21	5.21	
.7	Ceiling Finishes	Mineral fiber tile on concealed zee bars	S.F. Ceiling	3.63	3.63	
.9	Interior Surface/Exterior Wall	Painted gypsum board on furring 70% of wall	S.F. Wall	2.12	.36	
7.0 Conveying						
.1	Elevators	N/A	—	—	—	0.0%
.2	Special Conveyors	N/A	—	—	—	
8.0 Mechanical						
.1	Plumbing	Kitchen, bathroom and service fixtures, supply and drainage 1 Fixture/625 S.F. Floor	Each	2387	3.82	
.2	Fire Protection	Sprinklers, light hazard	S.F. Floor	1.44	1.44	
.3	Heating	Oil fired hot water, wall fin radiation	S.F. Floor	5.81	5.81	29.6%
.4	Cooling	Split systems with air cooled condensing units	S.F. Floor	8.14	8.14	
.5	Special Systems	N/A	—	—	—	
9.0 Electrical						
.1	Service & Distribution	800 ampere service, panel board and feeders	S.F. Floor	.85	.85	
.2	Lighting & Power	Fluorescent fixtures, receptacles, switches, A.C. and misc. power	S.F. Floor	6.86	6.86	13.8%
.4	Special Electrical	Alarm systems, communications systems and emergency lighting	S.F. Floor	1.24	1.24	
11.0 Special Construction						
.1	Specialties	Chalkboards	S.F. Floor	.90	.90	1.4%
12.0 Site Work						
.1	Earthwork	N/A	—	—	—	
.3	Utilities	N/A	—	—	—	0.0%
.5	Roads & Parking	N/A	—	—	—	
.7	Site Improvements	N/A	—	—	—	
			Sub-Total		64.82	**100%**
	CONTRACTOR FEES (General Requirements: 10%, Overhead: 5%, Profit: 10%)			25%	16.21	
	ARCHITECT FEES			7%	5.67	
			Total Building Cost		**86.70**	

Costs per square foot of floor area

Exterior Wall	S.F. Area	50000	70000	90000	110000	130000	150000	170000	190000	210000
	L.F. Perimeter	816	1083	1100	1300	1290	1450	1433	1566	1700
Face Brick with Concrete Block Back-up	Steel Frame	99.05	96.35	91.85	90.80	88.30	87.70	86.10	85.75	85.45
	R/Conc. Frame	102.30	99.85	95.50	94.55	92.10	91.55	90.00	89.65	89.35
Decorative Concrete Block	Steel Frame	95.15	92.85	89.10	88.20	86.15	85.65	84.30	84.00	83.70
	R/Conc. Frame	99.30	97.00	93.25	92.35	90.25	89.75	88.45	88.15	87.85
Limestone with Concrete Block Back-up	Steel Frame	103.45	100.70	95.30	94.20	91.15	90.55	88.60	88.15	87.85
	R/Conc. Frame	108.30	105.55	100.15	99.05	96.00	95.40	93.45	93.05	92.65
Perimeter Adj., Add or Deduct	Per 100 L.F.	2.15	1.50	1.20	.95	.80	.75	.65	.60	.50
Story Hgt. Adj., Add or Deduct	Per 1 Ft.	1.25	1.20	.95	.90	.75	.75	.65	.65	.60

For Basement, add $20.05 per square foot of basement area

The above costs were calculated using the basic specifications shown on the facing page. These costs should be adjusted where necessary for design alternatives and owner's requirements. Reported completed project costs, for this type of structure, range from $58.60 to $135.30 per S.F.

Common additives

Description	Unit	$ Cost
Bleachers, Telescoping, manual		
To 15 tier	Seat	79 - 109
16-20 tier	Seat	160 - 195
21-30 tier	Seat	170 - 205
For power operation, add	Seat	30 - 48
Carrels Hardwood	Each	725 - 940
Clock System		
20 room	Each	12,700
50 room	Each	30,800
Elevators, Hydraulic passenger, 2 stops		
1500# capacity	Each	42,225
2500# capacity	Each	43,425
Emergency Lighting, 25 watt, battery operated		
Lead battery	Each	289
Nickel cadmium	Each	655
Flagpoles, Complete		
Aluminum, 20' high	Each	1075
40' high	Each	2675
Fiberglass, 23' high	Each	1400
39'-5" high	Each	2950

Description	Unit	$ Cost
Kitchen Equipment		
Broiler	Each	4050
Cooler, 6 ft. long, reach-in	Each	3200
Dishwasher, 10-12 racks per hr.	Each	3050
Food warmer, counter, 1.2 KW	Each	715
Freezer, 44 C.F., reach-in	Each	8325
Lockers, Steel, single tier, 60" or 72"	Opening	125 - 220
2 tier, 60" or 72" total	Opening	70 - 119
5 tier, box lockers	Opening	40 - 60
Locker bench, lam. maple top only	L.F.	18.05
Pedestals, steel pipe	Each	58
Seating		
Auditorium chair, all veneer	Each	166
Veneer back, padded seat	Each	201
Upholstered, spring seat	Each	203
Classroom, movable chair & desk	Set	65 - 120
Lecture hall, pedestal type	Each	152 - 470
Sound System		
Amplifier, 250 watts	Each	1650
Speaker, ceiling or wall	Each	145
Trumpet	Each	271

Important: See the Reference Section for Location Factors

BUILDING TYPES

Model costs calculated for a 2 story building with 12' story height and 130,000 square feet of floor area

				Unit	Unit Cost	Cost Per S.F.	% Of Sub-Total
1.0 Foundations							
.1	Footings & Foundations	Poured concrete; strip and spread footings and 4' foundation wall		S.F. Ground	2.44	1.22	
.4	Piles & Caissons	N/A		—	—	—	2.6%
.9	Excavation & Backfill	Site preparation for slab and trench for foundation wall and footing		S.F. Ground	1.08	.54	
2.0 Substructure							
.1	Slab on Grade	4" reinforced concrete with vapor barrier and granular base		S.F. Slab	3.32	1.66	2.4%
.2	Special Substructures	N/A		—	—	—	
3.0 Superstructure							
.1	Columns & Beams	Concrete columns		L.F. Column	79	1.95	
.4	Structural Walls	N/A		—	—	—	
.5	Elevated Floors	Concrete slab without drop panel		S.F. Floor	10.24	5.12	17.8%
.7	Roof	Concrete slab without drop panel		S.F. Roof	9.85	4.93	
.9	Stairs	Concrete filled metal pan		Flight	5025	.23	
4.0 Exterior Closure							
.1	Walls	Face brick with concrete block backup	75% of wall	S.F. Wall	21	3.76	
.5	Exterior Wall Finishes	N/A		—	—	—	9.7%
.6	Doors	Metal and glass		Each	1262	.28	
.7	Windows & Glazed Walls	Window wall	25% of wall	S.F. Window	44	2.62	
5.0 Roofing							
.1	Roof Coverings	Built-up tar and gravel with flashing		S.F. Roof	1.98	.99	
.7	Insulation	Perlite/EPS composite		S.F. Roof	1.32	.66	2.5%
.8	Openings & Specialties	Gravel stop and hatches		S.F. Roof	.18	.09	
6.0 Interior Construction							
.1	Partitions	Concrete block, toilet partitions	25 S.F. Floor/L.F. Partition	S.F. Partition	5.90	2.85	
.4	Interior Doors	Single leaf kalamein fire doors	700 S.F. Floor/Door	Each	534	.76	
.5	Wall Finishes	75% paint, 15% glazed coating, 10% ceramic tile		S.F. Surface	2.28	1.82	21.3%
.6	Floor Finishes	70% vinyl composition tile, 20% carpet, 10% terrazzo		S.F. Floor	5.04	5.04	
.7	Ceiling Finishes	Mineral fiber tile on concealed zee bars		S.F. Ceiling	3.63	3.63	
.9	Interior Surface/Exterior Wall	Paint	75% of wall	S.F. Wall	3.02	.54	
7.0 Conveying							
.1	Elevators	One hydraulic passenger elevator		Each	50,700	.39	0.6%
.2	Special Conveyors	N/A		—	—	—	
8.0 Mechanical							
.1	Plumbing	Kitchen, bathroom and service fixtures, supply and drainage	1 Fixture/860 S.F. Floor	Each	2975	3.46	
.2	Fire Protection	Sprinklers, light hazard		S.F. Floor	1.28	1.28	
.3	Heating	Oil fired hot water, wall fin radiation		S.F. Floor	3.06	3.06	27.1%
.4	Cooling	Chilled water, cooling tower systems		S.F. Floor	10.93	10.93	
.5	Special Systems	N/A		—	—	—	
9.0 Electrical							
.1	Service & Distribution	2000 ampere service, panel board and feeders		S.F. Floor	.84	.84	
.2	Lighting & Power	Fluorescent fixtures, receptacles, switches, A.C. and misc. power		S.F. Floor	6.81	6.81	14.9%
.4	Special Electrical	Alarm systems, communications systems and emergency lighting		S.F. Floor	2.64	2.64	
11.0 Special Construction							
.1	Specialties	Chalkboards, laboratory counters, built-in athletic equipment		S.F. Floor	.76	.76	1.1%
12.0 Site Work							
.1	Earthwork	N/A		—	—	—	
.3	Utilities	N/A		—	—	—	
.5	Roads & Parking	N/A		—	—	—	0.0%
.7	Site Improvements	N/A		—	—	—	
				Sub-Total		68.86	100%
	CONTRACTOR FEES (General Requirements: 10%, Overhead: 5%, Profit: 10%)				25%	17.22	
	ARCHITECT FEES				7%	6.02	
				Total Building Cost		92.10	

BUILDING TYPES

Costs per square foot of floor area

Exterior Wall	S.F. Area	50000	65000	80000	95000	110000	125000	140000	155000	170000
	L.F. Perimeter	816	1016	1000	1150	1890	2116	2287	2438	2552
Face Brick with Concrete Block Back-up	Steel Frame	97.25	96.35	93.20	92.65	97.45	97.10	96.45	95.85	95.15
	Bearing Walls	93.35	92.45	89.25	88.75	93.50	93.20	92.55	91.95	91.25
Concrete Block Stucco Face	Steel Frame	93.55	92.80	90.30	89.90	93.50	93.25	92.75	92.30	91.75
	Bearing Walls	89.60	88.85	86.40	85.95	89.60	89.35	88.85	88.35	87.80
Decorative Concrete Block	Steel Frame	94.20	93.40	90.80	90.35	94.20	93.90	93.40	92.90	92.30
	Bearing Walls	89.85	89.00	86.45	85.95	89.85	89.55	89.00	88.55	87.95
Perimeter Adj., Add or Deduct	Per 100 L.F.	1.95	1.50	1.15	1.00	.90	.80	.70	.60	.55
Story Hgt. Adj., Add or Deduct	Per 1 Ft.	1.15	1.10	.85	.85	1.20	1.15	1.15	1.05	1.00
For Basement, add $20.85 per square foot of basement area										

The above costs were calculated using the basic specifications shown on the facing page. These costs should be adjusted where necessary for design alternatives and owner's requirements. Reported completed project costs, for this type of structure, range from $55.60 to $127.05 per S.F.

Common additives

Description	Unit	$ Cost	Description	Unit	$ Cost
Bleachers, Telescoping, manual			Kitchen Equipment		
To 15 tier	Seat	79 - 109	Broiler	Each	4050
16-20 tier	Seat	160 - 195	Cooler, 6 ft. long, reach-in	Each	3200
21-30 tier	Seat	170 - 205	Dishwasher, 10-12 racks per hr.	Each	3050
For power operation, add	Seat	30 - 48	Food warmer, counter, 1.2 KW	Each	715
Carrels Hardwood	Each	725 - 940	Freezer, 44 C.F., reach-in	Each	8325
Clock System			Lockers, Steel, single tier, 60" to 72"	Opening	125 - 220
20 room	Each	12,700	2 tier, 60" to 72" total	Opening	70 - 119
50 room	Each	30,800	5 tier, box lockers	Opening	40 - 60
Elevators, Hydraulic passenger, 2 stops			Locker bench, lam. maple top only	L.F.	18.05
1500# capacity	Each	42,225	Pedestals, steel pipe	Each	58
2500# capacity	Each	43,425	Seating		
Emergency Lighting, 25 watt, battery operated			Auditorium chair, all veneer	Each	166
Lead battery	Each	289	Veneer back, padded seat	Each	201
Nickel cadmium	Each	655	Upholstered, spring seat	Each	203
Flagpoles, Complete			Classroom, movable chair & desk	Set	65 - 120
Aluminum, 20' high	Each	1075	Lecture hall, pedestal type	Each	152 - 470
40' high	Each	2675	Sound System		
Fiberglass, 23' high	Each	1400	Amplifier, 250 watts	Each	1650
39'-5" high	Each	2950	Speaker, ceiling or wall	Each	145
			Trumpet	Each	271

Important: See the Reference Section for Location Factors

BUILDING TYPES

Model costs calculated for a 2 story building with 12' story height and 110,000 square feet of floor area

School, Jr High, 2-3 Story

			Unit	Unit Cost	Cost Per S.F.	% Of Sub-Total
1.0 Foundations						
.1	Footings & Foundations	Poured concrete; strip and spread footings and 4' foundation wall	S.F. Ground	3.36	1.68	3.0%
.4	Piles & Caissons	N/A	—	—	—	
.9	Excavation & Backfill	Site preparation for slab and trench for foundation wall and footing	S.F. Ground	1.08	.54	
2.0 Substructure						
.1	Slab on Grade	4" reinforced concrete with vapor barrier and granular base	S.F. Slab	3.32	1.66	2.3%
.2	Special Substructures	N/A	—	—	—	
3.0 Superstructure						
.1	Columns & Beams	Fireproofing, steel columns included in 3.5 and 3.7	L.F. Column	22	.32	15.6%
.4	Structural Walls	N/A	—	—	—	
.5	Elevated Floors	Open web steel joists, slab form, concrete, columns	S.F. Floor	15.30	7.65	
.7	Roof	Metal deck, open web steel joists, columns	S.F. Roof	6.28	3.14	
.9	Stairs	Concrete filled metal pan	Flight	5025	.27	
4.0 Exterior Closure						
.1	Walls	Face brick with concrete block backup · 75% of wall	S.F. Wall	21	6.51	14.1%
.5	Exterior Wall Finishes	N/A	—	—	—	
.6	Doors	Double aluminum & glass	Each	1385	.37	
.7	Windows & Glazed Walls	Window wall · 25% of wall	S.F. Window	32	3.38	
5.0 Roofing						
.1	Roof Coverings	Built-up tar and gravel with flashing	S.F. Roof	2.36	1.18	2.7%
.7	Insulation	Perlite/EPS composite	S.F. Roof	1.32	.66	
.8	Openings & Specialties	Gravel stop and hatches	S.F. Roof	.26	.13	
6.0 Interior Construction						
.1	Partitions	Concrete block, toilet partitions · 20 S.F. Floor/L.F. Partition	S.F. Partition	5.90	3.42	23.7%
.4	Interior Doors	Single leaf kalamein fire doors · 750 S.F. Floor/Door	Each	534	.71	
.5	Wall Finishes	50% paint, 40% glazed coatings, 10% ceramic tile	S.F. Surface	1.98	1.98	
.6	Floor Finishes	50% vinyl composition tile, 30% carpet, 20% terrrazzo	S.F. Floor	6.85	6.85	
.7	Ceiling Finishes	Mineral fiberboard on concealed zee bars	S.F. Ceiling	3.63	3.63	
.9	Interior Surface/Exterior Wall	Painted gypsum board on furring · 75% of wall	S.F. Wall	2.12	.66	
7.0 Conveying						
.1	Elevators	One hydraulic passenger elevator	Each	50,600	.46	0.6%
.2	Special Conveyors	N/A	—	—	—	
8.0 Mechanical						
.1	Plumbing	Kitchen, toilet and service fixtures, supply and drainage · 1 Fixture/1170 S.F. Floor	Each	2854	2.44	22.7%
.2	Fire Protection	Sprinklers, light hazard · 10% of area	S.F. Floor	.25	.25	
.3	Heating	Included in 8.4	—	—	—	
.4	Cooling	Multizone unit, gas heating, electric cooling	S.F. Floor	13.80	13.80	
.5	Special Systems	N/A	—	—	—	
9.0 Electrical						
.1	Service & Distribution	1600 ampere service, panel board and feeders	S.F. Floor	.81	.81	14.3%
.2	Lighting & Power	Fluorescent fixtures, receptacles, switches, A.C. and misc. power	S.F. Floor	6.89	6.89	
.4	Special Electrical	Alarm systems, communications systems and emergency lighting	S.F. Floor	2.73	2.73	
11.0 Special Construction						
.1	Specialties	Chalkboards, laboratory counters	S.F. Floor	.73	.73	1.0%
12.0 Site Work						
.1	Earthwork	N/A	—	—	—	0.0%
.3	Utilities	N/A	—	—	—	
.5	Roads & Parking	N/A	—	—	—	
.7	Site Improvements	N/A	—	—	—	
			Sub-Total		72.85	**100%**
	CONTRACTOR FEES (General Requirements: 10%, Overhead: 5%, Profit: 10%)			25%	18.21	
	ARCHITECT FEES			7%	6.39	
			Total Building Cost		**97.45**	

BUILDING TYPES

193

Costs per square foot of floor area

Exterior Wall	S.F. Area	20000	30000	40000	50000	60000	70000	80000	90000	100000
	L.F. Perimeter	400	500	685	700	800	900	1000	1100	1200
Face Brick with Concrete Block Back-up	Steel Frame	99.80	96.15	96.25	93.20	92.45	91.90	91.55	91.20	90.95
	Bearing Walls	96.95	93.30	93.40	90.35	89.60	89.10	88.70	88.40	88.15
Decorative Concrete Block	Steel Frame	94.15	91.45	91.45	89.25	88.70	88.30	88.00	87.75	87.55
	Bearing Walls	91.30	88.60	88.60	86.40	85.85	85.45	85.15	84.95	84.75
Steel Siding on Steel Studs	Steel Frame	91.40	89.10	89.05	87.25	86.80	86.50	86.25	86.05	85.90
Metal Sandwich Panel	Steel Frame	91.30	89.10	89.00	87.25	86.75	86.45	86.25	86.00	85.85
Perimeter Adj., Add or Deduct	Per 100 L.F.	4.65	3.05	2.30	1.85	1.55	1.35	1.10	1.05	.90
Story Hgt. Adj., Add or Deduct	Per 1 Ft.	1.35	1.10	1.10	.90	.85	.85	.80	.80	.80
For Basement, add $20.25 per square foot of basement area										

The above costs were calculated using the basic specifications shown on the facing page. These costs should be adjusted where necessary for design alternatives and owner's requirements. Reported completed project costs, for this type of structure, range from $49.50 to $141.25 per S.F.

Common additives

Description	Unit	$ Cost	Description	Unit	$ Cost
Carrels Hardwood	Each	725 - 940	Flagpoles, Complete		
Clock System			Aluminum, 20' high	Each	1075
20 room	Each	12,700	40' high	Each	2675
50 room	Each	30,800	Fiberglass, 23' high	Each	1400
Directory Boards, Plastic, glass covered			39'-5" high	Each	2950
30" x 20"	Each	565	Seating		
36" x 48"	Each	1025	Auditorium chair, all veneer	Each	166
Aluminum, 24" x 18"	Each	425	Veneer back, padded seat	Each	201
36" x 24"	Each	535	Upholstered, spring seat	Each	203
48" x 32"	Each	745	Classroom, movable chair & desk	Set	65 - 120
48" x 60"	Each	1600	Lecture hall, pedestal type	Each	152 - 470
Elevators, Hydraulic passenger, 2 stops			Shops & Workroom:		
1500# capacity	Each	42,225	Benches, metal	Each	395
2500# capacity	Each	43,425	Parts bins 6'-3" high, 3' wide, 12" deep, 72 bins	Each	480
3500# capacity	Each	47,225	Shelving, metal 1' x 3'	S.F.	12.90
Emergency Lighting, 25 watt, battery operated			Wide span 6' wide x 24" deep	S.F.	8.65
Lead battery	Each	289	Sound System		
Nickel cadmium	Each	655	Amplifier, 250 watts	Each	1650
			Speaker, ceiling or wall	Each	145
			Trumpet	Each	271

BUILDING TYPES

Model costs calculated for a 2 story building with 12' story height and 40,000 square feet of floor area

School, Vocational

BUILDING TYPES

				Unit	Unit Cost	Cost Per S.F.	% Of Sub-Total
1.0 Foundations							
.1	Footings & Foundations	Poured concrete; strip and spread footings and 4' foundation wall		S.F. Ground	3.48	1.74	
.4	Piles & Caissons	N/A		—	—	—	3.3%
.9	Excavation & Backfill	Site preparation for slab and trench for foundation wall and footing		S.F. Ground	1.08	.54	
2.0 Substructure							
.1	Slab on Grade	5" reinforced concrete with vapor barrier and granular base		S.F. Slab	6.48	3.24	4.6%
.2	Special Substructures	N/A		—	—	—	
3.0 Superstructure							
.1	Columns & Beams	Interior steel columns included in 3.5 and 3.7		—	—	—	
.4	Structural Walls	N/A		—	—	—	
.5	Elevated Floors	Open web steel joists, slab form, concrete, beams, columns		S.F. Floor	10.52	5.26	10.8%
.7	Roof	Metal deck, open web steel joists, beams, columns		S.F. Roof	3.57	1.79	
.9	Stairs	Concrete filled metal pan		Flight	5025	.50	
4.0 Exterior Closure							
.1	Walls	Face brick with concrete block backup	85% of wall	S.F. Wall	21	7.35	
.5	Exterior Wall Finishes	N/A		—	—	—	13.9%
.6	Doors	Metal and glass doors		Each	1647	.33	
.7	Windows & Glazed Walls	Steel outward projecting	15% of wall	S.F. Wall	32	2.03	
5.0 Roofing							
.1	Roof Coverings	Built-up tar and gravel with flashing		S.F. Roof	2.34	1.17	
.7	Insulation	Perlite/EPS composite		S.F. Roof	1.32	.66	2.9%
.8	Openings & Specialties	Gravel stop and hatches		S.F. Roof	.40	.20	
6.0 Interior Construction							
.1	Partitions	Concrete block, toilet partitions	20 S.F. Floor/L.F. Partition	S.F. Partition	5.90	3.59	
.4	Interior Doors	Single leaf kalamein fire doors	600 S.F. Floor/Door	Each	534	.89	
.5	Wall Finishes	50% paint, 40% glazed coating, 10% ceramic tile		S.F. Surface	1.98	1.98	
.6	Floor Finishes	70% vinyl composition tile, 20% carpet, 10% terrazzo		S.F. Floor	5.04	5.04	20.6%
.7	Ceiling Finishes	Mineral fiber tile on concealed zee bars	60% of area	S.F. Ceiling	3.63	2.18	
.9	Interior Surface/Exterior Wall	Painted gypsum board on furring	85% of wall	S.F. Wall	2.12	.74	
7.0 Conveying							
.1	Elevators	One hydraulic passenger elevator		Each	51,200	1.28	1.8%
.2	Special Conveyors	N/A		—	—	—	
8.0 Mechanical							
.1	Plumbing	Toilet and service fixtures, supply and drainage	1 Fixture/700 S.F. Floor	Each	2401	3.43	
.2	Fire Protection	Sprinklers, light hazard		S.F. Floor	.86	.86	
.3	Heating	Oil fired hot water, wall fin radiation and unit heaters		S.F. Floor	10.81	5.49	27.6%
.4	Cooling	Chilled water, cooling tower systems		S.F. Floor	9.47	9.47	
.5	Special Systems	N/A		—	—	—	
9.0 Electrical							
.1	Service & Distribution	800 ampere service, panel board and feeders		S.F. Floor	.95	.95	
.2	Lighting & Power	Fluorescent fixtures, receptacles, switches, A.C. and misc. power		S.F. Floor	6.90	6.90	13.5%
.4	Special Electrical	Alarm systems, communications systems and emergency lighting		S.F. Floor	1.55	1.55	
11.0 Special Construction							
.1	Specialties	Chalkboards		S.F. Floor	.69	.69	1.0%
12.0 Site Work							
.1	Earthwork	N/A		—	—	—	
.3	Utilities	N/A		—	—	—	
.5	Roads & Parking	N/A		—	—	—	0.0%
.7	Site Improvements	N/A		—	—	—	
				Sub-Total		69.85	**100%**

CONTRACTOR FEES (General Requirements: 10%, Overhead: 5%, Profit: 10%)		25%	17.46
ARCHITECT FEES		7%	6.09

Total Building Cost 93.40

195

Costs per square foot of floor area

Exterior Wall	S.F. Area	1000	2000	3000	4000	6000	8000	10000	12000	15000
	L.F. Perimeter	126	179	219	253	310	358	400	438	490
Wood Siding	Wood Frame	89.30	80.00	75.75	73.30	70.35	68.60	67.35	66.50	65.50
Face Brick Veneer	Wood Frame	108.50	93.30	86.40	82.35	77.50	74.65	72.65	71.20	69.65
Stucco on Concrete Block	Steel Frame	103.45	90.60	84.75	81.30	77.20	74.75	73.10	71.85	70.50
	Bearing Walls	101.20	88.35	82.50	79.05	74.95	72.50	70.85	69.60	68.25
Metal Sandwich Panel	Steel Frame	110.40	95.65	88.95	85.00	80.35	77.50	75.60	74.20	72.65
Precast Concrete	Steel Frame	115.00	98.60	91.15	86.80	81.55	78.45	76.30	74.75	73.00
Perimeter Adj., Add or Deduct	Per 100 L.F.	25.50	12.75	8.50	6.40	4.25	3.20	2.55	2.15	1.70
Story Hgt. Adj., Add or Deduct	Per 1 Ft.	1.85	1.30	1.05	.95	.75	.65	.60	.55	.50
For Basement, add $ 15.25 per square foot of basement area										

The above costs were calculated using the basic specifications shown on the facing page. These costs should be adjusted where necessary for design alternatives and owner's requirements. Reported completed project costs, for this type of structure, range from $ 40.75 to $ 141.30 per S.F.

Common additives

Description	Unit	$ Cost		Description	Unit	$ Cost
Check Out Counter				Refrigerated Food Cases, cont.		
Single belt	Each	2225		Frozen food, chest type, 12' long	Each	5475
Double belt	Each	3825		Glass door reach-in, 5 door	Each	10,400
Emergency Lighting, 25 watt, battery operated				Island case 12' long, single deck	Each	6175
Lead battery	Each	289		Multi deck	Each	12,900
Nickel cadmium	Each	655		Meat cases, 12' long, single deck	Each	4550
Refrigerators, Prefabricated, walk-in				Multi deck	Each	7700
7'-6" high, 6' x 6'	S.F.	120		Produce, 12' long single deck	Each	5950
10' x 10'	S.F.	95		Multi deck	Each	6625
12' x 14'	S.F.	83		Safe, Office type, 4 hour rating		
12' x 20'	S.F.	73		30" x 18" x 18"	Each	3125
Refrigerated Food Cases				62" x 33" x 20"	Each	6775
Dairy, multi deck, 12' long	Each	8025		Smoke Detectors		
Delicatessen case, single deck, 12' long	Each	5425		Ceiling type	Each	149
Multi deck, 18 S.F. shelf display	Each	6650		Duct type	Each	405
Freezer, self-contained chest type, 30 C.F.	Each	4025		Sound System		
Glass door upright, 78 C.F.	Each	7500		Amplifier, 250 watts	Each	1650
				Speaker, ceiling or wall	Each	145
				Trumpet	Each	271

Important: See the Reference Section for Location Factors

Model costs calculated for a 1 story building with 12' story height and 4,000 square feet of floor area

			Unit	Unit Cost	Cost Per S.F.	% Of Sub-Total
1.0 Foundations						
.1	Footings & Foundations	Poured concrete; strip and spread footings and 4' foundation wall	S.F. Ground	3.92	3.92	
.4	Piles & Caissons	N/A	—	—	—	9.5%
.9	Excavation & Backfill	Site preparation for slab and trench for foundation wall and footing	S.F. Ground	1.28	1.28	
2.0 Substructure						
.1	Slab on Grade	4" reinforced concrete with vapor barrier and granular base	S.F. Slab	3.32	3.32	6.1%
.2	Special Substructures	N/A	—	—	—	
3.0 Superstructure						
.1	Columns & Beams	N/A	—	—	—	
.4	Structural Walls	N/A	—	—	—	
.5	Elevated Floors	N/A	—	—	—	8.9%
.7	Roof	Wood truss with plywood sheathing	S.F. Ground	4.88	4.88	
.9	Stairs	N/A	—	—	—	
4.0 Exterior Closure						
.1	Walls	Wood siding on wood studs, insulated _80% of wall_	S.F. Wall	6.69	4.06	
.5	Exterior Wall Finishes	N/A	—	—	—	
.6	Doors	Double aluminum and glass, solid core wood	Each	2052	1.54	16.1%
.7	Windows & Glazed Walls	Storefront _20% of wall_	S.F. Window	32	3.24	
5.0 Roofing						
.1	Roof Coverings	Asphalt shingles	S.F. Roof	1.76	1.76	
.7	Insulation	Fiberglass sheets	S.F. Roof	1.00	1.00	5.2%
.8	Openings & Specialties	Gutters and downspouts	S.F. Roof	.10	.10	
6.0 Interior Construction						
.1	Partitions	Gypsum board on wood studs _60 S.F. Floor/L.F. Partition_	S.F. Partition	3.36	.56	
.4	Interior Doors	Single leaf wood, hollow metal _1300 S.F. Floor/Door_	Each	654	.50	
.5	Wall Finishes	Paint	S.F. Surface	.81	.27	
.6	Floor Finishes	Vinyl composition tile	S.F. Floor	2.91	2.91	14.0%
.7	Ceiling Finishes	Mineral fiber tile on wood furring	S.F. Ceiling	2.45	2.45	
.9	Interior Surface/Exterior Wall	Painted gypsum board on furring _80% of wall_	S.F. Wall	1.65	1.00	
7.0 Conveying						
.1	Elevators	N/A	—	—	—	0.0%
.2	Special Conveyors	N/A	—	—	—	
8.0 Mechanical						
.1	Plumbing	Toilet and service fixtures, supply and drainage _1 Fixture/1000 S.F. Floor_	Each	1860	1.86	
.2	Fire Protection	Sprinkler, ordinary hazard	S.F. Floor	2.27	2.27	
.3	Heating	Included in 8.4	—	—	—	18.6%
.4	Cooling	Single zone rooftop unit, gas heating, electric cooling	S.F. Floor	6.02	6.02	
.5	Special Systems	N/A	—	—	—	
9.0 Electrical						
.1	Service & Distribution	200 ampere service, panel board and feeders	S.F. Floor	1.81	1.81	
.2	Lighting & Power	Fluorescent fixtures, receptacles, switches, A.C. and misc. power	S.F. Floor	6.96	6.96	21.6%
.4	Special Electrical	Alarm systems and emergency lighting	S.F. Floor	3.08	3.08	
11.0 Special Construction						
.1	Specialties	N/A	—	—	—	0.0%
12.0 Site Work						
.1	Earthwork	N/A	—	—	—	
.3	Utilities	N/A	—	—	—	
.5	Roads & Parking	N/A	—	—	—	0.0%
.7	Site Improvements	N/A	—	—	—	
			Sub-Total		54.79	**100%**
	CONTRACTOR FEES (General Requirements: 10%, Overhead: 5%, Profit: 10%)			25%	13.70	
	ARCHITECT FEES			7%	4.81	
			Total Building Cost		**73.30**	

BUILDING TYPES

Costs per square foot of floor area

Exterior Wall	S.F. Area	50000	65000	80000	95000	110000	125000	140000	155000	170000
	L.F. Perimeter	920	1065	1167	1303	1333	1433	1533	1633	1733
Face Brick with Concrete Block Back-up	R/Conc. Frame	84.65	82.85	81.35	80.60	79.45	78.90	78.50	78.15	77.85
	Steel Frame	71.45	69.60	68.10	67.35	66.20	65.65	65.25	64.90	64.65
Decorative Concrete Block	R/Conc. Frame	81.20	79.75	78.60	78.00	77.15	76.70	76.40	76.15	75.95
	Steel Joists	68.60	67.10	65.85	65.25	64.30	63.90	63.55	63.25	63.05
Precast Concrete Panels	R/Conc. Frame	81.50	80.05	78.90	78.30	77.45	77.00	76.70	76.45	76.25
	Steel Joists	67.90	66.45	65.30	64.70	63.85	63.45	63.15	62.85	62.70
Perimeter Adj., Add or Deduct	Per 100 L.F.	1.25	.95	.75	.65	.55	.45	.40	.40	.35
Story Hgt. Adj., Add or Deduct	Per 1 Ft.	.65	.55	.50	.45	.40	.35	.40	.35	.35

For Basement, add $15.10 per square foot of basement area

The above costs were calculated using the basic specifications shown on the facing page. These costs should be adjusted where necessary for design alternatives and owner's requirements. Reported completed project costs, for this type of structure, range from $35.10 to $87.65 per S.F.

Common additives

Description	Unit	$ Cost
Closed Circuit Surveillance, One station		
Camera and monitor	Each	1375
For additional camera stations, add	Each	745
Directory Boards, Plastic, glass covered		
30" x 20"	Each	565
36" x 48"	Each	1025
Aluminum, 24" x 18"	Each	425
36" x 24"	Each	535
48" x 32"	Each	745
48" x 60"	Each	1600
Emergency Lighting, 25 watt, battery operated		
Lead battery	Each	289
Nickel cadmium	Each	655
Safe, Office type, 4 hour rating		
30" x 18" x 18"	Each	3125
62" x 33" x 20"	Each	6775
Sound System		
Amplifier, 250 watts	Each	1650
Speaker, ceiling or wall	Each	145
Trumpet	Each	271

BUILDING TYPES

Important: See the Reference Section for Location Factors

Model costs calculated for a 1 story building with 14' story height and 110,000 square feet of floor area

				Unit	Unit Cost	Cost Per S.F.	% Of Sub-Total
1.0 Foundations							
.1	Footings & Foundations	Poured concrete; strip and spread footings and 4' foundation wall		S.F. Ground	1.22	1.22	
.4	Piles & Caissons	N/A		—	—	—	3.7%
.9	Excavation & Backfill	Site preparation for slab and trench for foundation wall and footing		S.F. Ground	1.02	1.02	
2.0 Substructure							
.1	Slab on Grade	4" reinforced concrete with vapor barrier and granular base		S.F. Slab	3.32	3.32	5.5%
.2	Special Substructures	N/A		—	—	—	
3.0 Superstructure							
.1	Columns & Beams	Concrete columns		L.F. Column	46	.59	
.4	Structural Walls	N/A		—	—	—	
.5	Elevated Floors	N/A		—	—	—	26.5%
.7	Roof	Precast concrete beam and plank		S.F. Roof	15.30	15.30	
.9	Stairs	N/A		—	—	—	
4.0 Exterior Closure							
.1	Walls	Face brick with concrete block backup	90% of wall	S.F. Wall	21	3.23	
.5	Exterior Wall Finishes	N/A		—	—	—	7.1%
.6	Doors	Sliding electric operated entrance, hollow metal		Each	5025	.28	
.7	Windows & Glazed Walls	Storefront	10% of wall	S.F. Window	42	.72	
5.0 Roofing							
.1	Roof Coverings	Built-up tar and gravel with flashing		S.F. Roof	1.87	1.87	
.7	Insulation	Perlite/EPS composite		S.F. Roof	1.32	1.32	5.5%
.8	Openings & Specialties	Gravel stop and hatches		S.F. Roof	.11	.11	
6.0 Interior Construction							
.1	Partitions	Gypsum board on metal studs	60 S.F. Floor/L.F. Partition	S.F. Partition	4.14	.69	
.4	Interior Doors	Single leaf hollow metal	600 S.F. Floor/Door	Each	534	.89	
.5	Wall Finishes	Paint		S.F. Surface	.57	.19	26.4%
.6	Floor Finishes	50% ceramic tile, 50% carpet tile		S.F. Floor	12.06	12.06	
.7	Ceiling Finishes	Mineral fiber board on exposed grid system, suspended		S.F. Ceiling	1.56	1.56	
.9	Interior Surface/Exterior Wall	Painted gypsum board on furring	90% of wall	S.F. Wall	3.02	.46	
7.0 Conveying							
.1	Elevators	N/A		—	—	—	0.0%
.2	Special Conveyors	N/A		—	—	—	
8.0 Mechanical							
.1	Plumbing	Toilet and service fixtures, supply and drainage	1 Fixture/4075 S.F. Floor	Each	2852	.70	
.2	Fire Protection	Sprinklers, light hazard		S.F. Floor	1.44	1.44	
.3	Heating	Included in 8.4		—	—	—	14.6%
.4	Cooling	Single zone unit gas heating, electric cooling		S.F. Floor	6.54	6.54	
.5	Special Systems	N/A		—	—	—	
9.0 Electrical							
.1	Service & Distribution	1200 ampere service, panel board and feeders		S.F. Floor	.54	.54	
.2	Lighting & Power	Fluorescent fixtures, receptacles, switches, A.C. and misc. power		S.F. Floor	5.56	5.56	10.7%
.4	Special Electrical	Alarm systems and emergency lighting		S.F. Floor	.33	.33	
11.0 Special Construction							
.1	Specialties	N/A		—	—	—	0.0%
12.0 Site Work							
.1	Earthwork	N/A		—	—	—	
.3	Utilities	N/A		—	—	—	0.0%
.5	Roads & Parking	N/A		—	—	—	
.7	Site Improvements	N/A		—	—	—	
			Sub-Total			59.94	100%
	CONTRACTOR FEES (General Requirements: 10%, Overhead: 5%, Profit: 10%)				25%	14.99	
	ARCHITECT FEES				6%	4.52	
			Total Building Cost			79.45	

Costs per square foot of floor area

Exterior Wall	S.F. Area	50000	65000	80000	95000	110000	125000	140000	155000	170000
	L.F. Perimeter	533	593	670	715	778	840	871	923	976
Face Brick with Concrete Block Back-up	Steel Frame	94.65	90.95	89.05	87.15	86.10	85.20	84.20	83.55	83.10
	R/Conc. Frame	98.05	94.40	92.50	90.60	89.50	88.65	87.60	87.00	86.55
Face Brick on Steel Studs	Steel Frame	91.65	88.40	86.70	85.05	84.10	83.30	82.45	81.90	81.45
	R/Conc. Frame	96.30	93.05	91.35	89.70	88.75	87.95	87.10	86.55	86.15
Precast Concrete Panels Exposed Aggregate	Steel Frame	91.30	88.10	86.45	84.85	83.90	83.15	82.30	81.75	81.35
	R/Conc. Frame	95.55	92.40	90.75	89.10	88.20	87.40	86.55	86.00	85.60
Perimeter Adj., Add or Deduct	Per 100 L.F.	3.30	2.60	2.10	1.75	1.50	1.35	1.20	1.05	.95
Story Hgt. Adj., Add or Deduct	Per 1 Ft.	1.00	.90	.80	.75	.70	.65	.60	.55	.55
For Basement, add $25.50 per square foot of basement area										

The above costs were calculated using the basic specifications shown on the facing page. These costs should be adjusted where necessary for design alternatives and owner's requirements. Reported completed project costs, for this type of structure, range from $36.40 to $97.35 per S.F.

Common additives

Description	Unit	$ Cost	Description	Unit	$ Cost
Closed Circuit Surveillance, One station			Escalators, Metal		
Camera and monitor	Each	1375	32" wide, 10' story height	Each	88,400
For additional camera stations, add	Each	745	20' story height	Each	102,500
Directory Boards, Plastic, glass covered			48" wide, 10' story height	Each	92,900
30" x 20"	Each	565	20' story height	Each	107,000
36" x 48"	Each	1025	Glass		
Aluminum, 24" x 18"	Each	425	32" wide, 10' story height	Each	86,900
36" x 24"	Each	535	20' story height	Each	102,500
48" x 32"	Each	745	48" wide, 10' story height	Each	92,900
48" x 60"	Each	1600	20' story height	Each	107,000
Elevators, Hydraulic passenger, 2 stops			Safe, Office type, 4 hour rating		
1500# capacity	Each	42,225	30" x 18" x 18"	Each	3125
2500# capacity	Each	43,425	62" x 33" x 20"	Each	6775
3500# capacity	Each	47,225	Sound System		
Additional stop, add	Each	3650	Amplifier, 250 watts	Each	1650
Emergency Lighting, 25 watt, battery operated			Speaker, ceiling or wall	Each	145
Lead battery	Each	289	Trumpet	Each	271
Nickel cadmium	Each	655			

BUILDING TYPES

Important: See the Reference Section for Location Factors

Model costs calculated for a 3 story building with 16' story height and 95,000 square feet of floor area

				Unit	Unit Cost	Cost Per S.F.	% Of Sub-Total
1.0 Foundations							
.1	Footings & Foundations	Poured concrete; strip and spread footings and 4' foundation wall		S.F. Ground	3.60	1.20	
.4	Piles & Caissons	N/A		—	—	—	2.4%
.9	Excavation & Backfill	Site preparation for slab and trench for foundation wall and footing		S.F. Ground	1.08	.36	
2.0 Substructure							
.1	Slab on Grade	4" reinforced concrete with vapor barrier and granular base		S.F. Slab	3.32	1.11	1.7%
.2	Special Substructures	N/A		—			
3.0 Superstructure							
.1	Columns & Beams	Steel columns with sprayed fiber fireproofing		L.F. Column	104	1.24	
.4	Structural Walls	N/A		—	—	—	
.5	Elevated Floors	Concrete slab with metal deck and beams		S.F. Floor	14.25	9.50	20.3%
.7	Roof	Metal deck, open web steel joists, beams, columns		S.F. Roof	5.57	1.86	
.9	Stairs	Concrete filled metal pan		Flight	7000	.74	
4.0 Exterior Closure							
.1	Walls	Face brick with concrete block backup	90% of wall	S.F. Wall	21	6.88	
.5	Exterior Wall Finishes	N/A		—	—	—	14.0%
.6	Doors	Revolving and sliding panel, mall-front		Each	7955	1.17	
.7	Windows & Glazed Walls	Storefront	10% of wall	S.F. Window	31	1.14	
5.0 Roofing							
.1	Roof Coverings	Built-up tar and gravel with flashing		S.F. Roof	2.13	.71	
.7	Insulation	Perlite/EPS composite		S.F. Roof	1.32	.44	1.9%
.8	Openings & Specialties	Gravel stop and hatches		S.F. Roof	.27	.09	
6.0 Interior Construction							
.1	Partitions	Gypsum board on metal studs	60 S.F. Floor/L.F. Partition	S.F. Partition	4.14	.69	
.4	Interior Doors	Single leaf hollow metal	600 S.F. Floor/Door	Each	534	.89	
.5	Wall Finishes	70% paint, 20% vinyl wall covering, 10% ceramic tile		S.F. Surface	1.20	.40	27.6%
.6	Floor Finishes	50% carpet tile, 40% marble tile, 10% terrazzo		S.F. Floor	11.87	11.87	
.7	Ceiling Finishes	Mineral fiber tile on concealed zee bars		S.F. Ceiling	3.63	3.63	
.9	Interior Surface/Exterior Wall	Paint	90% of wall	S.F. Wall	2.12	.69	
7.0 Conveying							
.1	Elevators	One hydraulic passenger, one hydraulic freight		Each	149,150	1.57	8.4%
.2	Special Conveyors	Four escalators		Each	—	3.96	
8.0 Mechanical							
.1	Plumbing	Toilet and service fixtures, supply and drainage	1 Fixture/2570 S.F. Floor	Each	1644	.64	
.2	Fire Protection	Sprinklers, light hazard		S.F. Floor	1.21	1.21	
.3	Heating	Included in 8.4		—	—	—	12.7%
.4	Cooling	Multizone rooftop unit, gas heating, electric cooling		S.F. Floor	6.54	6.54	
.5	Special Systems	N/A		—	—	—	
9.0 Electrical							
.1	Service & Distribution	1200 ampere service, panel board and feeders		S.F. Floor	.82	.82	
.2	Lighting & Power	Fluorescent fixtures, receptacles, switches, A.C. and misc. power		S.F. Floor	5.87	5.87	11.0%
.4	Special Electrical	Alarm systems and emergency lighting		S.F. Floor	.56	.56	
11.0 Special Construction							
.1	Specialties	N/A		—	—	—	0.0%
12.0 Site Work							
.1	Earthwork	N/A		—	—	—	
.3	Utilities	N/A		—	—	—	0.0%
.5	Roads & Parking	N/A		—	—	—	
.7	Site Improvements	N/A		—	—	—	
				Sub-Total		65.78	**100%**
	CONTRACTOR FEES (General Requirements: 10%, Overhead: 5%, Profit: 10%)				25%	16.45	
	ARCHITECT FEES				6%	4.92	
				Total Building Cost		**87.15**	

Costs per square foot of floor area

Exterior Wall	S.F. Area	4000	6000	8000	10000	12000	15000	18000	20000	22000
	L.F. Perimeter	260	340	360	410	440	490	540	565	594
Split Face Concrete Block	Steel Joists	90.85	83.30	76.30	73.40	70.70	68.20	66.55	65.50	64.75
Stucco on Concrete Block	Steel Joists	88.75	81.45	74.85	72.10	69.55	67.15	65.60	64.60	63.90
Painted Concrete Block	Steel Joists	84.50	77.45	71.25	68.60	66.15	63.90	62.40	61.50	60.80
Face Brick on Concrete Block	Steel Joists	101.15	92.30	83.45	79.95	76.55	73.40	71.30	70.00	69.05
Painted Reinforced Concrete	Steel Joists	97.50	89.10	80.90	77.60	74.45	71.55	69.60	68.40	67.50
Tilt-up Concrete Panels	Steel Joists	91.25	83.65	76.60	73.70	70.95	68.40	66.75	65.70	64.95
Perimeter Adj., Add or Deduct	Per 100 L.F.	10.75	7.20	5.40	4.30	3.60	2.85	2.40	2.15	1.95
Story Hgt. Adj., Add or Deduct	Per 1 Ft.	1.35	1.20	.95	.85	.80	.70	.65	.60	.55
For Basement, add $21.10 per square foot of basement area										

The above costs were calculated using the basic specifications shown on the facing page. These costs should be adjusted where necessary for design alternatives and owner's requirements. Reported completed project costs, for this type of structure, range from $35.50 to $123.50 per S.F.

Common additives

Description	Unit	$ Cost
Emergency Lighting, 25 watt, battery operated		
Lead battery	Each	289
Nickel cadmium	Each	655
Safe, Office type, 4 hour rating		
30" x 18" x 18"	Each	3125
62" x 33" x 20"	Each	6775
Smoke Detectors		
Ceiling type	Each	149
Duct type	Each	405
Sound System		
Amplifier, 250 watts	Each	1650
Speaker, ceiling or wall	Each	145
Trumpet	Each	271

BUILDING TYPES

Important: See the Reference Section for Location Factors

Model costs calculated for a 1 story building with 14' story height and 8,000 square feet of floor area

				Unit	Unit Cost	Cost Per S.F.	% Of Sub-Total
1.0 Foundations							
	.1	Footings & Foundations	Poured concrete; strip and spread footings and 4' foundation wall	S.F. Ground	3.50	3.50	
	.4	Piles & Caissons	N/A	—	—	—	8.3%
	.9	Excavation & Backfill	Site preparation for slab and trench for foundation wall and footing	S.F. Ground	1.17	1.17	
2.0 Substructure							
	.1	Slab on Grade	4" reinforced concrete with vapor barrier and granular base	S.F. Slab	3.32	3.32	5.9%
	.2	Special Substructures	N/A	—	—	—	
3.0 Superstructure							
	.1	Columns & Beams	Interior columns included in 3.7	—	—	—	
	.4	Structural Walls	N/A	—	—	—	
	.5	Elevated Floors	N/A	—	—	—	7.0%
	.7	Roof	Metal deck, open web steel joists, beams, interior columns	S.F. Roof	3.97	3.97	
	.9	Stairs	N/A	—	—	—	
4.0 Exterior Closure							
	.1	Walls	Decorative concrete block 90% of wall	S.F. Wall	11.85	6.72	
	.5	Exterior Wall Finishes	N/A	—	—	—	16.0%
	.6	Doors	Sliding entrance door and hollow metal service doors	Each	1375	.34	
	.7	Windows & Glazed Walls	Storefront windows 10% of wall	S.F. Window	31	1.99	
5.0 Roofing							
	.1	Roof Coverings	Built-up tar and gravel with flashing	S.F. Roof	2.42	2.42	
	.7	Insulation	Perlite/EPS composite	S.F. Roof	1.32	1.32	7.2%
	.8	Openings & Specialties	Gravel stop and hatches	S.F. Roof	.35	.35	
6.0 Interior Construction							
	.1	Partitions	Gypsum board on metal studs 60 S.F. Floor/L.F. Partition	S.F. Partition	4.14	.69	
	.4	Interior Doors	Single leaf hollow metal 600 S.F. Floor/Door	Each	534	.89	
	.5	Wall Finishes	Paint	S.F. Surface	.57	.19	16.8%
	.6	Floor Finishes	Vinyl tile	S.F. Floor	2.91	2.91	
	.7	Ceiling Finishes	Mineral fiber tile on concealed zee bars	S.F. Ceiling	3.63	3.63	
	.9	Interior Surface/Exterior Wall	Paint 90% of wall	S.F. Wall	2.12	1.20	
7.0 Conveying							
	.1	Elevators	N/A	—	—	—	0.0%
	.2	Special Conveyors	N/A	—	—	—	
8.0 Mechanical							
	.1	Plumbing	Toilet and service fixtures, supply and drainage 1 Fixture/890 S.F. Floor	Each	3746	4.21	
	.2	Fire Protection	Wet pipe sprinkler system	S.F. Floor	2.21	2.21	
	.3	Heating	Included in 8.4	—	—	—	23.0%
	.4	Cooling	Single zone unit, gas heating, electric cooling	S.F. Floor	6.54	6.54	
	.5	Special Systems	N/A	—	—	—	
9.0 Electrical							
	.1	Service & Distribution	400 ampere service, panel board and feeders	S.F. Floor	1.66	1.66	
	.2	Lighting & Power	Fluorescent fixtures, receptacles, switches, A.C. and misc. power	S.F. Floor	6.84	6.84	15.8%
	.4	Special Electrical	Alarm systems and emergency lighting	S.F. Floor	.45	.45	
11.0 Special Construction							
	.1	Specialties	N/A	—	—	—	0.0%
12.0 Site Work							
	.1	Earthwork	N/A	—	—	—	
	.3	Utilities	N/A	—	—	—	
	.5	Roads & Parking	N/A	—	—	—	0.0%
	.7	Site Improvements	N/A	—	—	—	
				Sub-Total		56.52	100%
		CONTRACTOR FEES (General Requirements: 10%, Overhead: 5%, Profit: 10%)			25%	14.13	
		ARCHITECT FEES			8%	5.65	
				Total Building Cost		76.30	

BUILDING TYPES

Costs per square foot of floor area

Exterior Wall	S.F. Area	12000	16000	20000	26000	32000	38000	44000	52000	60000
	L.F. Perimeter	450	510	570	650	716	780	840	920	1020
Face Brick with Concrete Block Back-up	Steel Frame	89.20	83.30	79.70	76.15	73.60	71.75	70.40	69.05	68.30
	Bearing Walls	86.55	80.65	77.10	73.50	70.95	69.10	67.75	66.45	65.70
Stucco on Concrete Block	Steel Frame	82.30	77.40	74.45	71.55	69.50	68.00	66.90	65.80	65.15
	Bearing Walls	82.35	77.45	74.55	71.60	69.55	68.05	66.95	65.85	65.25
Precast Concrete Panels	Steel Frame	85.20	79.90	76.70	73.50	71.20	69.60	68.35	67.15	66.50
Metal Sandwich Panels	Steel Frame	76.60	72.55	70.15	67.75	66.05	64.85	64.00	63.10	62.60
Perimeter Adj., Add or Deduct	Per 100 L.F.	6.45	4.85	3.90	3.00	2.40	2.05	1.75	1.50	1.30
Story Hgt. Adj., Add or Deduct	Per 1 Ft.	1.35	1.15	1.00	.90	.80	.75	.65	.60	.60

For Basement, add $15.35 per square foot of basement area

The above costs were calculated using the basic specifications shown on the facing page. These costs should be adjusted where necessary for design alternatives and owner's requirements. Reported completed project costs, for this type of structure, range from $41.45 to $118.65 per S.F.

Common additives

Description	Unit	$ Cost
Check Out Counter		
Single belt	Each	2225
Double belt	Each	3825
Scanner, registers, guns & memory 2 lanes	Each	13,600
10 lanes	Each	129,000
Power take away	Each	4725
Emergency Lighting, 25 watt, battery operated		
Lead battery	Each	289
Nickel cadmium	Each	655
Refrigerators, Prefabricated, walk-in		
7'-6" High, 6' x 6'	S.F.	120
10' x 10'	S.F.	95
12' x 14'	S.F.	83
12' x 20'	S.F.	73
Refrigerated Food Cases		
Dairy, multi deck, 12' long	Each	8025
Delicatessen case, single deck, 12' long	Each	5425
Multi deck, 18 S.F. shelf display	Each	6650
Freezer, self-contained chest type, 30 C.F.	Each	4025
Glass door upright, 78 C.F.	Each	7500

Description	Unit	$ Cost
Refrigerated Food Cases, cont.		
Frozen food, chest type, 12' long	Each	5475
Glass door reach in, 5 door	Each	10,400
Island case 12' long, single deck	Each	6175
Multi deck	Each	12,900
Meat case 12' long, single deck	Each	4550
Multi deck	Each	7700
Produce, 12' long single deck	Each	5950
Multi deck	Each	6625
Safe, Office type, 4 hour rating		
30" x 18" x 18"	Each	3125
62" x 33" x 20"	Each	6775
Smoke Detectors		
Ceiling type	Each	149
Duct type	Each	405
Sound System		
Amplifier, 250 watts	Each	1650
Speaker, ceiling or wall	Each	145
Trumpet	Each	271

Important: See the Reference Section for Location Factors

BUILDING TYPES

Model costs calculated for a 1 story building with 18' story height and 44,000 square feet of floor area

Supermarket

			Unit	Unit Cost	Cost Per S.F.	% Of Sub-Total
1.0 Foundations						
.1	Footings & Foundations	Poured concrete; strip and spread footings and 4' foundation wall	S.F. Ground	1.70	1.70	
.4	Piles & Caissons	N/A	—	—	—	5.5%
.9	Excavation & Backfill	Site preparation for slab and trench for foundation wall and footing	S.F. Ground	1.08	1.08	
2.0 Substructure						
.1	Slab on Grade	4" reinforced concrete with vapor barrier and granular base	S.F. Slab	3.32	3.32	6.6%
.2	Special Substructures	N/A	—	—	—	
3.0 Superstructure						
.1	Columns & Beams	Interior columns included in 3.7	—	—	—	
.4	Structural Walls	N/A	—	—	—	
.5	Elevated Floors	N/A	—	—	—	8.5%
.7	Roof	Metal deck, open web steel joists, beams, interior columns	S.F. Roof	4.32	4.32	
.9	Stairs	N/A	—	—	—	
4.0 Exterior Closure						
.1	Walls	Face brick with concrete block backup 85% of wall	S.F. Wall	21	6.15	
.5	Exterior Wall Finishes	N/A	—	—	—	
.6	Doors	Sliding entrance doors with electrical operator, hollow metal	Each	3436	.86	18.6%
.7	Windows & Glazed Walls	Storefront windows 15% of wall	S.F. Window	46	2.41	
5.0 Roofing						
.1	Roof Coverings	Built-up tar and gravel with flashing	S.F. Roof	1.99	1.99	
.7	Insulation	Perlite/EPS composite	S.F. Roof	1.32	1.32	6.9%
.8	Openings & Specialties	Gravel stop and hatches	S.F. Roof	.19	.19	
6.0 Interior Construction						
.1	Partitions	50% concrete block, 50% gypsum board on metal studs 50 S.F. Floor/L.F. Partition	S.F. Partition	5.00	1.20	
.4	Interior Doors	Single leaf hollow metal 2000 S.F. Floor/Door	Each	534	.27	
.5	Wall Finishes	Paint	S.F. Surface	2.13	1.02	19.0%
.6	Floor Finishes	Vinyl composition tile	S.F. Floor	2.91	2.91	
.7	Ceiling Finishes	Mineral fiber tile on concealed zee bars	S.F. Ceiling	3.63	3.63	
.9	Interior Surface/Exterior Wall	Paint 85% of wall	S.F. Wall	2.12	.62	
7.0 Conveying						
.1	Elevators	N/A	—	—	—	0.0%
.2	Special Conveyors	N/A	—	—	—	
8.0 Mechanical						
.1	Plumbing	Toilet and service fixtures, supply and drainage 1 Fixture/1820 S.F. Floor	Each	1528	.84	
.2	Fire Protection	Sprinklers, light hazard	S.F. Floor	1.69	1.69	
.3	Heating	Included in 8.4	—	—	—	17.6%
.4	Cooling	Single zone rooftop unit, gas heating, electric cooling	S.F. Floor	6.36	6.36	
.5	Special Systems	N/A	—	—	—	
9.0 Electrical						
.1	Service & Distribution	600 ampere service, panel board and feeders	S.F. Floor	.78	.78	
.2	Lighting & Power	Fluorescent fixtures, receptacles, switches, A.C. and misc. power	S.F. Floor	7.84	7.84	17.3%
.4	Special Electrical	Alarm systems and emergency lighting	S.F. Floor	.17	.17	
11.0 Special Construction						
.1	Specialties	N/A	—	—	—	0.0%
12.0 Site Work						
.1	Earthwork	N/A	—	—	—	
.3	Utilities	N/A	—	—	—	
.5	Roads & Parking	N/A	—	—	—	0.0%
.7	Site Improvements	N/A	—	—	—	
			Sub-Total		50.67	**100%**
	CONTRACTOR FEES (General Requirements: 10%, Overhead: 5%, Profit: 10%)			25%	12.67	
	ARCHITECT FEES			7%	4.41	
			Total Building Cost		67.75	

BUILDING TYPES

205

BUILDING TYPES

Costs per square foot of floor area

Exterior Wall	S.F. Area	10000	16000	20000	22000	24000	26000	28000	30000	32000
	L.F. Perimeter	420	510	600	640	680	673	706	740	737
Face Brick with Concrete Block Back-up	Wood Truss	169.20	155.80	153.05	151.80	150.75	147.80	146.95	146.15	144.20
	Precast Conc.	182.90	166.80	163.55	162.05	160.80	157.20	156.15	155.25	152.90
Metal Sandwich Panel	Wood Truss	170.20	160.30	158.20	157.25	156.45	154.40	153.75	153.15	151.80
Precast Concrete Panel	Precast Conc.	165.60	153.60	151.10	149.95	149.00	146.45	145.65	144.95	143.25
Painted Concrete Block	Wood Frame	170.95	161.15	159.10	158.15	157.35	155.30	154.70	154.10	152.75
	Precast Conc.	167.90	155.45	152.85	151.70	150.70	148.00	147.20	146.45	144.70
Perimeter Adj., Add or Deduct	Per 100 L.F.	11.20	7.05	5.60	5.10	4.65	4.35	4.00	3.75	3.50
Story Hgt. Adj., Add or Deduct	Per 1 Ft.	1.40	1.05	1.00	1.00	.90	.90	.85	.85	.80
For Basement, add $22.85 per square foot of basement area										

The above costs were calculated using the basic specifications shown on the facing page. These costs should be adjusted where necessary for design alternatives and owner's requirements. Reported completed project costs, for this type of structure, range from $65.75 to $193.25 per S.F.

Common additives

Description	Unit	$ Cost		Description	Unit	$ Cost
Bleachers, Telescoping, manual				Sauna, Prefabricated, complete		
To 15 tier	Seat	79 - 109		6' x 4'	Each	4075
16-20 tier	Seat	160 - 195		6' x 6'	Each	4850
21-30 tier	Seat	170 - 205		6' x 9'	Each	5350
For power operation, add	Seat	30 - 48		8' x 8'	Each	6300
Emergency Lighting, 25 watt, battery operated				8' x 10'	Each	6950
Lead battery	Each	289		10' x 12'	Each	9125
Nickel cadmium	Each	655		Sound System		
Lockers, Steel, single tier, 60" or 72"	Opening	125 - 220		Amplifier, 250 watts	Each	1650
2 tier, 60" or 72" total	Opening	70 - 119		Speaker, ceiling or wall	Each	145
5 tier, box lockers	Opening	40 - 60		Trumpet	Each	271
Locker bench, lam. maple top only	L.F.	18.05		Steam Bath, Complete, to 140 C.F.	Each	1275
Pedestal, steel pipe	Each	58		To 300 C.F.	Each	1450
Pool Equipment				To 800 C.F.	Each	4625
Diving stand, 3 meter	Each	6925		To 2500 C.F.	Each	4925
1 meter	Each	4400				
Diving board, 16' aluminum	Each	1875				
Fiberglass	Each	1475				
Lifeguard chair, fixed	Each	1675				
Portable	Each	1825				
Lights, underwater, 12 volt, 300 watt	Each	1150				

Important: See the Reference Section for Location Factors

Model costs calculated for a 1 story building with 24' story height and 20,000 square feet of floor area

Swimming Pool, Enclosed

				Unit	Unit Cost	Cost Per S.F.	% Of Sub-Total
1.0 Foundations							
.1	Footings & Foundations	Poured concrete; strip and spread footings and 4' foundation wall		S.F. Ground	4.44	4.44	10.1%
.4	Piles & Caissons	N/A		—	—	—	
.9	Excavation & Backfill	Site preparation for slab and trench for foundation wall and footing		S.F. Ground	7.05	7.05	
2.0 Substructure							
.1	Slab on Grade	4" reinforced concrete with vapor barrier and granular base		S.F. Slab	3.32	3.32	5.3%
.2	Special Substructures	Pool walls		S.F. Ground	2.72	2.72	
3.0 Superstructure							
.1	Columns & Beams	Wood columns included in 3.7		—	—	—	
.4	Structural Walls	N/A		—	—	—	
.5	Elevated Floors	N/A		—	—	—	11.0%
.7	Roof	Wood deck on laminated wood truss		S.F. Ground	12.49	12.49	
.9	Stairs	N/A		—	—	—	
4.0 Exterior Closure							
.1	Walls	Face brick with concrete block backup	80% of wall	S.F. Wall	21	12.18	
.5	Exterior Wall Finishes	N/A		—	—	—	15.1%
.6	Doors	Double aluminum and glass, hollow metal		Each	1495	.37	
.7	Windows & Glazed Walls	Outward projecting steel	20% of wall	S.F. Window	31	4.55	
5.0 Roofing							
.1	Roof Coverings	Asphalt shingles with flashing		S.F. Ground	1.09	1.09	
.7	Insulation	Perlite/EPS composite		S.F. Ground	—	—	1.1%
.8	Openings & Specialties	Gutters and downspouts		S.F. Ground	.18	.18	
6.0 Interior Construction							
.1	Partitions	Concrete block, toilet partitions	100 S.F. Floor/L.F. Partition	S.F. Partition	5.90	.74	
.4	Interior Doors	Single leaf hollow metal	1000 S.F. Floor/Door	Each	534	.53	
.5	Wall Finishes	Acrylic glazed coating		S.F. Surface	.90	.18	15.6%
.6	Floor Finishes	70% terrazzo, 30% ceramic tile		S.F. Floor	14.70	14.70	
.7	Ceiling Finishes	Mineral fiber tile on concealed zee bars	20% of area	S.F. Ceiling	1.56	.31	
.9	Interior Surface/Exterior Wall	Paint	80% of wall	S.F. Wall	2.12	1.22	
7.0 Conveying							
.1	Elevators	N/A		—	—	—	0.0%
.2	Special Conveyors	N/A		—	—	—	
8.0 Mechanical							
.1	Plumbing	Toilet and service fixtures, supply and drainage	1 Fixture/210 S.F. Floor	Each	1978	9.42	
.2	Fire Protection	Sprinklers, light hazard		S.F. Floor	.85	.85	
.3	Heating	Terminal unit heaters	10% of area	S.F. Floor	.50	.50	19.4%
.4	Cooling	Single zone unit gas heating, electric cooling		S.F. Floor	11.16	11.16	
.5	Special Systems	N/A		—	—	—	
9.0 Electrical							
.1	Service & Distribution	400 ampere service, panel board and feeders		S.F. Floor	.69	.69	
.2	Lighting & Power	Fluorescent fixtures, receptacles, switches, A.C. and misc. power		S.F. Floor	6.07	6.07	6.2%
.4	Special Electrical	Alarm systems and emergency lighting		S.F. Floor	.30	.30	
11.0 Special Construction							
.1	Specialties	Swimming pool		—	18.31	18.31	16.2%
12.0 Site Work							
.1	Earthwork	N/A		—	—	—	
.3	Utilities	N/A		—	—	—	0.0%
.5	Roads & Parking	N/A		—	—	—	
.7	Site Improvements	N/A		—	—	—	
				Sub-Total		113.37	**100%**
	CONTRACTOR FEES (General Requirements: 10%, Overhead: 5%, Profit: 10%)				25%	28.34	
	ARCHITECT FEES				8%	11.34	
				Total Building Cost		**153.05**	

BUILDING TYPES

Costs per square foot of floor area

Exterior Wall	S.F. Area	2000	3000	4000	5000	6000	7000	8000	9000	10000
	L.F. Perimeter	180	220	260	286	320	353	368	397	425
Face Brick with Concrete Block Back-up	Steel Frame	135.05	120.70	113.60	107.45	104.25	101.90	98.65	97.10	95.85
	Bearing Walls	132.55	118.20	111.05	104.95	101.75	99.40	96.15	94.60	93.35
Limestone with Concrete Block Back-up	Steel Frame	151.10	133.80	125.20	117.65	113.80	110.90	106.85	105.00	103.45
	Bearing Walls	148.60	131.30	122.65	115.15	111.30	108.40	104.35	102.50	100.95
Decorative Concrete Block	Steel Frame	125.85	113.25	106.95	101.65	98.85	96.75	93.95	92.60	91.50
	Bearing Walls	123.35	110.75	104.45	99.10	96.35	94.25	91.45	90.10	89.00
Perimeter Adj., Add or Deduct	Per 100 L.F.	32.20	21.45	16.05	12.85	10.70	9.15	8.00	7.15	6.45
Story Hgt. Adj., Add or Deduct	Per 1 Ft.	3.80	3.10	2.75	2.40	2.25	2.10	1.90	1.85	1.80
For Basement, add $22.00 per square foot of basement area										

The above costs were calculated using the basic specifications shown on the facing page. These costs should be adjusted where necessary for design alternatives and owner's requirements. Reported completed project costs, for this type of structure, range from $57.60 to $203.45 per S.F.

Common additives

Description	Unit	$ Cost
Emergency Lighting, 25 watt, battery operated		
Lead battery	Each	289
Nickel cadmium	Each	655
Smoke Detectors		
Ceiling type	Each	149
Duct type	Each	405
Emergency Generators, complete system, gas		
15 kw	Each	12,800
85 kw	Each	28,400
170 kw	Each	71,500
Diesel, 50 kw	Each	24,500
150 kw	Each	42,300
350 kw	Each	67,500

Important: See the Reference Section for Location Factors

Model costs calculated for a 1 story building with 12' story height and 5,000 square feet of floor area

				Unit	Unit Cost	Cost Per S.F.	% Of Sub-Total
1.0 Foundations							
.1	Footings & Foundations	Poured concrete; strip and spread footings and 4' foundation wall		S.F. Ground	4.69	4.69	
.4	Piles & Caissons	N/A		—	—	—	7.7%
.9	Excavation & Backfill	Site preparation for slab and trench for foundation wall and footing		S.F. Ground	1.28	1.28	
2.0 Substructure							
.1	Slab on Grade	4" reinforced concrete with vapor barrier and granular base		S.F. Slab	3.32	3.32	4.3%
.2	Special Substructures	N/A		—	—	—	
3.0 Superstructure							
.1	Columns & Beams	Steel columns included in 3.7		—	—	—	
.4	Structural Walls	N/A		—	—	—	
.5	Elevated Floors	N/A		—	—	—	7.0%
.7	Roof	Metal deck, open web steel joists, beams, columns		S.F. Roof	5.42	5.42	
.9	Stairs	N/A		—	—	—	
4.0 Exterior Closure							
.1	Walls	Face brick with concrete block backup	80% of wall	S.F. Wall	21	11.56	
.5	Exterior Wall Finishes	N/A		—	—	—	
.6	Doors	Single aluminum glass with transom		Each	2425	.97	26.7%
.7	Windows & Glazed Walls	Outward projecting steel	20% of wall	Each	1190	8.17	
5.0 Roofing							
.1	Roof Coverings	Built-up tar and gravel with flashing		S.F. Roof	2.62	2.62	
.7	Insulation	Perlite/EPS composite		S.F. Roof	1.32	1.32	5.6%
.8	Openings & Specialties	Gravel stop and hatches		S.F. Roof	.37	.37	
6.0 Interior Construction							
.1	Partitions	Double layer gypsum board on metal studs, toilet partitions	15 S.F. Floor/L.F. Partition	S.F. Partition	5.67	3.78	
.4	Interior Doors	Single leaf hollow metal	150 S.F. Floor/Door	Each	534	3.56	
.5	Wall Finishes	Paint		S.F. Surface	.57	.76	
.6	Floor Finishes	90% carpet, 10% terrazzo		S.F. Floor	6.09	6.09	23.3%
.7	Ceiling Finishes	Fiberglass board on exposed grid system, suspended		S.F. Ceiling	2.69	2.69	
.9	Interior Surface/Exterior Wall	Paint	80% of wall	S.F. Floor	2.12	1.16	
7.0 Conveying							
.1	Elevators	N/A		—	—	—	0.0%
.2	Special Conveyors	N/A		—	—	—	
8.0 Mechanical							
.1	Plumbing	Kitchen, toilet and service fixtures, supply and drainage	1 Fixture/715 S.F. Floor	Each	3031	4.24	
.2	Fire Protection	Wet pipe sprinkler system		S.F. Floor	2.50	2.50	
.3	Heating	Included in 8.4		—	—	—	17.3%
.4	Cooling	Single zone unit, gas heating, electric cooling		S.F. Floor	6.71	6.71	
.5	Special Systems	N/A		—	—	—	
9.0 Electrical							
.1	Service & Distribution	200 ampere service, panel board and feeders		S.F. Floor	1.16	1.16	
.2	Lighting & Power	Fluorescent fixtures, receptacles, switches, A.C. and misc. power		S.F. Floor	4.01	4.01	8.1%
.4	Special Electrical	Alarm systems and emergency lighting		S.F. Floor	1.07	1.07	
11.0 Special Construction							
.1	Specialties	N/A		—	—	—	0.0%
12.0 Site Work							
.1	Earthwork	N/A		—	—	—	
.3	Utilities	N/A		—	—	—	
.5	Roads & Parking	N/A		—	—	—	0.0%
.7	Site Improvements	N/A		—	—	—	
				Sub-Total		77.45	**100%**
	CONTRACTOR FEES (General Requirements: 10%, Overhead: 5%, Profit: 10%)				25%	19.36	
	ARCHITECT FEES				11%	10.64	
				Total Building Cost		107.45	

BUILDING TYPES

BUILDING TYPES

Costs per square foot of floor area

Exterior Wall	S.F. Area	5000	6500	8000	9500	11000	14000	17500	21000	24000
	L.F. Perimeter	300	360	386	396	435	510	550	620	680
Face Brick with Concrete Block Back-up	Steel Joists	103.20	99.20	94.50	90.35	88.75	86.45	83.35	82.00	81.20
	Wood Joists	105.35	101.25	96.40	92.20	90.50	88.15	85.00	83.60	82.80
Stone with Concrete Block Back-up	Steel Joists	104.90	100.75	95.80	91.55	89.85	87.45	84.25	82.85	82.00
	Wood Joists	107.00	102.80	97.75	93.35	91.65	89.20	85.85	84.45	83.60
Brick Veneer	Wood Frame	99.25	95.50	91.20	87.45	85.90	83.80	81.00	79.80	79.05
E.I.F.S.	Wood Frame	94.45	91.05	87.30	84.15	82.75	80.90	78.50	77.40	76.80
Perimeter Adj., Add or Deduct	Per 100 L.F.	10.40	8.00	6.50	5.45	4.75	3.70	2.95	2.50	2.15
Story Hgt. Adj., Add or Deduct	Per 1 Ft.	1.90	1.75	1.55	1.30	1.30	1.15	1.00	.95	.90
For Basement, add $18.20 per square foot of basement area										

The above costs were calculated using the basic specifications shown on the facing page. These costs should be adjusted where necessary for design alternatives and owner's requirements. Reported completed project costs, for this type of structure, range from $50.95 to $143.85 per S.F.

Common additives

Description	Unit	$ Cost
Directory Boards, Plastic, glass covered		
30" x 20"	Each	565
36" x 48"	Each	1025
Aluminum, 24" x 18"	Each	425
36" x 24"	Each	535
48" x 32"	Each	745
48" x 60"	Each	1600
Emergency Lighting, 25 watt, battery operated		
Lead battery	Each	289
Nickel cadmium	Each	655
Flagpoles, Complete		
Aluminum, 20' high	Each	1075
40' high	Each	2675
70' high	Each	8250
Fiberglass, 23' high	Each	1400
39'-5" high	Each	2950
59' high	Each	7300
Safe, Office type, 4 hour rating		
30" x 18" x 18"	Each	3125
62" x 33" x 20"	Each	6775

Description	Unit	$ Cost
Smoke Detectors		
Ceiling type	Each	149
Duct type	Each	405
Vault Front, Door & frame		
1 Hour test, 32" x 78"	Opening	3550
2 Hour test, 32" door	Opening	4225
40" door	Opening	4625
4 Hour test, 32" door	Opening	4325
40" door	Opening	5150
Time lock movement; two movement	Each	1650

Important: See the Reference Section for Location Factors

Model costs calculated for a 1 story building with 12' story height and 11,000 square feet of floor area

Town Hall, 1 Story

BUILDING TYPES

				Unit	Unit Cost	Cost Per S.F.	% Of Sub-Total
1.0 Foundations							
.1	Footings & Foundations	Poured concrete; strip and spread footings and 4' foundation wall		S.F. Ground	3.09	3.09	
.4	Piles & Caissons	N/A		—	—	—	6.5%
.9	Excavation & Backfill	Site preparation for slab and trench for foundation wall and footing		S.F. Ground	1.17	1.17	
2.0 Substructure							
.1	Slab on Grade	4" reinforced concrete with vapor barrier and granular base		S.F. Slab	3.32	3.32	5.1%
.2	Special Substructures	N/A		—	—	—	
3.0 Superstructure							
.1	Columns & Beams	Steel columns included in 3.7		—	—	—	
.4	Structural Walls	N/A		—	—	—	
.5	Elevated Floors	N/A		—	—	—	6.3%
.7	Roof	Metal deck, open web steel joists, beams, interior columns		S.F. Roof	4.11	4.11	
.9	Stairs	N/A		—	—	—	
4.0 Exterior Closure							
.1	Walls	Face brick with concrete block backup	70% of wall	S.F. Wall	21	6.99	
.5	Exterior Wall Finishes	N/A		—	—	—	16.3%
.6	Doors	Metal and glass with transom		Each	1607	.59	
.7	Windows & Glazed Walls	Metal outward projecting	30% of wall	Each	493	3.05	
5.0 Roofing							
.1	Roof Coverings	Built-up tar and gravel with flashing		S.F. Roof	2.48	2.48	
.7	Insulation	Perlite/EPS composite		S.F. Roof	1.32	1.32	6.2%
.8	Openings & Specialties	Gravel stop and hatches		S.F. Roof	.25	.25	
6.0 Interior Construction							
.1	Partitions	Gypsum board on metal studs, toilet partition	20 S.F. Floor/L.F. Partition	S.F. Partition	4.12	2.46	
.4	Interior Doors	Wood solid core	200 S.F. Floor/Door	Each	427	2.14	
.5	Wall Finishes	90% paint, 10% ceramic tile		S.F. Surface	1.06	1.06	25.4%
.6	Floor Finishes	70% carpet tile, 15% terrazzo, 15% vinyl composition tile		S.F. Floor	6.22	6.22	
.7	Ceiling Finishes	Mineral fiber tile on concealed zee bars		S.F. Ceiling	3.63	3.63	
.9	Interior Surface/Exterior Wall	Painted gypsum board on furring	70% of wall	S.F. Wall	3.02	1.00	
7.0 Conveying							
.1	Elevators	N/A		—	—	—	0.0%
.2	Special Conveyors	N/A		—	—	—	
8.0 Mechanical							
.1	Plumbing	Kitchen, toilet and service fixtures, supply and drainage	1 Fixture/500 S.F. Floor	Each	2470	4.94	
.2	Fire Protection	Wet pipe sprinkler system		S.F. Floor	1.69	1.69	
.3	Heating	Included in 8.4		—	—	—	21.1%
.4	Cooling	Multizone unit, gas heating, electric cooling		S.F. Floor	7.11	7.11	
.5	Special Systems	N/A		—	—	—	
9.0 Electrical							
.1	Service & Distribution	400 ampere service, panel board and feeders		S.F. Floor	1.20	1.20	
.2	Lighting & Power	Fluorescent fixtures, receptacles, switches, A.C. and misc. power		S.F. Floor	6.73	6.73	13.1%
.4	Special Electrical	Alarm systems and emergency lighting		S.F. Floor	.57	.57	
11.0 Special Construction							
.1	Specialties	N/A		—	—	—	0.0%
12.0 Site Work							
.1	Earthwork	N/A		—	—	—	
.3	Utilities	N/A		—	—	—	
.5	Roads & Parking	N/A		—	—	—	0.0%
.7	Site Improvements	N/A		—	—	—	
				Sub-Total		65.12	**100%**
	CONTRACTOR FEES (General Requirements: 10%, Overhead: 5%, Profit: 10%)				25%	16.28	
	ARCHITECT FEES				9%	7.35	
				Total Building Cost		**88.75**	

Costs per square foot of floor area

Exterior Wall	S.F. Area	8000	10000	12000	15000	18000	24000	28000	35000	40000
	L.F. Perimeter	206	233	260	300	320	360	393	451	493
Face Brick with Concrete Block Back-up	Steel Frame	121.30	115.45	111.60	107.65	103.60	98.55	96.70	94.45	93.35
	R/Conc. Frame	129.05	123.25	119.35	115.40	111.40	106.30	104.45	102.25	101.10
Stone with Concrete Block Back-up	Steel Frame	116.50	111.40	107.90	104.40	100.80	96.25	94.60	92.60	91.65
	R/Conc. Frame	131.25	125.20	121.20	117.10	112.85	107.55	105.60	103.30	102.15
Limestone with Concrete Block Back-up	Steel Frame	133.15	126.20	121.55	116.85	111.80	105.45	103.10	100.40	99.00
	R/Conc. Frame	140.90	133.95	129.35	124.60	119.55	113.20	110.90	108.15	106.80
Perimeter Adj., Add or Deduct	Per 100 L.F.	16.00	12.80	10.65	8.55	7.15	5.35	4.60	3.65	3.20
Story Hgt. Adj., Add or Deduct	Per 1 Ft.	2.45	2.20	2.05	1.90	1.70	1.45	1.35	1.20	1.15
For Basement, add $17.75 per square foot of basement area										

The above costs were calculated using the basic specifications shown on the facing page. These costs should be adjusted where necessary for design alternatives and owner's requirements. Reported completed project costs, for this type of structure, range from $50.95 to $143.85 per S.F.

Common additives

Description	Unit	$ Cost
Directory Boards, Plastic, glass covered		
30" x 20"	Each	565
36" x 48"	Each	1025
Aluminum, 24" x 18"	Each	425
36" x 24"	Each	535
48" x 32"	Each	745
48" x 60"	Each	1600
Elevators, Hydraulic passenger, 2 stops		
1500# capacity	Each	42,225
2500# capacity	Each	43,425
3500# capacity	Each	47,225
Additional stop, add	Each	3650
Emergency Lighting, 25 watt, battery operated		
Lead battery	Each	289
Nickel cadmium	Each	655

Description	Unit	$ Cost
Flagpoles, Complete		
Aluminum, 20' high	Each	1075
40' high	Each	2675
70' high	Each	8250
Fiberglass, 23' high	Each	1400
39'-5" high	Each	2950
59' high	Each	7300
Safe, Office type, 4 hour rating		
30" x 18" x 18"	Each	3125
62" x 33" x 20"	Each	6775
Smoke Detectors		
Ceiling type	Each	149
Duct type	Each	405
Vault Front, Door & frame		
1 Hour test, 32" x 78"	Opening	3550
2 Hour test, 32" door	Opening	4225
40" door	Opening	4625
4 Hour test, 32" door	Opening	4325
40" door	Opening	5150
Time lock movement; two movement	Each	1650

Important: See the Reference Section for Location Factors

Model costs calculated for a 3 story building with 12' story height and 18,000 square feet of floor area

Town Hall, 2-3 Story

				Unit	Unit Cost	Cost Per S.F.	% Of Sub-Total
1.0 Foundations							
.1	Footings & Foundations	Poured concrete; strip and spread footings and 4' foundation wall		S.F. Ground	5.64	1.88	
.4	Piles & Caissons	N/A		—	—	—	3.0%
.9	Excavation & Backfill	Site preparation for slab and trench for foundation wall and footing		S.F. Ground	1.08	.36	
2.0 Substructure							
.1	Slab on Grade	4" reinforced concrete with vapor barrier and granular base		S.F. Slab	3.32	1.11	1.5%
.2	Special Substructures	N/A		—	—	—	
3.0 Superstructure							
.1	Columns & Beams	Wide flange steel columns with gypsum board fireproofing		L.F. Column	50	1.52	
.4	Structural Walls	N/A		—	—	—	
.5	Elevated Floors	Open web steel joists, slab form, concrete		S.F. Floor	12.09	8.06	17.7%
.7	Roof	Metal deck, open web steel joists, beams, interior columns		S.F. Roof	4.54	1.51	
.9	Stairs	Concrete filled metal pan		Flight	5975	1.99	
4.0 Exterior Closure							
.1	Walls	Stone with concrete block backup	70% of wall	S.F. Wall	23	10.53	
.5	Exterior Wall Finishes	N/A		—	—	—	17.0%
.6	Doors	Metal and glass with transoms		Each	1495	.41	
.7	Windows & Glazed Walls	Metal outward projecting	10% of wall	Each	705	1.63	
5.0 Roofing							
.1	Roof Coverings	Built-up tar and gravel with flashing		S.F. Roof	2.79	.93	
.7	Insulation	Perlite/EPS composite		S.F. Roof	1.32	.44	1.9%
.8	Openings & Specialties	N/A		—	—	—	
6.0 Interior Construction							
.1	Partitions	Gypsum board on metal studs, toilet partitions	20 S.F. Floor/L.F. Partition	S.F. Partition	4.12	2.30	
.4	Interior Doors	Wood solid core	200 S.F. Floor/Door	Each	427	2.14	
.5	Wall Finishes	90% paint, 10% ceramic tile		S.F. Surface	1.06	1.06	
.6	Floor Finishes	70% carpet tile, 15% terrazzo, 15% vinyl composition tile		S.F. Floor	6.22	6.22	22.6%
.7	Ceiling Finishes	Mineral fiber tile on concealed zee bars		S.F. Ceiling	3.63	3.63	
.9	Interior Surface/Exterior Wall	Painted gypsum board on furring	70% of wall	S.F. Wall	3.02	1.35	
7.0 Conveying							
.1	Elevators	Two hydraulic elevators		Each	66,960	7.44	10.1%
.2	Special Conveyors	N/A		—	—	—	
8.0 Mechanical							
.1	Plumbing	Toilet and service fixtures, supply and drainage	1 Fixture/1385 S.F. Floor	Each	2229	1.61	
.2	Fire Protection	Sprinklers, light hazard		S.F. Floor	1.63	1.63	
.3	Heating	Included in 8.4		—	—	—	13.9%
.4	Cooling	Multizone unit, gas heating, electric cooling		S.F. Floor	7.11	7.11	
.5	Special Systems	N/A		—	—	—	
9.0 Electrical							
.1	Service & Distribution	400 ampere service, panel board and feeders		S.F. Floor	1.03	1.03	
.2	Lighting & Power	Fluorescent fixtures, receptacles, switches, A.C. and misc. power		S.F. Floor	7.50	7.50	12.3%
.4	Special Electrical	Alarm systems and emergency lighting		S.F. Floor	.59	.59	
11.0 Special Construction							
.1	Specialties	N/A		—	—	—	0.0%
12.0 Site Work							
.1	Earthwork	N/A		—	—	—	
.3	Utilities	N/A		—	—	—	
.5	Roads & Parking	N/A		—	—	—	0.0%
.7	Site Improvements	N/A		—	—	—	
				Sub-Total		73.98	**100%**
	CONTRACTOR FEES (General Requirements: 10%, Overhead: 5%, Profit: 10%)				25%	18.50	
	ARCHITECT FEES				9%	8.32	
				Total Building Cost		**100.80**	

BUILDING TYPES

213

BUILDING TYPES

Costs per square foot of floor area

Exterior Wall	S.F. Area	10000	15000	20000	25000	30000	35000	40000	50000	60000
	L.F. Perimeter	410	500	600	700	700	766	833	966	1000
Brick with Concrete Block Back-up	Steel Frame	84.60	75.95	72.10	69.75	65.40	63.80	62.70	61.10	58.60
	Bearing Walls	83.10	74.25	70.35	67.90	63.45	61.85	60.70	59.05	56.55
Concrete Block	Steel Frame	68.65	62.90	60.35	58.75	56.20	55.20	54.50	53.50	52.05
	Bearing Walls	66.85	61.10	58.45	56.85	54.25	53.20	52.50	51.50	50.00
Galvanized Steel Siding	Steel Frame	72.05	66.20	63.55	61.95	59.35	58.30	57.60	56.55	55.05
Metal Sandwich Panels	Steel Frame	72.80	66.30	63.40	61.60	58.60	57.40	56.60	55.45	53.70
Perimeter Adj., Add or Deduct	Per 100 L.F.	8.60	5.70	4.30	3.45	2.85	2.45	2.15	1.70	1.40
Story Hgt. Adj., Add or Deduct	Per 1 Ft.	1.20	.95	.85	.85	.70	.65	.60	.55	.50
For Basement, add $17.05 per square foot of basement area										

The above costs were calculated using the basic specifications shown on the facing page. These costs should be adjusted where necessary for design alternatives and owner's requirements. Reported completed project costs, for this type of structure, range from $21.70 to $86.70 per S.F.

Common additives

Description	Unit	$ Cost		Description	Unit	$ Cost
Dock Leveler, 10 ton cap.				Sound System		
6' x 8'	Each	4900		Amplifier, 250 watts	Each	1650
7' x 8'	Each	4725		Speaker, ceiling or wall	Each	145
Emergency Lighting, 25 watt, battery operated				Trumpet	Each	271
Lead battery	Each	289		Yard Lighting, 20' aluminum pole	Each	2165
Nickel cadmium	Each	655		with 400 watt		
Fence, Chain link, 6' high				high pressure sodium		
9 ga. wire	L.F.	15.90		fixture.		
6 ga. wire	L.F.	21				
Gate	Each	287				
Flagpoles, Complete						
Aluminum, 20' high	Each	1075				
40' high	Each	2675				
70' high	Each	8250				
Fiberglass, 23' high	Each	1400				
39'-5" high	Each	2950				
59' high	Each	7300				
Paving, Bituminous						
Wearing course plus base course	S.Y.	5.60				
Sidewalks, Concrete 4" thick	S.F.	2.83				

Important: See the Reference Section for Location Factors

Model costs calculated for a 1 story building with 24' story height and 30,000 square feet of floor area

Warehouse

				Unit	Unit Cost	Cost Per S.F.	% Of Sub-Total
1.0 Foundations							
	.1	Footings & Foundations	Poured concrete; strip and spread footings and 4' foundation wall	S.F. Ground	2.47	2.47	
	.4	Piles & Caissons	N/A	—	—	—	8.8%
	.9	Excavation & Backfill	Site preparation for slab and trench for foundation wall and footing	S.F. Ground	1.08	1.08	
2.0 Substructure							
	.1	Slab on Grade	5" reinforced concrete with vapor barrier and granular base	S.F. Slab	6.48	6.48	16.0%
	.2	Special Substructures	N/A	—	—	—	
3.0 Superstructure							
	.1	Columns & Beams	Steel columns included in 3.5 and 3.7	—	—	—	
	.4	Structural Walls	N/A	—	—	—	
	.5	Elevated Floors	Mezzanine: open web steel joists, slab form, concrete beams, columns *10% of area*	S.F. Floor	9.43	1.23	13.4%
	.7	Roof	Metal deck, open web steel joists, beams, columns	S.F. Roof	3.90	3.90	
	.9	Stairs	Steel gate with rails	Flight	4800	.32	
4.0 Exterior Closure							
	.1	Walls	Concrete block *95% of wall*	S.F. Wall	7.99	4.25	
	.5	Exterior Wall Finishes	N/A	—	—	—	
	.6	Doors	Steel overhead, hollow metal *5% of wall*	Each	1751	.64	12.1%
	.7	Windows & Glazed Walls	N/A	—	—	—	
5.0 Roofing							
	.1	Roof Coverings	Built-up tar and gravel with flashing	S.F. Roof	2.06	2.06	
	.7	Insulation	Perlite/EPS composite	S.F. Roof	1.32	1.32	9.2%
	.8	Openings & Specialties	Gravel stop, hatches and skylight	S.F. Roof	.34	.34	
6.0 Interior Construction							
	.1	Partitions	Concrete block (office and washrooms) *100 S.F. Floor/L.F. Partition*	S.F. Partition	5.88	.47	
	.4	Interior Doors	Single leaf hollow metal *5000 S.F. Floor/Door*	Each	534	.11	
	.5	Wall Finishes	Paint	S.F. Surface	2.13	.34	
	.6	Floor Finishes	90% hardener, 10% vinyl composition tile	S.F. Floor	.97	.97	8.3%
	.7	Ceiling Finishes	Suspended mineral tile on zee channels in office area *10% of area*	S.F. Ceiling	3.63	.36	
	.9	Interior Surface/Exterior Wall	Paint *95% of wall*	S.F. Wall	2.12	1.13	
7.0 Conveying							
	.1	Elevators	N/A	—	—	—	0.0%
	.2	Special Conveyors	N/A	—	—	—	
8.0 Mechanical							
	.1	Plumbing	Toilet and service fixtures, supply and drainage *1 Fixture/2500 S.F. Floor*	Each	3675	1.47	
	.2	Fire Protection	Sprinklers, ordinary hazard	S.F. Floor	1.96	1.96	
	.3	Heating	Oil fired hot water, unit heaters *90% of area*	S.F. Floor	3.20	3.20	18.1%
	.4	Cooling	Single zone unit gas, heating, electric cooling *10% of area*	S.F. Floor	.72	.72	
	.5	Special Systems	N/A	—	—	—	
9.0 Electrical							
	.1	Service & Distribution	200 ampere service, panel board and feeders	S.F. Floor	.32	.32	
	.2	Lighting & Power	Fluorescent fixtures, receptacles, switches, A.C. and misc. power	S.F. Floor	3.25	3.25	9.5%
	.4	Special Electrical	Alarm systems	S.F. Floor	.30	.30	
11.0 Special Construction							
	.1	Specialties	Dock boards, dock levelers	S.F. Floor	1.88	1.88	4.6%
12.0 Site Work							
	.1	Earthwork	N/A	—	—	—	
	.3	Utilities	N/A	—	—	—	
	.5	Roads & Parking	N/A	—	—	—	0.0%
	.7	Site Improvements	N/A	—	—	—	
				Sub-Total		40.57	**100%**
		CONTRACTOR FEES (General Requirements: 10%, Overhead: 5%, Profit: 10%)			25%	10.14	
		ARCHITECT FEES			7%	3.54	
				Total Building Cost		**54.25**	

BUILDING TYPES

215

BUILDING TYPES

Costs per square foot of floor area

Exterior Wall	S.F. Area	2000	3000	5000	8000	12000	20000	30000	50000	100000
	L.F. Perimeter	180	220	300	420	580	900	1300	2100	4100
Concrete Block	Steel Frame	124.30	107.90	94.80	87.40	83.30	80.00	78.35	77.05	76.10
	R/Conc. Frame	102.40	93.55	86.45	82.45	80.25	78.45	77.60	76.85	76.30
Metal Sandwich Panel	Steel Frame	97.05	87.55	79.95	75.70	73.30	71.40	70.45	69.70	69.15
Tilt-up Concrete Panel	R/Conc. Frame	109.35	100.20	92.85	88.75	86.45	84.65	83.70	83.00	82.40
Precast Concrete Panel	Steel Frame	95.65	86.35	78.85	74.65	72.30	70.40	69.50	68.75	68.15
	R/Conc. Frame	113.00	103.05	95.05	90.60	88.05	86.10	85.10	84.30	83.70
Perimeter Adj., Add or Deduct	Per 100 L.F.	24.70	16.45	9.85	6.15	4.10	2.50	1.65	.95	.50
Story Hgt. Adj., Add or Deduct	Per 1 Ft.	1.90	1.55	1.25	1.10	1.00	.95	.90	.90	.85
Basement—Not Applicable										

The above costs were calculated using the basic specifications shown on the facing page. These costs should be adjusted where necessary for design alternatives and owner's requirements. Reported completed project costs, for this type of structure, range from $20.85 to $119.65 per S.F.

Common additives

Description	Unit	$ Cost	Description	Unit	$ Cost
Dock Leveler, 10 ton cap.			Sound System		
6' x 8'	Each	4900	Amplifier, 250 watts	Each	1650
7' x 8'	Each	4725	Speaker, ceiling or wall	Each	145
Emergency Lighting, 25 watt, battery operated			Trumpet	Each	271
Lead battery	Each	289	Yard Lighting,	Each	2165
Nickel cadmium	Each	655	20' aluminum pole with		
Fence, Chain link, 6' high			400 watt high pressure		
9 ga. wire	L.F.	15.90	sodium fixture		
6 ga. wire	L.F.	21			
Gate	Each	287			
Flagpoles, Complete					
Aluminum, 20' high	Each	1075			
40' high	Each	2675			
70' high	Each	8250			
Fiberglass, 23' high	Each	1400			
39'-5" high	Each	2950			
59' high	Each	7300			
Paving, Bituminous					
Wearing course plus base course	S.Y.	5.60			
Sidewalks, Concrete 4" thick	S.F.	2.83			

Model costs calculated for a 1 story building with 12' story height and 20,000 square feet of floor area

				Unit	Unit Cost	Cost Per S.F.	% Of Sub-Total
1.0 Foundations							
.1	Footings & Foundations	Poured concrete; strip and spread footings and 4' foundation wall		S.F. Ground	3.27	3.27	
.4	Piles & Caissons	N/A		—	—	—	7.4%
.9	Excavation & Backfill	Site preparation for slab and trench for foundation wall and footing		S.F. Ground	1.17	1.17	
2.0 Substructure							
.1	Slab on Grade	4" reinforced concrete with vapor barrier and granular base		S.F. Slab	5.56	5.56	9.3%
.2	Special Substructures	N/A		—	—	—	
3.0 Superstructure							
.1	Columns & Beams	Column fireproofing, steel columns included in 3.7		S.F. Floor	4.26	4.26	
.4	Structural Walls	N/A		—	—	—	
.5	Elevated Floors	N/A		—	—	—	15.4%
.7	Roof	Metal deck, open web steel joists, beams, columns		S.F. Roof	4.95	4.95	
.9	Stairs	N/A		—	—	—	
4.0 Exterior Closure							
.1	Walls	Concrete block	70% of wall	S.F. Wall	8.97	3.39	
.5	Exterior Wall Finishes	N/A		—	—	—	17.6%
.6	Doors	Steel overhead, hollow metal	25% of wall	Each	921	2.03	
.7	Windows & Glazed Walls	Aluminum projecting	5% of wall	Each	569	5.12	
5.0 Roofing							
.1	Roof Coverings	Built-up tar and gravel with flashing		S.F. Roof	2.35	2.35	
.7	Insulation	Perlite/EPS composite		S.F. Roof	.83	.83	5.3%
.8	Openings & Specialties	N/A		—	—	—	
6.0 Interior Construction							
.1	Partitions	Concrete block, gypsum board on metal studs	10.65 S.F. Floor/L.F. Partition	S.F. Partition	5.92	10.15	
.4	Interior Doors	Single leaf hollow metal	1835 S.F. Floor/Door	Each	861	2.87	
.5	Wall Finishes	Paint		—	—	—	
.6	Floor Finishes	N/A		—	—	—	21.8%
.7	Ceiling Finishes	N/A		—	—	—	
.9	Interior Surface/Exterior Wall	N/A		—	—	—	
7.0 Conveying							
.1	Elevators	N/A		—	—	—	0.0%
.2	Special Conveyors	N/A		—	—	—	
8.0 Mechanical							
.1	Plumbing	Toilet and service fixtures, supply and drainage	1 Fixture/5000 S.F. Floor	Each	5400	1.08	
.2	Fire Protection	Wet pipe sprinkler system		S.F. Floor	2.21	2.21	
.3	Heating	Oil fired hot water, unit heaters		S.F. Floor	5.39	5.39	14.5%
.4	Cooling	N/A		—	—	—	
.5	Special Systems	N/A		—	—	—	
9.0 Electrical							
.1	Service & Distribution	200 ampere service, panel board and feeders		S.F. Floor	1.04	1.04	
.2	Lighting & Power	Fluorescent fixtures, receptacles, switches and misc. power		S.F. Floor	3.78	3.78	8.7%
.4	Special Electrical	Alarm systems		S.F. Floor	.36	.36	
11.0 Special Construction							
.1	Specialties	N/A		—	—	—	0.0%
12.0 Site Work							
.1	Earthwork	N/A		—	—	—	
.3	Utilities	N/A		—	—	—	
.5	Roads & Parking	N/A		—	—	—	0.0%
.7	Site Improvements	N/A		—	—	—	
				Sub-Total		59.81	**100%**
	CONTRACTOR FEES (General Requirements: 10%, Overhead: 5%, Profit: 10%)				25%	14.95	
	ARCHITECT FEES				7%	5.24	
				Total Building Cost		**80.00**	

BUILDING TYPES

Deterioration occurs within the structure itself and is determined by the observation of both materials and equipment.

Curable deterioration can be remedied either by maintenance, repair or replacement, within prudent economic limits.

Incurable deterioration that has progressed to the point of actually affecting the structural integrity of the structure, making repair or replacement not economically feasible.

Actual Versus Observed Age

The observed age of a structure refers to the age that the structure appears to be. Periodic maintenance, remodeling and renovation all tend to reduce the amount of deterioration that has taken place, thereby decreasing the observed age. Actual age on the other hand relates solely to the year that the structure was built.

The Depreciation Table shown here relates to the observed age.

Obsolescence arises from conditions either occurring within the structure (functional) or caused by factors outside the limits of the structure (economic).

Functional obsolescence is any inadequacy caused by outmoded design, dated construction materials or oversized or undersized areas, all of which cause excessive operation costs.

Incurable is so costly as not to economically justify the capital expenditure required to correct the deficiency.

Economic obsolescence is caused by factors outside the limits of the structure. The prime causes of economic obsolescence are:
- zoning and environmental laws
- government legislation
- negative neighborhood influences
- business climate
- proximity to transportation facilities

Depreciation Table
Commercial/Industrial/Institutional

Observed Age (Years)	Building Material		
	Frame	Masonry On Wood	Masonry On Masonry or Steel
1	1%	0%	0%
2	2	1	0
3	3	2	1
4	4	3	2
5	6	5	3
10	20	15	8
15	25	20	15
20	30	25	20
25	35	30	25
30	40	35	30
35	45	40	35
40	50	45	40
45	55	50	45
50	60	55	50
55	65	60	55
60	70	65	60

DEPRECIATION

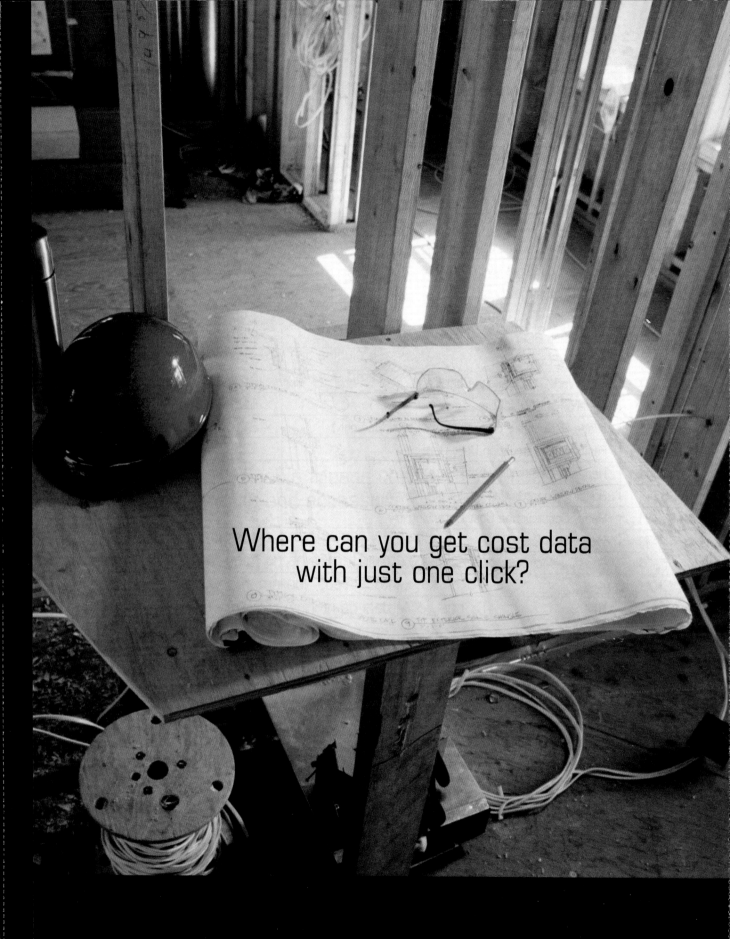

Where can you get cost data
with just one click?

Means CostWorks 2001 is the answer!

Just one CD is packed with massive amounts of cost data covering every detail from the ground up

- **18 detailed cost data books —** available individually, in specially priced packages, or in total.

- **Architects' First Source®** — featuring thousands of products listed by manufacturer.

- **The Construction Specifications Institute's SPEC-DATA®** for technical product information.

- **CSI's MANU-SPEC®** for manufacturers' complete product specifications.

Plus you get the productivity-enhancing tools to really put this valuable information to work.

Bonus

Get the Means Construction Dictionary with over 17,000 construction terms — a $99.95 value — FREE on the Means CostWorks 2001 CD!

Save hundreds on specially priced packages! Choose the one that's right for you...

Builder's Package
Includes:
- Residential Cost Data
- Light Commercial Cost Data
- Site Work & Landscape Cost Data
- Concrete & Masonry Cost Data
- Open Shop Building Construction Cost Data

Just $299.99

Save over $300 off the price of buying each book separately!

Building Professional's Package
Includes:
- Building Construction Cost Data
- Mechanical Cost Data
- Plumbing Cost Data
- Electrical Cost Data
- Square Foot Model Costs

Just $349.99

Save over $250 off the price of buying each book separately!

Facility Manager's Package
Includes:
- Facilities Construction Cost Data
- Facilities Maintenance & Repair
- Repair & Remodeling Cost Data
- Building Construction Cost Data

Just $449.99

Save over $300 off the price of buying each book separately!

Design Professional's Package
Includes:
- Building Construction Cost Data
- Square Foot Model Costs
- Interior Cost Data
- Assemblies Cost Data

Just $349.99

Save over $200 off the price of buying each book separately!

Stay current with online cost data updates — included in the cost of the Means CostWorks 2001 CD!

Your 2001 Annual Means CostWorks license includes four FREE quarterly updates from the Means CostWorks Web site

Assemblies Section

Table of Contents

Table of Contents

Introduction to the Assemblies Section

This section of the manual contains the technical description and installed cost of all components used in the commercial/industrial/institutional section. In most cases, there is an illustration of the component to aid in identification.

All Costs Include:

Materials purchased in lot sizes typical of normal construction projects with discounts appropriate to established contractors.

Installation work performed by union labor working under standard conditions at a normal pace.

Installing Contractor's Overhead & Profit

Standard installing contractor's overhead & profit are included in the assemblies costs.

These assemblies costs contain no provisions for General Contractor's overhead and profit or Architect's fees, nor do they include premiums for labor or materials or savings which may be realized under certain economic situations.

The assemblies tables are arranged by physical size (dimensions) of the component wherever possible.

How to Use the Assemblies Cost Tables

The following is a detailed explanation of a sample Assemblies Cost Table. Most Assembly Tables are separated into two parts: 1) an illustration of the system to be estimated with descriptive notes; and 2) the costs for similar systems with dimensional and/or size variations. Next to each bold number below is the item being described with the appropriate component of the sample entry following in parenthesis. In most cases, if the work is to be subcontracted, the general contractor will need to add an additional markup (R.S. Means suggests using 10%) to the "Total" figures.

System/Line Numbers (A2.1-200-2240)

Each Assemblies Cost Line has been assigned a unique identification number based on the UniFormat classification system.

UniFormat Division

2.1 200 2240

Means Subdivision
Means Major Classification
Means Individual Line Number

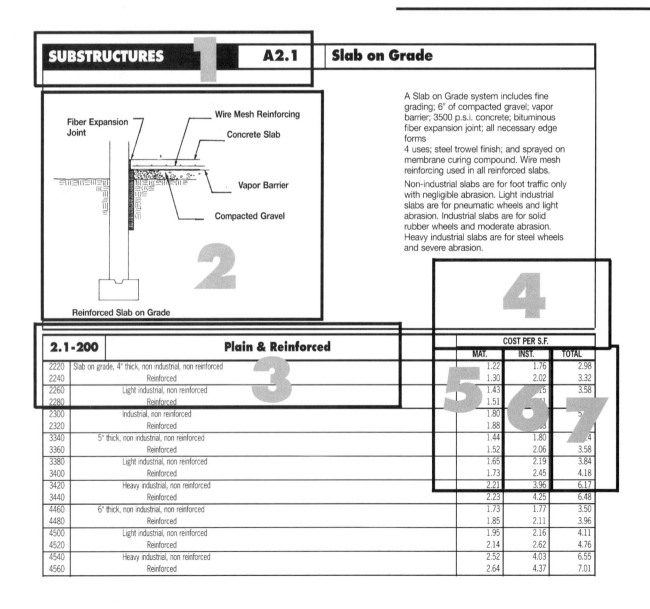

| SUBSTRUCTURES | A2.1 | Slab on Grade |

A Slab on Grade system includes fine grading; 6″ of compacted gravel; vapor barrier; 3500 p.s.i. concrete; bituminous fiber expansion joint; all necessary edge forms 4 uses; steel trowel finish; and sprayed on membrane curing compound. Wire mesh reinforcing used in all reinforced slabs.

Non-industrial slabs are for foot traffic only with negligible abrasion. Light industrial slabs are for pneumatic wheels and light abrasion. Industrial slabs are for solid rubber wheels and moderate abrasion. Heavy industrial slabs are for steel wheels and severe abrasion.

Reinforced Slab on Grade

(Diagram labels: Fiber Expansion Joint, Wire Mesh Reinforcing, Concrete Slab, Vapor Barrier, Compacted Gravel)

2.1-200	Plain & Reinforced	COST PER S.F.		
		MAT.	INST.	TOTAL
2220	Slab on grade, 4″ thick, non industrial, non reinforced	1.22	1.76	2.98
2240	Reinforced	1.30	2.02	3.32
2260	Light industrial, non reinforced	1.43	.15	3.58
2280	Reinforced	1.51	.1	
2300	Industrial, non reinforced	1.80		5
2320	Reinforced	1.88	.3	
3340	5″ thick, non industrial, non reinforced	1.44	1.80	.4
3360	Reinforced	1.52	2.06	3.58
3380	Light industrial, non reinforced	1.65	2.19	3.84
3400	Reinforced	1.73	2.45	4.18
3420	Heavy industrial, non reinforced	2.21	3.96	6.17
3440	Reinforced	2.23	4.25	6.48
4460	6″ thick, non industrial, non reinforced	1.73	1.77	3.50
4480	Reinforced	1.85	2.11	3.96
4500	Light industrial, non reinforced	1.95	2.16	4.11
4520	Reinforced	2.14	2.62	4.76
4540	Heavy industrial, non reinforced	2.52	4.03	6.55
4560	Reinforced	2.64	4.37	7.01

2 Illustration

At the top of most assembly pages is an illustration, a brief description, and the design criteria used to develop the cost.

3 System Description

The components of a typical system are listed in the description to show what has been included in the development of the total system price. The rest of the table contains prices for other similar systems with dimensional and/or size variations.

4 Unit of Measure for Each System (S.F.)

Costs shown in the three right hand columns have been adjusted by the component quantity and unit of measure for the entire system. In this example, "Cost per S.F." is the unit of measure for this system or "assembly."

5 Materials (1.30)

This column contains the Materials Cost of each component. These cost figures are bare costs plus 10% for profit.

6 Installation (2.02)

Installation includes labor and equipment plus the installing contractor's overhead and profit. Equipment costs are the bare rental costs plus 10% for profit. The labor overhead and profit is defined on the inside back cover of this book.

7 Total (3.32)

The figure in this column is the sum of the material and installation costs.

Material Cost	+	Installation Cost	=	Total
$1.30	+	$2.02	=	$3.32

Example

Assemblies costs can be used to calculate the cost for each component of a building and, accumulated with appropriate markups, produce a cost for the complete structure. Components from a model building with similar characteristics in conjunction with Assemblies components may be used to calculate costs for a complete structure.

Example:

Outline Specifications

General	Building size—60' x 100', 8 suspended floors, 12' floor to floor, 4' high parapet above roof, full basement 11'-8" floor to floor, bay size 25' x 30', ceiling heights - 9' in office area and 8' in core area.
1.0 Foundations	Concrete, spread and strip footings and concrete walls waterproofed.
2.0 Substructures	4" concrete slab on grade.
3.0 Superstructures	Columns, wide flange; 3 hr. fire rated; Floors, composite steel frame & deck with concrete slab; Roof, steel beams, open web joists and deck.
4.0 Exterior Closure	Walls; North, East & West, brick & lightweight concrete block with 2" cavity insulation, 25% window; South, 8" lightweight concrete block insulated, 10% window. Doors, aluminum & glass. Windows, aluminum, 3'-0" x 5'-4", insulating glass.
5.0 Roofing	Tar & gravel, 2" rigid insulation, R 12.5.
6.0 Interior Construction	Core—6" lightweight concrete block, full height with plaster on exposed faces to ceiling height.
	Corridors—1st & 2nd floor; 3-5/8" steel studs with F.R. gypsum board, full height.
	Exterior Wall—plaster, ceiling height.
	Doors—hollow metal.
	Wall Finishes—lobby, mahogany paneling on furring, remainder plaster & gypsum board, paint.
	Floor Finishes—1st floor lobby, corridors & toilet rooms, terrazzo; remainder, concrete, tenant developed. 2nd thru 8th, toilet rooms, ceramic tile; office & corridor, carpet.
	Ceiling Finishes—24" x 48" fiberglass board on Tee grid.
7.0 Conveying Systems	2-2500 lb. capacity, 200 F.P.M. geared elevators, 9 stops.
8.0 Mechanical	Fixtures, see sketch.
	Roof Drains—2-4" C.I. pipe.
	Fire Protection—4" standpipe, 9 hose cabinets.
	Heating—fin tube radiation, forced hot water.
	Air Conditioning—chilled water with water cooled condenser.
9.0 Electrical	Lighting, 1st thru 8th, 15 fluorescent fixtures/1000 S.F., 3 Watts/S.F.
	Basement, 10 fluorescent fixtures/1000 S.F., 2 Watts/S.F.
	Receptacles, 1st thru 8th, 16.5/1000 S.F., 2 Watts/S.F.
	Basement, 10 receptacles/1000 S.F., 1.2 Watts/S.F.
	Air Conditioning, 4 Watts/S.F.
	Miscellaneous Connections, 1.2 Watts/S.F.
	Elevator Power, 2-10 H.P., 230 volt motors.
	Wall Switches, 2/1000 S.F.
	Service, panel board & feeder, 2000 Amp.
	Fire Detection System, pull stations, signals, smoke and heat detectors.
	Emergency Lighting Generator, 30 KW.
10.0 General Conditions & Profit	See Summary Sheet.
11.0 Special Construction	Toilet Accessories & Directory Boards.
12.0 Site Work	NA.

Front Elevation

Basement Plan

Ground Floor Plan

Typical Floor Plan

Example

If spread footing & column sizes are unknown, develop approximate loads as follows. Enter tables with these loads to determine costs.

Superimposed Load Ranges

Apartments & Residential Structures	65	to	75 psf
Assembly Areas & Retail Stores	110	to	125 psf
Commercial & Manufacturing	150	to	250 psf
Offices	75	to	100 psf

Approximate loads/S.F. for roof & floors.
Roof. Assume 40 psf superimposed load.
Steel joists, beams & deck.
Table 3.7-420—Line 3900

3.7-420		Steel Joists, Beams, & Deck on Columns				COST PER S.F.		
	BAY SIZE (FT.)	SUPERIMPOSED LOAD (P.S.F.)	DEPTH (IN.)	TOTAL LOAD (P.S.F.)	COLUMN ADD	MAT.	INST.	TOTAL
3500	25x30	20	22	40		2.64	1.12	3.76
3600					columns	.55	.20	.75
3900		40	25	60		3.22	1.32	4.54
4000					columns	.66	.24	.90

3.5-540		Composite Beams, Deck & Slab				COST PER S.F.		
	BAY SIZE (FT.)	SUPERIMPOSED LOAD (P.S.F.)	SLAB THICKNESS (IN.)	TOTAL DEPTH (FT. - IN.)	TOTAL LOAD (P.S.F.)	MAT.	INST.	TOTAL
3400	25x30	40	5-1/2	1 - 11-1/2	83	6.05	3.96	10.01
3600		75	5-1/2	1 - 11-1/2	119	6.50	4.01	10.51
3900		125	5-1/2	1 - 11-1/2	170	7.55	4.54	12.09
4000		200	6-1/4	2 - 6-1/4	252	9.45	5.20	14.65

Floors–Total load, 119 psf.
Interior foundation load.
Roof

[(25' x 30' x 60 psf) + 8 floors x (25' x 30' x 119 psf)] x 1/1000 lb./Kip =	759 Kips
Approximate Footing Loads, Interior footing =	759 Kips
Exterior footing (1/2 bay) 759 k x .6 =	455 Kips
Corner footing (1/4 bay) 759 k x .45 =	342 Kips
[Factors to convert Interior load to Exterior & Corner loads]	
Approximate average Column load 759 k/2 =	379 Kips

PRELIMINARY ESTIMATE

PROJECT *Office Building*	TOTAL SITE AREA
BUILDING TYPE	OWNER
LOCATION	ARCHITECT
DATE OF CONSTRUCTION	ESTIMATED CONSTRUCTION PERIOD

BRIEF DESCRIPTION *Building size: 60' x 100' - 8 structural floors - 12' floor to floor*
4' high parapet above roof, full basement 11' - 8" floor to floor, bay size
25' x 30', ceiling heights - 9' in office area + 8' in core area

TYPE OF PLAN	TYPE OF CONSTRUCTION
QUALITY	BUILDING CAPACITY

Floor			Wall Area					
Below Grade Levels			Foundation Walls	L.F.		Ht.		S.F.
Area		S.F.	Frost Walls	L.F.		Ht.		S.F.
Area		S.F.	Exterior Closure		Total			S.F.
Total Area		S.F.	Comment					
Ground Floor			Fenestration			%		S.F.
Area		S.F.				%		S.F.
Area		S.F.	Exterior Wall			%		S.F.
Total Area		S.F.				%		S.F.
Supported Levels			Site Work					
Area			Parking		S.F. (For			Cars)
Area		S.F.	Access Roads		L.F. (X			Ft. Wide)
Area		S.F.	Sidewalk		L.F. (X			Ft. Wide)
Area		S.F.	Landscaping		S.F. (		% Unbuilt Site)	
Area		S.F.	Building Codes					
Total Area		S.F.	City			Country		
Miscellaneous			National			Other		
Area		S.F.	Loading					
Area		S.F.	Roof		psf	Ground Floor		psf
Area		S.F.	Supported Floors		psf	Corridor		psf
Area		S.F.	Balcony		psf	Partition, allow		psf
Total Area		S.F.	Miscellaneous					psf
Net Finished Area		S.F.	Live Load Reduction					
Net Floor Area		S.F.	Wind					
Gross Floor Area	54,000	S.F.	Earthquake			Zone		
Roof			Comment					
Total Area		S.F.	Soil Type					
Comments			Bearing Capacity					K.S.F.
			Frost Depth					Ft.
Volume			Frame					
Depth of Floor System			Type		Bay Spacing			
Minimum		In.	Foundation					
Maximum		In.	Special					
Foundation Wall Height		Ft.	Substructure					
Floor to Floor Height		Ft.	Comment					
Floor to Ceiling Height		Ft.	Superstructure, Vertical					
Subgrade Volume		C.F.	Fireproofing		☐ Columns			Hrs.
Above Grade Volume		C.F.	☐ Girders	Hrs.	☐ Beams			Hrs.
Total Building Volume	648,000	C.F.	☐ Floor	Hrs.	☐ None			

NUMBER		QTY.	UNIT	TOTAL COST UNIT	TOTAL COST TOTAL	COST PER S.F.
1.0	**Foundations**					
1.1-120-7900	Corner Footings 8'-6" SQ. x 27"	4	Ea.	1250	5,000	
-8010	Exterior 9'-6" SQ. x 30"	8		1665	13,320	
-8300	Interior 12" SQ.	3		3050	9,150	
1.1-140-2700	Strip 2' Wide x 1' Thick					
	320 L.F. [(4 x 8.5) + 8 x 9.5)] =	210	L.F.	24.90	5,229	
1.1-210-7262	Foundation Wall 12' High, 1' Thick	210		157.50	33,075	
1.1-292-2800	Foundation Waterproofing	210		12.62	2,650	
1.9-100-3440	Building Excavation + Backfill	6000	S.F.	4.47	26,820	
-3500	(Interpolated ; 12' Between					
-4620	8' and 16' ; 6,000 Between					
-4680	4,000 and 10,000 S.F.					
	Total				95,244	1.76
2.0	**Slab on Grade**					
2.1-200-2240	4", non-industrial, reinf.	6000	S.F.	3.32	19,920	
	Total				19,920	0.37
3.0	**Superstructure**					
3.1-130-5800	Columns: Load 379K Use 400K					
	Exterior 12 x 96' + Interior 3 x 108'	1476	V.L.F.	70.95	104,722	
3.1-190-3650	Column Fireproofing - Interior 4 sides					
-3700	Exterior 1/2 (Interpolated for 12")	900	V.L.F	23.16	20,844	
3.5-540-3600	Floors: Composite steel + lt. wt. conc.	48000	S.F.	10.51	504,480	
3.7-420-3900	Roof: Open web joists, beams + decks	6000	S.F.	4.54	27,240	
3.9-100-0760	Stairs: Steel w/conc. fill	18	Flt.	5975	107,550	
	Total				764,836	14.16
4.0	**Exterior Closure**					
4.1-273-1200	4" Brick + 6" Block - Insulated					
	75% NE + W Walls 220' x 100' x .75	16500	S.F.	19.75	325,875	
4.1-211-3410	8" Block - Insulated 90%					
	100' x 100' x .9	9000	S.F.	7.44	66,960	
4.6-100-6950	Double Aluminum + Glass Door	1	Pr.	3275	3,275	
-6300	Single	2	Ea.	1715	3,430	
4.7-110-8800	Aluminum windows - Insul. glass					
	(5,500 S.F. + 1,000 S.F.)/3 x 5.33	406	Ea.	660.50	268,163	
4.1-140-6776	Precast concrete coping	320	L.F.	26.15	8,368	
	Total				676,071	12.52
5.0	**Roofing**					
5.7-101-4020	Insulation: Perlite/Polyisocyanurate	6000	S.F.	1.36	8,160	
5.1-103-1400	Roof: 4 Ply T & G composite	6000		1.67	10,020	
5.1-620-0300	Flashing: Aluminum - fabric backed	640		2.28	1,459	
5.8-100-0500	Roof hatch	1	Ea.	781	781	
	Total				20,420	0.38
	Page Total					

ASSEMBLY NUMBER		QTY.	UNIT	TOTAL COST		COST PER S.F.
				UNIT	TOTAL	
6.0	**Interior Construction**					
6.1-210-5500	Core partitions: 6" Lt. Wt. concrete					
	block 288 L.F. x 11.5' x 8 Floors	26,449	S.F.	5.90	156,049	
6.1-680-0920	Plaster: [(196 L.F. x 8') + (144 L.F. x 9')] 8					
	+ Ext. Wall [(320 x 9 x 8 Floors) - 6500]	39,452	S.F.	2.16	85,216	
6.1-510-5400	Corridor partitions 1st + 2nd floors					
	steel studs + F.R. gypsum board	2,530	S.F.	2.81	7,109	
6.4-100-2600	Interior doors	66	Ea.	534	35,244	
	Wall finishes - Lobby: Mahogany w/furring					
6.1-580-0652	Furring: 150 L.F. x 9' + Ht.	1,350	S.F.	0.95	1,283	
6.5-100-1662	Mahogany paneling	1,350	S.F.	4.13	5,576	
	Paint, plaster + gypsum board					
6.5-100-0080	39,452 + [(220' x 9' x 2) - 1350] + 72	42,134	S.F.	0.80	33,707	
	Floor Finishes					
6.6-100-1100	1st floor lobby + terrazzo	2,175	S.F.	8.53	18,553	
	Remainder: Concrete - Tenant finished					
6.6-100-0060	2nd - 8th: Carpet - 4725 S.F. x 7	33,075	S.F.	3.90	128,993	
6.6-100-1720	Ceramic Tile - 300 S.F. x 7	2,100	S.F.	7.58	15,918	
6.7-810-2780	Suspended Ceiling Tiles- 5200 S.F. x 8	41,600	S.F.	1.45	60,320	
6.7-810-3260	Suspended Ceiling Grid- 5200 S.F. x 8	41,600	S.F.	0.82	34,112	
6.1-870-0700	Toilet partitions	31	Ea.	614	19,034	
-0760	Handicapped addition	16	Ea.	278	4,448	
	Total				605,561	11.21
7.0	**Conveying**					
	2 Elevators - 2500# 200'/min. Geared					
7.1-2001600	5 Floors $100,700					
-1800	15 Floors $ 187,500					
	Diff. $86,800/10 = 8,680/Flr.					
	$100,700 + (4 x 8,680) = $135,420/Ea.	2	Ea.	135,420	270,840	
	Total				270,840	5.02
8.0	**Mechanical System**					
8.1-433-2120	Plumbing - Lavatories	31	Ea.	900	27,900	
-434-4340	-Service Sink	8	Ea.	1500	12,000	
-450-2000	-Urinals	8	Ea.	925	7,400	
-470-2080	-Water Closets	31	Ea.	1160	35,960	
	Water Control, Waste Vent Piping	45%			37,467	
-310-4200	- Roof Drains, 4" C.I.	2	Ea.	945	1,890	
-310-4240	- Pipe, 9 Flr. x 12' x 12' Ea.	216	L.F.	22.35	4,828	
	Fire Protection					
8.2-310-0560	Wet Stand Pipe: 4" x 10' 1st floor	12/10	Ea.	4075	4,890	
-310-0580	Additional Floors: (12'/10 x 8)	9.6	Ea.	1120	10,752	
-390-8400	Cabinet Assembly	9	Ea.	661	5,949	
	Heating - Fin Tube Radiation					

ASSEMBLY NUMBER		QTY.	UNIT	TOTAL COST		COST PER S.F.
				UNIT	TOTAL	
8.3-161-2000	10,000 S.F. @ $5.81/S.F. Interpolate					
-2040	10,000 S.F. @ $2.66/S.F.	48,000	S.F.	4.24	203,520	
	Cooling - Chilled Water, Air Cool, Cond.					
8.4-120-4000	40,000 S.F. @8.84/S.F. Interpolate	48,000	S.F.	8.93	428,640	
-4040	60,000 S.F. @9.02/S.F.					
	Total				781,196	14.47
9.0	Electrical					
9.2-213-0280	Office Lighting, 15/1000 S.F. - 3 Watts/S.F.	48,000	S.F.	5.23	251,040	
-0240	Basement Lighting, 10/1000 S.F. - 2 Watts/S.F.	6,000	S.F.	3.48	20,880	
-522-0640	Office Receptacles 16.5/1000 S.F. - 2 Watts/S.F.	48,000	S.F.	3	144,000	
-0560	Basement Receptacles 10/1000 S.F. - 1.2 Watts/S.F.	6,000	S.F.	2.27	13,620	
-610-0280	Central A.C. - 4 Watts/S.F.	48,000	S.F.	0.38	18,240	
-582-0320	Misc. Connections - 1.2 Watts/S.F.	48,000	S.F.	0.22	10,560	
-710-0680	Elevator Motor Power - 10 H.P.	2	Ea.	2,075	4,150	
-542-0280	Wall Switches - 2/1000 S.F.	54,000	S.F.	0.28	15,120	
9.1-210-0560	2000 Amp Service	1	Ea.	26,025	26,025	
-410-0400	Switchgear	1	Ea.	37,200	37,200	
-310-0560	Feeder	50	L.F.	328	16,400	
9.4-100-0400	Fire Detection System - 50 Detectors	1	Ea.	21,875	21,875	
-310-0320	Emergency Generator - 30 kW	30	kW	436	13,080	
	Total				592,190	10.97
10.0	General Conditions					
11.0	Special Construction					
11.1-100-1100	Towel Dispenser	16	Ea.	63	1,008	
-1200	Grab Bar	32	Ea.	37.20	1,190	
-1300	Mirror	31	Ea.	122.25	3,790	
-1400	Toilet Tissue Dispenser	31	Ea.	24.60	763	
-2100	Directory Board	8	Ea.	239	1,912	
	Total				8,663	0.16
12.0	Site Work					
13.0	Miscellaneous					
			Page Total			

230

PRELIMINARY
ESTIMATE

PROJECT	*Office Building*		TOTAL AREA	54,000 S.F.	SHEET NO.	
LOCATION			TOTAL VOLUME	648,000 C.F.	ESTIMATE NO.	
ARCHITECT			COST PER S.F.		DATE	
OWNER			COST PER C.F.		NO. OF STORIES	
QUANTITIES BY			EXTENSIONS BY		CHECKED BY	

NO.		SUBTOTAL COST	COST/S.F.	%
1.0	Foundation	95,244	1.76	
2.0	Substructure	19,920	0.37	
3.0	Superstructure	764,836	14.16	
4.0	Exterior Closure	676,071	12.52	
5.0	Roofing	20,420	0.38	
6.0	Interior Construction	605,561	11.21	
7.0	Conveying	270,840	5.02	
8.0	Mechanical System	781,196	14.47	
9.0	Electrical	592,190	10.97	
10.0	General Conditions			
11.0	Special Construction	8,663	0.16	
12.0	Site Work			

	Building Subtotal	3,834,941		$ 3,834,941
Sales Tax	N/A	% x Subtotal $ N/A	/2	$
General Conditions (%)	10	% x Subtotal $ 3,834,941 = 383,494		
			General Conditions	$ 383,494
			Subtotal "A"	$ 4,218,435
Overhead	5	% x Subtotal "A" $ 4,218,435		$ 210,922
			Subtotal "B"	$ 4,429,357
Profit	10	% x Subtotal "B" $ 4,429,357		$ 442,936
			Subtotal "C"	$ 4,872,293
Location Factor	N/A	% x Subtotal "C" $		
			Adjusted Building Cost	$ 4,872,293
Architect's Fee	6.5	% x Adjusted Building Cost	4,872,293 =	$ 316,699
Contingency	N/A	% x Adjusted Building Cost	N/A =	$
			Total Cost	5,188,992
Square Foot Cost	$ 5,188,992 / 54,000 S.F. = 96.09	$/S.F.		
Cubic Foot Cost	$ 5,188,992 / 648,000 C.F. = 7.78	/C.F.		

231

Division 1
Foundations

Waterproofing

Spread Footing

Strip Footing

1.1-120	Spread Footings	COST EACH		
		MAT.	INST.	TOTAL
7090	Spread footings, 3000 psi concrete, chute delivered			
7100	Load 25K, soil capacity 3 KSF, 3'-0" sq. x 12" deep	41	79.50	120.50
7150	Load 50K, soil capacity 3 KSF, 4'-6" sq. x 12" deep	84	138	222
7200	Load 50K, soil capacity 6 KSF, 3'-0" sq. x 12" deep	41	79.50	120.50
7250	Load 75K, soil capacity 3 KSF, 5'-6" sq. x 13" deep	131	196	327
7300	Load 75K, soil capacity 6 KSF, 4'-0" sq. x 12" deep	68.50	118	186.50
7350	Load 100K, soil capacity 3 KSF, 6'-0" sq. x 14" deep	164	235	399
7410	Load 100K, soil capacity 6 KSF, 4'-6" sq. x 15" deep	103	163	266
7450	Load 125K, soil capacity 3 KSF, 7'-0" sq. x 17" deep	259	335	594
7500	Load 125K, soil capacity 6 KSF, 5'-0" sq. x 16" deep	131	196	327
7550	Load 150K, soil capacity 3 KSF 7'-6" sq. x 18" deep	310	395	705
7610	Load 150K, soil capacity 6 KSF, 5'-6" sq. x 18" deep	173	246	419
7650	Load 200K, soil capacity 3 KSF, 8'-6" sq. x 20" deep	440	525	965
7700	Load 200K, soil capacity 6 KSF, 6'-0" sq. x 20" deep	226	305	531
7750	Load 300K, soil capacity 3 KSF, 10'-6" sq. x 25" deep	805	850	1,655
7810	Load 300K, soil capacity 6 KSF, 7'-6" sq. x 25" deep	425	510	935
7850	Load 400K, soil capacity 3 KSF, 12'-6" sq. x 28" deep	1,275	1,275	2,550
7900	Load 400K, soil capacity 6 KSF, 8'-6" sq. x 27" deep	585	665	1,250
8010	Load 500K, soil capacity 6 KSF, 9'-6" sq. x 30" deep	800	865	1,665
8100	Load 600K, soil capacity 6 KSF, 10'-6" sq. x 33" deep	1,075	1,125	2,200
8200	Load 700K, soil capacity 6 KSF, 11'-6" sq. x 36" deep	1,375	1,375	2,750
8300	Load 800K, soil capacity 6 KSF, 12'-0" sq. x 37" deep	1,550	1,500	3,050
8400	Load 900K, soil capacity 6 KSF, 13'-0" sq. x 39" deep	1,900	1,775	3,675
8500	Load 1000K, soil capacity 6 KSF, 13'-6" sq. x 41" deep	2,150	2,000	4,150

1.1-140	Strip Footings	COST PER L.F.		
		MAT.	INST.	TOTAL
2100	Strip footing, load 2.6KLF, soil capacity 3KSF, 16"wide x 8"deep plain	4.58	9.40	13.98
2300	Load 3.9 KLF, soil capacity, 3 KSF, 24"wide x 8"deep, plain	5.80	10.45	16.25
2500	Load 5.1KLF, soil capacity 3 KSF, 24"wide x 12"deep, reinf.	9.15	15.75	24.90
2700	Load 11.1KLF, soil capacity 6 KSF, 24"wide x 12"deep, reinf.	9.15	15.75	24.90
2900	Load 6.8 KLF, soil capacity 3 KSF, 32"wide x 12"deep, reinf.	11.30	17.30	28.60
3100	Load 14.8 KLF, soil capacity 6 KSF, 32"wide x 12"deep, reinf.	11.30	17.30	28.60
3300	Load 9.3 KLF, soil capacity 3 KSF, 40"wide x 12"deep, reinf.	13.35	18.80	32.15
3500	Load 18.4 KLF, soil capacity 6 KSF, 40"wide x 12"deep, reinf.	13.45	18.90	32.35
4500	Load 10KLF, soil capacity 3 KSF, 48"wide x 16"deep, reinf.	19.10	23.50	42.60
4700	Load 22KLF, soil capacity 6 KSF, 48"wide, 16"deep, reinf.	19.50	24	43.50
5700	Load 15KLF, soil capacity 3 KSF, 72"wide x 20"deep, reinf.	33.50	33.50	67
5900	Load 33KLF, soil capacity 6 KSF, 72"wide x 20"deep, reinf.	35.50	36	71.50

1.1-210	Walls, Cast in Place							
	WALL HEIGHT (FT.)	PLACING METHOD	CONCRETE (C.Y./L.F.)	REINFORCING (LBS./L.F.)	WALL THICKNESS (IN.)	COST PER L.F.		
						MAT.	INST.	TOTAL
1500	4'	direct chute	.074	3.3	6	11.55	30.50	42.05
1520			.099	4.8	8	13.75	31.50	45.25
1540			.123	6.0	10	15.80	32	47.80
1561			.148	7.2	12	17.90	33	50.90
1580			.173	8.1	14	19.95	33.50	53.45
1600			.197	9.44	16	22	34.50	56.50
3000	6'	direct chute	.111	4.95	6	17.30	46	63.30
3020			.149	7.20	8	20.50	47.50	68
3040			.184	9.00	10	23.50	48.50	72
3061			.222	10.8	12	27	49.50	76.50
5000	8'	direct chute	.148	6.6	6	23	61.50	84.50
5020			.199	9.6	8	27.50	63.50	91
5040			.250	12	10	32	65	97
5061			.296	14.39	12	36	66.50	102.50
6020	10'	direct chute	.248	12	8	34.50	79.50	114
6040			.307	14.99	10	39.50	81	120.50
6061			.370	17.99	12	45	83	128
7220	12'	pumped	.298	14.39	8	41.50	98.50	140
7240			.369	17.99	10	47.50	100	147.50
7262			.444	21.59	12	53.50	104	157.50
9220	16'	pumped	.397	19.19	8	55	131	186
9240			.492	23.99	10	63	134	197
9260			.593	28.79	12	71.50	139	210.50

1.1-292	Foundation Dampproofing	COST PER L.F.		
		MAT.	INST.	TOTAL
1000	Foundation dampproofing, bituminous, 1 coat, 4' high	.28	2.96	3.24
1400	8' high	.56	5.90	6.46
1800	12' high	.84	9.15	9.99
2000	2 coats, 4' high	.44	3.68	4.12
2400	8' high	.88	7.35	8.23
2800	12' high	1.32	11.30	12.62
3000	Asphalt with fibers, 1/16" thick, 4' high	.68	3.68	4.36
3400	8' high	1.36	7.35	8.71
3800	12' high	2.04	11.30	13.34
4000	1/8" thick, 4' high	1.24	4.36	5.60
4400	8' high	2.48	8.70	11.18
4800	12' high	3.72	13.35	17.07
5000	Asphalt coated board and mastic, 1/4" thick, 4' high	2.48	4	6.48
5400	8' high	4.96	8	12.96
5800	12' high	7.45	12.30	19.75
6000	1/2" thick, 4' high	3.72	5.60	9.32
6400	8' high	7.45	11.15	18.60
6800	12' high	11.15	17	28.15
7000	Cementitious coating, on walls, 1/8" thick coating, 4' high	6.60	4.68	11.28
7400	8' high	13.20	9.40	22.60
7800	12' high	19.80	14	33.80
8000	Cementitious/metallic slurry, 2 coat, 1/4" thick, 2' high	38.50	134	172.50
8400	4' high	77	268	345
8800	6' high	116	400	516

FOUNDATIONS

1

Sand & Gravel 1:1

Clay 1/2:1

Line of Excavation

In general, the following items are accounted for in the table below.

Costs:
1) Excavation for building or other structure to depth and extent indicated.
2) Backfill compacted in place
3) Haul of excavated waste
4) Replacement of unsuitable backfill material with bank run gravel.

1.9-100	Building Excavation & Backfill	COST PER S.F.		
		MAT.	INST.	TOTAL
2220	Excav & fill, 1000 S.F. 4' sand, gravel, or common earth, on site storage		1.64	1.64
2240	Off site storage		3.50	3.50
2260	Clay excavation, bank run gravel borrow for backfill	2.51	3.12	5.63
2280	8' deep, sand, gravel, or common earth, on site storage		3.81	3.81
2300	Off site storage		8.95	8.95
2320	Clay excavation, bank run gravel borrow for backfill	6.05	7.15	13.20
2340	16' deep, sand, gravel, or common earth, on site storage		10.35	10.35
2350	Off site storage		22	22
2360	Clay excavation, bank run gravel borrow for backfill	16.80	18.30	35.10
3380	4000 S.F.,4' deep, sand, gravel, or common earth, on site storage		1.28	1.28
3400	Off site storage		2.13	2.13
3420	Clay excavation, bank run gravel borrow for backfill	1.17	1.97	3.14
3440	8' deep, sand, gravel, or common earth, on site storage		2.77	2.77
3460	Off site storage		5.05	5.05
3480	Clay excavation, bank run gravel borrow for backfill	2.77	4.32	7.09
3500	16' deep, sand, gravel, or common earth, on site storage		6.65	6.65
3520	Off site storage		13.80	13.80
3540	Clay, excavation, bank run gravel borrow for backfill	7.40	10.25	17.65
4560	10,000 S.F., 4' deep, sand gravel, or common earth, on site storage		1.17	1.17
4580	Off site storage		1.68	1.68
4600	Clay excavation, bank run gravel borrow for backfill	.72	1.59	2.31
4620	8' deep, sand, gravel, or common earth, on site storage		2.45	2.45
4640	Off site storage		3.80	3.80
4660	Clay excavation, bank run gravel borrow for backfill	1.67	3.39	5.06
4680	16' deep, sand, gravel, or common earth, on site storage		5.50	5.50
4700	Off site storage		9.70	9.70
4720	Clay excavation, bank run gravel borrow for backfill	4.44	7.70	12.14
5740	30,000 S.F., 4' deep, sand, gravel, or common earth, on site storage		1.08	1.08
5760	Off site storage		1.37	1.37
5780	Clay excavation, bank run gravel borrow for backfill	.40	1.32	1.72
5860	16' deep, sand, gravel, or common earth, on site storage		4.82	4.82
5880	Off site storage		7.05	7.05
5900	Clay excavation, bank run gravel borrow for backfill	2.47	6	8.47
6910	100,000 S.F., 4' deep, sand, gravel, or common earth, on site storage		1.02	1.02
6940	8' deep, sand, gravel, or common earth, on site storage		2.10	2.10
6970	16' deep, sand, gravel, or common earth, on site storage		4.41	4.41
6980	Off site storage		5.60	5.60
6990	Clay excavation, bank run gravel borrow for backfill	1.33	5.05	6.38

For information about Means Estimating Seminars, see yellow pages 11 and 12 in back of book

Division 2
Substructures

Fiber Expansion Joint

Wire Mesh Reinforcing

Concrete Slab

Vapor Barrier

Compacted Gravel

Reinforced Slab on Grade

A Slab on Grade system includes fine grading; 6" of compacted gravel; vapor barrier; 3500 p.s.i. concrete; bituminous fiber expansion joint; all necessary edge forms
4 uses; steel trowel finish; and sprayed on membrane curing compound. Wire mesh reinforcing used in all reinforced slabs.

Non-industrial slabs are for foot traffic only with negligible abrasion. Light industrial slabs are for pneumatic wheels and light abrasion. Industrial slabs are for solid rubber wheels and moderate abrasion. Heavy industrial slabs are for steel wheels and severe abrasion.

SUBSTRUCTURES 2

2.1-200	Plain & Reinforced	COST PER S.F.		
		MAT.	INST.	TOTAL
2220	Slab on grade, 4" thick, non industrial, non reinforced	1.22	1.76	2.98
2240	Reinforced	1.30	2.02	3.32
2260	Light industrial, non reinforced	1.43	2.15	3.58
2280	Reinforced	1.51	2.41	3.92
2300	Industrial, non reinforced	1.80	3.42	5.22
2320	Reinforced	1.88	3.68	5.56
3340	5" thick, non industrial, non reinforced	1.44	1.80	3.24
3360	Reinforced	1.52	2.06	3.58
3380	Light industrial, non reinforced	1.65	2.19	3.84
3400	Reinforced	1.73	2.45	4.18
3420	Heavy industrial, non reinforced	2.21	3.96	6.17
3440	Reinforced	2.23	4.25	6.48
4460	6" thick, non industrial, non reinforced	1.73	1.77	3.50
4480	Reinforced	1.85	2.11	3.96
4500	Light industrial, non reinforced	1.95	2.16	4.11
4520	Reinforced	2.14	2.62	4.76
4540	Heavy industrial, non reinforced	2.52	4.03	6.55
4560	Reinforced	2.64	4.37	7.01
5580	7" thick, non industrial, non reinforced	1.96	1.83	3.79
5600	Reinforced	2.12	2.20	4.32
5620	Light industrial, non reinforced	2.19	2.22	4.41
5640	Reinforced	2.35	2.59	4.94
5660	Heavy industrial, non reinforced	2.76	3.96	6.72
5680	Reinforced	2.88	4.30	7.18
6700	8" thick, non industrial, non reinforced	2.17	1.86	4.03
6720	Reinforced	2.30	2.17	4.47
6740	Light industrial, non reinforced	2.42	2.25	4.67
6760	Reinforced	2.55	2.56	5.11
6780	Heavy industrial, non reinforced	3	4.02	7.02
6800	Reinforced	3.19	4.35	7.54

For information about Means Estimating Seminars, see yellow pages 11 and 12 in back of book

Division 3
Superstructures

General: It is desirable for purposes of consistency and simplicity to maintain constant column sizes throughout building height. To do this, concrete strength may be varied (higher strength concrete at lower stories and lower strength concrete at upper stories), as well as varying the amount of reinforcing.

The table provides probably minimum column sizes with related costs and weight per lineal foot of story height.

3.1-114				C.I.P. Column, Square Tied				
						COST PER V.L.F.		
	LOAD (KIPS)	STORY HEIGHT (FT.)	COLUMN SIZE (IN.)	COLUMN WEIGHT (P.L.F.)	CONCRETE STRENGTH (PSI)	MAT.	INST.	TOTAL
0640	100	10	10	96	4000	7.30	31	38.30
0680		12	10	97	4000	7.15	30.50	37.65
0720		14	12	142	4000	9.25	37	46.25
0840	200	10	12	140	4000	9.35	37.50	46.85
0860		12	12	142	4000	9.30	37	46.30
0900		14	14	196	4000	11.70	42.50	54.20
0920	300	10	14	192	4000	12	43	55
0960		12	14	194	4000	11.85	43	54.85
0980		14	16	253	4000	13.40	47	60.40
1020	400	10	16	248	4000	14.60	49	63.60
1060		12	16	251	4000	14.45	49	63.45
1080		14	16	253	4000	14.35	48.50	62.85
1200	500	10	18	315	4000	19.25	58.50	77.75
1250		12	20	394	4000	19.70	61	80.70
1300		14	20	397	4000	19.60	61	80.60
1350	600	10	20	388	4000	23	67.50	90.50
1400		12	20	394	4000	22.50	66.50	89
1600		14	20	397	4000	22.50	66.50	89
3400	900	10	24	560	4000	32.50	87	119.50
3800		12	24	567	4000	32	86	118
4000		14	24	571	4000	32	85.50	117.50
7300	300	10	14	192	6000	11.85	43	54.85
7500		12	14	194	6000	11.75	42.50	54.25
7600		14	14	196	6000	11.70	42.50	54.20
8000	500	10	16	248	6000	14.60	49	63.60
8050		12	16	251	6000	14.45	49	63.45
8100		14	16	253	6000	14.35	48.50	62.85
8200	600	10	18	315	6000	17.60	56.50	74.10
8300		12	18	319	6000	17.40	56	73.40
8400		14	18	321	6000	17.30	55.50	72.80
8800	800	10	20	388	6000	19.90	61.50	81.40
8900		12	20	394	6000	19.70	61.50	81.20
9000		14	20	397	6000	19.60	61	80.60

Important: See the Reference Section for critical supporting data - Location Factors & Historical Cost Indexes

3.1-114	C.I.P. Column, Square Tied							
	LOAD (KIPS)	STORY HEIGHT (FT.)	COLUMN SIZE (IN.)	COLUMN WEIGHT (P.L.F.)	CONCRETE STRENGTH (PSI)	COST PER V.L.F.		
						MAT.	INST.	TOTAL
9100	900	10	20	388	6000	28	77	105
9300		12	20	394	6000	28	76	104
9600		14	20	397	6000	27.50	75.50	103

3.1-114	C.I.P. Column, Square Tied-Minimum Reinforcing							
	LOAD (KIPS)	STORY HEIGHT (FT.)	COLUMN SIZE (IN.)	COLUMN WEIGHT (P.L.F.)	CONCRETE STRENGTH (PSI)	COST PER V.L.F.		
						MAT.	INST.	TOTAL
9913	150	10-14	12	135	4000	9.10	37	46.10
9918	300	10-14	16	240	4000	13.30	46.50	59.80
9924	500	10-14	20	375	4000	19.40	60.50	79.90
9930	700	10-14	24	540	4000	27.50	78	105.50
9936	1000	10-14	28	740	4000	35	92.50	127.50
9942	1400	10-14	32	965	4000	46	107	153
9948	1800	10-14	36	1220	4000	55.50	124	179.50

SUPERSTRUCTURES

3

General: Data presented here is for plant produced members transported 50 miles to 100 miles to the site and erected.

Design and pricing assumptions:
Normal wt. concrete, f'c = 5 KSI

Main reinforcement, fy = 60 KSI
Ties, fy = 40 KSI

Minimum design eccentricity, 0.1t.

Concrete encased structural steel haunches are assumed where practical; otherwise galvanized rebar haunches are assumed.

Base plates are integral with columns.

Foundation anchor bolts, nuts and washers are included in price.

3.1-120 — Tied, Concentric Loaded Precast Concrete Columns

	LOAD (KIPS)	STORY HEIGHT (FT.)	COLUMN SIZE (IN.)	COLUMN WEIGHT (P.L.F.)	LOAD LEVELS	COST PER V.L.F. MAT.	COST PER V.L.F. INST.	COST PER V.L.F. TOTAL
0560	100	10	12x12	164	2	35	8.50	43.50
0570		12	12x12	162	2	34.50	7.10	41.60
0580		14	12x12	161	2	33.50	7.10	40.60
0590	150	10	12x12	166	3	34	7.10	41.10
0600		12	12x12	169	3	32	6.40	38.40
0610		14	12x12	162	3	33	6.40	39.40
0620	200	10	12x12	168	4	35.50	7.80	43.30
0630		12	12x12	170	4	35.50	7.10	42.60
0640		14	14x14	220	4	37.50	7.10	44.60

3.1-120 — Tied, Eccentric Loaded Precast Concrete Columns

	LOAD (KIPS)	STORY HEIGHT (FT.)	COLUMN SIZE (IN.)	COLUMN WEIGHT (P.L.F.)	LOAD LEVELS	COST PER V.L.F. MAT.	COST PER V.L.F. INST.	COST PER V.L.F. TOTAL
1130	100	10	12x12	161	2	32	8.50	40.50
1140		12	12x12	159	2	34	7.10	41.10
1150		14	12x12	159	2	33	7.10	40.10
1390	600	10	18x18	385	4	63.50	7.80	71.30
1400		12	18x18	380	4	61	7.10	68.10
1410		14	18x18	375	4	61	7.10	68.10
1480	800	10	20x20	490	4	81	7.80	88.80
1490		12	20x20	480	4	79.50	7.10	86.60
1500		14	20x20	475	4	79	7.10	86.10

SUPERSTRUCTURES 3

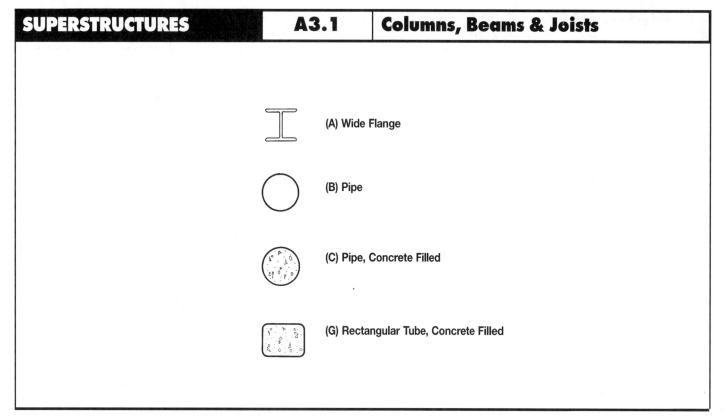

(A) Wide Flange

(B) Pipe

(C) Pipe, Concrete Filled

(G) Rectangular Tube, Concrete Filled

3.1-130				Steel Columns				
	LOAD (KIPS)	UNSUPPORTED HEIGHT (FT.)	WEIGHT (P.L.F.)	SIZE (IN.)	TYPE	COST PER V.L.F.		
						MAT.	INST.	TOTAL
1000	25	10	13	4	A	10.55	6.95	17.50
1020			7.58	3	B	8.70	6.95	15.65
1040			15	3-1/2	C	10.60	6.95	17.55
1120			20	4x3	G	8.30	6.95	15.25
1200		16	16	5	A	12	5.20	17.20
1220			10.79	4	B	11.50	5.20	16.70
1240			36	5-1/2	C	15.95	5.20	21.15
1320			64	8x6	G	16.90	5.20	22.10
1600	50	10	16	5	A	12.95	6.95	19.90
1620			14.62	5	B	16.80	6.95	23.75
1640			24	4-1/2	C	12.65	6.95	19.60
1720			28	6x3	G	11.05	6.95	18
1800		16	24	8	A	18	5.20	23.20
1840			36	5-1/2	C	15.95	5.20	21.15
1920			64	8x6	G	16.90	5.20	22.10
2000		20	28	8	A	19.90	5.20	25.10
2040			49	6-5/8	C	21.50	5.20	26.70
2120			64	8x6	G	16.05	5.20	21.25
2200	75	10	20	6	A	16.20	6.95	23.15
2240			36	4-1/2	C	32	6.95	38.95
2320			35	6x4	G	12.50	6.95	19.45
2400		16	31	8	A	23.50	5.20	28.70
2440			49	6-5/8	C	22.50	5.20	27.70
2520			64	8x6	G	16.90	5.20	22.10
2600		20	31	8	A	22	5.20	27.20
2640			81	8-5/8	C	32	5.20	37.20
2720			64	8x6	G	16.05	5.20	21.25
2800	100	10	24	8	A	19.45	6.95	26.40
2840			35	4-1/2	C	32	6.95	38.95
2920			46	8x4	G	15.25	6.95	22.20

	LOAD (KIPS)	UNSUPPORTED HEIGHT (FT.)	WEIGHT (P.L.F.)	SIZE (IN.)	TYPE	COST PER V.L.F.		
						MAT.	INST.	TOTAL
3000	100	16	31	8	A	23.50	5.20	28.70
3040			56	6-5/8	C	33.50	5.20	38.70
3120			64	8x6	G	16.90	5.20	22.10
3200		20	40	8	A	28.50	5.20	33.70
3240			81	8-5/8	C	32	5.20	37.20
3320			70	8x6	G	23	5.20	28.20
3400	125	10	31	8	A	25	6.95	31.95
3440			81	8	C	36.50	6.95	43.45
3520			64	8x6	G	18.20	6.95	25.15
3600		16	40	8	A	30	5.20	35.20
3640			81	8	C	34	5.20	39.20
3720			64	8x6	G	16.90	5.20	22.10
3800		20	48	8	A	34	5.20	39.20
3840			81	8	C	32	5.20	37.20
3920			60	8x6	G	23	5.20	28.20
4000	150	10	35	8	A	28.50	6.95	35.45
4040			81	8-5/8	C	36.50	6.95	43.45
4120			64	8x6	G	18.20	6.95	25.15
4200		16	45	10	A	34	5.20	39.20
4240			81	8-5/8	C	34	5.20	39.20
4320			70	8x6	G	24	5.20	29.20
4400		20	49	10	A	35	5.20	40.20
4440			123	10-3/4	C	46	5.20	51.20
4520			86	10x6	G	22.50	5.20	27.70
4600	200	10	45	10	A	36.50	6.95	43.45
4640			81	8-5/8	C	36.50	6.95	43.45
4720			70	8x6	G	26	6.95	32.95
4800		16	49	10	A	37	5.20	42.20
4840			123	10-3/4	C	48.50	5.20	53.70
4920			85	10x6	G	28	5.20	33.20
5200	300	10	61	14	A	49.50	6.95	56.45
5240			169	12-3/4	C	64	6.95	70.95
5320			86	10x6	G	39	6.95	45.95
5400		16	72	12	A	54	5.20	59.20
5440			169	12-3/4	C	59.50	5.20	64.70
5600		20	79	12	A	56	5.20	61.20
5640			169	12-3/4	C	56.50	5.20	61.70
5800	400	10	79	12	A	64	6.95	70.95
5840			178	12-3/4	C	84	6.95	90.95
6000		16	87	12	A	65.50	5.20	70.70
6040			178	12-3/4	C	77.50	5.20	82.70
6400	500	10	99	14	A	80.50	6.95	87.45
6600		16	109	14	A	82	5.20	87.20
6800		20	120	12	A	85	5.20	90.20
7000	600	10	120	12	A	97.50	6.95	104.45
7200		16	132	14	A	99	5.20	104.20
7400		20	132	14	A	94	5.20	99.20
7600	700	10	136	12	A	110	6.95	116.95
7800		16	145	14	A	109	5.20	114.20
8000		20	145	14	A	103	5.20	108.20
8200	800	10	145	14	A	118	6.95	124.95
8300		16	159	14	A	119	5.20	124.20
8400		20	176	14	A	125	5.20	130.20

Important: See the Reference Section for critical supporting data - Location Factors & Historical Cost Indexes

3.1-130	Steel Columns

	LOAD (KIPS)	UNSUPPORTED HEIGHT (FT.)	WEIGHT (P.L.F.)	SIZE (IN.)	TYPE	COST PER V.L.F.		
						MAT.	INST.	TOTAL
8800	900	10	159	14	A	129	6.95	135.95
8900		16	176	14	A	132	5.20	137.20
9000		20	193	14	A	137	5.20	142.20
9100	1000	10	176	14	A	143	6.95	149.95
9200		16	193	14	A	145	5.20	150.20
9300		20	211	14	A	150	5.20	155.20

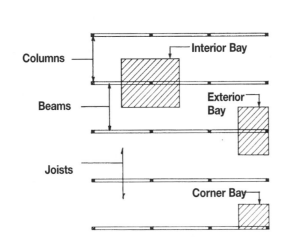

Description: Table below lists costs per S.F. of bay size for wood columns of various sizes and unsupported heights and the maximum allowable total load per S.F. per bay size.

SUPERSTRUCTURES 3

| 3.1-140 | Wood Columns | | | | | | | |

	NOMINAL COLUMN SIZE (IN.)	BAY SIZE (FT.)	UNSUPPORTED HEIGHT (FT.)	MATERIAL (BF/M.S.F.)	TOTAL LOAD (P.S.F.)	COST PER S.F.		
						MAT.	INST.	TOTAL
1000	4 x 4	10 x 8	8	133	100	.22	.16	.38
1050			10	167	60	.28	.20	.48
1200		10 x 10	8	106	80	.18	.13	.31
1250			10	133	50	.22	.16	.38
1400		10 x 15	8	71	50	.12	.09	.21
1450			10	88	30	.15	.11	.26
1600		15 x 15	8	47	30	.08	.06	.14
1650			10	59	15	.10	.07	.17
2000	6 x 6	10 x 15	8	160	230	.31	.18	.49
2050			10	200	210	.39	.23	.62
2200		15 x 15	8	107	150	.21	.12	.33
2250			10	133	140	.26	.15	.41
2400		15 x 20	8	80	110	.15	.09	.24
2450			10	100	100	.19	.11	.30
2600		20 x 20	8	60	80	.12	.07	.19
2650			10	75	70	.14	.08	.22
2800		20 x 25	8	48	60	.09	.05	.14
2850			10	60	50	.12	.07	.19
3400	8 x 8	20 x 20	8	107	160	.23	.11	.34
3450			10	133	160	.29	.14	.43
3600		20 x 25	8	85	130	.14	.10	.24
3650			10	107	130	.18	.13	.31
3800		25 x 25	8	68	100	.14	.07	.21
3850			10	85	100	.18	.08	.26
4200	10 x 10	20 x 25	8	133	210	.28	.13	.41
4250			10	167	210	.35	.16	.51
4400		25 x 25	8	107	160	.22	.10	.32
4450			10	133	160	.28	.13	.41
4700	12 x 12	20 x 25	8	192	310	.40	.17	.57
4750			10	240	310	.50	.22	.72
4900		25 x 25	8	154	240	.32	.14	.46
4950			10	192	240	.40	.17	.57

Steel Column Fireproofing

"T" Shaped Precast Beams

"L" Shaped Precast Beams

3.1-190 — Steel Column Fireproofing

	ENCASEMENT SYSTEM	COLUMN SIZE (IN.)	THICKNESS (IN.)	FIRE RATING (HRS.)	WEIGHT (P.L.F.)	COST PER V.L.F.		
						MAT.	INST.	TOTAL
3000	Concrete	8	1	1	110	4.24	23.50	27.74
3300		14	1	1	258	6.95	34	40.95
3400			2	3	325	8.35	38	46.35
3450	Gypsum board	8	1/2	2	8	2.35	14.10	16.45
3550	1 layer	14	1/2	2	18	2.58	15.05	17.63
3600	Gypsum board	8	1	3	14	3.43	18	21.43
3650	1/2" fire rated	10	1	3	17	3.71	19.10	22.81
3700	2 layers	14	1	3	22	3.86	19.65	23.51
3750	Gypsum board	8	1-1/2	3	23	4.71	22.50	27.21
3800	1/2" fire rated	10	1-1/2	3	27	5.35	25	30.35
3850	3 layers	14	1-1/2	3	35	5.95	27.50	33.45
3900	Sprayed fiber	8	1-1/2	2	6.3	2.98	5.20	8.18
3950	Direct application		2	3	8.3	4.11	7.20	11.31
4050		10	1-1/2	2	7.9	3.60	6.30	9.90
4200		14	1-1/2	2	10.8	4.48	7.85	12.33

3.1-224 — "T" Shaped Precast Beams

	SPAN (FT.)	SUPERIMPOSED LOAD (K.L.F.)	SIZE W X D (IN.)	BEAM WEIGHT (P.L.F.)	TOTAL LOAD (K.L.F.)	COST PER L.F.		
						MAT.	INST.	TOTAL
2300	15	2.8	12x16	260	3.06	105	15.15	120.15
2500		8.37	12x28	515	8.89	135	14.85	149.85
8900	45	3.31	12x60	1165	4.51	240	14.15	254.15
9900		6.5	24x60	1915	8.42	310	14.15	324.15

3.1-226 — "L" Shaped Precast Beams

	SPAN (FT.)	SUPERIMPOSED LOAD (K.L.F.)	SIZE W X D (IN.)	BEAM WEIGHT (P.L.F.)	TOTAL LOAD (K.L.F.)	COST PER L.F.		
						MAT.	INST.	TOTAL
2250	15	2.58	12x16	230	2.81	79.50	15.15	94.65
2400		5.92	12x24	370	6.29	97	14.15	111.15
4000	25	2.64	12x28	435	3.08	107	8.50	115.50
4450		6.44	18x36	790	7.23	146	10.65	156.65
5300	30	2.80	12x36	565	3.37	128	8.50	136.50
6400		8.66	24x44	1245	9.90	203	15.55	218.55

SUPERSTRUCTURES

3

Description: The table below lists costs, $/S.F., for channel girts with sag rods and connector angles top and bottom for various column spacings, building heights and wind loads. Additive costs are shown for wind columns.

3.4-300 — Metal Siding Support

	BLDG. HEIGHT (FT.)	WIND LOAD (P.S.F.)	COL. SPACING (FT.)		INTERMEDIATE COLUMNS	COST PER S.F.		
						MAT.	INST.	TOTAL
3000	18	20	20			1.11	2.69	3.80
3100					wind cols.	.57	.20	.77
3200		20	25			1.21	2.71	3.92
3300					wind cols.	.46	.16	.62
3400		20	30			1.34	2.77	4.11
3500					wind cols.	.38	.13	.51
3600		20	35			1.47	2.81	4.28
3700					wind cols.	.33	.12	.45
3800		30	20			1.23	2.73	3.96
3900					wind cols.	.57	.20	.77
4000		30	25			1.34	2.77	4.11
4100					wind cols.	.46	.16	.62
4200		30	30			1.48	2.81	4.29
4300					wind cols.	.52	.19	.71
4600	30	20	20			1.08	1.89	2.97
4700					wind cols.	.81	.29	1.10
4800		20	25			1.21	1.94	3.15
4900					wind cols.	.65	.23	.88
5000		20	30			1.37	1.99	3.36
5100					wind cols.	.64	.23	.87
5200		20	35			1.53	2.05	3.58
5300					wind cols.	.63	.23	.86
5400		30	20			1.23	1.94	3.17
5500					wind cols.	.96	.35	1.31
5600		30	25			1.36	1.99	3.35
5700					wind cols.	.91	.33	1.24
5800		30	30			1.54	2.05	3.59
5900					wind cols.	.86	.31	1.17

Cast in Place Floor Slab, One Way
General: Solid concrete slabs of uniform depth reinforced for flexure in one direction and for temperature and shrinkage in the other direction.

Cast in Place Beam & Slab, One Way
General: Solid concrete one way slab cast monolithically with reinforced concrete beams and girders.

3.5-110 — Cast in Place Slabs, One Way

	SLAB DESIGN & SPAN (FT.)	SUPERIMPOSED LOAD (P.S.F.)	THICKNESS (IN.)	TOTAL LOAD (P.S.F.)		COST PER S.F. MAT.	INST.	TOTAL
2500	Single 8	40	4	90		2.28	5.35	7.63
2600		75	4	125		2.36	5.80	8.16
2700		125	4-1/2	181		2.47	5.85	8.32
2800		200	5	262		2.75	6.05	8.80
3000	Single 10	40	4	90		2.43	5.75	8.18
3100		75	4	125		2.43	5.75	8.18
3200		125	5	188		2.72	5.90	8.62
3300		200	7-1/2	293		3.61	6.70	10.31
3500	Single 15	40	5-1/2	90		2.91	5.85	8.76
3600		75	6-1/2	156		3.24	6.15	9.39
3700		125	7-1/2	219		3.54	6.35	9.89
3800		200	8-1/2	306		3.85	6.50	10.35
4000	Single 20	40	7-1/2	115		3.51	6.20	9.71
4100		75	9	200		3.88	6.20	10.08
4200		125	10	250		4.29	6.45	10.74
4300		200	10	324		4.60	6.70	11.30

3.5-120 — Cast in Place Beam & Slab, One Way

	BAY SIZE (FT.)	SUPERIMPOSED LOAD (P.S.F.)	MINIMUM COL. SIZE (IN.)	SLAB THICKNESS (IN.)	TOTAL LOAD (P.S.F.)	COST PER S.F. MAT.	INST.	TOTAL
5000	20x25	40	12	5-1/2	121	3.27	7.35	10.62
5200		125	16	5-1/2	215	3.83	8.45	12.28
5500	25x25	40	12	6	129	3.44	7.25	10.69
5700		125	18	6	227	4.35	8.90	13.25
7500	30x35	40	16	8	158	4.28	8.15	12.43
7600		75	18	8	196	4.57	8.45	13.02
7700		125	22	8	254	5.10	9.45	14.55
7800		200	26	8	332	5.50	9.80	15.30
8000	35x35	40	16	9	169	4.78	8.50	13.28
8200		75	20	9	213	5.15	9.25	14.40
8400		125	24	9	272	5.65	9.60	15.25
8600		200	26	9	355	6.20	10.25	16.45

SUPERSTRUCTURES

3

General: Solid concrete two way slab cast monolithically with reinforced concrete support beams and girders.

General: Flat Slab: Solid uniform depth concrete two way slabs with drop panels at columns and no column capitals.

3.5-130 | Cast in Place Beam & Slab, Two Way

	BAY SIZE (FT.)	SUPERIMPOSED LOAD (P.S.F.)	MINIMUM COL. SIZE (IN.)	SLAB THICKNESS (IN.)	TOTAL LOAD (P.S.F.)	COST PER S.F.		
						MAT.	INST.	TOTAL
4000	20 x 25	40	12	7	141	3.76	7.45	11.21
4300		75	14	7	181	4.28	8.15	12.43
4500		125	16	7	236	4.37	8.40	12.77
5100	25 x 25	40	12	7-1/2	149	3.93	7.55	11.48
5200		75	16	7-1/2	185	4.29	8.10	12.39
5300		125	18	7-1/2	250	4.65	8.75	13.40
7600	30 x 35	40	16	10	188	5.20	8.55	13.75
7700		75	18	10	225	5.50	8.90	14.40
8000		125	22	10	282	6.10	9.60	15.70
8500	35 x 35	40	16	10-1/2	193	5.55	8.75	14.30
8600		75	20	10-1/2	233	5.80	9.05	14.85
9000		125	24	10-1/2	287	6.50	9.80	16.30

3.5-140 | Cast in Place Flat Slab with Drop Panels

	BAY SIZE (FT.)	SUPERIMPOSED LOAD (P.S.F.)	MINIMUM COL. SIZE (IN.)	SLAB & DROP (IN.)	TOTAL LOAD (P.S.F.)	COST PER S.F.		
						MAT.	INST.	TOTAL
1960	20 x 20	40	12	7 - 3	132	3.65	5.95	9.60
1980		75	16	7 - 4	168	3.84	6.10	9.94
2000		125	18	7 - 6	221	4.24	6.30	10.54
3200	25 x 25	40	12	8-1/2 - 5-1/2	154	4.24	6.25	10.49
4000		125	20	8-1/2 - 8-1/2	243	4.73	6.70	11.43
4400		200	24	9 - 8-1/2	329	4.95	6.85	11.80
5000	25 x 30	40	14	9-1/2 - 7	168	4.58	6.50	11.08
5200		75	18	9-1/2 - 7	203	4.85	6.75	11.60
5600		125	22	9-1/2 - 8	256	5.05	6.90	11.95
6400	30 x 30	40	14	10-1/2 - 7-1/2	182	4.93	6.65	11.58
6600		75	18	10-1/2 - 7-1/2	217	5.20	6.95	12.15
6800		125	22	10-1/2 - 9	269	5.45	7.10	12.55
7400	30 x 35	40	16	11-1/2 - 9	196	5.35	6.90	12.25
7900		75	20	11-1/2 - 9	231	5.65	7.20	12.85
8000		125	24	11-1/2 - 11	284	5.90	7.40	13.30
9000	35 x 35	40	16	12 - 9	202	5.50	7	12.50
9400		75	20	12 - 11	240	5.85	7.35	13.20
9600		125	24	12 - 11	290	6.05	7.50	13.55

Important: See the Reference Section for critical supporting data - Location Factors & Historical Cost Indexes

SUPERSTRUCTURES 3

Multispan Joist Slab

General: Flat Plates: Solid uniform depth concrete two way slab without drops or interior beams. Primary design limit is shear at columns.

General: Combination of thin concrete slab and monolithic ribs at uniform spacing to reduce dead weight and increase rigidity.

3.5-150 Cast in Place Flat Plate

	BAY SIZE (FT.)	SUPERIMPOSED LOAD (P.S.F.)	MINIMUM COL. SIZE (IN.)	SLAB THICKNESS (IN.)	TOTAL LOAD (P.S.F.)	COST PER S.F.		
						MAT.	INST.	TOTAL
3000	15 x 20	40	14	7	127	3.16	5.70	8.86
3400		75	16	7-1/2	169	3.36	5.85	9.21
3600		125	22	8-1/2	231	3.70	6	9.70
3800		175	24	8-1/2	281	3.72	6	9.72
4200	20 x 20	40	16	7	127	3.15	5.70	8.85
4400		75	20	7-1/2	175	3.39	5.85	9.24
4600		125	24	8-1/2	231	3.71	6	9.71
5000		175	24	8-1/2	281	3.74	6.05	9.79
5600	20 x 25	40	18	8-1/2	146	3.68	6	9.68
6000		75	20	9	188	3.81	6.05	9.86
6400		125	26	9-1/2	244	4.11	6.25	10.36
6600		175	30	10	300	4.26	6.35	10.61
7000	25 x 25	40	20	9	152	3.80	6.05	9.85
7400		75	24	9-1/2	194	4.04	6.20	10.24
7600		125	30	10	250	4.28	6.40	10.68

3.5-160 Cast in Place Multispan Joist Slab

	BAY SIZE (FT.)	SUPERIMPOSED LOAD (P.S.F.)	MINIMUM COL. SIZE (IN.)	RIB DEPTH (IN.)	TOTAL LOAD (P.S.F.)	COST PER S.F.		
						MAT.	INST.	TOTAL
2000	15 x 15	40	12	8	115	3.28	6.95	10.23
2100		75	12	8	150	3.30	7	10.30
2200		125	12	8	200	3.38	7.05	10.43
2300		200	14	8	275	3.50	7.30	10.80
2600	15 x 20	40	12	8	115	3.34	6.95	10.29
2800		75	12	8	150	3.42	7.10	10.52
3000		125	14	8	200	3.56	7.45	11.01
3300		200	16	8	275	3.73	7.60	11.33
3600	20 x 20	40	12	10	120	3.41	6.85	10.26
3900		75	14	10	155	3.60	7.25	10.85
4000		125	16	10	205	3.64	7.40	11.04
4100		200	18	10	280	3.83	7.70	11.53
6200	30 x 30	40	14	14	131	3.87	7.20	11.07
6400		75	18	14	166	4	7.45	11.45
6600		125	20	14	216	4.26	7.85	12.11
6700		200	24	16	297	4.60	8.15	12.75

For expanded coverage of these items see *Means Assemblies Cost Data 2001*

SUPERSTRUCTURES

3

Waffle Slab

3.5-170				Cast in Place Waffle Slab				
	BAY SIZE (FT.)	SUPERIMPOSED LOAD (P.S.F.)	MINIMUM COL. SIZE (IN.)	RIB DEPTH (IN.)	TOTAL LOAD (P.S.F.)	COST PER S.F.		
						MAT.	INST.	TOTAL
3900	20 x 20	40	12	8	144	5.15	7.40	12.55
4000		75	12	8	179	5.25	7.50	12.75
4100		125	16	8	229	5.35	7.55	12.90
4200		200	18	8	304	5.60	7.80	13.40
4400	20 x 25	40	12	8	146	5.25	7.40	12.65
4500		75	14	8	181	5.40	7.55	12.95
4600		125	16	8	231	5.50	7.65	13.15
4700		200	18	8	306	5.70	7.85	13.55
4900	25 x 25	40	12	10	150	5.40	7.50	12.90
5000		75	16	10	185	5.55	7.65	13.20
5300		125	18	10	235	5.70	7.80	13.50
5500		200	20	10	310	5.85	7.95	13.80
5700	25 x 30	40	14	10	154	5.50	7.55	13.05
5800		75	16	10	189	5.65	7.70	13.35
5900		125	18	10	239	5.80	7.80	13.60
6000		200	20	12	329	6.35	8.20	14.55
6400	30 x 30	40	14	12	169	5.90	7.75	13.65
6500		75	18	12	204	6	7.85	13.85
6600		125	20	12	254	6.10	7.95	14.05
6700		200	24	12	329	6.60	8.40	15
6900	30 x 35	40	16	12	169	6	7.80	13.80
7000		75	18	12	204	6	7.80	13.80
7100		125	22	12	254	6.25	8.05	14.30
7200		200	26	14	334	6.90	8.55	15.45
7400	35 x 35	40	16	14	174	6.35	8	14.35
7500		75	20	14	209	6.45	8.10	14.55
7600		125	24	14	259	6.60	8.25	14.85
7700		200	26	16	346	7.05	8.65	15.70
8000	35 x 40	40	18	14	176	6.50	8.15	14.65
8300		75	22	14	211	6.70	8.30	15
8500		125	26	16	271	7.05	8.50	15.55
8750		200	30	20	372	7.65	8.95	16.60
9200	40 x 40	40	18	14	176	6.70	8.30	15
9400		75	24	14	211	6.90	8.55	15.45
9500		125	26	16	271	7.10	8.60	15.70
9700	40 x 45	40	20	16	186	6.95	8.45	15.40
9800		75	24	16	221	7.20	8.70	15.90
9900		125	28	16	271	7.30	8.80	16.10

Important: See the Reference Section for critical supporting data - Location Factors & Historical Cost Indexes

SUPERSTRUCTURES 3

Precast Plank with No Topping

Precast Plank with 2″ Concrete Topping

3.5-210			Precast Plank with No Topping					
	SPAN (FT.)	SUPERIMPOSED LOAD (P.S.F.)	TOTAL DEPTH (IN.)	DEAD LOAD (P.S.F.)	TOTAL LOAD (P.S.F.)	COST PER S.F.		
						MAT.	INST.	TOTAL
0720	10	40	4	50	90	5.40	2.13	7.53
0750		75	6	50	125	5.20	1.83	7.03
0770		100	6	50	150	5.20	1.83	7.03
0800	15	40	6	50	90	5.20	1.83	7.03
0820		75	6	50	125	5.20	1.83	7.03
0850		100	6	50	150	5.20	1.83	7.03
0950	25	40	6	50	90	5.20	1.83	7.03
0970		75	8	55	130	5.80	1.60	7.40
1000		100	8	55	155	5.80	1.60	7.40
1200	30	40	8	55	95	5.80	1.60	7.40
1300		75	8	55	130	5.80	1.60	7.40
1400		100	10	70	170	6.55	1.41	7.96
1500	40	40	10	70	110	6.55	1.41	7.96
1600		75	12	70	145	6.75	1.21	7.96
1700	45	40	12	70	110	6.75	1.21	7.96

3.5-210			Precast Plank with 2″ Concrete Topping					
	SPAN (FT.)	SUPERIMPOSED LOAD (P.S.F.)	TOTAL DEPTH (IN.)	DEAD LOAD (P.S.F.)	TOTAL LOAD (P.S.F.)	COST PER S.F.		
						MAT.	INST.	TOTAL
2000	10	40	6	75	115	6	3.46	9.46
2100		75	8	75	150	5.80	3.16	8.96
2200		100	8	75	175	5.80	3.16	8.96
2500	15	40	8	75	115	5.80	3.16	8.96
2600		75	8	75	150	5.80	3.16	8.96
2700		100	8	75	175	5.80	3.16	8.96
3100	25	40	8	75	115	5.80	3.16	8.96
3200		75	8	75	150	5.80	3.16	8.96
3300		100	10	80	180	6.40	2.93	9.33
3400	30	40	10	80	120	6.40	2.93	9.33
3500		75	10	80	155	6.40	2.93	9.33
3600		100	10	80	180	6.40	2.93	9.33
4000	40	40	12	95	135	7.15	2.74	9.89
4500		75	14	95	170	7.35	2.54	9.89
5000	45	40	14	95	135	7.35	2.54	9.89

SUPERSTRUCTURES

3

Most widely used for moderate span floors and moderate and long span roofs. At shorter spans, they tend to be competitive with hollow core slabs. They are also used as wall panels.

Precast Double "T" Beams with No Topping

Precast Double "T" Beams with 2″ Topping

SUPERSTRUCTURES 3

3.5-230	Precast Double "T" Beams with No Topping							
	SPAN (FT.)	SUPERIMPOSED LOAD (P.S.F.)	DBL. "T" SIZE D (IN.) W (FT.)	CONCRETE "T" TYPE	TOTAL LOAD (P.S.F.)	COST PER S.F.		
						MAT.	INST.	TOTAL
4300	50	30	20x8	Lt. Wt.	66	5.20	1.09	6.29
4400		40	20x8	Lt. Wt.	76	5.55	1	6.55
4500		50	20x8	Lt. Wt.	86	5.85	1.20	7.05
4600		75	20x8	Lt. Wt.	111	6.10	1.38	7.48
5600	70	30	32x10	Lt. Wt.	78	6	.75	6.75
5750		40	32x10	Lt. Wt.	88	6.25	.92	7.17
5900		50	32x10	Lt. Wt.	98	6.45	1.06	7.51
6000		75	32x10	Lt. Wt.	123	6.80	1.29	8.09
6100		100	32x10	Lt. Wt.	148	7.45	1.75	9.20
6200	80	30	32x10	Lt. Wt.	78	6.45	1.05	7.50
6300		40	32x10	Lt. Wt.	88	6.80	1.29	8.09
6400		50	32x10	Lt. Wt.	98	7.10	1.52	8.62

3.5-230	Precast Double "T" Beams With 2″ Topping							
	SPAN (FT.)	SUPERIMPOSED LOAD (P.S.F.)	DBL. "T" SIZE D (IN.) W (FT.)	CONCRETE "T" TYPE	TOTAL LOAD (P.S.F.)	COST PER S.F.		
						MAT.	INST.	TOTAL
7100	40	30	18x8	Reg. Wt.	120	4.84	2.16	7
7200		40	20x8	Reg. Wt.	130	4.63	2.05	6.68
7300		50	20x8	Reg. Wt.	140	4.92	2.26	7.18
7400		75	20x8	Reg. Wt.	165	5.05	2.34	7.39
7500		100	20x8	Reg. Wt.	190	5.45	2.65	8.10
7550	50	30	24x8	Reg. Wt.	120	5.20	2.17	7.37
7600		40	24x8	Reg. Wt.	130	5.30	2.24	7.54
7750		50	24x8	Reg. Wt.	140	5.35	2.25	7.60
7800		75	24x8	Reg. Wt.	165	5.75	2.55	8.30
7900		100	32x10	Reg. Wt.	189	6.10	2.07	8.17

Precast Beam and Plank with No Topping

Precast Beam and Plank with 2″ Topping

3.5-242 — Precast Beam & Plank with No Topping

	BAY SIZE (FT.)	SUPERIMPOSED LOAD (P.S.F.)	PLANK THICKNESS (IN.)	TOTAL DEPTH (IN.)	TOTAL LOAD (P.S.F.)	COST PER S.F.		
						MAT.	INST.	TOTAL
6200	25x25	40	8	28	118	12.05	3.02	15.07
6400		75	8	36	158	12.60	3.02	15.62
6500		100	8	36	183	12.60	3.02	15.62
7000	25x30	40	8	36	110	11.50	3.02	14.52
7200		75	10	36	159	12.55	2.83	15.38
7400		100	12	36	188	13.35	2.63	15.98
7600	30x30	40	8	36	121	11.95	3.02	14.97
8000		75	10	44	140	12.55	3.02	15.57
8250		100	12	52	206	14.50	2.63	17.13
8500	30x35	40	12	44	135	12.40	2.63	15.03
8750		75	12	52	176	13.20	2.63	15.83
9000	35x35	40	12	52	141	13.25	2.63	15.88
9250		75	12	60	181	13.95	2.63	16.58
9500	35x40	40	12	52	137	12.65	3.34	15.99

3.5-244 — Precast Beam & Plank with 2″ Topping

	BAY SIZE (FT.)	SUPERIMPOSED LOAD (P.S.F.)	PLANK THICKNESS (IN.)	TOTAL DEPTH (IN.)	TOTAL LOAD (P.S.F.)	COST PER S.F.		
						MAT.	INST.	TOTAL
4300	20x20	40	6	22	135	12	4.55	16.55
4400		75	6	24	173	12.70	4.55	17.25
4500		100	6	28	200	13.15	4.55	17.70
4600	20x25	40	6	26	134	11.30	4.53	15.83
5000		75	8	30	177	12.40	4.30	16.70
5200		100	8	30	202	12.40	4.30	16.70
5400	25x25	40	6	38	143	12.65	4.50	17.15
5600		75	8	38	183	12.65	4.50	17.15
6000		100	8	46	216	14.25	4.27	18.52
6200	25x30	40	8	38	144	12.15	4.25	16.40
6400		75	10	46	200	13.75	4.06	17.81
6600		100	10	46	225	13.75	4.06	17.81
7000	30x30	40	8	46	150	13.15	4.24	17.39
7200		75	10	54	181	14.15	4.24	18.39
7600		100	10	54	231	14.15	4.24	18.39
7800	30x35	40	10	54	166	13.60	4.05	17.65
8000		75	12	54	200	13.55	3.85	17.40

SUPERSTRUCTURES

3

With Topping

General: Beams and double tees priced here are for plant produced prestressed members transported to the site and erected.

The 2″ structural topping is applied after the beams and double tees are in place and is reinforced with W.W.F.

Note: Deduct from prices 20% for Southern States. Add to prices 10% for Western States.

3.5-254	Precast Double "T" & 2″ Topping on Precast Beams							
	BAY SIZE (FT.)	SUPERIMPOSED LOAD (P.S.F.)	DEPTH (IN.)		TOTAL LOAD (P.S.F.)	COST PER S.F.		
						MAT.	INST.	TOTAL
3000	25x30	40	38		130	10.85	3.84	14.69
3100		75	38		168	10.85	3.84	14.69
3300		100	46		196	11.45	3.84	15.29
3600	30x30	40	46		150	11.90	3.82	15.72
3750		75	46		174	11.90	3.82	15.72
4000		100	54		203	12.55	3.82	16.37
4100	30x40	40	46		136	9.60	3.61	13.21
4300		75	54		173	10.15	3.61	13.76
4400		100	62		204	10.75	3.61	14.36
4600	30x50	40	54		138	9.15	3.49	12.64
4800		75	54		181	9.75	3.49	13.24
5000		100	54		219	10.70	3.28	13.98
5200	30x60	40	62		151	9.65	3.29	12.94
5400		75	62		192	10.30	3.29	13.59
5600		100	62		215	10.25	3.29	13.54
5800	35x40	40	54		139	10.40	3.60	14
6000		75	62		179	11.45	3.50	14.95
6250		100	62		212	11.80	3.50	15.30
6500	35x50	40	62		142	9.90	3.50	13.40
6750		75	62		186	10.50	3.50	14
7300		100	62		231	12.30	3.29	15.59
7600	35x60	40	54		154	11.05	3.20	14.25
7750		75	54		179	11.45	3.20	14.65
8000		100	62		224	12.10	3.20	15.30
8250	40x40	40	62		145	11.60	4.31	15.91
8400		75	62		187	12.25	4.30	16.55
8750		100	62		223	13.35	4.30	17.65
9000	40x50	40	62		151	10.85	4.19	15.04
9300		75	62		193	11.70	3.59	15.29
9800	40x60	40	62		164	13.85	3.73	17.58

Important: See the Reference Section for critical supporting data - Location Factors & Historical Cost Indexes

General: The following table is based upon structural wide flange (WF) beam and girder framing. Non-composite action is assumed between WF framing and decking. Deck costs not included.

The deck spans the short direction. The steel beams and girders are fireproofed with sprayed fiber fireproofing.

No columns included in price.

3.5-310	W Shape Beams & Girders							
	BAY SIZE (FT.) BEAM X GIRD	SUPERIMPOSED LOAD (P.S.F.)	STEEL FRAMING DEPTH (IN.)	FIREPROOFING (S.F./S.F.)	TOTAL LOAD (P.S.F.)	COST PER S.F.		
						MAT.	INST.	TOTAL
1350	15x20	40	12	.535	50	2.45	1.37	3.82
1400		40	16	.65	90	3.19	1.76	4.95
1450		75	18	.694	125	4.17	2.22	6.39
1500		125	24	.796	175	5.75	3.04	8.79
2000	20x20	40	12	.55	50	2.72	1.50	4.22
2050		40	14	.579	90	3.70	1.95	5.65
2100		75	16	.672	125	4.44	2.31	6.75
2150		125	16	.714	175	5.30	2.78	8.08
2900	20x25	40	16	.53	50	2.99	1.61	4.60
2950		40	18	.621	96	4.69	2.40	7.09
3000		75	18	.651	131	5.40	2.72	8.12
3050		125	24	.77	200	7.10	3.63	10.73
5200	25x25	40	18	.486	50	3.25	1.69	4.94
5300		40	18	.592	96	4.81	2.44	7.25
5400		75	21	.668	131	5.80	2.91	8.71
5450		125	24	.738	191	7.65	3.86	11.51
6300	25x30	40	21	.568	50	3.70	1.94	5.64
6350		40	21	.694	90	5	2.58	7.58
6400		75	24	.776	125	6.40	3.24	9.64
6450		125	30	.904	175	7.70	3.98	11.68
7700	30x30	40	21	.52	50	3.96	2.02	5.98
7750		40	24	.629	103	6.10	3.01	9.11
7800		75	30	.715	138	7.20	3.55	10.75
7850		125	36	.822	206	9.45	4.72	14.17
8250	30x35	40	21	.508	50	4.50	2.25	6.75
8300		40	24	.651	109	6.65	3.26	9.91
8350		75	33	.732	150	8.05	3.92	11.97
8400		125	36	.802	225	10	4.96	14.96
9550	35x35	40	27	.560	50	4.67	2.36	7.03
9600		40	36	.706	109	8.45	4.08	12.53
9650		75	36	.750	150	8.75	4.24	12.99
9820		125	36	.797	225	11.65	5.70	17.35

SUPERSTRUCTURES

3

Description: Table below lists costs for light gage CEE or PUNCHED DOUBLE joists to suit the span and loading with the minimum thickness subfloor required by the joist spacing.

SUPERSTRUCTURES 3

3.5-360	Light Gauge Steel Floor Systems							
	SPAN (FT.)	SUPERIMPOSED LOAD (P.S.F.)	FRAMING DEPTH (IN.)	FRAMING SPAC. (IN.)	TOTAL LOAD (P.S.F.)	COST PER S.F.		
						MAT.	INST.	TOTAL
1500	15	40	8	16	54	1.72	1.45	3.17
1550			8	24	54	1.85	1.48	3.33
1600		65	10	16	80	2.16	1.75	3.91
1650			10	24	80	2.20	1.70	3.90
1700		75	10	16	90	2.16	1.75	3.91
1750			10	24	90	2.20	1.70	3.90
1800		100	10	16	116	2.74	2.22	4.96
1850			10	24	116	2.20	1.70	3.90
1900		125	10	16	141	2.74	2.22	4.96
1950			10	24	141	2.20	1.70	3.90
2500	20	40	8	16	55	1.94	1.64	3.58
2550			8	24	55	1.85	1.48	3.33
2600		65	8	16	80	2.20	1.86	4.06
2650			10	24	80	2.21	1.72	3.93
2700		75	10	16	90	2.05	1.66	3.71
2750			12	24	90	2.43	1.51	3.94
2800		100	10	16	115	2.05	1.66	3.71
2850			10	24	116	2.73	1.93	4.66
2900		125	12	16	142	3.06	1.92	4.98
2950			12	24	141	2.93	2.03	4.96
3500	25	40	10	16	55	2.16	1.75	3.91
3550			10	24	55	2.20	1.70	3.90
3600		65	10	16	81	2.74	2.22	4.96
3650			12	24	81	2.65	1.64	4.29
3700		75	12	16	92	3.06	1.92	4.98
3750			12	24	91	2.93	2.03	4.96
3800		100	12	16	117	3.41	2.12	5.53
3850		125	12	16	143	3.85	2.72	6.57
4500	30	40	12	16	57	3.06	1.92	4.98
4550			12	24	56	2.64	1.64	4.28
4600		65	12	16	82	3.39	2.11	5.50
4650		75	12	16	92	3.39	2.11	5.50

Important: See the Reference Section for critical supporting data - Location Factors & Historical Cost Indexes

Description: The table below lists costs per S.F. for a floor system on bearing walls using open web steel joists, galvanized steel slab form and 2-1/2″ concrete slab reinforced with welded wire fabric. Costs of the bearing walls are not included.

3.5-420 — Deck & Joists on Bearing Walls

	SPAN (FT.)	SUPERIMPOSED LOAD (P.S.F.)	JOIST SPACING FT./IN.	DEPTH (IN.)	TOTAL LOAD (P.S.F.)	COST PER S.F. MAT.	COST PER S.F. INST.	COST PER S.F. TOTAL
1050	20	40	2-0	14-1/2	83	2.96	2.62	5.58
1070		65	2-0	16-1/2	109	3.23	2.77	6
1100		75	2-0	16-1/2	119	3.23	2.77	6
1120		100	2-0	18-1/2	145	3.25	2.79	6.04
1150		125	1-9	18-1/2	170	3.95	3.28	7.23
1170	25	40	2-0	18-1/2	84	3.56	3.05	6.61
1200		65	2-0	20-1/2	109	3.69	3.13	6.82
1220		75	2-0	20-1/2	119	3.62	2.98	6.60
1250		100	2-0	22-1/2	145	3.68	3	6.68
1270		125	1-9	22-1/2	170	4.24	3.29	7.53
1300	30	40	2-0	22-1/2	84	3.68	2.68	6.36
1320		65	2-0	24-1/2	110	4.01	2.80	6.81
1350		75	2-0	26-1/2	121	4.17	2.85	7.02
1370		100	2-0	26-1/2	146	4.47	2.96	7.43
1400		125	2-0	24-1/2	172	4.87	3.85	8.72
1420	35	40	2-0	26-1/2	85	4.59	3.69	8.28
1450		65	2-0	28-1/2	111	4.75	3.78	8.53
1470		75	2-0	28-1/2	121	4.75	3.78	8.53
1500		100	1-11	28-1/2	147	5.20	4.04	9.24
1520		125	1-8	28-1/2	172	5.70	4.35	10.05
1550	5/8″ gyp. fireproof.							
1560	On metal furring, add					.55	1.98	2.53

The table below lists costs for a floor system on exterior bearing walls and interior columns and beams using open web steel joists, galvanized steel slab form, 2-1/2" concrete slab reinforced with welded wire fabric.

Columns are sized to accommodate one floor plus roof loading but costs for columns are from suspended floor to slab on grade only. Costs of the bearing walls are not included.

Steel Joists and Concrete Slab on Walls and Beams

3.5-440 — Steel Joists on Beam & Wall

	BAY SIZE (FT.)	SUPERIMPOSED LOAD (P.S.F.)	DEPTH (IN.)	TOTAL LOAD (P.S.F.)	COLUMN ADD	COST PER S.F. MAT.	INST.	TOTAL
1720	25x25	40	23	84		4.35	3.28	7.63
1730					columns	.19	.08	.27
1750	25x25	65	29	110		4.58	3.40	7.98
1760					columns	.19	.08	.27
1770	25x25	75	26	120		4.76	3.34	8.10
1780					columns	.22	.09	.31
1800	25x25	100	29	145		5.40	3.66	9.06
1810					columns	.22	.09	.31
1820	25x25	125	29	170		5.65	3.78	9.43
1830					columns	.25	.11	.36
2020	30x30	40	29	84		4.69	3	7.69
2030					columns	.17	.08	.25
2050	30x30	65	29	110		5.30	3.24	8.54
2060					columns	.17	.08	.25
2070	30x30	75	32	120		5.50	3.30	8.80
2080					columns	.20	.08	.28
2100	30x30	100	35	145		6.05	3.53	9.58
2110					columns	.23	.10	.33
2120	30x30	125	35	172		6.65	4.51	11.16
2130					columns	.28	.12	.40
2170	30x35	40	29	85		5.35	3.24	8.59
2180					columns	.17	.07	.24
2200	30x35	65	29	111		6	4.22	10.22
2210					columns	.19	.08	.27
2220	30x35	75	32	121		6	4.21	10.21
2230					columns	.19	.08	.27
2250	30x35	100	35	148		6.50	3.68	10.18
2260					columns	.24	.10	.34
2320	35x35	40	32	85		5.50	3.29	8.79
2330					columns	.17	.08	.25
2350	35x35	65	35	111		6.30	4.38	10.68
2360					columns	.20	.09	.29
2370	35x35	75	35	121		6.45	4.43	10.88
2380					columns	.20	.09	.29
2400	35x35	100	38	148		6.70	4.59	11.29
2410					columns	.25	.11	.36
2460	5/8 gyp. fireproof.							
2475	On metal furring, add					.55	1.98	2.53

Important: See the Reference Section for critical supporting data - Location Factors & Historical Cost Indexes

SUPERSTRUCTURES 3

| **A3.5** | **Floors** |

The table below lists costs per S.F. for a floor system on steel columns and beams using open web steel joists, galvanized steel slab form, 2-1/2″ concrete slab reinforced with welded wire fabric.

Columns are sized to accommodate one floor plus roof loading but costs for columns are from floor to grade only.

Steel Joists and Concrete Slab on Steel Columns and Beams

3.5-460 — Steel Joists, Beams & Slab on Columns

	BAY SIZE (FT.)	SUPERIMPOSED LOAD (P.S.F.)	DEPTH (IN.)	TOTAL LOAD (P.S.F.)	COLUMN ADD	COST PER S.F.		
						MAT.	INST.	TOTAL
2350	15x20	40	17	83		4.17	3.04	7.21
2400					column	.63	.28	.91
2450	15x20	65	19	108		4.60	3.23	7.83
2500					column	.63	.28	.91
2550	15x20	75	19	119		4.81	3.32	8.13
2600					column	.69	.30	.99
2650	15x20	100	19	144		5.10	3.47	8.57
2700					column	.69	.30	.99
2750	15x20	125	19	170		5.70	3.88	9.58
2800					column	.92	.40	1.32
2850	20x20	40	19	83		4.51	3.18	7.69
2900					column	.52	.22	.74
2950	20x20	65	23	109		4.97	3.40	8.37
3000					column	.69	.30	.99
3100	20x20	75	26	119		5.25	3.52	8.77
3200					column	.69	.30	.99
3400	20x20	100	23	144		5.45	3.59	9.04
3450					column	.69	.30	.99
3500	20x20	125	23	170		6.05	3.89	9.94
3600					column	.83	.36	1.19
3700	20x25	40	44	83		5.15	3.62	8.77
3800					column	.55	.24	.79
3900	20x25	65	26	110		5.60	3.84	9.44
4000					column	.55	.24	.79
4100	20x25	75	26	120		5.55	3.68	9.23
4200					column	.66	.29	.95
4300	20x25	100	26	145		5.90	3.81	9.71
4400					column	.66	.29	.95
4500	20x25	125	29	170		6.60	4.17	10.77
4600					column	.77	.33	1.10
4700	25x25	40	23	84		5.50	3.77	9.27
4800					column	.53	.23	.76
4900	25x25	65	29	110		5.85	3.93	9.78
5000					column	.53	.23	.76
5100	25x25	75	26	120		6.10	3.92	10.02
5200					column	.62	.26	.88

SUPERSTRUCTURES

3

	BAY SIZE (FT.)	SUPERIMPOSED LOAD (P.S.F.)	DEPTH (IN.)	TOTAL LOAD (P.S.F.)	COLUMN ADD	COST PER S.F.		
						MAT.	INST.	TOTAL
5300	25x25	100	29	145		6.85	4.27	11.12
5400					column	.62	.26	.88
5500	25x25	125	32	170		7.20	4.44	11.64
5600					column	.69	.30	.99
5700	25x30	40	29	84		5.75	3.95	9.70
5800					column	.52	.22	.74
5900	25x30	65	29	110		6	4.09	10.09
6000					column	.52	.22	.74
6050	25x30	75	29	120		6.45	3.73	10.18
6100					column	.57	.25	.82
6150	25x30	100	29	145		7.05	3.95	11
6200					column	.57	.25	.82
6250	25x30	125	32	170		7.55	4.85	12.40
6300					column	.66	.29	.95
6350	30x30	40	29	84		6	3.56	9.56
6400					column	.48	.21	.69
6500	30x30	65	29	110		6.85	3.88	10.73
6600					column	.48	.21	.69
6700	30x30	75	32	120		7	3.94	10.94
6800					column	.55	.24	.79
6900	30x30	100	35	145		7.75	4.25	12
7000					column	.64	.28	.92
7100	30x30	125	35	172		8.50	5.30	13.80
7200					column	.71	.30	1.01
7300	30x35	40	29	85		6.80	3.86	10.66
7400					column	.41	.17	.58
7500	30x35	65	29	111		7.60	4.89	12.49
7600					column	.53	.23	.76
7700	30x35	75	32	121		7.60	4.89	12.49
7800					column	.54	.24	.78
7900	30x35	100	35	148		8.25	4.41	12.66
8000					column	.66	.29	.95
8100	30x35	125	38	173		9.15	4.77	13.92
8200					column	.67	.29	.96
8300	35x35	40	32	85		7	3.93	10.93
8400					column	.47	.20	.67
8500	35x35	65	35	111		8	5.10	13.10
8600					column	.56	.25	.81
9300	35x35	75	38	121		8.20	5.15	13.35
9400					column	.56	.25	.81
9500	35x35	100	38	148		8.80	5.50	14.30
9600					column	.70	.30	1
9750	35x35	125	41	173		9.50	4.96	14.46
9800					column	.71	.30	1.01
9810	5/8 gyp. fireproof.							
9815	On metal furring, add					.55	1.98	2.53

Important: See the Reference Section for critical supporting data - Location Factors & Historical Cost Indexes

General: Composite construction of wide flange beams and concrete slabs is most efficiently used when loads are heavy and spans are moderately long. It is stiffer with less deflection than non-composite construction of similar depth and spans.

Composite Beam & Cast in Place Slab

3.5-520	Composite Beam & Cast in Place Slab						
	BAY SIZE (FT.)	SUPERIMPOSED LOAD (P.S.F.)	SLAB THICKNESS (IN.)	TOTAL DEPTH (FT. - IN.)	TOTAL LOAD (P.S.F.)	COST PER S.F.		
						MAT.	INST.	TOTAL
3800	20x25	40	4	1 - 8	94	5.25	7	12.25
3900		75	4	1 - 8	130	6.10	7.50	13.60
4000		125	4	1 - 10	181	7.05	8.05	15.10
4100		200	5	2 - 2	272	9.15	9.15	18.30
4200	25x25	40	4-1/2	1 - 8-1/2	99	5.50	7.05	12.55
4300		75	4-1/2	1 - 10-1/2	136	6.60	7.70	14.30
4400		125	5-1/2	2 - 0-1/2	200	7.80	8.40	16.20
4500		200	5-1/2	2 - 2-1/2	278	9.60	9.40	19
4600	25x30	40	4-1/2	1 - 8-1/2	100	6.10	7.45	13.55
4700		75	4-1/2	1 - 10-1/2	136	7.10	7.95	15.05
4800		125	5-1/2	2 - 2-1/2	202	8.70	8.80	17.50
4900		200	5-1/2	2 - 5-1/2	279	10.35	9.70	20.05
5000	30x30	40	4	1 - 8	95	6.10	7.40	13.50
5200		75	4	2 - 1	131	7.05	7.90	14.95
5400		125	4	2 - 4	183	8.60	8.75	17.35
5600		200	5	2 - 10	274	11	9.95	20.95
5800	30x35	40	4	2 - 1	95	6.45	7.55	14
6000		75	4	2 - 4	139	7.70	8.20	15.90
6250		125	4	2 - 4	185	9.95	9.35	19.30
6500		200	5	2 - 11	276	12.15	10.55	22.70
8000	35x35	40	4	2 - 1	96	6.75	7.70	14.45
8250		75	4	2 - 4	133	8	8.35	16.35
8500		125	4	2 - 10	185	9.60	9.20	18.80
8750		200	5	3 - 5	276	12.45	10.65	23.10
9000	35x40	40	4	2 - 4	97	7.50	8.10	15.60
9250		75	4	2 - 4	134	8.70	8.60	17.30
9500		125	4	2 - 7	186	10.55	9.65	20.20
9750		200	5	3 - 5	278	13.65	11.15	24.80

SUPERSTRUCTURES

3

The table below lists costs per S.F. for floors using steel beams and girders, composite steel deck, concrete slab reinforced with W.W.F. and sprayed fiber fireproofing (non- asbestos) on the steel beams and girders and on the steel deck.

Wide Flange, Composite Deck & Slab

3.5-530	W Shape, Composite Deck, & Slab							
	BAY SIZE (FT.) BEAM X GIRD	SUPERIMPOSED LOAD (P.S.F.)	SLAB THICKNESS (IN.)	TOTAL DEPTH (FT.-IN.)	TOTAL LOAD (P.S.F.)	COST PER S.F.		
						MAT.	INST.	TOTAL
0540	15x20	40	5	1-7	89	6	4.62	10.62
0560		75	5	1-9	125	6.55	4.89	11.44
0580		125	5	1-11	176	7.60	5.35	12.95
0600		200	5	2-2	254	9.30	6.10	15.40
0700	20x20	40	5	1-9	90	6.45	4.82	11.27
0720		75	5	1-9	126	7.25	5.20	12.45
0740		125	5	1-11	177	8.20	5.65	13.85
0760		200	5	2-5	255	9.90	6.35	16.25
0780	20x25	40	5	1-9	90	6.65	4.76	11.41
0800		75	5	1-9	127	8.20	5.50	13.70
0820		125	5	1-11	180	9.85	6	15.85
0840		200	5	2-5	256	10.65	6.80	17.45
0940	25x25	40	5	1-11	91	7.45	5.10	12.55
0960		75	5	2-5	178	8.55	5.65	14.20
0980		125	5	2-5	181	10.50	6.25	16.75
1000		200	5-1/2	2-8-1/2	263	11.60	7.30	18.90
1400	25x30	40	5	2-5	91	7.35	5.25	12.60
1500		75	5	2-5	128	8.95	5.85	14.80
1600		125	5	2-8	180	10.05	6.50	16.55
1700		200	5	2-11	259	12.50	7.45	19.95
2200	30x30	40	5	2-2	92	8.15	5.60	13.75
2300		75	5	2-5	129	9.45	6.25	15.70
2400		125	5	2-11	182	11.15	7	18.15
2500		200	5	3-2	263	15	8.75	23.75
2600	30x35	40	5	2-5	94	8.85	5.95	14.80
2700		75	5	2-11	131	10.25	6.55	16.80
2800		125	5	3-2	183	11.95	7.35	19.30
2900		200	5-1/2	3-5-1/2	268	14.60	8.45	23.05
3800	35x35	40	5	2-8	94	9.15	5.90	15.05
3900		75	5	2-11	131	10.55	6.55	17.10
4000		125	5	3-5	184	12.60	7.50	20.10
4100		200	5-1/2	3-5-1/2	270	16.20	8.90	25.10

Important: See the Reference Section for critical supporting data - Location Factors & Historical Cost Indexes

The table below lists costs per S.F. for floors using composite steel beams with welded shear studs, composite steel deck and light weight concrete slab reinforced with W.W.F.

Composite Beam, Deck & Slab

| 3.5-540 | Composite Beams, Deck & Slab | | | | | | | |

	BAY SIZE (FT.)	SUPERIMPOSED LOAD (P.S.F.)	SLAB THICKNESS (IN.)	TOTAL DEPTH (FT. - IN.)	TOTAL LOAD (P.S.F.)	COST PER S.F.		
						MAT.	INST.	TOTAL
2400	20x25	40	5-1/2	1 - 5-1/2	80	5.90	4.19	10.09
2500		75	5-1/2	1 - 9-1/2	115	6.15	4.21	10.36
2750		125	5-1/2	1 - 9-1/2	167	7.60	4.97	12.57
2900		200	6-1/4	1 - 11-1/2	251	8.55	5.40	13.95
3000	25x25	40	5-1/2	1 - 9-1/2	82	5.90	4	9.90
3100		75	5-1/2	1 - 11-1/2	118	6.60	4.08	10.68
3200		125	5-1/2	2 - 2-1/2	169	6.90	4.42	11.32
3300		200	6-1/4	2 - 6-1/4	252	9.40	5.15	14.55
3400	25x30	40	5-1/2	1 - 11-1/2	83	6.05	3.96	10.01
3600		75	5-1/2	1 - 11-1/2	119	6.50	4.01	10.51
3900		125	5-1/2	1 - 11-1/2	170	7.55	4.54	12.09
4000		200	6-1/4	2 - 6-1/4	252	9.45	5.20	14.65
4200	30x30	40	5-1/2	1 - 11-1/2	81	5.95	4.11	10.06
4400		75	5-1/2	2 - 2-1/2	116	6.50	4.30	10.80
4500		125	5-1/2	2 - 5-1/2	168	7.85	4.84	12.69
4700		200	6-1/4	2 - 9-1/4	252	9.45	5.60	15.05
4900	30x35	40	5-1/2	2 - 2-1/2	82	6.25	4.25	10.50
5100		75	5-1/2	2 - 5-1/2	117	6.85	4.37	11.22
5300		125	5-1/2	2 - 5-1/2	169	8.10	4.93	13.03
5500		200	6-1/4	2 - 9-1/4	254	9.45	5.60	15.05
5750	35x35	40	5-1/2	2 - 5-1/2	84	6.75	4.28	11.03
6000		75	5-1/2	2 - 5-1/2	121	7.70	4.56	12.26
7000		125	5-1/2	2 - 8-1/2	170	9.05	5.20	14.25
7200		200	5-1/2	2 - 11-1/2	254	10.50	5.80	16.30
7400	35x40	40	5-1/2	2 - 5-1/2	85	7.45	4.57	12.02
7600		75	5-1/2	2 - 5-1/2	121	8.10	4.74	12.84
8000		125	5-1/2	2 - 5-1/2	171	9.25	5.30	14.55
9000		200	5-1/2	2 - 11-1/2	255	11.35	6.05	17.40

SUPERSTRUCTURES

3

Description: Table 3.5-580 lists S.F. costs for steel deck and concrete slabs for various spans.

Description: Table 3.5-710 lists the S.F. costs for wood joists and a minimum thickness plywood subfloor.

Description: Table 3.5-720 lists the S.F. costs, total load, and member sizes, for various bay sizes and loading conditions.

Metal Deck/Concrete Fill

Wood Joist

Wood Beam and Joist

3.5-580 — Metal Deck/Concrete Fill

	SUPERIMPOSED LOAD (P.S.F.)	DECK SPAN (FT.)	DECK GAGE DEPTH	SLAB THICKNESS (IN.)	TOTAL LOAD (P.S.F.)	COST PER S.F.		
						MAT.	INST.	TOTAL
0900	125	6	22 1-1/2	4	164	1.50	1.69	3.19
0920		7	20 1-1/2	4	164	1.63	1.78	3.41
0950		8	20 1-1/2	4	165	1.63	1.78	3.41
0970		9	18 1-1/2	4	165	1.88	1.78	3.66
1000		10	18 2	4	165	1.86	1.89	3.75
1020		11	18 3	5	169	2.33	2.03	4.36

3.5-710 — Wood Joist

		COST PER S.F.		
		MAT.	INST.	TOTAL
2902	Wood joist, 2" x 8", 12" O.C.	1.57	1.24	2.81
2950	16" O.C.	1.32	1.06	2.38
3000	24" O.C.	1.37	.98	2.35
3300	2"x10", 12" O.C.	2.05	1.41	3.46
3350	16" O.C.	1.68	1.19	2.87
3400	24" O.C.	1.59	1.06	2.65
3700	2"x12", 12" O.C.	2.35	1.42	3.77
3750	16" O.C.	1.91	1.19	3.10
3800	24" O.C.	1.75	1.07	2.82
4100	2"x14", 12" O.C.	2.72	1.56	4.28
4150	16" O.C.	2.19	1.30	3.49
4200	24" O.C.	1.94	1.14	3.08
7101	Note: Subfloor cost is included in these prices			

3.5-720 — Wood Beam & Joist

	BAY SIZE (FT.)	SUPERIMPOSED LOAD (P.S.F.)	GIRDER BEAM (IN.)	JOISTS (IN.)	TOTAL LOAD (P.S.F.)	COST PER S.F.		
						MAT.	INST.	TOTAL
2000	15x15	40	8 x 12 4 x 12	2 x 6 @ 16	53	5.10	2.86	7.96
2050		75	8 x 16 4 x 16	2 x 8 @ 16	90	6.65	3.14	9.79
2100		125	12 x 16 6 x 16	2 x 8 @ 12	144	10.55	4.03	14.58
2150		200	14 x 22 12 x 16	2 x 10 @ 12	227	19.70	6.15	25.85
3000	20x20	40	10 x 14 10 x 12	2 x 8 @ 16	63	7.50	2.87	10.37
3050		75	12 x 16 8 x 16	2 x 10 @ 16	102	9.40	3.24	12.64
3100		125	14 x 22 12 x 16	2 x 10 @ 12	163	15.90	5.15	21.05

Important: See the Reference Section for critical supporting data - Location Factors & Historical Cost Indexes

The table below lists the cost per S.F. for a roof system with steel columns, beams and deck using open web steel joists and 1-1/2" galvanized metal deck. Perimeter of system is supported on bearing walls.

Fireproofing is not included. Costs/S.F. are based on a building 4 bays long and 4 bays wide.

Column costs are additive. Costs for the bearing walls are not included.

Steel Joists, Beams and Deck on Bearing Walls

3.7-410	Steel Joists, Beams & Deck on Columns & Walls							
	BAY SIZE (FT.)	SUPERIMPOSED LOAD (P.S.F.)	DEPTH (IN.)	TOTAL LOAD (P.S.F.)	COLUMN ADD	COST PER S.F.		
						MAT.	INST.	TOTAL
3000	25x25	20	18	40		2.02	.99	3.01
3100					columns	.18	.07	.25
3200		30	22	50		2.29	1.15	3.44
3300					columns	.24	.08	.32
3400		40	20	60		2.42	1.16	3.58
3500					columns	.24	.08	.32
3600	25x30	20	22	40		2.16	.94	3.10
3700					columns	.20	.07	.27
3800		30	20	50		2.36	1.22	3.58
3900					columns	.20	.07	.27
4000		40	25	60		2.57	1.08	3.65
4100					columns	.24	.08	.32
4200	30x30	20	25	42		2.38	1.01	3.39
4300					columns	.17	.05	.22
4400		30	22	52		2.61	1.10	3.71
4500					columns	.20	.07	.27
4600		40	28	62		2.71	1.13	3.84
4700					columns	.20	.07	.27
4800	30x35	20	22	42		2.49	1.05	3.54
4900					columns	.17	.07	.24
5000		30	28	52		2.63	1.10	3.73
5100					columns	.17	.07	.24
5200		40	25	62		2.86	1.19	4.05
5300					columns	.20	.07	.27
5400	35x35	20	28	42		2.51	1.06	3.57
5500					columns	.15	.05	.20

SUPERSTRUCTURES

3

Description: The table below lists the cost per S.F. for a roof system with steel columns, beams, and deck, using open web steel joists and 1-1/2″ galvanized metal deck.

Column costs are additive. Fireproofing is not included.

Steel Joists, Beams and Deck on Columns

3.7-420 — Steel Joists, Beams, & Deck on Columns

	BAY SIZE (FT.)	SUPERIMPOSED LOAD (P.S.F.)	DEPTH (IN.)	TOTAL LOAD (P.S.F.)	COLUMN ADD	COST PER S.F.		
						MAT.	INST.	TOTAL
1100	15x20	20	16	40		2	.98	2.98
1200					columns	1.04	.37	1.41
1500		40	18	60		2.25	1.09	3.34
1600					columns	1.04	.37	1.41
2300	20x25	20	18	40		2.29	1.09	3.38
2400					columns	.62	.23	.85
2700		40	20	60		2.59	1.24	3.83
2800					columns	.83	.29	1.12
2900	25x25	20	18	40		2.67	1.23	3.90
3000					columns	.50	.17	.67
3100		30	22	50		2.89	1.39	4.28
3200					columns	.66	.24	.90
3300		40	20	60		3.11	1.41	4.52
3400					columns	.66	.24	.90
3500	25x30	20	22	40		2.64	1.12	3.76
3600					columns	.55	.20	.75
3900		40	25	60		3.22	1.32	4.54
4000					columns	.66	.24	.90
4100	30x30	20	25	42		2.99	1.23	4.22
4200					columns	.46	.16	.62
4300		30	22	52		3.31	1.35	4.66
4400					columns	.55	.20	.75
4500		40	28	62		3.46	1.41	4.87
4600					columns	.55	.20	.75
5300	35x35	20	28	42		3.28	1.34	4.62
5400					columns	.41	.15	.56
5500		30	25	52		3.67	1.48	5.15
5600					columns	.47	.17	.64
5700		40	28	62		3.97	1.60	5.57
5800					columns	.52	.19	.71

Important: See the Reference Section for critical supporting data - Location Factors & Historical Cost Indexes

Description: The table below lists the cost per S.F. for a roof system using open web steel joists and 1-1/2″ galvanized metal deck. The system is assumed supported on bearing walls or other suitable support. Costs for the supports are not included.

3.7-430 | Steel Joists & Deck on Bearing Walls

	BAY SIZE (FT.)	SUPERIMPOSED LOAD (P.S.F.)	DEPTH (IN.)	TOTAL LOAD (P.S.F.)		COST PER S.F. MAT.	INST.	TOTAL
1100	20	20	13-1/2	40		1.29	.71	2
1200		30	15-1/2	50		1.32	.72	2.04
1300		40	15-1/2	60		1.43	.78	2.21
1400	25	20	17-1/2	40		1.43	.79	2.22
1500		30	17-1/2	50		1.56	.85	2.41
1600		40	19-1/2	60		1.59	.86	2.45
1700	30	20	19-1/2	40		1.58	.86	2.44
1800		30	21-1/2	50		1.62	.88	2.50
1900		40	23-1/2	60		1.76	.95	2.71
2000	35	20	23-1/2	40		1.74	.79	2.53
2100		30	25-1/2	50		1.80	.81	2.61
2200		40	25-1/2	60		1.93	.85	2.78
2300	40	20	25-1/2	41		1.96	.86	2.82
2400		30	25-1/2	51		2.09	.92	3.01
2500		40	25-1/2	61		2.17	.95	3.12
2600	45	20	27-1/2	41		2.20	1.28	3.48
2700		30	31-1/2	51		2.34	1.36	3.70
2800		40	31-1/2	61		2.47	1.44	3.91
2900	50	20	29-1/2	42		2.48	1.45	3.93
3000		30	31-1/2	52		2.72	1.59	4.31
3100		40	31-1/2	62		2.90	1.70	4.60
3200	60	20	37-1/2	42		3.18	1.49	4.67
3300		30	37-1/2	52		3.55	1.66	5.21
3400		40	37-1/2	62		3.55	1.66	5.21
3500	70	20	41-1/2	42		3.54	1.65	5.19
3600		30	41-1/2	52		3.79	1.75	5.54
3700		40	41-1/2	64		4.65	2.14	6.79
3800	80	20	45-1/2	44		5.15	2.35	7.50
3900		30	45-1/2	54		5.15	2.35	7.50
4000		40	45-1/2	64		5.70	2.61	8.31
4400	100	20	57-1/2	44		4.52	1.97	6.49
4500		30	57-1/2	54		5.45	2.34	7.79
4600		40	57-1/2	65		6	2.58	8.58
4700	125	20	69-1/2	44		6.45	2.66	9.11
4800		30	69-1/2	56		7.60	3.09	10.69
4900		40	69-1/2	67		8.70	3.53	12.23

SUPERSTRUCTURES

3

Description: The table below lists costs for a roof system supported on exterior bearing walls and interior columns. Costs include bracing, joist girders, open web steel joists and 1-1/2″ galvanized metal deck.

Column costs are additive. Fireproofing is not included.

Costs/S.F. are based on a building 4 bays long and 4 bays wide. Costs for bearing walls are not included.

3.7-440   Steel Joists, Joist Girders & Deck on Columns & Walls

	BAY SIZE (FT.) GIRD X JOISTS	SUPERIMPOSED LOAD (P.S.F.)	DEPTH (IN.)	TOTAL LOAD (P.S.F.)	COLUMN ADD	COST PER S.F. MAT.	INST.	TOTAL
2350	30x35	20	32-1/2	40		1.93	1	2.93
2400					columns	.17	.06	.23
2550		40	36-1/2	60		2.19	1.11	3.30
2600					columns	.20	.07	.27
3000	35x35	20	36-1/2	40		2.11	1.24	3.35
3050					columns	.15	.05	.20
3200		40	36-1/2	60		2.40	1.34	3.74
3250					columns	.19	.07	.26
3300	35x40	20	36-1/2	40		2.15	1.14	3.29
3350					columns	.15	.05	.20
3500		40	36-1/2	60		2.46	1.25	3.71
3550					columns	.17	.05	.22
3900	40x40	20	40-1/2	41		2.41	1.45	3.86
3950					columns	.15	.05	.20
4100		40	40-1/2	61		2.72	1.60	4.32
4150					columns	.15	.05	.20
5100	45x50	20	52-1/2	41		2.72	1.67	4.39
5150					columns	.10	.04	.14
5300		40	52-1/2	61		3.33	2.02	5.35
5350					columns	.15	.05	.20
5400	50x45	20	56-1/2	41		2.63	1.61	4.24
5450					columns	.10	.04	.14
5600		40	56-1/2	61		3.43	2.05	5.48
5650					columns	.14	.05	.19
5700	50x50	20	56-1/2	42		2.97	1.82	4.79
5750					columns	.11	.04	.15
5900		40	59	64		4.09	2.05	6.14
5950					columns	.15	.05	.20
6300	60x50	20	62-1/2	43		3	1.84	4.84
6350					columns	.17	.05	.22
6500		40	71	65		4.20	2.09	6.29
6550					columns	.22	.08	.30

SUPERSTRUCTURES 3

Description: The table below lists the cost per S.F. for a roof system supported on columns. Costs include joist girders, open web steel joists and 1-1/2″ galvanized metal deck. Column costs are additive.

Fireproofing is not included. Costs/S.F. are based on a building 4 bays long and 4 bays wide.

Costs for wind columns are not included.

3.7-450 — Steel Joists & Joist Girders on Columns

	BAY SIZE (FT.) GIRD X JOISTS	SUPERIMPOSED LOAD (P.S.F.)	DEPTH (IN.)	TOTAL LOAD (P.S.F.)	COLUMN ADD	COST PER S.F. MAT.	INST.	TOTAL
2000	30x30	20	17-1/2	40		1.96	1.18	3.14
2050					columns	.56	.20	.76
2100		30	17-1/2	50		2.15	1.26	3.41
2150					columns	.56	.20	.76
2200		40	21-1/2	60		2.21	1.29	3.50
2250					columns	.56	.20	.76
2300	30x35	20	32-1/2	40		2.09	1.11	3.20
2350					columns	.48	.17	.65
2500		40	36-1/2	60		2.39	1.25	3.64
2550					columns	.56	.20	.76
3200	35x40	20	36-1/2	40		2.63	1.71	4.34
3250					columns	.42	.15	.57
3400		40	36-1/2	60		2.98	1.90	4.88
3450					columns	.46	.16	.62
3800	40x40	20	40-1/2	41		2.67	1.71	4.38
3850					columns	.40	.15	.55
4000		40	40-1/2	61		3.01	1.89	4.90
4050					columns	.40	.15	.55
4100	40x45	20	40-1/2	41		2.86	1.93	4.79
4150					columns	.36	.12	.48
4200		30	40-1/2	51		3.13	2.07	5.20
4250					columns	.36	.12	.48
4300		40	40-1/2	61		3.49	2.27	5.76
4350					columns	.41	.15	.56
5000	45x50	20	52-1/2	41		3.03	1.98	5.01
5050					columns	.29	.10	.39
5200		40	52-1/2	61		3.74	2.37	6.11
5250					columns	.37	.13	.50
5300	50x45	20	56-1/2	41		2.95	1.93	4.88
5350					columns	.29	.10	.39
5500		40	56-1/2	61		3.86	2.41	6.27
5550					columns	.37	.13	.50
5600	50x50	20	56-1/2	42		3.32	2.13	5.45
5650					columns	.29	.11	.40
5800		40	59	64		3.78	1.95	5.73
5850					columns	.41	.15	.56

SUPERSTRUCTURES

3

The table below lists prices per S.F. for roof rafters and sheathing by nominal size and spacing. Sheathing is 5/16" CDX for 12" and 16" spacing and 3/8" CDX for 24" spacing.

Factors for Converting Inclined to Horizontal

Roof Slope	Approx. Angle	Factor	Roof Slope	Approx. Angle	Factor
Flat	0°	1.000	12 in 12	45.0°	1.414
1 in 12	4.8°	1.003	13 in 12	47.3°	1.474
2 in 12	9.5°	1.014	14 in 12	49.4°	1.537
3 in 12	14.0°	1.031	15 in 12	51.3°	1.601
4 in 12	18.4°	1.054	16 in 12	53.1°	1.667
5 in 12	22.6°	1.083	17 in 12	54.8°	1.734
6 in 12	26.6°	1.118	18 in 12	56.3°	1.803
7 in 12	30.3°	1.158	19 in 12	57.7°	1.873
8 in 12	33.7°	1.202	20 in 12	59.0°	1.943
9 in 12	36.9°	1.250	21 in 12	60.3°	2.015
10 in 12	39.8°	1.302	22 in 12	61.4°	2.088
11 in 12	42.5°	1.357	23 in 12	62.4°	2.162

3.7-510	Wood/Flat or Pitched	COST PER S.F.		
		MAT.	INST.	TOTAL
2500	Flat rafter, 2"x4", 12" O.C.	.87	1.12	1.99
2550	16" O.C.	.75	.96	1.71
2600	24" O.C.	.67	.83	1.50
2900	2"x6", 12" O.C.	1.11	1.12	2.23
2950	16" O.C.	.93	.97	1.90
3000	24" O.C.	.79	.82	1.61
3300	2"x8", 12" O.C.	1.39	1.21	2.60
3350	16" O.C.	1.14	1.03	2.17
3400	24" O.C.	.94	.87	1.81
3700	2"x10", 12" O.C.	1.87	1.38	3.25
3750	16" O.C.	1.50	1.16	2.66
3800	24" O.C.	1.16	.95	2.11
4100	2"x12", 12" O.C.	2.17	1.39	3.56
4150	16" O.C.	1.73	1.16	2.89
4200	24" O.C.	1.32	.96	2.28
4500	2"x14", 12" O.C.	2.54	2.04	4.58
4550	16" O.C.	2.01	1.66	3.67
4600	24" O.C.	1.51	1.29	2.80
4900	3"x6", 12" O.C.	2.41	1.19	3.60
4950	16" O.C.	1.91	1.01	2.92
5000	24" O.C.	1.45	.86	2.31
5300	3"x8", 12" O.C.	3.09	1.33	4.42
5350	16" O.C.	2.41	1.12	3.53
5400	24" O.C.	1.78	.92	2.70
5700	3"x10", 12" O.C.	3.76	1.51	5.27
5750	16" O.C.	2.93	1.26	4.19
5800	24" O.C.	2.12	1.02	3.14
6100	3"x12", 12" O.C.	4.43	1.82	6.25
6150	16" O.C.	3.43	1.48	4.91
6200	24" O.C.	2.45	1.17	3.62
7001	Wood truss, 4 in 12 slope, 24" O.C., 24' to 29' span	3.01	1.71	4.72
7100	30' to 43' span	3.17	1.71	4.88
7200	44' to 60' span	3.35	1.71	5.06

The table below lists the cost per flight for 4'-0" wide stairs. Side walls are not included. Railings are included in the prices.

3.9-100	Stairs	COST PER FLIGHT		
		MAT.	INST.	TOTAL
0470	Stairs, C.I.P. concrete, w/o landing, 12 risers, w/o nosing	720	1,575	2,295
0480	With nosing	1,100	1,775	2,875
0550	W/landing, 12 risers, w/o nosing	805	1,925	2,730
0560	With nosing	1,175	2,150	3,325
0570	16 risers, w/o nosing	1,000	2,425	3,425
0580	With nosing	1,500	2,725	4,225
0590	20 risers, w/o nosing	1,200	2,925	4,125
0600	With nosing	1,825	3,300	5,125
0610	24 risers, w/o nosing	1,400	3,425	4,825
0620	With nosing	2,125	3,850	5,975
0630	Steel, grate type w/nosing & rails, 12 risers, w/o landing	1,800	565	2,365
0640	With landing	2,350	870	3,220
0660	16 risers, with landing	2,950	1,050	4,000
0680	20 risers, with landing	3,550	1,250	4,800
0700	24 risers, with landing	4,150	1,450	5,600
0701				
0710	Cement fill metal pan & picket rail, 12 risers, w/o landing	2,350	565	2,915
0720	With landing	3,100	970	4,070
0740	16 risers, with landing	3,875	1,150	5,025
0760	20 risers, with landing	4,650	1,325	5,975
0780	24 risers, with landing	5,450	1,550	7,000
0790	Cast iron tread & pipe rail, 12 risers, w/o landing	2,350	565	2,915
0800	With landing	3,100	970	4,070
1120	Wood, prefab box type, oak treads, wood rails 3'-6" wide, 14 risers	955	305	1,260
1150	Prefab basement type, oak treads, wood rails 3'-0" wide, 14 risers	735	243	978

For information about Means Estimating Seminars, see yellow pages 11 and 12 in back of book

SUPERSTRUCTURES

3

Division 4
Exterior Closure

Table 4.1-110 describes a concrete wall system for exterior closure. There are several types of wall finishes priced from plain finish to a finish with 3/4" rustication strip.

In Table 4.1-140, precast concrete wall panels are either solid or insulated. Prices below are based on delivery within 50 miles of a plant. Small jobs can double the prices below. For large, highly repetitive jobs, deduct up to 15%.

Cast in Place Concrete Wall

Flat Precast Concrete Wall

4.1-110	Cast In Place Concrete	COST PER S.F.		
		MAT.	INST.	TOTAL
2100	Conc wall reinforced, 8' high, 6" thick, plain finish, 3000 PSI	3.26	11.90	15.16
2700	Aged wood liner, 3000 PSI	5.15	12.35	17.50
3000	Sand blast light 1 side, 3000 PSI	3.49	12.75	16.24
3700	3/4" bevel rustication strip, 3000 PSI	3.43	14.25	17.68
4000	8" thick, plain finish, 3000 PSI	3.78	12.10	15.88
4100	4000 PSI	3.89	12.10	15.99
4300	Rub concrete 1 side, 3000 PSI	3.81	14	17.81
4550	8" thick, aged wood liner, 3000 PSI	5.65	12.60	18.25
4750	Sand blast light 1 side, 3000 PSI	4.01	13	17.01
5300	3/4" bevel rustication strip, 3000 PSI	3.95	14.50	18.45
5600	10" thick, plain finish, 3000 PSI	4.30	12.40	16.70
5900	Rub concrete 1 side, 3000 PSI	4.33	14.30	18.63
6200	Aged wood liner, 3000 PSI	6.15	12.90	19.05
6500	Sand blast light 1 side, 3000 PSI	4.53	13.25	17.78
7100	3/4" bevel rustication strip, 3000 PSI	4.47	14.75	19.22
7400	12" thick, plain finish, 3000 PSI	4.90	12.70	17.60
7700	Rub concrete 1 side, 3000 PSI	4.93	14.60	19.53
8000	Aged wood liner, 3000 PSI	6.75	13.20	19.95
8300	Sand blast light 1 side, 3000 PSI	5.15	13.60	18.75
8900	3/4" bevel rustication strip, 3000 PSI	5.05	15.05	20.10

4.1-140				Flat Precast Concrete			COST PER S.F.		
	THICKNESS (IN.)	PANEL SIZE (FT.)	FINISHES	RIGID INSULATION (IN)	TYPE	MAT.	INST.	TOTAL
3000	4	5x18	smooth gray	none	low rise	5.20	5.45	10.65
3050		6x18				4.35	4.54	8.89
3100		8x20				6.55	1.71	8.26
3150		12x20				6.15	1.61	7.76
3200	6	5x18	smooth gray	2	low rise	6	5.80	11.80
3250		6x18				5.15	4.90	10.05
3300		8x20				7.45	2.13	9.58
3350		12x20				6.80	1.95	8.75
3400	8	5x18	smooth gray	2	low rise	9.50	2.66	12.16
3450		6x18				9.05	2.54	11.59
3500		8x20				8.30	2.34	10.64
3550		12x20				7.60	2.16	9.76
3600	4	4x8	white face	none	low rise	15.95	3.13	19.08
3650		8x8				11.95	2.35	14.30
3700		10x10				10.50	2.06	12.56
3750		20x10				9.50	1.86	11.36

4.1-140   Flat Precast Concrete

	THICKNESS (IN.)	PANEL SIZE (FT.)	FINISHES	RIGID INSULATION (IN)	TYPE	COST PER S.F.		
						MAT.	INST.	TOTAL
3800	5	4x8	white face	none	low rise	16.30	3.20	19.50
3850		8x8				12.30	2.42	14.72
3900		10x10				10.90	2.14	13.04
3950		20x20				9.95	1.96	11.91
4000	6	4x8	white face	none	low rise	16.85	3.31	20.16
4050		8x8				12.80	2.52	15.32
4100		10x10				11.30	2.21	13.51
4150		20x10				10.35	2.04	12.39
4200	6	4x8	white face	2	low rise	17.75	3.72	21.47
4250		8x8				13.70	2.93	16.63
4300		10x10				12.15	2.62	14.77
4350		20x10				10.35	2.04	12.39
4400	7	4x8	white face	none	low rise	17.25	3.39	20.64
4450		8x8				13.25	2.60	15.85
4500		10x10				11.90	2.34	14.24
4550		20x10				10.90	2.14	13.04
4600	7	4x8	white face	2	low rise	18.15	3.80	21.95
4650		8x8				14.15	3.01	17.16
4700		10x10				12.75	2.75	15.50
4750		20x10				11.75	2.55	14.30
4800	8	4x8	white face	none	low rise	17.65	3.47	21.12
4850		8x8				13.60	2.67	16.27
4900		10x10				12.25	2.41	14.66
4950		20x10				11.30	2.21	13.51
5000	8	4x8	white face	2	low rise	18.55	3.88	22.43
5050		8x8				14.50	3.08	17.58
5100		10x10				13.10	2.82	15.92
5150		20x10				12.15	2.62	14.77

4.1-140   Fluted Window or Mullion Precast Concrete

	THICKNESS (IN.)	PANEL SIZE (FT.)	FINISHES	RIGID INSULATION (IN)	TYPE	COST PER S.F.		
						MAT.	INST.	TOTAL
5200	4	4x8	smooth gray	none	high rise	11.90	12.45	24.35
5250		8x8				8.50	8.90	17.40
5300		10x10				12.50	3.25	15.75
5350		20x10				10.95	2.84	13.79
5400	5	4x8	smooth gray	none	high rise	12.10	12.60	24.70
5450		8x8				8.80	9.20	18
5500		10x10				13	3.39	16.39
5550		20x10				11.50	3	14.50
5600	6	4x8	smooth gray	none	high rise	12.45	12.95	25.40
5650		8x8				9.10	9.50	18.60
5700		10x10				13.40	3.49	16.89
5750		20x10				11.90	3.09	14.99
5800	6	4x8	smooth gray	2	high rise	13.30	13.40	26.70
5850		8x8				9.95	9.90	19.85
5900		10x10				14.25	3.90	18.15
5950		20x10				12.75	3.50	16.25
6000	7	4x8	smooth gray	none	high rise	12.70	13.25	25.95
6050		8x8				9.35	9.80	19.15
6100		10x10				13.95	3.64	17.59
6150		20x10				12.25	3.19	15.44

EXTERIOR CLOSURE

4

4.1-140 | Fluted Window or Mullion Precast Concrete

	THICKNESS (IN.)	PANEL SIZE (FT.)	FINISHES	RIGID INSULATION (IN)	TYPE	COST PER S.F.		
						MAT.	INST.	TOTAL
6200	7	4x8	smooth gray	2	high rise	13.55	13.70	27.25
6250		8x8				10.25	10.20	20.45
6300		10x10				14.85	4.05	18.90
6350		20x10				13.15	3.60	16.75
6400	8	4x8	smooth gray	none	high rise	12.85	13.45	26.30
6450		8x8				9.60	10	19.60
6500		10x10				14.40	3.75	18.15
6550		20x10				12.85	3.35	16.20
6600	8	4x8	smooth gray	2	high rise	13.75	13.85	27.60
6650		8x8				10.45	10.40	20.85
6700		10x10				15.25	4.16	19.41
6750		20x10				13.75	3.76	17.51

4.1-140 | Precast Concrete Specialties

	TYPE	SIZE				COST PER L.F.		
						MAT.	INST.	TOTAL
6773	Coping, precast	6"wide				15.55	8.65	24.20
6774	Stock units	10"wide				11.10	9.30	20.40
6775		12"wide				16.65	10	26.65
6776		14" wide				15.30	10.85	26.15
6777	Window sills	6" wide				9.95	9.30	19.25
6778	Precast	10" wide				17.05	10.85	27.90
6779		14" wide				13.35	13	26.35

Important: See the Reference Section for critical supporting data - Location Factors & Historical Cost Indexes

Ribbed Precast Panel

4.1-140			Ribbed Precast Concrete					
	THICKNESS (IN.)	PANEL SIZE (FT.)	FINISHES	RIGID INSULATION(IN.)	TYPE	COST PER S.F.		
						MAT.	INST.	TOTAL
6800	4	4x8	aggregate	none	high rise	13.15	12.40	25.55
6850		8x8				9.60	9.10	18.70
6900		10x10				13.75	3.28	17.03
6950		20x10				12.15	2.90	15.05
7000	5	4x8	aggregate	none	high rise	13.40	12.60	26
7050		8x8				9.90	9.30	19.20
7100		10x10				14.25	3.40	17.65
7150		20x10				12.70	3.04	15.74
7200	6	4x8	aggregate	none	high rise	13.65	12.90	26.55
7250		8x8				10.15	9.60	19.75
7300		10x10				14.70	3.51	18.21
7350		20x10				13.20	3.15	16.35
7400	6	4x8	aggregate	2	high rise	14.50	13.30	27.80
7450		8x8				11.05	10	21.05
7500		10x10				15.60	3.92	19.52
7550		20x10				14.05	3.56	17.61
7600	7	4x8	aggregate	none	high rise	13.95	13.15	27.10
7650		8x8				10.40	9.80	20.20
7700		10x10				15.20	3.63	18.83
7750		20x10				13.55	3.24	16.79
7800	7	4x8	aggregate	2	high rise	14.85	13.60	28.45
7850		8x8				11.25	10.20	21.45
7900		10x10				16.05	4.04	20.09
7950		20x10				14.45	3.65	18.10
8000	8	4x8	aggregate	none	high rise	14.20	13.45	27.65
8050		8x8				10.70	10.15	20.85
8100		10x10				15.70	3.75	19.45
8150		20x10				14.20	3.39	17.59
8200	8	4x8	aggregate	2	high rise	15.05	13.85	28.90
8250		8x8				11.60	10.55	22.15
8300		10x10				16.60	4.16	20.76
8350		20x10				15.05	3.80	18.85

EXTERIOR CLOSURE

4

Tilt Up Concrete Panel

The advantage of tilt up construction is in the low cost of forms and placing of concrete and reinforcing. Tilt up has been used for several types of buildings, including warehouses, stores, offices, and schools. The panels are cast in forms on the ground, or floor slab. Most jobs use 5-1/2" thick solid reinforced concrete panels.

EXTERIOR CLOSURE 4

4.1-160	Tilt-Up Concrete Panel	COST PER S.F.		
		MAT.	INST.	TOTAL
3200	Tilt up conc panels, broom finish, 5-1/2" thick, 3000 PSI	2.70	4.05	6.75
3250	5000 PSI	2.82	3.98	6.80
3300	6" thick, 3000 PSI	2.98	4.15	7.13
3350	5000 PSI	3.11	4.07	7.18
3400	7-1/2" thick, 3000 PSI	3.79	4.32	8.11
3450	5000 PSI	3.95	4.24	8.19
3500	8" thick, 3000 PSI	4.07	4.42	8.49
3550	5000 PSI	4.25	4.34	8.59
3700	Steel trowel finish, 5-1/2" thick, 3000 PSI	2.71	4.12	6.83
3750	5000 PSI	2.82	4.05	6.87
3800	6" thick, 3000 PSI	2.98	4.22	7.20
3850	5000 PSI	3.11	4.14	7.25
3900	7-1/2" thick, 3000 PSI	3.79	4.39	8.18
3950	5000 PSI	3.95	4.31	8.26
4000	8" thick, 3000 PSI	4.07	4.49	8.56
4050	5000 PSI	4.25	4.41	8.66
4200	Exp. aggregate finish, 5-1/2" thick, 3000 PSI	6.70	4.13	10.83
4250	5000 PSI	6.85	4.05	10.90
4300	6" thick, 3000 PSI	7	4.23	11.23
4350	5000 PSI	7.10	4.15	11.25
4400	7-1/2" thick, 3000 PSI	7.80	4.40	12.20
4450	5000 PSI	7.95	4.32	12.27
4500	8" thick, 3000 PSI	8.10	4.49	12.59
4550	5000 PSI	8.25	4.42	12.67
4600	Exposed aggregate & vert. rustication 5-1/2" thick, 3000 PSI	8.10	6.80	14.90
4650	5000 PSI	8.20	6.70	14.90
4700	6" thick, 3000 PSI	8.40	6.90	15.30
4750	5000 PSI	8.50	6.80	15.30
4800	7-1/2" thick, 3000 PSI	9.20	7.10	16.30
4850	5000 PSI	9.35	7	16.35
4900	8" thick, 3000 PSI	9.45	7.20	16.65
4950	5000 PSI	9.65	7.10	16.75
5000	Vertical rib & light sandblast, 5-1/2" thick, 3000 PSI	4.81	4.92	9.73
5100	6" thick, 3000 PSI	5.10	5	10.10
5200	7-1/2" thick, 3000 PSI	5.90	5.20	11.10
5300	8" thick, 3000 PSI	6.20	5.30	11.50
6000	Broom finish w/2" urethane insulation, 6" thick, 3000 PSI	2.60	4.99	7.59
6100	Broom finish 2" fiberplank insulation, 6" thick, 3000 PSI	3.12	4.94	8.06
6200	Exposed aggregate w/2" urethane insulation, 6" thick, 3000 PSI	6.55	5.10	11.65
6300	Exposed aggregate 2" fiberplank insulation, 6" thick, 3000 PSI	7.10	5.05	12.15

Exterior concrete block walls are defined in the following terms; structural reinforcement, weight, percent solid, size, strength and insulation. Within each of these categories, two to four variations are shown. No costs are included for brick shelf or relieving angles.

4.1-211 — Concrete Block Wall - Regular Weight

	TYPE	SIZE (IN.)	STRENGTH (P.S.I.)	CORE FILL		COST PER S.F. MAT.	COST PER S.F. INST.	COST PER S.F. TOTAL
1200	Hollow	4x8x16	2,000	none		1.10	4.02	5.12
1250			4,500	none		1.06	4.02	5.08
1400		8x8x16	2,000	perlite		2.17	4.88	7.05
1410				styrofoam		2.60	4.61	7.21
1440				none		1.72	4.61	6.33
1450			4,500	perlite		2.04	4.88	6.92
1460				styrofoam		2.47	4.61	7.08
1490				none		1.59	4.61	6.20
2000	75% solid	4x8x16	2,000	none		1.13	4.07	5.20
2100	75% solid	6x8x16	2,000	perlite		1.66	4.48	6.14
2500	Solid	4x8x16	2,000	none		1.49	4.16	5.65
2700		8x8x16	2,000	none		2.55	4.80	7.35

4.1-211 — Concrete Block Wall - Lightweight

	TYPE	SIZE (IN.)	WEIGHT (P.C.F.)	CORE FILL		COST PER S.F. MAT.	COST PER S.F. INST.	COST PER S.F. TOTAL
3100	Hollow	8x4x16	105	perlite		1.46	4.60	6.06
3110				styrofoam		1.89	4.33	6.22
3200		4x8x16	105	none		1.25	3.93	5.18
3250			85	none		1.35	3.85	5.20
3300		6x8x16	105	perlite		2	4.43	6.43
3310				styrofoam		2.57	4.21	6.78
3340				none		1.69	4.21	5.90
3400		8x8x16	105	perlite		2.51	4.77	7.28
3410				styrofoam		2.94	4.50	7.44
3440				none		2.06	4.50	6.56
3450			85	perlite		2.31	4.66	6.97
4000	75% solid	4x8x16	105	none		1.14	3.98	5.12
4050			85	none		2.27	3.89	6.16
4100		6x8x16	105	perlite		1.68	4.37	6.05
4500	Solid	4x8x16	105	none		1.41	4.11	5.52
4700		8x8x16	105	none		2.53	4.73	7.26

4.1-211 — Reinforced Concrete Block Wall - Regular Weight

	TYPE	SIZE (IN.)	STRENGTH (P.S.I.)	VERT. REINF & GROUT SPACING		COST PER S.F. MAT.	INST.	TOTAL
5200	Hollow	4x8x16	2,000	#4 @ 48"		1.20	4.46	5.66
5300		6x8x16	2,000	#4 @ 48"		1.78	4.77	6.55
5330				#5 @ 32"		1.93	4.94	6.87
5340				#5 @ 16"		2.24	5.60	7.84
5350			4,500	#4 @ 28"		1.54	4.77	6.31
5390				#5 @ 16"		2	5.60	7.60
5400	Hollow	8x8x16	2,000	#4 @ 48"		1.96	5.10	7.06
5430				#5 @ 32"		2.10	5.35	7.45
5440				#5 @ 16"		2.48	6.15	8.63
5450		8x8x16	4,500	#4 @ 48"		1.81	5.15	6.96
5490				#5 @ 16"		2.35	6.15	8.50
5500		12x8x16	2,000	#4 @ 48"		2.79	6.50	9.29
5540				#5 @ 16"		3.53	7.55	11.08
6100	75% solid	6x8x16	2,000	#4 @ 48"		1.58	4.75	6.33
6140				#5 @ 16"		1.86	5.40	7.26
6150			4,500	#4 @ 48"		1.92	4.75	6.67
6190				#5 @ 16"		2.20	5.40	7.60
6200		8x8x16	2,000	#4 @ 48"		2.31	5.10	7.41
6230				#5 @ 32"		2.41	5.30	7.71
6240				#5 @ 16"		2.61	5.90	8.51
6250			4,500	#4 @ 48"		2.58	5.10	7.68
6280				#5 @ 32"		2.68	5.30	7.98
6290				#5 @ 16"		2.88	5.90	8.78
6500	Solid-double	2-4x8x16	2,000	#4 @ 48" E.W.		3.61	9.40	13.01
6530	Wythe			#5 @ 16" E.W.		4.01	10	14.01
6550			4,500	#4 @ 48" E.W.		3.11	9.30	12.41
6580				#5 @ 16" E.W.		3.51	9.90	13.41

4.1-211 — Reinforced Concrete Block Wall - Lightweight

	TYPE	SIZE (IN.)	WEIGHT (P.C.F.)	VERT REINF. & GROUT SPACING		COST PER S.F. MAT.	INST.	TOTAL
7100	Hollow	8x4x16	105	#4 @ 48"		1.23	4.87	6.10
7140				#5 @ 16"		1.77	5.85	7.62
7150			85	#4 @ 48"		3.24	4.77	8.01
7190				#5 @ 16"		3.78	5.75	9.53
7400		8x8x16	105	#4 @ 48"		2.28	5.05	7.33
7440				#5 @ 16"		2.82	6	8.82
7450		8x8x16	85	#4 @ 48"		2.08	4.93	7.01
7490				#5 @ 16"		2.62	5.90	8.52
7800		8x8x24	105	#4 @ 48"		1.73	5.40	7.13
7840				#5 @ 16"		2.27	6.40	8.67
7850			85	#4 @ 48"		3.54	4.63	8.17
7890				#5 @ 16"		4.08	5.60	9.68
8100	75% solid	6x8x16	105	#4 @ 48"		1.60	4.64	6.24
8130				#5 @ 32"		1.70	4.78	6.48
8150			85	#4 @ 48"		2.70	4.54	7.24
8180				#5 @ 32"		2.80	4.68	7.48
8200		8x8x16	105	#4 @ 48"		2.13	4.99	7.12
8230				#5 @ 32"		2.23	5.15	7.38
8250			85	#4 @ 48"		3.67	4.88	8.55
8280				#5 @ 32"		3.77	5.05	8.82

Important: See the Reference Section for critical supporting data - Location Factors & Historical Cost Indexes

4.1-211	Reinforced Concrete Block Wall - Lightweight

	TYPE	SIZE (IN.)	WEIGHT (P.C.F.)	VERT REINF. & GROUT SPACING		COST PER S.F.		
						MAT.	INST.	TOTAL
8500	Solid-double	2-4x8x16	105	#4 @ 48″		3.45	9.30	12.75
8530	Wythe		105	#5 @ 16″		3.85	9.90	13.75
8600		2-6x8x16	105	#4 @ 48″		4.42	9.95	14.37
8630				#5 @ 16″		4.82	10.55	15.37
8650			85	#4 @ 48″		6.30	9.55	15.85

EXTERIOR CLOSURE

4

Exterior split ribbed block walls are defined in the following terms; structural reinforcement, weight, percent solid, size, number of ribs and insulation. Within each of these categories two to four variations are shown. No costs are included for brick shelf or relieving angles. Costs include control joints every 20' and horizontal reinforcing.

EXTERIOR CLOSURE 4

4.1-212 — Split Ribbed Block Wall - Regular Weight

	TYPE	SIZE (IN.)	RIBS	CORE FILL		COST PER S.F. MAT.	INST.	TOTAL
1220	Hollow	4x8x16	4	none		2.18	4.98	7.16
1250			8	none		2.55	4.98	7.53
1280			16	none		2.07	5.05	7.12
1430		8x8x16	8	perlite		4.39	5.90	10.29
1440				styrofoam		4.82	5.60	10.42
1450				none		3.94	5.60	9.54
1530		12x8x16	8	perlite		5.50	7.85	13.35
1540				styrofoam		5.90	7.30	13.20
1550				none		4.78	7.30	12.08
2120	75% solid	4x8x16	4	none		2.73	5.05	7.78
2150			8	none		3.22	5.05	8.27
2180			16	none		2.62	5.10	7.72
2520	Solid	4x8x16	4	none		3.32	5.10	8.42
2550			8	none		3.89	5.10	8.99
2580			16	none		3.14	5.20	8.34

4.1-212 — Reinforced Split Ribbed Block Wall - Regular Weight

	TYPE	SIZE (IN.)	RIBS	VERT. REINF. & GROUT SPACING		COST PER S.F. MAT.	INST.	TOTAL
5200	Hollow	4x8x16	4	#4 @ 48"		2.28	5.40	7.68
5230			8	#4 @ 48"		2.65	5.40	8.05
5260			16	#4 @ 48"		2.17	5.50	7.67
5430		8x8x16	8	#4 @ 48"		4.16	6.15	10.31
5440				#5 @ 32"		4.32	6.40	10.72
5450				#5 @ 16"		4.70	7.15	11.85
5530		12x8x16	8	#4 @ 48"		5.10	7.85	12.95
5540				#5 @ 32"		5.30	8.10	13.40
5550				#5 @ 16"		5.85	8.90	14.75
6230	75% solid	6x8x16	8	#4 @ 48"		4.09	5.75	9.84
6240				#5 @ 32"		4.19	5.85	10.04
6250				#5 @ 16"		4.37	6.40	10.77
6330		8x8x16	8	#4 @ 48"		5.15	6.15	11.30
6340				#5 @ 32"		5.25	6.35	11.60
6350				#5 @ 16"		5.45	6.95	12.40

Exterior split face block walls are defined in the following terms; structural reinforcement, weight, percent solid, size, scores and insulation. Within each of these categories two to four variations are shown. No costs are included for brick shelf or relieving angles. Costs include control joints every 20' and horizontal reinforcing.

4.1-213   Split Face Block Wall - Regular Weight

	TYPE	SIZE (IN.)	SCORES	CORE FILL		MAT.	INST.	TOTAL
1200	Hollow	8x4x16	0	perlite		6.40	6.50	12.90
1210				styrofoam		6.85	6.20	13.05
1240				none		5.95	6.20	12.15
1250			1	perlite		6.85	6.50	13.35
1260				styrofoam		7.30	6.20	13.50
1290				none		6.40	6.20	12.60
1300		12x4x16	0	perlite		8.30	7.40	15.70
1310				styrofoam		8.70	6.85	15.55
1340				none		7.60	6.85	14.45
1350			1	perlite		8.80	7.40	16.20
1360				styrofoam		9.20	6.85	16.05
1390				none		8.10	6.85	14.95
1400		4x8x16	0	none		2.18	4.91	7.09
1450			1	none		2.46	4.98	7.44
1500		6x8x16	0	perlite		3.14	5.65	8.79
1510				styrofoam		3.71	5.45	9.16
1540				none		2.83	5.45	8.28
1550			1	perlite		3.42	5.70	9.12
1560				styrofoam		3.99	5.50	9.49
1590				none		3.11	5.50	8.61
1600		8x8x16	0	perlite		3.79	6.10	9.89
1610				styrofoam		4.22	5.80	10.02
1640				none		3.34	5.80	9.14
1650	Hollow	8x8x16	1	perlite		4.02	6.20	10.22
1660				styrofoam		4.45	5.90	10.35
1690				none		3.57	5.90	9.47
1700		12x8x16	0	perlite		4.87	7.95	12.82
1710				styrofoam		5.25	7.40	12.65
1740				none		4.13	7.40	11.53
1750			1	perlite		5.10	8.10	13.20
1760				styrofoam		5.45	7.55	13
1790				none		4.36	7.55	11.91

EXTERIOR CLOSURE

4

4.1-213 — Split Face Block Wall - Regular Weight

	TYPE	SIZE (IN.)	SCORES	CORE FILL		COST PER S.F. MAT.	INST.	TOTAL
1800	75% solid	8x4x16	0	perlite		7.75	6.45	14.20
1840				none		7.50	6.30	13.80
1852		8x4x16	1	perlite		8.20	6.45	14.65
1890				none		7.95	6.30	14.25
2000		4x8x16	0	none		2.73	4.98	7.71
2050			1	none		2.97	5.05	8.02
2400	Solid	8x4x16	0	none		9.15	6.45	15.60
2450			1	none		9.60	6.45	16.05
2900		12x8x16	0	none		6.30	7.70	14
2950			1	none		6.50	7.85	14.35

4.1-213 — Reinforced Split Face Block Wall - Regular Weight

	TYPE	SIZE (IN.)	SCORES	VERT. REINF. & GROUT SPACING		COST PER S.F. MAT.	INST.	TOTAL
5200	Hollow	8x4x16	0	#4 @ 48"		6.20	6.75	12.95
5210				#5 @ 32"		6.35	7	13.35
5240				#5 @ 16"		6.75	7.75	14.50
5250			1	#4 @ 48"		6.65	6.75	13.40
5260				#5 @ 32"		6.80	7	13.80
5290				#5 @ 16"		7.20	7.75	14.95
5700		12x8x16	0	#4 @ 48"		4.45	7.95	12.40
5710				#5 @ 32"		4.66	8.20	12.86
5740				#5 @ 16"		5.20	9	14.20
5750			1	#4 @ 48"		4.68	8.10	12.78
5760				#5 @ 32"		4.89	8.35	13.24
5790				#5 @ 16"		5.40	9.15	14.55
6000	75% solid	8x4x16	0	#4 @ 48"		7.60	6.75	14.35
6010				#5 @ 32"		7.70	6.95	14.65
6040				#5 @ 16"		7.90	7.55	15.45
6050			1	#4 @ 48"		8.05	6.75	14.80
6060				#5 @ 32"		8.15	6.95	15.10
6090				#5 @ 16"		8.35	7.55	15.90
6100		12x4x16	0	#4 @ 48"		9.80	7.50	17.30
6110				#5 @ 32"		9.95	7.65	17.60
6140				#5 @ 16"		10.20	8.15	18.35
6150			1	#4 @ 48"		10.20	7.50	17.70
6160				#5 @ 32"		10.35	7.65	18
6190				#5 @ 16"		10.65	8.30	18.95
6700	Solid-double	2-4x8x16	0	#4 @ 48" E.W.		7.25	11.20	18.45
6710	Wythe			#5 @ 32" E.W.		7.40	11.30	18.70
6740				#5 @ 16" E.W.		7.65	11.75	19.40
6750			1	#4 @ 48" E.W.		7.75	11.35	19.10
6760				#5 @ 32" E.W.		7.90	11.45	19.35
6790				#5 @ 16" E.W.		8.15	11.90	20.05
6800		2-6x8x16	0	#4 @ 48" E.W.		9.45	12.35	21.80
6810				#5 @ 32" E.W.		9.60	12.45	22.05
6840				#5 @ 16" E.W.		9.85	12.90	22.75
6850			1	#4 @ 48" E.W.		9.90	12.55	22.45
6860				#5 @ 32" E.W.		10.05	12.65	22.70
6890				#5 @ 16" E.W.		10.30	13.10	23.40

Important: See the Reference Section for critical supporting data - Location Factors & Historical Cost Indexes

Exterior solid brick walls are defined in the following terms; structural reinforcement, type of brick, thickness, and bond. Nine different types of face bricks are presented, with single wythes shown in four different bonds. Shelf angles are included in system components. These walls do not include ties and as such are not tied to a backup wall.

4.1-231			Solid Brick Walls - Single Wythe						
						COST PER S.F.			
	TYPE	THICKNESS (IN.)	BOND			MAT.	INST.	TOTAL	
1000	Common	4	running			2.80	9.15	11.95	
1010			common			3.35	10.45	13.80	
1050			Flemish			3.70	12.65	16.35	
1100			English			4.13	13.40	17.53	
1150	Standard	4	running			3.81	9.45	13.26	
1160			common			4.49	10.90	15.39	
1200			Flemish			4.97	13	17.97	
1250			English			5.55	13.80	19.35	
1300	Glazed	4	running			8.15	9.85	18	
1310			common			9.70	11.40	21.10	
1350			Flemish			10.75	13.80	24.55	
1400			English			12.05	14.70	26.75	
1600	Economy	4	running			3.68	7.25	10.93	
1610			common			4.33	8.30	12.63	
1650			Flemish			4.77	9.85	14.62	
1700			English			8.85	10.45	19.30	
1900	Fire	4-1/2	running			7.40	8.30	15.70	
1910			common			8.80	9.45	18.25	
1950			Flemish			9.75	11.40	21.15	
2000			English			10.95	12	22.95	
2050	King	3-1/2	running			3.10	7.45	10.55	
2060			common			3.63	8.55	12.18	
2100			Flemish			4.42	10.25	14.67	
2150			English			4.88	10.65	15.53	
2200	Roman	4	running			5.35	8.55	13.90	
2210			common			6.35	9.85	16.20	
2250			Flemish			7	11.70	18.70	
2300			English			7.90	12.65	20.55	
2350	Norman	4	running			4.01	7.10	11.11	
2360			common			4.73	8.05	12.78	
2400			Flemish			8.65	9.65	18.30	
2450			English			5.85	10.25	16.10	
2500	Norwegian	4	running			3.70	6.35	10.05	
2510			common			4.36	7.20	11.56	
2550			Flemish			4.81	8.55	13.36	
2600			English			5.40	9	14.40	

EXTERIOR CLOSURE

4

4.1-231 — Solid Brick Walls - Double Wythe

	TYPE	THICKNESS (IN.)	COLLAR JOINT THICKNESS (IN.)			COST PER S.F. MAT.	INST.	TOTAL
4100	Common	8	3/4			5.60	15.30	20.90
4150	Standard	8	1/2			7.45	15.80	23.25
4200	Glazed	8	1/2			16.15	16.40	32.55
4250	Engineer	8	1/2			7.30	14	21.30
4300	Economy	8	3/4			7.20	12	19.20
4350	Double	8	3/4			9.40	9.75	19.15
4400	Fire	8	3/4			14.65	14	28.65
4450	King	7	3/4			6.05	12.30	18.35
4500	Roman	8	1			10.55	14.40	24.95
4550	Norman	8	3/4			7.90	11.75	19.65
4600	Norwegian	8	3/4			7.25	10.45	17.70
4650	Utility	8	3/4			6.75	9.05	15.80
4700	Triple	8	3/4			5.30	8.15	13.45
4750	SCR	12	3/4			10.05	12	22.05
4800	Norwegian	12	3/4			8.75	10.60	19.35
4850	Jumbo	12	3/4			9.50	9.30	18.80

4.1-231 — Reinforced Brick Walls

	TYPE	THICKNESS (IN.)	WYTHE	REINF. & SPACING		COST PER S.F. MAT.	INST.	TOTAL
7200	Common	4"	1	#4 @ 48"vert		2.97	9.50	12.47
7220				#5 @ 32"vert		3.06	9.60	12.66
7230				#5 @ 16"vert		3.23	10.05	13.28
7700	King	9"	2	#4 @ 48" E.W.		6.40	12.90	19.30
7720				#5 @ 32" E.W.		6.55	13	19.55
7730				#5 @ 16" E.W.		6.80	13.35	20.15
7800	Common	10"	2	#4 @ 48" E.W.		5.90	15.90	21.80
7820				#5 @ 32" E.W.		6.05	16	22.05
7830				#5 @ 16" E.W.		6.30	16.35	22.65
7900	Standard	10"	2	#4 @ 48" E.W.		7.80	16.40	24.20
7920				#5 @ 32" E.W.		7.95	16.50	24.45
7930				#5 @ 16" E.W.		8.20	16.85	25.05
8100	Economy	10"	2	#4 @ 48" E.W.		7.55	12.60	20.15
8120				#5 @ 32" E.W.		7.70	12.70	20.40
8130				#5 @ 16" E.W.		7.95	13.05	21
8200	Double	10"	2	#4 @ 48" E.W.		9.75	10.35	20.10
8220				#5 @ 32" E.W.		9.90	10.45	20.35
8230				#5 @ 16" E.W.		10.15	10.80	20.95
8300	Fire	10"	2	#4 @ 48" E.W.		15	14.60	29.60
8320				#5 @ 32" E.W.		15.15	14.70	29.85
8330				#5 @ 16" E.W.		15.40	15.05	30.45
8400	Roman	10"	2	#4 @ 48" E.W.		10.90	15	25.90
8420				#5 @ 32" E.W.		11.05	15.10	26.15
8430				#5 @ 16" E.W.		11.30	15.45	26.75
8500	Norman	10"	2	#4 @ 48" E.W.		8.25	12.35	20.60
8520				#5 @ 32" E.W.		8.40	12.45	20.85
8530				#5 @ 16" E.W.		8.65	12.80	21.45
8600	Norwegian	10"	2	#4 @ 48" E.W.		7.60	11.05	18.65
8620				#5 @ 32" E.W.		7.75	11.15	18.90
8630				#5 @ 16" E.W.		8	11.50	19.50
8800	Triple	10"	2	#4 @ 48" E.W.		5.60	8.75	14.35
8820				#5 @ 32" E.W.		5.75	8.85	14.60
8830				#5 @ 16" E.W.		6	9.20	15.20

Important: See the Reference Section for critical supporting data - Location Factors & Historical Cost Indexes

The table below lists costs per S.F. for stone veneer walls on various backup using different stone.

Stone Veneer

4.1-242	Stone Veneer	MAT.	INST.	TOTAL
			COST PER S.F.	
2000	Ashlar veneer,4″, 2″x4″ stud backup,16″ O.C., 8′ high, low priced stone	7	12.15	19.15
2100	Metal stud backup, 8′ high, 16″ O.C.	7.20	12.35	19.55
2150	24″ O.C.	7	12.05	19.05
2200	Conc. block backup, 4″ thick	7.50	15	22.50
2300	6″ thick	8	15.20	23.20
2350	8″ thick	8.10	15.40	23.50
2400	10″ thick	8.75	15.50	24.25
2500	12″ thick	8.85	16.50	25.35
3100	High priced stone, wood stud backup, 10′ high, 16″ O.C.	12.60	13.70	26.30
3200	Metal stud backup, 10′ high, 16″ O.C.	12.70	13.90	26.60
3250	24″ O.C.	12.50	13.60	26.10
3300	Conc. block backup, 10′ high, 4″ thick	13	16.55	29.55
3350	6″ thick	13.50	16.60	30.10
3400	8″ thick	13.60	16.95	30.55
3450	10″ thick	14.25	17.05	31.30
3500	12″ thick	14.35	18.05	32.40
4000	Indiana limestone 2″ thick,sawn finish,wood stud backup,10′ high,16″ O.C.	14.70	10.20	24.90
4100	Metal stud backup, 10′ high, 16″ O.C.	14.90	10.40	25.30
4150	24″ O.C.	14.70	10.10	24.80
4200	Conc. block backup, 4″ thick	15.20	13.05	28.25
4250	6″ thick	15.70	13.25	28.95
4300	8″ thick	15.80	13.45	29.25
4350	10″ thick	16.45	13.55	30
4400	12″ thick	16.55	14.55	31.10
4450	2″ thick, smooth finish, wood stud backup, 8′ high, 16″ O.C.	14.70	10.20	24.90
4550	Metal stud backup, 8′ high, 16″ O.C.	14.90	10.25	25.15
4600	24″ O.C.	14.70	9.95	24.65
4650	Conc. block backup, 4″ thick	15.20	12.95	28.15
4700	6″ thick	15.70	13.10	28.80
4750	8″ thick	15.80	13.30	29.10
4800	10″ thick	16.45	13.55	30
4850	12″ thick	16.55	14.55	31.10
5350	4″ thick, smooth finish, wood stud backup, 8′ high, 16″ O.C.	19.80	10.20	30
5450	Metal stud backup, 8′ high, 16″ O.C.	20	10.40	30.40
5500	24″ O.C.	19.80	10.10	29.90
5550	Conc. block backup, 4″ thick	20.50	13.05	33.55
5600	6″ thick	21	13.25	34.25
5650	8″ thick	21	13.45	34.45
5700	10″ thick	21.50	13.55	35.05
5750	12″ thick	21.50	14.55	36.05

EXTERIOR CLOSURE

4

4.1-242	Stone Veneer	COST PER S.F.		
		MAT.	INST.	TOTAL
6000	Granite, grey or pink, 2" thick, wood stud backup, 8' high, 16" O.C.	18.75	17.55	36.30
6100	Metal studs, 8' high, 16" O.C.	18.95	17.75	36.70
6150	24" O.C.	18.75	17.45	36.20
6200	Conc. block backup, 4" thick	19.25	20.50	39.75
6250	6" thick	19.75	20.50	40.25
6300	8" thick	19.85	21	40.85
6350	10" thick	20.50	21	41.50
6400	12" thick	20.50	22	42.50
6900	4" thick, wood stud backup, 8' high, 16" O.C.	30	19.85	49.85
7000	Metal studs, 8' high, 16" O.C.	30.50	20	50.50
7050	24" O.C.	30	19.75	49.75
7100	Conc. block backup, 4" thick	30.50	22.50	53
7150	6" thick	31	23	54
7200	8" thick	31	23	54
7250	10" thick	32	23	55
7300	12" thick	32	24	56

Important: See the Reference Section for critical supporting data - Location Factors & Historical Cost Indexes

Exterior brick veneer/stud backup walls are defined in the following terms; type of brick and studs, stud spacing and bond. All systems include a brick shelf, ties to the backup and all necessary dampproofing and insulation.

4.1-252 — Brick Veneer/Wood Stud Backup

	FACE BRICK	STUD BACKUP	STUD SPACING (IN.)	BOND		COST PER S.F.		
						MAT.	INST.	TOTAL
1100	Standard	2x4-wood	16	running		5.20	11.15	16.35
1120				common		5.90	12.60	18.50
1140				Flemish		6.35	14.70	21.05
1160				English		6.95	15.50	22.45
1400		2x6-wood	16	running		5.40	11.20	16.60
1420				common		6.10	12.65	18.75
1440				Flemish		6.60	14.75	21.35
1460				English		7.15	15.55	22.70
1700	Glazed	2x4-wood	16	running		9.55	11.55	21.10
1720				common		11.10	13.10	24.20
1740				Flemish		12.15	15.50	27.65
1760				English		13.45	16.40	29.85
2300	Engineer	2x4-wood	16	running		5.10	10	15.10
2320				common		5.75	11.15	16.90
2340				Flemish		6.25	13.10	19.35
2360				English		6.80	13.70	20.50
2900	Roman	2x4-wood	16	running		6.75	10.25	17
2920				common		7.75	11.55	19.30
2940				Flemish		8.40	13.40	21.80
2960				English		9.30	14.35	23.65
4100	Norwegian	2x4-wood	16	running		5.10	8	13.10
4120				common		5.75	8.90	14.65
4140				Flemish		6.20	10.25	16.45
4160				English		6.75	10.70	17.45

EXTERIOR CLOSURE

4

4.1-252	Brick Veneer/Metal Stud Backup

	FACE BRICK	STUD BACKUP	STUD SPACING (IN.)	BOND		COST PER S.F.		
						MAT.	INST.	TOTAL
5100	Standard	25ga.x6"NLB	24	running		4.82	10.90	15.72
5120				common		5.50	12.35	17.85
5140				Flemish		5.75	14	19.75
5160				English		6.55	15.25	21.80
5200		20ga.x3-5/8"NLB	16	running		4.89	11.35	16.24
5220				common		5.55	12.80	18.35
5240				Flemish		6.05	14.90	20.95
5260				English		6.65	15.70	22.35
5400		16ga.x3-5/8"LB	16	running		5.25	11.50	16.75
5420				common		5.95	12.95	18.90
5440				Flemish		6.40	15.05	21.45
5460				English		7	15.85	22.85
5700	Glazed	25ga.x6"NLB	24	running		9.15	11.30	20.45
5720				common		10.70	12.85	23.55
5740				Flemish		11.75	15.25	27
5760				English		13.05	16.15	29.20
5800		20ga.x3-5/8"NLB	24	running		9.15	11.40	20.55
5820				common		10.70	12.95	23.65
5840				Flemish		11.75	15.35	27.10
5860				English		13.05	16.25	29.30
6000		16ga.x3-5/8"LB	16	running		9.60	11.90	21.50
6020				common		11.15	13.45	24.60
6040				Flemish		12.20	15.85	28.05
6060				English		13.50	16.75	30.25
6300	Engineer	25ga.x6"NLB	24	running		4.74	9.75	14.49
6320				common		5.40	10.90	16.30
6340				Flemish		5.85	12.85	18.70
6360				English		6.40	13.45	19.85
6400		20ga.x3-5/8"NLB	16	running		4.81	10.20	15.01
6420				common		5.45	11.35	16.80
6440				Flemish		5.90	13.30	19.20
6460				English		6.50	13.90	20.40
6900	Roman	25ga.x6"NLB	24	running		6.35	10	16.35
6920				common		7.35	11.30	18.65
6940				Flemish		8	13.15	21.15
6960				English		8.90	14.10	23
7000		20ga.x3-5/8"NLB	16	running		6.40	10.45	16.85
7020				common		7.45	11.75	19.20
7040				Flemish		8.10	13.60	21.70
7060				English		9	14.55	23.55
7500	Norman	25ga.x6"NLB	24	running		5	8.55	13.55
7520				common		5.75	9.50	15.25
7540				Flemish		9.65	11.10	20.75
7560				English		6.85	11.70	18.55
7600		20ga.x3-5/8"NLB	24	running		5	8.65	13.65
7620				common		5.75	9.60	15.35
7640				Flemish		9.65	11.20	20.85
7660				English		6.85	11.80	18.65
8100	Norwegian	25ga.x6"NLB	24	running		4.71	7.80	12.51
8120				common		5.35	8.65	14
8140				Flemish		5.80	10	15.80
8160				English		6.40	10.45	16.85

EXTERIOR CLOSURE 4

Important: See the Reference Section for critical supporting data - Location Factors & Historical Cost Indexes

4.1-252   Brick Veneer/Metal Stud Backup

	FACE BRICK	STUD BACKUP	STUD SPACING (IN.)	BOND		COST PER S.F.		
						MAT.	INST.	TOTAL
8400	Norwegian	16ga.x3-5/8"LB	16	running		5.15	8.40	13.55
8420				common		5.80	9.25	15.05
8440				Flemish		6.25	10.60	16.85
8460				English		6.80	11.05	17.85

EXTERIOR CLOSURE

4

Brick Face Composite Wall

4.1-272	Brick Face Composite Wall - Double Wythe							
	FACE BRICK	BACKUP MASONRY	BACKUP THICKNESS (IN.)	BACKUP CORE FILL		COST PER S.F.		
						MAT.	INST.	TOTAL
1000	Standard	common brick	4	none		6.45	17.30	23.75
1040		SCR brick	6	none		8.70	15.40	24.10
1080		conc. block	4	none		5.20	13.90	19.10
1120			6	perlite		6.05	14.40	20.45
1160				styrofoam		6.60	14.20	20.80
1200			8	perlite		6.30	14.75	21.05
1240				styrofoam		6.70	14.45	21.15
1520		glazed block	4	none		11.20	14.85	26.05
1560			6	perlite		11.90	15.30	27.20
1600				styrofoam		12.45	15.10	27.55
1640			8	perlite		12.40	15.65	28.05
1680				styrofoam		12.80	15.40	28.20
1720	Standard	clay tile	4	none		8.80	13.35	22.15
1760			6	none		8.45	13.75	22.20
1800			8	none		9.80	14.20	24
1840		glazed tile	4	none		10.40	17.60	28
1880								
2000	Glazed	common brick	4	none		10.75	17.70	28.45
2040		SCR brick	6	none		13.05	15.80	28.85
2080		conc. block	4	none		9.55	14.30	23.85
2200			8	perlite		10.60	15.15	25.75
2240				styrofoam		11.05	14.85	25.90
2280		L.W. block	4	none		9.70	14.20	23.90
2400			8	perlite		10.95	15.05	26
2520		glazed block	4	none		15.50	15.25	30.75
2560			6	perlite		16.25	15.70	31.95
2600				styrofoam		16.80	15.50	32.30
2640			8	perlite		16.70	16.05	32.75
2680				styrofoam		17.15	15.80	32.95
2720		clay tile	4	none		13.15	13.75	26.90
2760			6	none		12.80	14.15	26.95
2800			8	none		14.10	14.60	28.70
2840		glazed tile	4	none		14.70	18	32.70
3000	Engineer	common brick	4	none		6.35	16.15	22.50
3040		SCR brick	6	none		8.60	14.25	22.85

Important: See the Reference Section for critical supporting data - Location Factors & Historical Cost Indexes

4.1-272 | Brick Face Composite Wall - Double Wythe

	FACE BRICK	BACKUP MASONRY	BACKUP THICKNESS (IN.)	BACKUP CORE FILL		COST PER S.F.		
						MAT.	INST.	TOTAL
3080		conc. block	4	none		5.15	12.75	17.90
3200			8	perlite		6.20	13.60	19.80
3280		L.W. block	4	none		4.25	9.05	13.30
3322	Engineer	L.W. block	6	perlite		6.05	13.15	19.20
3520		glazed block	4	none		11.10	13.70	24.80
3560			6	perlite		11.80	14.15	25.95
3600				styrofoam		12.40	13.95	26.35
3640			8	perlite		12.30	14.50	26.80
3680				styrofoam		12.75	14.25	27
3720		clay tile	4	none		8.75	12.20	20.95
3800			8	none		9.70	13.05	22.75
3840		glazed tile	4	none		10.30	16.45	26.75
4000	Roman	common brick	4	none		7.95	16.40	24.35
4040		SCR brick	6	none		10.25	14.50	24.75
4080		conc. block	4	none		6.75	13	19.75
4120			6	perlite		7.55	13.50	21.05
4200			8	perlite		7.80	13.85	21.65
5000	Norman	common brick	4	none		6.65	14.95	21.60
5040		SCR brick	6	none		8.90	13.05	21.95
5280		L.W. block	4	none		5.55	11.45	17
5320			6	perlite		6.35	12.10	18.45
5720		clay tile	4	none		9	11	20
5760			6	none		8.65	11.40	20.05
5840		glazed tile	4	none		10.60	15.25	25.85
6000	Norwegian	common brick	4	none		6.30	14.15	20.45
6040		SCR brick	6	none		8.60	12.25	20.85
6080		conc. block	4	none		5.10	10.80	15.90
6120			6	perlite		5.90	11.30	17.20
6160				styrofoam		6.50	11.10	17.60
6200			8	perlite		6.15	11.65	17.80
6520		glazed block	4	none		11.05	11.75	22.80
6560			6	perlite		11.80	12.20	24
7000	Utility	common brick	4	none		6.05	13.45	19.50
7040		SCR brick	6	none		8.35	11.55	19.90
7080		conc. block	4	none		4.85	10.05	14.90
7120			6	perlite		5.65	10.55	16.20
7160				styrofoam		6.25	10.35	16.60
7200			8	perlite		5.90	10.90	16.80
7240				styrofoam		6.35	10.60	16.95
7280		L.W. block	4	none		5	9.95	14.95
7320			6	perlite		5.75	10.45	16.20
7520		glazed block	4	none		10.80	11	21.80
7560			6	perlite		11.50	11.45	22.95
7720		clay tile	4	none		8.45	9.50	17.95
7760			6	none		8.10	9.90	18
7840		glazed tile	4	none		10	13.75	23.75

4.1-272 | Brick Face Composite Wall - Triple Wythe

	FACE BRICK	MIDDLE WYTHE	INSIDE MASONRY	TOTAL THICKNESS (IN.)		COST PER S.F.		
						MAT.	INST.	TOTAL
8000	Standard	common brick	standard brick	12		10.05	24.50	34.55
8100		4" conc. brick	standard brick	12		9.80	25.50	35.30
8120		4" conc. brick	common brick	12		8.80	25	33.80

4.1-272	Brick Face Composite Wall - Triple Wythe

	FACE BRICK	MIDDLE WYTHE	INSIDE MASONRY	TOTAL THICKNESS (IN.)		COST PER S.F.		
						MAT.	INST.	TOTAL
8200	Glazed	common brick	standard brick	12		14.40	25	39.40
8300		4" conc. brick	standard brick	12		14.15	25.50	39.65
8320		4" conc. brick	glazed brick	12		13.15	25.50	38.65

EXTERIOR CLOSURE 4

Important: See the Reference Section for critical supporting data - Location Factors & Historical Cost Indexes

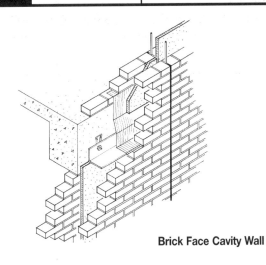

Brick Face Cavity Wall

4.1-273						Brick Face Cavity Wall				

	FACE BRICK	BACKUP MASONRY	TOTAL THICKNESS (IN.)	CAVITY INSULATION		COST PER S.F.		
						MAT.	INST.	TOTAL
1000	Standard	4"common brick	10	polystyrene		6.25	17.30	23.55
1020				none		6.15	16.85	23
1040		6"SCR brick	12	polystyrene		8.55	15.40	23.95
1060				none		8.40	14.95	23.35
1080		4"conc. block	10	polystyrene		5.05	13.95	19
1100				none		4.92	13.45	18.37
1120		6"conc. block	12	polystyrene		5.55	14.20	19.75
1140				none		5.45	13.75	19.20
1160		4"L.W. block	10	polystyrene		5.20	13.85	19.05
1180				none		5.05	13.40	18.45
1200		6"L.W. block	12	polystyrene		5.65	14.10	19.75
1220				none		5.50	13.65	19.15
1240		4"glazed block	10	polystyrene		11	14.90	25.90
1260				none		10.90	14.45	25.35
1280		6"glazed block	12	polystyrene		11.05	14.90	25.95
1300				none		10.90	14.45	25.35
1320		4"clay tile	10	polystyrene		8.65	13.40	22.05
1340				none		8.50	12.95	21.45
1360		4"glazed tile	10	polystyrene		10.20	17.60	27.80
1380				none		10.10	17.15	27.25
1500	Glazed	4" common brick	10	polystyrene		10.60	17.70	28.30
1520				none		10.45	17.25	27.70
1580		4" conc. block	10	polystyrene		9.40	14.35	23.75
1600				none		9.25	13.85	23.10
1660		4" L.W. block	10	polystyrene		9.55	14.25	23.80
1680				none		9.40	13.80	23.20
1740		4" glazed block	10	polystyrene		15.35	15.30	30.65
1760				none		15.20	14.85	30.05
1820		4" clay tile	10	polystyrene		13	13.80	26.80
1840				none		12.85	13.35	26.20
1860		4" glazed tile	10	polystyrene		12.65	14.15	26.80
1880				none		12.50	13.70	26.20
2000	Engineer	4" common brick	10	polystyrene		6.20	16.15	22.35
2020				none		6.05	15.70	21.75
2080		4" conc. block	10	polystyrene		4.98	12.80	17.78
2100				none		4.84	12.30	17.14
2162		4" L.W. block	10	polystyrene		5.15	12.70	17.85
2180				none		4.99	12.25	17.24

For expanded coverage of these items see *Means Assemblies Cost Data 2001*

	FACE BRICK	BACKUP MASONRY	TOTAL THICKNESS (IN.)	CAVITY INSULATION		COST PER S.F.		
						MAT.	INST.	TOTAL
2240	Engineer	4" glazed block	10	polystyrene		10.95	13.75	24.70
2260				none		10.80	13.30	24.10
2320		4" clay tile	10	polystyrene		8.60	12.25	20.85
2340				none		8.45	11.80	20.25
2360		4" glazed tile	10	polystyrene		10.15	16.45	26.60
2380				none		10	16	26
2500	Roman	4" common brick	10	polystyrene		7.80	16.40	24.20
2520				none		7.65	15.95	23.60
2580		4" conc. block	10	polystyrene		6.60	13.05	19.65
2600				none		6.45	12.55	19
2660		4" L.W. block	10	polystyrene		6.75	12.95	19.70
2680				none		6.60	12.50	19.10
2740		4" glazed block	10	polystyrene		12.55	14	26.55
2760				none		12.40	13.55	25.95
2820		4"clay tile	10	polystyrene		10.20	12.50	22.70
2840				none		10.05	12.05	22.10
2860		4"glazed tile	10	polystyrene		11.75	16.70	28.45
2880				none		11.60	16.25	27.85
3000	Norman	4" common brick	10	polystyrene		6.45	14.95	21.40
3020				none		6.35	14.50	20.85
3080		4" conc. block	10	polystyrene		5.25	11.60	16.85
3100				none		5.10	11.10	16.20
3160		4" L.W. block	10	polystyrene		5.40	11.50	16.90
3180				none		5.25	11.05	16.30
3240		4" glazed block	10	polystyrene		11.20	12.55	23.75
3260				none		11.10	12.10	23.20
3320		4" clay tile	10	polystyrene		8.85	11.05	19.90
3340				none		8.70	10.60	19.30
3360		4" glazed tile	10	polystyrene		10.40	15.25	25.65
3380				none		10.30	14.80	25.10
3500	Norwegian	4" common brick	10	polystyrene		6.15	14.20	20.35
3520				none		6	13.75	19.75
3580		4" conc. block	10	polystyrene		4.95	10.80	15.75
3600				none		4.81	10.35	15.16
3660		4" L.W. block	10	polystyrene		5.10	10.75	15.85
3680				none		4.96	10.25	15.21
3740		4" glazed block	10	polystyrene		10.90	11.80	22.70
3760				none		10.75	11.30	22.05
3820		4" clay tile	10	polystyrene		8.55	10.30	18.85
3840				none		8.40	9.80	18.20
3860		4" glazed tile	10	polystyrene		10.10	14.50	24.60
3880				none		9.95	14.05	24
4000	Utility	4" common brick	10	polystyrene		5.90	13.45	19.35
4020				none		5.75	13	18.75
4080		4" conc. block	10	polystyrene		4.69	10.10	14.79
4100				none		4.55	9.60	14.15
4160		4" L.W. block	10	polystyrene		4.84	10	14.84
4180				none		4.70	9.55	14.25
4240		4" glazed block	10	polystyrene		10.65	11.05	21.70
4260				none		10.50	10.60	21.10
4320		4" clay tile	10	polystyrene		8.30	9.55	17.85
4340				none		8.15	9.10	17.25
4360		4" glazed tile	10	polystyrene		9.85	13.75	23.60
4380				none		9.70	13.30	23

EXTERIOR CLOSURE 4

| 4.1-273 | | Brick Face Cavity Wall - Insulated Backup | | | | | | |

	FACE BRICK	BACKUP MASONRY	TOTAL THICKNESS (IN.)	BACKUP CORE FILL		COST PER S.F.		
						MAT.	INST.	TOTAL
5100	Standard	6" conc. block	10	perlite		5.75	14	19.75
5120				styrofoam		6.30	13.75	20.05
5180		6" L.W. block	10	perlite		5.80	13.90	19.70
5200				styrofoam		6.40	13.65	20.05
5260		6" glazed block	10	perlite		11.60	14.85	26.45
5280				styrofoam		12.15	14.65	26.80
5340		6" clay tile	10	none		8.15	13.30	21.45
5360		8" clay tile	12	none		9.50	13.75	23.25
5600	Glazed	6" conc. block	10	perlite		10.05	14.40	24.45
5620				styrofoam		10.65	14.15	24.80
5680		6" L.W. block	10	perlite		10.15	14.30	24.45
5700				styrofoam		10.70	14.05	24.75
5760		6" glazed block	10	perlite		15.95	15.25	31.20
5780				styrofoam		16.50	15.05	31.55
5840		6" clay tile	10	none		12.50	13.70	26.20
5860		8"clay tile	8	none		13.85	14.15	28
6100	Engineer	6" conc. block	10	perlite		5.65	12.85	18.50
6120				styrofoam		6.20	12.60	18.80
6180		6" L.W. block	10	perlite		5.75	12.75	18.50
6200				styrofoam		6.30	12.50	18.80
6260		6" glazed block	10	perlite		11.50	13.70	25.20
6280				styrofoam		12.10	13.50	25.60
6340		6" clay tile	10	none		8.10	12.15	20.25
6360		8" clay tile	12	none		9.40	12.60	22
6600	Roman	6" conc. block	10	perlite		7.25	13.10	20.35
6620				styrofoam		7.85	12.85	20.70
6680		6" L.W. block	10	perlite		7.35	13	20.35
6700				styrofoam		7.90	12.75	20.65
6760		6" glazed block	10	perlite		13.10	13.95	27.05
6780				styrofoam		13.70	13.75	27.45
6840		6" clay tile	10	none		9.70	12.40	22.10
6860		8" clay tile	12	none		11	12.85	23.85
7100	Norman	6" conc. block	10	perlite		5.95	11.65	17.60
7120				styrofoam		6.50	11.40	17.90
7180		6" L.W. block	10	perlite		6	11.55	17.55
7200				styrofoam		6.60	11.30	17.90
7260		6" glazed block	10	perlite		11.80	12.50	24.30
7280				styrofoam		12.35	12.30	24.65
7340		6" clay tile	10	none		8.35	10.95	19.30
7360		8" clay tile	12	none		9.70	11.40	21.10
7600	Norwegian	6" conc. block	10	perlite		5.60	10.85	16.45
7620				styrofoam		6.20	10.65	16.85
7680		6" L.W. block	10	perlite		5.70	10.75	16.45
7700				styrofoam		6.25	10.55	16.80
7760		6" glazed block	10	perlite		11.50	11.75	23.25
7780				styrofoam		12.05	11.55	23.60
7840		6" clay tile	10	none		8.05	10.20	18.25
7860		8" clay tile	12	none		9.40	10.65	20.05
8100	Utility	6" conc. block	10	perlite		5.35	10.15	15.50
8120				styrofoam		5.95	9.90	15.85
8180		6" L.W. block	10	perlite		5.45	10.05	15.50
8200				styrofoam		6	9.80	15.80
8260		6" glazed block	10	perlite		11.20	11	22.20
8280				styrofoam		11.80	10.80	22.60

EXTERIOR CLOSURE

4

4.1-273 Brick Face Cavity Wall - Insulated Backup

	FACE BRICK	BACKUP MASONRY	TOTAL THICKNESS (IN.)	BACKUP CORE FILL		COST PER S.F.		
						MAT.	INST.	TOTAL
8340	Utility	6" clay tile	10	none		7.80	9.45	17.25
8360		8" clay tile	12	none		9.10	9.90	19

Important: See the Reference Section for critical supporting data - Location Factors & Historical Cost Indexes

EXTERIOR CLOSURE 4

Glass Block

4.1-282	Glass Block	COST PER S.F.		
		MAT.	INST.	TOTAL
2300	Glass block 4" thick, 6"x6" plain, under 1,000 S.F.	14.10	16.15	30.25
2400	1,000 to 5,000 S.F.	14.25	14	28.25
2500	Over 5,000 S.F.	13.70	13.15	26.85
2600	Solar reflective, under 1,000 S.F.	19.70	22	41.70
2700	1,000 to 5,000 S.F.	19.90	18.95	38.85
2800	Over 5,000 S.F.	19.15	17.75	36.90
3500	8"x8" plain, under 1,000 S.F.	9.85	12.05	21.90
3600	1,000 to 5,000 S.F.	9.80	10.40	20.20
3700	Over 5,000 S.F.	8.90	9.40	18.30
3800	Solar reflective, under 1,000 S.F.	13.75	16.25	30
3900	1,000 to 5,000 S.F.	13.70	13.90	27.60
4000	Over 5,000 S.F.	12.45	12.50	24.95
5000	12"x12" plain, under 1,000 S.F.	12.05	11.15	23.20
5100	1,000 to 5,000 S.F.	12.15	9.40	21.55
5200	Over 5,000 S.F.	11.30	8.60	19.90
5300	Solar reflective, under 1,000 S.F.	16.85	14.95	31.80
5400	1,000 to 5,000 S.F.	17	12.50	29.50
5600	Over 5,000 S.F.	15.80	11.40	27.20
5800	3" thinline, 6"x6" plain, under 1,000 S.F.	12	16.15	28.15
5900	Over 5,000 S.F.	12	16.15	28.15
6000	Solar reflective, under 1,000 S.F.	16.75	22	38.75
6100	Over 5,000 S.F.	14.65	17.75	32.40
6200	8"x8" plain, under 1,000 S.F.	6.80	12.05	18.85
6300	Over 5,000 S.F.	6.55	9.40	15.95
6400	Solar reflective, under 1,000 S.F.	9.50	16.25	25.75
6500	Over 5,000 S.F.	9.15	12.50	21.65

EXTERIOR CLOSURE

4

The table below lists costs for metal siding of various descriptions, not including the steel frame, or the structural steel, of a building. Costs are per S.F. including all accessories and insulation.

Metal Siding

4.1-384	Metal Siding Panel	COST PER S.F.		
		MAT.	INST.	TOTAL
1400	Metal siding aluminum panel, corrugated, .024" thick, natural	1.52	2.64	4.16
1450	Painted	1.74	2.64	4.38
1500	.032" thick, natural	1.91	2.64	4.55
1550	Painted	2.29	2.64	4.93
1600	Ribbed 4" pitch, .032" thick, natural	1.97	2.64	4.61
1650	Painted	2.30	2.64	4.94
1700	.040" thick, natural	2.29	2.64	4.93
1750	Painted	2.63	2.64	5.27
1800	.050" thick, natural	2.61	2.64	5.25
1850	Painted	2.92	2.64	5.56
1900	8" pitch panel, .032" thick, natural	1.88	2.53	4.41
1950	Painted	2.20	2.55	4.75
2000	.040" thick, natural	2.20	2.55	4.75
2050	Painted	2.52	2.57	5.09
2100	.050" thick, natural	2.52	2.56	5.08
2150	Painted	2.84	2.58	5.42
3000	Steel, corrugated or ribbed, 29 Ga. .0135" thick, galvanized	1.29	2.35	3.64
3050	Colored	1.70	2.39	4.09
3100	26 Ga. .0179" thick, galvanized	1.33	2.36	3.69
3150	Colored	1.65	2.40	4.05
3200	24 Ga. .0239" thick, galvanized	1.41	2.37	3.78
3250	Colored	1.84	2.41	4.25
3300	22 Ga. .0299" thick, galvanized	1.61	2.38	3.99
3350	Colored	2.04	2.42	4.46
3400	20 Ga. .0359" thick, galvanized	1.61	2.38	3.99
3450	Colored	2.16	2.56	4.72
4100	Sandwich panels, factory fab., 1" polystyrene, steel core, 26 Ga., galv.	2.84	3.69	6.53
4200	Colored, 1 side	3.97	3.69	7.66
4300	2 sides	5.10	3.69	8.79
4400	2" polystyrene, steel core, 26 Ga., galvanized	3.43	3.69	7.12
4500	Colored, 1 side	4.56	3.69	8.25
4600	2 sides	5.70	3.69	9.39
4700	22 Ga., baked enamel exterior	7.55	3.89	11.44
4800	Polyvinyl chloride exterior	7.95	3.89	11.84
5100	Textured aluminum, 4' x 8' x 5/16" plywood backing, single face	2.40	2.21	4.61
5200	Double face	3.62	2.21	5.83

EXTERIOR CLOSURE 4

The table below lists costs per S.F. for exterior walls with wood siding. A variety of systems are presented using both wood and metal studs at 16″ and 24″ O.C.

Exterior Wall Siding

4.1-412	Wood & Other Siding	COST PER S.F.		
		MAT.	INST.	TOTAL
1400	Wood siding w/2″x4″studs, 16″O.C., insul. wall, 5/8″text 1-11 fir plywood	2.51	3.72	6.23
1450	5/8″ text 1-11 cedar plywood	3.24	3.59	6.83
1500	1″ x 4″ vert T.&G. redwood	4.49	5.05	9.54
1600	1″ x 8″ vert T.&G. redwood	4.08	4.59	8.67
1650	1″ x 5″ rabbetted cedar bev. siding	3.38	4.10	7.48
1700	1″ x 6″ cedar drop siding	3.42	4.13	7.55
1750	1″ x 12″ rough sawn cedar	2.79	3.75	6.54
1800	1″ x 12″ sawn cedar, 1″ x 4″ battens	3.78	4.04	7.82
1850	1″ x 10″ redwood shiplap siding	4.01	3.92	7.93
1900	18″ no. 1 red cedar shingles, 5-1/2″ exposed	3.37	4.91	8.28
1950	6″ exposed	3.24	4.75	7.99
2000	6-1/2″ exposed	3.11	4.58	7.69
2100	7″ exposed	2.98	4.42	7.40
2150	7-1/2″ exposed	2.85	4.26	7.11
3000	8″ wide aluminum siding	2.77	3.31	6.08
3150	8″ plain vinyl siding	2.18	3.32	5.50
3250	8″ insulated vinyl siding	2.26	3.32	5.58
3300				
3400	2″ x 6″ studs, 16″ O.C., insul. wall, w/ 5/8″ text 1-11 fir plywood	2.82	3.86	6.68
3500	5/8″ text 1-11 cedar plywood	3.55	3.86	7.41
3600	1″ x 4″ vert T.&G. redwood	4.80	5.20	10
3700	1″ x 8″ vert T.&G. redwood	4.39	4.73	9.12
3800	1″ x 5″ rabbetted cedar bev siding	3.69	4.24	7.93
3900	1″ x 6″ cedar drop siding	3.73	4.27	8
4000	1″ x 12″ rough sawn cedar	3.10	3.89	6.99
4200	1″ x 12″ sawn cedar, 1″ x 4″ battens	4.09	4.18	8.27
4500	1″ x 10″ redwood shiplap siding	4.32	4.06	8.38
4550	18″ no. 1 red cedar shingles, 5-1/2″ exposed	3.68	5.05	8.73
4600	6″ exposed	3.55	4.89	8.44
4650	6-1/2″ exposed	3.42	4.72	8.14
4700	7″ exposed	3.29	4.56	7.85
4750	7-1/2″ exposed	3.16	4.40	7.56
4800	8″ wide aluminum siding	3.08	3.45	6.53
4850	8″ plain vinyl siding	2.49	3.46	5.95
4900	8″ insulated vinyl siding	2.57	3.46	6.03
4910				
5000	2″ x 6″ studs, 24″ O.C., insul. wall, 5/8″ text 1-11, fir plywood	2.66	3.64	6.30
5050	5/8″ text 1-11 cedar plywood	3.39	3.64	7.03
5100	1″ x 4″ vert T.&G. redwood	4.64	4.99	9.63
5150	1″ x 8″ vert T.&G. redwood	4.23	4.51	8.74
5200	1″ x 5″ rabbetted cedar bev siding	3.53	4.02	7.55
5250	1″ x 6″ cedar drop siding	3.57	4.05	7.62

EXTERIOR CLOSURE

4

4.1-412	Wood & Other Siding	COST PER S.F.		
		MAT.	INST.	TOTAL
5300	1" x 12" rough sawn cedar	2.94	3.67	6.61
5400	1" x 12" sawn cedar, 1" x 4" battens	3.93	3.96	7.89
5450	1" x 10" redwood shiplap siding	4.16	3.84	8
5500	18" no. 1 red cedar shingles, 5-1/2" exposed	3.52	4.83	8.35
5550	6" exposed	3.39	4.67	8.06
5650	7" exposed	3.13	4.34	7.47
5700	7-1/2" exposed	3	4.18	7.18
5750	8" wide aluminum siding	2.92	3.23	6.15
5800	8" plain vinyl siding	2.33	3.24	5.57
5850	8" insulated vinyl siding	2.41	3.24	5.65
5900	3-5/8" metal studs, 16 Ga., 16" OC insul.wall, 5/8"text 1-11 fir plywood	2.69	3.92	6.61
5950	5/8" text 1-11 cedar plywood	3.42	3.92	7.34
6000	1" x 4" vert T.&G. redwood	4.67	5.25	9.92
6050	1" x 8" vert T.&G. redwood	4.26	4.79	9.05
6100	1" x 5" rabbetted cedar bev siding	3.56	4.30	7.86
6150	1" x 6" cedar drop siding	3.60	4.33	7.93
6200	1" x 12" rough sawn cedar	2.97	3.95	6.92
6250	1" x 12" sawn cedar, 1" x 4" battens	3.96	4.24	8.20
6300	1" x 10" redwood shiplap siding	4.19	4.12	8.31
6350	18" no. 1 red cedar shingles, 5-1/2" exposed	3.55	5.10	8.65
6500	6" exposed	3.42	4.95	8.37
6550	6-1/2" exposed	3.29	4.78	8.07
6600	7" exposed	3.16	4.62	7.78
6650	7-1/2" exposed	3.16	4.49	7.65
6700	8" wide aluminum siding	2.95	3.51	6.46
6750	8" plain vinyl siding	2.36	3.39	5.75
6800	8" insulated vinyl siding	2.44	3.39	5.83
7000	3-5/8" metal studs, 16 Ga. 24" OC insul wall, 5/8" text 1-11 fir plywood	2.50	3.48	5.98
7050	5/8" text 1-11 cedar plywood	3.23	3.48	6.71
7100	1" x 4" vert T.&G. redwood	4.48	4.96	9.44
7150	1" x 8" vert T.&G. redwood	4.07	4.48	8.55
7200	1" x 5" rabbetted cedar bev siding	3.37	3.99	7.36
7250	1" x 6" cedar drop siding	3.40	4.02	7.42
7300	1" x 12" rough sawn cedar	2.78	3.64	6.42
7350	1" x 12" sawn cedar 1" x 4" battens	3.77	3.93	7.70
7400	1" x 10" redwood shiplap siding	4	3.81	7.81
7450	18" no. 1 red cedar shingles, 5-1/2" exposed	3.49	4.96	8.45
7500	6" exposed	3.36	4.80	8.16
7550	6-1/2" exposed	3.23	4.64	7.87
7600	7" exposed	3.10	4.47	7.57
7650	7-1/2" exposed	2.84	4.15	6.99
7700	8" wide aluminum siding	2.76	3.20	5.96
7750	8" plain vinyl siding	2.17	3.21	5.38
7800	8" insul. vinyl siding	2.25	3.21	5.46

Important: See the Reference Section for critical supporting data - Location Factors & Historical Cost Indexes

The table below lists costs for some typical stucco walls including all the components as demonstrated in the component block below. Prices are presented for backup walls using wood studs, metal studs and CMU.

Exterior Stucco Wall

4.5-110	Stucco Wall	COST PER S.F.		
		MAT.	INST.	TOTAL
2100	Cement stucco, 7/8" th., plywood sheathing, stud wall, 2" x 4", 16" O.C.	2.19	6.05	8.24
2200	24" O.C.	2.08	5.90	7.98
2300	2" x 6", 16" O.C.	2.50	6.20	8.70
2400	24" O.C.	2.34	6	8.34
2500	No sheathing, metal lath on stud wall, 2" x 4", 16" O.C.	1.49	5.25	6.74
2600	24" O.C.	1.38	5.10	6.48
2700	2" x 6", 16" O.C.	1.80	5.40	7.20
2800	24" O.C.	1.64	5.20	6.84
2900	1/2" gypsum sheathing, 3-5/8" metal studs, 16" O.C.	1.80	5.50	7.30
2950	24" O.C.	1.61	5.15	6.76
3000	Cement stucco, 5/8" th., 2 coats on std. CMU block, 8"x 16", 8" thick	1.98	7.50	9.48
3100	10" Thick	2.67	7.70	10.37
3200	12" Thick	2.74	8.85	11.59
3300	Std. light Wt. block 8" x 16", 8" Thick	2.34	7.35	9.69
3400	10" Thick	2.95	7.50	10.45
3500	12" Thick	3.47	8.60	12.07
3600	3 coat stucco, self furring metal lath 3.4 Lb/SY, on 8" x 16", 8" thick	2.02	7.90	9.92
3700	10" Thick	2.71	8.10	10.81
3800	12" Thick	2.78	9.25	12.03
3900	Lt. Wt. block, 8" Thick	2.38	7.75	10.13
4000	10" Thick	2.99	7.90	10.89
4100	12" Thick	3.51	9	12.51

4.5-110	E.I.F.S.	COST PER S.F.		
		MAT.	INST.	TOTAL
5100	E.I.F.S., plywood sheathing, stud wall, 2" x 4", 16" O.C., 1" EPS	3.45	7.40	10.85
5110	2" EPS	3.69	7.40	11.09
5120	3" EPS	3.86	7.40	11.26
5130	4" EPS	4.08	7.40	11.48
5140	2" x 6", 16" O.C., 1" EPS	3.76	7.50	11.26
5150	2" EPS	4	7.50	11.50
5160	3" EPS	4.17	7.50	11.67
5170	4" EPS	4.39	7.50	11.89
5180	Cement board sheathing, 3-5/8" metal studs, 16" O.C., 1" EPS	4.09	8.80	12.89
5190	2" EPS	4.33	8.80	13.13
5200	3" EPS	4.50	8.80	13.30
5210	4" EPS	5.85	8.80	14.65
5220	6" metal studs, 16" O.C., 1" EPS	4.39	8.85	13.24
5230	2" EPS	4.63	8.85	13.48
5240	3" EPS	4.80	8.85	13.65
5250	4" EPS	6.15	8.85	15

EXTERIOR CLOSURE

4

4.5-110	E.I.F.S.		COST PER S.F.		
			MAT.	INST.	TOTAL
5260	CMU block, 8″ x 8″ x 16″, 1″ EPS		3.50	10.10	13.60
5270	2″ EPS		3.74	10.10	13.84
5280	3″ EPS		3.91	10.10	14.01
5290	4″ EPS		4.13	10.10	14.23
5300	8″ x 10″ x 16″, 1″ EPS		4.19	10.30	14.49
5310	2″ EPS		4.43	10.30	14.73
5320	3″ EPS		4.60	10.30	14.90
5330	4″ EPS		4.82	10.30	15.12
5340	8″ x 12″ x 16″, 1″ EPS		4.26	11.45	15.71
5350	2″ EPS		4.50	11.45	15.95
5360	3″ EPS		4.67	11.45	16.12
5370	4″ EPS		4.89	11.45	16.34

EXTERIOR CLOSURE 4

Important: See the Reference Section for critical supporting data - Location Factors & Historical Cost Indexes

Exterior Door System

The table below lists exterior door systems by material, type and size. Prices between sizes listed can be interpolated with reasonable accuracy. Prices are per opening for a complete door system including frame and required hardware.

Wood doors in this table are designed with wood frames and metal doors with hollow metal frames. Depending upon quality the total material and installation cost of a wood door frame is about the same as a hollow metal frame.

4.6-100 — Wood, Steel & Aluminum

	MATERIAL	TYPE	DOORS	SPECIFICATION	OPENING	MAT.	INST.	TOTAL
2350	Birch	solid core	single door	hinged	2'-6" x 6'-8"	855	198	1,053
2400					2'-6" x 7'-0"	860	199	1,059
2450					2'-8" x 7'-0"	865	199	1,064
2500					3'-0" x 7'-0"	875	203	1,078
2550			double door	hinged	2'-6" x 6'-8"	1,600	360	1,960
2600					2'-6" x 7'-0"	1,600	365	1,965
2650					2'-8" x 7'-0"	1,600	365	1,965
2700					3'-0" x 7'-0"	1,625	370	1,995
2750	Wood	combination	storm & screen	hinged	3'-0" x 6'-8"	272	48.50	320.50
2800					3'-0" x 7'-0"	299	53.50	352.50
2850		overhead	panels, H.D.	manual oper.	8'-0" x 8'-0"	510	365	875
2900					10'-0" x 10'-0"	765	405	1,170
2950					12'-0" x 12'-0"	1,100	485	1,585
3000					14'-0" x 14'-0"	1,700	560	2,260
3050					20'-0" x 16'-0"	3,500	1,125	4,625
3100				electric oper.	8'-0" x 8'-0"	1,025	545	1,570
3150					10'-0" x 10'-0"	1,275	585	1,860
3200					12'-0" x 12'-0"	1,625	665	2,290
3250					14'-0" x 14'-0"	2,225	740	2,965
3300					20'-0" x 16'-0"	4,200	1,500	5,700
3350	Steel 18 Ga.	hollow metal	1 door w/frame	no label	2'-6" x 7'-0"	845	206	1,051
3400					2'-8" x 7'-0"	845	206	1,051
3450					3'-0" x 7'-0"	845	206	1,051
3500					3'-6" x 7'-0"	915	216	1,131
3550	Steel 18 Ga.	hollow metal	1 door w/frame	no label	4'-0" x 8'-0"	1,025	217	1,242
3600			2 doors w/frame	no label	5'-0" x 7'-0"	1,650	380	2,030
3650					5'-4" x 7'-0"	1,650	380	2,030
3700					6'-0" x 7'-0"	1,650	380	2,030
3750					7'-0" x 7'-0"	1,775	405	2,180
3800					8'-0" x 8'-0"	2,000	405	2,405
3850			1 door w/frame	"A" label	2'-6" x 7'-0"	1,000	248	1,248
3900					2'-8" x 7'-0"	1,000	251	1,251
3950					3'-0" x 7'-0"	1,000	251	1,251
4000					3'-6" x 7'-0"	1,075	256	1,331
4050					4'-0" x 8'-0"	1,125	269	1,394
4100			2 doors w/frame	"A" label	5'-0" x 7'-0"	1,950	460	2,410
4150					5'-4" x 7'-0"	1,950	465	2,415
4200					6'-0" x 7'-0"	1,950	465	2,415

COST PER OPNG.

EXTERIOR CLOSURE

4

	MATERIAL	TYPE	DOORS	SPECIFICATION	OPENING	COST PER OPNG.		
						MAT.	INST.	TOTAL
4250	Steel 18 Ga.				7'-0" x 7'-0"	2,100	475	2,575
4300					8'-0" x 8'-0"	2,100	475	2,575
4350	Steel 24 Ga.	overhead	sectional	manual oper.	8'-0" x 8'-0"	415	365	780
4400					10'-0" x 10'-0"	570	405	975
4450					12'-0" x 12'-0"	770	485	1,255
4500					20'-0" x 14'-0"	1,800	1,050	2,850
4550				electric oper.	8'-0" x 8'-0"	935	545	1,480
4600					10'-0" x 10'-0"	1,100	585	1,685
4650					12'-0" x 12'-0"	1,300	665	1,965
4700					20'-0" x 14'-0"	2,500	1,425	3,925
4750	Steel	overhead	rolling	manual oper.	8'-0" x 8'-0"	765	595	1,360
4800					10'-0" x 10'-0"	1,000	680	1,680
4850					12'-0" x 12'-0"	1,325	795	2,120
4900					14'-0" x 14'-0"	1,750	1,200	2,950
4950					20'-0" x 12'-0"	2,125	1,050	3,175
5000					20'-0" x 16'-0"	2,475	1,600	4,075
5050				electric oper.	8'-0" x 8'-0"	1,500	785	2,285
5100					10'-0" x 10'-0"	1,750	870	2,620
5150					12'-0" x 12'-0"	2,075	985	3,060
5200					14'-0" x 14'-0"	2,500	1,400	3,900
5250					20'-0" x 12'-0"	2,825	1,250	4,075
5300					20'-0" x 16'-0"	3,175	1,800	4,975
5350				fire rated	10'-0" x 10'-0"	1,325	865	2,190
5400			rolling grill	manual oper.	10'-0" x 10'-0"	1,675	955	2,630
5450					15'-0" x 8'-0"	1,975	1,200	3,175
5500		vertical lift	1 door w/frame	motor operator	16'-0" x 16'-0"	16,900	3,850	20,750
5550					32'-0" x 24'-0"	33,100	2,575	35,675
5600	St. Stl. & glass	revolving	stock unit	manual oper.	6'-0" x 7'-0"	29,600	6,350	35,950
5650				auto Cntrls.	6'-10" x 7'-0"	41,500	6,750	48,250
5700	Bronze	revolving	stock unit	manual oper.	6'-10" x 7'-0"	34,600	12,700	47,300
5750				auto Cntrls.	6'-10" x 7'-0"	46,500	13,100	59,600
5800	St. Stl. & glass	balanced	standard	economy	3'-0" x 7'-0"	6,675	1,050	7,725
5850				premium	3'-0" x 7'-0"	11,600	1,375	12,975
6000	Aluminum	combination	storm & screen	hinged	3'-0" x 6'-8"	225	52	277
6050					3'-0" x 7'-0"	248	57	305
6100		overhead	rolling grill	manual oper.	12'-0" x 12'-0"	2,700	1,675	4,375
6150				motor oper.	12'-0" x 12'-0"	3,550	1,875	5,425
6200	Alum. & Fbrgls.	overhead	heavy duty	manual oper.	12'-0" x 12'-0"	1,425	485	1,910
6250				electric oper.	12'-0" x 12'-0"	1,950	665	2,615
6300	Alum. & glass	w/o transom	narrow stile	w/panic Hrdwre.	3'-0" x 7'-0"	1,025	690	1,715
6350				dbl. door, Hrdwre.	6'-0" x 7'-0"	1,875	1,150	3,025
6400			wide stile	hdwre.	3'-0" x 7'-0"	1,350	675	2,025
6450				dbl. door, Hdwre.	6'-0" x 7'-0"	2,650	1,350	4,000
6500			full vision	hdwre.	3'-0" x 7'-0"	1,525	1,075	2,600
6550				dbl. door, Hdwre.	6'-0" x 7'-0"	2,250	1,550	3,800
6600			non-standard	hdwre.	3'-0" x 7'-0"	955	675	1,630
6650				dbl. door, Hdwre.	6'-0" x 7'-0"	1,900	1,350	3,250
6700			bronze fin.	hdwre.	3'-0" x 7'-0"	1,025	675	1,700
6750				dbl. door, Hrdwre.	6'-0" x 7'-0"	2,025	1,350	3,375
6800			black fin.	hdwre.	3'-0" x 7'-0"	1,675	675	2,350
6850				dbl. door, Hdwre.	6'-0" x 7'-0"	3,350	1,350	4,700
6900		w/transom	narrow stile	hdwre.	3'-0" x 10'-0"	1,350	785	2,135
6950				dbl. door, Hdwre.	6'-0" x 10'-0"	1,900	1,375	3,275
7000			wide stile	hdwre.	3'-0" x 10'-0"	1,550	940	2,490

Important: See the Reference Section for critical supporting data - Location Factors & Historical Cost Indexes

	MATERIAL	TYPE	DOORS	SPECIFICATION	OPENING	COST PER OPNG.		
						MAT.	INST.	TOTAL
7050	Alum. & glass			dbl. door, Hdwre.	6'-0" x 10'-0"	2,050	1,625	3,675
7100			full vision	hdwre.	3'-0" x 10'-0"	1,725	1,050	2,775
7150				dbl. door, Hdwre.	6'-0" x 10'-0"	2,200	1,800	4,000
7200			non-standard	hdwre.	3'-0" x 10'-0"	1,000	730	1,730
7250				dbl. door, Hdwre.	6'-0" x 10'-0"	2,025	1,450	3,475
7300			bronze fin.	hdwre.	3'-0" x 10'-0"	1,075	730	1,805
7350				dbl. door, Hdwre.	6'-0" x 10'-0"	2,150	1,450	3,600
7400			black fin.	hdwre.	3'-0" x 10'-0"	1,725	730	2,455
7450				dbl. door, Hdwre.	6'-0" x 10'-0"	3,450	1,450	4,900
7500		revolving	stock design	minimum	6'-10" x 7'-0"	16,300	2,550	18,850
7550				average	6'-0" x 7'-0"	20,100	3,175	23,275
7600				maximum	6'-10" x 7'-0"	26,500	4,250	30,750
7650				min., automatic	6'-10" x 7'-0"	28,200	2,950	31,150
7700				avg., automatic	6'-10" x 7'-0"	32,000	3,575	35,575
7750				max., automatic	6'-10" x 7'-0"	38,400	4,650	43,050
7800		balanced	standard	economy	3'-0" x 7'-0"	5,100	1,050	6,150
7850				premium	3'-0" x 7'-0"	6,350	1,350	7,700
7900		mall front	sliding panels	alum. fin.	16'-0" x 9'-0"	2,475	535	3,010
7950					24'-0" x 9'-0"	3,600	990	4,590
8000				bronze fin.	16'-0" x 9'-0"	2,875	625	3,500
8050					24'-0" x 9'-0"	4,200	1,150	5,350
8100			fixed panels	alum. fin.	48'-0" x 9'-0"	6,675	770	7,445
8150				bronze fin.	48'-0" x 9'-0"	7,775	895	8,670
8200		sliding entrance	5' x 7' door	electric oper.	12'-0" x 7'-6"	6,300	990	7,290
8250		sliding patio	temp. glass	economy	6'-0" x 7'-0"	835	182	1,017
8300			temp. glass	economy	12'-0" x 7'-0"	2,100	243	2,343
8350				premium	6'-0" x 7'-0"	1,250	273	1,523
8400					12'-0" x 7'-0"	3,150	365	3,515

EXTERIOR CLOSURE

4

The table below lists window systems by material, type and size. Prices between sizes listed can be interpolated with reasonable accuracy. Prices include frame, hardware, and casing as illustrated in the component block below.

4.7-110 — Wood, Steel & Aluminum

	MATERIAL	TYPE	GLAZING	SIZE	DETAIL	MAT.	INST.	TOTAL
3000	Wood	double hung	std. glass	2'-8" x 4'-6"		173	159	332
3050				3'-0" x 5'-6"		228	183	411
3100			insul. glass	2'-8" x 4'-6"		185	159	344
3150				3'-0" x 5'-6"		245	183	428
3200		sliding	std. glass	3'-4" x 2'-7"		208	132	340
3250				4'-4" x 3'-3"		238	146	384
3300				5'-4" x 6'-0"		300	175	475
3350			insul. glass	3'-4" x 2'-7"		254	155	409
3400				4'-4" x 3'-3"		290	169	459
3450				5'-4" x 6'-0"		365	200	565
3500		awning	std. glass	2'-10" x 1'-9"		156	80	236
3600				4'-4" x 2'-8"		256	77.50	333.50
3700			insul. glass	2'-10" x 1'-9"		190	92	282
3800				4'-4" x 2'-8"		310	85	395
3900		casement	std. glass	1'-10" x 3'-2"	1 lite	199	105	304
3950				4'-2" x 4'-2"	2 lite	405	139	544
4000				5'-11" x 5'-2"	3 lite	630	179	809
4050				7'-11" x 6'-3"	4 lite	885	216	1,101
4100				9'-11" x 6'-3"	5 lite	1,150	251	1,401
4150			insul. glass	1'-10" x 3'-2"	1 lite	209	105	314
4200				4'-2" x 4'-2"	2 lite	430	139	569
4250				5'-11" x 5'-2"	3 lite	665	179	844
4300				7'-11" x 6'-3"	4 lite	940	216	1,156
4350				9'-11" x 6'-3"	5 lite	1,225	251	1,476
4400		picture	std. glass	4'-6" x 4'-6"		330	180	510
4450				5'-8" x 4'-6"		375	200	575
4500	Wood	picture	insul. glass	4'-6" x 4'-6"		400	209	609
4550				5'-8" x 4'-6"		455	232	687
4600		fixed bay	std. glass	8' x 5'		1,150	330	1,480
4650				9'-9" x 5'-4"		815	465	1,280
4700			insul. glass	8' x 5'		1,775	330	2,105
4750				9'-9" x 5'-4"		885	465	1,350
4800		casement bay	std. glass	8' x 5'		1,150	380	1,530
4850			insul. glass	8' x 5'		1,300	380	1,680
4900		vert. bay	std. glass	8' x 5'		1,300	380	1,680
4950			insul. glass	8' x 5'		1,350	380	1,730
5000	Steel	double hung	1/4" tempered	2'-8" x 4'-6"		585	126	711
5050				3'-4" x 5'-6"		895	193	1,088

Important: See the Reference Section for critical supporting data - Location Factors & Historical Cost Indexes

	MATERIAL	TYPE	GLAZING	SIZE	DETAIL	COST PER UNIT		
						MAT.	INST.	TOTAL
5100			insul. glass	2'-8" x 4'-6"		600	145	745
5150				3'-4" x 5'-6"		915	221	1,136
5202	Steel	horiz. pivoted	std. glass	2' x 2'		194	42	236
5250				3' x 3'		435	94.50	529.50
5300				4' x 4'		775	168	943
5350				6' x 4'		1,175	252	1,427
5400			insul. glass	2' x 2'		198	48.50	246.50
5450				3' x 3'		445	109	554
5500				4' x 4'		790	193	983
5550				6' x 4'		1,175	290	1,465
5600		picture window	std. glass	3' x 3'		261	94.50	355.50
5650				6' x 4'		695	252	947
5700			insul. glass	3' x 3'		269	109	378
5750				6' x 4'		720	290	1,010
5800		industrial security	std. glass	2'-9" x 4'-1"		560	118	678
5850				4'-1" x 5'-5"		1,100	233	1,333
5900			insul. glass	2'-9" x 4'-1"		570	135	705
5950				4'-1" x 5'-5"		1,125	267	1,392
6000		comm. projected	std. glass	3'-9" x 5'-5"		925	214	1,139
6050				6'-9" x 4'-1"		1,250	290	1,540
6100			insul. glass	3'-9" x 5'-5"		945	245	1,190
6150				6'-9" x 4'-1"		1,275	330	1,605
6200		casement	std. glass	4'-2" x 4'-2"	2 lite	665	183	848
6250			insul. glass	4'-2" x 4'-2"		685	209	894
6300			std. glass	5'-11" x 5'-2"	3 lite	1,350	320	1,670
6350			insul. glass	5'-11" x 5'-2"		1,375	370	1,745
6400	Aluminum	projecting	std. glass	3'-1" x 3'-2"		207	95.50	302.50
6450				4'-5" x 5'-3"		291	119	410
6500			insul. glass	3'-1" x 3'-2"		248	115	363
6550				4'-5" x 5'-3"		350	143	493
6600		sliding	std. glass	3' x 2'		156	95.50	251.50
6650				5' x 3'		198	106	304
6700				8' x 4'		286	159	445
6750				9' x 5'		430	238	668
6800			insul. glass	3' x 2'		173	95.50	268.50
6850				5' x 3'		278	106	384
6900				8' x 4'		460	159	619
6950				9' x 5'		690	238	928
7000		single hung	std. glass	2' x 3'		139	95.50	234.50
7050				2'-8" x 6'-8"		295	119	414
7100				3'-4" x 5'0"		190	106	296
7150			insul. glass	2' x 3'		168	95.50	263.50
7200				2'-8" x 6'-8"		380	119	499
7250				3'-4" x 5'		267	106	373
7300		double hung	std. glass	2' x 3'		207	63	270
7350				2'-8" x 6'-8"		615	187	802
7400				3'-4" x 5'		575	175	750
7450			insul. glass	2' x 3'		212	72.50	284.50
7500				2'-8" x 6'-8"		630	215	845
7550				3'-4" x 5'-0"		590	201	791
7600		casements	std. glass	3'-1" x 3'-2"		164	103	267
7650				4'-5" x 5'-3"		395	248	643
7700			insul. glass	3'-1" x 3'-2"		173	118	291
7750				4'-5" x 5'-3"		420	285	705

EXTERIOR CLOSURE

4

	MATERIAL	TYPE	GLAZING	SIZE	DETAIL	COST PER UNIT		
						MAT.	INST.	TOTAL
7800		hinged swing	std. glass	3' x 4'		370	126	496
7850				4' x 5'		620	210	830
7900			insul. glass	3' x 4'		385	145	530
7950				4' x 5'		640	241	881
8002	Aluminum	folding type	std. glass	3'-0" x 4'-0"		209	103	312
8050				4'-0" x 5'-0"		292	103	395
8100			insul. glass	3'-0" x 4'-0"		262	103	365
8150				4'-0" x 5'-0"		380	103	483
8200		picture unit	std. glass	2'-0" x 3'-0"		111	63	174
8250				2'-8" x 6'-8"		330	187	517
8300				3'-4" x 5'-0"		305	175	480
8350			insul. glass	2'-0" x 3'-0"		116	72.50	188.50
8400				2'-8" x 6'-8"		345	215	560
8450				3'-4" x 5'-0"		325	201	526
8500		awning type	std. glass	3'-0" x 3'-0"	2 lite	340	68	408
8550				3'-0" x 4'-0"	3 lite	400	95.50	495.50
8600				3'-0" x 5'-4"	4 lite	480	95.50	575.50
8650				4'-0" x 5'-4"	4 lite	530	106	636
8700			insul. glass	3'-0" x 3'-0"	2 lite	365	68	433
8750				3'-0" x 4'-0"	3 lite	460	95.50	555.50
8800				3'-0" x 5'-4"	4 lite	565	95.50	660.50
8850				4'-0" x 5'-4"	4 lite	635	106	741
8900		jalousie type	std. glass	1'-7" x 3'-2"		127	95.50	222.50
8950				2'-3" x 4'-0"		181	95.50	276.50
9000				3'-1" x 2'-0"		143	95.50	238.50
9050				3'-1" x 5'-3"		259	95.50	354.50
9051								
9052								

4.7-582 Tubular Aluminum Framing

		COST/S.F. OPNG.		
		MAT.	INST.	TOTAL
1100	Alum flush tube frame, for 1/4"glass, 1-3/4"x4", 5'x6'opng, no inter horizntls	8.90	8.50	17.40
1150	One intermediate horizontal	12.15	10	22.15
1200	Two intermediate horizontals	15.40	11.45	26.85
1250	5' x 20' opening, three intermediate horizontals	8	7.05	15.05
1400	1-3/4" x 4-1/2", 5' x 6' opening, no intermediate horizontals	10.10	8.50	18.60
1450	One intermediate horizontal	13.50	10	23.50
1500	Two intermediate horizontals	16.90	11.45	28.35
1550	5' x 20' opening, three intermediate horizontals	9	7.05	16.05
1700	For insulating glass, 2"x4-1/2", 5'x6' opening, no intermediate horizontals	11.35	8.95	20.30
1750	One intermediate horizontal	14.90	10.50	25.40
1800	Two intermediate horizontals	18.40	12.05	30.45
1850	5' x 20' opening, three intermediate horizontals	9.95	7.45	17.40
2000	Thermal break frame, 2-1/4"x4-1/2", 5'x6'opng, no intermediate horizontals	12.20	9.05	21.25
2050	One intermediate horizontal	16.40	10.90	27.30
2100	Two intermediate horizontals	20.50	12.75	33.25
2150	5' x 20' opening, three intermediate horizontals	11.15	7.75	18.90

Important: See the Reference Section for critical supporting data - Location Factors & Historical Cost Indexes

The table below lists costs of curtain wall and spandrel panels per S.F. Costs do not include structural framing used to hang the panels.

Glazing Panel   Plate Glass

Spandrel Glass   Polycarbonate   Sandwich Panel

4.7-584	Curtain Wall Panels	COST PER S.F.		
		MAT.	INST.	TOTAL
1000	Glazing panel, insulating, 1/2" thick, 2 lites 1/8" float, clear	6.90	7.30	14.20
1100	Tinted	10.25	7.30	17.55
1200	5/8" thick units, 2 lites 3/16" float, clear	8.30	7.70	16
1300	Tinted	8.55	7.70	16.25
1400	1" thick units, 2 lites, 1/4" float, clear	11.80	9.25	21.05
1500	Tinted	14.25	9.25	23.50
1600	Heat reflective film inside	16.65	8.15	24.80
1700	Light and heat reflective glass, tinted	19	8.15	27.15
2000	Plate glass, 1/4" thick, clear	5	5.75	10.75
2050	Tempered	5.95	5.75	11.70
2100	Tinted	4.75	5.75	10.50
2200	3/8" thick, clear	7.90	9.25	17.15
2250	Tempered	11.90	9.25	21.15
2300	Tinted	9.50	9.25	18.75
2400	1/2" thick, clear	15.50	12.60	28.10
2450	Tempered	17.80	12.60	30.40
2500	Tinted	16.65	12.60	29.25
2600	3/4" thick, clear	21.50	19.80	41.30
2650	Tempered	25	19.80	44.80
3000	Spandrel glass, panels, 1/4" plate glass insul w/fiberglass, 1" thick	10.15	5.75	15.90
3100	2" thick	11.85	5.75	17.60
3200	Galvanized steel backing, add	3.51		3.51
3300	3/8" plate glass, 1" thick	17	5.75	22.75
3400	2" thick	18.70	5.75	24.45
4000	Polycarbonate, masked, clear or colored, 1/8" thick	5.70	4.08	9.78
4100	3/16" thick	6.90	4.20	11.10
4200	1/4" thick	7.60	4.47	12.07
4300	3/8" thick	14.05	4.62	18.67
5000	Facing panel, textured al, 4' x 8' x 5/16" plywood backing, sgl face	2.40	2.21	4.61
5100	Double face	3.62	2.21	5.83
5200	4' x 10' x 5/16" plywood backing, single face	2.55	2.21	4.76
5300	Double face	3.75	2.21	5.96
5400	4' x 12' x 5/16" plywood backing, single face	3.29	2.21	5.50
5500	Sandwich panel, 22 Ga. galv., both sides 2" insulation, enamel exterior	7.55	3.89	11.44
5600	Polyvinylidene floride exterior finish	7.95	3.89	11.84
5700	26 Ga., galv. both sides, 1" insulation, colored 1 side	3.97	3.69	7.66
5800	Colored 2 sides	5.10	3.69	8.79

For information about Means Estimating Seminars, see yellow pages 11 and 12 in back of book

EXTERIOR CLOSURE

4

Division 5
Roofing

Multiple ply roofing is the most popular covering for minimum pitch roofs.

Built Up Ply

5.1-103	Built-Up	COST PER S.F.		
		MAT.	INST.	TOTAL
1200	Asphalt flood coat w/gravel; not incl. insul, flash., nailers			
1300				
1400	Asphalt base sheets & 3 plies #15 asphalt felt, mopped	.45	1.22	1.67
1500	On nailable deck	.49	1.27	1.76
1600	4 plies #15 asphalt felt, mopped	.63	1.34	1.97
1700	On nailable deck	.57	1.41	1.98
1800	Coated glass base sheet, 2 plies glass (type IV), mopped	.50	1.22	1.72
1900	For 3 plies	.59	1.34	1.93
2000	On nailable deck	.55	1.41	1.96
2300	4 plies glass fiber felt (type IV), mopped	.71	1.34	2.05
2400	On nailable deck	.64	1.41	2.05
2500	Organic base sheet & 3 plies #15 organic felt, mopped	.46	1.35	1.81
2600	On nailable deck	.49	1.41	1.90
2700	4 plies #15 organic felt, mopped	.60	1.22	1.82
2750				
2800	Asphalt flood coat, smooth surface			
2900	Asphalt base sheet & 3 plies #15 asphalt felt, mopped	.47	1.12	1.59
3000	On nailable deck	.44	1.17	1.61
3100	Coated glass fiber base sheet & 2 plies glass fiber felt, mopped	.44	1.08	1.52
3200	On nailable deck	.42	1.12	1.54
3300	For 3 plies, mopped	.53	1.17	1.70
3400	On nailable deck	.50	1.22	1.72
3700	4 plies glass fiber felt (type IV), mopped	.62	1.17	1.79
3800	On nailable deck	.59	1.22	1.81
3900	Organic base sheet & 3 plies #15 organic felt, mopped	.47	1.12	1.59
4000	On nailable decks	.43	1.17	1.60
4100	4 plies #15 organic felt, mopped	.54	1.22	1.76
4200	Coal tar pitch with gravel surfacing			
4300	4 plies #15 tarred felt, mopped	1.11	1.27	2.38
4400	3 plies glass fiber felt (type IV), mopped	.91	1.41	2.32
4500	Coated glass fiber base sheets 2 plies glass fiber felt, mopped	.92	1.41	2.33
4600	On nailable decks	.81	1.50	2.31
4800	3 plies glass fiber felt (type IV), mopped	1.25	1.27	2.52
4900	On nailable decks	1.15	1.34	2.49

ROOFING 5

Full Adhered
Single Ply Membrane

Preformed Metal

Flat Seam

Batten Seam

Standing Seam

5.1-220	Single Ply Membrane	COST PER S.F.		
		MAT.	INST.	TOTAL
1000	CSPE (Chlorosulfonated polyethylene), 35 mils, fully adhered	1.36	.70	2.06
2000	EPDM (Ethylene propylene diene monomer), 45 mils, fully adhered	.89	.70	1.59
4000	Modified bit., SBS modified, granule surface cap sheet, mopped, 150 mils	.48	1.34	1.82
4500	APP modified, granule surface cap sheet, torched, 180 mils	.54	.91	1.45
6000	Reinforced PVC, 48 mils, loose laid and ballasted with stone	1.03	.36	1.39
6200	Fully adhered with adhesive	1.28	.70	1.98

5.1-310	Preformed Metal Roofing	COST PER S.F.		
		MAT.	INST.	TOTAL
0200	Corrugated roofing, aluminum, mill finish, .0175" thick, .272 P.S.F.	.68	1.17	1.85
0250	.0215 thick, .334 P.S.F.	.88	1.17	2.05

5.1-330	Formed Metal	COST PER S.F.		
		MAT.	INST.	TOTAL
1000	Batten seam, formed copper roofing, 3"min slope, 16 oz., 1.2 P.S.F.	4.50	3.81	8.31
1100	18 oz., 1.35 P.S.F.	5	4.21	9.21
2000	Zinc copper alloy, 3" min slope, .020" thick, .88 P.S.F.	5.75	3.51	9.26
3000	Flat seam, copper, 1/4" min. slope, 16 oz., 1.2 P.S.F.	4	3.51	7.51
3100	18 oz., 1.35 P.S.F.	4.50	3.66	8.16
5000	Standing seam, copper, 2-1/2" min. slope, 16 oz., 1.25 P.S.F.	4.30	3.26	7.56
5100	18 oz., 1.40 P.S.F.	4.85	3.51	8.36
6000	Zinc copper alloy, 2-1/2" min. slope, .020" thick, .87 P.S.F.	5.65	3.51	9.16
6100	.032" thick, 1.39 P.S.F.	7.70	3.81	11.51

5 ROOFING

ROOFING | A5.1 | Roof Covers

Shingle and Tile

Roof Edges

Shingles and tiles are practical in applications where the roof slope is more than 3-1/2″ per foot of rise. Lines 1100 through 6000 list the various materials and the weight per square foot.

The table below lists the costs for various types of roof perimeter edge treatments.

Roof edge systems include the cost per L.F. for a 2″ x 8″ treated wood nailer fastened at 4′-0″ O.C. and a diagonally cut 4″ x 6″ treated wood cant.

Roof edge and base flashing are assumed to be made from the same material.

5.1-410	Shingle & Tile	COST PER S.F.		
		MAT.	INST.	TOTAL
1095	Asphalt roofing			
1100	Strip shingles,4″ slope,inorganic class A 210-235 lb/Sq.	.32	.74	1.06
1150	Organic, class C, 235-240 lb./sq.	.41	.81	1.22
1200	Premium laminated multi-layered, class A, 260-300 lb./Sq.	.56	1.11	1.67
1545	Metal roofing			
1550	Alum., shingles, colors, 3″min slope, .019″thick, 0.4 PSF	1.87	.79	2.66
1850	Steel, colors, 3″ min slope, 26 gauge, 1.0 PSF	2.18	1.68	3.86
2795	Slate roofing			
2800	4″ min. slope, shingles, 3/16″ thick, 8.0 PSF	6	2.10	8.10
3495	Wood roofing			
3500	4″ min slope, cedar shingles, 16″ x 5″, 5″ exposure 1.6 PSF	1.71	1.57	3.28
4000	Shakes, 18″, 8-1/2″ exposure, 2.8 PSF	1.12	1.93	3.05
5095	Tile roofing			
5100	Aluminum, mission, 3″ min slope, .019″ thick, 0.65 PSF	4.75	1.52	6.27
6000	Clay, Americana, 3″ minimum slope, 8 PSF	5.75	2.22	7.97

5.1-520		Roof Edges				COST PER L.F.		
	EDGE TYPE	DESCRIPTION	SPECIFICATION	FACE HEIGHT		MAT.	INST.	TOTAL
1000	Aluminum	mill finish	.050″ thick	4″		8.10	7.05	15.15
1100				6″		8.75	7.25	16
1300		duranodic	.050″ thick	4″		8.60	7.05	15.65
1400				6″		9.35	7.25	16.60
1600		painted	.050″ thick	4″		9.25	7.05	16.30
1700				6″		10.10	7.25	17.35
2000	Copper	plain	16 oz.	4″		6.20	7.05	13.25
2100				6″		7.05	7.25	14.30
2300			20 oz.	4″		6.75	8	14.75
2400				6″		7.45	7.70	15.15
2700	Sheet Metal	galvanized	20 Ga.	4″		6.90	8.30	15.20
2800				6″		8.15	8.30	16.45
3000			24 Ga.	4″		6.20	7.05	13.25
3100				6″		7.05	7.05	14.10

ROOFING 5

Important: See the Reference Section for critical supporting data - Location Factors & Historical Cost Indexes

5.1-620 — Flashing

	MATERIAL	BACKING	SIDES	SPECIFICATION	QUANTITY	COST PER S.F.		
						MAT.	INST.	TOTAL
0040	Aluminum	none		.019"		.85	2.86	3.71
0050				.032"		1.14	2.86	4
0300		fabric	2	.004"		1.02	1.26	2.28
0400		mastic		.004"		1.02	1.26	2.28
0700	Copper	none		16 oz.	<500 lbs.	2.40	3.60	6
0800				24 oz.	<500 lbs.	5.15	3.95	9.10
2000	Copper lead	fabric	1	2 oz.		1.55	1.26	2.81
3500	PVC black	none		.010"		.15	1.24	1.39
3700				.030"		.32	1.24	1.56
4200	Neoprene			1/16"		1.63	1.24	2.87
4500	Stainless steel	none		.015"	<500 lbs.	3.48	3.60	7.08
4600	Copper clad				>2000 lbs.	3.36	2.67	6.03
5000	Plain			32 ga.		2.38	2.67	5.05

ROOFING

5

5.7-101	Roof Deck Rigid Insulation	COST PER S.F.		
		MAT.	INST.	TOTAL
0100	Fiberboard low density, 1/2" thick, R1.39			
0150	1" thick R2.78	.36	.44	.80
0300	1 1/2" thick R4.17	.54	.44	.98
0350	2" thick R5.56	.73	.44	1.17
0370	Fiberboard high density, 1/2" thick R1.3	.21	.35	.56
0380	1" thick R2.5	.39	.44	.83
0390	1 1/2" thick R3.8	.63	.44	1.07
0410	Fiberglass, 3/4" thick R2.78	.50	.35	.85
0450	15/16" thick R3.70	.65	.35	1
0550	1-5/16" thick R5.26	1.12	.35	1.47
0650	2 7/16" thick R10	1.36	.44	1.80
1510	Polyisocyanurate 2#/CF density, 1" thick R7.14	.34	.25	.59
1550	1 1/2" thick R10.87	.37	.28	.65
1600	2" thick R14.29	.48	.32	.80
1650	2 1/2" thick R16.67	.54	.34	.88
1700	3" thick R21.74	.76	.35	1.11
1750	3 1/2" thick R25	.79	.35	1.14
1800	Tapered for drainage	.41	.25	.66
1810	Expanded polystyrene, 1#/CF density, 3/4" thick R2.89	.20	.24	.44
1820	2" thick R7.69	.37	.28	.65
1830	Extruded polystyrene, 15 PSI compressive strength, 1" thick R5	.24	.24	.48
1835	2" thick R10	.37	.28	.65
1840	3" thick R15	.83	.35	1.18
2550	40 PSI compressive strength, 1" thick R5	.37	.24	.61
2600	2" thick R10	.74	.28	1.02
2650	3" thick R15	1.08	.35	1.43
2700	4" thick R20	1.44	.35	1.79
2750	Tapered for drainage	.54	.25	.79
2810	60 PSI compressive strength, 1" thick R5	.45	.24	.69
2850	2" thick R10	.80	.29	1.09
2900	Tapered for drainage	.65	.25	.90
3050	Composites with 2" EPS			
3060	1" Fiberboard	.84	.37	1.21
3070	7/16" oriented strand board	.99	.44	1.43
3080	1/2" plywood	1.07	.44	1.51
3090	1" perlite	.88	.44	1.32
4000	Composites with 1-1/2" polyisocyanurate			
4010	1" fiberboard	.90	.44	1.34
4020	1" perlite	.94	.42	1.36
4030	7/16" oriented strand board	1.08	.44	1.52

ROOFING 5

Roof Hatch

Smoke Hatch

Skylight

5.8-100	Hatches	COST PER OPNG.		
		MAT.	INST.	TOTAL
0200	Roof hatches, with curb, and 1″ fiberglass insulation, 2′-6″x3′-0″,aluminum	435	140	575
0300	Galvanized steel 165 lbs.	375	140	515
0400	Primed steel 164 lbs.	390	140	530
0500	2′-6″x4′-6″ aluminum curb and cover, 150 lbs.	625	156	781
0600	Galvanized steel 220 lbs.	525	156	681
0650	Primed steel 218 lbs.	610	156	766
0800	2′x6″x8′-0″ aluminum curb and cover, 260 lbs.	1,200	212	1,412
0900	Galvanized steel, 360 lbs.	1,000	212	1,212
0950	Primed steel 358 lbs.	990	212	1,202
1200	For plexiglass panels, add to the above	380		380
2100	Smoke hatches, unlabeled not incl. hand winch operator, 2′-6″x3′, galv	455	169	624
2200	Plain steel, 160 lbs.	470	169	639
2400	2′-6″x8′-0″,galvanized steel, 360 lbs.	1,100	232	1,332
2500	Plain steel, 350 lbs.	1,075	232	1,307
3000	4′-0″x8′-0″, double leaf low profile, aluminum cover, 359 lb.	1,575	175	1,750
3100	Galvanized steel 475 lbs.	1,375	175	1,550
3200	High profile, aluminum cover, galvanized curb, 361 lbs.	1,425	175	1,600

5.8-100	Skylights	COST PER S.F.		
		MAT.	INST.	TOTAL
5100	Skylights, plastic domes, insul curbs, nom. size to 10 S.F., single glaze	13.55	8.75	22.30
5200	Double glazing	20.50	10.80	31.30
5300	10 S.F. to 20 S.F., single glazing	7.85	3.55	11.40
5400	Double glazing	15.75	4.45	20.20
5500	20 S.F. to 30 S.F., single glazing	10	3.01	13.01
5600	Double glazing	14.50	3.55	18.05
5700	30 S.F. to 65 S.F., single glazing	14.45	2.30	16.75
5800	Double glazing	10.65	3.01	13.66
6000	Sandwich panels fiberglass, 9-1/16″thick, 2 S.F. to 10 S.F.	15.35	7	22.35
6100	10 S.F. to 18 S.F.	13.75	5.30	19.05
6200	2-3/4″ thick, 25 S.F. to 40 S.F.	22	4.75	26.75
6300	40 S.F. to 70 S.F.	18.15	4.25	22.40
6301				

ROOFING

5

5.8-400 — Gutters

	SECTION	MATERIAL	THICKNESS	SIZE	FINISH	COST PER L.F.		
						MAT.	INST.	TOTAL
0050	Box	aluminum	.027"	5"	enameled	1.20	3.45	4.65
0100					mill	1.30	3.45	4.75
0200			.032"	5"	enameled	1.36	3.45	4.81
0500		copper	16 Oz.	4"	lead coated	7.80	3.45	11.25
0600					mill	3.81	3.45	7.26
1000		steel galv.	28 Ga.	5"	enameled	1.14	3.45	4.59
1200			26 Ga.	5"	mill	1.05	3.45	4.50
1800		vinyl		4"	colors	.94	3.32	4.26
1900				5"	colors	1.10	3.32	4.42
2300		hemlock or fir		4"x5"	treated	8	3.65	11.65
3000	Half round	copper	16 Oz.	4"	lead coated	5.15	3.45	8.60
3100					mill	3.77	3.45	7.22
3600		steel galv.	28 Ga.	5"	enameled	1.14	3.45	4.59
4102		stainless steel		5"	mill	5.50	3.45	8.95
5000		vinyl		4"	white	.75	3.32	4.07

5.8-500 — Downspouts

	MATERIALS	SECTION	SIZE	FINISH	THICKNESS	COST PER V.L.F.		
						MAT.	INST.	TOTAL
0100	Aluminum	rectangular	2"x3"	embossed mill	.020"	.81	2.18	2.99
0150				enameled	.020"	.99	2.18	3.17
0250			3"x4"	enameled	.024"	1.73	2.96	4.69
0300		round corrugated	3"	enameled	.020"	.87	2.18	3.05
0350			4"	enameled	.025"	1.66	2.96	4.62
0500	Copper	rectangular corr.	2"x3"	mill	16 Oz.	3.50	2.18	5.68
0600		smooth		mill	16 Oz.	5.25	2.18	7.43
0700		rectangular corr.	3"x4"	mill	16 Oz.	5.20	2.86	8.06
1300	Steel	rectangular corr.	2"x3"	galvanized	28 Ga.	.59	2.18	2.77
1350				epoxy coated	24 Ga.	1.11	2.18	3.29
1400		smooth		galvanized	28 Ga.	.69	2.18	2.87
1450		rectangular corr.	3"x4"	galvanized	28 Ga.	1.65	2.86	4.51
1500				epoxy coated	24 Ga.	1.84	2.86	4.70
1550		smooth		galvanized	28 Ga.	1.35	2.86	4.21
1652		round corrugated	3"	galvanized	28 Ga.	.80	2.18	2.98
1700			4"	galvanized	28 Ga.	1.18	2.86	4.04
1750			5"	galvanized	28 Ga.	1.54	3.19	4.73
2000	Steel pipe	round	4"	black	X.H.	4.93	20.50	25.43
2552	S.S. tubing sch.5	rectangular	3"x4"	mill		22.50	2.86	25.36

5.8-500 — Gravel Stop

	MATERIALS	SECTION	SIZE	FINISH	THICKNESS	COST PER L.F.		
						MAT.	INST.	TOTAL
5100	Aluminum	extruded	4"	mill	.050"	3.54	2.86	6.40
5200			4"	duranodic	.050"	4.06	2.86	6.92
5300			8"	mill	.050"	4.94	3.32	8.26
5400			8"	duranodic	.050"	5.50	3.32	8.82
6000			12"-2 pc.	duranodic	.050"	6.90	4.14	11.04
6100	Stainless	formed	6"	mill	24 Ga.	7.85	3.07	10.92

For information about Means Estimating Seminars, see yellow pages 11 and 12 in back of book

Important: See the Reference Section for critical supporting data - Location Factors & Historical Cost Indexes

Division 6
Interior Construction

The Concrete Block Partition Systems are defined by weight and type of block, thickness, type of finish and number of sides finished. System components include joint reinforcing on alternate courses and vertical control joints.

6.1-210 — Concrete Block Partitions - Regular Weight

	TYPE	THICKNESS (IN.)	TYPE FINISH	SIDES FINISHED		COST PER S.F.		
						MAT.	INST.	TOTAL
1000	Hollow	4	none	0		1.10	4.02	5.12
1010			gyp. plaster 2 coat	1		1.44	5.80	7.24
1020				2		1.79	7.65	9.44
1200			portland - 3 coat	1		1.34	6.15	7.49
1400			5/8" drywall	1		1.53	5.35	6.88
1500		6	none	0		1.61	4.31	5.92
1510			gyp. plaster 2 coat	1		1.95	6.10	8.05
1520				2		2.30	7.95	10.25
1700			portland - 3 coat	1		1.85	6.40	8.25
1900			5/8" drywall	1		2.04	5.65	7.69
1910				2		2.47	6.95	9.42
2000		8	none	0		1.72	4.61	6.33
2010			gyp. plaster 2 coat	1		2.06	6.40	8.46
2020			gyp. plaster 2 coat	2		2.41	8.25	10.66
2200			portland - 3 coat	1		1.96	6.70	8.66
2400			5/8" drywall	1		2.15	5.95	8.10
2410				2		2.58	7.25	9.83
2500		10	none	0		2.37	4.83	7.20
2510			gyp. plaster 2 coat	1		2.71	6.65	9.36
2520				2		3.06	8.50	11.56
2700			portland - 3 coat	1		2.61	6.95	9.56
2900			5/8" drywall	1		2.80	6.15	8.95
2910				2		3.23	7.45	10.68
3000	Solid	2	none	0		.98	3.98	4.96
3010			gyp. plaster	1		1.32	5.80	7.12
3020				2		1.67	7.65	9.32
3200			portland - 3 coat	1		1.22	6.10	7.32
3400			5/8" drywall	1		1.41	5.30	6.71
3410				2		1.84	6.60	8.44
3500		4	none	0		1.49	4.16	5.65
3510			gyp. plaster	1		1.90	6	7.90
3520				2		2.18	7.80	9.98
3700			portland - 3 coat	1		1.73	6.25	7.98
3900			5/8" drywall	1		1.92	5.50	7.42
3910				2		2.35	6.80	9.15

Important: See the Reference Section for critical supporting data - Location Factors & Historical Cost Indexes

INTERIOR CONSTRUCTION 6

6.1-210 — Concrete Block Partitions - Regular Weight

	TYPE	THICKNESS (IN.)	TYPE FINISH	SIDES FINISHED		COST PER S.F. MAT.	COST PER S.F. INST.	COST PER S.F. TOTAL
4002	Solid	6	none	0		1.73	4.48	6.21
4010			gyp. plaster	1		2.07	6.30	8.37
4020				2		2.42	8.15	10.57
4200			portland - 3 coat	1		1.97	6.60	8.57
4400			5/8" drywall	1		2.16	5.80	7.96
4410				2		2.59	7.10	9.69

6.1-210 — Concrete Block Partitions - Lightweight

	TYPE	THICKNESS (IN.)	TYPE FINISH	SIDES FINISHED		COST PER S.F. MAT.	COST PER S.F. INST.	COST PER S.F. TOTAL
5000	Hollow	4	none	0		1.25	3.93	5.18
5010			gyp. plaster	1		1.59	5.75	7.34
5020				2		1.94	7.60	9.54
5200			portland - 3 coat	1		1.49	6.05	7.54
5400			5/8" drywall	1		1.68	5.25	6.93
5410				2		2.11	6.55	8.66
5500		6	none	0		1.69	4.21	5.90
5510			gyp. plaster	1		2.03	6	8.03
5520			gyp. plaster	2		2.38	7.85	10.23
5700			portland - 3 coat	1		1.93	6.30	8.23
5900			5/8" drywall	1		2.12	5.55	7.67
5910				2		2.55	6.85	9.40
6000		8	none	0		2.06	4.50	6.56
6010			gyp. plaster	1		2.40	6.30	8.70
6020				2		2.75	8.15	10.90
6200			portland - 3 coat	1		2.30	6.60	8.90
6400			5/8" drywall	1		2.49	5.80	8.29
6410				2		2.92	7.15	10.07
6500		10	none	0		2.66	4.70	7.36
6510			gyp. plaster	1		3	6.50	9.50
6520				2		3.35	8.35	11.70
6700			portland - 3 coat	1		2.90	6.80	9.70
6900			5/8" drywall	1		3.09	6	9.09
6910				2		3.52	7.35	10.87
7000	Solid	4	none	0		1.41	4.11	5.52
7010			gyp. plaster	1		1.75	5.90	7.65
7020				2		2.10	7.75	9.85
7200			portland - 3 coat	1		1.65	6.20	7.85
7400			5/8" drywall	1		1.84	5.45	7.29
7410				2		2.27	6.75	9.02
7500		6	none	0		1.90	4.42	6.32
7510			gyp. plaster	1		2.29	6.25	8.54
7520				2		2.59	8.05	10.64
7700			portland - 3 coat	1		2.14	6.55	8.69
7900			5/8" drywall	1		2.33	5.75	8.08
7910				2		2.76	7.05	9.81
8000		8	none	0		2.53	4.73	7.26
8010			gyp. plaster	1		2.87	6.55	9.42
8020				2		3.22	8.40	11.62
8200			portland - 3 coat	1		2.77	6.85	9.62
8400			5/8" drywall	1		2.96	6.05	9.01
8410				2		3.39	7.35	10.74

6 INTERIOR CONSTRUCTION

Single Wythe

Structural facing tile
8W series
8" x 16"

Double Wythe

Single Wythe

Structural facing tile
6T series
5-1/3" x 12"

Double Wythe

6.1-270	Tile Partitions	COST PER S.F.		
		MAT.	INST.	TOTAL
1000	8W series 8"x16", 4" thick wall, reinf every 2 courses, glazed 1 side	6.65	4.83	11.48
1100	Glazed 2 sides	10.40	5.10	15.50
1200	Glazed 2 sides, using 2 wythes of 2" thick tile	11.70	9.25	20.95
1300	6" thick wall, horizontal reinf every 2 courses, glazed 1 side	10.20	5.05	15.25
1400	Glazed 2 sides, each face different color, 2" and 4" tile	12.50	9.45	21.95
1500	8" thick wall, glazed 2 sides using 2 wythes of 4" thick tile	13.30	9.65	22.95
1600	10" thick wall, glazed 2 sides using 1 wythe of 4" tile & 1 wythe of 6" tile	16.85	9.90	26.75
1700	Glazed 2 sides cavity wall, using 2 wythes of 4" thick tile	13.30	9.65	22.95
1800	12" thick wall, glazed 2 sides using 2 wythes of 6" thick tile	20.50	10.10	30.60
1900	Glazed 2 sides cavity wall, using 2 wythes of 4" thick tile	13.30	9.65	22.95
2100	6T series 5-1/3"x12" tile, 4" thick, non load bearing glazed one side,	6.10	7.55	13.65
2200	Glazed two sides	9.95	8.55	18.50
2300	Glazed two sides, using two wythes of 2" thick tile	10.40	14.80	25.20
2400	6" thick, glazed one side	10	7.95	17.95
2500	Glazed two sides	14.05	9	23.05
2600	Glazed two sides using 2" thick tile and 4" thick tile	11.30	14.95	26.25
2700	8" thick, glazed one side	12.90	9.25	22.15
2800	Glazed two sides using two wythes of 4" thick tile	12.20	15.10	27.30
2900	Glazed two sides using 6" thick tile and 2" thick tile	15.20	15.35	30.55
3000	10" thick cavity wall, glazed two sides using two wythes of 4" tile	12.20	15.10	27.30
3100	12" thick, glazed two sides using 4" thick tile and 8" thick tile	19	16.80	35.80
3200	2" thick facing tile, glazed one side, on 6" concrete block	7.30	8.80	16.10
3300	On 8" concrete block	7.40	9.05	16.45
3400	On 10" concrete block	8.05	9.25	17.30

Important: See the Reference Section for critical supporting data - Location Factors & Historical Cost Indexes

INTERIOR CONSTRUCTION 6

Gypsum board, single layer each side on wood studs.

Gypsum board, sound deadening board each side, with 1-1/2″ insulation on wood studs.

Gypsum board, two layers each side on wood studs.

Gypsum board, single layer each side on metal studs.

Gypsum board, sound deadening board each side on metal studs.

Gypsum board two layers one side, single layer opposite side, with 3-1/2″ insulation on metal studs.

INTERIOR CONSTRUCTION   6

6.1-510 — Drywall Partitions/Wood Stud Framing

	FACE LAYER	BASE LAYER	FRAMING	OPPOSITE FACE	INSULATION	COST PER S.F.		
						MAT.	INST.	TOTAL
1200	5/8″ FR drywall	none	2 x 4, @ 16″ O.C.	same	0	1.18	2.17	3.35
1250				5/8″ reg. drywall	0	1.18	2.17	3.35
1300				nothing	0	.82	1.45	2.27
1400		1/4″ SD gypsum	2 x 4 @ 16″ O.C.	same	1-1/2″ fiberglass	2.14	3.35	5.49
1450				5/8″ FR drywall	1-1/2″ fiberglass	1.88	2.94	4.82
1500				nothing	1-1/2″ fiberglass	1.52	2.22	3.74
1600		resil. channels	2 x 4 @ 16″, O.C.	same	1-1/2″ fiberglass	1.87	4.25	6.12
1650				5/8″ FR drywall	1-1/2″ fiberglass	1.74	3.39	5.13
1700				nothing	1-1/2″ fiberglass	1.38	2.67	4.05
1800		5/8″ FR drywall	2 x 4 @ 24″ O.C.	same	0	1.71	2.75	4.46
1850				5/8″ FR drywall	0	1.39	2.39	3.78
1900				nothing	0	1.03	1.67	2.70
2200		5/8″ FR drywall	2 rows-2 x 4	same	2″ fiberglass	2.76	3.98	6.74
2250			16″O.C.	5/8″ FR drywall	2″ fiberglass	2.44	3.62	6.06
2300				nothing	2″ fiberglass	2.08	2.90	4.98
2400	5/8″ WR drywall	none	2 x 4, @ 16″ O.C.	same	0	1.48	2.17	3.65
2450				5/8″ FR drywall	0	1.33	2.17	3.50
2500				nothing	0	.97	1.45	2.42
2600		5/8″ FR drywall	2 x 4, @ 24″ O.C.	same	0	2.01	2.75	4.76
2650				5/8″ FR drywall	0	1.54	2.39	3.93
2700				nothing	0	1.18	1.67	2.85
2800	5/8 VF drywall	none	2 x 4, @ 16″ O.C.	same	0	1.90	2.35	4.25
2850				5/8″ FR drywall	0	1.54	2.26	3.80
2900				nothing	0	1.18	1.54	2.72
3000		5/8″ FR drywall	2 x 4 , 24″ O.C.	same	0	2.43	2.93	5.36
3050				5/8″ FR drywall	0	1.75	2.48	4.23
3100				nothing	0	1.39	1.76	3.15

6.1-510 Drywall Partitions/Wood Stud Framing

	FACE LAYER	BASE LAYER	FRAMING	OPPOSITE FACE	INSULATION	COST PER S.F.		
						MAT.	INST.	TOTAL
3200	1/2" reg drywall	3/8" reg drywall	2 x 4, @ 16" O.C.	same	0	1.70	2.89	4.59
3252	1/2" reg. drywall	3/8" reg. drywall	2x4, @ 16"O.C.	5/8"FR drywall	0	1.44	2.53	3.97
3300				nothing	0	1.08	1.81	2.89

6.1-510 Drywall Partitions/Metal Stud Framing

	FACE LAYER	BASE LAYER	FRAMING	OPPOSITE FACE	INSULATION	COST PER S.F.		
						MAT.	INST.	TOTAL
5200	5/8" FR drywall	none	1-5/8" @ 24" O.C.	same	0	.84	1.92	2.76
5250				5/8" reg. drywall	0	.84	1.92	2.76
5300				nothing	0	.48	1.20	1.68
5400			3-5/8" @ 24" O.C.	same	0	.88	1.93	2.81
5450				5/8" reg. drywall	0	.88	1.93	2.81
5500				nothing	0	.52	1.21	1.73
5600		1/4" SD gypsum	1-5/8" @ 24" O.C.	same	0	1.36	2.74	4.10
5650				5/8" FR drywall	0	1.10	2.33	3.43
5700				nothing	0	.74	1.61	2.35
5800			2-1/2" @ 24" O.C.	same	0	1.37	2.75	4.12
5850				5/8" FR drywall	0	1.11	2.34	3.45
5900				nothing	0	.75	1.62	2.37
6000		5/8" FR drywall	2-1/2" @ 16" O.C.	same	0	1.66	3.10	4.76
6050				5/8" FR drywall	0	1.34	2.74	4.08
6100				nothing	0	.98	2.02	3
6200			3-5/8" @ 24" O.C.	same	0	1.52	2.65	4.17
6250				5/8"FR drywall	3-1/2" fiberglass	1.56	2.52	4.08
6300				nothing	0	.84	1.57	2.41
6400	5/8" WR drywall	none	1-5/8" @ 24" O.C.	same	0	1.14	1.92	3.06
6450				5/8" FR drywall	0	.99	1.92	2.91
6500				nothing	0	.63	1.20	1.83
6600			3-5/8" @ 24" O.C.	same	0	1.18	1.93	3.11
6650				5/8" FR drywall	0	1.03	1.93	2.96
6700				nothing	0	.67	1.21	1.88
6800		5/8" FR drywall	2-1/2" @ 16" O.C.	same	0	1.96	3.10	5.06
6850				5/8" FR drywall	0	1.49	2.74	4.23
6900				nothing	0	1.13	2.02	3.15
7000			3-5/8" @ 24" O.C.	same	0	1.82	2.65	4.47
7050				5/8"FR drywall	3-1/2" fiberglass	1.71	2.52	4.23
7100				nothing	0	.99	1.57	2.56
7200	5/8" VF drywall	none	1-5/8" @ 24" O.C.	same	0	1.56	2.10	3.66
7250				5/8" FR drywall	0	1.20	2.01	3.21
7300				nothing	0	.84	1.29	2.13
7400			3-5/8" @ 24" O.C.	same	0	1.60	2.11	3.71
7450				5/8" FR drywall	0	1.24	2.02	3.26
7500				nothing	0	.88	1.30	2.18
7600		5/8" FR drywall	2-1/2" @ 16" O.C.	same	0	2.38	3.28	5.66
7650				5/8" FR drywall	0	1.70	2.83	4.53
7700				nothing	0	1.34	2.11	3.45
7800			3-5/8" @ 24" O.C.	same	0	2.24	2.83	5.07
7850				5/8"FR drywall	3-1/2" fiberglass	1.92	2.61	4.53
7900				nothing	0	1.20	1.66	2.86

Important: See the Reference Section for critical supporting data - Location Factors & Historical Cost Indexes

6.1-580	Drywall Components	COST PER S.F.		
		MAT.	INST.	TOTAL
0060	Metal studs, 24″ O.C. including track, load bearing, 20 gage, 2-1/2″	.35	.68	1.03
0080	3-5/8″	.42	.70	1.12
0100	4″	.38	.71	1.09
0120	6″	.56	.72	1.28
0140	Metal studs, 24″ O.C. including track, load bearing, 18 gage, 2-1/2″	.35	.68	1.03
0160	3-5/8″	.42	.70	1.12
0180	4″	.38	.71	1.09
0200	6″	.56	.72	1.28
0220	16 gage, 2-1/2″	.41	.78	1.19
0240	3-5/8″	.49	.80	1.29
0260	4″	.52	.81	1.33
0280	6″	.66	.83	1.49
0300	Non load bearing, 25 gage, 1-5/8″	.12	.48	.60
0340	3-5/8″	.16	.49	.65
0360	4″	.19	.49	.68
0380	6″	.25	.50	.75
0400	20 gage, 2-1/2″	.22	.61	.83
0420	3-5/8″	.24	.62	.86
0440	4″	.30	.62	.92
0460	6″	.35	.63	.98
0540	Wood studs including blocking, shoe and double top plate, 2″x4″, 12″O.C.	.58	.91	1.49
0560	16″ O.C.	.46	.73	1.19
0580	24″ O.C.	.35	.59	.94
0600	2″x6″, 12″ O.C.	.85	1.04	1.89
0620	16″ O.C.	.68	.81	1.49
0640	24″ O.C.	.52	.64	1.16
0642	Furring one side only, steel channels, 3/4″, 12″ O.C.	.18	1.43	1.61
0644	16″ O.C.	.16	1.27	1.43
0646	24″ O.C.	.11	.96	1.07
0647	1-1/2″ , 12″ O.C.	.27	1.60	1.87
0648	16″ O.C.	.24	1.40	1.64
0649	24″ O.C.	.16	1.10	1.26
0650	Wood strips, 1″ x 3″, on wood, 12″ O.C.	.21	.66	.87
0651	16″ O.C.	.16	.50	.66
0652	On masonry, 12″ O.C.	.21	.74	.95
0653	16″ O.C.	.16	.56	.72
0654	On concrete, 12″ O.C.	.21	1.40	1.61
0655	16″ O.C.	.16	1.05	1.21
0665	Gypsum board, one face only, exterior sheathing, 1/2″	.31	.65	.96
0680	Interior, fire resistant, 1/2″	.26	.36	.62
0700	5/8″	.32	.36	.68
0720	Sound deadening board 1/4″	.26	.41	.67
0740	Standard drywall 3/8″	.29	.36	.65
0760	1/2″	.29	.36	.65
0780	5/8″	.32	.36	.68
0800	Tongue & groove coreboard 1″	.50	1.52	2.02
0820	Water resistant, 1/2″	.37	.36	.73
0840	5/8″	.47	.36	.83
0860	Add for the following:, foil backing	.11		.11
0880	Fiberglass insulation, 3-1/2″	.36	.23	.59
0900	6″	.44	.27	.71
0920	Rigid insulation 1″	.36	.36	.72
0940	Resilient furring @ 16″ O.C.	.16	1.14	1.30
0960	Taping and finishing	.04	.36	.40
0980	Texture spray	.06	.42	.48
1000	Thin coat plaster	.08	.46	.54
1040	2″x4″ staggered studs 2″x6″ plates & blocking	.66	.80	1.46

Gypsum plaster and gypsum lath on metal studs.

Gypsum plaster and diamond metal lath on metal studs.

Gypsum plaster and gypsum lath on wood studs.

Gypsum plaster and diamond metal lath on wood studs.

INTERIOR CONSTRUCTION 6

6.1-610 | Plaster Partitions/Metal Stud Framing

	TYPE	FRAMING	LATH	OPPOSITE FACE		COST PER S.F.		
						MAT.	INST.	TOTAL
1000	2 coat gypsum	2-1/2" @ 16"O.C.	3/8" gypsum	same		2.07	5.35	7.42
1010				nothing		1.16	3.11	4.27
1100		3-1/4" @ 24"O.C.	1/2" gypsum	same		2.05	5.15	7.20
1110				nothing		1.14	2.89	4.03
1500	2 coat vermiculite	2-1/2" @ 16"O.C.	3/8" gypsum	same		1.92	5.80	7.72
1510				nothing		1.09	3.35	4.44
1600		3-1/4" @ 24"O.C.	1/2" gypsum	same		1.90	5.65	7.55
1610				nothing		1.07	3.13	4.20
2000	3 coat gypsum	2-1/2" @ 16"O.C.	3/8" gypsum	same		1.96	6.05	8.01
2010				nothing		1.11	3.46	4.57
2020			3.4lb. diamond	same		1.63	6.05	7.68
2030				nothing		.95	3.46	4.41
2040			2.75lb. ribbed	same		1.63	6.05	7.68
2050				nothing		.95	3.46	4.41
2100		3-1/4" @ 24"O.C.	1/2" gypsum	same		1.94	5.85	7.79
2110				nothing		1.09	3.24	4.33
2120			3.4lb. ribbed	same		1.86	5.85	7.71
2130				nothing		1.05	3.24	4.29
3500	3 coat gypsum	2-1/2" @ 16"O.C.	3/8" gypsum	same		2.49	7.75	10.24
3510	W/med. Keenes			nothing		1.38	4.30	5.68
3520			3.4lb. diamond	same		2.16	7.75	9.91
3530				nothing		1.22	4.30	5.52
3540			2.75lb. ribbed	same		2.16	7.75	9.91
3550				nothing		1.22	4.30	5.52
3600		3-1/4" @ 24"O.C.	1/2" gypsum	same		2.47	7.60	10.07
3610				nothing		1.36	4.08	5.44
3620			3.4lb. ribbed	same		2.39	7.60	9.99
3630				nothing		1.32	4.08	5.40

Important: See the Reference Section for critical supporting data - Location Factors & Historical Cost Indexes

6.1-610 — Plaster Partitions/Metal Stud Framing

	TYPE	FRAMING	LATH	OPPOSITE FACE		COST PER S.F.		
						MAT.	INST.	TOTAL
4000	3 coat gypsum	2-1/2" @ 16"O.C.	3/8" gypsum	same		2.50	8.55	11.05
4010	W/hard Keenes			nothing		1.38	4.72	6.10
4022		2-1/2" @ 16"O.C.	3.4 lb. diamond	same		2.17	8.55	10.72
4032				nothing		1.22	4.72	5.94
4040			2.75lb. ribbed	same		2.17	8.55	10.72
4050				nothing		1.22	4.72	5.94
4100		3-1/4" @ 24"O.C.	1/2" gypsum	same		2.48	8.40	10.88
4110				nothing		1.36	4.50	5.86
4120			3.4lb. ribbed	same		2.40	8.40	10.80
4130				nothing		1.32	4.50	5.82

6.1-610 — Plaster Partitions/Wood Stud Framing

	TYPE	FRAMING	LATH	OPPOSITE FACE		COST PER S.F.		
						MAT.	INST.	TOTAL
5000	2 coat gypsum	2"x4" @ 16"O.C.	3/8" gypsum	same		2.33	5.20	7.53
5010				nothing		1.43	3.04	4.47
5100		2"x4" @ 24"O.C.	1/2" gypsum	same		2.22	5.10	7.32
5110				nothing		1.32	2.93	4.25
5500	2 coat vermiculite	2"x4" @ 16"O.C.	3/8" gypsum	same		2.18	5.70	7.88
5510				nothing		1.36	3.28	4.64
5600		2"x4" @ 24"O.C.	1/2" gypsum	same		2.07	5.60	7.67
5610				nothing		1.25	3.17	4.42
6000	3 coat gypsum	2"x4" @ 16"O.C.	3/8" gypsum	same		2.22	5.90	8.12
6010				nothing		1.38	3.39	4.77
6020			3.4lb. diamond	same		1.91	5.95	7.86
6030				nothing		1.23	3.42	4.65
6040			2.75lb. ribbed	same		1.89	6	7.89
6050				nothing		1.22	3.43	4.65
6100		2"x4" @ 24"O.C.	1/2" gypsum	same		2.11	5.80	7.91
6110				nothing		1.27	3.28	4.55
6120			3.4lb. ribbed	same		1.80	5.90	7.70
6130				nothing		1.12	3.31	4.43
7500	3 coat gypsum	2"x4" @ 16"O.C.	3/8" gypsum	same		2.75	7.65	10.40
7510	W/med Keenes			nothing		1.65	4.23	5.88
7520			3.4lb. diamond	same		2.44	7.70	10.14
7530				nothing		1.50	4.26	5.76
7540			2.75lb. ribbed	same		2.42	7.70	10.12
7550				nothing		1.49	4.27	5.76
7600		2"x4" @ 24"O.C.	1/2" gypsum	same		2.64	7.55	10.19
7610				nothing		1.54	4.12	5.66
7620			3.4lb. ribbed	same		2.58	7.70	10.28
7630				nothing		1.51	4.18	5.69
8000	3 coat gypsum	2"x4" @ 16"O.C.	3/8" gypsum	same		2.76	8.45	11.21
8010	W/hard Keenes			nothing		1.65	4.65	6.30
8020			3.4lb. diamond	same		2.45	8.50	10.95
8030				nothing		1.50	4.68	6.18
8040			2.75lb. ribbed	same		2.43	8.50	10.93
8050				nothing		1.49	4.69	6.18
8100		2"x4" @ 24"O.C.	1/2" gypsum	same		2.65	8.35	11
8110				nothing		1.54	4.54	6.08
8120			3.4lb. ribbed	same		2.59	8.50	11.09
8130				nothing		1.51	4.60	6.11

6 INTERIOR CONSTRUCTION

6.1-680	Plaster Partition Components	COST PER S.F.		
		MAT.	INST.	TOTAL
0060	Metal studs, 16" O.C., including track, non load bearing, 25 gage, 1-5/8"	.18	.74	.92
0080	2-1/2"	.18	.74	.92
0100	3-1/4"	.21	.76	.97
0120	3-5/8"	.21	.76	.97
0140	4"	.26	.77	1.03
0160	6"	.33	.78	1.11
0180	Load bearing, 20 gage, 2-1/2"	.48	.95	1.43
0200	3-5/8"	.57	.96	1.53
0220	4"	.60	.99	1.59
0240	6"	.76	1	1.76
0260	16 gage 2-1/2"	.56	1.08	1.64
0280	3-5/8"	.68	1.11	1.79
0300	4"	.71	1.12	1.83
0320	6"	.90	1.14	2.04
0340	Wood studs, including blocking, shoe and double plate, 2"x4" , 12" O.C.	.58	.91	1.49
0360	16" O.C.	.46	.73	1.19
0380	24" O.C.	.35	.59	.94
0400	2"x6" , 12" O.C.	.85	1.04	1.89
0420	16" O.C.	.68	.81	1.49
0440	24" O.C.	.52	.64	1.16
0460	Furring one face only, steel channels, 3/4", 12" O.C.	.18	1.43	1.61
0480	16" O.C.	.16	1.27	1.43
0500	24" O.C.	.11	.96	1.07
0520	1-1/2", 12" O.C.	.27	1.60	1.87
0540	16" O.C.	.24	1.40	1.64
0560	24"O.C.	.16	1.10	1.26
0580	Wood strips 1"x3", on wood., 12" O.C.	.21	.66	.87
0600	16"O.C.	.16	.50	.66
0620	On masonry, 12" O.C.	.21	.74	.95
0640	16" O.C.	.16	.56	.72
0660	On concrete, 12" O.C.	.21	1.40	1.61
0680	16" O.C.	.16	1.05	1.21
0700	Gypsum lath. plain or perforated, nailed to studs, 3/8" thick	.43	.44	.87
0720	1/2" thick	.43	.47	.90
0740	Clipped to studs, 3/8" thick	.44	.50	.94
0760	1/2" thick	.44	.53	.97
0780	Metal lath, diamond painted, nailed to wood studs, 2.5 lb.	.18	.44	.62
0800	3.4 lb.	.28	.47	.75
0820	Screwed to steel studs, 2.5 lb.	.18	.47	.65
0840	3.4 lb.	.28	.50	.78
0860	Rib painted, wired to steel, 2.75 lb	.28	.50	.78
0880	3.4 lb	.40	.53	.93
0900	4.0 lb	.41	.58	.99
0910				
0920	Gypsum plaster, 2 coats	.42	1.74	2.16
0940	3 coats	.58	2.09	2.67
0960	Perlite or vermiculite plaster, 2 coats	.40	1.98	2.38
0980	3 coats	.66	2.49	3.15
1000	Stucco, 3 coats, 1" thick, on wood framing	.45	3.50	3.95
1020	On masonry	.25	2.72	2.97
1100	Metal base galvanized and painted 2-1/2" high	.49	1.40	1.89

INTERIOR CONSTRUCTION 6

Important: See the Reference Section for critical supporting data - Location Factors & Historical Cost Indexes

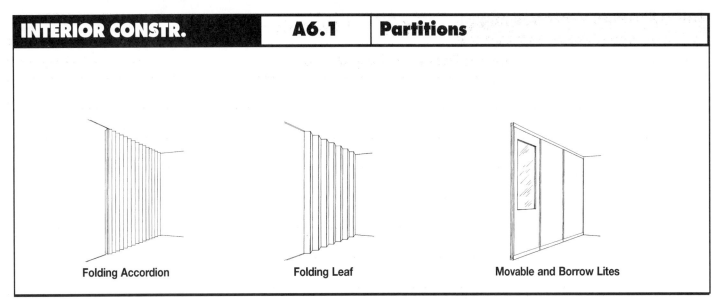

Folding Accordion   **Folding Leaf**   **Movable and Borrow Lites**

6.1-820	Partitions	COST PER S.F.		
		MAT.	INST.	TOTAL
0360	Folding accordion, vinyl covered, acoustical, 3 lb. S.F., 17 ft max. hgt	21.50	7.30	28.80
0380	5 lb. per S.F. 27 ft max height	29.50	7.70	37.20
0400	5.5 lb. per S.F., 17 ft. max height	33	8.10	41.10
0420	Commercial, 1.75 lb per S.F., 8 ft. max height	14.85	3.24	18.09
0440	2.0 Lb per S.F., 17 ft. max height	15.95	4.86	20.81
0460	Industrial, 4.0 lb. per S.F. 27 ft max height	27	9.75	36.75
0480	Vinyl clad wood or steel, electric operation 6 psf	38.50	4.56	43.06
0500	Wood, non acoustic, birch or mahogany	19.80	2.43	22.23
0560	Folding leaf, aluminum framed acoustical 12 ft.high.,5.5 lb per S.F.,min.	29.50	12.15	41.65
0580	Maximum	36	24.50	60.50
0600	6.5 lb. per S.F., minimum	31.50	12.15	43.65
0620	Maximum	38.50	24.50	63
0640	Steel acoustical, 7.5 per S.F., vinyl faced, minimum	44	12.15	56.15
0660	Maximum	54	24.50	78.50
0680	Wood acoustic type, vinyl faced to 18' high 6 psf, minimum	41.50	12.15	53.65
0700	Average	49.50	16.20	65.70
0720	Maximum	64	24.50	88.50
0740	Formica or hardwood faced, minimum	42.50	12.15	54.65
0760	Maximum	45.50	24.50	70
0780	Wood, low acoustical type to 12 ft. high 4.5 psf	31	14.60	45.60
0840	Demountable, trackless wall, cork finish, semi acous, 1-5/8"th, min	28.50	2.24	30.74
0860	Maximum	27	3.84	30.84
0880	Acoustic, 2" thick, minimum	23	2.39	25.39
0900	Maximum	40	3.24	43.24
0920	In-plant modular office system, w/prehung steel door			
0940	3" thick honeycomb core panels			
0960	12' x 12', 2 wall	8.85	.45	9.30
0970	4 wall	8.25	.60	8.85
0980	16' x 16', 2 wall	8.30	.32	8.62
0990	4 wall	5.75	.32	6.07
1000	Gypsum, demountable, 3" to 3-3/4" thick x 9' high, vinyl clad	4.44	1.69	6.13
1020	Fabric clad	11.10	1.84	12.94
1040	1.75 system, vinyl clad hardboard, paper honeycomb core panel			
1060	1-3/4" to 2-1/2" thick x 9' high	7.50	1.69	9.19
1080	Unitized gypsum panel system, 2" to 2-1/2" thick x 9' high			
1100	Vinyl clad gypsum	9.65	1.69	11.34
1120	Fabric clad gypsum	15.85	1.84	17.69
1140	Movable steel walls, modular system			
1160	Unitized panels, 48" wide x 9' high			
1180	Baked enamel, pre-finished	10.90	1.35	12.25
1200	Fabric clad	15.65	1.45	17.10

Toilet Units   Entrance Screens   Urinal Screens

6.1-870	Toilet Partitions	COST PER UNIT		
		MAT.	INST.	TOTAL
0380	Toilet partitions, cubicles, ceiling hung, marble	1,450	360	1,810
0400	Painted metal	400	182	582
0420	Plastic laminate	545	182	727
0460	Stainless steel	1,100	182	1,282
0480	Handicap addition	320		320
0520	Floor and ceiling anchored, marble	1,575	289	1,864
0540	Painted metal	405	146	551
0560	Plastic laminate	515	146	661
0600	Stainless steel	1,275	146	1,421
0620	Handicap addition	278		278
0660	Floor mounted marble	935	241	1,176
0680	Painted metal	375	104	479
0700	Plastic laminate	510	104	614
0740	Stainless steel	1,300	104	1,404
0760	Handicap addition	278		278
0780	Juvenile deduction	38.50		38.50
0820	Floor mounted with handrail marble	900	241	1,141
0840	Painted metal	405	122	527
0860	Plastic laminate	695	122	817
0900	Stainless steel	1,250	122	1,372
0920	Handicap addition	278		278
0960	Wall hung, painted metal	510	104	614
1020	Stainless steel	1,225	104	1,329
1040	Handicap addition	278		278
1080	Entrance screens, floor mounted, 54" high, marble	585	80	665
1100	Painted metal	182	48.50	230.50
1140	Stainless steel	670	48.50	718.50
1300	Urinal screens, floor mounted, 24" wide, laminated plastic	232	91	323
1320	Marble	520	108	628
1340	Painted metal	185	91	276
1380	Stainless steel	530	91	621
1428	Wall mounted wedge type, painted metal	221	73	294
1460	Stainless steel	455	73	528

Single Leaf

Sliding Entrance

Rolling Overhead

6.4-100	Special Doors	COST PER OPNG.		
		MAT.	INST.	TOTAL
2500	Single leaf, wood, 3'-0"x7'-0"x1 3/8", birch, solid core	290	137	427
2510	Hollow core	253	131	384
2530	Hollow core, lauan	236	131	367
2540	Louvered pine	355	131	486
2550	Paneled pine	365	131	496
2600	Hollow metal, comm. quality, flush, 3'-0"x7'-0"x1-3/8"	390	144	534
2650	3'-0"x10'-0" openings with panel	635	186	821
2700	Metal fire, comm. quality, 3'-0"x7'-0"x1-3/8"	465	149	614
2800	Kalamein fire, comm. quality, 3'-0"x7'-0"x1-3/4"	385	274	659
3200	Double leaf, wood, hollow core, 2 - 3'-0"x7'-0"x1-3/8"	405	251	656
3300	Hollow metal, comm. quality, B label, 2'-3'-0"x7'-0"x1-3/8"	870	315	1,185
3400	6'-0"x10'-0" opening, with panel	1,225	390	1,615
3500	Double swing door system, 12'-0"x7'-0", mill finish	6,100	2,075	8,175
3700	Black finish	6,650	2,125	8,775
3800	Sliding entrance door and system mill finish	7,100	1,750	8,850
3900	Bronze finish	7,800	1,900	9,700
4000	Black finish	8,125	1,975	10,100
4100	Sliding panel mall front, 16'x9' opening, mill finish	2,475	535	3,010
4200	Bronze finish	3,225	695	3,920
4300	Black finish	3,950	855	4,805
4400	24'x9' opening mill finish	3,600	990	4,590
4500	Bronze finish	4,675	1,275	5,950
4600	Black finish	5,750	1,575	7,325
4700	48'x9' opening mill finish	6,675	770	7,445
4800	Bronze finish	8,675	1,000	9,675
4900	Black finish	10,700	1,225	11,925
5000	Rolling overhead steel door, manual, 8' x 8' high	765	595	1,360
5100	10' x 10' high	1,000	680	1,680
5200	20' x 10' high	2,075	955	3,030
5300	12' x 12' high	1,325	795	2,120
5400	Motor operated, 8' x 8' high	1,500	785	2,285
5500	10' x 10' high	1,750	870	2,620
5600	20' x 10' high	2,825	1,150	3,975
5700	12' x 12' high	2,075	985	3,060
5800	Roll up grille, aluminum, manual, 10' x 10' high, mill finish	1,875	1,175	3,050
5900	Bronze anodized	3,000	1,175	4,175
6000	Motor operated, 10' x 10' high, mill finish	2,725	1,350	4,075
6100	Bronze anodized	3,850	1,350	5,200
6200	Steel, manual, 10' x 10' high	1,675	955	2,630
6300	15' x 8' high	1,975	1,200	3,175
6400	Motor operated, 10' x 10' high	2,525	1,150	3,675
6500	15' x 8' high	2,825	1,400	4,225

INTERIOR CONSTRUCTION

6

6.5-100	Paint & Covering	COST PER S.F.		
		MAT.	INST.	TOTAL
0060	Painting, interior on plaster and drywall, brushwork, primer & 1 coat	.10	.49	.59
0080	Primer & 2 coats	.15	.65	.80
0100	Primer & 3 coats	.20	.80	1
0120	Walls & ceilings, roller work, primer & 1 coat	.10	.33	.43
0140	Primer & 2 coats	.15	.42	.57
0160	Woodwork incl. puttying, brushwork, primer & 1 coat	.10	.71	.81
0180	Primer & 2 coats	.15	.94	1.09
0200	Primer & 3 coats	.20	1.27	1.47
0260	Cabinets and casework, enamel, primer & 1 coat	.10	.80	.90
0280	Primer & 2 coats	.15	.98	1.13
0300	Masonry or concrete, latex, brushwork, primer & 1 coat	.18	.66	.84
0320	Primer & 2 coats	.24	.95	1.19
0340	Addition for block filler	.11	.82	.93
0380	Fireproof paints, intumescent, 1/8" thick 3/4 hour	1.77	.65	2.42
0400	3/16" thick 1 hour	3.94	.98	4.92
0420	7/16" thick 2 hour	5.10	2.27	7.37
0440	1-1/16" thick 3 hour	8.30	4.54	12.84
0480	Miscellaneous metal brushwork, exposed metal, primer & 1 coat	.08	.80	.88
0500	Gratings, primer & 1 coat	.19	.99	1.18
0600	Pipes over 12" diameter	.48	3.18	3.66
0700	Structural steel, brushwork, light framing 300-500 S.F./Ton	.06	1.27	1.33
0720	Heavy framing 50-100 S.F./Ton	.06	.64	.70
0740	Spraywork, light framing 300-500 S.F./Ton	.06	.28	.34
0760	Heavy framing 50-100 S.F./Ton	.06	.31	.37
0800	Varnish, interior wood trim, no sanding sealer & 1 coat	.07	.80	.87
0820	Hardwood floor, no sanding 2 coats	.13	.17	.30
0840	Wall coatings, acrylic glazed coatings, minimum	.28	.61	.89
0860	Maximum	.57	1.04	1.61
0880	Epoxy coatings, minimum	.35	.61	.96
0900	Maximum	1.09	1.87	2.96
0940	Exposed epoxy aggregate, troweled on, 1/16" to 1/4" aggregate, minimum	.54	1.35	1.89
0960	Maximum	1.17	2.45	3.62
0980	1/2" to 5/8" aggregate, minimum	1.08	2.45	3.53
1000	Maximum	1.84	3.98	5.82
1020	1" aggregate, minimum	1.87	3.53	5.40
1040	Maximum	2.86	5.80	8.66
1060	Sprayed on, minimum	.51	1.08	1.59
1080	Maximum	.92	2.19	3.11
1100	High build epoxy 50 mil, minimum	.59	.82	1.41
1120	Maximum	1.02	3.35	4.37
1140	Laminated epoxy with fiberglass minimum	.65	1.08	1.73
1160	Maximum	1.16	2.19	3.35
1180	Sprayed perlite or vermiculite 1/16" thick, minimum	.23	.11	.34
1200	Maximum	.66	.50	1.16
1250	Wall coatings, vinyl plastic, minimum	.30	.43	.73
1280	Maximum	.73	1.32	2.05
1300	Urethane on smooth surface, 2 coats, minimum	.22	.28	.50
1320	Maximum	.50	.48	.98
1340	3 coats, minimum	.30	.38	.68
1360	Maximum	.66	.68	1.34
1380	Ceramic-like glazed coating, cementitious, minimum	.43	.72	1.15
1400	Maximum	.72	.92	1.64
1420	Resin base, minimum	.30	.50	.80
1440	Maximum	.48	.96	1.44
1460	Wall coverings, aluminum foil	.88	1.16	2.04
1480	Copper sheets, .025" thick, phenolic backing	6.10	1.33	7.43
1500	Vinyl backing	4.70	1.33	6.03
1520	Cork tiles, 12"x12", light or dark, 3/16" thick	2.68	1.33	4.01
1540	5/16" thick	3.12	1.36	4.48
1560	Basketweave, 1/4" thick	4.80	1.33	6.13

Important: See the Reference Section for critical supporting data - Location Factors & Historical Cost Indexes

6.5-100	Paint & Covering	COST PER S.F.		
		MAT.	INST.	TOTAL
1580	Natural, non-directional, 1/2" thick	6.75	1.33	8.08
1600	12"x36", granular, 3/16" thick	1.03	.83	1.86
1620	1" thick	1.34	.86	2.20
1640	12"x12", polyurethane coated, 3/16" thick	3.23	1.33	4.56
1660	5/16" thick	4.60	1.36	5.96
1661	Paneling, prefinished plywood, birch	1.23	1.74	2.97
1662	Mahogany, African	2.31	1.82	4.13
1663	Philippine (lauan)	.99	1.46	2.45
1664	Oak or cherry	2.97	1.82	4.79
1665	Rosewood	4.21	2.28	6.49
1666	Teak	2.97	1.82	4.79
1667	Chestnut	4.39	1.95	6.34
1668	Pecan	1.89	1.82	3.71
1669	Walnut	4.80	1.82	6.62
1670	Wood board, knotty pine, finished	1.39	2.43	3.82
1671	Rough sawn cedar	1.77	2.43	4.20
1672	Redwood	4.14	2.43	6.57
1673	Aromatic cedar	3.19	2.65	5.84
1680	Cork wallpaper, paper backed, natural	1.84	.67	2.51
1700	Color	2.28	.67	2.95
1720	Gypsum based, fabric backed, minimum	.72	.40	1.12
1740	Average	1.06	.44	1.50
1760	Maximum	1.18	.50	1.68
1780	Vinyl wall covering, fabric back, light weight	.59	.50	1.09
1800	Medium weight	.74	.67	1.41
1820	Heavy weight	1.19	.74	1.93
1840	Wall paper, double roll, solid pattern, avg. workmanship	.31	.50	.81
1860	Basic pattern, avg. workmanship	.67	.60	1.27
1880	Basic pattern, quality workmanship	1.61	.74	2.35
1900	Grass cloths with lining paper, minimum	.67	.80	1.47
1920	Maximum	2.15	.91	3.06
1940	Ceramic tile, thin set, 4-1/4" x 4-1/4"	2.30	3.16	5.46
1942				

6.5-100	Paint Trim	COST PER L.F.		
		MAT.	INST.	TOTAL
2040	Painting, wood trim, to 6" wide, enamel, primer & 1 coat	.10	.40	.50
2060	Primer & 2 coats	.15	.50	.65
2080	Misc. metal brushwork, ladders	.39	3.98	4.37
2100	Pipes, to 4" dia.	.06	.84	.90
2120	6" to 8" dia.	.13	1.67	1.80
2140	10" to 12" dia.	.38	2.50	2.88
2160	Railings, 2" pipe	.14	1.99	2.13
2180	Handrail, single	.10	.80	.90

INTERIOR CONSTRUCTION

3

6.6-100	Tile & Covering	COST PER S.F.		
		MAT.	INST.	TOTAL
0060	Carpet tile, nylon, fusion bonded, 18" x 18" or 24" x 24", 24 oz.	3.44	.46	3.90
0080	35 oz.	4	.46	4.46
0100	42 oz.	4.77	.46	5.23
0140	Carpet, tufted, nylon, roll goods, 12' wide, 26 oz.	3.11	.53	3.64
0160	36 oz.	4.94	.53	5.47
0180	Woven, wool, 36 oz.	7.85	.53	8.38
0200	42 oz.	7.95	.53	8.48
0220	Padding, add to above, minimum	.42	.25	.67
0240	Maximum	.73	.25	.98
0260	Composition flooring, acrylic, 1/4" thick	1.36	3.60	4.96
0280	3/8" thick	1.79	4.16	5.95
0300	Epoxy, minimum	2.41	2.77	5.18
0320	Maximum	2.93	3.82	6.75
0340	Epoxy terrazzo, minimum	4.88	3.81	8.69
0360	Maximum	8	5.10	13.10
0380	Mastic, hot laid, 1-1/2" thick, minimum	3.53	2.71	6.24
0400	Maximum	4.53	3.60	8.13
0420	Neoprene 1/4" thick, minimum	3.48	3.43	6.91
0440	Maximum	4.79	4.35	9.14
0460	Polyacrylate with ground granite 1/4", minimum	2.72	2.54	5.26
0480	Maximum	5.25	3.89	9.14
0500	Polyester with colored quart 2 chips 1/16", minimum	2.64	1.76	4.40
0520	Maximum	4.43	2.77	7.20
0540	Polyurethane with vinyl chips, minimum	6.80	1.76	8.56
0560	Maximum	9.75	2.18	11.93
0600	Concrete topping, granolithic concrete, 1/2" thick	.18	1.61	1.79
0620	1" thick	.36	1.65	2.01
0640	2" thick	.72	1.90	2.62
0660	Heavy duty 3/4" thick, minimum	2.31	2.50	4.81
0680	Maximum	2.31	2.97	5.28
0700	For colors, add to above, minimum	.33	.58	.91
0720	Maximum	.66	.63	1.29
0740	Exposed aggregate finish, minimum	3.96	.53	4.49
0760	Maximum	12.55	.71	13.26
0780	Abrasives, .25 P.S.F. add to above, minimum	.17	.39	.56
0800	Maximum	.20	.39	.59
0820	Dust on coloring, add, minimum	.64	.26	.90
0840	Maximum	2.23	.53	2.76
0860	1/2" integral, minimum	.21	1.61	1.82
0880	Maximum	.21	1.61	1.82
0900	Dustproofing, add, minimum	.08	.17	.25
0920	Maximum	.14	.26	.40
0930	Paint	.24	.95	1.19
0940	Hardeners, metallic add, minimum	.17	.39	.56
0960	Maximum	.38	.58	.96
0980	Non-metallic, minimum	.19	.39	.58
1000	Maximum	.52	.58	1.10
1020	Integral topping, 3/16" thick	.06	.95	1.01
1040	1/2" thick	.17	1	1.17
1060	3/4" thick	.26	1.12	1.38
1080	1" thick	.34	1.27	1.61
1100	Terrazzo, minimum	2.68	5.85	8.53
1120	Maximum	5	12.75	17.75
1280	Resilient, asphalt tile, 1/8" thick on concrete, minimum	1.06	.83	1.89
1300	Maximum	1.17	.83	2
1320	On wood, add for felt underlay	.20		.20
1340	Cork tile, minimum	3.80	1.06	4.86
1360	Maximum	9.05	1.06	10.11
1380	Polyethylene, in rolls, minimum	2.54	1.21	3.75
1400	Maximum	4.94	1.21	6.15

   Important: See the Reference Section for critical supporting data - Location Factors & Historical Cost Indexes

INTERIOR CONSTRUCTION 6

6.6-100	Tile & Covering	COST PER S.F.		
		MAT.	INST.	TOTAL
1420	Polyurethane, thermoset, minimum	3.91	3.33	7.24
1440	Maximum	4.64	6.65	11.29
1460	Rubber, sheet goods, minimum	3.50	2.77	6.27
1480	Maximum	5.75	3.70	9.45
1500	Tile, minimum	3.92	.83	4.75
1520	Maximum	6.65	1.21	7.86
1580	Vinyl, composition tile, minimum	.78	.67	1.45
1600	Maximum	2.24	.67	2.91
1620	Tile, minimum	1.75	.67	2.42
1640	Maximum	4.93	.67	5.60
1660	Sheet goods, minimum	2.04	1.33	3.37
1680	Maximum	3.93	1.66	5.59
1720	Tile, ceramic natural clay	4.29	3.29	7.58
1730	Marble, synthetic 12"x12"x5/8"	9.65	10	19.65
1740	Porcelain type, minimum	4.61	3.29	7.90
1760	Maximum	6.35	3.88	10.23
1800	Quarry tile, mud set, minimum	3.16	4.30	7.46
1820	Maximum	5.65	5.45	11.10
1840	Thin set, deduct		.86	.86
1860	Terrazzo precast, minimum	3.89	4.44	8.33
1880	Maximum	8.60	4.44	13.04
1900	Non-slip, minimum	16.20	22.50	38.70
1920	Maximum	18.65	31	49.65
1960	Wood, block, end grain factory type, creosoted, 2" thick	3.09	1.24	4.33
1980	2-1/2" thick	3.20	2.92	6.12
2000	3" thick	3.15	2.92	6.07
2020	Natural finish, 2" thick	3.19	2.92	6.11
2040	Fir, vertical grain, 1"x4", no finish, minimum	2.38	1.43	3.81
2060	Maximum	2.53	1.43	3.96
2080	Prefinished white oak, prime grade, 2-1/4" wide	6.45	2.15	8.60
2100	3-1/4" wide	8.25	1.97	10.22
2120	Maple strip, sanded and finished, minimum	3.64	3.12	6.76
2140	Maximum	4.30	3.12	7.42
2160	Oak strip, sanded and finished, minimum	3.69	3.12	6.81
2180	Maximum	4.57	3.12	7.69
2200	Parquetry, sanded and finished, minimum	3.22	3.25	6.47
2220	Maximum	6.35	4.62	10.97
2260	Add for sleepers on concrete, treated, 24" O.C., 1"x2"	.65	1.88	2.53
2280	1"x3"	.81	1.45	2.26
2300	2"x4"	.87	.74	1.61
2340	Underlayment, plywood, 3/8" thick	.64	.49	1.13
2350	1/2" thick	.81	.50	1.31
2360	5/8" thick	.77	.52	1.29
2370	3/4" thick	.99	.56	1.55
2380	Particle board, 3/8" thick	.42	.49	.91
2390	1/2" thick	.44	.50	.94
2400	5/8" thick	.59	.52	1.11
2410	3/4" thick	.64	.56	1.20
2420	Hardboard, 4' x 4', .215" thick	.45	.49	.94

INTERIOR CONSTRUCTION

6

Plaster Partitions are defined as follows: type of plaster, type and spacing of framing, type of lath and treatment of opposite face.

Included in the system components are expansion joints. Metal studs are assumed to be nonload bearing.

2 Coats of Plaster on Gypsum Lath on Wood Furring

Fiberglass Board on Exposed Suspended Grid System

Plaster and Metal Lath on Metal Furring

6.7-100 Plaster Ceilings

	TYPE	LATH	FURRING	SUPPORT		COST PER S.F. MAT.	INST.	TOTAL
2400	2 coat gypsum	3/8" gypsum	1"x3" wood, 16" O.C.	wood		1.11	3.70	4.81
2500	Painted			masonry		1.11	3.78	4.89
2600				concrete		1.11	4.23	5.34
2700	3 coat gypsum	3.4# metal	1"x3" wood, 16" O.C.	wood		1.12	3.95	5.07
2800	Painted			masonry		1.12	4.03	5.15
2900				concrete		1.12	4.48	5.60
3000	2 coat perlite	3/8" gypsum	1"x3" wood, 16" O.C.	wood		1.09	3.85	4.94
3100	Painted			masonry		1.09	3.93	5.02
3200				concrete		1.09	4.38	5.47
3300	3 coat perlite	3.4# metal	1"x3" wood, 16" O.C.	wood		.94	3.94	4.88
3400	Painted			masonry		.94	4.02	4.96
3500				concrete		.94	4.47	5.41
3600	2 coat gypsum	3/8" gypsum	3/4" CRC, 12" O.C.	1-1/2" CRC, 48"O.C.		1.13	4.52	5.65
3700	Painted		3/4" CRC, 16" O.C.	1-1/2" CRC, 48"O.C.		1.11	4.08	5.19
3800			3/4" CRC, 24" O.C.	1-1/2" CRC, 48"O.C.		1.06	3.72	4.78
3900	2 coat perlite	3/8" gypsum	3/4" CRC, 12" O.C.	1-1/2" CRC, 48"O.C		1.11	4.84	5.95
4000	Painted		3/4" CRC, 16" O.C.	1-1/2" CRC, 48"O.C.		1.09	4.40	5.49
4100			3/4" CRC, 24" O.C.	1-1/2" CRC, 48"O.C.		1.04	4.04	5.08
4200	3 coat gypsum	3.4# metal	3/4" CRC, 12" O.C.	1-1/2" CRC, 36" O.C.		1.47	5.90	7.37
4300	Painted		3/4" CRC, 16" O.C.	1-1/2" CRC, 36" O.C.		1.45	5.45	6.90
4400			3/4" CRC, 24" O.C.	1-1/2" CRC, 36" O.C.		1.40	5.05	6.45
4500	3 coat perlite	3.4# metal	3/4" CRC, 12" O.C.	1-1/2" CRC,36" O.C.		1.55	6.45	8
4600	Painted		3/4" CRC, 16" O.C.	1-1/2" CRC, 36" O.C.		1.53	6	7.53
4700			3/4" CRC, 24" O.C.	1-1/2" CRC, 36" O.C.		1.48	5.65	7.13

6.7-100 Drywall Ceilings

	TYPE	FINISH	FURRING	SUPPORT		COST PER S.F. MAT.	INST.	TOTAL
4800	1/2" F.R. drywall	painted and textured	1"x3" wood, 16" O.C.	wood		.63	2.29	2.92
4900				masonry		.63	2.37	3
5000				concrete		.63	2.82	3.45
5100	5/8" F.R. drywall	painted and textured	1"x3" wood, 16" O.C.	wood		.68	2.29	2.97
5200				masonry		.68	2.37	3.05
5300				concrete		.68	2.82	3.50
5400	1/2" F.R. drywall	painted and textured	7/8"resil. channels	24" O.C.		.57	2.23	2.80
5500			1"x2" wood	stud clips		.72	2.15	2.87
5602		painted	1-5/8" metal studs	24" O.C.		.59	1.99	2.58

Important: See the Reference Section for critical supporting data - Location Factors & Historical Cost Indexes

6.7-100 Drywall Ceilings

	TYPE	FINISH	FURRING	SUPPORT		COST PER S.F.		
						MAT.	INST.	TOTAL
5700 5702	5/8" F.R. drywall	painted and textured	1-5/8"metal studs	24" O.C.		.64	1.99	2.63

6.7-100 Acoustical Ceilings

	TYPE	TILE	GRID	SUPPORT		COST PER S.F.		
						MAT.	INST.	TOTAL
5800	5/8" fiberglass board	24" x 48"	tee	suspended		.94	1.05	1.99
5900		24" x 24"	tee	suspended		1.02	1.15	2.17
6000	3/4" fiberglass board	24" x 48"	tee	suspended		1.61	1.08	2.69
6100		24" x 24"	tee	suspended		1.69	1.18	2.87
6500	5/8" mineral fiber	12" x 12"	1"x3" wood, 12" O.C.	wood		1.05	1.40	2.45
6600				masonry		1.05	1.50	2.55
6700				concrete		1.05	2.10	3.15
6800	3/4" mineral fiber	12" x 12"	1"x3" wood, 12" O.C.	wood		1.54	1.40	2.94
6900				masonry		1.54	1.40	2.94
7000				concrete		1.54	1.40	2.94
7100 7102	3/4"mineral fiber on 5/8" F.R. drywall	12" x 12"	25 ga. channels	runners		1.96	1.91	3.87
7200 7201 7202	5/8" plastic coated Mineral fiber	12" x 12"		adhesive backed		1.20	.36	1.56
7300 7301 7302	3/4" plastic coated Mineral fiber	12" x 12"		adhesive backed		1.69	.36	2.05
7400 7401 7402	3/4" mineral fiber	12" x 12"	conceal 2" bar & channels	suspended		1.78	1.85	3.63

6.7-810 Acoustical Ceilings

		COST PER S.F.		
		MAT.	INST.	TOTAL
2480	Ceiling boards, eggcrate, acrylic, 1/2" x 1/2" x 1/2" cubes	1.55	.73	2.28
2500	Polystyrene, 3/8" x 3/8" x 1/2" cubes	1.30	.72	2.02
2520	1/2" x 1/2" x 1/2" cubes	1.74	.73	2.47
2540	Fiberglass boards, plain, 5/8" thick	.57	.58	1.15
2560	3/4" thick	1.24	.61	1.85
2580	Grass cloth faced, 3/4" thick	1.85	.73	2.58
2600	1" thick	1.99	.75	2.74
2620	Luminous panels, prismatic, acrylic	1.88	.91	2.79
2640	Polystyrene	.96	.91	1.87
2660	Flat or ribbed, acrylic	3.28	.91	4.19
2680	Polystyrene	2.24	.91	3.15
2700	Drop pan, white, acrylic	4.81	.91	5.72
2720	Polystyrene	4.02	.91	4.93
2740	Mineral fiber boards, 5/8" thick, standard	.67	.54	1.21
2760	Plastic faced	1.05	.91	1.96
2780	2 hour rating	.91	.54	1.45
2800	Perforated aluminum sheets, .024 thick, corrugated painted	1.91	.74	2.65
2820	Plain	2.38	.73	3.11
3080	Mineral fiber, plastic coated, 12" x 12" or 12" x 24", 5/8" thick	.84	.36	1.20
3100	3/4" thick	1.33	.36	1.69
3120	Fire rated, 3/4" thick, plain faced	1.13	.36	1.49
3140	Mylar faced	1.20	.36	1.56
3160	Add for ceiling primer	.13		.13
3180	Add for ceiling cement	.36		.36
3240	Suspension system, furring, 1" x 3" wood 12" O.C.	.21	1.04	1.25
3260	T bar suspension system, 2' x 4' grid	.36	.46	.82

For expanded coverage of these items see *Means Assemblies Cost Data 2001*

INTERIOR CONSTRUCTION

6

6.7-810	Acoustical Ceilings	COST PER S.F.		
		MAT.	INST.	TOTAL
3280	2' x 2' grid	.44	.56	1
3300	Concealed Z bar suspension system 12" module	.40	.70	1.10
3320	Add to above for 1-1/2" carrier channels 4' O.C.	.24	.78	1.02
3340	Add to above for carrier channels for recessed lighting	.37	.79	1.16

6.7-820	Plaster Ceilings	COST PER S.F.		
		MAT.	INST.	TOTAL
0060	Plaster, gypsum incl. finish, 2 coats			
0080	3 coats	.58	2.31	2.89
0100	Perlite, incl. finish, 2 coats	.40	2.30	2.70
0120	3 coats	.66	2.89	3.55
0140	Thin coat on drywall	.08	.46	.54
0200	Lath, gypsum, 3/8" thick	.43	.61	1.04
0220	1/2" thick	.43	.64	1.07
0240	5/8" thick	.48	.75	1.23
0260	Metal, diamond, 2.5 lb.	.18	.50	.68
0280	3.4 lb.	.28	.53	.81
0300	Flat rib, 2.75 lb.	.28	.50	.78
0320	3.4 lb.	.40	.53	.93
0440	Furring, steel channels, 3/4" galvanized , 12" O.C.	.18	1.60	1.78
0460	16" O.C.	.16	1.16	1.32
0480	24" O.C.	.11	.80	.91
0500	1-1/2" galvanized , 12" O.C.	.27	1.77	2.04
0520	16" O.C.	.24	1.30	1.54
0540	24" O.C.	.16	.86	1.02
0560	Wood strips, 1"x3", on wood, 12" O.C.	.21	1.04	1.25
0580	16" O.C.	.16	.78	.94
0600	24" O.C.	.11	.52	.63
0620	On masonry, 12" O.C.	.21	1.14	1.35
0640	16" O.C.	.16	.86	1.02
0660	24" O.C.	.11	.57	.68
0680	On concrete, 12" O.C.	.21	1.74	1.95
0700	16" O.C.	.16	1.31	1.47
0720	24" O.C.	.11	.87	.98
0940	Paint on plaster or drywall, roller work, primer + 1 coat	.10	.33	.43
0960	Primer + 2 coats	.15	.42	.57

For information about Means Estimating Seminars, see yellow pages 11 and 12 in back of book

INTERIOR CONSTRUCTION 6

Important: See the Reference Section for critical supporting data - Location Factors & Historical Cost Indexes

Division 7
Conveying Systems

Hydraulic   Traction Geared   Traction Gearless

7.1-100	Hydraulic	COST EACH		
		MAT.	INST.	TOTAL
1300	Pass. elev., 1500 lb., 2 Floors, 100 FPM	33,400	8,825	42,225
1400	5 Floors, 100 FPM	44,900	23,500	68,400
1600	2000 lb., 2 Floors, 100 FPM	33,900	8,825	42,725
1700	5 floors, 100 FPM	45,400	23,500	68,900
1900	2500 lb., 2 Floors, 100 FPM	34,600	8,825	43,425
2000	5 floors, 100 FPM	46,100	23,500	69,600
2200	3000 lb., 2 Floors, 100 FPM	36,300	8,825	45,125
2300	5 floors, 100 FPM	47,800	23,500	71,300
2500	3500 lb., 2 Floors, 100 FPM	38,400	8,825	47,225
2600	5 floors, 100 FPM	49,900	23,500	73,400
2800	4000 lb., 2 Floors, 100 FPM	39,200	8,825	48,025
2900	5 floors, 100 FPM	50,500	23,500	74,000
3100	4500 lb., 2 Floors, 100 FPM	40,400	8,825	49,225
3200	5 floors, 100 FPM	52,000	23,500	75,500
4000	Hospital elevators, 3500 lb., 2 Floors, 100 FPM	49,700	8,825	58,525
4100	5 floors, 100 FPM	74,000	23,500	97,500
4300	4000 lb., 2 Floors, 100 FPM	49,700	8,825	58,525
4400	5 floors, 100 FPM	74,000	23,500	97,500
4600	4500 lb., 2 Floors, 100 FPM	55,500	8,825	64,325
4800	5 floors, 100 FPM	79,500	23,500	103,000
4900	5000 lb., 2 Floors, 100 FPM	58,000	8,825	66,825
5000	5 floors, 100 FPM	82,500	23,500	106,000
6700	Freight elevators (Class "B"), 3000 lb., 2 Floors, 50 FPM	51,500	11,200	62,700
6800	5 floors, 100 FPM	75,000	29,500	104,500
7000	4000 lb., 2 Floors, 50 FPM	54,000	11,200	65,200
7100	5 floors, 100 FPM	77,500	29,500	107,000
7500	10,000 lb., 2 Floors, 50 FPM	67,500	11,200	78,700
7600	5 floors, 100 FPM	91,000	29,500	120,500
8100	20,000 lb., 2 Floors, 50 FPM	82,500	11,200	93,700
8200	5 Floors, 100 FPM	106,000	29,500	135,500

7.1-200	Traction Geared Elevators	COST EACH		
		MAT.	INST.	TOTAL
1300	Passenger, 2000 Lb., 5 floors, 200 FPM	75,500	22,200	97,700
1500	15 floors, 350 FPM	117,500	67,000	184,500
1600	2500 Lb., 5 floors, 200 FPM	78,500	22,200	100,700
1800	15 floors, 350 FPM	120,500	67,000	187,500
1900	3000 Lb., 5 floors, 200 FPM	80,000	22,200	102,200
2100	15 floors, 350 FPM	122,000	67,000	189,000
2200	3500 Lb., 5 floors, 200 FPM	81,500	22,200	103,700
2400	15 floors, 350 FPM	123,500	67,000	190,500
2500	4000 Lb., 5 floors, 200 FPM	81,500	22,200	103,700
2700	15 floors, 350 FPM	124,000	67,000	191,000
2800	4500 Lb., 5 floors, 200 FPM	83,500	22,200	105,700
3000	15 floors, 350 FPM	126,000	67,000	193,000

Important: See the Reference Section for critical supporting data - Location Factors & Historical Cost Indexes

7.1-200   Traction Geared Elevators

		MAT.	INST.	TOTAL
3100	5000 Lb., 5 floors, 200 FPM	86,000	22,200	108,200
3300	15 floors, 350 FPM	128,000	67,000	195,000
4000	Hospital, 3500 Lb., 5 floors, 200 FPM	91,500	22,200	113,700
4200	15 floors, 350 FPM	157,500	67,000	224,500
4300	4000 Lb., 5 floors, 200 FPM	91,500	22,200	113,700
4500	15 floors, 350 FPM	157,500	67,000	224,500
4600	4500 Lb., 5 floors, 200 FPM	96,500	22,200	118,700
4800	15 floors, 350 FPM	162,500	67,000	229,500
4900	5000 Lb., 5 floors, 200 FPM	98,000	22,200	120,200
5100	15 floors, 350 FPM	164,000	67,000	231,000
6000	Freight, 4000 Lb., 5 floors, 50 FPM class 'B'	81,500	22,900	104,400
6200	15 floors, 200 FPM class 'B'	151,000	80,000	231,000
6300	8000 Lb., 5 floors, 50 FPM class 'B'	98,500	22,900	121,400
6500	15 floors, 200 FPM class 'B'	167,500	80,000	247,500
7000	10,000 Lb., 5 floors, 50 FPM class 'B'	114,000	22,900	136,900
7200	15 floors, 200 FPM class 'B'	306,500	80,000	386,500
8000	20,000 Lb., 5 floors, 50 FPM class 'B'	126,000	22,900	148,900
8200	15 floors, 200 FPM class 'B'	319,000	80,000	399,000

7.1-300   Traction Gearless Elevators

		MAT.	INST.	TOTAL
1700	Passenger, 2500 Lb., 10 floors, 200 FPM	151,000	58,000	209,000
1900	30 floors, 600 FPM	263,500	147,500	411,000
2000	3000 Lb., 10 floors, 200 FPM	152,500	58,000	210,500
2200	30 floors, 600 FPM	265,000	147,500	412,500
2300	3500 Lb., 10 floors, 200 FPM	154,000	58,000	212,000
2500	30 floors, 600 FPM	266,500	147,500	414,000
2700	50 floors, 800 FPM	348,000	237,500	585,500
2800	4000 lb., 10 floors, 200 FPM	154,500	58,000	212,500
3000	30 floors, 600 FPM	266,500	147,500	414,000
3200	50 floors, 800 FPM	348,000	237,500	585,500
3300	4500 lb., 10 floors, 200 FPM	156,000	58,000	214,000
3500	30 floors, 600 FPM	268,500	147,500	416,000
3700	50 floors, 800 FPM	350,000	237,500	587,500
3800	5000 lb., 10 floors, 200 FPM	158,500	58,000	216,500
4000	30 floors, 600 FPM	271,000	147,500	418,500
4200	50 floors, 800 FPM	352,000	237,500	589,500
6000	Hospital, 3500 Lb., 10 floors, 200 FPM	176,000	58,000	234,000
6200	30 floors, 600 FPM	336,000	147,500	483,500
6400	4000 Lb., 10 floors, 200 FPM	176,000	58,000	234,000
6600	30 floors, 600 FPM	336,000	147,500	483,500
6800	4500 Lb., 10 floors, 200 FPM	181,000	58,000	239,000
7000	30 floors, 600 FPM	341,000	147,500	488,500
7200	5000 Lb., 10 floors, 200 FPM	182,500	58,000	240,500
7400	30 floors, 600 FPM	342,500	147,500	490,000

CONVEYING SYSTEMS

7

For information about Means Estimating Seminars, see yellow pages 11 and 12 in back of book

Division 8
Mechanical

8.1-040	Piping - Installed - Unit Costs	COST PER L.F.		
		MAT.	INST.	TOTAL
0840	Cast iron, soil, B & S, service weight, 2″ diameter	5.20	11.90	17.10
0860	3″ diameter	5.10	12.50	17.60
0880	4″ diameter	8.75	13.60	22.35
0900	5″ diameter	11.65	15.35	27
0920	6″ diameter	10.05	15.95	26
0940	8″ diameter	22	27	49
0960	10″ diameter	37	29.50	66.50
0980	12″ diameter	51.50	33	84.50
1040	No hub, 1-1/2″ diameter	5.55	10.55	16.10
1060	2″ diameter	5.60	11.20	16.80
1080	3″ diameter	7.25	11.70	18.95
1100	4″ diameter	8.95	12.90	21.85
1120	5″ diameter	12.50	14.05	26.55
1140	6″ diameter	15.60	14.75	30.35
1160	8″ diameter	24.50	23	47.50
1180	10″ diameter	40.50	26	66.50
1220	Copper tubing, hard temper, solder, type K, 1/2″ diameter	1.50	5.35	6.85
1260	3/4″ diameter	2.17	5.60	7.77
1280	1″ diameter	2.64	6.30	8.94
1300	1-1/4″ diameter	3.17	7.45	10.62
1320	1-1/2″ diameter	3.88	8.30	12.18
1340	2″ diameter	5.75	10.40	16.15
1360	2-1/2″ diameter	8.35	12.50	20.85
1380	3″ diameter	11.30	13.85	25.15
1400	4″ diameter	17.55	19.70	37.25
1480	5″ diameter	46	23.50	69.50
1500	6″ diameter	66	30.50	96.50
1520	8″ diameter	117	34.50	151.50
1560	Type L, 1/2″ diameter	1.38	5.15	6.53
1600	3/4″ diameter	1.74	5.45	7.19
1620	1″ diameter	2.23	6.10	8.33
1640	1-1/4″ diameter	2.80	7.15	9.95
1660	1-1/2″ diameter	3.37	8	11.37
1680	2″ diameter	4.92	9.90	14.82
1700	2-1/2″ diameter	7.15	12.10	19.25
1720	3″ diameter	9.50	13.35	22.85
1740	4″ diameter	14.90	19.20	34.10
1760	5″ diameter	41.50	22	63.50
1780	6″ diameter	52	29	81
1800	8″ diameter	90	32.50	122.50
1840	Type M, 1/2″ diameter	1.16	4.95	6.11
1880	3/4″ diameter	1.47	5.35	6.82
1900	1″ diameter	1.87	5.95	7.82
1920	1-1/4″ diameter	2.39	6.95	9.34
1940	1-1/2″ diameter	3.05	7.70	10.75
1960	2″ diameter	4.59	9.45	14.04
1980	2-1/2″ diameter	6.35	11.70	18.05
2000	3″ diameter	8.05	12.90	20.95
2020	4″ diameter	13.40	18.70	32.10
2060	6″ diameter	51	27.50	78.50
2080	8″ diameter	84.50	30.50	115
2120	Type DWV, 1-1/4″ diameter	2.36	6.95	9.31
2160	1-1/2″ diameter	2.79	7.70	10.49
2180	2″ diameter	3.51	9.45	12.96
2200	3″ diameter	5.75	12.90	18.65
2220	4″ diameter	9.85	18.70	28.55
2240	5″ diameter	28.50	21	49.50
2260	6″ diameter	40	27.50	67.50

Important: See the Reference Section for critical supporting data - Location Factors & Historical Cost Indexes

8.1-040	Piping - Installed - Unit Costs	COST PER L.F.		
		MAT.	INST.	TOTAL
2280	8″ diameter	88	30.50	118.50
2800	Plastic,PVC, DWV, schedule 40, 1-1/4″ diameter	2.57	9.90	12.47
2820	1-1/2″ diameter	2.69	11.55	14.24
2830	2″ diameter	2.76	12.70	15.46
2840	3″ diameter	4.78	14.15	18.93
2850	4″ diameter	5.20	15.60	20.80
2890	6″ diameter	8.95	19.20	28.15
3010	Pressure pipe 200 PSI, 1/2″ diameter	2.41	7.70	10.11
3030	3/4″ diameter	2.43	8.15	10.58
3040	1″ diameter	2.59	9.05	11.64
3050	1-1/4″ diameter	2.84	9.90	12.74
3060	1-1/2″ diameter	2.97	11.55	14.52
3070	2″ diameter	3.20	12.70	15.90
3080	2-1/2″ diameter	4.72	13.35	18.07
3090	3″ diameter	5.20	14.15	19.35
3100	4″ diameter	6.50	15.60	22.10
3110	6″ diameter	11.45	19.20	30.65
3120	8″ diameter	15.65	24.50	40.15
4000	Steel, schedule 40, threaded, black, 1/2″ diameter	1.35	6.60	7.95
4020	3/4″ diameter	1.50	6.80	8.30
4030	1″ diameter	1.91	7.85	9.76
4040	1-1/4″ diameter	2.24	8.40	10.64
4050	1-1/2″ diameter	2.51	9.35	11.86
4060	2″ diameter	3.18	11.70	14.88
4070	2-1/2″ diameter	5.05	15	20.05
4080	3″ diameter	6.35	17.40	23.75
4090	4″ diameter	9.40	21	30.40
4100	5″ diameter	13.80	29	42.80
4110	6″ diameter	18.15	37.50	55.65
4120	8″ diameter	24.50	43	67.50
4130	10″ diameter	43	50.50	93.50
4140	12″ diameter	54.50	64.50	119
4200	Galvanized, 1/2″ diameter	1.51	6.60	8.11
4220	3/4″ diameter	1.68	6.80	8.48
4230	1″ diameter	1.99	7.85	9.84
4240	1-1/4″ diameter	2.37	8.40	10.77
4250	1-1/2″ diameter	2.63	9.35	11.98
4260	2″ diameter	3.34	11.70	15.04
4270	2-1/2″ diameter	4.97	15	19.97
4280	3″ diameter	6.15	17.40	23.55
4290	4″ diameter	8.85	21	29.85
4300	5″ diameter	16.40	29	45.40
4310	6″ diameter	22.50	37.50	60
4320	8″ diameter	36.50	43	79.50
4330	10″ diameter	53	50.50	103.50
4340	12″ diameter	73.50	64.50	138
5010	Flanged, black, 1″ diameter	6.65	12.30	18.95
5020	1-1/4″ diameter	7.35	13.45	20.80
5030	1-1/2″ diameter	7.55	14.80	22.35
5040	2″ diameter	8.50	19.10	27.60
5050	2-1/2″ diameter	10.40	24	34.40
5060	3″ diameter	11.35	27	38.35
5070	4″ diameter	14.90	33.50	48.40
5080	5″ diameter	24.50	41	65.50
5090	6″ diameter	28.50	51	79.50
5100	8″ diameter	43	67.50	110.50
5110	10″ diameter	74	80	154
5120	12″ diameter	101	91	192
5720	Grooved joints, black, 3/4″ diameter	2.11	5.85	7.96
5730	1″ diameter	2.24	6.60	8.84

For expanded coverage of these items see *Means Mechanical or Plumbing Cost Data 2001*

8.1-040	Piping - Installed - Unit Costs	COST PER L.F.		
		MAT.	INST.	TOTAL
5740	1-1/4" diameter	2.76	7.15	9.91
5750	1-1/2" diameter	3.06	8.15	11.21
5760	2" diameter	3.54	10.40	13.94
5770	2-1/2" diameter	5.20	13.15	18.35
5900	3" diameter	5.85	15	20.85
5910	4" diameter	8.30	16.65	24.95
5920	5" diameter	14	20	34
5930	6" diameter	18.20	27.50	45.70
5940	8" diameter	27.50	31.50	59
5950	10" diameter	41	37.50	78.50
5960	12" diameter	54	43	97

MECHANICAL 8

Important: See the Reference Section for critical supporting data - Location Factors & Historical Cost Indexes

Installation includes piping and fittings within 10' of heater. Gas heaters require vent piping (not included with these units).

Gas Fired

Oil Fired

8.1-120	Gas Fired Water Heaters - Residential Systems	COST EACH		
		MAT.	INST.	TOTAL
2200	Gas fired water heater, residential, 100° F rise			
2220	20 gallon tank, 25 GPH	415	845	1,260
2260	30 gallon tank, 32 GPH	575	860	1,435
2300	40 gallon tank, 32 GPH	635	965	1,600
2340	50 gallon tank, 63 GPH	785	965	1,750
2380	75 gallon tank, 63 GPH	905	1,075	1,980
2420	100 gallon tank, 63 GPH	1,200	1,125	2,325
2422				

8.1-130	Oil Fired Water Heaters - Residential Systems	COST EACH		
		MAT.	INST.	TOTAL
2200	Oil fired water heater, residential, 100° F rise			
2220	30 gallon tank, 103 GPH	1,025	800	1,825
2260	50 gallon tank, 145 GPH	1,375	895	2,270
2300	70 gallon tank, 164 GPH	1,800	1,000	2,800
2340	85 gallon tank, 181 GPH	4,075	1,025	5,100

MECHANICAL

8

Systems below include piping and fittings within 10' of heater. Electric water heaters do not require venting. Gas fired heaters require vent piping (not included in these prices).

Electric

Gas Fired

8.1-160	Electric Water Heaters - Commercial Systems	COST EACH		
		MAT.	INST.	TOTAL
1800	Electric water heater, commercial, 100° F rise			
1820	50 gallon tank, 9 KW 37 GPH	2,350	725	3,075
1860	80 gal, 12 KW 49 GPH	2,950	890	3,840
1900	36 KW 147 GPH	4,025	965	4,990
1940	120 gal, 36 KW 147 GPH	4,325	1,050	5,375
1980	150 gal, 120 KW 490 GPH	13,500	1,125	14,625
2020	200 gal, 120 KW 490 GPH	14,300	1,150	15,450
2060	250 gal, 150 KW 615 GPH	15,800	1,350	17,150
2100	300 gal, 180 KW 738 GPH	17,300	1,400	18,700
2140	350 gal, 30 KW 123 GPH	12,800	1,525	14,325
2180	180 KW 738 GPH	17,800	1,525	19,325
2220	500 gal, 30 KW 123 GPH	16,700	1,800	18,500
2260	240 KW 984 GPH	24,300	1,800	26,100
2300	700 gal, 30 KW 123 GPH	20,100	2,050	22,150
2340	300 KW 1230 GPH	29,900	2,050	31,950
2380	1000 gal, 60 KW 245 GPH	24,200	2,850	27,050
2420	480 KW 1970 GPH	24,800	2,875	27,675
2460	1500 gal, 60 KW 245 GPH	35,500	3,525	39,025
2500	480 KW 1970 GPH	48,800	3,525	52,325

8.1-170	Gas Fired Water Heaters - Commercial Systems	COST EACH		
		MAT.	INST.	TOTAL
1760	Gas fired water heater, commercial, 100° F rise			
1780	75.5 MBH input, 63 GPH	1,700	1,100	2,800
1820	95 MBH input, 86 GPH	2,725	1,100	3,825
1860	100 MBH input, 91 GPH	2,925	1,150	4,075
1900	115 MBH input, 110 GPH	2,500	1,200	3,700
1980	155 MBH input, 150 GPH	3,525	1,350	4,875
2020	175 MBH input, 168 GPH	3,200	1,425	4,625
2060	200 MBH input, 192 GPH	3,275	1,625	4,900
2100	240 MBH input, 230 GPH	3,450	1,775	5,225
2140	300 MBH input, 278 GPH	3,800	2,025	5,825
2180	390 MBH input, 374 GPH	4,450	2,050	6,500
2220	500 MBH input, 480 GPH	5,950	2,200	8,150
2260	600 MBH input, 576 GPH	9,650	2,375	12,025

Important: See the Reference Section for critical supporting data - Location Factors & Historical Cost Indexes

MECHANICAL 8

Oil fired water heater systems include piping and fittings within 10′ of heater. Oil fired heaters require vent piping (not included in these systems).

Oil Fired

8.1-180	Oil Fired Water Heaters - Commercial Systems	COST EACH		
		MAT.	INST.	TOTAL
1800	Oil fired water heater, commercial, 100° F rise			
1820	103 MBH output, 116 GPH	1,175	975	2,150
1900	134 MBH output, 161 GPH	1,950	1,250	3,200
1940	161 MBH output, 192 GPH	2,175	1,425	3,600
1980	187 MBH output, 224 GPH	2,425	1,650	4,075
2060	262 MBH output, 315 GPH	2,850	1,900	4,750
2100	341 MBH output, 409 GPH	3,500	2,025	5,525
2140	420 MBH output, 504 GPH	3,925	2,200	6,125
2180	525 MBH output, 630 GPH	5,350	2,475	7,825
2220	630 MBH output, 756 GPH	5,550	2,475	8,025
2260	735 MBH output, 880 GPH	6,300	2,875	9,175
2300	840 MBH output, 1000 GPH	7,125	2,875	10,000
2340	1050 MBH output, 1260 GPH	7,950	2,950	10,900
2380	1365 MBH output, 1640 GPH	9,675	3,350	13,025
2420	1680 MBH output, 2000 GPH	10,900	4,200	15,100
2460	2310 MBH output, 2780 GPH	14,000	5,175	19,175
2500	2835 MBH output, 3400 GPH	16,400	5,175	21,575
2540	3150 MBH output, 3780 GPH	17,900	7,125	25,025

MECHANICAL

8

Design Assumptions: Vertical conductor size is based on a maximum rate of rainfall of 4" per hour. To convert roof area to other rates multiply "Max. S.F. Roof Area" shown by four and divide the result by desired local rate. The answer is the local roof area that may be handled by the indicated pipe diameter.

Basic cost is for roof drain, 10' of vertical leader and 10' of horizontal, plus connection to the main.

Pipe Dia.	Max. S.F. Roof Area	Gallons per Min.
2"	544	23
3"	1610	67
4"	3460	144
5"	6280	261
6"	10,200	424
8"	22,000	913

8.1-310	Roof Drain Systems	COST PER SYSTEM		
		MAT.	INST.	TOTAL
1880	Roof drain, DWV PVC, 2" diam., piping, 10' high	110	415	525
1920	For each additional foot add	2.76	12.70	15.46
1960	3" diam., 10' high	163	485	648
2000	For each additional foot add	4.78	14.15	18.93
2040	4" diam., 10' high	186	545	731
2080	For each additional foot add	5.20	15.60	20.80
2120	5" diam., 10' high	395	630	1,025
2160	For each additional foot add	8.50	17.40	25.90
2200	6" diam., 10' high	585	700	1,285
2240	For each additional foot add	8.95	19.20	28.15
2280	8" diam., 10' high	1,375	1,200	2,575
2320	For each additional foot add	14.40	24.50	38.90
3940	C.I., soil, single hub, service wt., 2" diam. piping, 10' high	247	455	702
3980	For each additional foot add	5.20	11.90	17.10
4120	3" diam., 10' high	310	495	805
4160	For each additional foot add	5.10	12.50	17.60
4200	4" diam., 10' high	405	540	945
4240	For each additional foot add	8.75	13.60	22.35
4280	5" diam., 10' high	450	595	1,045
4320	For each additional foot add	11.65	15.35	27
4360	6" diam., 10' high	610	635	1,245
4400	For each additional foot add	10.05	15.95	26
4440	8" diam., 10' high	1,500	1,300	2,800
4480	For each additional foot add	22	27	49
6040	Steel galv. sch 40 threaded, 2" diam. piping, 10' high	246	440	686
6080	For each additional foot add	3.34	11.70	15.04
6120	3" diam., 10' high	460	635	1,095
6160	For each additional foot add	6.15	17.40	23.55
6200	4" diam., 10' high	650	820	1,470
6240	For each additional foot add	8.85	21	29.85
6280	5" diam., 10' high	775	1,050	1,825
6320	For each additional foot add	16.40	29	45.40
6360	6" diam, 10' high	1,425	1,275	2,700
6400	For each additional foot add	22.50	37.50	60
6440	8" diam., 10' high	2,900	1,725	4,625
6480	For each additional foot add	36.50	43	79.50

MECHANICAL 8

Reference-Minimum Plumbing Fixture Requirements

Type of Building/Use	Water Closets		Urinals		Lavatories		Bathtubs or Showers		Drinking Fountain	Other
	Persons	Fixtures	Persons	Fixtures	Persons	Fixtures	Persons	Fixtures	Fixtures	Fixtures
Assembly Halls Auditoriums Theater Public assembly	1-100 101-200 201-400	1 2 3	1-200 201-400 401-600	1 2 3	1-200 201-400 401-750	1 2 3			1 for each 1000 persons	1 service sink
	Over 400 add 1 fixt. for ea. 500 men; 1 fixt. for ea. 300 women		Over 600 add 1 fixture for each 300 men		Over 750 add 1 fixture for each 500 persons					
Assembly Public Worship	300 men 150 women	1 1	300 men	1	men women	1 1			1	
Dormitories	Men: 1 for each 10 persons Women: 1 for each 8 persons		1 for each 25 men; over 150 add 1 fixture for each 50 men		1 for ea. 12 persons 1 separate dental lav. for each 50 persons recom.		1 for ea. 8 persons For women add 1 additional for each 30. Over 150 persons add 1 for each 20.		1 for each 75 persons	Laundry trays 1 for each 50 serv. sink 1 for ea. 100
Dwellings Apartments and homes	1 fixture for each unit				1 fixture for each unit		1 fixture for each unit			
Hospitals Indiv. Room Ward Waiting room	8 persons	1 1 1			10 persons	1 1 1	20 persons	1 1	1 for 100 patients	1 service sink per floor
Industrial Mfg. plants Warehouses	1-10 11-25 26-50 51-75 76-100	1 2 3 4 5	0-30 31-80 81-160 161-240	1 2 3 4	1-100 over 100	1 for ea. 10 1 for ea. 15	1 Shower for each 15 persons subject to excessive heat or occupation- al hazard		1 for each 75 persons	
	1 fixture for each additional 30 persons									
Public Buildings Businesses Offices	1-15 16-35 36-55 56-80 81-110 111-150	1 2 3 4 5 6	Urinals may be provided in place of water closets but may not replace more than 1/3 required number of men's water closets		1-15 16-35 36-60 61-90 91-125	1 2 3 4 5			1 for each 75 persons	1 service sink per floor
	1 fixture for ea. additional 40 persons				1 fixture for ea. additional 45 persons					
Schools Elementary	1 for ea. 30 boys 1 for ea. 25 girls		1 for ea. 25 boys		1 for ea. 35 boys 1 for ea. 35 girls		For gym or pool shower room 1/5 of a class		1 for each 40 pupils	
Schools Secondary	1 for ea. 40 boys 1 for ea. 30 girls		1 for ea. 25 boys		1 for ea. 40 boys 1 for ea. 40 girls		For gym or pool shower room 1/5 of a class		1 for each 50 pupils	

MECHANICAL

8

Recessed Bathtub   **Corner Bathtub**

Systems are complete with trim and rough-in (supply, waste and vent) to connect to supply branches and waste mains.

Drinking Fountain

Drinking Fountain

8.1-410	Bathtub Systems	COST EACH		
		MAT.	**INST.**	**TOTAL**
1960	Bathtub, recessed, P.E. on CI., 42" x 37"	900	510	1,410
2000	48" x 42"	1,275	550	1,825
2040	72" x 36"	1,425	610	2,035
2080	Mat bottom, 5' long	515	530	1,045
2120	5'-6" long	1,075	550	1,625
2160	Corner, 48" x 42"	1,525	530	2,055
2200	Formed steel, enameled, 4'-6" long	425	490	915
2240	5' long	410	500	910

8.1-420	Drinking Fountain Systems	COST EACH		
		MAT.	**INST.**	**TOTAL**
1740	Drinking fountain, one bubbler, wall mounted			
1760	Non recessed			
1800	Bronze, no back	1,150	291	1,441
1840	Cast iron, enameled, low back	510	291	801
1880	Fiberglass, 12" back	625	291	916
1920	Stainless steel, no back	915	291	1,206
1960	Semi-recessed, poly marble	750	291	1,041
2040	Stainless steel	870	291	1,161
2080	Vitreous china	515	291	806
2120	Full recessed, poly marble	840	291	1,131
2200	Stainless steel	735	291	1,026
2240	Floor mounted, pedestal type, aluminum	520	395	915
2320	Bronze	1,300	395	1,695
2360	Stainless steel	1,300	395	1,695

MECHANICAL 8

Systems are complete with trim and rough-in (supply, waste and vent) to connect to supply branches and waste mains.

Counter Top Single Bowl

Counter Top Double Bowl

Single Compartment Sink

Double Compartment Sink

8.1-431	Kitchen Sink Systems	COST EACH		
		MAT.	INST.	TOTAL
1720	Kitchen sink w/trim, countertop, PE on CI, 24"x21", single bowl	274	485	759
1760	30" x 21" single bowl	430	485	915
1800	32" x 21" double bowl	370	525	895
1840	42" x 21" double bowl	565	530	1,095
1880	Stainless steel, 19" x 18" single bowl	380	485	865
1920	25" x 22" single bowl	410	485	895
1960	33" x 22" double bowl	565	525	1,090
2000	43" x 22" double bowl	640	530	1,170
2040	44" x 22" triple bowl	915	550	1,465
2080	44" x 24" corner double bowl	620	530	1,150
2120	Steel, enameled, 24" x 21" single bowl	179	485	664
2160	32" x 21" double bowl	214	525	739
2240	Raised deck, PE on CI, 32" x 21", dual level, double bowl	475	665	1,140
2280	42" x 21" dual level, triple bowl	670	720	1,390

8.1-432	Laundry Sink Systems	COST EACH		
		MAT.	INST.	TOTAL
1740	Laundry sink w/trim, PE on CI, black iron frame			
1760	24" x 20", single compartment	440	475	915
1840	48" x 21" double compartment	775	515	1,290
1920	Molded stone, on wall, 22" x 21" single compartment	199	475	674
1960	45"x 21" double compartment	345	515	860
2040	Plastic, on wall or legs, 18" x 23" single compartment	161	465	626
2080	20" x 24" single compartment	189	465	654
2120	36" x 23" double compartment	216	505	721
2160	40" x 24" double compartment	282	505	787
2200	Stainless steel, countertop, 22" x 17" single compartment	365	475	840
2240	19" x 22" single compartment	445	475	920
2280	33" x 22" double compartment	420	515	935

MECHANICAL

8

Systems are complete with trim and rough-in (supply, waste and vent) to connect to supply branches and waste mains.

Vanity Top

Wall Hung

Laboratory Sink

Service Sink

8.1-433	Lavatory Systems	COST EACH		
		MAT.	INST.	TOTAL
1560	Lavatory w/trim, vanity top, PE on CI, 20" x 18", Vanity top by others.	234	445	679
1600	19" x 16" oval	234	445	679
1640	18" round	221	445	666
1680	Cultured marble, 19" x 17"	173	445	618
1720	25" x 19"	203	445	648
1760	Stainless, self-rimming, 25" x 22"	240	445	685
1800	17" x 22"	235	445	680
1840	Steel enameled, 20" x 17"	155	455	610
1880	19" round	153	455	608
1920	Vitreous china, 20" x 16"	246	465	711
1960	19" x 16"	246	465	711
2000	22" x 13"	256	465	721
2040	Wall hung, PE on CI, 18" x 15"	535	490	1,025
2080	19" x 17"	525	490	1,015
2120	20" x 18"	410	490	900
2160	Vitreous china, 18" x 15"	355	500	855
2200	19" x 17"	340	500	840
2240	24" x 20"	465	500	965
2241				
2243				

8.1-434	Laboratory Sink Systems	COST EACH		
		MAT.	INST.	TOTAL
1580	Laboratory sink w/trim, polyethylene, single bowl,			
1600	Double drainboard, 54" x 24" O.D.	935	620	1,555
1640	Single drainboard, 47" x 24"O.D.	975	620	1,595
1680	70" x 24" O.D.	995	620	1,615
1760	Flanged, 14-1/2" x 14-1/2" O.D.	370	560	930
1800	18-1/2" x 18-1/2" O.D.	325	560	885
1840	23-1/2" x 20-1/2" O.D.	380	560	940
1920	Polypropylene, cup sink, oval, 7" x 4" O.D.	168	495	663
1960	10" x 4-1/2" O.D.	179	495	674
1961				

8.1-434	Service Sink Systems	COST EACH		
		MAT.	INST.	TOTAL
4260	Service sink w/trim, PE on CI, corner floor, 28" x 28", w/rim guard	665	625	1,290
4300	Wall hung w/rim guard, 22" x 18"	730	725	1,455
4340	24" x 20"	775	725	1,500
4380	Vitreous china, wall hung 22" x 20"	705	725	1,430

Important: See the Reference Section for critical supporting data - Location Factors & Historical Cost Indexes

MECHANICAL 8

Square Shower Stall

Corner Angle Shower Stall

Systems are complete with trim and rough-in (supply, waste and vent) to connect to supply branches and waste mains.

Wall Hung Urinal

Stall Type Urinal

Wall Hung Water Cooler

Floor Mounted Water Cooler

8.1-440	Shower Systems	COST EACH		
		MAT.	INST.	TOTAL
1560	Shower, stall, baked enamel, molded stone receptor, 30" square	440	740	1,180
1600	32" square	410	740	1,150
1640	Terrazzo receptor, 32" square	1,175	740	1,915
1680	36" square	970	780	1,750
1720	36" corner angle	890	780	1,670
1800	Fiberglass one piece, three walls, 32" square	385	675	1,060
1840	36" square	430	675	1,105
1880	Polypropylene, molded stone receptor, 30" square	475	740	1,215
1920	32" square	460	740	1,200
1960	Built-in head, arm, bypass, stops and handles	88	193	281

8.1-450	Urinal Systems	COST EACH		
		MAT.	INST.	TOTAL
2000	Urinal, vitreous china, wall hung	390	535	925
2040	Stall type	605	590	1,195

8.1-460	Water Cooler Systems	COST EACH		
		MAT.	INST.	TOTAL
1840	Water cooler, electric, wall hung, 8.2 GPH	630	375	1,005
1880	Dual height, 14.3 GPH	935	385	1,320
1920	Wheelchair type, 7.5 G.P.H.	1,575	375	1,950
1960	Semi recessed, 8.1 G.P.H.	900	375	1,275
2000	Full recessed, 8 G.P.H.	1,375	400	1,775
2040	Floor mounted, 14.3 G.P.H.	665	325	990
2080	Dual height, 14.3 G.P.H.	985	395	1,380
2120	Refrigerated compartment type, 1.5 G.P.H.	1,225	325	1,550

MECHANICAL

8

One Piece Wall Hung Water Closet

Circular Wash Fountain

Side By Side Water Closet Group

Floor Mount Water Closet

Semi-Circular Wash Fountain

Back to Back Water Closet Group

8.1-470	Water Closet Systems	COST EACH		
		MAT.	INST.	TOTAL
1800	Water closet, vitreous china, elongated			
1840	Tank type, wall hung, one piece	750	435	1,185
1880	Close coupled two piece	805	435	1,240
1920	Floor mount, one piece	675	470	1,145
1960	One piece low profile	735	470	1,205
2000	Two piece close coupled	291	470	761
2040	Bowl only with flush valve			
2080	Wall hung	670	490	1,160
2120	Floor mount	480	475	955
2122				

8.1-510	Water Closets, Group	COST EACH		
		MAT.	INST.	TOTAL
1760	Water closets, battery mount, wall hung, side by side, first closet	705	505	1,210
1800	Each additional water closet, add	670	480	1,150
3000	Back to back, first pair of closets	1,275	685	1,960
3100	Each additional pair of closets, back to back	1,250	675	1,925

8.1-560	Group Wash Fountain Systems	COST EACH		
		MAT.	INST.	TOTAL
1740	Group wash fountain, precast terrazzo			
1760	Circular, 36" diameter	2,600	800	3,400
1800	54" diameter	3,125	875	4,000
1840	Semi-circular, 36" diameter	2,350	800	3,150
1880	54" diameter	2,875	875	3,750
1960	Stainless steel, circular, 36" diameter	3,000	745	3,745
2000	54" diameter	3,925	825	4,750
2040	Semi-circular, 36" diameter	2,600	745	3,345
2080	54" diameter	3,400	825	4,225
2160	Thermoplastic, circular, 36" diameter	2,350	605	2,955
2200	54" diameter	2,750	705	3,455
2240	Semi-circular, 36" diameter	2,200	605	2,805
2280	54" diameter	2,600	705	3,305

Two Fixture　　　　　Three Fixture

*Common wall is with adjacent bathroom

| 8.1-620 | Two Fixture Bathroom, Two Wall Plumbing | COST EACH | | |
		MAT.	INST.	TOTAL
1180	Bathroom, lavatory & water closet, 2 wall plumbing, stand alone	795	1,225	2,020
1200	Share common plumbing wall*	750	1,050	1,800

| 8.1-620 | Two Fixture Bathroom, One Wall Plumbing | COST EACH | | |
		MAT.	INST.	TOTAL
2220	Bathroom, lavatory & water closet, one wall plumbing, stand alone	760	1,100	1,860
2240	Share common plumbing wall*	680	930	1,610

| 8.1-630 | Three Fixture Bathroom, One Wall Plumbing | COST EACH | | |
		MAT.	INST.	TOTAL
1150	Bathroom, three fixture, one wall plumbing			
1160	Lavatory, water closet & bathtub			
1170	Stand alone	1,175	1,425	2,600
1180	Share common plumbing wall *	995	1,025	2,020

| 8.1-630 | Three Fixture Bathroom, Two Wall Plumbing | COST EACH | | |
		MAT.	INST.	TOTAL
2130	Bathroom, three fixture, two wall plumbing			
2140	Lavatory, water closet & bathtub			
2160	Stand alone	1,175	1,450	2,625
2180	Long plumbing wall common *	1,050	1,150	2,200
3610	Lavatory, bathtub & water closet			
3620	Stand alone	1,250	1,650	2,900
3640	Long plumbing wall common *	1,200	1,475	2,675
4660	Water closet, corner bathtub & lavatory			
4680	Stand alone	2,200	1,450	3,650
4700	Long plumbing wall common *	2,075	1,100	3,175
6100	Water closet, stall shower & lavatory			
6120	Stand alone	1,175	1,875	3,050
6140	Long plumbing wall common *	1,125	1,750	2,875
7060	Lavatory, corner stall shower & water closet			
7080	Stand alone	1,575	1,700	3,275
7100	Short plumbing wall common *	1,450	1,225	2,675

MECHANICAL

8

Four Fixture   Five Fixture

*Common wall is with adjacent bathroom

8.1-640	Four Fixture Bathroom, Two Wall Plumbing	COST EACH		
		MAT.	INST.	TOTAL
1140	Bathroom, four fixture, two wall plumbing			
1150	Bathtub, water closet, stall shower & lavatory			
1160	Stand alone	1,400	1,800	3,200
1180	Long plumbing wall common *	1,300	1,425	2,725
2260	Bathtub, lavatory, corner stall shower & water closet			
2280	Stand alone	1,900	1,825	3,725
2320	Long plumbing wall common *	1,775	1,475	3,250
3620	Bathtub, stall shower, lavatory & water closet			
3640	Stand alone	1,600	2,200	3,800
3660	Long plumbing wall (opp. door) common *	1,475	1,850	3,325
4680	Bathroom, four fixture, three wall plumbing			
4700	Bathtub, stall shower, lavatory & water closet			
4720	Stand alone	2,125	2,425	4,550
4761	Long plumbing wall (opposite door) common*	2,075	2,275	4,350

8.1-650	Five Fixture Bathroom, Two Wall Plumbing	COST EACH		
		MAT.	INST.	TOTAL
1320	Bathroom, five fixture, two wall plumbing			
1340	Bathtub, water closet, stall shower & two lavatories			
1360	Stand alone	2,000	2,750	4,750
1400	One short plumbing wall common *	1,900	2,375	4,275
2360	Bathroom, five fixture, three wall plumbing			
2380	Water closet, bathtub, two lavatories & stall shower			
2400	Stand alone	2,475	2,775	5,250
2440	One short plumbing wall common *	2,375	2,425	4,800
4080	Bathroom, five fixture, one wall plumbing			
4100	Bathtub, two lavatories, corner stall shower & water closet			
4120	Stand alone	2,350	2,525	4,875
4160	Share common wall *	1,975	1,725	3,700

Reference-Sprinkler Systems (Automatic)

Sprinkler systems may be classified by type as follows:

1. **Wet Pipe System.** A system employing automatic sprinklers attached to a piping system containing water and connected to a water supply so that water discharges immediately from sprinklers opened by a fire.

2. **Dry Pipe System.** A system employing automatic sprinklers attached to a piping system containing air under pressure, the release of which as from the opening of sprinklers permits the water pressure to open a valve known as a "dry pipe valve". The water then flows into the piping system and out the opened sprinklers.

3. **Pre-Action System.** A system employing automatic sprinklers attached to a piping system containing air that may or may not be under pressure, with a supplemental heat responsive system of generally more sensitive characteristics than the automatic sprinklers themselves, installed in the same areas as the sprinklers; actuation of the heat responsive system, as from a fire, opens a valve which permits water to flow into the sprinkler piping system and to be discharged from any sprinklers which may be open.

4. **Deluge System.** A system employing open sprinklers attached to a piping system connected to a water supply through a valve which is opened by the operation of a heat responsive system installed in the same areas as the sprinklers. When this valve opens, water flows into the piping system and discharges from all sprinklers attached thereto.

5. **Combined Dry Pipe and Pre-Action Sprinkler System.** A system employing automatic sprinklers attached to a piping system containing air under pressure with a supplemental heat responsive system of generally more sensitive characteristics than the automatic sprinklers themselves, installed in the same areas as the sprinklers; operation of the heat responsive system, as from a fire, actuates tripping devices which open dry pipe valves simultaneously and without loss of air pressure in the system. Operation of the heat responsive system also opens

approved air exhaust valves at the end of the feed main which facilitates the filling of the system with water which usually precedes the opening of sprinklers. The heat responsive system also serves as an automatic fire alarm system.

6. **Limited Water Supply System.** A system employing automatic sprinklers and conforming to these standards but supplied by a pressure tank of limited capacity.

7. **Chemical Systems.** Systems using halon, carbon dioxide, dry chemical or high expansion foam as selected for special requirements. Agent may extinguish flames by chemically inhibiting flame propagation, suffocate flames by excluding oxygen, interrupting chemical action of oxygen uniting with fuel or sealing and cooling the combustion center.

8. **Firecycle System.** Firecycle is a fixed fire protection sprinkler system utilizing water as its extinguishing agent. It is a time delayed, recycling, preaction type which automatically shuts the water off when heat is reduced below the detector operating temperature and turns the water back on when that temperature is exceeded. The system senses a fire condition through a closed circuit electrical detector system which controls water flow to the fire automatically. Batteries supply up to 90 hour emergency power supply for system operation. The piping system is dry (until water is required) and is monitored with pressurized air. Should any leak in the system piping occur, an alarm will sound, but water will not enter the system until heat is sensed by a firecycle detector.

Area coverage sprinkler systems may be laid out and fed from the supply in any one of several patterns as shown below. It is desirable, if possible, to utilize a central feed and achieve a shorter flow path from the riser to the furthest sprinkler. This permits use of the smallest sizes of pipe possible with resulting savings.

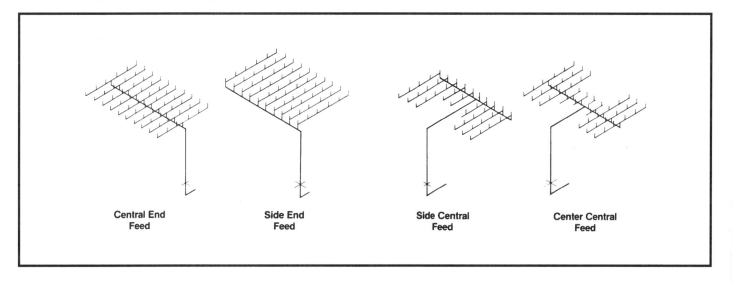

| Central End Feed | Side End Feed | Side Central Feed | Center Central Feed |

MECHANICAL

8

Reference-System Classification
System Classification

Rules for installation of sprinkler systems vary depending on the classification of occupancy falling into one of three categories as follows:

Light Hazard Occupancy

The protection area allotted per sprinkler should not exceed 200 S.F. with the maximum distance between lines and sprinklers on lines being 15'. The sprinklers do not need to be staggered. Branch lines should not exceed eight sprinklers on either side of a cross main. Each large area requiring more than 100 sprinklers and without a sub-dividing partition should be supplied by feed mains or risers sized for ordinary hazard occupancy.

Included in this group are:

Auditoriums	Museums
Churches	Nursing Homes
Clubs	Offices
Educational	Residential
Hospitals	Restaurants
Institutional	Schools
Libraries	Theaters
(except large stack rooms)	

Ordinary Hazard Occupancy

The protection area allotted per sprinkler shall not exceed 130 S.F. of noncombustible ceiling and 120 S.F. of combustible ceiling. The maximum allowable distance between sprinkler lines and sprinklers on line is 15'. Sprinklers shall be staggered if the distance between heads exceeds 12'. Branch lines should not exceed eight sprinklers on either side of a cross main.

Included in this group are:

Automotive garages	Electric generating stations
Bakeries	Feed mills
Beverage manufacturing	Grain elevators
Bleacheries	Ice manufacturing
Boiler houses	Laundries
Canneries	Machine shops
Cement plants	Mercantiles
Clothing factories	Paper mills
Cold storage warehouses	Printing and Publishing
Dairy products manufacturing	Shoe factories
Distilleries	Warehouses
Dry cleaning	Wood product assembly

Extra Hazard Occupancy

The protection area allotted per sprinkler shall not exceed 90 S.F. of noncombustible ceiling and 80 S.F. of combustible ceiling. The maximum allowable distance between lines and between sprinklers on lines is 12'. Sprinklers on alternate lines shall be staggered if the distance between sprinklers on lines exceeds 8'. Branch lines should not exceed six sprinklers on either side of a cross main.

Included in this group are:

Aircraft hangars	Paint shops
Chemical works	Shade cloth manufacturing
Explosives manufacturing	Solvent extracting
Linoleum manufacturing	Varnish works
Linseed oil mills	Volatile flammable
Oil refineries	liquid manufacturing & use

Wet Pipe System. A system employing automatic sprinklers attached to a piping system containing water and connected to a water supply so that water discharges immediately from sprinklers opened by heat from a fire.

All areas are assumed to be open.

8.2-110	Wet Pipe Sprinkler Systems	COST PER S.F.		
		MAT.	INST.	TOTAL
0520	Wet pipe sprinkler systems, steel, black, sch. 40 pipe			
0530	Light hazard, one floor, 500 S.F.	1.11	1.90	3.01
0560	1000 S.F.	1.72	1.97	3.69
0580	2000 S.F.	1.80	1.99	3.79
0600	5000 S.F.	.86	1.41	2.27
0620	10,000 S.F.	.53	1.16	1.69
0640	50,000 S.F.	.36	1.08	1.44
0660	Each additional floor, 500 S.F.	.54	1.61	2.15
0680	1000 S.F.	.51	1.50	2.01
0700	2000 S.F.	.47	1.36	1.83
0720	5000 S.F.	.33	1.15	1.48
0740	10,000 S.F.	.30	1.06	1.36
0760	50,000 S.F.	.26	.86	1.12
1000	Ordinary hazard, one floor, 500 S.F.	1.21	2.04	3.25
1020	1000 S.F.	1.70	1.95	3.65
1040	2000 S.F.	1.85	2.10	3.95
1060	5000 S.F.	.97	1.53	2.50
1080	10,000 S.F.	.66	1.55	2.21
1100	50,000 S.F.	.60	1.54	2.14
1140	Each additional floor, 500 S.F.	.64	1.82	2.46
1160	1000 S.F.	.49	1.49	1.98
1180	2000 S.F.	.54	1.53	2.07
1200	5000 S.F.	.54	1.43	1.97
1220	10,000 S.F.	.43	1.45	1.88
1240	50,000 S.F.	.46	1.36	1.82
1500	Extra hazard, one floor, 500 S.F.	3.23	3.14	6.37
1520	1000 S.F.	2.12	2.73	4.85
1540	2000 S.F.	1.96	2.78	4.74
1560	5000 S.F.	1.21	2.45	3.66
1580	10,000 S.F.	1.12	2.33	3.45
1600	50,000 S.F.	1.05	2.26	3.31
1660	Each additional floor, 500 S.F.	.83	2.24	3.07
1680	1000 S.F.	.83	2.12	2.95
1700	2000 S.F.	.72	2.14	2.86
1720	5000 S.F.	.60	1.88	2.48
1740	10,000 S.F.	.71	1.76	2.47
1760	50,000 S.F.	.68	1.66	2.34
2020	Grooved steel, black sch. 40 pipe, light hazard, one floor, 2000 S.F.	1.83	1.66	3.49
2060	10,000 S.F.	.70	1.02	1.72
2100	Each additional floor, 2000 S.F.	.52	1.09	1.61
2150	10,000 S.F.	.34	.87	1.21
2200	Ordinary hazard, one floor, 2000 S.F.	1.87	1.79	3.66

8.2-110	Wet Pipe Sprinkler Systems	COST PER S.F.		
		MAT.	INST.	TOTAL
2250	10,000 S.F.	.65	1.31	1.96
2300	Each additional floor, 2000 S.F.	.56	1.22	1.78
2350	10,000 S.F.	.42	1.21	1.63
2400	Extra hazard, one floor, 2000 S.F.	2.01	2.26	4.27
2450	10,000 S.F.	.96	1.70	2.66
2500	Each additional floor, 2000 S.F.	.79	1.74	2.53
2550	10,000 S.F.	.66	1.52	2.18
3050	Grooved steel black sch. 10 pipe, light hazard, one floor, 2000 S.F.	1.81	1.65	3.46
3100	10,000 S.F.	.56	.96	1.52
3150	Each additional floor, 2000 S.F.	.50	1.08	1.58
3200	10,000 S.F.	.33	.86	1.19
3250	Ordinary hazard, one floor, 2000 S.F.	1.85	1.78	3.63
3300	10,000 S.F.	.64	1.27	1.91
3350	Each additional floor, 2000 S.F.	.54	1.21	1.75
3400	10,000 S.F.	.41	1.17	1.58
3450	Extra hazard, one floor, 2000 S.F.	1.99	2.26	4.25
3500	10,000 S.F.	.92	1.69	2.61
3550	Each additional floor, 2000 S.F.	.77	1.74	2.51
3600	10,000 S.F.	.65	1.51	2.16
4050	Copper tubing, type M, light hazard, one floor, 2000 S.F.	1.72	1.66	3.38
4100	10,000 S.F.	.55	.99	1.54
4150	Each additional floor, 2000 S.F.	.42	1.11	1.53
4200	10,000 S.F.	.32	.89	1.21
4250	Ordinary hazard, one floor, 2000 S.F.	1.77	1.86	3.63
4300	10,000 S.F.	.64	1.20	1.84
4350	Each additional floor, 2000 S.F.	.47	1.23	1.70
4400	10,000 S.F.	.40	1.07	1.47
4450	Extra hazard, one floor, 2000 S.F.	1.89	2.29	4.18
4500	10,000 S.F.	1.08	1.84	2.92
4550	Each additional floor, 2000 S.F.	.67	1.77	2.44
4600	10,000 S.F.	.68	1.65	2.33
5050	Copper tubing, type M, T-drill system, light hazard, one floor			
5060	2000 S.F.	1.72	1.53	3.25
5100	10,000 S.F.	.53	.83	1.36
5150	Each additional floor, 2000 S.F.	.42	.98	1.40
5200	10,000 S.F.	.30	.73	1.03
5250	Ordinary hazard, one floor, 2000 S.F.	1.73	1.56	3.29
5300	10,000 S.F.	.62	1.06	1.68
5350	Each additional floor, 2000 S.F.	.42	.99	1.41
5400	10,000 S.F.	.39	.96	1.35
5450	Extra hazard, one floor, 2000 S.F.	1.80	1.87	3.67
5500	10,000 S.F.	.91	1.33	2.24
5550	Each additional floor, 2000 S.F.	.62	1.38	2
5600	10,000 S.F.	.51	1.14	1.65

Important: See the Reference Section for critical supporting data - Location Factors & Historical Cost Indexes

Dry Pipe System: A system employing automatic sprinklers attached to a piping system containing air under pressure, the release of which as from the opening of sprinklers permits the water pressure to open a valve known as a "dry pipe valve." The water then flows into the piping system and out the opened sprinklers.

All areas are assumed to be open.

8.2-120	Dry Pipe Sprinkler Systems	COST PER S.F.		
		MAT.	INST.	TOTAL
0520	Dry pipe sprinkler systems, steel, black, sch. 40 pipe			
0530	Light hazard, one floor, 500 S.F.	4.45	3.72	8.17
0560	1000 S.F.	2.41	2.18	4.59
0580	2000 S.F.	2.15	2.20	4.35
0600	5000 S.F.	1.07	1.50	2.57
0620	10,000 S.F.	.70	1.22	1.92
0640	50,000 S.F.	.49	1.10	1.59
0660	Each additional floor, 500 S.F.	.77	1.79	2.56
0680	1000 S.F.	.64	1.48	2.12
0700	2000 S.F.	.61	1.37	1.98
0720	5000 S.F.	.48	1.17	1.65
0740	10,000 S.F.	.43	1.08	1.51
0760	50,000 S.F.	.40	.99	1.39
1000	Ordinary hazard, one floor, 500 S.F.	4.51	3.77	8.28
1020	1000 S.F.	2.45	2.21	4.66
1040	2000 S.F.	2.20	2.31	4.51
1060	5000 S.F.	1.22	1.62	2.84
1080	10,000 S.F.	.89	1.61	2.50
1100	50,000 S.F.	.81	1.61	2.42
1140	Each additional floor, 500 S.F.	.83	1.84	2.67
1160	1000 S.F.	.72	1.66	2.38
1180	2000 S.F.	.73	1 55	2.28
1200	5000 S.F.	.66	1.31	1.97
1220	10,000 S.F.	.57	1.27	1.84
1240	50,000 S.F.	.58	1.18	1.76
1500	Extra hazard, one floor, 500 S.F.	6.10	4.69	10.79
1520	1000 S.F.	3.53	3.38	6.91
1540	2000 S.F.	2.39	2.93	5.32
1560	5000 S.F.	1.39	2.23	3.62
1580	10,000 S.F.	1.37	2.12	3.49
1600	50,000 S.F.	1.40	2.06	3.46
1660	Each additional floor, 500 S.F.	1.11	2.28	3.39
1680	1000 S.F.	1.11	2.16	3.27
1700	2000 S.F.	1	2.18	3.18
1720	5000 S.F.	.84	1.89	2.73
1740	10,000 S.F.	.98	1.75	2.73
1760	50,000 S.F.	.99	1.68	2.67
2020	Grooved steel, black, sch. 40 pipe, light hazard, one floor, 2000 S.F.	2.13	1.86	3.99
2060	10,000 S.F.	.74	1.03	1.77
2100	Each additional floor, 2000 S.F.	.66	1.10	1.76
2150	10,000 S.F.	.47	.89	1.36
2200	Ordinary hazard, one floor, 2000 S.F.	2.22	2	4.22

8.2-120	Dry Pipe Sprinkler Systems	COST PER S.F.		
		MAT.	INST.	TOTAL
2250	10,000 S.F.	.88	1.37	2.25
2300	Each additional floor, 2000 S.F.	.75	1.24	1.99
2350	10,000 S.F.	.61	1.23	1.84
2400	Extra hazard, one floor, 2000 S.F.	2.45	2.49	4.94
2450	10,000 S.F.	1.28	1.77	3.05
2500	Each additional floor, 2000 S.F.	1.07	1.78	2.85
2550	10,000 S.F.	.94	1.55	2.49
3050	Grooved steel black sch. 10 pipe, light hazard, one floor, 2000 S.F.	2.11	1.85	3.96
3100	10,000 S.F.	.73	1.02	1.75
3150	Each additional floor, 2000 S.F.	.64	1.09	1.73
3200	10,000 S.F.	.46	.88	1.34
3250	Ordinary hazard, one floor, 2000 S.F.	2.20	1.99	4.19
3300	10,000 S.F.	.87	1.33	2.20
3350	Each additional floor, 2000 S.F.	.73	1.23	1.96
3400	10,000 S.F.	.60	1.19	1.79
3450	Extra hazard, one floor, 2000 S.F.	2.43	2.49	4.92
3500	10,000 S.F.	1.24	1.76	3
3550	Each additional floor, 2000 S.F.	1.05	1.78	2.83
3600	10,000 S.F.	.93	1.54	2.47
4050	Copper tubing, type M, light hazard, one floor, 2000 S.F.	2.02	1.86	3.88
4100	10,000 S.F.	.72	1.05	1.77
4150	Each additional floor, 2000 S.F.	.56	1.12	1.68
4200	10,000 S.F.	.45	.91	1.36
4250	Ordinary hazard, one floor, 2000 S.F.	2.12	2.07	4.19
4300	10,000 S.F.	.87	1.26	2.13
4350	Each additional floor, 2000 S.F.	.70	1.29	1.99
4400	10,000 S.F.	.59	1.09	1.68
4450	Extra hazard, one floor, 2000 S.F.	2.33	2.52	4.85
4500	10,000 S.F.	1.41	1.91	3.32
4550	Each additional floor, 2000 S.F.	.95	1.81	2.76
4600	10,000 S.F.	.96	1.68	2.64
5050	Copper tubing, type M, T-drill system, light hazard, one floor			
5060	2000 S.F.	2.02	1.73	3.75
5100	10,000 S.F.	.70	.89	1.59
5150	Each additional floor, 2000 S.F.	.56	.99	1.55
5200	10,000 S.F.	.43	.75	1.18
5250	Ordinary hazard, one floor, 2000 S.F.	2.08	1.77	3.85
5300	10,000 S.F.	.85	1.12	1.97
5350	Each additional floor, 2000 S.F.	.61	1.01	1.62
5400	10,000 S.F.	.55	.93	1.48
5450	Extra hazard, one floor, 2000 S.F.	2.24	2.10	4.34
5500	10,000 S.F.	1.24	1.40	2.64
5550	Each additional floor, 2000 S.F.	.86	1.39	2.25
5600	10,000 S.F.	.79	1.17	1.96

Preaction System: A system employing automatic sprinklers attached to a piping system containing air that may or may not be under pressure, with a supplemental heat responsive system of generally more sensitive characteristics than the automatic sprinklers themselves, installed in the same areas as the sprinklers. Actuation of the heat responsive system, as from a fire, opens a valve which permits water to flow into the sprinkler piping system and to be discharged from those sprinklers which were opened by heat from the fire.

All areas are assumed to be opened.

8.2-130	Preaction Sprinkler Systems	COST PER S.F.		
		MAT.	INST.	TOTAL
0520	Preaction sprinkler systems, steel, black, sch. 40 pipe			
0530	Light hazard, one floor, 500 S.F.	4.42	2.97	7.39
0560	1000 S.F.	2.50	2.23	4.73
0580	2000 S.F.	2.18	2.19	4.37
0600	5000 S.F.	1.10	1.49	2.59
0620	10,000 S.F.	.72	1.21	1.93
0640	50,000 S.F.	.51	1.09	1.60
0660	Each additional floor, 500 S.F.	.97	1.60	2.57
0680	1000 S.F.	.72	1.48	2.20
0700	2000 S.F.	.69	1.38	2.07
0720	5000 S.F.	.51	1.16	1.67
0740	10,000 S.F.	.45	1.07	1.52
0760	50,000 S.F.	.45	1.01	1.46
1000	Ordinary hazard, one floor, 500 S.F.	1.66	2.18	3.84
1020	1000 S.F.	2.48	2.21	4.69
1040	2000 S.F.	2.34	2.31	4.65
1060	5000 S.F.	1.21	1.61	2.82
1080	10,000 S.F.	.85	1.60	2.45
1100	50,000 S.F.	.76	1.58	2.34
1140	Each additional floor, 500 S.F.	1.08	1.85	2.93
1160	1000 S.F.	.71	1.51	2.22
1180	2000 S.F.	.65	1.54	2.19
1200	5000 S.F.	.71	1.42	2.13
1220	10,000 S.F.	.58	1.46	2.04
1240	50,000 S.F.	.60	1.37	1.97
1500	Extra hazard, one floor, 500 S.F.	6.05	4.12	10.17
1520	1000 S.F.	3.35	3.08	6.43
1540	2000 S.F.	2.33	2.91	5.24
1560	5000 S.F.	1.39	2.39	3.78
1580	10,000 S.F.	1.30	2.35	3.65

MECHANICAL

8

8.2-130	Preaction Sprinkler Systems	COST PER S.F.		
		MAT.	INST.	TOTAL
1600	50,000 S.F.	1.30	2.28	3.58
1660	Each additional floor, 500 S.F.	1.27	2.27	3.54
1680	1000 S.F.	1.05	2.14	3.19
1700	2000 S.F.	.94	2.16	3.10
1720	5000 S.F.	.78	1.89	2.67
1740	10,000 S.F.	.86	1.77	2.63
1760	50,000 S.F.	.83	1.66	2.49
2020	Grooved steel, black, sch. 40 pipe, light hazard, one floor, 2000 S.F.	2.21	1.87	4.08
2060	10,000 S.F.	.76	1.02	1.78
2100	Each additional floor of 2000 S.F.	.74	1.11	1.85
2150	10,000 S.F.	.49	.88	1.37
2200	Ordinary hazard, one floor, 2000 S.F.	2.25	2	4.25
2250	10,000 S.F.	.84	1.36	2.20
2300	Each additional floor, 2000 S.F.	.78	1.24	2.02
2350	10,000 S.F.	.57	1.22	1.79
2400	Extra hazard, one floor, 2000 S.F.	2.39	2.47	4.86
2450	10,000 S.F.	1.16	1.75	2.91
2500	Each additional floor, 2000 S.F.	1.01	1.76	2.77
2550	10,000 S.F.	.81	1.53	2.34
3050	Grooved steel, black, sch. 10 pipe light hazard, one floor, 2000 S.F.	2.19	1.86	4.05
3100	10,000 S.F.	.75	1.01	1.76
3150	Each additional floor, 2000 S.F.	.72	1.10	1.82
3200	10,000 S.F.	.48	.87	1.35
3250	Ordinary hazard, one floor, 2000 S.F.	2.20	1.86	4.06
3300	10,000 S.F.	.72	1.31	2.03
3350	Each additional floor, 2000 S.F.	.76	1.23	1.99
3400	10,000 S.F.	.56	1.18	1.74
3450	Extra hazard, one floor, 2000 S.F.	2.37	2.47	4.84
3500	10,000 S.F.	1.11	1.74	2.85
3550	Each additional floor, 2000 S.F.	.99	1.76	2.75
3600	10,000 S.F.	.80	1.52	2.32
4050	Copper tubing, type M, light hazard, one floor, 2000 S.F.	2.10	1.87	3.97
4100	10,000 S.F.	.74	1.04	1.78
4150	Each additional floor, 2000 S.F.	.64	1.13	1.77
4200	10,000 S.F.	.36	.89	1.25
4250	Ordinary hazard, one floor, 2000 S.F.	2.15	2.07	4.22
4300	10,000 S.F.	.83	1.25	2.08
4350	Each additional floor, 2000 S.F.	.63	1.15	1.78
4400	10,000 S.F.	.51	.99	1.50
4450	Extra hazard, one floor, 2000 S.F.	2.27	2.50	4.77
4500	10,000 S.F.	1.27	1.89	3.16
4550	Each additional floor, 2000 S.F.	.89	1.79	2.68
4600	10,000 S.F.	.83	1.66	2.49
5050	Copper tubing, type M, T-drill system, light hazard, one floor			
5060	2000 S.F.	2.10	1.74	3.84
5100	10,000 S.F.	.72	.88	1.60
5150	Each additional floor, 2000 S.F.	.64	1	1.64
5200	10,000 S.F.	.45	.74	1.19
5250	Ordinary hazard, one floor, 2000 S.F.	2.11	1.77	3.88
5300	10,000 S.F.	.81	1.11	1.92
5350	Each additional floor, 2000 S.F.	.65	1.02	1.67
5400	10,000 S.F.	.54	.97	1.51
5450	Extra hazard, one floor, 2000 S.F.	2.18	2.08	4.26
5500	10,000 S.F.	1.10	1.38	2.48
5550	Each additional floor, 2000 S.F.	.80	1.37	2.17
5600	10,000 S.F.	.66	1.15	1.81

Important: See the Reference Section for critical supporting data - Location Factors & Historical Cost Indexes

Deluge System: A system employing open sprinklers attached to a piping system connected to a water supply through a valve which is opened by the operation of a heat responsive system installed in the same areas as the sprinklers. When this valve opens, water flows into the piping system and discharges from all sprinklers attached thereto.

8.2-140	Deluge Sprinkler Systems	COST PER S.F.		
		MAT.	INST.	TOTAL
0520	Deluge sprinkler systems, steel, black, sch. 40 pipe			
0530	Light hazard, one floor, 500 S.F.	5.65	3	8.65
0560	1000 S.F.	3.10	2.15	5.25
0580	2000 S.F.	2.60	2.20	4.80
0600	5000 S.F.	1.27	1.49	2.76
0620	10,000 S.F.	.80	1.21	2.01
0640	50,000 S.F.	.52	1.09	1.61
0660	Each additional floor, 500 S.F.	.97	1.60	2.57
0680	1000 S.F.	.72	1.48	2.20
0700	2000 S.F.	.69	1.38	2.07
0720	5000 S.F.	.51	1.16	1.67
0740	10,000 S.F.	.45	1.07	1.52
0760	50,000 S.F.	.45	1.01	1.46
1000	Ordinary hazard, one floor, 500 S.F.	6.05	3.44	9.49
1020	1000 S.F.	3.10	2.23	5.33
1040	2000 S.F.	2.75	2.32	5.07
1060	5000 S.F.	1.38	1.61	2.99
1080	10,000 S.F.	.93	1.60	2.53
1100	50,000 S.F.	.80	1.60	2.40
1140	Each additional floor, 500 S.F.	1.08	1.85	2.93
1160	1000 S.F.	.71	1.51	2.22
1180	2000 S.F.	.65	1.54	2.19
1200	5000 S.F.	.65	1.30	1.95
1220	10,000 S.F.	.58	1.28	1.86
1240	50,000 S.F.	.57	1.26	1.83
1500	Extra hazard, one floor, 500 S.F.	7.25	4.15	11.40
1520	1000 S.F.	4.17	3.21	7.38
1540	2000 S.F.	2.74	2.92	5.66
1560	5000 S.F.	1.48	2.20	3.68
1580	10,000 S.F.	1.34	2.15	3.49
1600	50,000 S.F.	1.33	2.09	3.42
1660	Each additional floor, 500 S.F.	1.27	2.27	3.54
1680	1000 S.F.	1.05	2.14	3.19
1700	2000 S.F.	.94	2.16	3.10

MECHANICAL

8

8.2-140 Deluge Sprinkler Systems

		COST PER S.F.		
		MAT.	INST.	TOTAL
1720	5000 S.F.	.78	1.89	2.67
1740	10,000 S.F.	.87	1.83	2.70
1760	50,000 S.F.	.86	1.77	2.63
2000	Grooved steel, black, sch. 40 pipe, light hazard, one floor			
2020	2000 S.F.	2.63	1.88	4.51
2060	10,000 S.F.	.85	1.03	1.88
2100	Each additional floor, 2,000 S.F.	.74	1.11	1.85
2150	10,000 S.F.	.49	.88	1.37
2200	Ordinary hazard, one floor, 2000 S.F.	2.25	2	4.25
2250	10,000 S.F.	.92	1.36	2.28
2300	Each additional floor, 2000 S.F.	.78	1.24	2.02
2350	10,000 S.F.	.57	1.22	1.79
2400	Extra hazard, one floor, 2000 S.F.	2.80	2.48	5.28
2450	10,000 S.F.	1.25	1.76	3.01
2500	Each additional floor, 2000 S.F.	1.01	1.76	2.77
2550	10,000 S.F.	.81	1.53	2.34
3000	Grooved steel, black, sch. 10 pipe, light hazard, one floor			
3050	2000 S.F.	2.32	1.79	4.11
3100	10,000 S.F.	.83	1.01	1.84
3150	Each additional floor, 2000 S.F.	.72	1.10	1.82
3200	10,000 S.F.	.48	.87	1.35
3250	Ordinary hazard, one floor, 2000 S.F.	2.64	2	4.64
3300	10,000 S.F.	.80	1.31	2.11
3350	Each additional floor, 2000 S.F.	.76	1.23	1.99
3400	10,000 S.F.	.56	1.18	1.74
3450	Extra hazard, one floor, 2000 S.F.	2.78	2.48	5.26
3500	10,000 S.F.	1.19	1.74	2.93
3550	Each additional floor, 2000 S.F.	.99	1.76	2.75
3600	10,000 S.F.	.80	1.52	2.32
4000	Copper tubing, type M, light hazard, one floor			
4050	2000 S.F.	2.51	1.88	4.39
4100	10,000 S.F.	.82	1.04	1.86
4150	Each additional floor, 2000 S.F.	.64	1.12	1.76
4200	10,000 S.F.	.36	.89	1.25
4250	Ordinary hazard, one floor, 2000 S.F.	2.56	2.08	4.64
4300	10,000 S.F.	.91	1.25	2.16
4350	Each additional floor, 2000 S.F.	.63	1.15	1.78
4400	10,000 S.F.	.51	.99	1.50
4450	Extra hazard, one floor, 2000 S.F.	2.68	2.51	5.19
4500	10,000 S.F.	1.37	1.90	3.27
4550	Each additional floor, 2000 S.F.	.89	1.79	2.68
4600	10,000 S.F.	.83	1.66	2.49
5000	Copper tubing, type M, T-drill system, light hazard, one floor			
5050	2000 S.F.	2.51	1.75	4.26
5100	10,000 S.F.	.80	.88	1.68
5150	Each additional floor, 2000 S.F.	.69	1.01	1.70
5200	10,000 S.F.	.45	.74	1.19
5250	Ordinary hazard, one floor, 2000 S.F.	2.52	1.78	4.30
5300	10,000 S.F.	.89	1.11	2
5350	Each additional floor, 2000 S.F.	.64	1.01	1.65
5400	10,000 S.F.	.54	.97	1.51
5450	Extra hazard, one floor, 2000 S.F.	2.59	2.09	4.68
5500	10,000 S.F.	1.18	1.38	2.56
5550	Each additional floor, 2000 S.F.	.80	1.37	2.17
5600	10,000 S.F.	.66	1.15	1.81

MECHANICAL 8

Important: See the Reference Section for critical supporting data - Location Factors & Historical Cost Indexes

Firecycle is a fixed fire protection sprinkler system utilizing water as its extinguishing agent. It is a time delayed, recycling, preaction type which automatically shuts the water off when heat is reduced below the detector operating temperature and turns the water back on when that temperature is exceeded.

The system senses a fire condition through a closed circuit electrical detector system which controls water flow to the fire automatically. Batteries supply up to 90 hours emergency power supply for system operation. The piping system is dry (until water is required) and is monitored with pressurized air. Should any leak in the system piping occur, an alarm will sound, but water will not enter the system until heat is sensed by a Firecycle detector.

8.2-150	Firecycle Sprinkler Systems	COST PER S.F.		
		MAT.	INST.	TOTAL
0520	Firecycle sprinkler systems, steel black sch. 40 pipe			
0530	Light hazard, one floor, 500 S.F.	18.90	5.90	24.80
0560	1000 S.F.	9.70	3.68	13.38
0580	2000 S.F.	5.75	2.70	8.45
0600	5000 S.F.	2.53	1.70	4.23
0620	10,000 S.F.	1.46	1.32	2.78
0640	50,000 S.F.	.68	1.10	1.78
0660	Each additional floor of 500 S.F.	1	1.61	2.61
0680	1000 S.F.	.74	1.48	2.22
0700	2000 S.F.	.59	1.37	1.96
0720	5000 S.F.	.52	1.17	1.69
0740	10,000 S.F.	.49	1.08	1.57
0760	50,000 S.F.	.47	1.01	1.48
1000	Ordinary hazard, one floor, 500 S.F.	19.05	6.15	25.20
1020	1000 S.F.	9.70	3.66	13.36
1040	2000 S.F.	5.80	2.82	8.62
1060	5000 S.F.	2.64	1.82	4.46
1080	10,000 S.F.	1.59	1.71	3.30
1100	50,000 S.F.	1.05	1.79	2.84
1140	Each additional floor, 500 S.F.	1.11	1.86	2.97
1160	1000 S.F.	.73	1.51	2.24
1180	2000 S.F.	.75	1.41	2.16
1200	5000 S.F.	.66	1.31	1.97
1220	10,000 S.F.	.57	1.27	1.84
1240	50,000 S.F.	.59	1.19	1.78
1500	Extra hazard, one floor, 500 S.F.	20.50	7.05	27.55
1520	1000 S.F.	10.50	4.52	15.02
1540	2000 S.F.	5.90	3.42	9.32
1560	5000 S.F.	2.74	2.41	5.15
1580	10,000 S.F.	2.02	2.45	4.47
1600	50,000 S.F.	1.61	2.69	4.30
1660	Each additional floor, 500 S.F.	1.30	2.28	3.58

MECHANICAL

8

8.2-150	Firecycle Sprinkler Systems	COST PER S.F.		
		MAT.	INST.	TOTAL
1680	1000 S.F.	1.07	2.14	3.21
1700	2000 S.F.	.96	2.16	3.12
1720	5000 S.F.	.79	1.90	2.69
1740	10,000 S.F.	.90	1.78	2.68
1760	50,000 S.F.	.88	1.71	2.59
2020	Grooved steel, black, sch. 40 pipe, light hazard, one floor			
2030	2000 S.F.	5.75	2.38	8.13
2060	10,000 S.F.	1.62	1.59	3.21
2100	Each additional floor, 2000 S.F.	.76	1.11	1.87
2150	10,000 S.F.	.53	.89	1.42
2200	Ordinary hazard, one floor, 2000 S.F.	5.80	2.51	8.31
2250	10,000 S.F.	1.71	1.55	3.26
2300	Each additional floor, 2000 S.F.	.80	1.24	2.04
2350	10,000 S.F.	.61	1.23	1.84
2400	Extra hazard, one floor, 2000 S.F.	5.95	2.98	8.93
2450	10,000 S.F.	1.88	1.85	3.73
2500	Each additional floor, 2000 S.F.	1.03	1.76	2.79
2550	10,000 S.F.	.85	1.54	2.39
3050	Grooved steel, black, sch. 10 pipe light hazard, one floor,			
3060	2000 S.F.	5.75	2.37	8.12
3100	10,000 S.F.	1.49	1.12	2.61
3150	Each additional floor, 2000 S.F.	.74	1.10	1.84
3200	10,000 S.F.	.52	.88	1.40
3250	Ordinary hazard, one floor, 2000 S.F.	5.80	2.50	8.30
3300	10,000 S.F.	1.57	1.43	3
3350	Each additional floor, 2000 S.F.	.78	1.23	2.01
3400	10,000 S.F.	.60	1.19	1.79
3450	Extra hazard, one floor, 2000 S.F.	5.90	2.98	8.88
3500	10,000 S.F.	1.84	1.84	3.68
3550	Each additional floor, 2000 S.F.	1.01	1.76	2.77
3600	10,000 S.F.	.84	1.53	2.37
4060	Copper tubing, type M, light hazard, one floor, 2000 S.F.	5.65	2.38	8.03
4100	10,000 S.F.	1.48	1.15	2.63
4150	Each additional floor, 2000 S.F.	.66	1.13	1.79
4200	10,000 S.F.	.51	.91	1.42
4250	Ordinary hazard, one floor, 2000 S.F.	5.70	2.58	8.28
4300	10,000 S.F.	1.57	1.36	2.93
4350	Each additional floor, 2000 S.F.	.65	1.15	1.80
4400	10,000 S.F.	.54	.99	1.53
4450	Extra hazard, one floor, 2000 S.F.	5.80	3.01	8.81
4500	10,000 S.F.	2.07	2.01	4.08
4550	Each additional floor, 2000 S.F.	.91	1.79	2.70
4600	10,000 S.F.	.87	1.67	2.54
5060	Copper tubing, type M, T-drill system, light hazard, one floor 2000 S.F.	5.65	2.25	7.90
5100	10,000 S.F.	1.46	.99	2.45
5150	Each additional floor, 2000 S.F.	.75	1.05	1.80
5200	10,000 S.F.	.49	.75	1.24
5250	Ordinary hazard, one floor, 2000 S.F.	5.65	2.28	7.93
5300	10,000 S.F.	1.55	1.22	2.77
5350	Each additional floor, 2000 S.F.	.66	1.01	1.67
5400	10,000 S.F.	.58	.98	1.56
5450	Extra hazard, one floor, 2000 S.F.	5.75	2.59	8.34
5500	10,000 S.F.	1.83	1.48	3.31
5550	Each additional floor, 2000 S.F.	.82	1.37	2.19
5600	10,000 S.F.	.70	1.16	1.86

Important: See the Reference Section for critical supporting data - Location Factors & Historical Cost Indexes

Roof

Roof connections with hose gate valves (for combustible roof)

Hose connections on each floor (size based on class of service)

Check valve

Siamese inlet connections (for fire department use)

8.2-310	Wet Standpipe Risers, Class I	COST PER FLOOR		
		MAT.	INST.	TOTAL
0550	Wet standpipe risers, Class I, steel black sch. 40, 10' height			
0560	4" diameter pipe, one floor	2,000	2,075	4,075
0580	Additional floors	475	645	1,120
0600	6" diameter pipe, one floor	3,475	3,700	7,175
0620	Additional floors	850	1,050	1,900
0640	8" diameter pipe, one floor	5,150	4,475	9,625
0660	Additional floors	1,150	1,275	2,425

8.2-310	Wet Standpipe Risers, Class II	COST PER FLOOR		
		MAT.	INST.	TOTAL
1030	Wet standpipe risers, Class II, steel black sch. 40, 10' height			
1040	2" diameter pipe, one floor	845	745	1,590
1060	Additional floors	278	289	567
1080	2-1/2" diameter pipe, one floor	1,100	1,100	2,200
1100	Additional floors	310	335	645

8.2-310	Wet Standpipe Risers, Class III	COST PER FLOOR		
		MAT.	INST.	TOTAL
1530	Wet standpipe risers, Class III, steel black sch. 40, 10' height			
1540	4" diameter pipe, one floor	2,050	2,075	4,125
1560	Additional floors	400	540	940
1580	6" diameter pipe, one floor	3,525	3,700	7,225
1600	Additional floors	880	1,050	1,930
1620	8" diameter pipe, one floor	5,225	4,475	9,700
1640	Additional floors	1,175	1,275	2,450

MECHANICAL

8

Roof

Roof connections with hose gate valves (for combustible roof)

Hose connections on each floor (size based on class of service)

Check valve

Siamese inlet connections (for fire department use)

8.2-320	Dry Standpipe Risers, Class I	COST PER FLOOR		
		MAT.	INST.	TOTAL
0530	Dry standpipe riser, Class I, steel black sch. 40, 10' height			
0540	4" diameter pipe, one floor	1,275	1,700	2,975
0560	Additional floors	430	610	1,040
0580	6" diameter pipe, one floor	2,525	2,950	5,475
0600	Additional floors	805	1,000	1,805
0620	8" diameter pipe, one floor	3,725	3,600	7,325
0640	Additional floors	1,100	1,225	2,325

8.2-320	Dry Standpipe Risers, Class II	COST PER FLOOR		
		MAT.	INST.	TOTAL
1030	Dry standpipe risers, Class II, steel black sch. 40, 10' height			
1040	2" diameter pipe, one floor	690	780	1,470
1060	Additional floor	233	254	487
1080	2-1/2" diameter pipe, one floor	825	910	1,735
1100	Additional floors	263	300	563

8.2-320	Dry Standpipe Risers, Class III	COST PER FLOOR		
		MAT.	INST.	TOTAL
1530	Dry standpipe risers, Class III, steel black sch. 40, 10' height			
1540	4" diameter pipe, one floor	1,300	1,650	2,950
1560	Additional floors	360	550	910
1580	6" diameter pipe, one floor	2,550	2,950	5,500
1600	Additional floors	835	1,000	1,835
1620	8" diameter pipe, one floor	3,750	3,600	7,350
1640	Additional floor	1,125	1,225	2,350

MECHANICAL 8

Important: See the Reference Section for critical supporting data - Location Factors & Historical Cost Indexes

8.2-390	Standpipe Equipment	COST EACH		
		MAT.	INST.	TOTAL
0100	Adapters, reducing, 1 piece, FxM, hexagon, cast brass, 2-1/2" x 1-1/2"	30.50		30.50
0200	Pin lug, 1-1/2" x 1"	9.70		9.70
0250	3" x 2-1/2"	38		38
0300	For polished chrome, add 75% mat.			
0400	Cabinets, D.S. glass in door, recessed, steel box, not equipped			
0500	Single extinguisher, steel door & frame	62	94	156
0550	Stainless steel door & frame	109	94	203
0600	Valve, 2-1/2" angle, steel door & frame	67.50	62.50	130
0650	Aluminum door & frame	90	62.50	152.50
0700	Stainless steel door & frame	118	62.50	180.50
0750	Hose rack assy, 2-1/2" x 1-1/2" valve & 100' hose, steel door & frame	137	125	262
0800	Aluminum door & frame	203	125	328
0850	Stainless steel door & frame	264	125	389
0900	Hose rack assy,& extinguisher,2-1/2"x1-1/2" valve & hose,steel door & frame	171	150	321
0950	Aluminum	259	150	409
1000	Stainless steel	305	150	455
1550	Compressor, air, dry pipe system, automatic, 200 gal., 1/3 H.P.	770	320	1,090
1600	520 gal., 1 H.P.	805	320	1,125
1650	Alarm, electric pressure switch (circuit closer)	144	16.05	160.05
2500	Couplings, hose, rocker lug, cast brass, 1-1/2"	28.50		28.50
2550	2-1/2"	37.50		37.50
3000	Escutcheon plate, for angle valves, polished brass, 1-1/2"	11.30		11.30
3050	2-1/2"	27		27
3500	Fire pump, electric, w/controller, fittings, relief valve			
3550	4" pump, 30 H.P., 500 G.P.M.	14,900	2,350	17,250
3600	5" pump, 40 H.P., 1000 G.P.M.	21,800	2,650	24,450
3650	5" pump, 100 H.P., 1000 G.P.M.	24,400	2,950	27,350
3700	For jockey pump system, add	2,675	375	3,050
5000	Hose, per linear foot, synthetic jacket, lined,			
5100	300 lb. test, 1-1/2" diameter	1.58	.29	1.87
5150	2-1/2" diameter	2.64	.34	2.98
5200	500 lb. test, 1-1/2" diameter	1.64	.29	1.93
5250	2-1/2" diameter	2.85	.34	3.19
5500	Nozzle, plain stream, polished brass, 1-1/2" x 10"	23.50		23.50
5550	2-1/2" x 15" x 13/16" or 1-1/2"	47.50		47.50
5600	Heavy duty combination adjustable fog and straight stream w/handle 1-1/2"	273		273
5650	2-1/2" direct connection	390		390
6000	Rack, for 1-1/2" diameter hose 100 ft. long, steel	35.50	37.50	73
6050	Brass	55	37.50	92.50
6500	Reel, steel, for 50 ft. long 1-1/2" diameter hose	74	53.50	127.50
6550	For 75 ft. long 2-1/2" diameter hose	119	53.50	172.50
7050	Siamese, w/plugs & chains, polished brass, sidewalk, 4" x 2-1/2" x 2-1/2"	340	300	640
7100	6" x 2-1/2" x 2-1/2"	565	375	940
7200	Wall type, flush, 4" x 2-1/2" x 2-1/2"	291	150	441
7250	6" x 2-1/2" x 2-1/2"	395	163	558
7300	Projecting, 4" x 2-1/2" x 2-1/2"	266	150	416
7350	6" x 2-1/2" x 2-1/2"	435	163	598
7400	For chrome plate, add 15% mat.			
8000	Valves, angle, wheel handle, 300 Lb., rough brass, 1-1/2"	29	34.50	63.50
8050	2-1/2"	50.50	59.50	110
8100	Combination pressure restricting, 1-1/2"	46	34.50	80.50
8150	2-1/2"	98	59.50	157.50
8200	Pressure restricting, adjustable, satin brass, 1-1/2"	76	34.50	110.50
8250	2-1/2"	107	59.50	166.50
8300	Hydrolator, vent and drain, rough brass, 1-1/2"	45	34.50	79.50
8350	2-1/2"	45	34.50	79.50
8400	Cabinet assy, incls. adapter, rack, hose, and nozzle	435	226	661

MECHANICAL

8

General: Automatic fire protection (suppression) systems other than water sprinklers may be desired for special environments, high risk areas, isolated locations or unusual hazards. Some typical applications would include:

1. Paint dip tanks
2. Securities vaults
3. Electronic data processing
4. Tape and data storage
5. Transformer rooms
6. Spray booths
7. Petroleum storage
8. High rack storage

Piping and wiring costs are highly variable and are not included.

8.2-810	FM200 Fire Suppression	COST EACH		
		MAT.	INST.	TOTAL
0020	Detectors with brackets			
0040	Fixed temperature heat detector	31	51	82
0060	Rate of temperature rise detector	37	51	88
0080	Ion detector (smoke) detector	82.50	66	148.50
0200	Extinguisher agent			
0240	200 lb FM200, container	6,375	187	6,562
0280	75 lb carbon dioxide cylinder	1,050	125	1,175
0320	Dispersion nozzle			
0340	FM200 1-1/2" dispersion nozzle	55	29.50	84.50
0380	Carbon dioxide 3" x 5" dispersion nozzle	55	23	78
0420	Control station			
0440	Single zone control station with batteries	1,400	410	1,810
0470	Multizone (4) control station with batteries	2,700	820	3,520
0500	Electric mechanical release	138	206	344
0550	Manual pull station	49.50	69.50	119
0640	Battery standby power 10" x 10" x 17"	760	102	862
0740	Bell signalling device	54.50	51	105.50

8.2-810	FM200 Systems	COST PER C.F.		
		MAT.	INST.	TOTAL
0820	Average FM200 system, minimum			1.38
0840	Maximum			2.75

MECHANICAL 8

Small Electric Boiler Systems Considerations:

1. Terminal units are fin tube baseboard radiation rated at 720 BTU/hr with 200° water temperature or 820 BTU/hr steam.
2. Primary use being for residential or smaller supplementary areas, the floor levels are based on 7-1/2″ ceiling heights.
3. All distribution piping is copper for boilers through 205 MBH. All piping for larger systems is steel pipe.

Large Electric Boiler System Considerations:

1. Terminal units are all unit heaters of the same size. Quantities are varied to accommodate total requirements.
2. All air is circulated through the heaters a minimum of three times per hour.
3. As the capacities are adequate for commercial use, gross output rating by floor levels are based on 10′ ceiling height.
4. All distribution piping is black steel pipe.

8.3-110	Small Heating Systems, Hydronic, Electric Boilers	COST PER S.F.		
		MAT.	INST.	TOTAL
1100	Small heating systems, hydronic, electric boilers			
1120	Steam, 1 floor, 1480 S.F., 61 M.B.H.	8.30	5.20	13.50
1160	3,000 S.F., 123 M.B.H.	4.80	4.55	9.35
1200	5,000 S.F., 205 M.B.H.	3.60	4.20	7.80
1240	2 floors, 12,400 S.F., 512 M.B.H.	2.56	4.17	6.73
1280	3 floors, 24,800 S.F., 1023 M.B.H.	2.21	4.13	6.34
1320	34,750 S.F., 1,433 M.B.H.	1.95	4	5.95
1360	Hot water, 1 floor, 1,000 S.F., 41 M.B.H.	7.75	2.91	10.66
1400	2,500 S.F., 103 M.B.H.	4.60	5.20	9.80
1440	2 floors, 4,850 S.F., 205 M.B.H.	4	6.20	10.20
1480	3 floors, 9,700 S.F., 410 M.B.H.	3.71	6.45	10.16

8.3-120	Large Heating Systems, Hydronic, Electric Boilers	COST PER S.F.		
		MAT.	INST.	TOTAL
1230	Large heating systems, hydronic, electric boilers			
1240	9,280 S.F., 150 K.W., 510 M.B.H., 1 floor	2.95	2.01	4.96
1280	14,900 S.F., 240 K.W., 820 M.B.H., 2 floors	3.03	3.30	6.33
1320	18,600 S.F., 296 K.W., 1,010 M.B.H., 3 floors	2.93	3.60	6.53
1360	26,100 S.F., 420 K.W., 1,432 M.B.H., 4 floors	3.06	3.55	6.61
1400	39,100 S.F., 666 K.W., 2,273 M.B.H., 4 floors	2.71	2.97	5.68
1440	57,700 S.F., 900 K.W., 3,071 M.B.H., 5 floors	2.48	2.91	5.39
1480	111,700 S.F., 1,800 K.W., 6,148 M.B.H., 6 floors	2.19	2.48	4.67
1520	149,000 S.F., 2,400 K.W., 8,191 M.B.H., 8 floors	2.13	2.47	4.60
1560	223,300 S.F., 3,600 K.W., 12,283 M.B.H., 14 floors	2.14	2.82	4.96

MECHANICAL

8

Boiler Selection: The maximum allowable working pressures are limited by ASME "Code for Heating Boilers" to 15 PSI for steam and 160 PSI for hot water heating boilers, with a maximum temperature limitation of 250° F. Hot water boilers are generally rated for a working pressure of 30 PSI. High pressure boilers are governed by the ASME "Code for Power Boilers" which is used almost universally for boilers operating over 15 PSIG. High pressure boilers used for a combination of heating/ process loads are usually designed for 150 PSIG.

Boiler ratings are usually indicated as either Gross or Net Output. The Gross Load is equal to the Net Load plus a piping and pickup allowance. When this allowance cannot be determined, divide the gross output rating by 1.25 for a value equal to or greater than the next heat loss requirement of the building.

Table below lists installed cost per boiler and includes insulating jacket, standard controls, burner and safety controls. Costs do not include piping or boiler base pad. Outputs are Gross.

8.3-130	Boilers, Hot Water & Steam	COST EACH		
		MAT.	INST.	TOTAL
0600	Boiler, electric, steel, hot water, 12 K.W., 41 M.B.H.	3,725	900	4,625
0620	30 K.W., 103 M.B.H.	4,100	975	5,075
0640	60 K.W., 205 M.B.H.	5,200	1,050	6,250
0660	120 K.W., 410 M.B.H.	6,625	1,300	7,925
0680	210 K.W., 716 M.B.H.	11,000	1,950	12,950
0700	510 K.W., 1,739 M.B.H.	20,800	3,600	24,400
0720	720 K.W., 2,452 M.B.H.	26,200	4,075	30,275
0740	1,200 K.W., 4,095 M.B.H.	37,000	4,675	41,675
0760	2,100 K.W., 7,167 M.B.H.	58,000	5,875	63,875
0780	3,600 K.W., 12,283 M.B.H.	79,500	9,925	89,425
0820	Steam, 6 K.W., 20.5 M.B.H.	8,700	975	9,675
0840	24 K.W., 81.8 M.B.H.	9,250	1,050	10,300
0860	60 K.W., 205 M.B.H.	10,700	1,175	11,875
0880	150 K.W., 512 M.B.H.	13,900	1,800	15,700
0900	510 K.W., 1,740 M.B.H.	22,600	4,400	27,000
0920	1,080 K.W., 3,685 M.B.H.	34,700	6,350	41,050
0940	2,340 K.W., 7,984 M.B.H.	65,500	9,925	75,425
0980	Gas, cast iron, hot water, 80 M.B.H.	1,125	1,100	2,225
1000	100 M.B.H.	1,300	1,200	2,500
1020	163 M.B.H.	1,750	1,600	3,350
1040	280 M.B.H.	2,475	1,775	4,250
1060	544 M.B.H.	4,175	3,150	7,325
1080	1,088 M.B.H.	7,025	4,025	11,050
1100	2,000 M.B.H.	12,100	6,275	18,375
1120	2,856 M.B.H.	16,700	8,025	24,725
1140	4,720 M.B.H.	48,300	11,100	59,400
1160	6,970 M.B.H.	61,500	18,000	79,500
1180	For steam systems under 2,856 M.B.H., add 8%			
1240	Steel, hot water, 72 M.B.H.	1,925	590	2,515
1260	101 M.B.H.	2,200	655	2,855
1280	132 M.B.H.	2,500	695	3,195
1300	150 M.B.H.	2,900	785	3,685
1320	240 M.B.H.	4,450	905	5,355
1340	400 M.B.H.	6,350	1,475	7,825
1360	640 M.B.H.	8,625	1,975	10,600
1380	800 M.B.H.	10,100	2,350	12,450
1400	960 M.B.H.	12,500	2,625	15,125
1420	1,440 M.B.H.	17,400	3,375	20,775
1440	2,400 M.B.H.	28,100	5,900	34,000
1460	3,000 M.B.H.	34,700	7,850	42,550

8.3-130	Boilers, Hot Water & Steam	COST EACH		
		MAT.	INST.	TOTAL
1520	Oil, cast iron, hot water, 109 M.B.H.	1,525	1,350	2,875
1540	173 M.B.H.	1,900	1,600	3,500
1560	236 M.B.H.	2,975	1,900	4,875
1580	1,084 M.B.H.	6,975	4,275	11,250
1600	1,600 M.B.H.	9,250	6,125	15,375
1620	2,480 M.B.H.	13,700	7,825	21,525
1640	3,550 M.B.H.	16,800	9,400	26,200
1660	Steam systems same price as hot water			
1700	Steel, hot water, 103 M.B.H.	1,075	735	1,810
1720	137 M.B.H.	2,700	865	3,565
1740	225 M.B.H.	3,000	970	3,970
1760	315 M.B.H.	3,925	1,225	5,150
1780	420 M.B.H.	4,575	1,700	6,275
1800	630 M.B.H.	6,000	2,250	8,250
1820	735 M.B.H.	6,200	2,450	8,650
1840	1,050 M.B.H.	11,300	3,225	14,525
1860	1,365 M.B.H.	11,300	3,650	14,950
1880	1,680 M.B.H.	12,800	4,100	16,900
1900	2,310 M.B.H.	14,400	5,650	20,050
1920	2,835 M.B.H.	18,600	6,925	25,525
1940	3,150 M.B.H.	19,800	9,075	28,875

MECHANICAL

8

Unit Heater

Fossil Fuel Boiler System Considerations:

1. Terminal units are horizontal unit heaters. Quantities are varied to accommodate total heat loss per building.
2. Unit heater selection was determined by their capacity to circulate the building volume a minimum of three times per hour in addition to the BTU output.
3. Systems shown are forced hot water. Steam boilers cost slightly more than hot water boilers. However, this is compensated for by the smaller size or fewer terminal units required with steam.
4. Floor levels are based on 10' story heights.
5. MBH requirements are gross boiler output.

8.3-141	Heating Systems, Unit Heaters	COST PER S.F.		
		MAT.	**INST.**	**TOTAL**
1260	Heating systems, hydronic, fossil fuel, terminal unit heaters,			
1280	Cast iron boiler, gas, 80 M.B.H., 1,070 S.F. bldg.	5.50	6.25	11.75
1320	163 M.B.H., 2,140 S.F. bldg.	3.70	4.23	7.93
1360	544 M.B.H., 7,250 S.F. bldg.	2.57	3.08	5.65
1400	1,088 M.B.H., 14,500 S.F. bldg.	2.26	2.93	5.19
1440	3,264 M.B.H., 43,500 S.F. bldg.	1.86	2.22	4.08
1480	5,032 M.B.H., 67,100 S.F. bldg.	2.24	2.27	4.51
1520	Oil, 109 M.B.H., 1,420 S.F. bldg.	5.40	5.55	10.95
1560	235 M.B.H., 3,150 S.F. bldg.	4.02	4.09	8.11
1600	940 M.B.H., 12,500 S.F. bldg.	2.71	2.68	5.39
1640	1,600 M.B.H., 21,300 S.F. bldg.	2.62	2.56	5.18
1680	2,480 M.B.H., 33,100 S.F. bldg.	2.64	2.32	4.96
1720	3,350 M.B.H., 44,500 S.F. bldg.	2.28	2.36	4.64
1760	Coal, 148 M.B.H., 1,975 S.F. bldg.	4.63	3.63	8.26
1800	300 M.B.H., 4,000 S.F. bldg.	3.55	2.85	6.40
1840	2,360 M.B.H., 31,500 S.F. bldg.	2.50	2.36	4.86
1880	Steel boiler, gas, 72 M.B.H., 1,020 S.F. bldg.	5.50	4.61	10.11
1920	240 M.B.H., 3,200 S.F. bldg.	3.86	3.77	7.63
1960	480 M.B.H., 6,400 S.F. bldg.	3.15	2.78	5.93
2000	800 M.B.H., 10,700 S.F. bldg.	2.68	2.48	5.16
2040	1,960 M.B.H., 26,100 S.F. bldg.	2.38	2.24	4.62
2080	3,000 M.B.H., 40,000 S.F. bldg.	2.34	2.29	4.63
2120	Oil, 97 M.B.H., 1,300 S.F. bldg.	4.90	5.25	10.15
2160	315 M.B.H., 4,550 S.F. bldg.	3.31	2.68	5.99
2200	525 M.B.H., 7,000 S.F. bldg.	3.50	2.78	6.28
2240	1,050 M.B.H., 14,000 S.F. bldg.	3.07	2.80	5.87
2280	2,310 M.B.H. 30,800 S.F. bldg.	2.66	2.41	5.07
2320	3,150 M.B.H., 42,000 S.F. bldg.	2.42	2.47	4.89

MECHANICAL 8

Fossil Fuel Boiler System Considerations:

1. Terminal units are commercial steel fin tube radiation. Quantities are varied to accommodate total heat loss per building.
2. Systems shown are forced hot water. Steam boilers cost slightly more than hot water boilers. However, this is compensated for by the smaller size or fewer terminal units required with steam.
3. Floor levels are based on 10' story heights.
4. MBH requirements are gross boiler output.

Fin Tube Radiator

8.3-142	Heating System, Fin Tube Radiation	COST PER S.F.		
		MAT.	INST.	TOTAL
3230	Heating systems, hydronic, fossil fuel, fin tube radiation			
3240	Cast iron boiler, gas, 80 MBH, 1,070 S.F. bldg.	6.70	9.30	16
3280	169 M.B.H., 2,140 S.F. bldg.	4.22	5.90	10.12
3320	544 M.B.H., 7,250 S.F. bldg.	3.47	5.15	8.62
3360	1,088 M.B.H., 14,500 S.F. bldg.	3.22	5.05	8.27
3400	3,264 M.B.H., 43,500 S.F. bldg.	2.91	4.43	7.34
3440	5,032 M.B.H., 67,100 S.F. bldg.	3.31	4.49	7.80
3480	Oil, 109 M.B.H., 1,420 S.F. bldg.	7.65	10.15	17.80
3520	235 M.B.H., 3,150 S.F. bldg.	4.92	6.10	11.02
3560	940 M.B.H., 12,500 S.F. bldg.	3.70	4.83	8.53
3600	1,600 M.B.H., 21,300 S.F. bldg.	3.67	4.79	8.46
3640	2,480 M.B.H., 33,100 S.F. bldg.	3.71	4.54	8.25
3680	3,350 M.B.H., 44,500 S.F. bldg.	3.34	4.59	7.93
3720	Coal, 148 M.B.H., 1,975 S.F. bldg.	5.50	5.65	11.15
3760	300 M.B.H., 4,000 S.F. bldg.	4.41	4.84	9.25
3800	2,360 M.B.H., 31,500 S.F. bldg.	3.54	4.55	8.09
3840	Steel boiler, gas, 72 M.B.H., 1,020 S.F. bldg.	7.70	8.85	16.55
3880	240 M.B.H., 3,200 S.F. bldg.	4.81	5.90	10.71
3920	480 M.B.H., 6,400 S.F. bldg.	4.08	4.84	8.92
3960	800 M.B.H., 10,700 S.F. bldg.	3.97	5.15	9.12
4000	1,960 M.B.H., 26,100 S.F. bldg.	3.41	4.43	7.84
4040	3,000 M.B.H., 40,000 S.F. bldg.	3.35	4.45	7.80
4080	Oil, 97 M.B.H., 1,300 S.F. bldg.	5.40	8.35	13.75
4120	315 M.B.H., 4,550 S.F. bldg.	4.15	4.57	8.72
4160	525 M.B.H., 7,000 S.F. bldg.	4.51	4.94	9.45
4200	1,050 M.B.H., 14,000 S.F. bldg.	4.08	4.96	9.04
4240	2,310 M.B.H., 30,800 S.F. bldg.	3.68	4.57	8.25
4280	3,150 M.B.H., 42,000 S.F. bldg.	3.44	4.64	8.08

MECHANICAL

8

Forced Hot Water Heating System

Fin Tube Radiation

Terminal Unit Heater

8.3-151	Apartment Building Heating - Fin Tube Radiation	COST PER S.F.		
		MAT.	INST.	TOTAL
1740	Heating systems, fin tube radiation, forced hot water			
1760	1,000 S.F. area, 10,000 C.F. volume	4.10	4.07	8.17
1800	10,000 S.F. area, 100,000 C.F. volume	1.21	2.44	3.65
1840	20,000 S.F. area, 200,000 C.F. volume	1.36	2.76	4.12
1880	30,000 S.F. area, 300,000 C.F. volume	1.25	2.66	3.91

8.3-161	Commercial Building Heating - Fin Tube Radiation	COST PER S.F.		
		MAT.	INST.	TOTAL
1940	Heating systems, fin tube radiation, forced hot water			
1960	1,000 S.F. bldg, one floor	8.25	9.15	17.40
2000	10,000 S.F., 100,000 C.F., total two floors	2.30	3.51	5.81
2040	100,000 S.F., 1,000,000 C.F., total three floors	1.04	1.62	2.66
2080	1,000,000 S.F., 10,000,000 C.F., total five floors	.51	.85	1.36

8.3-162	Commercial Bldg. Heating - Terminal Unit Heaters	COST PER S.F.		
		MAT.	INST.	TOTAL
1860	Heating systems, terminal unit heaters, forced hot water			
1880	1,000 S.F. bldg., one floor	8.10	8.40	16.50
1920	10,000 S.F. bldg., 100,000 C.F. total two floors	2.08	2.92	5
1960	100,000 S.F. bldg., 1,000,000 C.F. total three floors	1.07	1.49	2.56
2000	1,000,000 S.F. bldg., 10,000,000 C.F. total five floors	.68	.96	1.64

Chilled Water Supply & Return Piping

Air Cooled Water Chiller Unit

Roof

Insulate

Return →⌇→ | Fan Coil Unit | →⌇→ Supply

Finish Ceiling

*Cooling requirements would lead to a choice of multiple chillers.

8.4-110	Chilled Water, Air Cooled Condenser Systems	COST PER S.F.		
		MAT.	INST.	TOTAL
1180	Packaged chiller, air cooled, with fan coil unit			
1200	Apartment corridors, 3,000 S.F., 5.50 ton	4.28	5.10	9.38
1240	6,000 S.F., 11.00 ton	3.39	4.12	7.51
1280	10,000 S.F., 18.33 ton	3	3.13	6.13
1320	20,000 S.F., 36.66 ton	2.45	2.27	4.72
1360	40,000 S.F., 73.33 ton	2.93	2.29	5.22
1440	Banks and libraries, 3,000 S.F., 12.50 ton	6.50	6.05	12.55
1480	6,000 S.F., 25.00 ton	6.10	4.91	11.01
1520	10,000 S.F., 41.66 ton	5	3.43	8.43
1560	20,000 S.F., 83.33 ton	5.40	3.12	8.52
1600	40,000 S.F., 167 ton*			
1680	Bars and taverns, 3,000 S.F., 33.25 ton	12.55	7.15	19.70
1720	6,000 S.F., 66.50 ton	11.85	5.55	17.40
1760	10,000 S.F., 110.83 ton	9.80	1.78	11.58
1800	20,000 S.F., 220 ton*			
1840	40,000 S.F., 440 ton*			
1920	Bowling alleys, 3,000 S.F., 17.00 ton	8.35	6.80	15.15
1960	6,000 S.F., 34.00 ton	6.80	4.77	11.57
2000	10,000 S.F., 56.66 ton	6.25	3.47	9.72
2040	20,000 S.F., 113.33 ton	6.05	3.15	9.20
2080	40,000 S.F., 227 ton*			
2160	Department stores, 3,000 S.F., 8.75 ton	6.20	5.70	11.90
2200	6,000 S.F., 17.50 ton	4.57	4.43	9
2240	10,000 S.F., 29.17 ton	3.84	3.20	7.04
2280	20,000 S.F., 58.33 ton	3.45	2.36	5.81
2320	40,000 S.F., 116.66 ton	3.77	2.34	6.11
2400	Drug stores, 3,000 S.F., 20.00 ton	9.60	7	16.60
2440	6,000 S.F., 40.00 ton	8.05	5.20	13.25
2480	10,000 S.F., 66.66 ton	8.40	4.48	12.88
2520	20,000 S.F., 133.33 ton	7.40	3.33	10.73
2560	40,000 S.F., 267 ton*			
2640	Factories, 2,000 S.F., 10.00 ton	5.60	5.80	11.40
2680	6,000 S.F., 20.00 ton	5.20	4.67	9.87
2720	10,000 S.F., 33.33 ton	4.23	3.27	7.50
2760	20,000 S.F., 66.66 ton	4.62	2.95	7.57
2800	40,000 S.F., 133.33 ton	4.15	2.41	6.56
2880	Food supermarkets, 3,000 S.F., 8.50 ton	6.05	5.70	11.75
2920	6,000 S.F., 17.00 ton	4.48	4.41	8.89
2960	10,000 S.F., 28.33 ton	3.66	3.10	6.76
3000	20,000 S.F., 56.66 ton	3.32	2.31	5.63
3040	40,000 S.F., 113.33 ton	3.64	2.35	5.99
3120	Medical centers, 3,000 S.F., 7.00 ton	5.35	5.55	10.90
3160	6,000 S.F., 14.00 ton	3.94	4.26	8.20
3200	10,000 S.F., 23.33 ton	3.59	3.25	6.84

MECHANICAL

8

8.4-110	Chilled Water, Air Cooled Condenser Systems	COST PER S.F.		
		MAT.	INST.	TOTAL
3240	20,000 S.F., 46.66 ton	2.99	2.38	5.37
3280	40,000 S.F., 93.33 ton	3.23	2.30	5.53
3360	Offices, 3,000 S.F., 9.50 ton	5.20	5.65	10.85
3400	6,000 S.F., 19.00 ton	5	4.63	9.63
3440	10,000 S.F., 31.66 ton	4.08	3.25	7.33
3480	20,000 S.F., 63.33 ton	4.57	3.02	7.59
3520	40,000 S.F., 126.66 ton	4.06	2.44	6.50
3600	Restaurants, 3,000 S.F., 15.00 ton	7.45	6.25	13.70
3640	6,000 S.F., 30.00 ton	6.35	4.77	11.12
3680	10,000 S.F., 50.00 ton	5.85	3.52	9.37
3720	20,000 S.F., 100.00 ton	6.05	3.29	9.34
3760	40,000 S.F., 200 ton*			
3840	Schools and colleges, 3,000 S.F., 11.50 ton	6.15	5.95	12.10
3880	6,000 S.F., 23.00 ton	5.75	4.82	10.57
3920	10,000 S.F., 38.33 ton	4.69	3.37	8.06
3960	20,000 S.F., 76.66 ton	5.20	3.15	8.35
4000	40,000 S.F., 153 ton*			

Important: See the Reference Section for critical supporting data - Location Factors & Historical Cost Indexes

MECHANICAL 8

Reciprocating Package Chiller — Condenser Water — Cooling Tower — Cooling Tower Water Makeup — Chilled Water Supply & Return Piping — Roof Structure — Finish Ceiling — Insulate — Return — Supply — Fan Coil Unit

*Cooling requirements would lead to a choice of multiple chillers

8.4-120	Chilled Water, Cooling Tower Systems	COST PER S.F.		
		MAT.	INST.	TOTAL
1300	Packaged chiller, water cooled, with fan coil unit			
1320	Apartment corridors, 4,000 S.F., 7.33 ton	5.35	5	10.35
1360	6,000 S.F., 11.00 ton	4.22	4.33	8.55
1400	10,000 S.F., 18.33 ton	3.53	3.20	6.73
1440	20,000 S.F., 26.66 ton	2.80	2.39	5.19
1480	40,000 S.F., 73.33 ton	3.14	2.46	5.60
1520	60,000 S.F., 110.00 ton	3.07	2.53	5.60
1600	Banks and libraries, 4,000 S.F., 16.66 ton	8.05	5.50	13.55
1640	6,000 S.F., 25.00 ton	6.50	4.85	11.35
1680	10,000 S.F., 41.66 ton	5.20	3.62	8.82
1720	20,000 S.F., 83.33 ton	5.85	3.46	9.31
1760	40,000 S.F., 166.66 ton	5.65	4.32	9.97
1800	60,000 S.F., 250.00 ton	5.55	4.57	10.12
1880	Bars and taverns, 4,000 S.F., 44.33 ton	12.65	6.95	19.60
1920	6,000 S.F., 66.50 ton	12.95	7.20	20.15
1960	10,000 S.F., 110.83 ton	12.75	5.70	18.45
2000	20,000 S.F., 221.66 ton	11.90	6.20	18.10
2040	40,000 S.F., 440 ton*			
2080	60,000 S.F., 660 ton*			
2160	Bowling alleys, 4,000 S.F., 22.66 ton	9.45	6.05	15.50
2200	6,000 S.F., 34.00 ton	7.95	5.35	13.30
2240	10,000 S.F., 56.66 ton	6.50	3.92	10.42
2280	20,000 S.F., 113.33 ton	6.90	3.66	10.56
2320	40,000 S.F., 226.66 ton	6.65	4.45	11.10
2360	60,000 S.F., 340 ton			
2440	Department stores, 4,000 S.F., 11.66 ton	6.05	5.45	11.50
2480	6,000 S.F., 17.50 ton	5.85	4.49	10.34
2520	10,000 S.F., 29.17 ton	4.25	3.35	7.60
2560	20,000 S.F., 58.33 ton	3.29	2.49	5.78
2600	40,000 S.F., 116.66 ton	3.96	2.58	6.54
2640	60,000 S.F., 175.00 ton	4.49	4.28	8.77
2720	Drug stores, 4,000 S.F., 26.66 ton	9.90	6.25	16.15
2760	6,000 S.F., 40.00 ton	8.25	5.35	13.60
2800	10,000 S.F., 66.66 ton	8.15	4.87	13.02
2840	20,000 S.F., 133.33 ton	7.95	3.83	11.78
2880	40,000 S.F., 266.67 ton	7.75	4.90	12.65
2920	60,000 S.F., 400 ton*			
3000	Factories, 4,000 S.F., 13.33 ton	6.80	5.25	12.05
3040	6,000 S.F., 20.00 ton	5.90	4.50	10.40
3080	10,000 S.F., 33.33 ton	4.71	3.45	8.16
3120	20,000 S.F., 66.66 ton	4.44	3.10	7.54
3160	40,000 S.F., 133.33 ton	4.42	2.65	7.07
3200	60,000 S.F., 200.00 ton	4.85	4.38	9.23
3280	Food supermarkets, 4,000 S.F., 11.33 ton	5.95	5.40	11.35
3320	6,000 S.F., 17.00 ton	5.15	4.42	9.57
3360	10,000 S.F., 28.33 ton	4.15	3.33	7.48

MECHANICAL

8

8.4-120	Chilled Water, Cooling Tower Systems	COST PER S.F.		
		MAT.	INST.	TOTAL
3400	20,000 S.F., 56.66 ton	3.38	2.50	5.88
3440	40,000 S.F., 113.33 ton	3.91	2.58	6.49
3480	60,000 S.F., 170.00 ton	4.42	4.27	8.69
3560	Medical centers, 4.000 S.F., 9.33 ton	5.05	4.95	10
3600	6,000 S.F., 14.00 ton	4.96	4.31	9.27
3640	10,000 S.F., 23.33 ton	3.82	3.21	7.03
3680	20,000 S.F., 46.66 ton	2.98	2.43	5.41
3720	40,000 S.F., 93.33 ton	3.57	2.52	6.09
3760	60,000 S.F., 140.00 ton	4.06	4.21	8.27
3840	Offices, 4,000 S.F., 12.66 ton	6.55	5.20	11.75
3880	6,000 S.F., 19.00 ton	5.75	4.63	10.38
3920	10,000 S.F., 31.66 ton	4.63	3.50	8.13
3960	20,000 S.F., 63.33 ton	4.35	3.12	7.47
4000	40,000 S.F., 126.66 ton	4.70	4.14	8.84
4040	60,000 S.F., 190.00 ton	4.68	4.34	9.02
4120	Restaurants, 4,000 S.F., 20.00 ton	8.45	5.60	14.05
4160	6,000 S.F., 30.00 ton	7.15	5	12.15
4200	10,000 S.F., 50.00 ton	5.90	3.76	9.66
4240	20,000 S.F., 100.00 ton	6.65	3.65	10.30
4280	40,000 S.F., 200.00 ton	5.90	4.19	10.09
4320	60,000 S.F., 300.00 ton	6.25	4.73	10.98
4400	Schools and colleges, 4,000 S.F., 15.33 ton	7.55	5.40	12.95
4440	6,000 S.F., 23.00 ton	6.10	4.76	10.86
4480	10,000 S.F., 38.33 ton	4.85	3.54	8.39
4520	20,000 S.F., 76.66 ton	5.55	3.43	8.98
4560	40,000 S.F., 153.33 ton	5.25	4.22	9.47
4600	60,000 S.F., 230.00 ton	5.10	4.40	9.50

MECHANICAL 8

Important: See the Reference Section for critical supporting data - Location Factors & Historical Cost Indexes

Roof — Roof Top Unit

Return Duct

Fan Coil Unit —

Insulated Supply Duct

Return Grille

Supply Diff.

Finish Ceiling

*Above normal capacity

Rooftop, Single Zone System

8.4-210	Rooftop Single Zone Unit Systems	COST PER S.F.		
		MAT.	INST.	TOTAL
1260	Rooftop, single zone, air conditioner			
1280	Apartment corridors, 500 S.F., .92 ton	4.79	2.42	7.21
1320	1,000 S.F., 1.83 ton	4.76	2.40	7.16
1360	1500 S.F., 2.75 ton	2.80	1.99	4.79
1400	3,000 S.F., 5.50 ton	2.42	1.92	4.34
1440	5,000 S.F., 9.17 ton	2.44	1.75	4.19
1480	10,000 S.F., 18.33 ton	2.60	1.64	4.24
1560	Banks or libraries, 500 S.F., 2.08 ton	10.80	5.45	16.25
1600	1,000 S.F., 4.17 ton	6.35	4.53	10.88
1640	1,500 S.F., 6.25 ton	5.50	4.36	9.86
1680	3,000 S.F., 12.50 ton	5.55	3.97	9.52
1720	5,000 S.F., 20.80 ton	5.90	3.72	9.62
1760	10,000 S.F., 41.67 ton	5.55	3.71	9.26
1840	Bars and taverns, 500 S.F. 5.54 ton	13	7.30	20.30
1880	1,000 S.F., 11.08 ton	13.10	6.25	19.35
1920	1,500 S.F., 16.62 ton	11.80	5.80	17.60
1960	3,000 S.F., 33.25 ton	13.40	5.55	18.95
2000	5,000 S.F., 55.42 ton	12.80	5.55	18.35
2040	10,000 S.F., 110.83 ton*			
2080	Bowling alleys, 500 S.F., 2.83 ton	8.65	6.15	14.80
2120	1,000 S.F., 5.67 ton	7.45	5.90	13.35
2160	1,500 S.F., 8.50 ton	7.55	5.40	12.95
2200	3,000 S.F., 17.00 ton	6.85	5.15	12
2240	5,000 S.F., 28.33 ton	7.70	5.05	12.75
2280	10,000 S.F., 56.67 ton	7.35	5.05	12.40
2360	Department stores, 500 S.F., 1.46 ton	7.60	3.83	11.43
2400	1,000 S.F., 2.92 ton	4.45	3.17	7.62
2480	3,000 S.F., 8.75 ton	3.87	2.78	6.65
2520	5,000 S.F., 14.58 ton	3.52	2.66	6.18
2560	10,000 S.F., 29.17 ton	3.95	2.59	6.54
2640	Drug stores, 500 S.F., 3.33 ton	10.15	7.25	17.40
2680	1,000 S.F., 6.67 ton	8.80	6.95	15.75
2720	1,500 S.F., 10.00 ton	8.85	6.35	15.20
2760	3,000 S.F., 20.00 ton	9.45	5.95	15.40
2800	5,000 S.F., 33.33 ton	9.05	5.95	15
2840	10,000 S.F., 66.67 ton	8.65	5.95	14.60
2920	Factories, 500 S.F., 1.67 ton	8.65	4.37	13.02
3000	1,500 S.F., 5.00 ton	4.39	3.48	7.87
3040	3,000 S.F., 10.00 ton	4.43	3.17	7.60
3080	5,000 S.F., 16.67 ton	4.03	3.04	7.07
3120	10,000 S.F., 33.33 ton	4.52	2.96	7.48
3200	Food supermarkets, 500 S.F., 1.42 ton	7.35	3.72	11.07
3240	1,000 S.F., 2.83 ton	4.29	3.07	7.36
3280	1,500 S.F., 4.25 ton	3.74	2.97	6.71

MECHANICAL

8

8.4-210	Rooftop Single Zone Unit Systems	COST PER S.F.		
		MAT.	INST.	TOTAL
3320	3,000 S.F., 8.50 ton	3.77	2.70	6.47
3360	5,000 S.F., 14.17 ton	3.43	2.59	6.02
3400	10,000 S.F., 28.33 ton	3.84	2.52	6.36
3480	Medical centers, 500 S.F., 1.17 ton	6.05	3.06	9.11
3520	1,000 S.F., 2.33 ton	6.05	3.06	9.11
3560	1,500 S.F., 3.50 ton	3.56	2.54	6.10
3640	5,000 S.F., 11.67 ton	3.10	2.22	5.32
3680	10,000 S.F., 23.33 ton	3.31	2.09	5.40
3760	Offices, 500 S.F., 1.58 ton	8.25	4.15	12.40
3800	1,000 S.F., 3.17 ton	4.84	3.45	8.29
3840	1,500 S.F., 4.75 ton	4.18	3.31	7.49
3880	3,000 S.F., 9.50 ton	4.21	3.01	7.22
3920	5,000 S.F., 15.83 ton	3.82	2.89	6.71
3960	10,000 S.F., 31.67 ton	4.30	2.81	7.11
4000	Restaurants, 500 S.F., 2.50 ton	13	6.55	19.55
4040	1,000 S.F., 5.00 ton	6.60	5.25	11.85
4080	1,500 S.F., 7.50 ton	6.65	4.77	11.42
4120	3,000 S.F., 15.00 ton	6.05	4.57	10.62
4160	5,000 S.F., 25.00 ton	7.10	4.48	11.58
4200	10,000 S.F., 50.00 ton	6.50	4.45	10.95
4240	Schools and colleges, 500 S.F., 1.92 ton	9.95	5.05	15
4280	1,000 S.F., 3.83 ton	5.85	4.17	10.02
4360	3,000 S.F., 11.50 ton	5.10	3.65	8.75
4400	5,000 S.F., 19.17 ton	5.45	3.43	8.88

Important: See the Reference Section for critical supporting data , Location Factors , Historical Cost Indexes

*Note A: Small single zone unit recommended.

*Note B: A combination of multizone units recommended.

8.4-220	Rooftop Multizone Unit Systems	COST PER S.F.		
		MAT.	INST.	TOTAL
1240	Rooftop, multizone, air conditioner			
1260	Apartment corridors, 1,500 S.F., 2.75 ton. See Note A.			
1280	3,000 S.F., 5.50 ton	7.20	3.14	10.34
1320	10,000 S.F., 18.30 ton	5.35	3.03	8.38
1360	15,000 S.F., 27.50 ton	4.49	3.01	7.50
1400	20,000 S.F., 36.70 ton	4.61	3.01	7.62
1440	25,000 S.F., 45.80 ton	4.40	3.03	7.43
1520	Banks or libraries, 1,500 S.F., 6.25 ton	16.35	7.15	23.50
1560	3,000 S.F., 12.50 ton	13.90	7	20.90
1600	10,000 S.F., 41.67 ton	10	6.90	16.90
1640	15,000 S.F., 62.50 ton	8.60	6.85	15.45
1680	20,000 S.F., 83.33 ton	8.60	6.85	15.45
1720	25,000 S.F., 104.00 ton	8.15	6.80	14.95
1800	Bars and taverns, 1,500 S.F., 16.62 ton	34.50	10.25	44.75
1840	3,000 S.F., 33.24 ton	25.50	9.90	35.40
1880	10,000 S.F., 110.83 ton	19.35	9.85	29.20
1920	15,000 S.F., 165 ton, See Note B			
1960	20,000 S.F., 220 ton, See Note B			
2000	25,000 S.F., 275 ton, See Note B			
2080	Bowling alleys, 1,500 S.F., 8.50 ton	22.50	9.70	32.20
2120	3,000 S.F., 17.00 ton	18.95	9.50	28.45
2160	10,000 S.F., 56.70 ton	13.60	9.40	23
2200	15,000 S.F., 85.00 ton	11.70	9.30	21
2240	20,000 S.F., 113.00 ton	11.05	9.25	20.30
2280	25,000 S.F., 140.00 ton see Note B			
2360	Department stores, 1,500 S.F., 4.37 ton, See Note A.			
2400	3,000 S.F., 8.75 ton	11.45	4.99	16.44
2440	10,000 S.F., 29.17 ton	7.35	4.80	12.15
2520	20,000 S.F., 58.33 ton	6	4.79	10.79
2560	25,000 S.F., 72.92 ton	6	4.80	10.80
2640	Drug stores, 1,500 S.F., 10.00 ton	26	11.40	37.40
2680	3,000 S.F., 20.00 ton	19.45	11	30.45
2720	10,000 S.F., 66.66 ton	13.75	10.95	24.70
2760	15,000 S.F., 100.00 ton	13	10.95	23.95
2800	20,000 S.F., 135 ton, See Note B			
2840	25,000 S.F., 165 ton, See Note B			
2920	Factories, 1,500 S.F., 5 ton, See Note A			
3000	10,000 S.F., 33.33 ton	8.40	5.50	13.90
3040	15,000 S.F., 50.00 ton	8	5.50	13.50
3080	20,000 S.F., 66.66 ton	6.90	5.45	12.35
3120	25,000 S.F., 83.33 ton	6.90	5.50	12.40
3200	Food supermarkets, 1,500 S.F., 4.25 ton, See Note A			

MECHANICAL

8

8.4-220	Rooftop Multizone Unit Systems	COST PER S.F.		
		MAT.	INST.	TOTAL
3240	3,000 S.F., 8.50 ton	11.15	4.85	16
3280	10,000 S.F., 28.33 ton	6.95	4.65	11.60
3320	15,000 S.F., 42.50 ton	6.80	4.69	11.49
3360	20,000 S.F., 56.67 ton	5.85	4.65	10.50
3400	25,000 S.F., 70.83 ton	5.85	4.65	10.50
3480	Medical centers, 1,500 S.F., 3.5 ton, See Note A			
3520	3,000 S.F., 7.00 ton	9.15	3.99	13.14
3560	10,000 S.F., 23.33 ton	5.95	3.84	9.79
3600	15,000 S.F., 35.00 ton	5.85	3.83	9.68
3640	20,000 S.F., 46.66 ton	5.60	3.86	9.46
3680	25,000 S.F., 58.33 ton	4.82	3.83	8.65
3760	Offices, 1,500 S.F., 4.75 ton, See Note A			
3800	3,000 S.F., 9.50 ton	12.45	5.40	17.85
3840	10,000 S.F., 31.66 ton	7.95	5.20	13.15
3920	20,000 S.F., 63.33 ton	6.55	5.20	11.75
3960	25,000 S.F., 79.16 ton	6.55	5.20	11.75
4000	Restaurants, 1,500 S.F., 7.50 ton	19.65	8.55	28.20
4040	3,000 S.F., 15.00 ton	16.70	8.40	25.10
4080	10,000 S.F., 50.00 ton	12	8.25	20.25
4120	15,000 S.F., 75.00 ton	10.35	8.20	18.55
4160	20,000 S.F., 100.00 ton	9.75	8.20	17.95
4200	25,000 S.F., 125 ton, See Note B			
4240	Schools and colleges, 1,500 S.F., 5.75 ton	15.05	6.55	21.60
4320	10,000 S.F., 38.33 ton	9.20	6.35	15.55
4360	15,000 S.F., 57.50 ton	7.90	6.30	14.20
4400	20,000 S.F., 76.66 ton	7.90	6.30	14.20
4440	25,000 S.F., 95.83 ton	7.50	6.30	13.80

MECHANICAL 8

Important: See the Reference Section for critical supporting data - Location Factors & Historical Cost Indexes

Self-Contained Water Cooled System

8.4-230	Self-contained, Water Cooled Unit Systems	COST PER S.F.		
		MAT.	INST.	TOTAL
1280	Self-contained, water cooled unit	2.69	1.93	4.62
1300	Apartment corridors, 500 S.F., .92 ton	2.68	1.92	4.60
1320	1,000 S.F., 1.83 ton	2.68	1.91	4.59
1360	3,000 S.F., 5.50 ton	2.04	1.63	3.67
1400	5,000 S.F., 9.17 ton	2.07	1.52	3.59
1440	10,000 S.F., 18.33 ton	1.89	1.35	3.24
1520	Banks or libraries, 500 S.F., 2.08 ton	5.70	1.89	7.59
1560	1,000 S.F., 4.17 ton	4.64	3.72	8.36
1600	3,000 S.F., 12.50 ton	4.70	3.45	8.15
1640	5,000 S.F., 20.80 ton	4.29	3.07	7.36
1680	10,000 S.F., 41.66 ton	3.75	3.08	6.83
1760	Bars and taverns, 500 S.F., 5.54 ton	11.15	3.33	14.48
1800	1,000 S.F., 11.08 ton	11.85	5.90	17.75
1840	3,000 S.F., 33.25 ton	9.80	4.65	14.45
1880	5,000 S.F., 55.42 ton	9.20	4.85	14.05
1920	10,000 S.F., 110.00 ton	9	4.79	13.79
2000	Bowling alleys, 500 S.F., 2.83 ton	7.75	2.59	10.34
2040	1,000 S.F., 5.66 ton	6.30	5.05	11.35
2080	3,000 S.F., 17.00 ton	5.85	4.19	10.04
2120	5,000 S.F., 28.33 ton	5.30	4.05	9.35
2160	10,000 S.F., 56.66 ton	4.98	4.14	9.12
2200	Department stores, 500 S.F., 1.46 ton	3.99	1.33	5.32
2240	1,000 S.F., 2.92 ton	3.24	2.60	5.84
2280	3,000 S.F., 8.75 ton	3.28	2.42	5.70
2320	5,000 S.F., 14.58 ton	3	2.16	5.16
2360	10,000 S.F., 29.17 ton	2.73	2.09	4.82
2440	Drug stores, 500 S.F., 3.33 ton	9.10	3.05	12.15
2480	1,000 S.F., 6.66 ton	7.40	5.95	13.35
2520	3,000 S.F., 20.00 ton	6.85	4.94	11.79
2560	5,000 S.F., 33.33 ton	7.20	4.88	12.08
2600	10,000 S.F., 66.66 ton	5.85	4.88	10.73
2680	Factories, 500 S.F., 1.66 ton	4.55	1.51	6.06
2720	1,000 S.F. 3.37 ton	3.74	3	6.74
2760	3,000 S.F., 10.00 ton	3.76	2.76	6.52
2800	5,000 S.F., 16.66 ton	3.43	2.46	5.89
2840	10,000 S.F., 33.33 ton	3.12	2.38	5.50
2920	Food supermarkets, 500 S.F., 1.42 ton	3.86	1.30	5.16
2960	1,000 S.F., 2.83 ton	4.14	2.97	7.11
3000	3,000 S.F., 8.50 ton	3.15	2.53	5.68
3040	5,000 S.F., 14.17 ton	3.19	2.35	5.54

8.4-230	Self-contained, Water Cooled Unit Systems	COST PER S.F.		
		MAT.	INST.	TOTAL
3080	10,000 S.F., 28.33 ton	2.66	2.03	4.69
3160	Medical centers, 500 S.F., 1.17 ton	3.18	1.06	4.24
3200	1,000 S.F., 2.33 ton	3.42	2.44	5.86
3240	3,000 S.F., 7.00 ton	2.60	2.08	4.68
3280	5,000 S.F., 11.66 ton	2.63	1.94	4.57
3320	10,000 S.F., 23.33 ton	2.40	1.73	4.13
3400	Offices, 500 S.F., 1.58 ton	4.33	1.45	5.78
3440	1,000 S.F., 3.17 ton	4.64	3.32	7.96
3480	3,000 S.F., 9.50 ton	3.57	2.63	6.20
3520	5,000 S.F., 15.83 ton	3.26	2.34	5.60
3560	10,000 S.F., 31.67 ton	2.97	2.27	5.24
3640	Restaurants, 500 S.F., 2.50 ton	6.85	2.29	9.14
3680	1,000 S.F., 5.00 ton	5.55	4.47	10.02
3720	3,000 S.F., 15.00 ton	5.65	4.16	9.81
3760	5,000 S.F., 25.00 ton	5.15	3.71	8.86
3800	10,000 S.F., 50.00 ton	3.27	3.42	6.69
3880	Schools and colleges, 500 S.F., 1.92 ton	5.25	1.75	7
3920	1,000 S.F., 3.83 ton	4.25	3.42	7.67
3960	3,000 S.F., 11.50 ton	4.31	3.18	7.49
4000	5,000 S.F., 19.17 ton	3.94	2.84	6.78
4040	10,000 S.F., 38.33 ton	3.44	2.84	6.28

MECHANICAL 8

Self-Contained Air Cooled System

8.4-240	Self-contained, Air Cooled Unit Systems	COST PER S.F.		
		MAT.	INST.	TOTAL
1300	Self-contained, air cooled unit			
1320	Apartment corridors, 500 S.F., .92 ton	4.19	2.48	6.67
1360	1,000 S.F., 1.83 ton	4.13	2.46	6.59
1400	3,000 S.F., 5.50 ton	3.40	2.32	5.72
1440	5,000 S.F., 9.17 ton	2.89	2.20	5.09
1480	10,000 S.F., 18.33 ton	2.41	2.03	4.44
1560	Banks or libraries, 500 S.F., 2.08 ton	8.95	3.12	12.07
1600	1,000 S.F., 4.17 ton	7.70	5.25	12.95
1640	3,000 S.F., 12.50 ton	6.60	5	11.60
1680	5,000 S.F., 20.80 ton	5.50	4.59	10.09
1720	10,000 S.F., 41.66 ton	5.05	4.50	9.55
1800	Bars and taverns, 500 S.F., 5.54 ton	16.40	6.85	23.25
1840	1,000 S.F., 11.08 ton	16.95	10.05	27
1880	3,000 S.F., 33.25 ton	13.05	8.70	21.75
1920	5,000 S.F., 55.42 ton	12.50	8.75	21.25
1960	10,000 S.F., 110.00 ton	12.65	8.70	21.35
2040	Bowling alleys, 500 S.F., 2.83 ton	12.25	4.26	16.51
2080	1,000 S.F., 5.66 ton	10.50	7.15	17.65
2120	3,000 S.F., 17.00 ton	7.45	6.25	13.70
2160	5,000 S.F., 28.33 ton	6.95	6.10	13.05
2200	10,000 S.F., 56.66 ton	6.65	6.15	12.80
2240	Department stores, 500 S.F., 1.46 ton	6.30	2.20	8.50
2280	1,000 S.F., 2.92 ton	5.40	3.68	9.08
2320	3,000 S.F., 8.75 ton	4.59	3.50	8.09
2360	5,000 S.F., 14.58 ton	4.59	3.50	8.09
2400	10,000 S.F., 29.17 ton	3.57	3.14	6.71
2480	Drug stores, 500 S.F., 3.33 ton	14.40	5	19.40
2520	1,000 S.F., 6.66 ton	12.30	8.40	20.70
2560	3,000 S.F., 20.00 ton	8.80	7.35	16.15
2600	5,000 S.F., 33.33 ton	8.15	7.20	15.35
2640	10,000 S.F., 66.66 ton	7.90	7.25	15.15
2720	Factories, 500 S.F., 1.66 ton	7.30	2.54	9.84
2760	1,000 S.F., 3.33 ton	6.20	4.22	10.42
2800	3,000 S.F., 10.00 ton	5.25	4.01	9.26
2840	5,000 S.F., 16.66 ton	4.35	3.68	8.03
2880	10,000 S.F., 33.33 ton	4.07	3.60	7.67
2960	Food supermarkets, 500 S.F., 1.42 ton	6.15	2.14	8.29
3000	1,000 S.F., 2.83 ton	6.35	3.80	10.15
3040	3,000 S.F., 8.50 ton	5.25	3.58	8.83
3080	5,000 S.F., 14.17 ton	4.47	3.40	7.87
3120	10,000 S.F., 28.33 ton	3.47	3.06	6.53
3200	Medical centers, 500 S.F., 1.17 ton	5.05	1.77	6.82
3240	1,000 S.F., 2.33 ton	5.30	3.15	8.45
3280	3,000 S.F., 7.00 ton	4.33	2.95	7.28

MECHANICAL

8

8.4-240	Self-contained, Air Cooled Unit Systems	COST PER S.F.		
		MAT.	INST.	TOTAL
3320	5,000 S.F., 16.66 ton	3.70	2.81	6.51
3360	10,000 S.F., 23.33 ton	3.08	2.58	5.66
3440	Offices, 500 S.F., 1.58 ton	6.85	2.38	9.23
3480	1,000 S.F., 3.16 ton	7.20	4.25	11.45
3520	3,000 S.F., 9.50 ton	5	3.80	8.80
3560	5,000 S.F., 15.83 ton	4.18	3.50	7.68
3600	10,000 S.F., 31.66 ton	3.88	3.41	7.29
3680	Restaurants, 500 S.F., 2.50 ton	10.75	3.75	14.50
3720	1,000 S.F., 5.00 ton	9.25	6.30	15.55
3760	3,000 S.F., 15.00 ton	7.90	6	13.90
3800	5,000 S.F., 25.00 ton	6.10	5.40	11.50
3840	10,000 S.F., 50.00 ton	6.10	5.35	11.45
3920	Schools and colleges, 500 S.F., 1.92 ton	8.25	2.88	11.13
3960	1,000 S.F., 3.83 ton	7.15	4.84	11.99
4000	3,000 S.F., 11.50 ton	6.05	4.61	10.66
4040	5,000 S.F., 19.17 ton	5.05	4.24	9.29
4080	10,000 S.F., 38.33 ton	4.64	4.14	8.78

Important: See the Reference Section for critical supporting data - Location Factors & Historical Cost Indexes

Air Cooled Condensing Unit

Refrigerant Piping

Roof

Supply Duct

Finish Ceiling

Return Grille

DX Air Handling Unit

Supply Diffuser

*Cooling requirements would lead to more than one system.

8.4-250	Split Systems With Air Cooled Condensing Units	COST PER S.F.		
		MAT.	INST.	TOTAL
1260	Split system, air cooled condensing unit			
1280	Apartment corridors, 1,000 S.F., 1.83 ton	1.62	1.56	3.18
1320	2,000 S.F., 3.66 ton	1.32	1.57	2.89
1360	5,000 S.F., 9.17 ton	1.62	1.98	3.60
1400	10,000 S.F., 18.33 ton	1.86	2.16	4.02
1440	20,000 S.F., 36.66 ton	1.68	2.19	3.87
1520	Banks and libraries, 1,000 S.F., 4.17 ton	3.02	3.58	6.60
1560	2,000 S.F., 8.33 ton	3.67	4.49	8.16
1600	5,000 S.F., 20.80 ton	4.21	4.89	9.10
1640	10,000 S.F., 41.66 ton	3.81	4.98	8.79
1680	20,000 S.F., 83.32 ton	3.71	5.15	8.86
1760	Bars and taverns, 1,000 S.F., 11.08 ton	8.95	7.05	16
1800	2,000 S.F., 22.16 ton	12.65	8.45	21.10
1840	5,000 S.F., 55.42 ton	9.10	7.90	17
1880	10,000 S.F., 110.84 ton	9.25	8.25	17.50
1920	20,000 S.F., 220 ton*			
2000	Bowling alleys, 1,000 S.F., 5.66 ton	4.22	6.70	10.92
2040	2,000 S.F., 11.33 ton	5	6.10	11.10
2080	5,000 S.F., 28.33 ton	5.75	6.65	12.40
2120	10,000 S.F., 56.66 ton	5.15	6.80	11.95
2160	20,000 S.F., 113.32 ton	5.45	7.30	12.75
2320	Department stores, 1,000 S.F., 2.92 ton	2.13	2.46	4.59
2360	2,000 S.F., 5.83 ton	2.17	3.46	5.63
2400	5,000 S.F., 14.58 ton	2.57	3.14	5.71
2440	10,000 S.F., 29.17 ton	2.95	3.43	6.38
2480	20,000 S.F., 58.33 ton	2.67	3.49	6.16
2560	Drug stores, 1,000 S.F., 6.66 ton	4.96	7.90	12.86
2600	2,000 S.F., 13.32 ton	5.85	7.20	13.05
2640	5,000 S.F., 33.33 ton	6.10	8	14.10
2680	10,000 S.F., 66.66 ton	5.85	8.30	14.15
2720	20,000 S.F., 133.32 ton*			
2800	Factories, 1,000 S.F., 3.33 ton	2.43	2.81	5.24
2840	2,000 S.F., 6.66 ton	2.47	3.95	6.42
2880	5,000 S.F., 16.66 ton	3.37	3.92	7.29
2920	10,000 S.F., 33.33 ton	3.05	3.98	7.03
2960	20,000 S.F., 66.66 ton	2.91	4.15	7.06
3040	Food supermarkets, 1,000 S.F., 2.83 ton	2.07	2.38	4.45
3080	2,000 S.F., 5.66 ton	2.10	3.35	5.45
3120	5,000 S.F., 14.66 ton	2.49	3.05	5.54
3160	10,000 S.F., 28.33 ton	2.86	3.34	6.20
3200	20,000 S.F., 56.66 ton	2.59	3.39	5.98
3280	Medical centers, 1,000 S.F., 2.33 ton	1.73	1.93	3.66
3320	2,000 S.F., 4.66 ton	1.72	2.76	4.48
3360	5,000 S.F., 11.66 ton	2.05	2.52	4.57

MECHANICAL

8

8.4-250	Split Systems With Air Cooled Condensing Units	COST PER S.F.		
		MAT.	INST.	TOTAL
3400	10,000 S.F., 23.33 ton	2.36	2.75	5.11
3440	20,000 S.F., 46.66 ton	2.14	2.79	4.93
3520	Offices, 1,000 S.F., 3.17 ton	2.31	2.67	4.98
3560	2,000 S.F., 6.33 ton	2.36	3.76	6.12
3600	5,000 S.F., 15.83 ton	2.79	3.41	6.20
3640	10,000 S.F., 31.66 ton	3.20	3.73	6.93
3680	20,000 S.F., 63.32 ton	2.77	3.96	6.73
3760	Restaurants, 1,000 S.F., 5.00 ton	3.73	5.95	9.68
3800	2,000 S.F., 10.00 ton	4.42	5.40	9.82
3840	5,000 S.F., 25.00 ton	5.05	5.90	10.95
3880	10,000 S.F., 50.00 ton	4.57	6	10.57
3920	20,000 S.F., 100.00 ton	4.82	6.50	11.32
4000	Schools and colleges, 1,000 S.F., 3.83 ton	2.77	3.28	6.05
4040	2,000 S.F., 7.66 ton	3.38	4.13	7.51
4080	5,000 S.F., 19.17 ton	3.87	4.52	8.39
4120	10,000 S.F., 38.33 ton	3.50	4.59	8.09

Important: See the Reference Section for critical supporting data - Location Factors & Historical Cost Indexes

Vitrified Clay Garage Exhaust System

Dual Exhaust System

8.5-110	Garage Exhaust Systems	COST PER BAY		
		MAT.	INST.	TOTAL
1040	Garage, single exhaust, 3" outlet, cars & light trucks, one bay	1,625	835	2,460
1060	Additional bays up to seven bays	305	122	427
1500	4" outlet, trucks, one bay	1,625	835	2,460
1520	Additional bays up to six bays	315	122	437
1600	5" outlet, diesel trucks, one bay	1,675	835	2,510
1650	Additional single bays up to six	375	142	517
1700	Two adjoining bays	1,675	835	2,510
2000	Dual exhaust, 3" outlets, pair of adjoining bays	1,900	930	2,830
2100	Additional pairs of adjoining bays	570	142	712

For information about Means Estimating Seminars, see yellow pages 11 and 12 in back of book

MECHANICAL

8

Division 9
Electrical

Electric Service

Feeder Installation

Switchgear

9.1-210	Electric Service, 3 Phase - 4 Wire	COST EACH		
		MAT.	INST.	TOTAL
0200	Service installation, includes breakers, metering, 20' conduit & wire			
0220	3 phase, 4 wire, 120/208 volts, 60 A	590	630	1,220
0240	100 A	735	760	1,495
0280	200 A	1,050	1,175	2,225
0320	400 A	2,300	2,150	4,450
0360	600 A	4,525	2,900	7,425
0400	800 A	5,900	3,500	9,400
0440	1000 A	7,525	4,025	11,550
0480	1200 A	9,075	4,100	13,175
0520	1600 A	17,300	5,925	23,225
0560	2000 A	19,300	6,725	26,025
0570	Add 25% for 277/480 volt			

9.1-310	Feeder Installation	COST PER L.F.		
		MAT.	INST.	TOTAL
0200	Feeder installation 600 V, including RGS conduit and XHHW wire, 60 A	3.37	7.60	10.97
0240	100 A	6.10	10.15	16.25
0280	200 A	12.80	15.65	28.45
0320	400 A	25.50	31.50	57
0360	600 A	53	51	104
0400	800 A	67	61	128
0440	1000 A	86	78	164
0480	1200 A	99.50	80	179.50
0520	1600 A	134	122	256
0560	2000 A	172	156	328
1200	Branch installation 600 V, including EMT conduit and THW wire, 15 A	.68	3.89	4.57
1240	20 A	.68	3.89	4.57
1280	30 A	1.05	4.79	5.84
1320	50 A	1.71	5.50	7.21
1360	65 A	2.05	5.85	7.90
1400	85 A	3.12	6.95	10.07
1440	100 A	3.90	7.35	11.25
1480	130 A	5.05	8.25	13.30
1520	150 A	6.05	9.45	15.50
1560	200 A	7.80	10.65	18.45

9.1-410	Switchgear	COST EACH		
		MAT.	INST.	TOTAL
0200	Switchgear inst., incl. swbd., panels & circ bkr, 400 A, 120/208volt	3,375	2,575	5,950
0240	600 A	8,575	3,500	12,075
0280	800 A	10,700	4,950	15,650
0320	1200 A	13,700	7,600	21,300

ELECTRICAL 9

9.1-410	Switchgear		COST EACH		
			MAT.	INST.	TOTAL
0360	1600 A		18,600	10,600	29,200
0400	2000 A		23,600	13,600	37,200
0410	Add 20% for 277/480 volt				

Fluorescent Fixture

Incandescent Fixture

9.2-213	Fluorescent Fixtures (by Wattage)	COST PER S.F.		
		MAT.	INST.	TOTAL
0190	Fluorescent fixtures recess mounted in ceiling			
0200	1 watt per S.F., 20 FC, 5 fixtures per 1000 S.F.	.56	1.20	1.76
0240	2 watts per S.F., 40 FC, 10 fixtures per 1000 S.F.	1.11	2.37	3.48
0280	3 watts per S.F., 60 FC, 15 fixtures per 1000 S.F	1.66	3.57	5.23
0320	4 watts per S.F., 80 FC, 20 fixtures per 1000 S.F.	2.21	4.72	6.93
0400	5 watts per S.F., 100 FC, 25 fixtures per 1000 S.F.	2.77	5.90	8.67

9.2-223	Incandescent Fixture (by Wattage)	COST PER S.F.		
		MAT.	INST.	TOTAL
0190	Incandescent fixture recess mounted, type A			
0200	1 watt per S.F., 8 FC, 6 fixtures per 1000 S.F.	.61	.96	1.57
0240	2 watt per S.F., 16 FC, 12 fixtures per 1000 S.F.	1.20	1.94	3.14
0280	3 watt per S.F., 24 FC, 18 fixtures, per 1000 S.F.	1.81	2.87	4.68
0320	4 watt per S.F., 32 FC, 24 fixtures per 1000 S.F.	2.40	3.82	6.22
0400	5 watt per S.F., 40 FC, 30 fixtures per 1000 S.F.	3.01	4.80	7.81

9.2-235	H.I.D. Fixture, High Bay (by Wattage)	COST PER S.F.		
		MAT.	INST.	TOTAL
0190	High intensity discharge fixture, 16' above work plane			
0200	1 watt/S.F., type D, 23 FC, 1 fixture/1000 S.F.	.69	.97	1.66
0240	Type E, 42 FC, 1 fixture/1000 S.F.	.82	1.02	1.84
0280	Type G, 52 FC, 1 fixture/1000 S.F.	.82	1.02	1.84
0320	Type C, 54 FC, 2 fixture/1000 S.F.	.98	1.13	2.11
0400	2 watt/S.F., type D, 45 FC, 2 fixture/1000 S.F.	1.40	1.94	3.34
0440	Type E, 84 FC, 2 fixture/1000 S.F.	1.66	2.06	3.72
0480	Type G, 105 FC, 2 fixture/1000 S.F.	1.66	2.06	3.72
0520	Type C, 108 FC, 4 fixture/1000 S.F.	1.94	2.26	4.20
0600	3 watt/S.F., type D, 68 FC, 3 fixture/1000 S.F.	2.07	2.87	4.94
0640	Type E, 126 FC, 3 fixture/1000 S.F.	2.47	3.08	5.55
0680	Type G, 157 FC, 3 fixture/1000 S.F.	2.47	3.08	5.55
0720	Type C, 162 FC, 6 fixture/1000 S.F.	2.92	3.39	6.31
0800	4 watt/ S.F., type D, 91 FC, 4 fixture/1000 S.F.	3.01	4.53	7.54
0840	Type E, 168 FC, 4 fixture/1000 S.F.	3.31	4.11	7.42
0880	Type G, 210 FC, 4 fixture/1000 S.F.	3.31	4.11	7.42
0920	Type C, 243 FC, 9 fixture/1000 S.F.	4.26	4.71	8.97
1000	5 watt/S.F., type D, 113 FC, 5 fixture/1000 S.F.	3.47	4.81	8.28
1040	Type E, 210 FC, 5 fixture/1000 S.F.	4.13	5.15	9.28
1080	Type G, 262 FC, 5 fixture/1000 S.F.	4.13	5.15	9.28
1120	Type C, 297 FC, 11 fixture/1000 S.F.	5.25	5.85	11.10

Important: See the Reference Section for critical supporting data - Location Factors & Historical Cost Indexes

ELECTRICAL 9

9.2-239	H.I.D. Fixture, High Bay (by Wattage)	COST PER S.F.		
		MAT.	INST.	TOTAL
0190	High intensity discharge fixture, 30' above work plane			
0200	1 watt/S.F., type D, 23 FC, 1 fixture/1000 S.F.	.78	1.25	2.03
0240	Type E, 37 FC, 1 fixture/1000 S.F.	.90	1.29	2.19
0280	Type G, 45 FC., 1 fixture/1000 S.F.	.90	1.29	2.19
0320	Type F, 50 FC, 1 fixture/1000 S.F.	.77	1.01	1.78
0400	2 watt/S.F., type D, 40 FC, 2 fixtures/1000 S.F.	1.55	2.44	3.99
0440	Type E, 74 FC, 2 fixtures/1000 S.F.	1.81	2.56	4.37
0480	Type G, 92 FC, 2 fixtures/1000 S.F.	1.81	2.56	4.37
0520	Type F, 100 FC, 2 fixtures/1000 S.F.	1.56	2.04	3.60
0600	3 watt/S.F., type D, 60 FC, 3 fixtures/1000 S.F.	2.33	3.69	6.02
0640	Type E, 110 FC, 3 fixtures/1000 S.F.	2.72	3.89	6.61
0680	Type G, 138FC, 3 fixtures/1000 S.F.	2.72	3.89	6.61
0720	Type F, 150 FC, 3 fixtures/1000 S.F.	2.33	3.05	5.38
0800	4 watt/ S.F., type D, 80 FC, 4 fixtures/1000 S.F.	3.10	4.87	7.97
0840	Type E, 148 FC, 4 fixtures/1000 S.F.	3.62	5.15	8.77
0880	Type G, 185 FC, 4 fixtures/1000 S.F.	3.62	5.15	8.77
0920	Type F, 200 FC, 4 fixtures/1000 S.F.	3.11	4.09	7.20
1000	5 watt/ S.F., type D, 100 FC 5 fixtures/1000 S.F.	3.87	6.10	9.97
1040	Type E, 185 FC, 5 fixtures/1000 S.F.	4.52	6.45	10.97
1080	Type G, 230 FC, 5 fixtures/1000 S.F.	4.52	6.45	10.97
1120	Type F, 250 FC, 5 fixtures/1000 S.F.	3.88	5.10	8.98

ELECTRICAL

9

High Bay Fixture

Low Bay Fixture

9.2-242	H.I.D. Fixture, Low Bay (by Wattage)	COST PER S.F.		
		MAT.	INST.	TOTAL
0190	High intensity discharge fixture, 8'-10' above work plane			
0200	1 watt/S.F., type H, 19 FC, 4 fixtures/1000 S.F.	1.68	2.06	3.74
0240	Type J, 30 FC, 4 fixtures/1000 S.F.	2.01	2.09	4.10
0280	Type K, 29 FC, 5 fixtures/1000 S.F.	1.93	1.88	3.81
0360	2 watt/S.F. type H, 33 FC, 7 fixtures/1000 S.F.	3.07	3.99	7.06
0400	Type J, 52 FC, 7 fixtures/1000 S.F.	3.58	3.84	7.42
0440	Type K, 63 FC, 11 fixtures/1000 S.F.	4.19	3.95	8.14
0520	3 watt/S.F., type H, 51 FC, 11 fixtures/1000 S.F.	4.75	6.10	10.85
0560	Type J, 81 FC, 11 fixtures/1000 S.F.	5.55	5.80	11.35
0600	Type K, 92 FC, 16 fixtures/1000 S.F.	6.10	5.80	11.90
0680	4 watt/S.F., type H, 65 FC, 14 fixtures/1000 S.F.	6.15	8	14.15
0720	Type J, 103 FC, 14 fixtures/1000 S.F.	7.15	7.60	14.75
0760	Type K, 127 FC, 22 fixtures/1000 S.F.	8.35	7.90	16.25
0840	5 watt/S.F., type H, 84 FC, 18 fixtures/1000 S.F.	7.80	10.05	17.85
0880	Type J, 133 FC, 18 fixtures/1000 S.F.	9.10	9.60	18.70
0920	Type K, 155 FC, 27 fixtures/1000 S.F.	10.30	9.75	20.05

Important: See the Reference Section for critical supporting data - Location Factors & Historical Cost Indexes

9.2-244	H.I.D. Fixture, Low Bay (by Wattage)	COST PER S.F.		
		MAT.	INST.	TOTAL
0190	High intensity discharge fixture, mounted 16' above work plane			
0200	1 watt/S.F., type H, 19 FC, 4 fixtures/1000 S.F.	1.77	2.35	4.12
0240	Type J, 28 FC, 4 fixt./1000 S.F.	2.09	2.36	4.45
0280	Type K, 27 FC, 5 fixt./1000 S.F.	2.17	2.66	4.83
0360	2 watts/S.F., type H, 30 FC, 7 fixt/1000 S.F.	3.24	4.56	7.80
0400	Type J, 48 FC, 7 fixt/1000 S.F.	3.82	4.59	8.41
0440	Type K, 58 FC, 11 fixt/1000 S.F.	4.66	5.45	10.11
0520	3 watts/S.F., type H, 47 FC, 11 fixt/1000 S.F.	5	6.90	11.90
0560	Type J, 75 FC, 11 fixt/1000 S.F.	5.90	6.95	12.85
0600	Type K, 85 FC, 16 fixt/1000 S.F.	6.80	8.10	14.90
0680	4 watts/S.F., type H, 60 FC, 14 fixt/1000 S.F.	6.50	9.10	15.60
0720	Type J, 95 FC, 14 fixt/1000 S.F.	7.65	9.15	16.80
0760	Type K, 117 FC, 22 fixt/1000 S.F.	9.30	10.85	20.15
0840	5 watts/S.F., type H, 77 FC, 18 fixt/1000 S.F.	8.35	11.80	20.15
0880	Type J, 122 FC, 18 fixt/1000 S.F.	9.70	11.55	21.25
0920	Type K, 143 FC, 27 fixt/1000 S.F.	11.50	13.50	25

ELECTRICAL

9

Light Pole

9.2-252	Light Pole (Installed)	COST EACH		
		MAT.	INST.	TOTAL
0200	Light pole, aluminum, 20' high, 1 arm bracket	810	740	1,550
0240	2 arm brackets	900	740	1,640
0280	3 arm brackets	990	765	1,755
0320	4 arm brackets	1,075	765	1,840
0360	30' high, 1 arm bracket	1,475	935	2,410
0400	2 arm brackets	1,575	935	2,510
0440	3 arm brackets	1,650	960	2,610
0480	4 arm brackets	1,750	960	2,710
0680	40' high, 1 arm bracket	1,775	1,225	3,000
0720	2 arm brackets	1,875	1,225	3,100
0760	3 arm brackets	1,975	1,275	3,250
0800	4 arm brackets	2,050	1,275	3,325
0840	Steel, 20' high, 1 arm bracket	1,000	785	1,785
0880	2 arm brackets	1,075	785	1,860
0920	3 arm brackets	1,100	810	1,910
0960	4 arm brackets	1,175	810	1,985
1000	30' high, 1 arm bracket	1,150	990	2,140
1040	2 arm brackets	1,225	990	2,215
1080	3 arm brackets	1,250	1,025	2,275
1120	4 arm brackets	1,350	1,025	2,375
1320	40' high, 1 arm bracket	1,500	1,350	2,850
1360	2 arm brackets	1,575	1,350	2,925
1400	3 arm brackets	1,600	1,375	2,975
1440	4 arm brackets	1,700	1,375	3,075

Important: See the Reference Section for critical supporting data - Location Factors & Historical Cost Indexes

Duplex Wall Receptacle

Undercarpet Receptacle System

9.2-522	Receptacle (by Wattage)	COST PER S.F.		
		MAT.	INST.	TOTAL
0190	Receptacles include plate, box, conduit, wire & transformer when required			
0200	2.5 per 1000 S.F., .3 watts per S.F.	.26	.92	1.18
0240	With transformer	.30	.97	1.27
0280	4 per 1000 S.F., .5 watts per S.F.	.30	1.07	1.37
0320	With transformer	.36	1.14	1.50
0360	5 per 1000 S.F., .6 watts per S.F.	.36	1.26	1.62
0400	With transformer	.44	1.35	1.79
0440	8 per 1000 S.F., .9 watts per S.F.	.37	1.38	1.75
0480	With transformer	.47	1.51	1.98
0520	10 per 1000 S.F., 1.2 watts per S.F.	.38	1.51	1.89
0560	With transformer	.55	1.72	2.27
0600	16.5 per 1000 S.F., 2.0 watts per S.F.	.46	1.90	2.36
0640	With transformer	.75	2.25	3
0680	20 per 1000 S.F.,2.4 watts per S.F.	.49	2.07	2.56
0720	With transformer	.83	2.48	3.31

9.2-524	Receptacles	COST PER S.F.		
		MAT.	INST.	TOTAL
0200	Receptacle systems, underfloor duct, 5' on center, low density	3.87	2.01	5.88
0240	High density	4.18	2.59	6.77
0280	7' on center, low density	3.05	1.72	4.77
0320	High density	3.36	2.30	5.66
0400	Poke thru fittings, low density	.87	.92	1.79
0440	High density	1.73	1.82	3.55
0520	Telepoles, using Romex, low density	.63	.60	1.23
0560	High density	1.27	1.22	2.49
0600	Using EMT, low density	.66	.80	1.46
0640	High density	1.34	1.61	2.95
0720	Conduit system with floor boxes, low density	.70	.69	1.39
0760	High density	1.41	1.39	2.80
0840	Undercarpet power system, 3 conductor with 5 conductor feeder, low density	1.26	.24	1.50
0880	High density	2.46	.50	2.96

ELECTRICAL

9

Description: Table 9.2-542 includes the cost for switch, plate, box, conduit in slab or EMT exposed and copper wire. Add 20% for exposed conduit.

No power required for switches.

Federal energy guidelines recommend the maximum lighting area controlled per switch shall not exceed 1000 S.F. and that areas over 500 S.F. shall be so controlled that total illumination can be reduced by at least 50%.

9.2-542	Wall Switch by Sq. Ft.	COST PER S.F.		
		MAT.	INST.	TOTAL
0200	Wall switches, 1.0 per 1000 S.F.	.04	.15	.19
0240	1.2 per 1000 S.F.	.04	.16	.20
0280	2.0 per 1000 S.F.	.05	.23	.28
0320	2.5 per 1000 S.F.	.08	.30	.38
0360	5.0 per 1000 S.F.	.18	.63	.81
0400	10.0 per 1000 S.F.	.35	1.28	1.63

9.2-582	Miscellaneous Power	COST PER S.F.		
		MAT.	INST.	TOTAL
0200	Miscellaneous power, to .5 watts	.02	.07	.09
0240	.8 watts	.03	.11	.14
0280	1 watt	.04	.13	.17
0320	1.2 watts	.05	.17	.22
0360	1.5 watts	.06	.19	.25
0400	1.8 watts	.07	.22	.29
0440	2 watts	.09	.27	.36
0480	2.5 watts	.10	.32	.42
0520	3 watts	.12	.38	.50

9.2-610	Central A. C. Power (by Wattage)	COST PER S.F.		
		MAT.	INST.	TOTAL
0200	Central air conditioning power, 1 watt	.05	.16	.21
0220	2 watts	.06	.19	.25
0240	3 watts	.07	.21	.28
0280	4 watts	.11	.27	.38
0320	6 watts	.18	.38	.56
0360	8 watts	.23	.40	.63
0400	10 watts	.30	.46	.76

Motor Installation

9.2-710	Motor Installation	COST EACH		
		MAT.	INST.	TOTAL
0200	Motor installation, single phase, 115V, to and including 1/3 HP motor size	445	625	1,070
0240	To and incl. 1 HP motor size	465	625	1,090
0280	To and incl. 2 HP motor size	500	665	1,165
0320	To and incl. 3 HP motor size	560	675	1,235
0360	230V, to and including 1 HP motor size	445	630	1,075
0400	To and incl. 2 HP motor size	470	630	1,100
0440	To and incl. 3 HP motor size	525	680	1,205
0520	Three phase, 200V, to and including 1-1/2 HP motor size	520	695	1,215
0560	To and incl. 3 HP motor size	555	755	1,310
0600	To and incl. 5 HP motor size	600	840	1,440
0640	To and incl. 7-1/2 HP motor size	615	860	1,475
0680	To and incl. 10 HP motor size	1,000	1,075	2,075
0720	To and incl. 15 HP motor size	1,325	1,200	2,525
0760	To and incl. 20 HP motor size	1,625	1,375	3,000
0800	To and incl. 25 HP motor size	1,650	1,375	3,025
0840	To and incl. 30 HP motor size	2,625	1,625	4,250
0880	To and incl. 40 HP motor size	3,175	1,925	5,100
0920	To and incl. 50 HP motor size	5,575	2,250	7,825
0960	To and incl. 60 HP motor size	5,725	2,375	8,100
1000	To and incl. 75 HP motor size	7,250	2,725	9,975
1040	To and incl. 100 HP motor size	15,000	3,200	18,200
1080	To and incl. 125 HP motor size	15,200	3,500	18,700
1120	To and incl. 150 HP motor size	18,400	4,125	22,525
1160	To and incl. 200 HP motor size	22,300	5,025	27,325
1240	230V, to and including 1-1/2 HP motor size	495	685	1,180
1280	To and incl. 3 HP motor size	535	745	1,280
1320	To and incl. 5 HP motor size	575	830	1,405
1360	To and incl. 7-1/2 HP motor size	575	830	1,405
1400	To and incl. 10 HP motor size	905	1,025	1,930
1440	To and incl. 15 HP motor size	1,025	1,100	2,125
1480	To and incl. 20 HP motor size	1,525	1,350	2,875
1520	To and incl. 25 HP motor size	1,625	1,375	3,000
1560	To and incl. 30 HP motor size	1,675	1,375	3,050
1600	To and incl. 40 HP motor size	3,125	1,875	5,000
1640	To and incl. 50 HP motor size	3,225	2,000	5,225
1680	To and incl. 60 HP motor size	5,575	2,250	7,825
1720	To and incl. 75 HP motor size	6,600	2,550	9,150
1760	To and incl. 100 HP motor size	7,550	2,850	10,400
1800	To and incl. 125 HP motor size	15,200	3,300	18,500
1840	To and incl. 150 HP motor size	16,300	3,750	20,050
1880	To and incl. 200 HP motor size	17,700	4,175	21,875
1960	460V, to and including 2 HP motor size	600	690	1,290
2000	To and incl. 5 HP motor size	635	755	1,390
2040	To and incl. 10 HP motor size	665	830	1,495
2080	To and incl. 15 HP motor size	890	950	1,840
2120	To and incl. 20 HP motor size	925	1,025	1,950
2160	To and incl. 25 HP motor size	1,000	1,075	2,075
2200	To and incl. 30 HP motor size	1,300	1,150	2,450

9.2-710	Motor Installation	COST EACH		
		MAT.	INST.	TOTAL
2240	To and incl. 40 HP motor size	1,625	1,250	2,875
2280	To and incl. 50 HP motor size	1,800	1,375	3,175
2320	To and incl. 60 HP motor size	2,775	1,625	4,400
2360	To and incl. 75 HP motor size	3,125	1,800	4,925
2400	To and incl. 100 HP motor size	3,400	2,000	5,400
2440	To and incl. 125 HP motor size	5,750	2,250	8,000
2480	To and incl. 150 HP motor size	7,075	2,525	9,600
2520	To and incl. 200 HP motor size	8,125	2,850	10,975
2600	575V, to and including 2 HP motor size	600	690	1,290
2640	To and incl. 5 HP motor size	635	755	1,390
2680	To and incl. 10 HP motor size	665	830	1,495
2720	To and incl. 20 HP motor size	890	950	1,840
2760	To and incl. 25 HP motor size	925	1,025	1,950
2800	To and incl. 30 HP motor size	1,300	1,150	2,450
2840	To and incl. 50 HP motor size	1,375	1,200	2,575
2880	To and incl. 60 HP motor size	2,725	1,600	4,325
2920	To and incl. 75 HP motor size	2,775	1,625	4,400
2960	To and incl. 100 HP motor size	3,125	1,800	4,925
3000	To and incl. 125 HP motor size	5,675	2,225	7,900
3040	To and incl. 150 HP motor size	5,750	2,250	8,000
3080	To and incl. 200 HP motor size	7,175	2,575	9,750

9.2-720	Motor Feeder	COST PER L.F.		
		MAT.	INST.	TOTAL
0200	Motor feeder systems, single phase, feed up to 115V 1HP or 230V 2 HP	1.51	4.84	6.35
0240	115V 2HP, 230V 3HP	1.59	4.92	6.51
0280	115V 3HP	1.76	5.10	6.86
0360	Three phase, feed to 200V 3HP, 230V 5HP, 460V 10HP, 575V 10HP	1.57	5.20	6.77
0440	200V 5HP, 230V 7.5HP, 460V 15HP, 575V 20HP	1.69	5.35	7.04
0520	200V 10HP, 230V 10HP, 460V 30HP, 575V 30HP	1.94	5.65	7.59
0600	200V 15HP, 230V 15HP, 460V 40HP, 575V 50HP	2.54	6.45	8.99
0680	200V 20HP, 230V 25HP, 460V 50HP, 575V 60HP	3.65	8.20	11.85
0760	200V 25HP, 230V 30HP, 460V 60HP, 575V 75HP	4.43	8.30	12.73
0840	200V 30HP	4.49	8.60	13.09
0920	230V 40HP, 460V 75HP, 575V 100HP	5.70	9.35	15.05
1000	200V 40HP	6.30	10	16.30
1080	230V 50HP, 460V 100HP, 575V 125HP	7.45	11.10	18.55
1160	200V 50HP, 230V 60HP, 460V 125HP, 575V 150HP	8.60	11.75	20.35
1240	200V 60HP, 460V 150HP	10.65	13.80	24.45
1320	230V 75HP, 575V 200HP	12.30	14.35	26.65
1400	200V 75HP	13.55	14.70	28.25
1480	230V 100HP, 460V 200HP	19.05	17.10	36.15
1560	200V 100HP	26	21.50	47.50
1640	230V 125HP	29.50	23	52.50
1720	200V 125HP, 230V 150HP	29.50	26.50	56
1800	200V 150HP	34.50	29	63.50
1880	200V 200HP	51.50	42.50	94
1960	230V 200HP	45	32	77

Important: See the Reference Section for critical supporting data - Location Factors & Historical Cost Indexes

9.4-100	Communication & Alarm Systems	COST EACH		
		MAT.	INST.	TOTAL
0200	Communication & alarm systems, includes outlets, boxes, conduit & wire			
0210	Sound system, 6 outlets	4,375	5,175	9,550
0220	12 outlets	6,175	8,275	14,450
0240	30 outlets	10,800	15,600	26,400
0280	100 outlets	32,300	52,500	84,800
0320	Fire detection systems, 12 detectors	2,250	4,300	6,550
0360	25 detectors	3,950	7,275	11,225
0400	50 detectors	7,575	14,300	21,875
0440	100 detectors	13,800	25,700	39,500
0480	Intercom systems, 6 stations	2,475	3,550	6,025
0560	25 stations	8,550	13,600	22,150
0640	100 stations	32,700	49,800	82,500
0680	Master clock systems, 6 rooms	3,800	5,800	9,600
0720	12 rooms	5,675	9,850	15,525
0760	20 rooms	7,600	13,900	21,500
0800	30 rooms	12,200	25,700	37,900
0840	50 rooms	19,500	43,400	62,900
0920	Master TV antenna systems, 6 outlets	2,150	3,650	5,800
0960	12 outlets	4,025	6,825	10,850
1000	30 outlets	8,025	15,800	23,825
1040	100 outlets	26,600	51,500	78,100

ELECTRICAL

9

Generator System

A: Engine
B: Battery
C: Charger
D: Transfer Switch
E: Muffler

9.4-310	Generators (by kW)	COST PER KW		
		MAT.	INST.	TOTAL
0190	Generator sets, include battery, charger, muffler & transfer switch			
0200	Gas/gasoline operated, 3 phase, 4 wire, 277/480 volt, 7.5 kW	880	188	1,068
0240	11.5 kW	815	143	958
0280	20 kW	550	92.50	642.50
0320	35 kW	375	61	436
0360	80 kW	283	36.50	319.50
0400	100 kW	248	36	284
0440	125 kW	405	33.50	438.50
0480	185 kW	360	25.50	385.50
0560	Diesel engine with fuel tank, 30 kW	585	71	656
0600	50 kW	435	56	491
0640	75 kW	375	44.50	419.50
0680	100 kW	315	38	353
0760	150 kW	252	30	282
0840	200 kW	213	24.50	237.50
0880	250 kW	200	20.50	220.50
0960	350 kW	176	16.75	192.75
1040	500 kW	190	13	203

For information about Means Estimating Seminars, see yellow pages 11 and 12 in back of book

ELECTRICAL 9

Important: See the Reference Section for critical supporting data - Location Factors & Historical Cost Indexes

Division 11
Special Construction

11.1-100	Architectural Specialties/Each	COST EACH		
		MAT.	INST.	TOTAL
1000	Specialties, bathroom accessories, st. steel, curtain rod, 5' long, 1" diam	26.50	28	54.50
1100	Dispenser, towel, surface mounted	40	23	63
1200	Grab bar, 1-1/4" diam., 12" long	22	15.20	37.20
1300	Mirror, framed with shelf, 18" x 24"	104	18.25	122.25
1340	72" x 24"	277	61	338
1400	Toilet tissue dispenser, surface mounted, single roll	12.45	12.15	24.60
1500	Towel bar, 18" long	33.50	15.85	49.35
1600	Canopies, wall hung, prefinished aluminum, 8' x 10'	1,525	1,125	2,650
1700	Chutes, linen or refuse incl. sprinklers, galv. steel, 18" diam., per floor	780	237	1,017
1740	Aluminized steel, 36" diam., per floor	1,100	296	1,396
1800	Mail, 8-3/4" x 3-1/2", aluminum & glass, per floor	605	166	771
1840	Bronze or stainless, per floor	940	184	1,124
1900	Control boards, magnetic, porcelain finish, framed, 24" x 18"	160	91	251
1940	96" x 48"	865	146	1,011
2000	Directory boards, outdoor, black plastic, 36" x 24"	345	365	710
2040	36" x 36"	725	485	1,210
2100	Indoor, economy, open faced, 18" x 24"	135	104	239
2300	Disappearing stairways, folding, pine, 8'-6" ceiling	97	91	188
2400	Fire escape, galvanized steel, 8'-0" to 10'-6" ceiling	1,225	730	1,955
2500	Automatic electric, wood, 8' to 9' ceiling	6,075	730	6,805
2600	Display cases, freestanding, glass and aluminum, 3'-6" x 3' x 1'-0" deep	455	91	546
2700	Wall mounted, glass and aluminum, 3' x 4' x 1'-4" deep	1,100	146	1,246
2900	Fireplace prefabricated, freestanding or wall hung, economy	1,050	281	1,331
2940	Deluxe	3,050	405	3,455
3000	Woodburning stoves, cast iron, economy	800	560	1,360
3040	Deluxe	2,400	910	3,310
3100	Flagpoles, on grade, aluminum, tapered, 20' high	655	425	1,080
3140	70' high	7,175	1,075	8,250
3240	59' high	6,350	950	7,300
3300	Concrete, internal halyard, 20' high	1,275	340	1,615
3340	100' high	12,800	855	13,655
3400	Lockers, steel, single tier, 5' to 6' high, per opening, min.	95.50	29.50	125
3440	Maximum	185	34.50	219.50
3700	Mail boxes, horizontal, rear loaded, aluminum, 5" x 6" x 15" deep	33.50	10.75	44.25
3740	Front loaded, aluminum, 10" x 12" x 15" deep	116	18.25	134.25
3800	Vertical, front loaded, aluminum, 15" x 5" x 6" deep	25.50	10.75	36.25
3840	Bronze, duranodic finish	47.50	10.75	58.25
3900	Letter slot, post office	210	45.50	255.50
4000	Mail counter, window, post office, with grille	565	182	747
4100	Medicine cabinets, sliding mirror doors, 20" x 16" x 4-3/4", unlighted	93.50	52	145.50
4140	24" x 19" x 8-1/2", lighted	147	73	220
4400	Partitions, shower stall, single wall, painted steel, 2'-8" x 2'-8"	685	166	851
4440	Fiberglass, 2'-8" x 2'-8"	560	184	744
4500	Double wall, enameled steel, 2'-8" x 2'-8"	700	166	866
4540	Stainless steel, 2'-8" x 2'-8"	1,225	166	1,391
4700	Tub enclosure, sliding panels, tempered glass, aluminum frame	300	207	507
4740	Chrome/brass frame-deluxe	865	276	1,141
5400	Projection screens, wall hung, manual operation, 50 S.F., economy	243	73	316
5440	Electric operation, 100 S.F., deluxe	1,650	365	2,015
5500	Scales, dial type, built in floor, 5 ton capacity, 8' x 6' platform	6,025	2,200	8,225
5540	10 ton capacity, 9' x 7' platform	9,625	3,125	12,750
5600	Truck (including weigh bridge), 20 ton capacity, 24' x 10'	9,225	3,650	12,875
5900	Security gates-scissors type, painted steel, single, 6' high, 5-1/2' wide	125	238	363
5940	Double gate, 7-1/2' high, 14' wide	445	475	920
6000	Shelving, metal industrial, braced, 3' wide, 1' deep	30.50	8.15	38.65
6040	2' deep	47.50	8.65	56.15
6200	Signs, interior electric exit sign, wall mounted, 6"	59	51	110
6240	Street, reflective alum., dbl. face, 4 way, w/bracket	116	24.50	140.50

Important: See the Reference Section for critical supporting data - Location Factors & Historical Cost Indexes

11.1-100	Architectural Specialties/Each	COST EACH		
		MAT.	INST.	TOTAL
6300	Letters, cast aluminum, 1/2" deep, 4" high	15.45	20.50	35.95
6340	1" deep, 10" high	32.50	20.50	53
6400	Plaques, cast aluminum, 20" x 30"	855	182	1,037
6440	Cast bronze, 36" x 48"	3,350	365	3,715
6700	Turnstiles, one way, 4' arm, 46" diam., manual	280	146	426
6740	Electric	935	610	1,545
6800	3 arm, 5'-5' diam. & 7' high, manual	2,425	730	3,155
6840	Electric	3,150	1,225	4,375

11.1-100	Architectural Specialties/S.F.	COST PER S.F.		
		MAT.	INST.	TOTAL
7100	Bulletin board, cork sheets, no frame, 1/4" thick	6.40	2.52	8.92
7200	Aluminum frame, 1/4" thick, 3' x 5'	7.75	3.05	10.80
7500	Chalkboards, wall hung, alum, frame & chalktrough	8.75	1.61	10.36
7540	Wood frame & chalktrough	7.95	1.74	9.69
7600	Sliding board, one board with back panel	31	1.56	32.56
7640	Two boards with back panel	48	1.56	49.56
7700	Liquid chalk type, alum. frame & chalktrough	10.55	1.61	12.16
7740	Wood frame & chalktrough	18.15	1.61	19.76

11.1-100	Architectural Specialties/L.F.	COST PER L.F.		
		MAT.	INST.	TOTAL
8600	Partitions, hospital curtain, ceiling hung, polyester oxford cloth	14.60	3.56	18.16
8640	Designer oxford cloth	27.50	4.51	32.01

11.1-200	Architectural Equipment/Each	COST EACH		
		MAT.	INST.	TOTAL
0200	Arch. equip., appliances, range, cook top, 4 burner, economy	208	68.50	276.50
0240	Built in, single oven 30" wide, economy	345	68.50	413.50
0300	Standing, single oven-21" wide, economy	310	57	367
0340	Double oven-30" wide, deluxe	1,550	57	1,607
0400	Compactor, residential, economy	385	73	458
0440	Deluxe	420	122	542
0500	Dish washer, built-in, 2 cycles, economy	271	206	477
0540	4 or more cycles, deluxe	560	415	975
0600	Garbage disposer, sink type, economy	41.50	82.50	124
0640	Deluxe	196	82.50	278.50
0700	Refrigerator, no frost, 10 to 12 C.F., economy	465	57	522
0740	21 to 29 C.F., deluxe	2,950	191	3,141
0800	Automotive equipment, compressors, electric, 1-1/2 H.P., std. controls	345	685	1,030
0840	5 H.P., dual controls	1,800	1,025	2,825
0900	Hoists, single post, 4 ton capacity, swivel arms	3,850	2,575	6,425
0940	Dual post, 12 ton capacity, adjustable frame	6,600	6,850	13,450
1000	Lube equipment, 3 reel type, with pumps	6,600	2,050	8,650
1040	Product dispenser, 6 nozzles, w/vapor recovery, not incl. piping, installed	16,500		16,500
1100	Bank equipment, drive up window, drawer & mike, no glazing, economy	4,025	955	4,980
1140	Deluxe	7,625	1,900	9,525
1200	Night depository, economy	6,800	955	7,755
1240	Deluxe	10,800	1,900	12,700
1300	Pneumatic tube systems, 2 station, standard	20,800	3,100	23,900
1340	Teller, automated, 24 hour, single unit	39,200	3,100	42,300
1400	Teller window, bullet proof glazing, 44" x 60"	2,600	575	3,175
1440	Pass through, painted steel, 72" x 40"	2,775	1,200	3,975
1500	Barber equipment, chair, hydraulic, economy	450	15.20	465.20
1540	Deluxe	2,975	23	2,998
1700	Church equipment, altar, wood, custom, plain	1,825	261	2,086
1740	Granite, custom, deluxe	23,300	3,600	26,900
1800	Baptistry, fiberglass, economy	2,675	940	3,615
1840	Bells & carillons, keyboard operation	10,800	6,025	16,825

SPECIAL CONSTRUCTION

11

11.1-200	Architectural Equipment/Each	COST EACH		
		MAT.	INST.	TOTAL
1900	Confessional, wood, single, economy	2,325	610	2,935
1940	Double, deluxe	14,600	1,825	16,425
2000	Steeples, translucent fiberglas, 30" square, 15' high	3,500	1,200	4,700
2100	Checkout counter, single belt	2,175	57	2,232
2140	Double belt, power take-away	3,750	63.50	3,813.50
2600	Dental equipment, central suction system, economy	2,975	345	3,320
2640	Compressor-air, deluxe	22,700	750	23,450
2700	Chair, hydraulic, economy	3,750	750	4,500
2740	Deluxe	7,925	1,500	9,425
2800	Drill console with accessories, economy	3,375	234	3,609
2840	Deluxe	9,625	234	9,859
2900	X-ray unit, portable	4,500	93.50	4,593.50
2940	Panoramic unit	20,400	625	21,025
3000	Detention equipment, cell front rolling door, 7/8" bars, 5' x 7' high	4,600	1,025	5,625
3040	Cells, prefab., including front, 5' x 7' x 7' deep	8,150	1,350	9,500
3100	Doors and frames, 3' x 7', single plate	3,425	510	3,935
3140	Double plate	4,225	510	4,735
3200	Toilet apparatus, incl wash basin	2,275	625	2,900
3240	Visitor cubicle, vision panel, no intercom	2,600	1,025	3,625
3300	Dock bumpers, rubber blocks, 4-1/2" thick, 10" high, 14" long	41.50	14.05	55.55
3340	6" thick, 20" high, 11" long	115	28	143
3400	Dock boards, H.D., 5' x 5', aluminum, 5000 lb. capacity	1,150		1,150
3440	16,000 lb. capacity	1,325		1,325
3500	Dock levelers, hydraulic, 7' x 8', 10 ton capacity	7,275	995	8,270
3540	Dock lifters, platform, 6' x 6', portable, 3000 lb. capacity	7,150		7,150
3600	Dock shelters, truck, scissor arms, economy	1,150	365	1,515
3640	Deluxe	1,700	730	2,430
3700	Kitchen equipment, bake oven, single deck	4,125	93.50	4,218.50
3740	Broiler, without oven	3,950	93.50	4,043.50
3800	Commercial dish washer, semiautomatic, 50 racks/hr.	5,900	575	6,475
3840	Automatic, 275 racks/hr.	24,400	2,325	26,725
3900	Cooler, beverage, reach-in, 6 ft. long	3,075	125	3,200
3940	Food warmer, counter, 1.65 kw	715		715
4000	Fryers, with submerger, single	3,200	107	3,307
4040	Double	4,325	150	4,475
4100	Kettles, steam jacketed, 20 gallons	6,225	174	6,399
4140	Range, restaurant type, burners, 2 ovens and 24" griddle	4,900	125	5,025
4200	Range hood, incl. carbon dioxide system, economy	3,175	250	3,425
4240	Deluxe	23,200	750	23,950
4300	Laboratory equipment, glassware washer, distilled water, economy	6,825	460	7,285
4340	Deluxe	8,275	825	9,100
4440	Radio isotope	12,100		12,100
4600	Laundry equipment, dryers, gas fired, residential, 16 lb. capacity	570	139	709
4640	Commercial, 30 lb. capacity, single	2,625	139	2,764
4700	Dry cleaners, electric, 20 lb. capacity	30,700	4,125	34,825
4740	30 lb. capacity	42,100	5,500	47,600
4800	Ironers, commercial, 120" with canopy, 8 roll	150,000	11,800	161,800
4840	Institutional, 110", single roll	26,600	2,050	28,650
4900	Washers, residential, 4 cycle	655	139	794
4940	Commercial, coin operated, deluxe	2,750	139	2,889
5000	Library equipment, carrels, metal, economy	215	73	288
5040	Hardwood, deluxe	850	91	941
5100	Medical equipment, autopsy table, standard	7,150	415	7,565
5140	Deluxe	14,400	695	15,095
5200	Incubators, economy	2,925		2,925
5240	Deluxe	16,200		16,200
5300	Station, scrub-surgical, single, economy	1,075	139	1,214
5340	Dietary, medium, with ice	13,100		13,100
5400	Sterilizers, general purpose, single door, 20" x 20" x 28"	12,500		12,500
5440	Floor loading, double door, 28" x 67" x 52"	166,500		166,500

Important: See the Reference Section for critical supporting data - Location Factors & Historical Cost Indexes

11.1-200	Architectural Equipment/Each	COST EACH		
		MAT.	INST.	TOTAL
5500	Surgery tables, standard	11,300	680	11,980
5540	Deluxe	25,700	955	26,655
5600	Tables, standard, with base cabinets, economy	1,075	243	1,318
5640	Deluxe	3,150	365	3,515
5700	X-ray, mobile, economy	10,900		10,900
5740	Stationary, deluxe	178,000		178,000
5800	Movie equipment, changeover, economy	385		385
5840	Film transport, incl. platters and autowind, economy	4,175		4,175
5900	Lamphouses, incl. rectifiers, xenon, 1000W	5,275	205	5,480
5940	4000W	7,475	273	7,748
6000	Projector mechanisms, 35 mm, economy	9,250		9,250
6040	Deluxe	12,700		12,700
6100	Sound systems, incl. amplifier, single, economy	2,750	455	3,205
6140	Dual, Dolby/super sound	13,800	1,025	14,825
6200	Seating, painted steel, upholstered, economy	110	21	131
6240	Deluxe	350	26	376
6300	Parking equipment, automatic gates, 8 ft. arm, one way	2,975	745	3,720
6340	Traffic detectors, single treadle	2,225	340	2,565
6400	Booth for attendant, economy	4,675		4,675
6440	Deluxe	23,200		23,200
6500	Ticket printer/dispenser, rate computing	7,425	585	8,010
6540	Key station on pedestal	825	200	1,025
6700	Frozen food, chest type, 12 ft. long	5,250	230	5,480
7000	Safe, office type, 1 hr. rating, 34" x 20" x 20"	1,575		1,575
7040	4 hr. rating, 62" x 33" x 20"	6,775		6,775
7100	Data storage, 4 hr. rating, 63" x 44" x 16"	9,375		9,375
7140	Jewelers, 63" x 44" x 16"	16,000		16,000
7200	Money, "B" label, 9" x 14" x 14"	490		490
7240	Tool and torch resistive, 24" x 24" x 20"	7,000	143	7,143
7300	Sauna, prefabricated, incl. heater and controls, 7' high, 6' x 4'	3,525	555	4,080
7340	10' x 12'	7,900	1,225	9,125
7400	Heaters, wall mounted, to 200 C.F.	555		555
7440	Floor standing, to 1000 C.F., 12500 W	1,725	137	1,862
7500	School equipment, basketball backstops, wall mounted, wood, fixed	990	640	1,630
7540	Suspended type, electrically operated	3,500	1,225	4,725
7600	Bleachers-telescoping, manual operation, 15 tier, economy (per seat)	56	23	79
7640	Power operation, 30 tier, deluxe (per seat)	213	40.50	253.50
7700	Weight lifting gym, universal, economy	2,500	570	3,070
7740	Deluxe	13,900	1,150	15,050
7800	Scoreboards, basketball, 1 side, economy	2,175	565	2,740
7840	4 sides, deluxe	24,000	7,800	31,800
8300	Vocational shop equipment, benches, metal	248	146	394
8340	Wood	440	146	586
8400	Dust collector, not incl. ductwork, 6' diam.	2,725	375	3,100
8440	Planer, 13" x 6"	1,300	182	1,482
8500	Waste handling, compactors, single bag, 250 lbs./hr., hand fed	6,250	430	6,680
8540	Heavy duty industrial, 5 C.Y. capacity	15,400	2,050	17,450
8600	Incinerator, electric, 100 lbs./hr., economy	10,000	2,050	12,050
8640	Gas, 2000 lbs./hr., deluxe	171,000	15,900	186,900
8700	Shredder, no baling, 35 tons/hr.	211,000		211,000
8740	Incl. baling, 50 tons/day	422,000		422,000

SPECIAL CONSTRUCTION

11

11.1-200	Architectural Equipment/S.F.	COST PER S.F.		
		MAT.	INST.	TOTAL
8910	Arch. equip., lab equip., counter tops, acid proof, economy	22.50	8.90	31.40
8940	Stainless steel	72.50	8.90	81.40
9000	Movie equipment, projection screens, rigid in wall, acrylic, 1/4" thick	35	3.55	38.55
9040	1/2" thick	40.50	5.35	45.85
9100	School equipment, gym mats, naugahyde cover, 2" thick	3.45		3.45
9140	Wrestling, 1" thick, heavy duty	4.62		4.62
9200	Stage equipment, curtains, velour, medium weight	6.60	1.22	7.82
9240	Silica based yarn, fireproof	13.20	14.60	27.80
9300	Stages, portable with steps, folding legs, 8" high	16.70		16.70
9340	Telescoping platforms, aluminum, deluxe	30	18.95	48.95

11.1-200	Architectural Equipment/L.F.	COST PER L.F.		
		MAT.	INST.	TOTAL
9410	Arch. equip., church equip. pews, bench type, hardwood, economy	64	18.25	82.25
9440	Deluxe	128	24.50	152.50
9500	Laboratory equipment, cabinets, wall, open	97	36.50	133.50
9540	Base, drawer units	305	40.50	345.50
9600	Fume hoods, not incl. HVAC, economy	555	135	690
9640	Deluxe incl. fixtures	1,300	305	1,605
9700	Library equipment, book shelf, metal, single face, 90" high x 10" shelf	165	30.50	195.50
9740	Double face, 90" high x 10" shelf	214	65.50	279.50
9800	Charging desk, built-in, with counter, plastic laminate	455	52	507
9900	Stage equipment, curtain track, heavy duty	41.50	40.50	82
9940	Lights, border, quartz, colored	152	20.50	172.50

11.1-500	Furnishings/Each	COST EACH		
		MAT.	INST.	TOTAL
1000	Furnishings, blinds, exterior, aluminum, louvered, 1'-4" wide x 3'-0" long	43.50	36.50	80
1040	1'-4" wide x 6'-8" long	87	40.50	127.50
1100	Hemlock, solid raised, 1'-4" wide x 3'-0" long	57	36.50	93.50
1140	1'-4" wide x 6'-9" long	107	40.50	147.50
1200	Polystyrene, louvered, 1'-3" wide x 3'-3" long	44	36.50	80.50
1240	1'-3" wide x 6'-8" long	95.50	40.50	136
1300	Interior, wood folding panels, louvered, 7" x 20" (per pair)	41.50	21.50	63
1340	18" x 40" (per pair)	129	21.50	150.50
1800	Hospital furniture, beds, manual, economy	910		910
1840	Deluxe	1,575		1,575
1900	All electric, economy	1,525		1,525
1940	Deluxe	3,775		3,775
2000	Patient wall systems, no utilities, economy, per room	910		910
2040	Deluxe, per room	1,675		1,675
2200	Hotel furnishings, standard room set, economy, per room	1,625		1,625
2240	Deluxe, per room	8,025		8,025
2400	Office furniture, standard employee set, economy, per person	375		375
2440	Deluxe, per person	2,225		2,225
2800	Posts, portable, pedestrian traffic control, economy	98.50		98.50
2840	Deluxe	315		315
3000	Restaurant furniture, booth, molded plastic, stub wall and 2 seats, economy	345	182	527
3040	Deluxe	1,525	243	1,768
3100	Upholstered seats, foursome, single-economy	1,175	73	1,248
3140	Foursome, double-deluxe	2,425	122	2,547
3300	Seating, lecture hall, pedestal type, economy	119	33	152
3340	Deluxe	420	50.50	470.50
3400	Auditorium chair, veneer construction	133	33	166
3440	Fully upholstered, spring seat	170	33	203

Important: See the Reference Section for critical supporting data - Location Factors & Historical Cost Indexes

SPECIAL CONSTRUCTION 11

11.1-500	Furnishings/S.F.	COST PER S.F.		
		MAT.	INST.	TOTAL
4010	Furnishings, blinds-interior, venetian-aluminum, stock, 2″ slats, economy	1.67	.62	2.29
4040	Custom, 1″ slats, deluxe	7.25	.83	8.08
4100	Vertical, PVC or cloth, T&B track, economy	7.30	.79	8.09
4140	Deluxe	9.75	.91	10.66
4300	Draperies, unlined, economy	2.22		2.22
4440	Lightproof, deluxe	6.65		6.65
4700	Floor mats, recessed, inlaid black rubber, 3/8″ thick, solid	21.50	1.85	23.35
4740	Colors, 1/2″ thick, perforated	35	1.85	36.85
4800	Link-including nosings, steel-galvanized, 3/8″ thick	7.05	1.85	8.90
4840	Vinyl, in colors	18.90	1.85	20.75
5000	Shades, mylar, wood roller, single layer, non-reflective	5.60	.53	6.13
5040	Metal roller, triple layer, heat reflective	7.80	.53	8.33
5100	Vinyl, light weight, 4 ga.	.42	.53	.95
5140	Heavyweight, 6 ga.	1.32	.53	1.85
5200	Vinyl coated cotton, lightproof decorator shades	1.53	.53	2.06
5300	Woven aluminum, 3/8″ thick, light and fireproof	4.33	1.04	5.37

11.1-500	Furnishings/L.F.	COST PER L.F.		
		MAT.	INST.	TOTAL
5510	Furnishings, cabinets, hospital, base, laminated plastic	208	73	281
5540	Stainless steel	260	73	333
5600	Counter top, laminated plastic, no backsplash	36	18.25	54.25
5640	Stainless steel	99.50	18.25	117.75
5700	Nurses station, door type, laminated plastic	241	73	314
5740	Stainless steel	278	73	351
5900	Household, base, hardwood, one top drawer & one door below x 12″ wide	138	29.50	167.50
5940	Four drawer x 24″ wide	385	32.50	417.50
6000	Wall, hardwood, 30″ high with one door x 12″ wide	116	33	149
6040	Two doors x 48″ wide	282	39.50	321.50
6100	Counter top-laminated plastic, stock, economy	5.40	12.15	17.55
6140	Custom-square edge, 7/8″ thick	11.55	27.50	39.05
6300	School, counter, wood, 32″ high	165	36.50	201.50
6340	Metal, 84″ high	255	48.50	303.50
6500	Dormitory furniture, desk top (built-in),laminated plastc, 24″deep, economy	26	14.60	40.60
6540	30″ deep, deluxe	144	18.25	162.25
6600	Dressing unit, built-in, economy	193	61	254
6640	Deluxe	575	91	666
7000	Restaurant furniture, bars, built-in, back bar	154	73	227
7040	Front bar	212	73	285
7200	Wardrobes & coatracks, standing, steel, single pedestal, 30″ x 18″ x 63″	61		61
7300	Double face rack, 39″ x 26″ x 70″	63		63
7340	Wall mounted rack, steel frame & shelves, 12″ x 15″ x 26″	56.50	5.20	61.70
7400	12″ x 15″ x 50″	44.50	2.71	47.21

SPECIAL CONSTRUCTION

11.1-700	Special Construction/Each	COST EACH		
		MAT.	INST.	TOTAL
1000	Special construction, bowling alley incl. pinsetter, scorer etc., economy	35,500	7,300	42,800
1040	Deluxe	40,400	8,100	48,500
1100	For automatic scorer, economy, add	6,600		6,600
1140	Deluxe, add	7,475		7,475
1200	Chimney, metal, high temp. steel jacket, factory lining, 24" diameter	9,550	3,475	13,025
1240	60" diameter	69,500	15,100	84,600
1300	Poured concrete, brick lining, 10' diam., 200' high			1,200,000
1340	20' diam., 500' high			5,350,000
1400	Radial brick, 3'-6" I.D., 75' high			197,000
1440	7' I.D., 175' high			590,500
1500	Control tower, modular, 12' x 10', incl. instrumentation, economy			450,000
1540	Deluxe			600,000
1600	Garage costs, residential, prefab, wood, single car economy	2,800	730	3,530
1640	Two car deluxe	8,400	1,450	9,850
1700	Grandstands, permanent, closed deck, steel, economy (per seat)			33
1740	Deluxe (per seat)			88
1800	Composite design, economy (per seat)			82.50
1840	Deluxe (per seat)			154
1900	Hangars, prefab, galv. steel, bottom rolling doors, economy (per plane)	9,250	3,600	12,850
1940	Electrical bi-folding doors, deluxe (per plane)	12,900	4,950	17,850
2000	Ice skating rink, 85' x 200', 55° system, 5 mos., 100 ton			451,000
2040	90° system, 12 mos., 135 ton			500,500
2100	Dash boards, acrylic screens, polyethylene coated plywood	126,500	24,700	151,200
2140	Fiberglass and aluminum construction	176,000	24,700	200,700
2200	Integrated ceilings, radiant electric, 2' x 4' panel, manila finish	88	16.40	104.40
2240	ABS plastic finish	103	31.50	134.50
2300	Kiosks, round, 5' diam., 1/4" fiberglass wall, 8' high	6,050		6,050
2340	Rectangular, 5' x 9', 1" insulated dbl. wall fiberglass, 7'-6" high	10,500		10,500
2400	Portable booth, acoustical, 27 db 1000 hz., 15 S.F. floor	3,175		3,175
2440	55 S.F. flr.	6,500		6,500
2500	Radio towers, guyed, 40 lb. section, 50' high, 70 MPH basic wind speed	1,725	955	2,680
2540	90 lb. section, 400' high, wind load 70 MPH basic wind speed	22,400	10,500	32,900
2600	Self supporting, 60' high, 70 MPH basic wind speed	3,600	1,825	5,425
2640	190' high, wind load 90 MPH basic wind speed	21,400	7,375	28,775
2700	Shelters, aluminum frame, acrylic glazing, 8' high, 3' x 9'	2,800	835	3,635
2740	9' x 12'	4,675	1,300	5,975
2800	Shielding, lead x-ray protection, radiography room, 1/16" lead, economy	5,050	2,700	7,750
2840	Deluxe	6,600	4,500	11,100
2900	Deep therapy x-ray, 1/4" lead, economy	17,100	8,425	25,525
2940	Deluxe	23,100	11,200	34,300
3000	Shooting range incl. bullet traps, controls, separators, ceilings, economy	12,200	4,825	17,025
3040	Deluxe	21,900	8,125	30,025
3100	Silos, concrete stave, industrial, 12' diam., 35' high	17,300	15,100	32,400
3140	25' diam., 75' high	56,500	33,300	89,800
3200	Steel prefab, 30,000 gal., painted, economy	12,100	3,975	16,075
3240	Epoxy-lined, deluxe	25,100	7,900	33,000
3300	Sport court, squash, regulation, in existing building, economy			14,500
3340	Deluxe			27,100
3400	Racketball, regulation, in existing building, economy	1,925	6,900	8,825
3440	Deluxe	25,700	13,800	39,500
3500	Swimming pool equipment, diving stand, stainless steel, 1 meter	4,125	270	4,395
3540	3 meter	5,100	1,825	6,925
3600	Diving boards, 16 ft. long, aluminum	1,600	270	1,870
3640	Fiberglass	1,200	270	1,470
3700	Filter system, sand, incl. pump, 6000 gal./hr.	1,150	460	1,610
3800	Lights, underwater, 12 volt with transformer, 300W	128	1,025	1,153
3900	Slides, fiberglass with aluminum handrails & ladder, 6' high, straight	2,350	455	2,805
3940	12' high, straight with platform	1,550	610	2,160
4000	Tanks, steel, ground level, 100,000 gal.			98,000
4040	10,000,000 gal.			1,937,500

SPECIAL CONSTRUCTION 11

11.1-700	Special Construction/Each	MAT.	INST.	TOTAL
4100	Elevated water, 50,000 gal.		129,500	180,000
4140	1,000,000 gal.		604,000	840,500
4200	Cypress wood, ground level, 3,000 gal.	6,350	7,275	13,625
4240	Redwood, ground level, 45,000 gal.	49,100	19,700	68,800

11.1-700	Special Construction/S.F.	MAT.	INST.	TOTAL
4500	Special construction, acoustical, enclosure, 4" thick, 8 psf panels	27	15.20	42.20
4540	Reverb chamber, 4" thick, parallel walls	38.50	18.25	56.75
4600	Sound absorbing panels, 2'-6" x 8', painted metal	9.95	5.10	15.05
4640	Vinyl faced	8	4.56	12.56
4700	Flexible transparent curtain, clear	6.15	5.80	11.95
4740	With absorbing foam, 75% coverage	8.60	5.80	14.40
4800	Strip entrance, 2/3 overlap	4.14	9.20	13.34
4840	Full overlap	5.10	10.80	15.90
4900	Audio masking system, plenum mounted, over 10,000 S.F.	.59	.19	.78
4940	Ceiling mounted, under 5,000 S.F.	1.06	.34	1.40
5000	Air supported struc., polyester vinyl fabric, 24oz., warehouse, 5000 S.F.	16.50	.23	16.73
5040	50,000 S.F.	7.55	.18	7.73
5100	Tennis, 7,200 S.F.	15.40	.19	15.59
5140	24,000 S.F.	10.45	.19	10.64
5200	Woven polyethylene, 6 oz., shelter, 3,000 S.F.	6.50	.38	6.88
5240	24,000 S.F.	5.50	.19	5.69
5300	Teflon coated fiberglass, stadium cover, economy	39.50	.10	39.60
5340	Deluxe	46	.14	46.14
5400	Air supported storage tank covers, reinf. vinyl fabric, 12 oz., 400 S.F.	14.85	.32	15.17
5440	18,000 S.F.	4.57	.29	4.86
5500	Anechoic chambers, 7' high, 100 cps cutoff, 25 S.F.			2,000
5540	200 cps cutoff, 100 S.F.			1,025
5600	Audiometric rooms, under 500 S.F.	44	14.90	58.90
5640	Over 500 S.F.	42	12.15	54.15
5700	Comfort stations, prefab, mobile on steel frame, economy	41		41
5740	Permanent on concrete slab, deluxe	220	32.50	252.50
5800	Darkrooms, shell, not including door, 240 S.F., 8' high	37.50	6.10	43.60
5840	64 S.F., 12' high	86.50	11.40	97.90
5900	Domes, bulk storage, wood framing, wood decking, 50' diam.	27.50	1.20	28.70
5940	116' diam.	16.50	1.39	17.89
6000	Steel framing, metal decking, 150' diam.	29.50	8.25	37.75
6040	400' diam.	24	6.30	30.30
6100	Geodesic, wood framing, wood panels, 30' diam.	18.30	1.33	19.63
6140	60' diam.	14.40	.85	15.25
6200	Aluminum framing, acrylic panels, 40' diam.			82.50
6240	Aluminum panels, 400' diam.			33
6300	Garden house, prefab, wood, shell only, 48 S.F.	16.75	3.65	20.40
6340	200 S.F.	30.50	15.20	45.70
6400	Greenhouse, shell-stock, residential, lean-to, 8'-6" long x 3'-10" wide	34	21.50	55.50
6440	Freestanding, 8'-6" long x 13'-6" wide	26.50	6.75	33.25
6500	Commercial-truss frame, under 2000 S.F., deluxe			38
6540	Over 5,000 S.F., economy			23
6600	Institutional-rigid frame, under 500 S.F., deluxe			99
6640	Over 2,000 S.F., economy			39
6700	Hangar, prefab, galv. roof and walls, bottom rolling doors, economy	8.85	3.26	12.11
6740	Electric bifolding doors, deluxe	10.45	4.25	14.70
6800	Integrated ceilings, Luminaire, suspended, 5' x 5' modules, 50% lighted	3.88	8.65	12.53
6840	100% lighted	5.80	15.55	21.35
6900	Dimensionaire, 2' x 4' module tile system, no air bar	2.35	1.46	3.81
6940	With air bar, deluxe	3.40	1.46	4.86
7000	Music practice room, modular, perforated steel, under 500 S.F.	26.50	10.40	36.90
7040	Over 500 S.F.	23	9.10	32.10

SPECIAL CONSTRUCTION

11

11.1-700	Special Construction/S.F.	COST PER S.F.		
		MAT.	INST.	TOTAL
7100	Pedestal access floors, stl pnls, no stringers, vinyl covering, >6000 S.F.	11.55	1.62	13.17
7140	With stringers, high pressure laminate covering, under 6000 S.F.	10.20	1.82	12.02
7200	Carpet covering, under 6000 S.F.	11.80	1.82	13.62
7240	Aluminum panels, no stringers, no covering	23	1.46	24.46
7300	Refrigerators, prefab, walk-in, 7'-6" high, 6' x 6'	107	13.30	120.30
7340	12' x 20'	67	6.65	73.65
7400	Shielding, lead, gypsum board, 5/8" thick, 1/16" lead	5.25	4.33	9.58
7440	1/8" lead	10.75	4.95	15.70
7500	Lath, 1/16" thick	5.05	4.99	10.04
7540	1/8" thick	10.50	5.60	16.10
7600	Radio frequency, copper, prefab screen type, economy	26.50	4.05	30.55
7640	Deluxe	34	5.05	39.05
7700	Swimming pool enclosure, transluscent, freestanding, economy	12.10	3.65	15.75
7740	Deluxe	305	10.40	315.40
7800	Swimming pools, residential, vinyl liner, metal sides	9.55	4.89	14.44
7840	Concrete sides	11.45	9.25	20.70
7900	Gunite shell, plaster finish, 350 S.F.	18.95	19.10	38.05
7940	800 S.F.	15.25	11.10	26.35
8000	Motel, gunite shell, plaster finish	23.50	24	47.50
8040	Municipal, gunite shell, tile finish, formed gutters	97.50	42	139.50
8100	Tension structures, steel frame, polyester vinyl fabric, 12,000 S.F.	9.85	1.66	11.51
8140	20,800 S.F.	10.35	1.49	11.84

11.1-700	Special Construction/L.F.	COST PER L.F.		
		MAT.	INST.	TOTAL
8500	Spec. const., air curtains, shipping & receiving, 8'high x 5'wide, economy	204	166	370
8540	20' high x 8' wide, heated, deluxe	630	320	950
8600	Customer entrance, 10' high x 5' wide, economy	208	166	374
8640	12' high x 4' wide, heated, deluxe	320	296	616

For information about Means Estimating Seminars, see yellow pages 11 and 12 in back of book

SPECIAL CONSTRUCTION 11

Division 12
Site Work

12.3-110	Trenching	COST PER L.F.		
		MAT.	INST.	TOTAL
1310	Trenching, backhoe, 0 to 1 slope, 2' wide, 2' deep, 3/8 C.Y. bucket		2.48	2.48
1330	4' deep, 3/8 C.Y. bucket		4.29	4.29
1360	10' deep, 1 C.Y. bucket		8.68	8.68
1400	4' wide, 2' deep, 3/8 C.Y. bucket		5.09	5.09
1420	4' deep, 1/2 C.Y. bucket		7.29	7.29
1450	10' deep, 1 C.Y. bucket		17.55	17.55
1480	18' deep, 2-1/2 C.Y. bucket		27	27
1520	6' wide, 6' deep, 5/8 C.Y. bucket		16.90	16.90
1540	10' deep, 1 C.Y. bucket		23.60	23.60
1570	20' deep, 3-1/2 C.Y. bucket		37.15	37.15
1640	8' wide, 12' deep, 1-1/4 C.Y. bucket		28.15	28.15
1680	24' deep, 3-1/2 C.Y. bucket		83	83
1730	10' wide, 20' deep, 3-1/2 C.Y. bucket		65.50	65.50
1740	24' deep, 3-1/2 C.Y. bucket		104.50	104.50
3500	1 to 1 slope, 2' wide, 2' deep, 3/8 C.Y. bucket		3.78	3.78
3540	4' deep, 3/8 C.Y. bucket		8.86	8.86
3600	10' deep, 1 C.Y. bucket		37.75	37.75
3800	4' wide, 2' deep, 3/8 C.Y. bucket		6.46	6.46
3840	4' deep, 1/2 C.Y. bucket		10.55	10.55
3900	10' deep, 1 C.Y. bucket		39.75	39.75
4030	6' wide, 6' deep, 5/8 C.Y. bucket		22.85	22.85
4050	10' deep, 1 C.Y. bucket		47.50	47.50
4080	20' deep, 3-1/2 C.Y. bucket		121.50	121.50
4500	8' wide, 12' deep, 1-1/4 C.Y. bucket		54	54
4650	24' deep, 3-1/2 C.Y. bucket		253	253
4800	10' wide, 20' deep, 3-1/2 C.Y. bucket		147	147
4850	24' deep, 3-1/2 C.Y. bucket		270	270

12.3-310	Pipe Bedding	COST PER L.F.		
		MAT.	INST.	TOTAL
1440	Pipe bedding, side slope 0 to 1, 1' wide, pipe size 6" diameter	.26	.45	.71
1460	2' wide, pipe size 8" diameter	.58	.99	1.57
1500	Pipe size 12" diameter	.61	1.06	1.67
1600	4' wide, pipe size 20" diameter	1.52	2.61	4.13
1660	Pipe size 30" diameter	1.61	2.77	4.38
1680	6' wide, pipe size 32" diameter	2.81	4.85	7.66
1740	8' wide, pipe size 60" diameter	4.69	8.05	12.74
1780	12' wide, pipe size 84" diameter	9.20	15.85	25.05

12.3-710	Manholes & Catch Basins	COST PER EACH		
		MAT.	INST.	TOTAL
1920	Manhole/catch basin, brick, 4' I.D. riser, 4' deep	680	1,125	1,805
1980	10' deep	1,500	2,650	4,150
3200	Block, 4' I.D. riser, 4' deep	630	910	1,540
3260	10' deep	1,225	2,175	3,400
4620	Concrete, cast-in-place, 4' I.D. riser, 4' deep	760	1,600	2,360
4680	10' deep	1,725	3,800	5,525
5820	Concrete, precast, 4' I.D. riser, 4' deep	715	835	1,550
5880	10' deep	1,425	1,950	3,375
6200	6' I.D. riser, 4' deep	1,300	1,200	2,500
6260	10' deep	2,625	2,825	5,450

Important: See the Reference Section for critical supporting data - Location Factors & Historical Cost Indexes

SITE WORK 12

12.5-110	Roadway Pavement	COST PER L.F.		
		MAT.	INST.	TOTAL
1500	Roadways, bituminous conc. paving, 2-1/2" thick, 20' wide	37	40	77
1580	30' wide	45.50	46	91.50
1800	3" thick, 20' wide	39	39	78
1880	30' wide	48	46	94
2100	4" thick, 20' wide	41.50	39	80.50
2180	30' wide	52.50	46	98.50
2400	5" thick, 20' wide	48.50	40	88.50
2480	30' wide	62.50	47	109.50
3000	6" thick, 20' wide	67.50	40.50	108
3080	30' wide	91	48.50	139.50
3300	8" thick 20' wide	83	41	124
3380	30' wide	114	49	163
3600	12" thick 20' wide	102	43	145
3700	32' wide	151	54	205

12.5-510	Parking Lots	COST PER CAR		
		MAT.	INST.	TOTAL
1500	Parking lot, 90° angle parking, 3" bituminous paving, 6" gravel base	305	219	524
1540	10" gravel base	360	255	615
1560	4" bituminous paving, 6" gravel base	350	217	567
1600	10" gravel base	405	253	658
1620	6" bituminous paving, 6" gravel base	450	226	676
1660	10" gravel base	505	263	768
1800	60° angle parking, 3" bituminous paving, 6" gravel base	350	239	589
1840	10" gravel base	415	281	696
1860	4" bituminous paving, 6" gravel base	400	237	637
1900	10" gravel base	465	280	745
1920	6" bituminous paving, 6" gravel base	520	248	768
1960	10" gravel base	585	290	875
2200	45° angle parking, 3" bituminous paving, 6" gravel base	395	259	654
2240	10" gravel base	470	305	775
2260	4" bituminous paving, 6" gravel base	455	257	712
2300	10" gravel base	530	305	835
2320	6" bituminous paving, 6" gravel base	590	270	860
2360	10" gravel base	660	320	980

For information about Means Estimating Seminars, see yellow pages 11 and 12 in back of book

SITE WORK

12

Reference Section

All the reference information is in one section making it easy to find what you need to know . . . and easy to use the book on a daily basis. This section is visually identified by a vertical gray bar on the edge of pages.

In this Reference Section, we've included General Conditions; Historical Cost Indexes for cost comparisons over time; Location Factors; a Glossary; and an explanation of all Abbreviations used in the book.

Table of Contents

429

General Conditions, Overhead & Profit

The total building costs in the Commercial/Industrial/Institutional section include a 10% allowance for general conditions and a 15% allowance for the general contractor's overhead and profit and contingencies.

General contractor overhead includes indirect costs such as permits, Workers' Compensation, insurances, supervision and bonding fees. Overhead will vary with the size of project, the contractor's operating procedures and location. Profits will vary with economic activity and local conditions.

Contingencies provide for unforeseen construction difficulties which include material shortages and weather. In all situations, the appraiser should give consideration to possible adjustment of the 25% factor used in developing the Commercial/Industrial/Institutional models.

Architectural Fees

Tabulated below are typical percentage fees by project size, for good professional architectural service. Fees may vary from those listed depending upon degree of design difficulty and economic conditions in any particular area.

Rates can be interpolated horizontally and vertically. Various portions of the same project requiring different rates should be adjusted proportionately. For alterations, add 50% to the fee for the first $500,000 of project cost and add 25% to the fee for project cost over $500,000.

Architectural fees tabulated below include Engineering fees.

Insurance Exclusions

Many insurance companies exclude from coverage such items as architect's fees, excavation, foundations below grade, underground piping and site preparation. Since exclusions vary among insurance companies, it is recommended that for greatest accuracy each exclusion be priced separately using the unit-in-place section.

As a rule of thumb, exclusions can be calculated at 9% of total building cost plus the appropriate allowance for architect's fees.

Building Types	Total Project Size in Thousands of Dollars						
	100	250	500	1,000	5,000	10,000	50,000
Factories, garages, warehouses, repetitive housing	9.0%	8.0%	7.0%	6.2%	5.3%	4.9%	4.5%
Apartments, banks, schools, libraries, offices, municipal buildings	12.2	12.3	9.2	8.0	7.0	6.6	6.2
Churches, hospitals, homes, laboratories, museums, research	15.0	13.6	12.7	11.9	9.5	8.8	8.0
Memorials, monumental work, decorative furnishings	—	16.0	14.5	13.1	10.0	9.0	8.3

Location Factors

Costs shown in *Means cost data publications* are based on National Averages for materials and installation. To adjust these costs to a specific location, simply multiply the base cost by the factor for that city. The data is arranged alphabetically by state and postal zip code numbers. For a city not listed, use the factor for a nearby city with similar economic characteristics.

STATE/ZIP	CITY	Residential	Commercial
ALABAMA			
350-352	Birmingham	.86	.87
354	Tuscaloosa	.81	.79
355	Jasper	.77	.78
356	Decatur	.80	.81
357-358	Huntsville	.82	.83
359	Gadsden	.80	.81
360-361	Montgomery	.83	.81
362	Anniston	.74	.75
363	Dothan	.80	.78
364	Evergreen	.80	.78
365-366	Mobile	.82	.83
367	Selma	.80	.78
368	Phenix City	.83	.81
369	Butler	.79	.77
ALASKA			
995-996	Anchorage	1.26	1.25
997	Fairbanks	1.25	1.24
998	Juneau	1.25	1.24
999	Ketchikan	1.31	1.30
ARIZONA			
850,853	Phoenix	.92	.89
852	Mesa/Tempe	.87	.85
855	Globe	.88	.85
856-857	Tucson	.90	.87
859	Show Low	.90	.86
860	Flagstaff	.93	.89
863	Prescott	.90	.86
864	Kingman	.90	.86
865	Chambers	.89	.85
ARKANSAS			
716	Pine Bluff	.80	.80
717	Camden	.71	.71
718	Texarkana	.75	.74
719	Hot Springs	.70	.70
720-722	Little Rock	.81	.81
723	West Memphis	.80	.80
724	Jonesboro	.80	.80
725	Batesville	.76	.76
726	Harrison	.77	.77
727	Fayetteville	.69	.67
728	Russellville	.78	.75
729	Fort Smith	.82	.79
CALIFORNIA			
900-902	Los Angeles	1.08	1.08
903-905	Inglewood	1.06	1.06
906-908	Long Beach	1.07	1.07
910-912	Pasadena	1.06	1.06
913-916	Van Nuys	1.08	1.08
917-918	Alhambra	1.08	1.08
919-921	San Diego	1.10	1.06
922	Palm Springs	1.10	1.06
923-924	San Bernardino	1.09	1.05
925	Riverside	1.12	1.08
926-927	Santa Ana	1.09	1.06
928	Anaheim	1.11	1.09
930	Oxnard	1.14	1.09
931	Santa Barbara	1.10	1.07
932-933	Bakersfield	1.11	1.06
934	San Luis Obispo	1.14	1.08
935	Mojave	1.09	1.05
936-938	Fresno	1.12	1.08
939	Salinas	1.12	1.12
940-941	San Francisco	1.20	1.23
942,956-958	Sacramento	1.11	1.10
943	Palo Alto	1.14	1.17
944	San Mateo	1.14	1.17
945	Vallejo	1.12	1.15
946	Oakland	1.15	1.18
947	Berkeley	1.15	1.18
948	Richmond	1.14	1.17
949	San Rafael	1.25	1.19
950	Santa Cruz	1.15	1.14
951	San Jose	1.22	1.20
952	Stockton	1.13	1.09
953	Modesto	1.14	1.10

STATE/ZIP	CITY	Residential	Commercial
CALIFORNIA (CONT'D)			
954	Santa Rosa	1.14	1.17
955	Eureka	1.11	1.10
959	Marysville	1.10	1.09
960	Redding	1.10	1.09
961	Susanville	1.11	1.10
COLORADO			
800-802	Denver	.99	.95
803	Boulder	.89	.85
804	Golden	.97	.93
805	Fort Collins	.98	.92
806	Greeley	.91	.85
807	Fort Morgan	.98	.92
808-809	Colorado Springs	.94	.92
810	Pueblo	.94	.92
811	Alamosa	.90	.88
812	Salida	.90	.88
813	Durango	.88	.86
814	Montrose	.86	.84
815	Grand Junction	.91	.86
816	Glenwood Springs	.96	.91
CONNECTICUT			
060	New Britain	1.04	1.05
061	Hartford	1.04	1.05
062	Willimantic	1.04	1.05
063	New London	1.05	1.04
064	Meriden	1.03	1.04
065	New Haven	1.04	1.05
066	Bridgeport	1.02	1.05
067	Waterbury	1.06	1.06
068	Norwalk	1.01	1.05
069	Stamford	1.04	1.08
D.C.			
200-205	Washington	.93	.95
DELAWARE			
197	Newark	1.00	1.01
198	Wilmington	1.00	1.01
199	Dover	1.00	1.01
FLORIDA			
320,322	Jacksonville	.84	.83
321	Daytona Beach	.88	.87
323	Tallahassee	.76	.78
324	Panama City	.71	.72
325	Pensacola	.85	.83
326,344	Gainesville	.85	.82
327-328,347	Orlando	.88	.86
329	Melbourne	.91	.90
330-332,340	Miami	.84	.86
333	Fort Lauderdale	.84	.86
334,349	West Palm Beach	.87	.84
335-336,346	Tampa	.81	.83
337	St. Petersburg	.82	.84
338	Lakeland	.80	.82
339,341	Fort Myers	.80	.80
342	Sarasota	.80	.81
GEORGIA			
300-303,399	Atlanta	.84	.89
304	Statesboro	.65	.67
305	Gainesville	.71	.75
306	Athens	.78	.82
307	Dalton	.68	.67
308-309	Augusta	.77	.79
310-312	Macon	.81	.81
313-314	Savannah	.81	.82
315	Waycross	.74	.74
316	Valdosta	.76	.76
317	Albany	.77	.79
318-319	Columbus	.79	.79
HAWAII			
967	Hilo	1.26	1.22
968	Honolulu	1.27	1.23

Location Factors

STATE/ZIP	CITY	Residential	Commercial
STATES & POSS.			
969	Guam	1.43	1.38
IDAHO			
832	Pocatello	.94	.93
833	Twin Falls	.80	.79
834	Idaho Falls	.84	.83
835	Lewiston	1.09	1.01
836-837	Boise	.95	.94
838	Coeur d'Alene	.96	.89
ILLINOIS			
600-603	North Suburban	1.10	1.09
604	Joliet	1.07	1.06
605	South Suburban	1.09	1.08
606	Chicago	1.12	1.11
609	Kankakee	.99	.99
610-611	Rockford	1.05	1.04
612	Rock Island	1.06	.97
613	La Salle	1.05	.98
614	Galesburg	1.06	.99
615-616	Peoria	1.07	1.01
617	Bloomington	1.04	.99
618-619	Champaign	1.04	1.00
620-622	East St. Louis	.99	.99
623	Quincy	.97	.95
624	Effingham	1.00	.97
625	Decatur	1.00	.97
626-627	Springfield	1.01	.98
628	Centralia	.98	.98
629	Carbondale	.96	.96
INDIANA			
460	Anderson	.94	.92
461-462	Indianapolis	.97	.95
463-464	Gary	1.03	1.01
465-466	South Bend	.93	.91
467-468	Fort Wayne	.90	.91
469	Kokomo	.92	.91
470	Lawrenceburg	.92	.89
471	New Albany	.92	.88
472	Columbus	.95	.92
473	Muncie	.93	.92
474	Bloomington	.96	.93
475	Washington	.93	.93
476-477	Evansville	.95	.95
478	Terre Haute	.95	.94
479	Lafayette	.91	.91
IOWA			
500-503,509	Des Moines	.97	.92
504	Mason City	.87	.81
505	Fort Dodge	.84	.79
506-507	Waterloo	.88	.83
508	Creston	.90	.85
510-511	Sioux City	.95	.89
512	Sibley	.80	.78
513	Spencer	.81	.79
514	Carroll	.85	.80
515	Council Bluffs	.95	.89
516	Shenandoah	.83	.78
520	Dubuque	.99	.89
521	Decorah	.89	.80
522-524	Cedar Rapids	1.00	.92
525	Ottumwa	.95	.87
526	Burlington	.92	.87
527-528	Davenport	.98	.96
KANSAS			
660-662	Kansas City	.96	.94
664-666	Topeka	.86	.85
667	Fort Scott	.86	.84
668	Emporia	.82	.81
669	Belleville	.87	.81
670-672	Wichita	.89	.86
673	Independence	.82	.79
674	Salina	.85	.81
675	Hutchinson	.80	.76
676	Hays	.85	.81
677	Colby	.85	.81
678	Dodge City	.85	.82
679	Liberal	.78	.76
KENTUCKY			
400-402	Louisville	.95	.92
403-405	Lexington	.88	.85

STATE/ZIP	CITY	Residential	Commercial
KENTUCKY (CONT'D)			
406	Frankfort	.93	.87
407-409	Corbin	.78	.73
410	Covington	.98	.95
411-412	Ashland	.97	.98
413-414	Campton	.77	.74
415-416	Pikeville	.83	.84
417-418	Hazard	.77	.73
420	Paducah	.97	.92
421-422	Bowling Green	.96	.91
423	Owensboro	.91	.89
424	Henderson	.96	.94
425-426	Somerset	.76	.72
427	Elizabethtown	.94	.90
LOUISIANA			
700-701	New Orleans	.87	.86
703	Thibodaux	.86	.86
704	Hammond	.84	.83
705	Lafayette	.85	.82
706	Lake Charles	.83	.83
707-708	Baton Rouge	.83	.82
710-711	Shreveport	.81	.81
712	Monroe	.79	.79
713-714	Alexandria	.78	.78
MAINE			
039	Kittery	.77	.79
040-041	Portland	.88	.90
042	Lewiston	.89	.90
043	Augusta	.79	.79
044	Bangor	.92	.92
045	Bath	.77	.77
046	Machias	.83	.83
047	Houlton	.82	.82
048	Rockland	.83	.83
049	Waterville	.79	.78
MARYLAND			
206	Waldorf	.88	.88
207-208	College Park	.90	.90
209	Silver Spring	.90	.90
210-212	Baltimore	.92	.92
214	Annapolis	.89	.90
215	Cumberland	.88	.88
216	Easton	.73	.74
217	Hagerstown	.90	.88
218	Salisbury	.77	.78
219	Elkton	.83	.84
MASSACHUSETTS			
010-011	Springfield	1.04	1.02
012	Pittsfield	.98	.98
013	Greenfield	1.01	.99
014	Fitchburg	1.08	1.04
015-016	Worcester	1.10	1.06
017	Framingham	1.06	1.07
018	Lowell	1.08	1.08
019	Lawrence	1.08	1.08
020-022, 024	Boston	1.14	1.15
023	Brockton	1.06	1.08
025	Buzzards Bay	1.02	1.04
026	Hyannis	1.05	1.06
027	New Bedford	1.06	1.07
MICHIGAN			
480,483	Royal Oak	1.02	1.01
481	Ann Arbor	1.05	1.04
482	Detroit	1.07	1.06
484-485	Flint	.99	1.00
486	Saginaw	.96	.97
487	Bay City	.96	.97
488-489	Lansing	1.01	.98
490	Battle Creek	1.01	.94
491	Kalamazoo	1.00	.93
492	Jackson	1.00	.97
493,495	Grand Rapids	.89	.86
494	Muskegon	.95	.92
496	Traverse City	.88	.85
497	Gaylord	.88	.89
498-499	Iron Mountain	.98	.95
MINNESOTA			
550-551	Saint Paul	1.13	1.10
553-555	Minneapolis	1.15	1.12

STATE/ZIP	CITY	Residential	Commercial
556-558	Duluth	1.06	1.07
559	Rochester	1.06	1.03
560	Mankato	1.02	1.01
561	Windom	.92	.91
562	Willmar	.95	.94
563	St. Cloud	1.13	1.05
564	Brainerd	1.08	1.01
565	Detroit Lakes	.90	.97
566	Bemidji	.93	1.00
567	Thief River Falls	.89	.96
MISSISSIPPI			
386	Clarksdale	.70	.67
387	Greenville	.81	.78
388	Tupelo	.71	.72
389	Greenwood	.72	.69
390-392	Jackson	.81	.78
393	Meridian	.77	.76
394	Laurel	.73	.69
395	Biloxi	.85	.81
396	Mccomb	.69	.67
397	Columbus	.71	.72
MISSOURI			
630-631	St. Louis	1.00	1.03
633	Bowling Green	.92	.95
634	Hannibal	1.00	.94
635	Kirksville	.87	.91
636	Flat River	.95	.98
637	Cape Girardeau	.93	.96
638	Sikeston	.91	.93
639	Poplar Bluff	.90	.92
640-641	Kansas City	1.03	1.00
644-645	St. Joseph	.89	.93
646	Chillicothe	.82	.86
647	Harrisonville	.98	.96
648	Joplin	.84	.86
650-651	Jefferson City	.98	.92
652	Columbia	.99	.93
653	Sedalia	.99	.92
654-655	Rolla	.96	.90
656-658	Springfield	.85	.87
MONTANA			
590-591	Billings	.98	.96
592	Wolf Point	.98	.96
593	Miles City	.97	.95
594	Great Falls	.97	.96
595	Havre	.96	.95
596	Helena	.97	.96
597	Butte	.96	.95
598	Missoula	.95	.94
599	Kalispell	.94	.93
NEBRASKA			
680-681	Omaha	.92	.91
683-685	Lincoln	.88	.83
686	Columbus	.74	.73
687	Norfolk	.84	.83
688	Grand Island	.88	.83
689	Hastings	.82	.78
690	McCook	.80	.76
691	North Platte	.87	.82
692	Valentine	.78	.74
693	Alliance	.75	.72
NEVADA			
889-891	Las Vegas	1.06	1.05
893	Ely	.94	.95
894-895	Reno	.95	1.00
897	Carson City	.96	.99
898	Elko	.92	.94
NEW HAMPSHIRE			
030	Nashua	.93	.94
031	Manchester	.93	.94
032-033	Concord	.92	.93
034	Keene	.79	.80
035	Littleton	.82	.83
036	Charleston	.77	.78
037	Claremont	.77	.77
038	Portsmouth	.92	.91

STATE/ZIP	CITY	Residential	Commercial
NEW JERSEY			
070-071	Newark	1.14	1.12
072	Elizabeth	1.11	1.09
073	Jersey City	1.13	1.12
074-075	Paterson	1.12	1.12
076	Hackensack	1.11	1.11
077	Long Branch	1.11	1.09
078	Dover	1.12	1.10
079	Summit	1.10	1.08
080,083	Vineland	1.12	1.08
081	Camden	1.12	1.09
082,084	Atlantic City	1.11	1.08
085-086	Trenton	1.13	1.11
087	Point Pleasant	1.12	1.10
088-089	New Brunswick	1.12	1.10
NEW MEXICO			
870-872	Albuquerque	.89	.91
873	Gallup	.90	.92
874	Farmington	.90	.92
875	Santa Fe	.89	.91
877	Las Vegas	.89	.91
878	Socorro	.89	.91
879	Truth/Consequences	.88	.88
880	Las Cruces	.86	.86
881	Clovis	.91	.91
882	Roswell	.92	.92
883	Carrizozo	.92	.92
884	Tucumcari	.91	.91
NEW YORK			
100-102	New York	1.34	1.34
103	Staten Island	1.29	1.29
104	Bronx	1.28	1.28
105	Mount Vernon	1.17	1.17
106	White Plains	1.16	1.16
107	Yonkers	1.20	1.20
108	New Rochelle	1.17	1.17
109	Suffern	1.15	1.15
110	Queens	1.29	1.29
111	Long Island City	1.30	1.30
112	Brooklyn	1.30	1.30
113	Flushing	1.31	1.31
114	Jamaica	1.30	1.30
115,117,118	Hicksville	1.25	1.25
116	Far Rockaway	1.31	1.31
119	Riverhead	1.27	1.27
120-122	Albany	.97	.97
123	Schenectady	.98	.98
124	Kingston	1.11	1.09
125-126	Poughkeepsie	1.14	1.12
127	Monticello	1.09	1.07
128	Glens Falls	.95	.93
129	Plattsburgh	.95	.93
130-132	Syracuse	.98	.96
133-135	Utica	.91	.94
136	Watertown	.93	.96
137-139	Binghamton	.94	.94
140-142	Buffalo	1.06	1.02
143	Niagara Falls	1.06	1.02
144-146	Rochester	.99	1.00
147	Jamestown	.97	.94
148-149	Elmira	.96	.94
NORTH CAROLINA			
270,272-274	Greensboro	.75	.76
271	Winston-Salem	.75	.76
275-276	Raleigh	.77	.77
277	Durham	.75	.76
278	Rocky Mount	.69	.69
279	Elizabeth City	.70	.70
280	Gastonia	.74	.75
281-282	Charlotte	.74	.75
283	Fayetteville	.76	.76
284	Wilmington	.73	.75
285	Kinston	.68	.68
286	Hickory	.67	.67
287-288	Asheville	.73	.75
289	Murphy	.67	.68
NORTH DAKOTA			
580-581	Fargo	.79	.84
582	Grand Forks	.78	.83
583	Devils Lake	.77	.82
584	Jamestown	.77	.82
585	Bismarck	.81	.85

STATE/ZIP	CITY	Residential	Commercial
NORTH DAKOTA (CONT'D)			
586	Dickinson	.78	.82
587	Minot	.80	.84
588	Williston	.77	.81
OHIO			
430-432	Columbus	.98	.96
433	Marion	.91	.92
434-436	Toledo	1.00	.99
437-438	Zanesville	.92	.91
439	Steubenville	.98	.98
440	Lorain	1.04	.98
441	Cleveland	1.10	1.03
442-443	Akron	1.01	1.00
444-445	Youngstown	1.00	.97
446-447	Canton	.97	.96
448-449	Mansfield	.97	.95
450	Hamilton	1.00	.94
451-452	Cincinnati	1.01	.95
453-454	Dayton	.94	.93
455	Springfield	.95	.93
456	Chillicothe	1.02	.96
457	Athens	.88	.87
458	Lima	.95	.94
OKLAHOMA			
730-731	Oklahoma City	.82	.83
734	Ardmore	.83	.82
735	Lawton	.85	.84
736	Clinton	.80	.82
737	Enid	.83	.82
738	Woodward	.82	.81
739	Guymon	.69	.69
740-741	Tulsa	.85	.82
743	Miami	.86	.83
744	Muskogee	.76	.73
745	Mcalester	.76	.78
746	Ponca City	.82	.81
747	Durant	.79	.81
748	Shawnee	.79	.81
749	Poteau	.85	.81
OREGON			
970-972	Portland	1.09	1.07
973	Salem	1.07	1.06
974	Eugene	1.07	1.06
975	Medford	1.06	1.05
976	Klamath Falls	1.07	1.06
977	Bend	1.07	1.06
978	Pendleton	1.04	1.02
979	Vale	.99	.97
PENNSYLVANIA			
150-152	Pittsburgh	1.03	1.01
153	Washington	1.02	1.00
154	Uniontown	1.01	.99
155	Bedford	1.03	.97
156	Greensburg	1.02	1.00
157	Indiana	1.05	.98
158	Dubois	1.04	.97
159	Johnstown	1.04	.98
160	Butler	1.01	.98
161	New Castle	1.01	.98
162	Kittanning	1.02	.99
163	Oil City	.91	.96
164-165	Erie	.99	.97
166	Altoona	1.04	.96
167	Bradford	1.00	.98
168	State College	.97	.97
169	Wellsboro	.94	.95
170-171	Harrisburg	.97	.96
172	Chambersburg	.96	.95
173-174	York	.97	.95
175-176	Lancaster	.96	.94
177	Williamsport	.92	.91
178	Sunbury	.96	.95
179	Pottsville	.96	.95
180	Lehigh Valley	1.02	1.01
181	Allentown	1.02	1.01
182	Hazleton	.97	.96
183	Stroudsburg	1.03	1.02
184-185	Scranton	.96	.99
186-187	Wilkes-Barre	.93	.96
188	Montrose	.94	.97
189	Doylestown	.95	1.06

STATE/ZIP	CITY	Residential	Commercial
PENNSYLVANIA (CONT'D)			
190-191	Philadelphia	1.13	1.11
193	Westchester	1.07	1.05
194	Norristown	1.09	1.07
195-196	Reading	.97	.98
PUERTO RICO			
009	San Juan	.88	.88
RHODE ISLAND			
028	Newport	1.02	1.04
029	Providence	1.02	1.04
SOUTH CAROLINA			
290-292	Columbia	.72	.75
293	Spartanburg	.71	.74
294	Charleston	.74	.76
295	Florence	.71	.73
296	Greenville	.71	.74
297	Rock Hill	.65	.67
298	Aiken	.65	.68
299	Beaufort	.68	.70
SOUTH DAKOTA			
570-571	Sioux Falls	.88	.82
572	Watertown	.84	.78
573	Mitchell	.84	.78
574	Aberdeen	.85	.79
575	Pierre	.85	.79
576	Mobridge	.85	.78
577	Rapid City	.85	.79
TENNESSEE			
370-372	Nashville	.86	.86
373-374	Chattanooga	.82	.81
375,380-381	Memphis	.86	.86
376	Johnson City	.80	.79
377-379	Knoxville	.80	.80
382	Mckenzie	.69	.69
383	Jackson	.68	.75
384	Columbia	.76	.76
385	Cookeville	.68	.68
TEXAS			
750	Mckinney	.89	.82
751	Waxahackie	.82	.82
752-753	Dallas	.89	.85
754	Greenville	.78	.73
755	Texarkana	.88	.77
756	Longview	.84	.74
757	Tyler	.91	.80
758	Palestine	.73	.73
759	Lufkin	.77	.77
760-761	Fort Worth	.84	.83
762	Denton	.88	.79
763	Wichita Falls	.80	.80
764	Eastland	.74	.73
765	Temple	.78	.77
766-767	Waco	.81	.80
768	Brownwood	.73	.72
769	San Angelo	.79	.75
770-772	Houston	.87	.88
773	Huntsville	.74	.74
774	Wharton	.76	.77
775	Galveston	.86	.87
776-777	Beaumont	.82	.84
778	Bryan	.81	.82
779	Victoria	.79	.79
780	Laredo	.77	.78
781-782	San Antonio	.82	.83
783-784	Corpus Christi	.81	.80
785	Mc Allen	.79	.77
786-787	Austin	.79	.82
788	Del Rio	.68	.68
789	Giddings	.73	.72
790-791	Amarillo	.81	.81
792	Childress	.76	.78
793-794	Lubbock	.78	.80
795-796	Abilene	.77	.77
797	Midland	.78	.79
798-799,885	El Paso	.80	.79
UTAH			
840-841	Salt Lake City	.91	.90
842,844	Ogden	.91	.89

Location Factors

STATE/ZIP	CITY	Residential	Commercial
UTAH (CONT'D)			
843	Logan	.92	.90
845	Price	.82	.81
846-847	Provo	.91	.90
VERMONT			
050	White River Jct.	.73	.72
051	Bellows Falls	.74	.73
052	Bennington	.72	.71
053	Brattleboro	.74	.74
054	Burlington	.85	.86
056	Montpelier	.83	.84
057	Rutland	.86	.85
058	St. Johnsbury	.75	.75
059	Guildhall	.73	.74
VIRGINIA			
220-221	Fairfax	.89	.90
222	Arlington	.89	.90
223	Alexandria	.90	.91
224-225	Fredericksburg	.84	.85
226	Winchester	.79	.79
227	Culpeper	.79	.80
228	Harrisonburg	.75	.76
229	Charlottesville	.84	.82
230-232	Richmond	.86	.84
233-235	Norfolk	.83	.83
236	Newport News	.83	.82
237	Portsmouth	.82	.82
238	Petersburg	.86	.84
239	Farmville	.75	.73
240-241	Roanoke	.77	.76
242	Bristol	.80	.75
243	Pulaski	.73	.72
244	Staunton	.77	.75
245	Lynchburg	.81	.77
246	Grundy	.73	.73
WASHINGTON			
980-981,987	Seattle	.99	1.04
982	Everett	.97	1.03
983-984	Tacoma	1.05	1.03
985	Olympia	1.05	1.03
986	Vancouver	1.10	1.04
988	Wenatchee	.94	.98
989	Yakima	1.02	1.00
990-992	Spokane	.99	.98
993	Richland	1.01	1.00
994	Clarkston	1.00	.99
WEST VIRGINIA			
247-248	Bluefield	.90	.90
249	Lewisburg	.91	.91
250-253	Charleston	.94	.94
254	Martinsburg	.76	.77
255-257	Huntington	.95	.97
258-259	Beckley	.92	.92
260	Wheeling	.93	.95
261	Parkersburg	.94	.96
262	Buckhannon	.97	.94
263-264	Clarksburg	.97	.94
265	Morgantown	.97	.94
266	Gassaway	.94	.94
267	Romney	.92	.92
268	Petersburg	.96	.93
WISCONSIN			
530,532	Milwaukee	1.01	1.00
531	Kenosha	1.01	1.00
534	Racine	1.05	1.00
535	Beloit	1.00	.98
537	Madison	1.00	.98
538	Lancaster	.92	.90
539	Portage	.99	.96
540	New Richmond	1.03	.95
541-543	Green Bay	1.00	.97
544	Wausau	.99	.95
545	Rhinelander	.99	.95
546	La Crosse	.98	.95
547	Eau Claire	1.04	.96
548	Superior	1.04	.98
549	Oshkosh	.97	.94

STATE/ZIP	CITY	Residential	Commercial
WYOMING			
820	Cheyenne	.86	.82
821	Yellowstone Nat. Pk.	.81	.78
822	Wheatland	.83	.79
823	Rawlins	.82	.78
824	Worland	.79	.76
825	Riverton	.82	.79
826	Casper	.87	.83
827	Newcastle	.80	.76
828	Sheridan	.84	.81
829-831	Rock Springs	.83	.79
CANADIAN FACTORS (reflect Canadian currency)			
ALBERTA			
	Calgary	1.00	.97
	Edmonton	1.00	.97
	Fort McMurray	.99	.96
	Lethbridge	.99	.96
	Lloydminster	.99	.96
	Medicine Hat	.99	.96
	Red Deer	.99	.96
BRITISH COLUMBIA			
	Kamloops	1.03	1.04
	Prince George	1.05	1.06
	Vancouver	1.06	1.07
	Victoria	1.05	1.06
MANITOBA			
	Brandon	.98	.97
	Portage la Prairie	.98	.97
	Winnipeg	.97	.97
NEW BRUNSWICK			
	Bathurst	.93	.91
	Dalhousie	.93	.91
	Fredericton	.96	.94
	Moncton	.93	.91
	Newcastle	.93	.91
	Saint John	.97	.95
NEWFOUNDLAND			
	Corner Brook	.95	.94
	St. John's	.95	.94
NORTHWEST TERRITORIES			
	Yellowknife	.92	.91
NOVA SCOTIA			
	Dartmouth	.97	.96
	Halifax	.97	.96
	New Glasgow	.97	.96
	Sydney	.95	.94
	Yarmouth	.97	.96
ONTARIO			
	Barrie	1.09	1.07
	Brantford	1.11	1.09
	Cornwall	1.09	1.07
	Hamilton	1.12	1.08
	Kingston	1.09	1.07
	Kitchener	1.05	1.03
	London	1.08	1.06
	North Bay	1.07	1.05
	Oshawa	1.09	1.07
	Ottawa	1.09	1.07
	Owen Sound	1.08	1.06
	Peterborough	1.08	1.06
	Sarnia	1.11	1.09
	St. Catharines	1.04	1.02
	Sudbury	1.04	1.02
	Thunder Bay	1.05	1.03
	Toronto	1.12	1.11
	Windsor	1.06	1.04
PRINCE EDWARD ISLAND			
	Charlottetown	.93	.91
	Summerside	.93	.91

STATE/ZIP	CITY	Residential	Commercial
QUEBEC			
	Cap-de-la-Madeleine	1.04	1.03
	Charlesbourg	1.04	1.03
	Chicoutimi	1.03	1.02
	Gatineau	1.02	1.01
	Laval	1.04	1.02
	Montreal	1.09	1.03
	Quebec	1.11	1.04
	Sherbrooke	1.04	1.02
	Trois Rivieres	1.04	1.03
SASKATCHEWAN			
	Moose Jaw	.92	.92
	Prince Albert	.92	.92
	Regina	.92	.92
	Saskatoon	.92	.92
YUKON			
	Whitehorse	.92	.91

The following tables are the revised Historical Cost Indexes based on a 30-city national average with a base of 100 on January 1, 1993.

The indexes may be used to:

1. Estimate and compare construction costs for different years in the same city.
2. Estimate and compare construction costs in different cities for the same year.
3. Estimate and compare construction costs in different cities for different years.
4. Compare construction trends in any city with the national average.

EXAMPLES

1. Estimate and compare construction costs for different years in the same city.

   A. To estimate the construction cost of a building in Lexington, KY in 1970, knowing that it cost $900,000 in 2001.

   Index Lexington, KY in 1970 = 26.9
   Index Lexington, KY in 2001 = 103.6

   $$\frac{\text{Index } 1970}{\text{Index } 2001} \quad \text{x} \quad \text{Cost } 2001 \quad = \quad \text{Cost } 1970$$

   $$\frac{26.9}{103.6} \quad \text{x} \quad \$900,000 \quad = \quad \$233,500$$

   Construction Cost in Lexington, KY in 1970 = $233,500

   B. To estimate the current construction cost of a building in Boston, MA that was built in 1978 for $900,000.

   Index Boston, MA in 1978 = 54.0
   Index Boston, MA in 2001 = 140.5

   $$\frac{\text{Index } 2001}{\text{Index } 1978} \quad \text{x} \quad \text{Cost } 1978 \quad = \quad \text{Cost } 2001$$

   $$\frac{140.5}{54.0} \quad \text{x} \quad \$900,000 \quad = \quad \$2,341,500$$

   Construction Cost in Boston in 2001 = $2,341,500

2. Estimate and compare construction costs in different cities for the same year.

   To compare the construction cost of a building in Topeka, KS in 2001 with the known cost of $800,000 in Baltimore, MD in 2001

   Index Topeka, KS in 2001 = 103.1
   Index Baltimore, MD in 2001 = 112.1

   $$\frac{\text{Index Topeka}}{\text{Index Baltimore}} \quad \text{x} \quad \text{Cost Baltimore} \quad = \quad \text{Cost Topeka}$$

   $$\frac{103.1}{112.1} \quad \text{x} \quad \$800,000 \quad = \quad \$736,000$$

   Construction Cost in Topeka in 2001 = $736,000

3. Estimate and compare construction costs in different cities for different years.

   To compare the construction cost of a building in Detroit, MI in 2001 with the known construction cost of $4,000,000 for the same building in San Francisco, CA in 1978.

   Index Detroit, MI in 2001 = 129.5
   Index San Francisco, CA in 1978 = 62.6

   $$\frac{\text{Index Detroit } 2001}{\text{Index San Francisco } 1978} \quad \text{x} \quad \text{Cost San Francisco } 1978 \quad = \quad \text{Cost Detroit } 2001$$

   $$\frac{129.5}{62.6} \quad \text{x} \quad \$4,000,000 \quad = \quad \$8,275,000$$

   Construction Cost in Detroit in 2001 = $8,275,000

4. Compare construction trends in any city with the national average.

   To compare the construction cost in Las Vegas, NV from 1975 to 2001 with the increase in the National Average during the same time period.

   Index Las Vegas, NV for 1975 = 42.8   For 2001 = 128.0
   Index 30 City Average for 1975 = 43.7   For 2001 = 121.8

   A. National Average escalation From 1975 to 2001 = $\dfrac{\text{Index} - \text{30 City } 2001}{\text{Index} - \text{30 City } 1975}$

   $$= \frac{121.8}{43.7}$$

   National Average escalation From 1975 to 2001 = 2.79   or 279%

   B. Escalation for Las Vegas, NV From 1975 to 2001 = $\dfrac{\text{Index Las Vegas, NV } 2001}{\text{Index Las Vegas, NV } 1975}$

   $$= \frac{128.0}{42.8}$$

   Las Vegas escalation 1975 — 2001 = 2.99   or 299%

   Conclusion: Construction costs in Las Vegas are higher than National average costs and increased at a greater rate from 1975 to 2001 than the National Average.

Historical Cost Indexes

Year	National 30 City Average	Alabama Birmingham	Alabama Huntsville	Alabama Mobile	Alabama Montgomery	Alabama Tuscaloosa	Alaska Anchorage	Arizona Phoenix	Arizona Tuscon	Arkansas Fort Smith	Arkansas Little Rock	California Anaheim	California Bakersfield	California Fresno	California Los Angeles	California Oxnard
Jan 2001	121.8E	106.6E	101.0E	101.3E	98.8E	96.7E	151.8E	109.0E	106.7E	96.5E	97.8E	132.1E	129.0E	131.9E	132.1E	131.9E
2000	118.9	104.1	98.9	99.1	94.2	94.6	148.3	106.9	104.9	94.4	95.7	129.4	125.2	129.4	129.9	129.7
1999	116.6	101.2	97.4	97.7	92.5	92.8	145.9	105.5	103.3	93.1	94.4	127.9	123.6	126.9	128.7	128.2
1998	113.6	96.2	94.0	94.8	90.3	89.8	143.8	102.1	101.0	90.6	91.4	125.2	120.3	123.9	125.8	124.7
1997	111.5	94.6	92.4	93.3	88.8	88.3	142.0	101.8	100.7	89.3	90.1	124.0	119.1	122.3	124.6	123.5
1996	108.9	90.9	91.4	92.3	87.5	86.5	140.4	98.3	97.4	86.5	86.7	121.7	117.2	120.2	122.4	121.5
1995	105.6	87.8	88.0	88.8	84.5	83.5	138.0	96.1	95.5	85.0	85.6	120.1	115.7	117.5	120.9	120.0
1994	103.0	85.9	86.1	86.8	82.6	81.7	134.0	93.7	93.1	82.4	83.9	118.1	113.6	114.5	119.0	117.5
1993	100.0	82.8	82.7	86.1	82.1	78.7	132.0	90.9	90.9	80.9	82.4	115.0	111.3	112.9	115.6	115.4
1992	97.9	81.7	81.5	84.9	80.9	77.6	128.6	88.8	89.4	79.7	81.2	113.5	108.1	110.3	113.7	113.7
1991	95.7	80.5	78.9	83.9	79.8	76.6	127.4	88.1	88.5	78.3	80.0	111.0	105.8	108.2	110.9	111.4
1990	93.2	79.4	77.6	82.7	78.4	75.2	125.8	86.4	87.0	77.1	77.9	107.7	102.7	103.3	107.5	107.4
1989	91.0	77.5	76.1	81.1	76.8	73.7	123.4	85.3	85.6	75.6	76.4	105.6	101.0	101.7	105.3	105.4
1988	88.5	75.7	74.7	79.7	75.4	72.3	121.4	84.4	84.3	74.2	75.0	102.7	97.6	99.2	102.6	102.3
1987	85.7	74.0	73.8	77.9	74.5	71.7	119.3	79.7	80.6	72.2	72.8	100.9	96.1	98.0	100.0	101.1
1986	83.7	72.8	71.7	76.7	72.3	69.4	117.3	78.9	78.8	70.7	72.3	99.2	94.2	93.8	97.8	100.4
1985	81.8	71.1	70.5	72.7	70.9	67.9	116.0	78.1	77.7	69.6	71.0	95.4	92.2	92.6	94.6	96.6
1984	80.6	69.7	69.0	75.2	69.4	66.3	113.8	79.4	79.2	69.1	70.3	93.4	89.8	90.6	92.1	94.0
1983	78.2	67.4	68.8	72.9	69.4	65.5	104.5	77.5	77.9	66.8	68.7	90.9	88.8	88.3	89.7	91.8
1982	72.1	63.5	63.1	67.3	64.4	61.8	96.1	72.3	71.7	62.2	64.6	83.1	83.0	82.5	80.9	83.4
1981	66.1	60.0	58.1	62.2	61.3	58.1	91.5	69.0	67.5	57.7	60.2	75.7	76.5	75.2	74.8	77.1
1980	60.7	55.2	54.1	56.8	56.8	54.0	91.4	63.7	62.4	53.1	55.8	68.7	69.4	68.7	67.4	69.9
1979	54.9	49.9	48.9	52.5	50.8	48.7	82.5	55.9	56.5	47.8	49.5	62.9	61.9	62.5	61.7	62.9
1978	51.3	46.7	45.5	48.8	46.9	45.0	75.3	51.9	52.3	44.8	45.4	57.4	57.1	57.7	57.0	58.6
1975	43.7	40.0	40.9	41.8	40.1	37.8	57.3	44.5	45.2	39.0	38.7	47.6	46.6	47.7	48.3	47.0
1970	27.8	24.1	25.1	25.8	25.4	24.2	43.0	27.2	28.5	24.3	22.3	31.0	30.8	31.1	29.0	31.0
1965	21.5	19.6	19.3	19.6	19.5	18.7	34.9	21.8	22.0	18.7	18.5	23.9	23.7	24.0	22.7	23.9
1960	19.5	17.9	17.5	17.8	17.7	16.9	31.7	19.9	20.0	17.0	16.8	21.7	21.5	21.8	20.6	21.7
1955	16.3	14.8	14.7	14.9	14.9	14.2	26.6	16.7	16.7	14.3	14.5	18.2	18.1	18.3	17.3	18.2
1950	13.5	12.2	12.1	12.3	12.3	11.7	21.9	13.8	13.8	11.8	11.6	15.1	15.0	15.1	14.3	15.1
1945	8.6	7.8	7.7	7.8	7.8	7.5	14.0	8.8	8.8	7.5	7.4	9.6	9.5	9.6	9.1	9.6
1940	6.6	6.0	6.0	6.1	6.0	5.8	10.8	6.8	6.8	5.8	5.7	7.4	7.4	7.4	7.0	7.4

Year	National 30 City Average	California Riverside	California Sacramento	California San Diego	California San Francisco	California Santa Barbara	California Stockton	California Vallejo	Colorado Colorado Springs	Colorado Denver	Colorado Pueblo	Connecticut Bridge-Port	Connecticut Bristol	Connecticut Hartford	Connecticut New Britain	Connecticut New Haven
Jan 2001	121.8E	131.5E	134.0E	129.5E	149.6E	130.9E	133.1E	140.2E	112.6E	116.1E	112.3E	128.2E	128.1E	128.4E	128.3E	128.6E
2000	118.9	128.0	131.5	127.1	146.9	128.7	130.7	137.1	109.8	111.8	108.8	122.7	122.6	122.9	122.4	122.7
1999	116.6	126.5	129.4	124.9	145.1	127.2	127.9	135.3	107.0	109.1	107.1	121.1	121.3	121.2	121.1	121.3
1998	113.6	123.7	125.9	121.3	141.9	123.7	124.7	132.5	103.3	106.5	103.7	119.1	119.4	120.0	119.7	120.0
1997	111.5	122.6	124.7	120.3	139.2	122.4	123.3	130.6	101.1	104.4	102.0	119.2	119.5	119.9	119.7	120.0
1996	108.9	120.6	122.4	118.4	136.8	120.5	121.4	128.1	98.5	101.4	99.7	117.4	117.6	117.9	117.8	118.1
1995	105.6	119.2	119.5	115.4	133.8	119.0	119.0	122.5	96.1	98.9	96.8	116.0	116.5	116.9	116.3	116.5
1994	103.0	116.6	114.8	113.4	131.4	116.4	115.5	119.7	94.2	95.9	94.6	114.3	115.0	115.3	114.7	114.8
1993	100.0	114.3	112.5	111.3	129.6	114.3	115.2	117.5	92.1	93.8	92.6	108.7	107.8	108.4	106.3	106.1
1992	97.9	111.8	110.8	109.5	127.9	112.2	112.7	115.2	90.6	91.5	90.9	106.7	106.0	106.6	104.5	104.4
1991	95.7	109.4	108.5	107.7	125.8	110.0	111.0	113.4	88.9	90.4	89.4	97.6	97.3	98.0	97.3	97.9
1990	93.2	107.0	104.9	105.6	121.8	106.4	105.4	111.4	86.9	88.8	88.8	96.3	95.9	96.6	95.9	96.5
1989	91.0	105.2	103.1	103.6	119.2	104.6	103.7	109.8	85.6	88.7	87.4	94.5	94.2	94.9	94.2	94.6
1988	88.5	102.6	100.5	101.0	115.2	101.4	101.2	107.2	83.8	87.0	85.6	92.8	92.6	93.3	92.6	93.0
1987	85.7	100.3	98.7	99.0	111.0	99.3	99.6	103.2	81.6	84.8	83.8	92.4	93.0	93.3	93.0	92.6
1986	83.7	98.6	94.4	96.9	108.0	97.0	96.1	99.1	81.9	83.1	82.7	88.5	88.7	89.4	88.6	88.8
1985	81.8	94.8	92.2	94.2	106.2	93.2	93.7	97.0	79.6	81.0	80.4	86.1	86.2	87.2	86.1	86.3
1984	80.6	91.8	93.8	92.0	102.8	90.6	91.9	95.6	79.8	84.1	80.5	83.5	83.4	84.4	83.0	83.2
1983	78.2	89.4	92.0	90.3	101.0	88.8	91.0	93.0	77.3	80.5	77.4	79.6	79.9	81.1	79.5	79.3
1982	72.1	82.1	84.9	83.8	91.9	81.8	84.9	85.7	71.2	73.4	75.0	71.9	71.2	73.2	71.4	72.0
1981	66.1	75.5	77.7	74.5	82.8	75.9	77.4	78.5	65.5	66.3	65.4	67.0	66.3	67.3	66.3	67.0
1980	60.7	68.7	71.3	68.1	75.2	71.1	71.2	71.9	60.7	60.9	59.5	61.5	60.7	61.9	60.7	61.4
1979	54.9	62.2	64.0	61.6	67.5	65.0	64.2	65.2	54.9	56.0	54.0	56.0	55.3	56.4	55.4	55.8
1978	51.3	57.7	60.0	58.3	62.6	59.2	59.5	59.9	51.1	52.0	50.6	52.5	50.9	51.9	51.8	52.0
1975	43.7	47.3	49.1	47.7	49.8	46.1	47.6	46.5	43.1	42.7	42.5	45.2	45.5	46.0	45.2	46.0
1970	27.8	31.0	32.1	30.7	31.6	31.3	31.8	31.8	27.6	26.1	27.3	29.2	28.2	29.6	28.2	29.3
1965	21.5	23.9	24.8	24.0	23.7	24.1	24.5	24.5	21.3	20.9	21.0	22.4	21.7	22.6	21.7	23.2
1960	19.5	21.7	22.5	21.7	21.5	21.9	22.3	22.2	19.3	19.0	19.1	20.0	19.8	20.0	19.8	20.0
1955	16.3	18.2	18.9	18.2	18.0	18.4	18.7	18.6	16.2	15.9	16.0	16.8	16.6	16.8	16.6	16.8
1950	13.5	15.0	15.6	15.0	14.9	15.2	15.4	15.4	13.4	13.2	13.2	13.9	13.7	13.8	13.7	13.9
1945	8.6	9.6	10.0	9.6	9.5	9.7	9.9	9.8	8.5	8.4	8.4	8.8	8.7	8.8	8.7	8.9
1940	6.6	7.4	7.7	7.4	7.3	7.5	7.6	7.6	6.6	6.5	6.5	6.8	6.8	6.8	6.8	6.8

Historical Cost Indexes

Year	National 30 City Average	Connecticut Norwalk	Stamford	Waterbury	Delaware Wilmington	D.C. Washington	Florida Fort Lauderdale	Jacksonville	Miami	Orlando	Tallahassee	Tampa	Georgia Albany	Atlanta	Columbus	Macon
Jan 2001	121.8E	128.1E	131.6E	128.7E	122.7E	115.6E	104.8E	101.0E	104.9E	104.4E	95.4E	101.0E	96.9E	108.8E	96.0E	99.1E
2000	118.9	121.5	126.4	123.2	117.4	113.8	102.4	99.0	101.8	101.2	93.6	98.9	94.9	106.1	94.1	97.0
1999	116.6	120.0	122.0	121.2	116.6	111.5	101.4	98.0	100.8	100.1	92.5	97.9	93.5	102.9	92.8	95.8
1998	113.6	118.8	120.8	120.1	112.3	109.6	99.4	96.2	99.0	98.4	90.9	96.3	91.4	100.8	90.4	93.3
1997	111.5	118.9	120.9	120.2	110.7	106.4	98.6	95.4	98.2	97.2	89.9	95.5	89.9	98.5	88.7	91.6
1996	108.9	117.0	119.0	118.4	108.6	105.4	95.9	92.6	95.9	95.1	88.0	93.6	86.6	94.3	83.9	88.3
1995	105.6	115.5	117.9	117.3	106.1	102.3	94.0	90.9	93.7	93.5	86.5	92.2	85.0	92.0	82.6	86.8
1994	103.0	113.9	116.4	115.8	105.0	99.6	92.2	88.9	91.8	91.5	84.5	90.2	82.3	89.6	80.6	83.7
1993	100.0	108.8	110.6	104.8	101.5	96.3	87.4	86.1	87.1	88.5	82.1	87.7	79.5	85.7	77.8	80.9
1992	97.9	107.2	109.0	103.1	100.3	94.7	85.7	84.0	85.3	87.1	80.8	86.2	78.2	84.3	76.5	79.6
1991	95.7	100.6	103.2	96.5	94.5	92.9	85.1	82.8	85.2	85.5	79.7	86.3	76.3	82.6	75.4	78.4
1990	93.2	96.3	98.9	95.1	92.5	90.4	83.9	81.1	84.0	82.9	78.4	85.0	75.0	80.4	74.0	76.9
1989	91.0	94.4	97.0	93.4	89.5	87.5	82.4	79.7	82.5	81.6	76.9	83.5	73.4	78.6	72.4	75.3
1988	88.5	92.3	94.9	91.8	87.7	85.0	80.9	78.0	81.0	80.1	75.4	81.9	71.8	76.9	70.8	73.6
1987	85.7	92.0	92.7	92.5	85.1	82.1	78.8	76.0	77.9	76.6	74.4	79.4	72.2	73.6	70.3	72.3
1986	83.7	88.2	89.7	87.8	83.8	80.8	78.9	75.0	79.9	76.2	72.3	79.1	68.5	72.0	67.5	69.8
1985	81.8	85.3	86.8	85.6	81.1	78.8	76.7	73.4	78.3	73.9	70.6	77.3	66.9	70.3	66.1	68.1
1984	80.6	82.6	83.7	82.5	79.7	79.1	73.8	72.6	75.6	73.0	69.6	76.5	65.9	68.6	65.2	67.5
1983	78.2	78.5	79.8	78.7	76.3	76.0	71.5	70.4	72.9	71.1	67.6	73.6	65.6	68.6	64.7	65.3
1982	72.1	71.7	72.0	71.8	69.1	69.4	65.4	65.2	65.7	66.0	62.8	67.7	60.1	61.9	59.3	60.0
1981	66.1	66.2	66.2	67.3	63.4	64.9	60.3	61.0	60.7	62.0	58.6	62.1	56.2	58.3	55.7	56.1
1980	60.7	60.7	60.9	62.3	58.5	59.6	55.3	55.8	56.5	56.7	53.5	57.2	51.7	54.0	51.1	51.3
1979	54.9	55.2	55.6	57.0	53.6	53.9	50.0	51.7	50.8	51.8	48.9	51.8	46.5	48.3	46.1	46.4
1978	51.3	51.5	51.6	52.9	50.0	51.5	47.0	47.7	47.6	48.0	45.4	48.4	42.7	45.0	42.5	42.4
1975	43.7	44.7	45.0	46.3	42.9	43.7	42.1	40.3	43.2	41.5	38.1	41.3	37.5	38.4	36.2	36.5
1970	27.8	28.1	28.2	28.9	27.0	26.3	25.7	22.8	27.0	26.2	24.5	24.2	23.8	25.2	22.8	23.4
1965	21.5	21.6	21.7	22.2	20.9	21.8	19.8	17.4	19.3	20.2	18.9	18.6	18.3	19.8	17.6	18.0
1960	19.5	19.7	19.7	20.2	18.9	19.4	18.0	15.8	17.6	18.3	17.2	16.9	16.7	17.1	16.0	16.4
1955	16.3	16.5	16.5	17.0	15.9	16.3	15.1	13.2	14.7	15.4	14.4	14.1	14.0	14.4	13.4	13.7
1950	13.5	13.6	13.7	14.0	13.1	13.4	12.5	11.0	12.2	12.7	11.9	11.7	11.5	11.9	11.0	11.3
1945	8.6	8.7	8.7	8.9	8.4	8.6	7.9	7.0	7.8	8.1	7.6	7.5	7.4	7.6	7.0	7.2
1940	6.6	6.7	6.7	6.9	6.4	6.6	6.1	5.4	6.0	6.2	5.8	5.7	5.7	5.8	5.5	5.6

Year	National 30 City Average	Georgia Savannah	Hawaii Honolulu	Idaho Boise	Pocatello	Illinois Chicago	Decatur	Joliet	Peoria	Rockford	Springfield	Indiana Anderson	Evansville	Fort Wayne	Gary	Indianapolis
Jan 2001	121.8E	99.6E	149.6E	114.5E	113.7E	135.9E	118.2E	129.7E	123.2E	126.7E	119.6E	112.8E	115.4E	111.1E	122.8E	115.8E
2000	118.9	97.5	144.8	112.9	112.1	131.2	115.1	124.6	119.0	122.2	116.2	109.8	111.5	108.4	117.8	113.2
1999	116.6	96.0	143.0	110.2	109.6	129.6	113.0	122.6	116.4	120.7	113.8	107.1	109.3	106.8	112.8	110.6
1998	113.6	93.7	140.4	107.4	107.0	125.2	110.1	119.8	113.8	115.5	111.1	105.0	107.2	104.5	111.1	108.0
1997	111.5	92.0	139.8	104.6	104.7	121.3	107.8	117.5	111.5	113.1	108.9	101.9	104.4	101.8	110.3	105.2
1996	108.9	88.6	134.5	102.2	102.1	118.8	106.6	116.2	109.3	111.5	106.5	100.0	102.1	99.9	107.5	102.7
1995	105.6	87.4	130.3	99.5	98.2	114.2	98.5	110.5	102.3	103.6	98.1	96.4	97.2	95.0	100.7	100.1
1994	103.0	85.3	124.0	94.8	95.0	111.3	97.3	108.9	100.9	102.2	97.0	93.6	95.8	93.6	99.1	97.1
1993	100.0	82.0	122.0	92.2	92.1	107.6	95.6	106.8	98.9	99.6	95.2	91.2	94.3	91.5	96.7	93.9
1992	97.9	80.8	120.0	91.0	91.0	104.3	94.4	104.2	97.3	98.2	94.0	89.5	92.9	89.9	95.0	91.5
1991	95.7	79.5	106.1	89.5	89.4	100.9	92.3	100.0	95.9	95.8	91.5	87.8	91.4	88.3	93.3	89.1
1990	93.2	77.9	104.7	88.2	88.1	98.4	90.9	98.4	93.7	94.0	90.1	84.6	89.3	83.4	88.4	87.1
1989	91.0	76.0	102.8	86.6	86.5	93.7	89.4	92.8	91.6	92.1	88.6	82.3	87.8	81.7	86.5	85.1
1988	88.5	74.5	101.1	83.9	83.7	90.6	87.5	89.8	88.5	87.9	86.8	80.8	85.5	80.0	84.6	83.1
1987	85.7	72.0	99.1	81.4	81.5	86.6	84.4	86.7	86.3	85.2	85.0	78.8	82.4	78.1	81.7	80.4
1986	83.7	70.8	97.5	80.6	80.3	84.4	83.5	85.3	85.1	84.5	83.4	77.0	80.9	76.5	79.6	78.6
1985	81.8	68.9	94.7	78.0	78.0	82.4	81.9	83.4	83.7	83.0	81.5	75.2	79.8	75.0	77.8	77.1
1984	80.6	67.9	90.7	76.6	76.8	80.2	80.4	82.2	83.6	80.6	80.1	73.5	77.4	73.5	77.3	75.9
1983	78.2	66.3	87.2	76.0	75.8	79.0	78.8	80.6	81.5	78.9	78.8	70.9	75.0	71.2	75.2	74.0
1982	72.1	61.1	79.3	71.0	70.1	75.0	72.7	74.4	75.3	72.6	72.7	66.4	69.8	67.1	70.5	68.2
1981	66.1	57.1	73.4	65.4	64.8	68.6	67.2	68.8	70.3	67.3	67.0	61.5	64.3	61.5	65.3	62.4
1980	60.7	52.2	68.9	60.3	59.5	62.8	62.3	63.4	64.5	61.6	61.1	56.5	59.0	56.7	59.8	57.9
1979	54.9	47.2	63.0	54.4	53.7	56.5	56.0	57.0	58.4	54.8	55.6	50.8	53.3	51.2	54.0	51.9
1978	51.3	43.6	58.9	50.0	49.9	52.9	51.9	52.7	53.8	50.4	51.5	46.7	49.1	46.9	49.4	48.7
1975	43.7	36.9	44.6	40.8	40.5	45.7	43.1	44.5	44.7	42.7	42.4	39.5	41.7	39.9	41.9	40.6
1970	27.8	21.0	30.4	26.7	26.6	29.1	28.0	28.6	29.0	27.5	27.6	25.4	26.4	25.5	27.1	26.2
1965	21.5	16.4	21.8	20.6	20.5	22.7	21.5	22.1	22.4	21.2	21.3	19.5	20.4	19.7	20.8	20.7
1960	19.5	14.9	19.8	18.7	18.6	20.2	19.6	20.0	20.3	19.2	19.3	17.7	18.7	17.9	18.9	18.4
1955	16.3	12.5	16.6	15.7	15.6	16.9	16.4	16.8	17.0	16.1	16.2	14.9	15.7	15.0	15.9	15.5
1950	13.5	10.3	13.7	13.0	12.9	14.0	13.6	13.9	14.0	13.3	13.4	12.3	12.9	12.4	13.1	12.8
1945	8.6	6.6	8.8	8.3	8.2	8.9	8.6	8.9	9.0	8.5	8.6	7.8	8.3	7.9	8.4	8.1
1940	6.6	5.1	6.8	6.4	6.3	6.9	6.7	6.8	6.9	6.5	6.6	6.0	6.4	6.1	6.5	6.3

Year	National 30 City Average	Indiana Muncie	Indiana South Bend	Indiana Terre Haute	Iowa Cedar Rapids	Iowa Daven-port	Iowa Des Moines	Iowa Sioux City	Iowa Water-loo	Kansas Topeka	Kansas Wichita	Kentucky Lexing-ton	Kentucky Louis-ville	Louisiana Baton Rouge	Louisiana Lake Charles	Louisiana New Orleans
Jan 2001	121.8E	112.0E	111.4E	115.2E	111.6E	117.3E	112.8E	108.0E	100.9E	103.1E	105.1E	103.6E	112.0E	99.6E	101.4E	104.3E
2000	118.9	109.1	106.9	110.8	108.8	112.6	108.9	99.0	98.1	101.0	101.1	101.4	109.3	97.8	99.7	102.1
1999	116.6	105.7	103.7	107.9	104.1	109.2	107.6	96.7	96.4	98.7	99.3	99.7	106.6	96.1	97.6	99.5
1998	113.6	103.6	102.3	106.0	102.5	106.8	103.8	95.1	94.8	97.4	97.4	97.4	101.5	94.7	96.1	97.7
1997	111.5	101.3	101.2	104.6	101.2	105.6	102.5	93.8	93.5	96.3	96.2	96.1	99.9	93.3	96.8	96.2
1996	108.9	99.4	99.1	102.1	99.1	102.0	99.1	90.9	90.7	93.6	93.8	94.4	98.3	91.5	94.9	94.3
1995	105.6	95.6	94.6	97.2	95.4	96.6	94.4	88.2	88.9	91.1	91.0	91.6	94.6	89.6	92.7	91.6
1994	103.0	93.2	93.0	95.8	93.0	92.3	92.4	85.9	86.8	89.4	88.1	89.6	92.2	87.7	89.9	89.5
1993	100.0	91.0	90.7	94.4	91.1	90.5	90.7	84.1	85.2	87.4	86.2	87.3	89.4	86.4	88.5	87.8
1992	97.9	89.4	89.3	93.1	89.8	89.3	89.4	82.9	83.8	86.2	85.0	85.8	88.0	85.2	87.3	86.6
1991	95.7	87.7	87.5	91.7	88.5	88.0	88.4	81.8	81.6	84.4	83.9	84.1	84.4	83.2	85.3	85.8
1990	93.2	83.9	85.1	89.1	87.1	86.5	86.9	80.4	80.3	83.2	82.6	82.8	82.6	82.0	84.1	84.5
1989	91.0	81.9	83.5	86.7	85.3	84.9	85.3	79.0	78.8	81.6	81.2	81.3	80.1	80.6	82.7	83.4
1988	88.5	80.4	82.1	84.9	83.4	83.1	83.6	76.8	77.2	80.1	79.5	79.4	78.2	79.0	81.1	82.0
1987	85.7	78.5	79.6	83.0	82.4	81.1	81.2	75.4	75.6	78.9	78.4	77.3	76.3	77.1	78.0	81.3
1986	83.7	76.9	77.5	81.1	79.5	80.0	79.8	73.8	73.7	76.9	76.2	76.5	75.3	76.1	78.1	79.2
1985	81.8	75.2	76.0	79.2	75.9	77.6	77.1	72.1	72.3	75.0	74.7	75.5	74.5	74.9	78.5	78.2
1984	80.6	73.6	75.1	78.0	80.3	77.8	76.6	74.4	73.7	75.1	74.6	75.6	73.7	77.3	78.3	77.5
1983	78.2	71.2	74.5	76.1	79.6	77.0	75.5	74.6	73.0	73.2	72.4	74.9	74.1	75.1	76.6	74.7
1982	72.1	66.0	68.3	69.9	73.5	71.7	71.1	70.1	67.7	68.4	66.1	69.4	69.2	69.3	70.5	69.2
1981	66.1	61.0	63.1	65.1	68.6	66.7	67.1	65.5	63.5	63.0	62.2	64.7	65.1	64.0	64.8	62.7
1980	60.7	56.1	58.3	59.7	62.7	59.6	61.8	59.3	57.7	58.9	58.0	59.3	59.8	59.1	60.0	57.2
1979	54.9	50.7	52.6	54.0	56.6	54.1	55.6	53.6	52.0	53.5	52.9	53.2	54.5	53.5	54.5	52.6
1978	51.3	46.8	48.2	49.9	52.3	50.0	51.1	49.2	48.1	50.0	48.9	49.2	50.0	49.2	50.2	48.5
1975	43.7	39.2	40.3	41.9	43.1	41.0	43.1	41.0	40.0	42.0	43.1	42.7	42.5	40.4	40.6	41.5
1970	27.8	25.3	26.2	27.0	28.2	26.9	27.6	26.6	25.9	27.0	25.5	26.9	25.9	25.0	26.7	27.2
1965	21.5	19.5	20.2	20.9	21.7	20.8	21.7	20.5	20.0	20.8	19.6	20.7	20.3	19.4	20.6	20.4
1960	19.5	17.8	18.3	18.9	19.7	18.8	19.5	18.6	18.2	18.9	17.8	18.8	18.4	17.6	18.7	18.5
1955	16.3	14.9	15.4	15.9	16.6	15.8	16.3	15.6	15.2	15.8	15.0	15.8	15.4	14.8	15.7	15.6
1950	13.5	12.3	12.7	13.1	13.7	13.1	13.5	12.9	12.6	13.1	12.4	13.0	12.8	12.2	13.0	12.8
1945	8.6	7.8	8.1	8.4	8.7	8.3	8.6	8.2	8.0	8.3	7.9	8.3	8.1	7.8	8.3	8.2
1940	6.6	6.0	6.3	6.5	6.7	6.4	6.6	6.3	6.2	6.4	6.1	6.4	6.3	6.0	6.4	6.3

Year	National 30 City Average	Louisiana Shreve-port	Maine Lewis-ton	Maine Portland	Maryland Balti-more	Massachusetts Boston	Massachusetts Brockton	Massachusetts Fall River	Massachusetts Law-rence	Massachusetts Lowell	Massachusetts New Bedford	Massachusetts Pitts-field	Massachusetts Spring-field	Massachusetts Wor-cester	Michigan Ann Arbor	Michigan Dear-born
Jan 2001	121.8E	98.2E	109.8E	109.6E	112.1E	140.5E	132.0E	130.8E	132.2E	132.1E	130.7E	119.8E	124.0E	129.6E	126.7E	130.0E
2000	118.9	96.2	105.7	105.4	107.7	138.9	129.4	128.4	129.7	130.3	128.3	116.7	121.0	127.3	124.3	125.8
1999	116.6	94.8	105.0	104.7	106.4	136.2	126.7	126.3	127.3	127.4	126.2	115.0	118.8	123.8	117.5	122.7
1998	113.6	92.0	102.8	102.5	104.1	132.8	125.0	124.7	125.0	125.3	124.6	114.2	117.1	122.6	116.0	119.7
1997	111.5	90.1	101.7	101.4	102.2	132.1	124.4	124.7	125.1	125.6	124.7	114.6	117.4	122.9	113.5	117.9
1996	108.9	88.5	99.5	99.2	99.6	128.7	121.6	122.2	121.7	122.1	122.2	112.7	115.0	120.2	112.9	116.2
1995	105.6	86.7	96.8	96.5	96.1	128.6	119.6	117.7	120.5	119.6	117.2	110.7	112.7	114.8	106.1	110.5
1994	103.0	85.0	95.2	94.9	94.4	124.9	114.2	113.7	116.8	116.9	111.6	109.2	111.1	112.9	105.0	109.0
1993	100.0	83.6	93.0	93.0	93.1	121.1	111.7	111.5	114.9	114.3	109.4	107.1	108.9	110.3	102.8	105.8
1992	97.9	82.3	91.7	91.7	90.9	118.0	110.0	109.8	110.9	110.2	107.7	105.7	107.2	108.6	101.5	103.2
1991	95.7	81.6	89.8	89.9	89.1	115.2	105.9	104.7	107.3	105.5	105.1	100.6	103.2	105.7	95.1	98.3
1990	93.2	80.3	88.5	88.6	85.6	110.9	103.7	102.9	105.2	102.8	102.6	98.7	101.4	103.2	93.2	96.5
1989	91.0	78.8	86.7	86.7	83.5	107.2	100.4	99.7	102.9	99.7	99.8	94.7	96.4	99.1	89.6	94.6
1988	88.5	77.0	84.0	84.1	81.2	102.5	96.7	96.4	97.7	96.6	96.4	91.9	92.7	94.4	85.8	91.4
1987	85.7	74.5	81.3	81.4	78.6	97.3	94.5	94.8	94.9	94.8	95.0	89.4	90.5	92.2	87.4	88.7
1986	83.7	74.1	79.0	79.0	75.7	95.1	91.2	90.8	92.5	90.8	90.7	87.1	87.8	89.8	81.7	85.3
1985	81.8	73.6	76.7	77.0	72.7	92.8	88.8	88.7	89.4	88.2	88.6	85.0	85.6	86.7	80.1	82.7
1984	80.6	73.3	75.0	75.1	72.4	88.1	85.5	85.8	86.8	84.1	84.8	82.8	83.5	83.6	78.9	81.1
1983	78.2	72.2	73.1	72.9	70.6	84.0	82.5	82.2	82.7	80.9	81.3	79.5	80.6	81.3	77.7	79.4
1982	72.1	67.0	67.4	67.4	64.7	76.9	75.7	75.0	74.5	73.6	74.2	72.3	73.7	73.1	73.7	75.8
1981	66.1	62.5	62.2	63.1	59.0	67.8	68.7	69.2	68.4	67.1	68.7	66.3	67.0	66.7	68.6	70.1
1980	60.7	58.7	57.3	58.5	53.6	64.0	63.7	64.1	63.4	62.7	63.1	61.8	62.0	62.3	62.9	64.0
1979	54.9	53.1	52.3	52.6	48.2	57.9	58.0	57.5	57.3	57.0	57.4	56.2	55.9	56.0	57.0	57.8
1978	51.3	49.2	48.6	48.8	45.9	54.0	53.4	53.3	53.5	53.1	53.2	52.6	52.3	52.2	52.5	54.1
1975	43.7	40.5	41.9	42.1	39.8	46.6	45.8	45.7	46.2	45.7	46.1	45.5	45.8	46.0	44.1	44.9
1970	27.8	26.4	26.5	25.8	25.1	29.2	29.1	29.2	29.1	28.9	29.0	28.6	28.5	28.7	28.5	28.9
1965	21.5	20.3	20.4	19.4	20.2	23.0	22.5	22.5	22.5	22.2	22.4	22.0	22.4	22.1	22.0	22.3
1960	19.5	18.5	18.6	17.6	17.5	20.5	20.4	20.4	20.4	20.2	20.3	20.0	20.1	20.1	20.0	20.2
1955	16.3	15.5	15.6	14.7	14.7	17.2	17.1	17.1	17.1	16.9	17.1	16.8	16.9	16.8	16.7	16.9
1950	13.5	12.8	12.9	12.2	12.1	14.2	14.1	14.1	14.1	14.0	14.1	13.8	14.0	13.9	13.8	14.0
1945	8.6	8.1	8.2	7.8	7.7	9.1	9.0	9.0	9.0	8.9	9.0	8.9	8.9	8.9	8.8	8.9
1940	6.6	6.3	6.3	6.0	6.0	7.0	6.9	7.0	7.0	6.9	6.9	6.8	6.9	6.8	6.8	6.9

Historical Cost Indexes

Year	National 30 City Average	Michigan						Minnesota			Mississippi		Missouri			
		Detroit	Flint	Grand Rapids	Kala-mazoo	Lansing	Sagi-naw	Duluth	Minne-apolis	Roches-ter	Biloxi	Jackson	Kansas City	St. Joseph	St. Louis	Spring-field
Jan 2001	121.8E	129.5E	122.2E	104.7E	113.8E	119.8E	118.1E	130.6E	136.1E	125.3E	99.0E	94.5E	122.1E	114.1E	126.0E	106.7E
2000	118.9	125.3	119.8	102.7	111.6	117.6	115.9	124.1	131.1	120.1	97.2	92.9	118.2	111.9	122.4	104.3
1999	116.6	122.6	113.7	100.9	106.1	111.5	110.1	120.3	126.5	117.1	95.7	91.8	114.9	106.1	119.8	101.1
1998	113.6	119.5	112.3	99.7	104.9	110.1	108.7	117.7	124.6	115.5	92.1	89.5	108.2	104.2	115.9	98.9
1997	111.5	117.6	110.8	98.9	104.2	108.7	107.5	115.9	121.9	114.1	90.9	88.3	106.4	102.4	113.2	97.3
1996	108.9	116.0	109.7	93.9	103.5	107.8	106.9	115.0	120.4	113.5	87.1	85.4	103.2	99.9	110.1	94.6
1995	105.6	110.1	104.1	91.1	96.4	98.3	102.3	100.3	111.9	102.5	84.2	83.5	99.7	96.1	106.3	89.5
1994	103.0	108.5	102.9	89.7	95.0	97.1	101.1	99.1	109.3	101.1	82.4	81.7	97.3	92.8	103.2	88.2
1993	100.0	105.4	100.7	87.7	92.7	95.3	98.8	99.8	106.7	99.9	80.0	79.4	94.5	90.9	99.9	86.2
1992	97.9	102.9	99.4	86.4	91.4	94.0	97.4	98.5	105.3	98.6	78.8	78.2	92.9	89.5	98.6	84.9
1991	95.7	97.6	93.6	85.3	90.0	92.1	90.3	96.0	102.9	97.3	77.6	76.9	90.9	88.1	96.4	83.9
1990	93.2	96.0	91.7	84.0	87.4	90.2	88.9	94.3	100.5	95.6	76.4	75.6	89.5	86.8	94.0	82.6
1989	91.0	94.0	90.2	82.4	85.8	88.6	87.4	92.5	97.4	93.7	75.0	74.1	87.3	85.1	91.8	80.9
1988	88.5	90.8	87.8	80.7	84.1	86.3	85.6	90.5	94.6	91.9	73.5	72.9	84.9	82.9	89.0	79.2
1987	85.7	87.8	85.4	79.7	82.6	85.2	84.5	88.5	92.0	90.6	72.4	71.3	81.7	82.7	85.5	78.2
1986	83.7	84.3	82.8	77.5	80.9	82.7	81.5	87.2	89.7	88.4	70.6	69.9	79.9	79.4	83.5	75.6
1985	81.8	81.6	80.7	75.8	79.4	80.0	80.5	85.2	87.9	86.5	69.4	68.5	78.2	77.3	80.8	73.2
1984	80.6	79.4	79.5	74.3	78.7	79.0	79.9	84.9	86.9	86.0	68.6	67.5	77.7	76.7	77.7	72.7
1983	78.2	77.0	77.4	74.1	76.2	77.1	78.0	81.6	81.4	82.6	68.0	67.3	76.2	76.8	76.2	71.6
1982	72.1	74.8	73.5	69.9	72.3	73.2	73.7	74.6	75.2	75.6	63.1	62.6	70.2	70.3	69.2	66.5
1981	66.1	68.6	68.2	64.6	67.1	67.5	68.5	68.8	69.6	69.8	58.7	59.1	63.5	65.7	64.5	61.4
1980	60.7	62.5	63.1	59.8	61.7	60.3	63.3	63.4	64.1	64.8	54.3	54.3	59.1	60.4	59.7	56.7
1979	54.9	56.2	56.4	53.7	55.5	55.8	56.8	59.2	58.5	58.7	49.3	49.3	54.4	54.6	54.9	51.3
1978	51.3	52.6	52.0	49.1	51.7	51.4	53.2	53.1	54.1	53.3	45.0	45.8	50.1	51.4	51.1	47.9
1975	43.7	45.8	44.9	41.8	43.7	44.1	44.8	45.2	46.0	45.3	37.9	37.7	42.7	45.4	44.8	41.1
1970	27.8	29.7	28.5	26.7	28.1	27.8	28.7	28.9	29.5	28.9	24.4	21.3	25.3	28.3	28.4	26.0
1965	21.5	22.1	21.9	20.6	21.7	21.5	22.2	22.3	23.4	22.3	18.8	16.4	20.6	21.8	21.8	20.0
1960	19.5	20.1	20.0	18.7	19.7	19.5	20.1	20.3	20.5	20.2	17.1	14.9	19.0	19.8	19.5	18.2
1955	16.3	16.8	16.7	15.7	16.5	16.3	16.9	17.0	17.2	17.0	14.3	12.5	16.0	16.6	16.3	15.2
1950	13.5	13.9	13.8	13.0	13.6	13.5	13.9	14.0	14.2	14.0	11.8	10.3	13.2	13.7	13.5	12.6
1945	8.6	8.9	8.8	8.3	8.7	8.6	8.9	8.9	9.0	8.9	7.6	6.6	8.4	8.8	8.6	8.0
1940	6.6	6.8	6.8	6.4	6.7	6.6	6.9	6.9	7.0	6.9	5.8	5.1	6.5	6.7	6.7	6.2

Year	National 30 City Average	Montana		Nebraska		Nevada		New Hamphire		New Jersey					NM	NY
		Billings	Great Falls	Lincoln	Omaha	Las Vegas	Reno	Man-chester	Nashua	Camden	Jersey City	Newark	Pater-son	Trenton	Albu-querque	Albany
Jan 2001	121.8E	116.9E	117.4E	101.4E	110.5E	128.0E	121.1E	114.5E	114.5E	132.4E	136.5E	137.0E	136.8E	135.3E	111.2E	118.5E
2000	118.9	113.7	113.9	98.8	107.0	125.8	118.2	111.9	111.9	128.4	130.5	132.6	132.4	130.6	109.0	116.5
1999	116.6	112.1	112.7	96.6	104.8	121.9	114.4	109.6	109.6	125.3	128.8	131.6	129.5	129.6	106.7	114.6
1998	113.6	109.7	109.1	94.9	101.2	118.1	111.4	110.1	110.0	124.3	127.7	128.9	128.5	127.9	103.8	113.0
1997	111.5	107.4	107.6	93.3	99.5	114.6	109.8	108.6	108.6	121.9	125.1	126.4	126.4	125.2	100.8	110.0
1996	108.9	108.0	107.5	91.4	97.4	111.8	108.9	106.5	106.4	119.1	122.5	122.5	123.8	121.8	98.6	108.3
1995	105.6	104.7	104.9	85.6	93.4	108.5	105.0	100.9	100.8	107.0	112.2	111.9	112.1	111.2	96.3	103.6
1994	103.0	100.2	100.7	84.3	91.0	105.3	102.2	97.8	97.7	105.4	110.6	110.1	110.6	108.2	93.4	102.4
1993	100.0	97.9	97.8	82.3	88.7	102.8	99.9	95.4	95.4	103.7	109.0	108.2	109.0	106.4	90.1	99.8
1992	97.9	95.5	96.4	81.1	87.4	99.4	98.4	90.4	90.4	102.0	107.5	107.0	107.8	103.9	87.5	98.5
1991	95.7	94.2	95.1	80.1	86.4	97.5	95.8	87.8	87.8	95.0	98.5	95.6	100.0	96.6	86.2	96.1
1990	93.2	92.9	93.8	78.8	85.0	96.3	94.5	86.3	86.3	93.0	93.5	93.8	97.2	94.5	84.9	93.2
1989	91.0	91.3	92.2	77.3	83.6	94.8	92.3	84.8	84.8	90.4	91.4	91.8	95.5	91.9	83.3	88.4
1988	88.5	89.5	90.4	75.8	82.0	93.0	90.5	83.2	83.2	87.7	89.5	89.7	92.5	89.5	81.7	86.8
1987	85.7	85.4	87.3	75.3	79.8	91.5	88.3	82.4	82.5	86.1	88.3	88.7	90.3	87.9	78.1	84.5
1986	83.7	86.2	87.3	72.6	78.8	90.1	87.2	79.7	79.7	84.6	86.1	86.7	87.8	86.1	78.9	81.7
1985	81.8	83.9	84.3	71.5	77.5	87.6	85.0	78.1	78.1	81.3	83.3	83.5	84.5	82.8	76.7	79.5
1984	80.6	83.2	82.9	70.9	77.6	85.9	83.3	76.4	75.5	78.2	80.3	80.1	81.3	78.5	75.9	77.3
1983	78.2	80.3	80.0	72.1	77.3	83.0	81.9	73.0	72.2	74.6	76.5	76.7	76.5	74.2	73.1	74.2
1982	72.1	74.3	74.1	67.8	72.5	76.9	75.8	67.0	66.7	67.9	69.8	70.4	70.1	69.1	67.1	69.2
1981	66.1	69.5	70.3	64.1	68.2	70.2	68.5	61.5	61.1	62.5	65.0	65.1	64.8	63.4	63.3	64.4
1980	60.7	63.9	64.6	58.5	63.5	64.6	63.0	56.6	56.0	58.6	60.6	60.1	60.0	58.9	59.0	59.5
1979	54.9	57.5	58.9	52.9	56.2	58.4	56.7	51.2	50.8	53.5	55.6	55.3	54.7	54.0	54.3	54.2
1978	51.3	53.4	54.0	49.3	52.2	53.9	51.9	47.5	47.1	50.1	51.7	51.4	51.7	50.8	49.8	50.6
1975	43.7	43.1	43.8	40.9	43.2	42.8	41.9	41.3	40.8	42.3	43.4	44.2	43.9	43.8	40.3	43.9
1970	27.8	28.5	28.9	26.4	26.8	29.4	28.0	26.2	25.6	27.2	27.8	29.0	27.8	27.4	26.4	28.3
1965	21.5	22.0	22.3	20.3	20.6	22.4	21.6	20.6	19.7	20.9	21.4	23.8	21.4	21.3	20.6	22.3
1960	19.5	20.0	20.3	18.5	18.7	20.2	19.6	18.0	17.9	19.0	19.4	19.4	19.4	19.2	18.5	19.3
1955	16.3	16.7	17.0	15.5	15.7	16.9	16.4	15.1	15.0	16.0	16.3	16.3	16.3	16.1	15.6	16.2
1950	13.5	13.9	14.0	12.8	13.0	14.0	13.6	12.5	12.4	13.2	13.5	13.5	13.5	13.3	12.9	13.4
1945	8.6	8.8	9.0	8.1	8.3	8.9	8.7	8.0	7.9	8.4	8.6	8.6	8.6	8.5	8.2	8.5
1940	6.6	6.8	6.9	6.3	6.4	6.9	6.7	6.2	6.1	6.5	6.6	6.6	6.6	6.6	6.3	6.6

Historical Cost Indexes

Year	National 30 City Average	New York Binghamton	Buffalo	New York	Rochester	Schenectady	Syracuse	Utica	Yonkers	North Carolina Charlotte	Durham	Greensboro	Raleigh	Winston-Salem	N. Dakota Fargo	Ohio Akron
Jan 2001	121.8E	114.3E	124.6E	164.0E	122.3E	119.5E	117.2E	114.4E	147.0E	91.8E	93.1E	93.1E	93.4E	92.5E	101.9E	122.3E
2000	118.9	112.4	122.3	159.2	120.0	117.5	115.1	112.4	144.8	90.3	91.6	91.6	91.9	91.0	97.9	117.8
1999	116.6	108.6	120.2	155.9	116.8	114.7	113.7	108.5	140.6	89.3	90.2	90.3	90.5	90.1	96.8	116.0
1998	113.6	109.0	119.1	154.4	117.2	114.2	113.6	108.6	141.4	88.2	89.1	89.2	89.4	89.0	95.2	113.1
1997	111.5	107.2	115.7	150.3	115.2	111.2	110.6	107.0	138.8	86.8	87.7	87.8	87.9	87.6	93.5	110.6
1996	108.9	105.5	114.0	148.0	113.3	109.5	108.2	105.2	137.2	85.0	85.9	86.0	86.1	85.8	91.7	107.9
1995	105.6	99.3	110.1	140.7	106.6	104.6	104.0	97.7	129.4	81.8	82.6	82.6	82.7	82.6	88.4	103.4
1994	103.0	98.1	107.2	137.1	105.2	103.5	102.3	96.5	128.1	80.3	81.1	81.0	81.2	81.1	87.0	102.2
1993	100.0	95.7	102.2	133.3	102.0	100.8	99.6	94.1	126.3	78.2	78.9	78.9	78.9	78.8	85.8	100.3
1992	97.9	93.7	100.1	128.2	99.3	99.3	98.1	90.5	123.9	77.1	77.7	77.8	77.8	77.6	83.1	98.0
1991	95.7	89.5	96.8	124.4	96.0	96.7	95.5	88.7	121.5	76.0	76.6	76.8	76.7	76.6	82.6	96.8
1990	93.2	87.0	94.1	118.1	94.6	93.9	91.0	85.6	111.4	74.8	75.4	75.5	75.5	75.3	81.3	94.6
1989	91.0	85.4	91.8	114.8	92.6	89.6	88.4	84.1	102.1	73.3	74.0	74.0	74.0	73.8	79.7	92.9
1988	88.5	83.6	89.4	106.5	87.9	87.7	86.5	82.4	99.9	71.5	72.2	72.2	72.2	72.0	78.2	91.1
1987	85.7	82.4	85.8	102.6	85.8	85.3	85.1	82.1	98.9	70.6	71.2	71.2	71.1	71.0	77.4	90.1
1986	83.7	80.2	84.4	99.8	83.7	82.4	83.3	79.2	96.6	68.4	69.1	69.1	69.1	68.9	75.4	87.7
1985	81.8	77.5	83.2	94.9	81.6	80.1	81.0	77.0	92.8	66.9	67.6	67.7	67.6	67.5	73.4	86.8
1984	80.6	75.4	81.3	91.1	80.6	78.5	79.0	76.1	89.5	66.3	66.6	66.8	66.2	66.0	72.2	82.8
1983	78.2	73.2	78.2	86.5	77.1	75.3	76.5	74.5	85.4	64.6	65.1	65.7	64.9	64.6	70.5	79.4
1982	72.1	67.5	70.3	78.3	71.3	69.8	70.2	68.4	77.8	58.7	60.0	60.5	59.5	59.4	66.1	73.2
1981	66.1	62.6	65.2	71.6	65.6	64.7	64.6	63.5	71.0	55.3	56.6	56.7	55.9	56.3	61.7	67.7
1980	60.7	58.0	60.6	66.0	60.5	60.3	61.6	58.5	65.9	51.1	52.2	52.5	51.7	50.8	57.4	62.3
1979	54.9	52.8	56.0	60.2	55.0	54.9	56.2	53.2	60.0	45.9	46.9	47.1	46.4	45.9	52.2	56.3
1978	51.3	50.0	52.6	56.4	51.7	50.8	52.2	49.1	54.7	41.9	43.0	42.9	42.4	41.9	47.8	52.1
1975	43.7	42.5	45.1	49.5	44.8	43.7	44.8	42.7	47.1	36.1	37.0	37.0	37.3	36.1	39.3	44.7
1970	27.8	27.0	28.9	32.8	29.2	27.8	28.5	26.9	30.0	20.9	23.7	23.6	23.4	23.0	25.8	28.3
1965	21.5	20.8	22.2	25.5	22.8	21.4	21.9	20.7	23.1	16.0	18.2	18.2	18.0	17.7	19.9	21.8
1960	19.5	18.9	19.9	21.5	19.7	19.5	19.9	18.8	21.0	14.4	16.6	16.6	16.4	16.1	18.1	19.9
1955	16.3	15.8	16.7	18.1	16.5	16.3	16.7	15.8	17.6	12.1	13.9	13.9	13.7	13.5	15.2	16.6
1950	13.5	13.1	13.8	14.9	13.6	13.5	13.8	13.0	14.5	10.0	11.5	11.5	11.4	11.2	12.5	13.7
1945	8.6	8.3	8.8	9.5	8.7	8.6	8.8	8.3	9.3	6.4	7.3	7.3	7.2	7.1	8.0	8.8
1940	6.6	6.4	6.8	7.4	6.7	6.7	6.8	6.4	7.2	4.9	5.6	5.6	5.6	5.5	6.2	6.8

Year	National 30 City Average	Ohio Canton	Cincinnati	Cleveland	Columbus	Dayton	Lorain	Springfield	Toledo	Youngstown	Oklahoma Lawton	Oklahoma City	Tulsa	Oregon Eugene	Portland	PA Allentown
Jan 2001	121.8E	117.2E	115.5E	125.5E	116.5E	113.5E	119.4E	113.5E	120.8E	118.8E	102.0E	101.8E	100.0E	128.7E	130.1E	123.2E
2000	118.9	112.7	110.1	121.3	112.5	109.0	115.0	109.2	115.7	114.1	98.7	98.9	97.5	126.3	127.4	119.9
1999	116.6	110.6	107.9	118.7	109.5	107.1	112.0	106.4	113.6	111.9	97.5	97.4	96.2	120.9	124.3	117.8
1998	113.6	108.5	105.0	114.8	106.8	104.5	109.4	104.1	111.2	109.0	94.3	94.5	94.5	120.0	122.2	115.7
1997	111.5	106.4	102.9	112.9	104.7	102.6	107.4	102.2	108.5	107.2	92.9	93.2	93.0	118.1	119.6	113.9
1996	108.9	103.2	100.2	110.1	101.1	98.8	103.8	98.4	105.1	104.1	90.9	91.3	91.2	114.4	116.1	112.0
1995	105.6	98.8	97.1	106.4	99.1	94.6	97.1	92.0	100.6	100.1	85.3	88.0	89.0	112.2	114.3	108.3
1994	103.0	97.7	95.0	104.8	95.4	93.0	96.0	90.1	99.3	98.9	84.0	86.5	87.6	107.6	109.2	106.4
1993	100.0	95.9	92.3	101.9	93.9	90.6	93.9	87.7	98.3	97.2	81.3	83.9	84.8	107.2	108.8	103.6
1992	97.9	94.5	90.6	98.7	92.6	89.2	92.2	86.4	97.1	96.0	80.1	82.7	83.4	101.1	102.6	101.6
1991	95.7	93.4	88.6	97.2	90.6	87.7	91.1	84.9	94.2	92.7	78.3	80.7	81.4	99.5	101.1	98.9
1990	93.2	92.1	86.7	95.1	88.1	85.9	89.4	83.4	92.9	91.8	77.1	79.9	80.0	98.0	99.4	95.0
1989	91.0	90.3	84.6	93.6	85.8	82.6	87.9	81.0	91.4	88.4	75.8	78.5	78.4	95.2	97.0	92.4
1988	88.5	89.1	82.9	92.1	83.9	81.0	85.2	79.5	89.6	86.9	74.3	77.0	76.8	93.5	95.3	89.8
1987	85.7	87.7	80.9	89.6	81.5	79.5	86.9	78.0	86.1	85.4	72.6	74.4	74.7	91.4	91.9	86.9
1986	83.7	84.9	78.8	87.3	79.7	78.0	81.6	76.1	84.6	83.8	71.6	74.1	73.9	90.0	91.7	84.7
1985	81.8	83.7	78.2	86.2	77.7	76.3	80.7	74.3	84.7	82.7	71.2	73.9	73.8	88.7	90.1	81.9
1984	80.6	81.3	77.4	82.5	76.1	75.9	79.5	73.9	83.5	80.3	70.6	72.9	72.8	89.5	89.3	78.4
1983	78.2	76.9	74.9	77.9	74.5	71.6	77.2	71.9	80.4	77.3	69.1	71.5	72.2	89.0	89.2	75.0
1982	72.1	70.8	70.1	71.6	68.6	65.2	70.8	66.5	74.6	71.7	63.5	65.2	66.2	82.3	83.6	68.2
1981	66.1	65.8	65.3	66.0	63.9	60.6	65.7	61.3	69.4	67.2	57.0	60.3	61.5	74.2	74.5	62.7
1980	60.7	60.6	59.8	61.0	58.6	56.6	60.8	56.2	64.0	61.5	52.2	55.5	57.2	68.9	68.4	58.7
1979	54.9	55.2	54.3	54.8	52.7	51.2	55.2	51.0	57.9	56.0	47.7	49.8	51.4	61.9	60.6	54.1
1978	51.3	51.1	50.4	51.3	49.3	47.2	50.3	46.9	54.0	52.2	44.5	46.3	48.0	57.2	56.0	50.4
1975	43.7	44.0	43.7	44.6	42.2	40.5	42.7	40.0	44.9	44.5	38.6	38.6	39.2	44.6	44.9	42.3
1970	27.8	27.8	28.2	29.6	26.7	27.0	27.5	25.4	29.1	29.6	24.1	23.4	24.1	30.4	30.0	27.3
1965	21.5	21.5	20.7	21.1	20.2	20.0	21.1	19.6	21.3	21.0	18.5	17.8	20.6	23.4	22.6	21.0
1960	19.5	19.5	19.3	19.6	18.7	18.1	19.2	17.8	19.4	19.1	16.9	16.1	18.1	21.2	21.1	19.1
1955	16.3	16.3	16.2	16.5	15.7	15.2	16.1	14.9	16.2	16.0	14.1	13.5	15.1	17.8	17.7	16.0
1950	13.5	13.5	13.3	13.6	13.0	12.5	13.3	12.3	13.4	13.2	11.7	11.2	12.5	14.7	14.6	13.2
1945	8.6	8.6	8.5	8.7	8.3	8.0	8.5	7.8	8.6	8.4	7.4	7.1	8.0	9.4	9.3	8.4
1940	6.6	6.7	6.5	6.7	6.4	6.2	6.5	6.1	6.6	6.5	5.7	5.5	6.1	7.2	7.2	6.5

HISTORICAL COST INDEXES

Historical Cost Indexes

Year	National 30 City Average	Pennsylvania						RI	South Carolina		South Dakota			Tennessee		
		Erie	Harrisburg	Philadelphia	Pittsburgh	Reading	Scranton	Providence	Charleston	Columbia	Rapid City	Sioux Falls	Chattanooga	Knoxville	Memphis	Nashville
Jan 2001	121.8E	118.9E	116.9E	135.9E	123.7E	120.0E	120.7E	126.9E	92.5E	91.6E	96.0E	100.0E	98.9E	97.2E	104.9E	104.5E
2000	118.9	114.6	114.0	132.1	120.9	115.9	117.7	122.8	89.9	89.1	94.2	98.0	96.9	95.0	100.8	100.8
1999	116.6	113.8	112.8	129.8	119.6	114.8	116.3	121.6	89.0	88.1	92.4	95.8	95.9	93.4	99.7	98.6
1998	113.6	109.8	110.5	126.6	117.1	112.5	113.7	120.3	88.0	87.2	90.7	93.6	94.9	92.4	97.2	96.8
1997	111.5	108.5	108.8	123.3	113.9	110.8	112.3	118.9	86.5	85.6	89.3	92.1	93.6	90.8	96.1	94.9
1996	108.9	106.8	105.7	120.3	110.8	108.7	109.9	117.2	84.9	84.1	87.2	90.0	91.6	88.8	94.0	91.9
1995	105.6	99.8	100.6	117.1	106.3	103.6	103.8	111.1	82.7	82.2	84.0	84.7	89.2	86.0	91.2	87.6
1994	103.0	98.2	99.4	115.2	103.7	102.2	102.6	109.6	81.2	80.6	82.7	83.1	87.4	84.1	89.0	84.8
1993	100.0	94.9	96.6	107.4	99.0	98.6	99.8	108.2	78.4	77.9	81.2	81.9	85.1	82.3	86.8	81.9
1992	97.9	92.1	94.8	105.3	96.5	96.7	97.8	106.9	77.1	76.8	80.0	80.7	83.6	77.7	85.4	80.7
1991	95.7	90.5	92.5	101.7	93.2	94.1	94.8	96.1	75.0	75.8	78.7	79.7	81.9	76.6	83.0	79.1
1990	93.2	88.5	89.5	98.5	91.2	90.8	91.3	94.1	73.7	74.5	77.2	78.4	79.9	75.1	81.3	77.1
1989	91.0	86.6	86.5	94.2	89.4	87.9	88.8	92.4	72.1	72.8	75.7	77.0	78.5	73.7	81.2	74.8
1988	88.5	84.9	84.0	89.8	87.7	85.3	86.4	89.1	70.5	71.3	74.2	75.5	77.0	72.1	79.7	73.1
1987	85.7	82.6	81.8	86.8	85.6	82.9	83.3	86.3	70.2	70.2	73.6	74.9	74.4	70.2	77.5	71.0
1986	83.7	81.5	79.6	84.9	83.6	79.7	81.3	85.2	67.4	68.1	71.0	72.3	74.2	69.2	75.3	68.1
1985	81.8	79.6	77.2	82.2	81.5	77.7	80.0	83.0	65.9	66.9	69.7	71.2	72.5	67.7	74.3	66.7
1984	80.6	78.3	75.4	79.0	78.9	75.9	78.8	80.3	64.3	65.5	68.7	70.4	71.4	66.4	73.3	66.3
1983	78.2	76.3	72.2	74.4	75.5	74.0	75.0	76.3	65.3	65.2	67.7	69.7	69.3	64.1	72.8	65.1
1982	72.1	71.0	66.3	69.0	70.9	67.7	68.4	70.0	59.9	60.0	64.4	67.6	64.5	59.8	66.5	62.2
1981	66.1	64.6	61.7	63.4	66.3	62.5	62.3	64.3	56.3	55.9	59.7	63.6	59.9	55.9	60.3	57.3
1980	60.7	59.4	56.9	58.7	61.3	57.7	58.4	59.2	50.6	51.1	54.8	57.1	55.0	51.6	55.9	53.1
1979	54.9	54.0	52.6	54.2	55.6	53.8	53.5	53.3	45.7	44.4	49.7	51.5	49.8	46.4	51.0	47.0
1978	51.3	50.2	49.6	51.3	51.4	49.7	50.0	50.2	42.1	40.7	46.0	47.4	45.9	42.8	47.4	43.9
1975	43.7	43.4	42.2	44.5	44.5	43.6	41.9	42.7	35.0	36.4	37.7	39.6	39.1	37.3	40.7	37.0
1970	27.8	27.5	25.8	27.5	28.7	27.1	27.0	27.3	22.8	22.9	24.8	25.8	24.9	22.0	23.0	22.8
1965	21.5	21.1	20.1	21.7	22.4	20.9	20.8	21.9	17.6	17.6	19.1	19.9	19.2	17.1	18.3	17.4
1960	19.5	19.1	18.6	19.4	19.7	19.0	18.9	19.1	16.0	16.0	17.3	18.1	17.4	15.5	16.6	15.8
1955	16.3	16.1	15.6	16.3	16.5	15.9	15.9	16.0	13.4	13.4	14.5	15.1	14.6	13.0	13.9	13.3
1950	13.5	13.3	12.9	13.5	13.6	13.2	13.1	13.2	11.1	11.1	12.0	12.5	12.1	10.7	11.5	10.9
1945	8.6	8.5	8.2	8.6	8.7	8.4	8.3	8.4	7.1	7.1	7.7	8.0	7.7	6.8	7.3	7.0
1940	6.6	6.5	6.3	6.6	6.7	6.4	6.5	6.5	5.4	5.5	5.9	6.2	6.0	5.3	5.6	5.4

Year	National 30 City Average	Texas														Utah
		Abilene	Amarillo	Austin	Beaumont	Corpus Christi	Dallas	El Paso	Fort Worth	Houston	Lubbock	Odessa	San Antonio	Waco	Wichita Falls	Ogden
Jan 2001	121.8E	94.3E	99.2E	100.5E	103.0E	97.8E	103.9E	96.5E	100.7E	107.2E	98.5E	94.3E	101.3E	98.4E	98.1E	108.2E
2000	118.9	93.4	98.1	99.1	101.6	96.9	102.7	92.4	99.9	106.0	97.6	93.4	99.4	97.3	96.9	104.6
1999	116.6	91.8	94.5	96.0	99.7	94.0	101.0	90.7	97.6	104.6	96.0	92.1	98.0	94.8	95.5	103.3
1998	113.6	89.8	92.7	94.2	97.9	91.8	97.9	88.4	94.5	101.3	93.3	90.1	94.8	92.7	92.9	98.5
1997	111.5	88.4	91.3	92.8	96.8	90.3	96.1	87.0	93.3	100.1	91.9	88.8	93.4	91.4	91.5	96.1
1996	108.9	86.8	89.6	90.9	95.3	88.5	94.1	86.7	91.5	97.9	90.2	87.1	92.3	89.7	89.9	94.1
1995	105.6	85.2	87.4	89.3	93.7	87.4	91.4	85.2	89.5	95.9	88.4	85.6	88.9	86.4	86.8	92.2
1994	103.0	83.3	85.5	87.0	91.8	84.6	89.6	82.2	87.4	93.4	87.0	83.9	87.0	84.9	85.4	89.4
1993	100.0	81.4	83.4	84.9	90.0	82.8	87.8	80.2	85.5	91.1	84.8	81.9	85.0	83.0	83.5	87.1
1992	97.9	80.3	82.3	83.8	88.9	81.6	86.2	79.0	84.1	89.8	83.6	80.7	83.9	81.8	82.4	85.1
1991	95.7	79.2	81.1	82.8	87.8	80.6	85.9	78.0	83.3	87.9	82.7	79.8	83.3	80.6	81.5	84.1
1990	93.2	78.0	80.1	81.3	86.5	79.3	84.5	76.7	82.1	85.4	81.5	78.6	80.7	79.6	80.3	83.4
1989	91.0	76.6	78.7	79.7	85.1	77.8	82.5	75.2	80.6	84.0	80.0	77.0	78.7	78.1	78.7	81.9
1988	88.5	75.0	77.2	78.3	83.9	76.3	81.1	73.6	79.8	82.5	78.4	75.5	77.1	76.5	77.4	80.4
1987	85.7	75.9	76.4	76.0	81.3	75.6	79.9	72.2	77.7	81.3	77.3	74.6	75.7	75.2	77.4	79.1
1986	83.7	72.5	74.1	75.3	80.5	73.5	78.9	70.7	76.7	80.3	75.4	72.4	74.3	72.8	74.5	77.3
1985	81.8	71.1	72.5	74.5	79.3	72.3	77.6	69.4	75.1	79.6	74.0	71.2	73.9	71.7	73.3	75.2
1984	80.6	70.5	71.6	72.8	78.7	71.6	79.8	68.3	77.1	80.7	72.7	69.8	73.1	71.3	72.4	74.9
1983	78.2	68.3	70.6	71.0	75.0	70.2	77.8	66.3	74.9	79.8	71.0	69.0	71.8	69.4	70.1	76.1
1982	72.1	62.7	65.5	64.9	65.7	64.7	70.7	62.6	68.2	72.1	65.6	62.5	66.0	64.3	64.8	69.7
1981	66.1	57.9	60.1	59.3	62.4	59.6	63.1	58.6	61.0	65.1	61.0	58.3	60.5	59.2	60.0	65.3
1980	60.7	53.4	55.2	54.5	57.6	54.5	57.9	53.1	57.0	59.4	55.6	57.2	55.0	54.9	55.4	62.2
1979	54.9	48.6	49.8	49.0	52.3	48.7	51.5	48.5	51.4	53.3	50.3	51.1	49.2	49.7	49.4	53.3
1978	51.3	44.7	45.8	46.2	48.0	44.9	48.2	45.3	47.5	50.2	46.5	43.9	46.0	46.4	47.1	49.6
1975	43.7	37.6	39.0	39.0	39.6	38.1	40.7	38.0	40.4	41.2	38.9	37.9	39.0	38.6	38.0	40.0
1970	27.8	24.5	24.9	24.9	25.7	24.5	25.5	23.7	25.9	25.4	25.1	24.6	23.3	24.8	24.5	26.8
1965	21.5	18.9	19.2	19.2	19.9	18.9	19.9	19.0	19.9	20.0	19.4	19.0	18.5	19.2	18.9	20.6
1960	19.5	17.1	17.4	17.4	18.1	17.1	18.2	17.0	18.1	18.2	17.6	17.3	16.8	17.4	17.2	18.8
1955	16.3	14.4	14.6	14.6	15.1	14.4	15.3	14.3	15.2	15.2	14.8	14.5	14.1	14.6	14.4	15.7
1950	13.5	11.9	12.1	12.1	12.5	11.9	12.6	11.8	12.5	12.6	12.2	12.0	11.6	12.1	11.9	13.0
1945	8.6	7.6	7.7	7.7	8.0	7.6	8.0	7.5	8.0	8.0	7.8	7.6	7.4	7.7	7.6	8.3
1940	6.6	5.9	5.9	5.9	6.1	5.8	6.2	5.8	6.2	6.2	6.0	5.9	5.7	5.9	5.8	6.4

Historical Cost Indexes

Year	National 30 City Average	Utah Salt Lake City	Vermont Burlington	Vermont Rutland	Virginia Alexandria	Virginia Newport News	Virginia Norfolk	Virginia Richmond	Virginia Roanoke	Washington Seattle	Washington Spokane	Washington Tacoma	West Virginia Charleston	West Virginia Huntington	Wisconsin Green Bay	Wisconsin Kenosha
Jan 2001	121.8E	109.3E	104.0E	103.5E	110.5E	100.3E	100.8E	102.7E	92.4E	127.3E	120.5E	125.4E	115.2E	117.9E	118.2E	122.2E
2000	118.9	106.5	98.9	98.3	108.1	96.5	97.6	100.2	90.7	124.6	118.3	122.9	111.5	114.4	114.6	119.1
1999	116.6	104.5	98.2	97.7	106.1	95.6	96.5	98.8	89.8	123.3	116.7	121.6	110.6	113.4	112.1	115.8
1998	113.6	99.5	97.8	97.3	104.1	93.7	93.9	97.0	88.3	119.4	114.3	118.3	106.7	109.0	109.5	112.9
1997	111.5	97.2	96.6	96.3	101.2	91.6	91.7	92.9	86.9	118.1	111.7	117.2	105.3	107.7	105.6	109.1
1996	108.9	94.9	95.1	94.8	99.7	90.2	90.4	91.6	85.5	115.2	109.2	114.3	103.1	104.8	103.8	106.4
1995	105.6	93.1	91.1	90.8	96.3	86.0	86.4	87.8	82.8	113.7	107.4	112.8	95.8	97.2	97.6	97.9
1994	103.0	90.2	89.5	89.3	93.9	84.6	84.8	86.3	81.4	109.9	104.0	108.3	94.3	95.3	96.3	96.2
1993	100.0	87.9	87.6	87.6	91.6	82.9	83.0	84.3	79.5	107.3	103.9	106.7	92.6	93.5	94.0	94.3
1992	97.9	86.0	86.1	86.1	90.1	81.0	81.6	82.0	78.3	105.1	101.4	103.7	91.4	92.3	92.0	92.1
1991	95.7	84.9	84.2	84.2	88.2	77.6	77.9	79.8	77.3	102.2	100.0	102.2	89.7	88.6	88.6	89.8
1990	93.2	84.3	83.0	82.9	86.1	76.3	76.7	77.6	76.1	100.1	98.5	100.5	86.1	86.8	86.7	87.8
1989	91.0	82.8	81.4	81.3	83.4	74.9	75.2	76.0	74.2	96.1	96.8	98.4	84.5	84.8	84.3	85.6
1988	88.5	81.3	79.7	79.7	81.0	73.4	73.7	74.1	72.3	94.2	95.0	96.6	82.8	83.1	82.0	83.0
1987	85.7	79.8	79.0	79.0	77.9	71.0	71.7	72.7	70.2	91.9	92.4	92.9	81.1	81.3	80.2	81.7
1986	83.7	78.1	76.4	76.4	76.8	70.3	70.5	71.0	67.8	90.5	91.9	92.8	79.9	80.2	77.8	79.3
1985	81.8	75.9	74.8	74.9	75.1	68.7	68.8	69.5	67.2	88.3	89.0	91.2	77.7	77.7	76.7	77.4
1984	80.6	75.2	73.7	73.7	75.0	67.9	68.3	68.8	66.2	89.2	88.1	90.0	75.4	75.8	75.0	75.1
1983	78.2	74.5	70.9	71.5	72.9	65.9	66.5	68.9	66.0	87.6	86.9	88.8	73.8	74.4	73.4	73.2
1982	72.1	68.1	64.9	65.4	67.0	60.6	60.9	63.7	61.0	80.7	80.6	81.7	67.6	68.4	67.5	69.1
1981	66.1	61.9	59.3	59.7	61.6	56.0	56.8	58.2	55.6	75.7	72.9	73.8	62.6	63.3	63.6	63.5
1980	60.7	57.0	55.3	58.3	57.3	52.5	52.4	54.3	51.3	67.9	66.3	66.7	57.7	58.3	58.6	58.3
1979	54.9	52.5	49.8	51.2	51.7	47.6	47.6	49.1	46.8	61.1	60.1	60.0	51.8	52.5	52.7	53.2
1978	51.3	49.0	46.1	47.2	48.9	44.0	44.9	46.0	43.6	56.7	55.4	55.6	48.2	48.5	48.7	49.5
1975	43.7	40.1	41.8	43.9	41.7	37.2	36.9	37.1	37.1	44.9	44.4	44.5	41.0	40.0	40.9	40.5
1970	27.8	26.1	25.4	26.8	26.2	23.9	21.5	22.0	23.7	28.8	29.3	29.6	26.1	25.8	26.4	26.5
1965	21.5	20.0	19.8	20.6	20.2	18.4	17.1	17.2	18.3	22.4	22.5	22.8	20.1	19.9	20.3	20.4
1960	19.5	18.4	18.0	18.8	18.4	16.7	15.4	15.6	16.6	20.4	20.8	20.8	18.3	18.1	18.4	18.6
1955	16.3	15.4	15.1	15.7	15.4	14.0	12.9	13.1	13.9	17.1	17.4	17.4	15.4	15.2	15.5	15.6
1950	13.5	12.7	12.4	13.0	12.7	11.6	10.7	10.8	11.5	14.1	14.4	14.4	12.7	12.5	12.8	12.9
1945	8.6	8.1	7.9	8.3	8.1	7.4	6.8	6.9	7.3	9.0	9.2	9.2	8.1	8.0	8.1	8.2
1940	6.6	6.3	6.1	6.4	6.2	5.7	5.3	5.3	5.7	7.0	7.1	7.1	6.2	6.2	6.3	6.3

Year	National 30 City Average	Wisconsin Madison	Wisconsin Milwaukee	Wisconsin Racine	Wyoming Cheyenne	Calgary	Edmonton	Hamilton	London	Montreal	Ottawa	Quebec	Toronto	Vancouver	Winnipeg
Jan 2001	121.8E	120.8E	122.4E	121.9E	99.5E	118.0E	118.0E	132.3E	129.8E	125.1E	131.0E	126.3E	135.5E	130.8E	117.6E
2000	118.9	116.6	120.5	118.7	98.1	115.9	115.8	130.0	127.5	122.8	128.8	124.1	133.1	128.4	115.6
1999	116.6	115.9	117.4	115.5	96.9	115.3	115.2	128.1	125.6	120.8	126.8	121.9	131.2	127.1	115.2
1998	113.6	110.8	113.4	112.7	95.4	112.5	112.4	126.3	123.9	119.0	124.7	119.6	128.5	123.8	113.7
1997	111.5	106.1	110.1	109.3	93.2	110.7	110.6	124.4	121.9	114.6	122.8	115.4	125.7	121.9	111.4
1996	108.9	104.4	107.1	106.5	91.1	109.1	109.0	122.6	120.2	112.9	121.0	113.6	123.9	119.0	109.7
1995	105.6	96.5	103.9	97.8	87.6	107.4	107.4	119.9	117.5	110.8	118.2	111.5	121.6	116.2	107.6
1994	103.0	94.5	100.6	96.1	85.4	106.7	106.6	116.5	114.2	109.5	115.0	110.2	117.8	115.1	105.5
1993	100.0	91.3	96.7	93.8	82.9	104.7	104.5	113.7	111.9	106.9	112.0	107.0	114.9	109.2	102.8
1992	97.9	89.2	93.9	91.7	81.7	103.4	103.2	112.4	110.7	104.2	110.8	103.6	113.7	108.0	101.6
1991	95.7	86.2	91.6	89.3	80.3	102.1	102.0	108.2	106.7	101.8	106.9	100.4	109.0	106.8	98.6
1990	93.2	84.3	88.9	87.3	79.1	98.0	97.1	103.8	101.4	99.0	102.7	96.8	104.6	103.2	95.1
1989	91.0	81.8	86.4	85.0	77.8	95.6	94.7	98.2	96.5	94.9	98.5	92.5	98.5	97.6	92.9
1988	88.5	79.9	84.1	82.4	76.3	93.9	93.0	95.4	93.2	90.6	94.0	88.3	94.8	95.9	90.0
1987	85.7	78.1	81.1	81.1	76.7	90.2	89.3	89.7	90.1	87.2	89.6	85.0	90.4	94.2	87.1
1986	83.7	76.1	78.9	78.6	73.4	91.2	90.1	88.9	87.9	84.8	87.7	82.4	89.3	93.2	85.3
1985	81.8	74.3	77.4	77.0	72.3	90.2	89.1	85.8	84.9	82.4	83.9	79.9	86.5	89.8	83.4
1984	80.6	72.5	76.3	74.7	73.8	89.6	88.1	85.1	84.1	81.6	82.9	80.0	85.2	89.2	82.5
1983	78.2	71.9	74.0	73.0	73.8	84.6	82.8	80.1	79.1	76.4	77.6	75.8	79.9	83.3	77.9
1982	72.1	65.9	70.5	68.6	68.3	76.2	74.1	73.7	71.8	70.2	72.3	69.6	71.8	76.4	70.7
1981	66.1	61.4	64.9	63.3	62.7	70.6	68.1	68.8	67.1	64.6	65.8	64.3	67.5	70.3	65.4
1980	60.7	56.8	58.8	58.1	56.9	64.9	63.3	63.7	61.9	59.2	60.9	59.3	60.9	65.0	61.7
1979	54.9	51.4	53.0	52.8	51.2	58.9	58.5	58.1	56.6	54.4	55.5	53.9	56.0	59.2	56.1
1978	51.3	47.3	49.9	49.2	47.5	54.9	54.4	54.0	52.6	50.4	51.7	49.7	51.9	55.1	51.7
1975	43.7	40.7	43.3	40.7	40.6	42.2	41.6	42.9	41.6	39.7	41.5	39.0	42.2	42.4	39.2
1970	27.8	26.5	29.4	26.5	26.0	28.9	28.6	28.5	27.8	25.6	27.6	26.0	25.6	26.0	23.1
1965	21.5	20.6	21.8	20.4	20.0	22.3	22.0	22.0	21.4	18.7	21.2	20.1	19.4	20.5	17.5
1960	19.5	18.1	19.0	18.6	18.2	20.2	20.0	20.0	19.5	17.0	19.3	18.2	17.6	18.6	15.8
1955	16.3	15.2	15.2	15.6	15.2	17.0	16.8	16.7	16.3	14.3	16.2	15.3	14.8	15.5	13.3
1950	13.5	12.5	13.2	12.9	12.6	14.0	13.9	13.8	13.5	11.8	13.4	12.6	12.2	12.8	10.9
1945	8.6	8.0	8.4	8.2	8.0	9.0	8.8	8.8	8.6	7.5	8.5	8.0	7.8	8.2	7.0
1940	6.6	6.2	6.5	6.3	6.2	6.9	6.8	6.8	6.6	5.8	6.6	6.2	6.0	6.3	5.4

Accent lighting–Fixtures or directional beams of light arranged to bring attention to an object or area.

Acoustical material–A material fabricated for the sole purpose of absorbing sound.

Addition–An expansion to an existing structure generally in the form of a room, floor(s) or wing(s). An increase in the floor area or volume of a structure.

Aggregate–Materials such as sand, gravel, stone, vermiculite, perlite and fly ash (slag) which are essential components in the production of concrete, mortar or plaster.

Air conditioning system–An air treatment to control the temperature, humidity and cleanliness of air and to provide for its distribution throughout the structure.

Air curtain–A stream of air directed downward to prevent the loss of hot or cool air from the structure and inhibit the entrance of dust and insects. Generally installed at loading platforms.

Anodized aluminum–Aluminum treated by an electrolytic process to produce an oxide film that is corrosion resistant.

Arcade–A covered passageway between buildings often with shops and offices on one or both sides.

Ashlar–A square-cut building stone or a wall constructed of cut stone.

Asphalt paper–A sheet paper material either coated or saturated with asphalt to increase its strength and resistance to water.

Asphalt shingles–Shingles manufactured from saturated roofing felts, coated with asphalt and topped with mineral granules to prevent weathering.

Assessment ratio–The ratio between the market value and assessed valuation of a property.

Back-up–That portion of a masonry wall behind the exterior facing-usually load bearing.

Balcony–A platform projecting from a building either supported from below or cantilevered. Usually protected by railing.

Bay–Structural component consisting of beams and columns occurring consistently throughout the structure.

Beam–A horizontal structural framing member that transfers loads to vertical members (columns) or bearing walls.

Bid–An offer to perform work described in a contract at a specified price.

Board foot–A unit or measure equal in volume to a board one foot long, one foot wide and one inch thick.

Booster pump–A supplemental pump installed to increase or maintain adequate pressure in the system.

Bowstring roof–A roof supported by trusses fabricated in the shape of a bow and tied together by a straight member.

Brick veneer–A facing of brick laid against, but not bonded to, a wall.

Bridging–A method of bracing joists for stiffness, stability and load distribution.

Broom finish–A method of finishing concrete by lightly dragging a broom over freshly placed concrete.

Built-up roofing–Installed on flat or extremely low-pitched roofs, a roof covering composed of plies or laminations of saturated roofing felts alternated with layers of coal tar pitch or asphalt and surfaced with a layer of gravel or slag in a thick coat of asphalt and finished with a capping sheet.

Caisson–A watertight chamber to expedite work on foundations or structure below water level.

Cantilever–A structural member supported only at one end.

Carport–An automobile shelter having one or more sides open to the weather.

Casement window–A vertical opening window having one side fixed.

Caulking–A resilient compound generally having a silicone or rubber base used to prevent infiltration of water or outside air.

Cavity wall–An exterior wall usually of masonry having an inner and outer wall separated by a continuous air space for thermal insulation.

Cellular concrete–A lightweight concrete consisting of cement mixed with gas-producing materials which, in turn, forms bubbles resulting in good insulating qualities.

Chattel mortgage–A secured interest in a property as collateral for payment of a note.

Clapboard–A wood siding used as exterior covering in frame construction. It is applied horizontally with grain running lengthwise. The thickest section of the board is on the bottom.

Clean room–An environmentally controlled room usually found in medical facilities or precision manufacturing spaces where it is essential to eliminate dust, lint or pathogens.

Close studding–A method of construction whereby studs are spaced close together and the intervening spaces are plastered.

Cluster housing–A closely grouped series of houses resulting in a high density land use.

Cofferdam–A watertight enclosure used for foundation construction in waterfront areas. Water is pumped out of the cofferdam allowing free access to the work area.

Collar joint–Joint between the collar beam and roof rafters.

Column–A vertical structural member supporting horizontal members (beams) along the direction of its longitudinal axis.

Combination door (windows)–Door (windows) having interchangeable screens and glass for seasonal use.

Common area–Spaces either inside or outside the building designated for use by the occupant of the building but not the general public.

Common wall–A wall used jointly by two dwelling units.

Compound wall–A wall constructed of more than one material.

Concrete–A composite material consisting of sand, coarse aggregate (gravel, stone or slag), cement and water that when mixed and allowed to harden forms a hard stone-like material.

Concrete floor hardener–A mixture of chemicals applied to the surface of concrete to produce a dense, wear-resistant bearing surface.

Conduit–A tube or pipe used to protect electric wiring.

Coping–The top cover or capping on a wall.

Craneway–Steel or concrete column and beam supports and rails on which a crane travels.

Curtain wall–A non-bearing exterior wall not supported by beams or girders of the steel frame.

Dampproofing–Coating of a surface to prevent the passage of water or moisture.

Dead load–Total weight of all structural components plus permanently attached fixtures and equipment.

Decibel–Unit of acoustical measurement.

Decorative block–A concrete masonry unit having a special treatment on its face.

Deed restriction–A restriction on the use of a property as set forth in the deed.

Depreciation–A loss in property value caused by physical aging, functional or economic obsolescence.

Direct heating–Heating of spaces by means of exposed heated surfaces (stove, fire, radiators, etc.).

Distributed load–A load that acts evenly over a structural member.

Dock bumper–A resilient material attached to a loading dock to absorb the impact of trucks backing in.

Dome–A curved roof shape spanning an area.

Dormer–A structure projecting from a sloping roof.

Double-hung window–A window having two vertical sliding sashes-one covering the upper section and one covering the lower.

Downspout–A vertical pipe for carrying rain water from the roof to the ground.

Drain tile–A hollow tile used to drain water-soaked soil.

Dressed size–In lumber about 3/8" - 1/2" less than nominal size after planing and sawing.

Drop panel–The depressed surface on the bottom side of a flat concrete slab which surrounds a column.

Dry pipe sprinkler system–A sprinkler system that is activated with water only in case of fire. Used in areas susceptible to freezing or to avoid the hazards of leaking pipes.

Drywall–An interior wall constructed of gypsum board, plywood or wood paneling. No water is required for application.

Duct–Pipe for transmitting warm or cold air. A pipe containing electrical cable or wires.

Dwelling–A structure designed as living quarters for one or more families.

Easement–A right of way or free access over land owned by another.

Eave–The lower edge of a sloping roof that overhangs the side wall of the structure.

Economic rent–That rent on a property sufficient to pay all operating costs exclusive of services and utilities.

Economic life–The term during which a structure is expected to be profitable. Generally shorter than the physical life of the structure.

Economic obsolescence–Loss in value due to unfavorable economic influences occurring from outside the structure itself.

Effective age–The age a structure appears to be based on observed physical condition determined by degree of maintenance and repair.

Elevator–A mechanism for vertical transport of personnel or freight equipped with car or platform.

Ell–A secondary wing or addition to a structure at right angles to the main structure.

Eminent domain–The right of the state to take private property for public use.

Envelope–The shape of a building indicating volume.

Equity–Value of an owner's interest calculated by subtracting outstanding mortgages and expenses from the value of the property.

Escheat–The assumption of ownership by the state, of property whose owner cannot be determined.

Facade–The exterior face of a building sometimes decorated with elaborate detail.

Face brick–Brick manufactured to present an attractive appearance.

Facing block–A concrete masonry unit having a decorative exterior finish.

Feasibility study–A detailed evaluation of a proposed project to determine its financial potential.

Felt paper–Paper sheathing used on walls as an insulator and to prevent infiltration of moisture.

Fenestration–Pertaining to the density and arrangement of windows in a structure.

Fiberboard–A building material composed of wood fiber compressed with a binding agent, produced in sheet form.

Fiberglass–Fine spun filaments of glass processed into various densities to produce thermal and acoustical insulation.

Field house–A long structure used for indoor athletic events.

Finish floor–The top or wearing surface of the floor system.

Fireproofing–The use of fire-resistant materials for the protection of structural members to ensure structural integrity in the event of fire.

Fire stop–A material or member used to seal an opening to prevent the spread of fire.

Flashing–A thin, impervious material such as copper or sheet metal used to prevent air or water penetration.

Float finish–A concrete finish accomplished by using a flat tool with a handle on the back.

Floor drain–An opening installed in a floor for removing excess water into a plumbing system.

Floor load–The live load the floor system has been designed for and which may be applied safely.

Flue–A heat-resistant enclosed passage in a chimney to remove gaseous products of combustion from a fireplace or boiler.

Footing–The lowest portion of the foundation wall that transmits the load directly to the soil.

Foundation–Below grade wall system that supports the structure.

Foyer–A portion of the structure that serves as a transitional space between the interior and exterior.

Frontage–That portion of a lot that is placed facing a street, public way or body of water.

Frost action–The effects of freezing and thawing on materials and the resultant structural damage.

Functional obsolescence–An inadequacy caused by outmoded design, dated construction materials or over or undersized areas, all of which cause excessive operating costs.

Furring strips–Wood or metal channels used for attaching gypsum or metal lath to masonry walls as a finish or for leveling purposes.

Gambrel roof (mansard)–A roof system having two pitches on each side.

Garden apartment–Two or three story apartment building with common outside areas.

General contractor–The prime contractor responsible for work on the construction site.

Girder–A principal horizontal supporting member.

Girt–A horizontal framing member for adding rigid support to columns which also acts as a support for sheathing or siding.

Grade beam–That portion of the foundation system that directly supports the exterior walls of the building.

Gross area–The total enclosed floor area of a building.

Ground area–The area computed by the exterior dimensions of the structure.

Ground floor–The floor of a building in closest proximity to the ground.

Grout–A mortar containing a high water content used to fill joints and cavities in masonry work.

Gutter–A wood or sheet metal conduit set along the building eaves used to channel rainwater to leaders or downspouts.

Gunite–A concrete mix placed pneumatically.

Gypsum–Hydrated calcium sulphate used as both a retarder in Portland cement and as a major ingredient in plaster of Paris. Used in sheets as a substitute for plaster.

Hall–A passageway providing access to various parts of a building–a large room for entertainment or assembly.

Hangar–A structure for the storage or repair of aircraft.

Head room–The distance between the top of the finished floor to the bottom of the finished ceiling.

Hearth–The floor of a fireplace and the adjacent area of fireproof material.

Heat pump–A mechanical device for providing either heating or air conditioning.

Hip roof–A roof whose four sides meet at a common point with no gabled ends.

I-beam–A structural member having a cross-section resembling the letter "I".

Insulation–Material used to reduce the effects of heat, cold or sound.

Jack rafter–An unusually short rafter generally found in hip roofs.

Jalousie–Adjustable glass louvers which pivot simultaneously in a common frame.

Jamb–The vertical member on either side of a door frame or window frame.

Joist–Parallel beams of timber, concrete or steel used to support floor and ceiling.

Junction box–A box that protects splices or joints in electrical wiring.

Kalamein door–Solid core wood doors clad with galvanized sheet metal.

Kip–A unit of weight equal to 1,000 pounds.

Lally column–A concrete-filled steel pipe used as a vertical support.

Laminated beam–A beam built up by gluing together several pieces of timber.

Landing–A platform between flights of stairs.

Lath–Strips of wood or metal used as a base for plaster.

Lead-lined door, sheetrock–Doors or sheetrock internally lined with sheet lead to provide protection from X-ray radiation.

Lean-to–A small shed or building addition with a single pitched roof attached to the exterior wall of the main building.

Lintel–A horizontal framing member used to carry a load over a wall opening.

Live load–The moving or movable load on a structure composed of furnishings, equipment or personnel weight.

Load bearing partition–A partition that supports a load in addition to its own weight.

Loading dock leveler–An adjustable platform for handling off-on loading of trucks.

Loft building–A commercial/industrial type building containing large, open unpartitioned floor areas.

Louver window–A window composed of a series of sloping, overlapping blades or slats that may be adjusted to admit varying degrees of air or light.

Main beam–The principal load bearing beam used to transmit loads directly to columns.

Mansard roof–A roof having a double pitch on all four sides, the lower level having the steeper pitch.

Mansion–An extremely large and imposing residence.

Masonry–The utilization of brick, stone, concrete or block for walls and other building components.

Mastic–A sealant or adhesive compound generally used as either a binding agent or floor finish.

Membrane fireproofing–A coating of metal lath and plaster to provide resistance to fire and heat.

Mesh reinforcement–An arrangement of wire tied or welded at their intersection to provide strength and resistance to cracking.

Metal lath–A diamond-shaped metallic base for plaster.

Mezzanine–A low story situated between two main floors.

Mill construction–A heavy timber construction that achieves fire resistance by using large wood structural members, noncombustible bearing and non-bearing walls and omitting concealed spaces under floors and roof.

Mixed occupancy–Two or more classes of occupancy in a single structure.

Molded brick–A specially shaped brick used for decorative purposes.

Monolithic concrete–Concrete poured in a continuous process so there are no joints.

Movable partition–A non-load bearing demountable partition that can be relocated and can be either ceiling height or partial height.

Moving walk–A continually moving horizontal passenger carrying device.

Multi-zone system–An air conditioning system that is capable of handling several individual zones simultaneously.

Net floor area–The usable, occupied area of a structure excluding stairwells, elevator shafts and wall thicknesses.

Non-combustible construction–Construction in which the walls, partitions and the structural members are of non-combustible materials.

Nurses call system–An electrically operated system for use by patients or personnel for summoning a nurse.

Occupancy rate–The number of persons per room, per dwelling unit, etc.

One-way joist connection–A framing system for floors and roofs in a concrete building consisting of a series of parallel joists supported by girders between columns.

Open web joist–A lightweight prefabricated metal chord truss.

Parapet–A low guarding wall at the point of a drop. That portion of the exterior wall that extends above the roof line.

Parging–A thin coat of mortar applied to a masonry wall used primarily for waterproofing purposes.

Parquet–Inlaid wood flooring set in a simple design.

Peaked roof–A roof of two or more slopes that rises to a peak.

Penthouse–A structure occupying usually half the roof area and used to house elevator, HVAC equipment, or other mechanical or electrical systems.

Pier–A column designed to support a concentrated load.

Pilaster–A column usually formed of the same material and integral with, but projecting from, a wall.

Pile–A concrete, wood or steel column usually less than 2′ in diameter which is driven or otherwise introduced into the soil to carry a vertical load or provide vertical support.

Pitched roof–A roof having one or more surfaces with a pitch greater than 10°.

Plenum–The space between the suspended ceiling and the floor above.

Plywood–Structural wood made of three or more layers of veneer and bonded together with glue.

Porch–A structure attached to a building to provide shelter for an entranceway or to serve as a semi-enclosed space.

Post and beam framing–A structural framing system where beams rest on posts rather than bearing walls.

Post-tensioned concrete–Concrete that has the reinforcing tendons tensioned after the concrete has set.

Pre-cast concrete–Concrete structural components fabricated at a location other than in-place.

Pre-stressed concrete–Concrete that has the reinforcing tendons tensioned prior to the concrete setting.

Purlins–A horizontal structural member supporting the roof deck and resting on the trusses, girders, beams or rafters.

Rafters–Structural members supporting the roof deck and covering.

Resilient flooring–A manufactured interior floor covering material in either sheet or tile form, that is resilient.

Ridge–The horizontal line at the junction of two sloping roof edges.

Rigid frame–A structural framing system in which all columns and beams are rigidly connected; there are no hinged joints.

Roof drain–A drain designed to accept rainwater and discharge it into a leader or downspout.

Rough floor–A layer of boards or plywood nailed to the floor joists that serves as a base for the finished floor.

Sanitary sewer–A sewer line designed to carry only liquid or waterborne waste from the structure to a central treatment plant.

Sawtooth roof–Roof shape found primarily in industrial roofs that creates the appearance of the teeth of a saw.

Semi-rigid frame–A structural system wherein the columns and beams are so attached that there is some flexibility at the joints.

Septic tank–A covered tank in which waste matter is decomposed by natural bacterial action.

Service elevator–A combination passenger and freight elevator.

Sheathing–The first covering of exterior studs by boards, plywood or particle board.

Glossary

Shoring–Temporary bracing for structural components during construction.

Span–The horizontal distance between supports.

Specification–A detailed list of materials and requirements for construction of a building.

Storm sewer–A system of pipes used to carry rainwater or surface waters.

Stucco–A cement plaster used to cover exterior wall surfaces usually applied over a wood or metal lath base.

Stud–A vertical wooden structural component.

Subfloor–A system of boards, plywood or particle board laid over the floor joists to form a base.

Superstructure–That portion of the structure above the foundation or ground level.

Terrazzo–A durable floor finish made of small chips of colored stone or marble, embedded in concrete, then polished to a high sheen.

Tile–A thin piece of fired clay, stone or concrete used for floor, roof or wall finishes.

Unit cost–The cost per unit of measurement.

Vault–A room especially designed for storage.

Veneer–A thin surface layer covering a base of common material.

Vent–An opening serving as an outlet for air.

Wainscot–The lower portion of an interior wall whose surface differs from that of the upper wall.

Wall bearing construction–A structural system where the weight of the floors and roof are carried directly by the masonry walls rather than the structural framing system.

Waterproofing–Any of a number of materials applied to various surfaces to prevent the infiltration of water.

Weatherstrip–A thin strip of metal, wood or felt used to cover the joint between the door or window sash and the jamb, casing or sill to keep out air, dust, rain, etc.

Wing–A building section or addition projecting from the main structure.

X-ray protection–Lead encased in sheetrock or plaster to prevent the escape of radiation.

GLOSSARY

Abbreviations

A	Area Square Feet; Ampere	Cab.	Cabinet	d.f.u.	Drainage Fixture Units
ABS	Acrylonitrile Butadiene Stryrene;	Cair.	Air Tool Laborer	D.H.	Double Hung
	Asbestos Bonded Steel	Calc	Calculated	DHW	Domestic Hot Water
A.C.	Alternating Current;	Cap.	Capacity	Diag.	Diagonal
	Air-Conditioning;	Carp.	Carpenter	Diam.	Diameter
	Asbestos Cement;	C.B.	Circuit Breaker	Distrib.	Distribution
	Plywood Grade A & C	C.C.A.	Chromate Copper Arsenate	Dk.	Deck
A.C.I.	American Concrete Institute	C.C.F.	Hundred Cubic Feet	D.L.	Dead Load; Diesel
AD	Plywood, Grade A & D	cd	Candela	DLH	Deep Long Span Bar Joist
Addit.	Additional	cd/sf	Candela per Square Foot	Do.	Ditto
Adj.	Adjustable	CD	Grade of Plywood Face & Back	Dp.	Depth
af	Audio-frequency	CDX	Plywood, Grade C & D, exterior	D.P.S.T.	Double Pole, Single Throw
A.G.A.	American Gas Association		glue	Dr.	Driver
Agg.	Aggregate	Cefi.	Cement Finisher	Drink.	Drinking
A.H.	Ampere Hours	Cem.	Cement	D.S.	Double Strength
A hr.	Ampere-hour	CF	Hundred Feet	D.S.A.	Double Strength A Grade
A.H.U.	Air Handling Unit	C.F.	Cubic Feet	D.S.B.	Double Strength B Grade
A.I.A.	American Institute of Architects	CFM	Cubic Feet per Minute	Dty.	Duty
AIC	Ampere Interrupting Capacity	c.g.	Center of Gravity	DWV	Drain Waste Vent
Allow.	Allowance	CHW	Chilled Water;	DX	Deluxe White, Direct Expansion
alt.	Altitude		Commercial Hot Water	dyn	Dyne
Alum.	Aluminum	C.I.	Cast Iron	e	Eccentricity
a.m.	Ante Meridiem	C.I.P.	Cast in Place	E	Equipment Only; East
Amp.	Ampere	Circ.	Circuit	Ea.	Each
Anod.	Anodized	C.L.	Carload Lot	E.B.	Encased Burial
Approx.	Approximate	Clab.	Common Laborer	Econ.	Economy
Apt.	Apartment	C.L.F.	Hundred Linear Feet	EDP	Electronic Data Processing
Asb.	Asbestos	CLF	Current Limiting Fuse	EIFS	Exterior Insulation Finish System
A.S.B.C.	American Standard Building Code	CLP	Cross Linked Polyethylene	E.D.R.	Equiv. Direct Radiation
Asbe.	Asbestos Worker	cm	Centimeter	Eq.	Equation
A.S.H.R.A.E.	American Society of Heating,	CMP	Corr. Metal Pipe	Elec.	Electrician; Electrical
	Refrig. & AC Engineers	C.M.U.	Concrete Masonry Unit	Elev.	Elevator; Elevating
A.S.M.E.	American Society of Mechanical	CN	Change Notice	EMT	Electrical Metallic Conduit;
	Engineers	Col.	Column		Thin Wall Conduit
A.S.T.M.	American Society for Testing and	CO_2	Carbon Dioxide	Eng.	Engine, Engineered
	Materials	Comb.	Combination	EPDM	Ethylene Propylene Diene
Attchmt.	Attachment	Compr.	Compressor		Monomer
Avg.	Average	Conc.	Concrete	EPS	Expanded Polystyrene
A.W.G.	American Wire Gauge	Cont.	Continuous; Continued	Eqhv.	Equip. Oper., Heavy
AWWA	American Water Works Assoc.	Corr.	Corrugated	Eqlt.	Equip. Oper., Light
Bbl.	Barrel	Cos	Cosine	Eqmd.	Equip. Oper., Medium
B. & B.	Grade B and Better;	Cot	Cotangent	Eqmm.	Equip. Oper., Master Mechanic
	Balled & Burlapped	Cov.	Cover	Eqol.	Equip. Oper., Oilers
B. & S.	Bell and Spigot	C/P	Cedar on Paneling	Equip.	Equipment
B. & W.	Black and White	CPA	Control Point Adjustment	ERW	Electric Resistance Welded
b.c.c.	Body-centered Cubic	Cplg.	Coupling	E.S.	Energy Saver
B.C.Y.	Bank Cubic Yards	C.P.M.	Critical Path Method	Est.	Estimated
BE	Bevel End	CPVC	Chlorinated Polyvinyl Chloride	esu	Electrostatic Units
B.F.	Board Feet	C.Pr.	Hundred Pair	E.W.	Each Way
Bg. cem.	Bag of Cement	CRC	Cold Rolled Channel	EWT	Entering Water Temperature
BHP	Boiler Horsepower;	Creos.	Creosote	Excav.	Excavation
	Brake Horsepower	Crpt.	Carpet & Linoleum Layer	Exp.	Expansion, Exposure
B.I.	Black Iron	CRT	Cathode-ray Tube	Ext.	Exterior
Bit.; Bitum.	Bituminous	CS	Carbon Steel, Constant Shear Bar	Extru.	Extrusion
Bk.	Backed		Joist	f.	Fiber stress
Bkrs.	Breakers	Csc	Cosecant	F	Fahrenheit; Female; Fill
Bldg.	Building	C.S.F.	Hundred Square Feet	Fab.	Fabricated
Blk.	Block	CSI	Construction Specifications	FBGS	Fiberglass
Bm.	Beam		Institute	F.C.	Footcandles
Boil.	Boilermaker	C.T.	Current Transformer	f.c.c.	Face-centered Cubic
B.P.M.	Blows per Minute	CTS	Copper Tube Size	f'c.	Compressive Stress in Concrete;
BR	Bedroom	Cu	Copper, Cubic		Extreme Compressive Stress
Brg.	Bearing	Cu. Ft.	Cubic Foot	F.E.	Front End
Brhe.	Bricklayer Helper	cw	Continuous Wave	FEP	Fluorinated Ethylene Propylene
Bric.	Bricklayer	C.W.	Cool White; Cold Water		(Teflon)
Brk.	Brick	Cwt.	100 Pounds	F.G.	Flat Grain
Brng.	Bearing	C.W.X.	Cool White Deluxe	F.H.A.	Federal Housing Administration
Brs.	Brass	C.Y.	Cubic Yard (27 cubic feet)	Fig.	Figure
Brz.	Bronze	C.Y./Hr.	Cubic Yard per Hour	Fin.	Finished
Bsn.	Basin	Cyl.	Cylinder	Fixt.	Fixture
Btr.	Better	d	Penny (nail size)	Fl. Oz.	Fluid Ounces
BTU	British Thermal Unit	D	Deep; Depth; Discharge	Flr.	Floor
BTUH	BTU per Hour	Dis.;Disch.	Discharge	F.M.	Frequency Modulation;
B.U.R.	Built-up Roofing	Db.	Decibel		Factory Mutual
BX	Interlocked Armored Cable	Dbl.	Double	Fmg.	Framing
c	Conductivity, Copper Sweat	DC	Direct Current	Fndtn.	Foundation
C	Hundred; Centigrade	DDC	Direct Digital Control	Fori.	Foreman, Inside
C/C	Center to Center, Cedar on Cedar	Demob.	Demobilization	Foro.	Foreman, Outside

449

Abbreviation	Meaning
Fount.	Fountain
FPM	Feet per Minute
FPT	Female Pipe Thread
Fr.	Frame
F.R.	Fire Rating
FRK	Foil Reinforced Kraft
FRP	Fiberglass Reinforced Plastic
FS	Forged Steel
FSC	Cast Body; Cast Switch Box
Ft.	Foot; Feet
Ftng.	Fitting
Ftg.	Footing
Ft. Lb.	Foot Pound
Furn.	Furniture
FVNR	Full Voltage Non-Reversing
FXM	Female by Male
Fy.	Minimum Yield Stress of Steel
g	Gram
G	Gauss
Ga.	Gauge
Gal.	Gallon
Gal./Min.	Gallon per Minute
Galv.	Galvanized
Gen.	General
G.F.I.	Ground Fault Interrupter
Glaz.	Glazier
GPD	Gallons per Day
GPH	Gallons per Hour
GPM	Gallons per Minute
GR	Grade
Gran.	Granular
Grnd.	Ground
H	High; High Strength Bar Joist; Henry
H.C.	High Capacity
H.D.	Heavy Duty; High Density
H.D.O.	High Density Overlaid
Hdr.	Header
Hdwe.	Hardware
Help.	Helpers Average
HEPA	High Efficiency Particulate Air Filter
Hg	Mercury
HIC	High Interrupting Capacity
HM	Hollow Metal
H.O.	High Output
Horiz.	Horizontal
H.P.	Horsepower; High Pressure
H.P.F.	High Power Factor
Hr.	Hour
Hrs./Day	Hours per Day
HSC	High Short Circuit
Ht.	Height
Htg.	Heating
Htrs.	Heaters
HVAC	Heating, Ventilation & Air-Conditioning
Hvy.	Heavy
HW	Hot Water
Hyd.;Hydr.	Hydraulic
Hz.	Hertz (cycles)
I.	Moment of Inertia
I.C.	Interrupting Capacity
ID	Inside Diameter
I.D.	Inside Dimension; Identification
I.F.	Inside Frosted
I.M.C.	Intermediate Metal Conduit
In.	Inch
Incan.	Incandescent
Incl.	Included; Including
Int.	Interior
Inst.	Installation
Insul.	Insulation/Insulated
I.P.	Iron Pipe
I.P.S.	Iron Pipe Size
I.P.T.	Iron Pipe Threaded
I.W.	Indirect Waste
J	Joule
J.I.C.	Joint Industrial Council
K	Thousand; Thousand Pounds; Heavy Wall Copper Tubing, Kelvin
K.A.H.	Thousand Amp. Hours
KCMIL	Thousand Circular Mils
KD	Knock Down
K.D.A.T.	Kiln Dried After Treatment
kg	Kilogram
kG	Kilogauss
kgf	Kilogram Force
kHz	Kilohertz
Kip.	1000 Pounds
KJ	Kiljoule
K.L.	Effective Length Factor
K.L.F.	Kips per Linear Foot
Km	Kilometer
K.S.F.	Kips per Square Foot
K.S.I.	Kips per Square Inch
kV	Kilovolt
kVA	Kilovolt Ampere
K.V.A.R.	Kilovar (Reactance)
KW	Kilowatt
KWh	Kilowatt-hour
L	Labor Only; Length; Long; Medium Wall Copper Tubing
Lab.	Labor
lat	Latitude
Lath.	Lather
Lav.	Lavatory
lb.; #	Pound
L.B.	Load Bearing; L Conduit Body
L. & E.	Labor & Equipment
lb./hr.	Pounds per Hour
lb./L.F.	Pounds per Linear Foot
lbf/sq.in.	Pound-force per Square Inch
L.C.L.	Less than Carload Lot
Ld.	Load
LE	Lead Equivalent
LED	Light Emitting Diode
L.F.	Linear Foot
Lg.	Long; Length; Large
L & H	Light and Heat
LH	Long Span Bar Joist
L.H.	Labor Hours
L.L.	Live Load
L.L.D.	Lamp Lumen Depreciation
L-O-L	Lateralolet
lm	Lumen
lm/sf	Lumen per Square Foot
lm/W	Lumen per Watt
L.O.A.	Length Over All
log	Logarithm
L.P.	Liquefied Petroleum; Low Pressure
L.P.F.	Low Power Factor
LR	Long Radius
L.S.	Lump Sum
Lt.	Light
Lt. Ga.	Light Gauge
L.T.L.	Less than Truckload Lot
Lt. Wt.	Lightweight
L.V.	Low Voltage
M	Thousand; Material; Male; Light Wall Copper Tubing
M²CA	Meters Squared Contact Area
m/hr; M.H.	Man-hour
mA	Milliampere
Mach.	Machine
Mag. Str.	Magnetic Starter
Maint.	Maintenance
Marb.	Marble Setter
Mat; Mat'l.	Material
Max.	Maximum
MBF	Thousand Board Feet
MBH	Thousand BTU's per hr.
MC	Metal Clad Cable
M.C.F.	Thousand Cubic Feet
M.C.F.M.	Thousand Cubic Feet per Minute
M.C.M.	Thousand Circular Mils
M.C.P.	Motor Circuit Protector
MD	Medium Duty
M.D.O.	Medium Density Overlaid
Med.	Medium
MF	Thousand Feet
M.F.B.M.	Thousand Feet Board Measure
Mfg.	Manufacturing
Mfrs.	Manufacturers
mg	Milligram
MGD	Million Gallons per Day
MGPH	Thousand Gallons per Hour
MH, M.H.	Manhole; Metal Halide; Man-Hour
MHz	Megahertz
Mi.	Mile
MI	Malleable Iron; Mineral Insulated
mm	Millimeter
Mill.	Millwright
Min., min.	Minimum, minute
Misc.	Miscellaneous
ml	Milliliter, Mainline
M.L.F.	Thousand Linear Feet
Mo.	Month
Mobil.	Mobilization
Mog.	Mogul Base
MPH	Miles per Hour
MPT	Male Pipe Thread
MRT	Mile Round Trip
ms	Millisecond
M.S.F.	Thousand Square Feet
Mstz.	Mosaic & Terrazzo Worker
M.S.Y.	Thousand Square Yards
Mtd.	Mounted
Mthe.	Mosaic & Terrazzo Helper
Mtng.	Mounting
Mult.	Multi; Multiply
M.V.A.	Million Volt Amperes
M.V.A.R.	Million Volt Amperes Reactance
MV	Megavolt
MW	Megawatt
MXM	Male by Male
MYD	Thousand Yards
N	Natural; North
nA	Nanoampere
NA	Not Available; Not Applicable
N.B.C.	National Building Code
NC	Normally Closed
N.E.M.A.	National Electrical Manufacturers Assoc.
NEHB	Bolted Circuit Breaker to 600V.
N.L.B.	Non-Load-Bearing
NM	Non-Metallic Cable
nm	Nanometer
No.	Number
NO	Normally Open
N.O.C.	Not Otherwise Classified
Nose.	Nosing
N.P.T.	National Pipe Thread
NQOD	Combination Plug-on/Bolt on Circuit Breaker to 240V.
N.R.C.	Noise Reduction Coefficient
N.R.S.	Non Rising Stem
ns	Nanosecond
nW	Nanowatt
OB	Opposing Blade
OC	On Center
OD	Outside Diameter
O.D.	Outside Dimension
ODS	Overhead Distribution System
O.G.	Ogee
O.H.	Overhead
O & P	Overhead and Profit
Oper.	Operator
Opng.	Opening
Orna.	Ornamental
OSB	Oriented Strand Board
O. S. & Y.	Outside Screw and Yoke
Ovhd.	Overhead
OWG	Oil, Water or Gas

Abbreviations

Oz.	Ounce	S.	Suction; Single Entrance; South	THHN	Nylon Jacketed Wire
P.	Pole; Applied Load; Projection	SCFM	Standard Cubic Feet per Minute	THW.	Insulated Strand Wire
p.	Page	Scaf.	Scaffold	THWN;	Nylon Jacketed Wire
Pape.	Paperhanger	Sch.; Sched.	Schedule	T.L.	Truckload
P.A.P.R.	Powered Air Purifying Respirator	S.C.R.	Modular Brick	T.M.	Track Mounted
PAR	Weatherproof Reflector	S.D.	Sound Deadening	Tot.	Total
Pc., Pcs.	Piece, Pieces	S.D.R.	Standard Dimension Ratio	T-O-L	Threadolet
P.C.	Portland Cement; Power Connector	S.E.	Surfaced Edge	T.S.	Trigger Start
P.C.F.	Pounds per Cubic Foot	Sel.	Select	Tr.	Trade
P.C.M.	Phase Contract Microscopy	S.E.R.;	Service Entrance Cable	Transf.	Transformer
P.E.	Professional Engineer;	S.E.U.	Service Entrance Cable	Trhv.	Truck Driver, Heavy
	Porcelain Enamel;	S.F.	Square Foot	Trlr	Trailer
	Polyethylene; Plain End	S.F.C.A.	Square Foot Contact Area	Trlt.	Truck Driver, Light
Perf.	Perforated	S.F.G.	Square Foot of Ground	TV	Television
Ph.	Phase	S.F. Hor.	Square Foot Horizontal	T.W.	Thermoplastic Water Resistant
P.I.	Pressure Injected	S.F.R.	Square Feet of Radiation		Wire
Pile.	Pile Driver	S.F. Shlf.	Square Foot of Shelf	UCI	Uniform Construction Index
Pkg.	Package	S4S	Surface 4 Sides	UF	Underground Feeder
Pl.	Plate	Shee.	Sheet Metal Worker	UGND	Underground Feeder
Plah.	Plasterer Helper	Sin.	Sine	U.H.F.	Ultra High Frequency
Plas.	Plasterer	Skwk.	Skilled Worker	U.L.	Underwriters Laboratory
Pluh.	Plumbers Helper	SL	Saran Lined	Unfin.	Unfinished
Plum.	Plumber	S.L.	Slimline	URD	Underground Residential
Ply.	Plywood	Sldr.	Solder		Distribution
p.m.	Post Meridiem	SLH	Super Long Span Bar Joist	US	United States
Pntd.	Painted	S.N.	Solid Neutral	USP	United States Primed
Pord.	Painter, Ordinary	S-O-L	Socketolet	UTP	Unshielded Twisted Pair
pp	Pages	sp	Standpipe	V	Volt
PP; PPL	Polypropylene	S.P.	Static Pressure; Single Pole; Self-	V.A.	Volt Amperes
P.P.M.	Parts per Million		Propelled	V.C.T.	Vinyl Composition Tile
Pr.	Pair	Spri.	Sprinkler Installer	VAV	Variable Air Volume
P.E.S.B.	Pre-engineered Steel Building	spwg	Static Pressure Water Gauge	VC	Veneer Core
Prefab.	Prefabricated	Sq.	Square; 100 Square Feet	Vent.	Ventilation
Prefin.	Prefinished	S.P.D.T.	Single Pole, Double Throw	Vert.	Vertical
Prop.	Propelled	SPF	Spruce Pine Fir	V.F.	Vinyl Faced
PSF; psf	Pounds per Square Foot	S.P.S.T.	Single Pole, Single Throw	V.G.	Vertical Grain
PSI; psi	Pounds per Square Inch	SPT	Standard Pipe Thread	V.H.F.	Very High Frequency
PSIG	Pounds per Square Inch Gauge	Sq. Hd.	Square Head	VHO	Very High Output
PSP	Plastic Sewer Pipe	Sq. In.	Square Inch	Vib.	Vibrating
Pspr.	Painter, Spray	S.S.	Single Strength; Stainless Steel	V.L.F.	Vertical Linear Foot
Psst.	Painter, Structural Steel	S.S.B.	Single Strength B Grade	Vol.	Volume
P.T.	Potential Transformer	sst	Stainless Steel	VRP	Vinyl Reinforced Polyester
P. & T.	Pressure & Temperature	Sswk.	Structural Steel Worker	W	Wire; Watt; Wide; West
Ptd.	Painted	Sswl.	Structural Steel Welder	w/	With
Ptns.	Partitions	St.; Stl.	Steel	W.C.	Water Column; Water Closet
Pu	Ultimate Load	S.T.C.	Sound Transmission Coefficient	W.F.	Wide Flange
PVC	Polyvinyl Chloride	Std.	Standard	W.G.	Water Gauge
Pvmt.	Pavement	STK	Select Tight Knot	Wldg.	Welding
Pwr.	Power	STP	Standard Temperature & Pressure	W. Mile	Wire Mile
Q	Quantity Heat Flow	Stpi.	Steamfitter, Pipefitter	W-O-L	Weldolet
Quan.; Qty.	Quantity	Str.	Strength; Starter; Straight	W.R.	Water Resistant
Q.C.	Quick Coupling	Strd.	Stranded	Wrck.	Wrecker
r	Radius of Gyration	Struct.	Structural	W.S.P.	Water, Steam, Petroleum
R	Resistance	Sty.	Story	WT., Wt.	Weight
R.C.P.	Reinforced Concrete Pipe	Subj.	Subject	WWF	Welded Wire Fabric
Rect.	Rectangle	Subs.	Subcontractors	XFER	Transfer
Reg.	Regular	Surf.	Surface	XFMR	Transformer
Reinf.	Reinforced	Sw.	Switch	XHD	Extra Heavy Duty
Req'd.	Required	Swbd.	Switchboard	XHHW; XLPE	Cross-Linked Polyethylene Wire
Res.	Resistant	S.Y.	Square Yard		Insulation
Resi.	Residential	Syn.	Synthetic	XLP	Cross-linked Polyethylene
Rgh.	Rough	S.Y.P.	Southern Yellow Pine	Y	Wye
RGS	Rigid Galvanized Steel	Sys.	System	yd	Yard
R.H.W.	Rubber, Heat & Water Resistant;	t.	Thickness	yr	Year
	Residential Hot Water	T	Temperature; Ton	Δ	Delta
rms	Root Mean Square	Tan	Tangent	%	Percent
Rnd.	Round	T.C.	Terra Cotta	~	Approximately
Rodm.	Rodman	T & C	Threaded and Coupled	∅	Phase
Rofc.	Roofer, Composition	T.D.	Temperature Difference	@	At
Rofp.	Roofer, Precast	T.E.M.	Transmission Electron Microscopy	#	Pound; Number
Rohe.	Roofer Helpers (Composition)	TFE	Tetrafluoroethylene (Teflon)	<	Less Than
Rots.	Roofer, Tile & Slate	T. & G.	Tongue & Groove;	>	Greater Than
R.O.W.	Right of Way		Tar & Gravel		
RPM	Revolutions per Minute	Th.; Thk.	Thick		
R.R.	Direct Burial Feeder Conduit	Thn.	Thin		
R.S.	Rapid Start	Thrded	Threaded		
Rsr	Riser	Tilf.	Tile Layer, Floor		
RT	Round Trip	Tilh.	Tile Layer, Helper		

RESIDENTIAL COST ESTIMATE

OWNER'S NAME: _____   APPRAISER: _____

RESIDENCE ADDRESS: _____   PROJECT: _____

CITY, STATE, ZIP CODE: _____   DATE: _____

CLASS OF CONSTRUCTION
- ☐ ECONOMY
- ☐ AVERAGE
- ☐ CUSTOM
- ☐ LUXURY

RESIDENCE TYPE
- ☐ 1 STORY
- ☐ 1-1/2 STORY
- ☐ 2 STORY
- ☐ 2-1/2 STORY
- ☐ 3 STORY
- ☐ BI-LEVEL
- ☐ TRI-LEVEL

CONFIGURATION
- ☐ DETACHED
- ☐ TOWN/ROW HOUSE
- ☐ SEMI-DETACHED

OCCUPANCY
- ☐ ONE STORY
- ☐ TWO FAMILY
- ☐ THREE FAMILY
- ☐ OTHER _____

EXTERIOR WALL SYSTEM
- ☐ WOOD SIDING—WOOD FRAME
- ☐ BRICK VENEER—WOOD FRAME
- ☐ STUCCO ON WOOD FRAME
- ☐ PAINTED CONCRETE BLOCK
- ☐ SOLID MASONRY (AVERAGE & CUSTOM)
- ☐ STONE VENEER—WOOD FRAME
- ☐ SOLID BRICK (LUXURY)
- ☐ SOLID STONE (LUXURY)

*LIVING AREA (Main Building)

First Level	_____ S.F.
Second Level	_____ S.F.
Third Level	_____ S.F.
Total	_____ S.F.

*LIVING AREA (Wing or Ell) (   )

First Level	_____ S.F.
Second Level	_____ S.F.
Third Level	_____ S.F.
Total	_____ S.F.

*LIVING AREA (Wing or Ell) (   )

First Level	_____ S.F.
Second Level	_____ S.F.
Third Level	_____ S.F.
Total	_____ S.F.

*Basement Area is not part of living area.

MAIN BUILDING	COSTS PER S.F. LIVING AREA
Cost per Square Foot of Living Area, from Page _____	$
Basement Addition: _____ % Finished, _____ % Unfinished	+
Roof Cover Adjustment: _____ Type, Page _____ (Add or Deduct)	( )
Central Air Conditioning: ☐ Separate Ducts ☐ Heating Ducts, Page _____	+
Heating System Adjustment: _____ Type, Page _____ (Add or Deduct)	( )
Main Building: Adjusted Cost per S.F. of Living Area	$

MAIN BUILDING TOTAL COST

$ /S.F.	x	S.F.	x		=	$
Cost per S.F. Living Area		Living Area		Town/Row House Multiplier (Use 1 for Detached)		TOTAL COST

WING OR ELL ( ) _____ STORY	COSTS PER S.F. LIVING AREA
Cost per Square Foot of Living Area, from Page _____	$
Basement Addition: _____ % Finished, _____ % Unfinished	+
Roof Cover Adjustment: _____ Type, Page _____ (Add or Deduct)	( )
Central Air Conditioning: ☐ Separate Ducts ☐ Heating Ducts, Page _____	+
Heating System Adjustment: _____ Type, Page _____ (Add or Deduct)	( )
Wing or Ell ( ): Adjusted Cost per S.F. of Living Area	$

WING OR ELL (   ) TOTAL COST

$ /S.F.	x	S.F.	=	$
Cost per S.F. Living Area		Living Area		TOTAL COST

WING OR ELL ( ) _____ STORY	COSTS PER S.F. LIVING AREA
Cost per Square Foot of Living Area, from Page _____	$
Basement Addition: _____ % Finished, _____ % Unfinished	+
Roof Cover Adjustment: _____ Type, Page _____ (Add or Deduct)	( )
Central Air Conditioning: ☐ Separate Ducts ☐ Heating Ducts, Page _____	+
Heating System Adjustment: _____ Type, Page _____ (Add or Deduct)	( )
Wing or Ell ( ): Adjusted Cost per S.F. of Living Area	$

WING OR ELL (   ) TOTAL COST

$ /S.F.	x	S.F.	=	$
Cost per S.F. Living Area		Living Area		TOTAL COST

TOTAL THIS PAGE [_____]

Page 1 of 2

RESIDENTIAL
COST ESTIMATE

		QUANTITY	UNIT COST	
Total Page 1				$
Additional Bathrooms: _____ Full, _____ Half				
Finished Attic: _____ Ft. x _____ Ft.		S.F.		+
Breezeway: ☐ Open ☐ Enclosed _____ Ft. x _____ Ft.		S.F.		+
Covered Porch: ☐ Open ☐ Enclosed _____ Ft. x _____ Ft.		S.F.		+
Fireplace: ☐ Interior Chimney ☐ Exterior Chimney ☐ No. of Flues ☐ Additional Fireplaces				+
Appliances:				+
Kitchen Cabinets Adjustment: (+/−)				
☐ Garage ☐ Carport: _____ Car(s) Description _____ (+/−)				
Miscellaneous:				+

ADJUSTED TOTAL BUILDING COST $ _____

REPLACEMENT COST	
ADJUSTED TOTAL BUILDING COST	$ _____
Site Improvements	
(A) Paving & Sidewalks	$ _____
(B) Landscaping	$ _____
(C) Fences	$ _____
(D) Swimming Pool	$ _____
(E) Miscellaneous	$ _____
TOTAL	$ _____
Location Factor	x _____
Location Replacement Cost	$ _____
Depreciation	−$ _____
LOCAL DEPRECIATED COST	$ _____

INSURANCE COST	
ADJUSTED TOTAL BUILDING COST	$ _____
Insurance Exclusions	
(A) Footings, Site Work, Underground Piping	−$ _____
(B) Architects' Fees	−$ _____
Total Building Cost Less Exclusion	$ _____
Location Factor	x _____
LOCAL INSURABLE REPLACEMENT COST	$ _____

SKETCH AND ADDITIONAL CALCULATIONS

CII APPRAISAL

1. SUBJECT PROPERTY: _____

2. BUILDING: _____

3. ADDRESS: _____

4. BUILDING USE: _____

5. DATE: _____

6. APPRAISER: _____

7. YEAR BUILT: _____

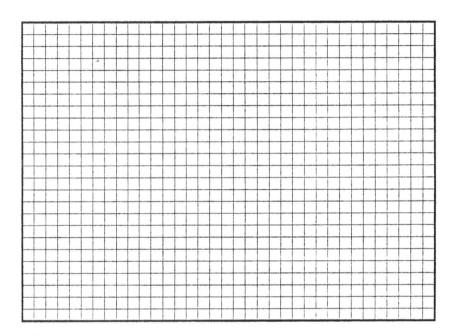

8. EXTERIOR WALL CONSTRUCTION: _____

9. FRAME: _____

10. GROUND FLOOR AREA: _____ S.F.   11. GROSS FLOOR AREA (EXCL. BASEMENT): _____ S.F.

12. NUMBER OF STORIES: _____   13. STORY HEIGHT: _____

14. PERIMETER: _____ L.F.   15. BASEMENT AREA: _____ S.F.

16. GENERAL COMMENTS: _____
_____
_____
_____
_____
_____
_____

SQUARE FOOT AREA *(EXCLUDING BASEMENT)* FROM ITEM 11 _____ S.F. _____

PERIMETER FROM ITEM 14 _____ L.F. _____

ITEM 17– MODEL SQUARE FOOT COSTS *(FROM MODEL SUB-TOTAL)* $ _____

Field Description & Calculation Section

NO.	SYSTEM/COMPONENT		DESCRIPTION	UNIT	UNIT COST	NEW S.F. COST	MODEL S.F. COST	+/– CHANGE
1.0	**FOUNDATION**							
.1	Bldg. Excavation	Depth						
		Area		S.F.				
	Trench Excavation	Depth Width	Length	L.F.				
.2	Footings: Strip Width	L.F. Length		L.F.				
	Footings: Spread	Bay Size		S.F. Gnd.				
		Other						
.3	Foundation Wall	Material						
		Height Thickness		L.F. Wall				
.4	Slab on Grade	Material Thickness		S.F. Gnd.				
3.0	**SUPERSTRUCTURE**							
.1	Elevated Floors	Bay Size Material						
		Member Size		S.F. Floor				
.2	Roof Structure	Material						
		Bay Size						
		Member Size		S.F. Roof				
.3	Column/Bearing Wall							
	Column	Size		L.F. Col.				
		Bay Size						
	Bearing Wall	Material						
		Thickness		L.F. Wall				
.4	Fireproofing	Material		S.F. Surf.				
4.0	**EXTERIOR WALLS**		Building Ht. _____ Ft.					
.1	Outer Wall	Material						
		Thickness		S.F. Wall				
.2	Interior Finish			S.F. Wall				
.3	Windows	Type						
		% of Wall		S.F. Wind.				
.4	Doors	Type						
		Density		S.F. Door				
5.0	**ROOFING**							
.1	Roof Covering	Material		S.F. Roof				

NO.	SYSTEM/COMPONENT		DESCRIPTION	UNIT	UNIT COST	NEW S.F. COST	MODEL S.F. COST	+/– CHANGE
6.0	**INTERIOR CONSTRUCTION**							
.1	Partitions	Material						
		Density		S.F. Part.				
.2	Doors	Type						
		Density		S.F. Door				
.3	Floor Finish	Material						
		% of Floor		S.F. Floor				
.4	Ceiling Finish	Material						
		% of Ceiling		S.F. Ceil.				
.5	Partition Finish	Material Size		S.F. Surf.				
7.0	**CONVEYING SYSTEM**							
.1	Vertical	Type		Each				
		Capacity						
		Stops						
8.0	**MECHANICAL SYSTEMS**							
.1	Plumbing			Each				
.2	Fire Protection			S.F.				
.3	Heating	Type		S.F.				
.4	Air Conditioning			S.F.				
9.0	**ELECTRICAL**							
.1	Lighting			S.F.				
10.0	**MISCELLANEOUS**							
11.0	**SPECIALTIES**							

Item   Total Change

18. ADJUSTED S.F. COST $ _____ ITEM 17+/–CHANGES

19. BUILDING AREA – FROM ITEM 11 _____ S.F. X ADJUSTED S.F. COST $ .... $ _____

20. BASEMENT AREA – FROM ITEM 15 _____ S.F. X S.F. COST $ .... $ _____

21. BASE BUILDING SUB-TOTAL – ITEM 20 + ITEM 19 .... $ _____

22. MISCELLANEOUS ADDITION (QUALITY, ETC.) .... $ _____

23. SUB-TOTAL – ITEM 22 + ITEM 21 .... $ _____

24. GENERAL CONDITIONS – 15% OF ITEM 23 .... $ _____

25. SUB-TOTAL – ITEM 24 + ITEM 23 .... $ _____

26. ARCHITECT'S FEES _____ % OF ITEM 25 .... $ _____

27. SUB-TOTAL – ITEM 26 + ITEM 25 .... $ _____

28. LOCATION MODIFIER ....   X _____

29. LOCAL REPLACEMENT COST – ITEM 28 X ITEM 27 .... $ _____

30. DEPRECIATION _____ % OF ITEM 29 .... $ _____

31. DEPRECIATED LOCAL REPLACEMENT COST – ITEM 29 LESS ITEM 30 .... $ _____

32. EXCLUSIONS .... $ _____

33. NET DEPRECIATED REPLACEMENT COST – ITEM 31 LESS ITEM 32 .... $ _____

Base Cost per square foot floor area: *(from square foot table)*

Specify source:

Page: _____ , Model # _____ , Area _____ S.F.,
Exterior wall _____ , Frame _____

Adjustments for exterior wall variation:

Size Adjustment:
   (Interpolate)

Height Adjustment: _____ + _____ = _____

Adjusted Base Cost per square foot:

Building Cost $ _____ x _____ = _____
                   Adjusted Base Cost   *Floor Area*
                   per square foot

Basement Cost $ _____ x _____ = _____
                      Basement Cost   *Basement Area*

Lump Sum Additions

TOTAL BUILDING COST *(Sum of above costs)*   _____

Modifications: *(complexity, workmanship, size)*   +/- _____ %   _____

Location Modifier: City _____ Date _____   x   _____

   Local cost of replacement   _____

Less depreciation: _____   -   _____

   Local cost of replacement less depreciation $ _____

Means Project Cost Report

By filling out and returning the Project Description, you can receive a discount of $20.00 off any one of the Means products advertised in the following pages. The cost information required includes all items marked (✔) except those where no costs occurred. The sum of all major items should equal the Total Project Cost.

$20.00 Discount per product for each report you submit.

DISCOUNT PRODUCTS AVAILABLE—FOR U.S. CUSTOMERS ONLY—STRICTLY CONFIDENTIAL

Project Description (No remodeling projects, please.)

✔ Type Building _____

✔ Location _____

  Capacity _____

✔ Frame _____

✔ Exterior _____

✔ Basement: full ☐ partial ☐ none ☐ crawl ☐

✔ Height in Stories _____

✔ Total Floor Area _____

  Ground Floor Area _____

✔ Volume in C.F. _____

  % Air Conditioned _____ Tons _____

  Comments _____

Owner _____

Architect _____

General Contractor _____

✔ Bid Date _____

  Typical Bay Size _____

✔ Labor Force: _____ % Union _____ % Non-Union

✔ Project Description (Circle one number in each line)
1. Economy 2. Average 3. Custom 4. Luxury
1. Square 2. Rectangular 3. Irregular 4. Very Irregular

	✔ **Total Project Cost**		$	
A	✔ **General Conditions**		$	
B	✔ **Site Work**		$	
BS	**Site Clearing & Improvement**			
BE	Excavation	(	C.Y.)	
BF	Caissons & Piling	(	L.F.)	
BU	Site Utilities			
BP	Roads & Walks Exterior Paving	(	S.Y.)	
C	✔ **Concrete**		$	
C	Cast in Place	(	C.Y.)	
CP	Precast	(	S.F.)	
D	✔ **Masonry**		$	
DB	Brick	(	M)	
DC	Block	(	M)	
DT	Tile	(	S.F.)	
DS	Stone	(	S.F.)	
E	✔ **Metals**		$	
ES	Structural Steel	(	Tons)	
EM	Misc. & Ornamental Metals			
F	✔ **Wood & Plastics**		$	
FR	Rough Carpentry	(	MBF)	
FF	Finish Carpentry			
FM	Architectural Millwork			
G	✔ **Thermal & Moisture Protection**		$	
GW	Waterproofing-Dampproofing	(	S.F.)	
GN	Insulation	(	S.F.)	
GR	Roofing & Flashing	(	S.F.)	
GM	Metal Siding/Curtain Wall	(	S.F.)	
H	✔ **Doors and Windows**		$	
HD	Doors	(	Ea.)	
HW	Windows	(	S.F.)	
HH	Finish Hardware			
HG	Glass & Glazing	(	S.F.)	
HS	Storefronts	(	S.F.)	

J	✔ **Finishes**		$	
JL	Lath & Plaster	(	S.Y.)	
JD	Drywall	(	S.F.)	
JM	Tile & Marble	(	S.F.)	
JT	Terrazzo	(	S.F.)	
JA	Acoustical Treatment	(	S.F.)	
JC	Carpet	(	S.Y.)	
JF	Hard Surface Flooring	(	S.F.)	
JP	Painting & Wall Covering	(	S.F.)	
K	✔ **Specialties**		$	
KB	Bathroom Partitions & Access.	(	S.F.)	
KF	Other Partitions	(	S.F.)	
KL	Lockers	(	Ea.)	
L	✔ **Equipment**		$	
LK	Kitchen			
LS	School			
LO	Other			
M	✔ **Furnishings**		$	
MW	Window Treatment			
MS	Seating	(	Ea.)	
N	✔ **Special Construction**		$	
NA	Acoustical	(	S.F.)	
NB	Prefab. Bldgs.	(	S.F.)	
NO	Other			
P	✔ **Conveying Systems**		$	
PE	Elevators	(	Ea.)	
PS	Escalators	(	Ea.)	
PM	Material Handling			
Q	✔ **Mechanical**		$	
QP	Plumbing	(No. of fixtures	)	
QS	Fire Protection (Sprinklers)			
QF	Fire Protection (Hose Standpipes)			
QB	Heating, Ventilating & A.C.			
QH	Heating & Ventilating	(BTU Output	)	
QA	Air Conditioning	(	Tons)	
R	✔ **Electrical**		$	
RL	Lighting	(	S.F.)	
RP	Power Service			
RD	Power Distribution			
RA	Alarms			
RG	Special Systems			
S	✔ **Mech./Elec. Combined**		$	

Product Name _____

Product Number _____

Your Name _____

Title _____

Company _____

  ☐ Company

  ☐ Home Street Address _____

City, State, Zip _____

☐ Please send _____ forms.

Please specify the Means product you wish to receive. Complete the address information as requested and return this form with your check (product cost less $20.00) to address below.

R.S. Means Company, Inc.,
Square Foot Costs Department
P.O. Box 800
Kingston, MA 02364-9988

R.S. Means Company, Inc. . . a tradition of excellence in Construction Cost Information and Services since 1942.

Table of Contents

Book Selection Guide

The following table provides definitive information on the content of each cost data publication. The number of lines of data provided in each unit price or assemblies division, as well as the number of reference tables and crews is listed for each book. The presence of other elements such as an historical cost index, city cost indexes, square foot models or cross-referenced index is also indicated. You can use the table to help select the Means' book that has the quantity and type of information you most need in your work.

Unit Cost Divisions	Building Construction Costs	Mechanical	Electrical	Repair & Remodel.	Square Foot	Site Work Landsc.	Assemblies	Interior	Concrete Masonry	Open Shop	Heavy Construc.	Resi-dential	Light Commercial	Facil. Construc.	Plumbing	Western Construction Costs
1	1098	586	667	862		1089		491	987	1096	1132	416	621	1612	659	1091
2	3141	1467	509	1881		9149		852	1655	3090	5621	1064	984	5015	1826	3114
3	1516	91	71	768		1321		198	1937	1510	1494	268	233	1378	43	1514
4	871	27	0	688		751		636	1174	853	651	313	396	1124	0	849
5	1857	177	174	955		803		985	667	1824	1056	779	809	1849	95	1841
6	1388	97	84	1314		493		1336	339	1379	612	1532	1473	1411	59	1772
7	1365	180	91	1329		490		546	451	1365	353	805	1036	1357	188	1364
8	1899	60	0	1904		337		1821	726	1880	9	1133	1184	2032	0	1900
9	1650	50	0	1473		188		1746	327	1598	113	1251	1390	1845	50	1644
10	991	58	31	565		217		822	196	995	0	250	467	996	249	991
11	1158	435	213	622		151		917	34	1052	95	116	237	1221	371	1051
12	352	0	0	48		228		1536	30	344	0	72	68	1538	0	343
13	1384	1221	498	587		443		1075	106	1358	302	237	562	2094	1083	1339
14	364	43	0	261		36		330	0	364	40	9	18	362	17	362
15	2510	14742	763	2243		1809		1477	80	2515	2028	1087	1553	12312	10902	2545
16	1517	541	10191	1200		879		1292	62	1535	916	706	1290	9872	481	1459
17	421	0		421		0		421	421	460	0	421	421	421	0	421
Totals	23482	19775	13292	17121		18384		16508	9192	23218	14422	10459	12742	46439	16023	23600

Assembly Divisions	Building Construction Costs	Mechanical	Electrical	Repair & Remodel.	Square Foot	Site Work Landsc.	Assemblies	Interior	Concrete Masonry	Open Shop	Heavy Construc.	Resi-dential	Light Commercial	Facil. Construc.	Plumbing	Western Construction Costs
1		0	0	202	131	738	775	0	689		752	841	131	89	0	
2		0	0	40	33	35	48	0	40		0	584	32	0	0	
3		0	0	443	1114	0	3064	228	1245		0	1546	805	174	0	
4		0	0	714	1382	0	3201	255	1273		0	2050	1200	26	0	
5		0	0	288	227	0	459	0	0		0	1081	223	25	0	
6		0	0	1006	843	0	1295	1723	152		0	1077	738	330	0	
7		0	0	42	89	0	179	159	0		0	709	33	71	0	
8		2257	149	998	1689	0	2718	926	0		0	1686	1189	1114	2084	
9		0	1383	355	367	0	1320	306	0		0	238	358	319	0	
10		0	0	0	0	0	0	0	0		0	0	0	0	0	
11		0	0	365	465	0	724	153	0		0	0	466	201	0	
12		501	160	539	84	2392	699	0	698		541	0	84	119	663	
Totals		2758	1692	4992	6424	3165	14482	3750	4106		1293	9812	5259	2468	2747	

Reference Section	Building Construction Costs	Mechanical	Electrical	Repair & Remodel.	Square Foot	Site Work Landsc.	Assemblies	Interior	Concrete Masonry	Open Shop	Heavy Construc.	Resi-dential	Light Commercial	Facil. Construc.	Plumbing	Western Construction Costs
Tables	150	46	84	66	4	84	223	59	83	146	55	49	70	86	49	148
Models					102								32	43		
Crews	408	408	408	389		408		408	408	391	408	391	391	389	408	408
City Cost Indexes	yes	yes	yes	yes	yes	yes	yes	yes	yes	yes	yes	yes	yes	yes	yes	yes
Historical Cost Indexes	yes	yes	yes	yes	yes	yes	yes	yes	yes	yes	yes	no	yes	yes	yes	yes
Index	yes	yes	yes	yes	no	yes	yes	yes	yes	yes	yes	yes	yes	yes	yes	yes

1

Annual Cost Guides

For more information
visit Means Web Site
at www.rsmeans.com

Means Building Construction Cost Data 2001

Available in Both Softbound and Looseleaf Editions

The "Bible" of the industry comes in the standard softcover edition or the looseleaf edition.

Many customers enjoy the convenience and flexibility of the looseleaf binder, which increases the usefulness of *Means Building Construction Cost Data 2001* by making it easy to add and remove pages. You can insert your own cost information pages, so everything is in one place. Copying pages for faxing is easier also. Whichever edition you prefer, softbound or the convenient looseleaf edition, you'll get the *DesignBuildIntelligence* newsletter at no extra cost.

$89.95 per copy, Softbound
Catalog No. 60011

$116.95 per copy, Looseleaf
Catalog No. 61011

Means Building Construction Cost Data 2001

Offers you unchallenged unit price reliability in an easy-to-use arrangement. Whether used for complete, finished estimates or for periodic checks, it supplies more cost facts better and faster than any comparable source. Over 23,000 unit prices for 2001. The City Cost Indexes cover over 930 areas, for indexing to any project location in North America. Order and get the *DesignBuildIntelligence* newsletter sent to you FREE. You'll have year-long access to the Means Estimating **Hotline** FREE with your subscription. Expert assistance when using Means data is just a phone call away.

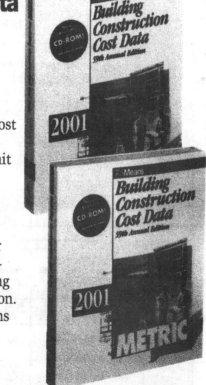

$89.95 per copy
Over 650 pages, illustrated, available Oct. 2000
Catalog No. 60011

Means Building Construction Cost Data 2001
Metric Version

The Federal Government has stated that all federal construction projects must now use metric documentation. The *Metric Version* of *Means Building Construction Cost Data 2001* is presented in metric measurements covering all construction areas. Don't miss out on these billion dollar opportunities. Make the switch to metric today.

$89.95 per copy
Over 650 pages, illustrated, available Nov. 2000
Catalog No. 63011

For more information
visit Means Web Site
at www.rsmeans.com

Annual Cost Guides

Means Mechanical Cost Data 2001

· HVAC · Controls

Total unit and systems price guidance for mechanical construction . . . materials, parts, fittings, and complete labor cost information. Includes prices for piping, heating, air conditioning, ventilation, and all related construction.

Plus new 2001 unit costs for:

· Over 2500 installed HVAC/controls assemblies
· "On Site" Location Factors for over 930 cities and towns in the U.S. and Canada
· Crews, labor and equipment

$89.95 per copy
Over 600 pages, illustrated, available Oct. 2000
Catalog No. 60021

Means Plumbing Cost Data 2001

Comprehensive unit prices and assemblies for plumbing, irrigation systems, commercial and residential fire protection, point-of-use water heaters, and the latest approved materials. This publication and its companion, *Means Mechanical Cost Data*, provide full-range cost estimating coverage for all the mechanical trades.

$89.95 per copy
Over 500 pages, illustrated, available Nov. 2000
Catalog No. 60211

Means Electrical Cost Data 2001

Pricing information for every part of electrical cost planning: More than 15,000 unit and systems costs with design tables; clear specifications and drawings; engineering guides and illustrated estimating procedures; complete labor-hour and materials costs for better scheduling and procurement; the latest electrical products and construction methods.

· A Variety of Special Electrical Systems including Cathodic Protection
· Costs for maintenance, demolition, HVAC/ mechanical, specialties, equipment, and more

$89.95 per copy
Over 450 pages, illustrated, available Oct. 2000
Catalog No. 60031

Means Electrical Change Order Cost Data 2001

You are provided with electrical unit prices exclusively for pricing change orders—based on the recent, direct experience of contractors and suppliers. Analyze and check your own change order estimates against the experience others have had doing the same work. It also covers productivity analysis and change order cost justifications. With useful information for calculating the effects of change orders and dealing with their administration.

$89.95 per copy
Over 450 pages, available Oct. 2000
Catalog No. 60231

Means Facilities Maintenance & Repair Cost Data 2001

Published in a looseleaf format, *Means Facilities Maintenance & Repair Cost Data* gives you a complete system to manage and plan your facility repair and maintenance costs and budget efficiently. Guidelines for auditing a facility and developing an annual maintenance plan. Budgeting is included, along with reference tables on cost and management and information on frequency and productivity of maintenance operations.

The only nationally recognized source of maintenance and repair costs. Developed in cooperation with the Army Corps of Engineers.

$199.95 per copy
Over 600 pages, illustrated, available Dec. 2000
Catalog No. 60301

Means Square Foot Costs 2001

It's Accurate and Easy To Use!

· **Updated 2001 price information,** based on nationwide figures from suppliers, estimators, labor experts and contractors.

· "How-to-Use" Sections, with **clear examples** of commercial, residential, industrial, and institutional structures.

· Realistic graphics, offering true-to-life illustrations of building projects.

· Extensive information on using square foot cost data, including **sample estimates** and **alternate pricing methods.**

$99.95 per copy
Over 450 pages, illustrated, available Oct. 2000
Catalog No. 60051

Annual Cost Guides

For more information
visit Means Web Site
at www.rsmeans.com

Means Repair & Remodeling
Cost Data 2001
Commercial/Residential

You can use this valuable tool to estimate
commercial and residential renovation and
remodeling.

**Includes: New costs for hundreds of unique
methods, materials and conditions that only come
up in repair and remodeling. PLUS:**

· Unit costs for over 16,000 construction
  components
· Installed costs for over 90 assemblies
· Costs for 300+ construction crews
· Over 930 "On Site" localization factors for the
  U.S. and Canada.

$79.95 per copy
Over 600 pages, illustrated, available Nov. 2000
Catalog No. 60041

Means Facilities
Construction
Cost Data 2001

For the maintenance and construction of
commercial, industrial, municipal, and institutional
properties. Costs are shown for new and remodeling
construction and are broken down into materials,
labor, equipment, overhead, and profit. Special
emphasis is given to sections on mechanical,
electrical, furnishings, site work, building
maintenance, finish work, and demolition. More
than 45,000 unit costs plus assemblies and
reference sections are included.

$219.95 per copy
Over 1150 pages, illustrated, available Nov. 2000
Catalog No. 60201

Means Residential
Cost Data 2001

Contains square foot costs for 30 basic home
models with the look of today—plus hundreds of
custom additions and modifications you can quote
right off the page. With costs for the 100 residential
systems you're most likely to use in the year ahead.
Complete with blank estimating forms, sample
estimates and step-by-step instructions.

$79.95 per copy
Over 550 pages, illustrated, available Dec. 2000
Catalog No. 60171

Means Light Commercial
Cost Data 2001

Specifically addresses the light commercial market,
which is an increasingly specialized niche in the
industry. Aids you, the owner/designer/contractor,
in preparing all types of estimates, from budgets to
detailed bids. Includes new advances in methods
and materials. Assemblies section allows you to
evaluate alternatives in the early stages of
design/planning.

Over 13,000 unit costs for 2001 ensure you have
the prices you need... when you need them.

$79.95 per copy
Over 600 pages, illustrated, available Dec. 2000
Catalog No. 60181

Means Assemblies
Cost Data 2001

Means Assemblies Cost Data 2001 takes the
guesswork out of preliminary or conceptual
estimates. Now you don't have to try to calculate
the assembled cost by working up individual
components costs. We've done all the work for you.

Presents detailed illustrations, descriptions,
specifications and costs for every conceivable
building assembly—240 types in all—arranged in
the easy-to-use UniFormat system. Each illustrated
"assembled" cost includes a complete grouping of
materials and associated installation costs including
the installing contractor's overhead and profit.

$149.95 per copy
Over 550 pages, illustrated, available Oct. 2000
Catalog No. 60061

Means Site Work & Landscape
Cost Data 2001

Means Site Work & Landscape Cost Data 2001 is
organized to assist you in all your estimating needs.
Hundreds of fact-filled pages help you make
accurate cost estimates efficiently.

Updated for 2001!

· Demolition features—including
  ceilings, doors, electrical, flooring, HVAC,
  millwork, plumbing, roofing, walls and windows
· State-of-the-art segmental retaining walls
· Flywheel trenching costs and details
· Updated Wells section
· Thousands of landscape materials, flowers,
  shrubs and trees

$89.95 per copy
Over 600 pages, illustrated, available Oct. 2000
Catalog No. 60281

For more information
visit Means Web Site
at www.rsmeans.com

Annual Cost Guides

Means Open Shop Building Construction Cost Data 2001

The latest costs for accurate budgeting and estimating of new commercial and residential construction... renovation work... change orders... cost engineering. *Means Open Shop BCCD* will assist you to...
· Develop benchmark prices for change orders
· Plug gaps in preliminary estimates, budgets
· Estimate complex projects
· Substantiate invoices on contracts
· Price ADA-related renovations

$89.95 per copy
Over 650 pages, illustrated, available Nov. 2000
Catalog No. 60151

Means Heavy Construction Cost Data 2001

A comprehensive guide to heavy construction costs. Includes costs for highly specialized projects such as tunnels, dams, highways, airports, and waterways. Information on different labor rates, equipment, and material costs is included. Has unit price costs, systems costs, and numerous reference tables for costs and design. Valuable not only to contractors and civil engineers, but also to government agencies and city/town engineers.

$89.95 per copy
Over 450 pages, illustrated, available Nov. 2000
Catalog No. 60161

Means Building Construction Cost Data 2001

Western Edition

This regional edition provides more precise cost information for western North America. Labor rates are based on union rates from 13 western states and western Canada. Included are western practices and materials not found in our national edition: tilt-up concrete walls, glu-lam structural systems, specialized timber construction, seismic restraints, landscape and irrigation systems.

$89.95 per copy
Over 600 pages, illustrated, available Dec. 2000
Catalog No. 60221

Means Heavy Construction Cost Data 2001

Metric Version

Make sure you have the Means industry standard metric costs for the federal, state, municipal and private marketplace. With thousands of up-to-date metric unit prices in tables by CSI standard divisions. Supplies you with assemblies costs using the metric standard for reliable cost projections in the design stage of your project. Helps you determine sizes, material amounts, and has tips for handling metric estimates.

$89.95 per copy
Over 450 pages, illustrated, available Nov. 2000
Catalog No. 63161

Means Construction Cost Indexes 2001

Who knows what 2001 holds? What materials and labor costs will change unexpectedly? By how much?
· Breakdowns for 305 major cities.
· National averages for 30 key cities.
· Expanded five major city indexes.
· Historical construction cost indexes.

$198.00 per year/$49.50 individual quarters
Catalog No. 60141

Means Interior Cost Data 2001

Provides you with prices and guidance needed to make accurate interior work estimates. Contains costs on materials, equipment, hardware, custom installations, furnishings, labor costs . . . every cost factor for new and remodel commercial and industrial interior construction, including updated information on office furnishings, plus more than 50 reference tables. For contractors, facility managers, owners.

$89.95 per copy
Over 550 pages, illustrated, available Oct. 2000
Catalog No. 60091

Means Concrete & Masonry Cost Data 2001

Provides you with cost facts for virtually all concrete/masonry estimating needs, from complicated formwork to various sizes and face finishes of brick and block, all in great detail. The comprehensive unit cost section contains more than 8,500 selected entries. Also contains an assemblies cost section, and a detailed reference section which supplements the cost data.

$83.95 per copy
Over 450 pages, illustrated, available Nov. 2000
Catalog No. 60111

Means Labor Rates for the Construction Industry 2001

Complete information for estimating labor costs, making comparisons and negotiating wage rates by trade for over 300 cities (United States and Canada). With 46 construction trades listed by local union number in each city, and historical wage rates included for comparison. No similar book is available through the trade.

Each city chart lists the county and is alphabetically arranged with handy visual flip tabs for quick reference.

$199.95 per copy
Over 300 pages, available Dec. 2000
Catalog No. 60121

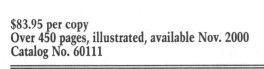

Reference Books

For more information
visit Means Web Site
at www.rsmeans.com

Project Scheduling & Management for Construction

New 2nd Edition

By David R. Pierce, Jr.

A comprehensive, yet easy-to-follow guide to construction project scheduling and control—from vital project management principles through the latest scheduling, tracking, and controlling techniques. The author is a leading authority on scheduling with years of field and teaching experience at leading academic institutions. Spend a few hours with this book and come away with a solid understanding of this essential management topic.

$64.95 per copy
Over 250 pages; illustrated, Hardcover
Catalog No. 67247A

Residential & Light Commercial Construction Standards

A Unique Collection of Industry Standards That Define Quality in Construction

For Contractors & Subcontractors, Owners, Developers, Architects & Engineers, Attorneys & Insurance Personnel

Compiled from the nation's major building codes, professional associations, and product manufacturer institutes, this unique resource enables you to:

• Set a standard for subcontractors and employees
• Protect yourself against defect claims
• Resolve disputes
• Answer client questions with authority

$59.95 per copy
Over 500 pages, illustrated, Softcover
Catalog No. 67322

The Building Professional's Guide to Contract Documents

New 3rd Edition

By Waller S. Poage, AIA, CSI, SAVE

This comprehensive treatment of Contract Documents is an important reference for owners, design professionals, contractors, and students.

• Structure your Documents for Maximum Efficiency
• Understand the Roles and Responsibilities of Construction Professionals
• Improve Methods of Project Delivery

$64.95 per copy, 400 pages
Diagrams and construction forms, Hardcover
Catalog No. 67261A

Cyberplaces II: The Internet Guide for AECs & Facility Managers 2nd Edition

By Paul Doherty

With an added section on the New Economy and e-commerce—such as AEC arbitrage, aggregate purchasing, auctions, e-supply chains, and more. Plus the best Knowledge Management and other Internet tools, including PDAs and the newest Web software for scheduling and project management.

The **Web site** keeps you current on the best Internet tools and applications for building design, construction and management—with workshops to put it all into practice.

$59.95 per copy
Over 700 pages, illustrated, Softcover
Catalog No. 67317A

Value Engineering: Practical Applications

... For Design, Construction, Maintenance & Operations

By Alphonse Dell'Isola, PE, leading authority on VE in construction

A tool for immediate application—for engineers, architects, facility managers, owners and contractors. Includes: Making the Case for VE—The Management Briefing, Integrating VE into Planning and Budgeting, Conducting Life Cycle Costing, Integrating VE into the Design Process, Using VE Methodology in Design Review and Consultant Selection, Case Studies, VE Workbook, and a Life Cycle Costing program on disk.

$79.95 per copy
Over 450 pages, illustrated, Hardcover
Catalog No. 67319

Means Landscape Estimating Methods

3rd Edition

By Sylvia H. Fee

This revised edition offers expert guidance for preparing accurate estimates for new landscape construction and grounds maintenance. Includes a complete project estimate featuring the latest equipment and methods, and **two totally new chapters—Life Cycle Costing and Landscape Maintenance Estimating.**

$62.95 per copy
Over 300 pages, illustrated, Hardcover
Catalog No. 67295A

For more information
visit Means Web Site
at www.rsmeans.com

Reference Books

Preventive Maintenance Guidelines for School Facilities

NEW! By John C. Maciha

This new publication gives you a complete program for school maintenance that ensures: sustained security, safety, property integrity, facility acceptance, user satisfaction, and reasonable ongoing expenditures.

Includes schedules for weekly, monthly, half-yearly and annual maintenance. 3-ring binder with hard copy forms, electronic forms on disk, and laminated wall chart.

$149.95 per copy
Over 150 pages, Hardcover
Catalog No. 67326

Means Environmental Remediation Estimating Methods By Richard R. Rast

Guidelines for estimating 50 standard remediation technologies. Use it to: prepare preliminary budgets, develop detailed estimates, compare costs and solutions, estimate liability, review quotes, negotiate settlements. A valuable support tool for *Means Environmental Remediation Unit Price* and *Assemblies books.*

$99.95 per copy
Over 600 pages, illustrated, Hardcover
Catalog No. 64777

Means Facilities Maintenance Standards By Roger W. Liska, PE, AIC

Unique features of this one-of-a-kind working guide for facilities maintenance

A working encyclopedia that points the way to solutions to every kind of maintenance and repair dilemma. With a labor-hours section to provide productivity figures for over 180 maintenance tasks. Included are ready-to-use forms, checklists, worksheets and comparisons, as well as analysis of materials systems and remedies for deterioration and wear.

$159.95 per copy, 600 pages, 205 tables, checklists and diagrams, Hardcover
Catalog No. 67246

HVAC: Design Criteria, Options, Selection
Expanded Second Edition

By William H. Rowe III, AIA, PE

Includes Indoor Air Quality, CFC Removal, Energy Efficient Systems and Special Systems by Building Type. Helps you solve a wide range of HVAC system design and selection problems effectively and economically. Gives you clear explanations of the latest ASHRAE standards.

$84.95 per copy
Over 600 pages, illustrated, Hardcover
Catalog No. 67306

The Facilities Manager's Reference

By Harvey H. Kaiser, PhD

The tasks and tools the facility manager needs to accomplish the organization's objectives, and develop individual and staff skills. Includes Facilities and Property Management, Administrative Control, Planning and Operations, Support Services, and a complete building audit with forms and instructions, widely used by facilities managers nationwide.

$86.95 per copy, over 250 pages, with prototype forms and graphics, Hardcover
Catalog No. 67264

Facilities Maintenance Management

By Gregory H. Magee, PE

Now you can get successful management methods and techniques for all aspects of facilities maintenance. This comprehensive reference explains and demonstrates successful management techniques for all aspects of maintenance, repair and improvements for buildings, machinery, equipment and grounds. Plus, guidance for outsourcing and managing internal staffs.

$86.95 per copy
Over 280 pages with illustrations, Hardcover
Catalog No. 67249

Cost Planning & Estimating for Facilities Maintenance

In this unique book, a team of facilities management authorities shares their expertise at:
· Evaluating and budgeting maintenance operations
· Maintaining & repairing key building components
· Applying *Means Facilities Maintenance & Repair Cost Data* to your estimating

With the special maintenance requirements of the 10 major building types.

$82.95 per copy
Over 475 pages, Hardcover
Catalog No. 67314

The ADA in Practice

By Deborah S. Kearney, PhD

Helps you meet and budget for the requirements of the Americans with Disabilities Act. Shows how to do the job right by understanding what the law requires, allows, and enforces. Includes a "buyers guide" for 70 ADA-compliant products.

*Winner of IFMA's "Distinguished Author of the Year" award.

See page 9 for another ADA resource.

$72.95 per copy
Over 600 pages, illustrated, Softcover
Catalog No. 67147A

Reference Books

For more information visit Means Web Site at www.rsmeans.com

Basics for Builders: Plan Reading & Material Takeoff
By Wayne J. DelPico

For Residential and Light Commercial Construction

A valuable tool for understanding plans and specs, and accurately calculating material quantities. Step-by-step instructions and takeoff procedures based on a full set of working drawings.

$35.95 per copy
Over 420 pages, Softcover
Catalog No. 67307

Planning & Managing Interior Projects New 2nd Edition, By Carol E. Farren, CFM

Addresses changes in technology and business, guiding you through commercial design and construction from initial client meetings to post-project administration. Includes: evaluating space requirements, alternative work models, telecommunications and data management, and environmental issues.

$69.95 per copy
Over 400 pages, illustrated, Hardcover
Catalog No. 67245A

Superintending for Contractors:
How to Bring Jobs in On-time, On-Budget
By Paul J. Cook

This book examines the complex role of the superintendent/field project manager, and provides guidelines for the efficient organization of this job. Includes administration of contracts, change orders, purchase orders, and more.

$35.95 per copy
Over 220 pages, illustrated, Softcover
Catalog No. 67233

Means Forms for Contractors
For general and specialty contractors

Means editors have created and collected the most needed forms as requested by contractors of various-sized firms and specialties. This book covers all project phases. Includes sample correspondence and personnel administration.
Full-size forms on durable paper for photocopying or reprinting.

$79.95 per copy
Over 400 pages, three-ring binder, more than 80 forms
Catalog No. 67288

Total Productive Facilities Management

By Richard W. Sievert, Jr.

The best of today's cost and project management, quality, and value engineering principles. Includes Benchmarking, Value Engineering, and Scheduling.

$79.95 per copy
Over 270 pages, illustrated, Hardcover
Catalog No. 67321

Means Heavy Construction Handbook

Informed guidance for planning, estimating and performing today's heavy construction projects. Provides expert advice on every aspect of heavy construction work including hazardous waste remediation and estimating. To assist planning, estimating, performing, or overseeing work.

$74.95 per copy
Over 430 pages, illustrated, Hardcover
Catalog No. 67148

Estimating for Contractors:
How to Make Estimates that Win Jobs
By Paul J. Cook

Estimating for Contractors is a reference that will be used over and over, whether to check a specific estimating procedure, or to take a complete course in estimating.

$35.95 per copy
Over 225 pages, illustrated, Softcover
Catalog No. 67160

HVAC Systems Evaluation

By Harold R. Colen, PE

You get direct comparisons of how each type of system works, with the relative costs of installation, operation, maintenance and applications by type of building. With requirements for hooking up electrical power to HVAC components. Contains experienced advice for repairing operational problems in existing HVAC systems, ductwork, fans, cooling coils, and much more!

$84.95 per copy
Over 500 pages, illustrated, Hardcover
Catalog No. 67281

Quantity Takeoff for Contractors:
How to Get Accurate Material Counts
By Paul J. Cook

Contractors who are new to material takeoffs or want to be sure they are using the best techniques will find helpful information in this book, organized by CSI MasterFormat division.

Now $17.98 per copy, limited quantity
Over 250 pages, illustrated, Softcover
Catalog No. 67262

Roofing: Design Criteria, Options, Selection

By R.D. Herbert, III

This book is required reading for those who specify, install or have to maintain roofing systems. It covers all types of roofing technology and systems. You'll get the facts needed to intelligently evaluate and select both traditional and new roofing systems.

Now $31.48 per copy
Over 225 pages with illustrations, Hardcover
Catalog No. 67253

For more information
visit Means Web Site
at www.rsmeans.com

Reference Books

Means Estimating Handbook

This comprehensive reference covers a full spectrum of
technical data for estimating, with information on
sizing, productivity, equipment requirements, codes,
design standards and engineering factors.
Means Estimating Handbook will help you: evaluate
architectural plans and specifications, prepare accurate
quantity takeoffs, prepare estimates from conceptual to
detailed, and evaluate change orders.

$99.95 per copy
Over 900 pages, Hardcover
Catalog No. 67276

Means Repair and Remodeling Estimating Third Edition

By Edward B. Wetherill & R.S. Means

Focuses on the unique problems of estimating
renovations of existing structures. It helps you
determine the true costs of remodeling through careful
evaluation of architectural details and a site visit.
New section on disaster restoration costs.

$69.95 per copy
Over 450 pages, illustrated, Hardcover
Catalog No. 67265A

Successful Estimating Methods:

From Concept to Bid

By John D. Bledsoe, PhD, PE

A highly practical, all-in-one guide to the tips and
practices of today's successful estimator. Presents
techniques for all types of estimates, *and* advanced
topics such as life cycle cost analysis, value engineering,
and automated estimating.
Estimate spreadsheets available at Means Web site.

$64.95 per copy
Over 300 pages, illustrated, Hardcover
Catalog No. 67287

Means Productivity Standards for Construction

Expanded Edition (*Formerly* Man-Hour Standards)

Here is the working encyclopedia of labor productivity
information for construction professionals, with labor
requirements for thousands of construction functions in
CSI MasterFormat.
Completely updated, with over 3,000 new work items.

$159.95 per copy
Over 800 pages, Hardcover
Catalog No. 67236A

Means Electrical Estimating Methods Second Edition

Expanded version includes sample estimates and cost
information in keeping with the latest version of the
CSI MasterFormat. Contains new coverage of Fiber
Optic and Uninterruptible Power Supply electrical
systems, broken down by components and explained
in detail. A practical companion to *Means Electrical
Cost Data.*

$64.95 per copy
Over 325 pages, Hardcover
Catalog No. 67230A

Means Mechanical Estimating Methods Second Edition

This guide assists you in making a review of plans,
specs and bid packages with suggestions for takeoff
procedures, listings, substitutions and pre-bid
scheduling. Includes suggestions for budgeting labor and
equipment usage. Compares materials and construction
methods to allow you to select the best option.

$64.95 per copy
Over 350 pages, illustrated, Hardcover
Catalog No. 67294

Means Scheduling Manual

Third Edition

By F. William Horsley

Fast, convenient expertise for keeping your scheduling
skills right in step with today's cost-conscious times.
Covers bar charts, PERT, precedence and CPM
scheduling methods. Now updated to include computer
applications.

$64.95 per copy
Over 200 pages, spiral-bound, Softcover
Catalog No. 67291

Maintenance Management Audit

This annual audit program is essential for every
organization in need of a proper assessment of its
maintenance operation. Downloadable electronic forms
from Means Web Site allow managers to identify and
correct problems and enhance productivity.

Now $32.48 per copy, limited quantity
125 pages, spiral bound, illustrated, Hardcover
Catalog No. 67299

Means Square Foot Estimating Methods Second Edition

By Billy J. Cox and F. William Horsley

Proven techniques for conceptual and design-stage cost
planning. Steps you through the square foot cost
process, demonstrating faster, better ways to relate the
design to the budget. Now updated to the latest version
of UniFormat.

$69.95 per copy
Over 300 pages, illustrated, Hardcover
Catalog No. 67145A

Means ADA Compliance Pricing Guide

Gives you detailed cost estimates for budgeting
modification projects, including estimates for each
of 260 alternates. You get the 75 most commonly
needed modifications for ADA compliance, each an
assembly estimate with detailed cost breakdown.

$72.95 per copy
Over 350 pages, illustrated, Softcover
Catalog No. 67310

Reference Books

For more information
visit Means Web Site
at www.rsmeans.com

Means Unit Price Estimating Methods
2nd Edition
$59.95 per copy
Catalog No. 67303

Legal Reference for Design & Construction
By Charles R. Heuer, Esq., AIA
Now $54.98 per copy, limited quantity
Catalog No. 67266

Means Plumbing Estimating Methods
New 2nd Edition
By Joseph J. Galeno & Sheldon T. Greene
$59.95 per copy
Catalog No. 67283A

Structural Steel Estimating
By S. Paul Bunea, PhD
Now $39.98 per copy, limited quantity
Catalog No. 67241

Business Management for Contractors
How to Make Profits in Today's Market
By Paul J. Cook
Now $17.98 per copy, limited quantity
Catalog No. 67250

Understanding Legal Aspects of Design/Build
By Timothy R. Twomey, Esq., AIA
$79.95 per copy
Catalog No. 67259

Risk Management for Building Professionals
By Thomas E. Papageorge, RA
Now $29.98 per copy, limited quantity
Catalog No. 67254

Contractor's Business Handbook
By Michael S. Milliner
Now $21.48 per copy, limited quantity
Catalog No. 67255

Basics for Builders: How to Survive and Prosper in Construction
By Thomas N. Frisby
$34.95 per copy
Catalog No. 67273

Successful Interior Projects Through Effective Contract Documents
By Joel Downey & Patricia K. Gilbert
Now $34.98 per copy, limited quantity
Catalog No. 67313

Understanding Building Automation Systems
By Reinhold A. Carlson, PE & Robert Di Giandomenico
$39.98 per copy, limited quantity
Catalog No. 67284

Illustrated Construction Dictionary, Condensed
$59.95 per copy
Catalog No. 67282

Managing Construction Purchasing
By John G. McConville, CCC, CPE
Now $31.48 per copy, limited quantity
Catalog No. 67302

Hazardous Material & Hazardous Waste
By Francis J. Hopcroft, PE, David L. Vitale, M. Ed., & Donald L. Anglehart, Esq.
Now $44.98 per copy, limited quantity
Catalog No. 67258

Fundamentals of the Construction Process
By Kweku K. Bentil, AIC
Now $34.98 per copy, limited quantity
Catalog No. 67260

Construction Delays
By Theodore J. Trauner, Jr., PE, PP
$59.95 per copy
Catalog No. 67278

Basics for Builders: Framing & Rough Carpentry
By Scot Simpson
$24.95 per copy
Catalog No. 67298

Interior Home Improvement Costs
New 7th Edition
$19.95 per copy
Catalog No. 67308B

Exterior Home Improvement Costs
New 7th Edition
$19.95 per copy
Catalog No. 67309B

Concrete Repair and Maintenance Illustrated
By Peter H. Emmons
$69.95 per copy
Catalog No. 67146

How to Estimate with Metric Units
Now $24.98 per copy, limited quantity
Catalog No. 67304

For more information
visit Means Web Site
at www.rsmeans.com

Seminars

Developing Facility Assessment Programs

This two-day program concentrates on the management process required for planning, conducting, and documenting the physical condition and functional adequacy of buildings and other facilities. Regular facilities condition inspections are one of the facility department's most important duties. However, gathering reliable data hinges on the design of the overall program used to identify and gauge deferred maintenance requirements. Knowing where to look . . . and reporting results effectively are the keys. This seminar is designed to give the facility executive essential steps for conducting facilities inspection programs.

Inspection Program Requirements • Where is the deficiency? • What is the nature of the problem? • How can it be remedied? • How much will it cost in labor, equipment and materials? • When should it be accomplished? • Who is best suited to do the work?

Note: Because of its management focus, this course will not address trade practices and procedures.

Mechanical and Electrical Estimating

This seminar is tailored to fit the needs of those seeking to develop or improve their skills and to have a better understanding of how mechanical and electrical estimates are prepared during the conceptual, planning, budgeting and bidding stages. Learn how to avoid costly omissions and overlaps between these two interrelated specialties by preparing complete and thorough cost estimates for both trades. Featured are order of magnitude, assemblies, and unit price estimating. In combination with the use of **Means Mechanical Cost Data**, **Means Plumbing Cost Data** and **Means Electrical Cost Data**, this seminar will ensure more accurate and complete Mechanical/Electrical estimates for both unit price and preliminary estimating procedures.

Square Foot Cost Estimating

Learn how to make better preliminary estimates with a limited amount of budget and design information. You will benefit from examples of a wide range of systems estimates with specifications limited to building use requirements, budget, building codes, and type of building. And yet, with minimal information, you will obtain a remarkable degree of accuracy.

Workshop sessions will provide you with model square foot estimating problems and other skill-building exercises. The exclusive Means building assemblies square foot cost approach shows how to make very reliable estimates using preliminary budget and design information.

Facilities Maintenance and Repair Estimating

With our Facilities Maintenance and Repair Estimating seminar, you'll learn how to plan, budget, and estimate the cost of ongoing and preventive maintenance and repair for all your buildings and grounds. Based on R.S. Means' groundbreaking cost estimating book, this two-day seminar will show you how to decide to either contract out or retain maintenance and repair work in-house. In addition, you'll learn how to prepare budgets and schedules that help cut down on unplanned and costly emergency repair projects. Facilities Maintenance and Repair Estimating crystallizes what facilities professionals have learned over the years, but never had time to organize or document. This program covers a variety of maintenance and repair projects, from underground storage tank removal, roof repair and maintenance, exterior wall renovations, and energy source conversions, to service upgrades and estimating energy-saving alternatives.

Repair and Remodeling Estimating

Repair and remodeling work is becoming increasingly competitive as more professionals enter the market. Recycling existing buildings can pose difficult estimating problems. Labor costs, energy use concerns, building codes, and the limitations of working with an existing structure place enormous importance on the development of accurate estimates. Using the exclusive techniques associated with Means' widely acclaimed **Repair & Remodeling Cost Data**, this seminar sorts out and discusses solutions to the problems of building alteration estimating. Attendees will receive two intensive days of eye-opening methods for handling virtually every kind of repair and remodeling situation . . . from demolition and removal to final restoration.

Unit Price Estimating

This seminar shows how today's advanced estimating techniques and cost information sources can be used to develop more reliable unit price estimates for projects of any size. It demonstrates how to organize data, use plans efficiently, and avoid embarrassing errors by using better methods of checking.

You'll get down-to-earth help and easy-to-apply guidance for:
- making maximum use of construction cost information sources
- organizing estimating procedures in order to save time and reduce mistakes
- sorting out and identifying unusual job requirements to improve estimating accuracy.

Scheduling and Project Management

This seminar helps you successfully establish project priorities, develop realistic schedules, and apply today's advanced management techniques to your construction projects. Hands-on exercises familiarize participants with network approaches such as the Critical Path Method. Special emphasis is placed on cost control, including use of computer-based systems. Through this seminar you'll perfect your scheduling and management skills, ensuring completion of your projects *on time* and *within budget*. Includes hands-on application of **Means Building Construction Cost Data.**

Managing Facilities Construction and Maintenance

In you're involved in new facility construction, renovation or maintenance projects and are concerned about getting quality work done on time and on or below budget, in Means' seminar **Managing Facilities Construction and Maintenance** you'll learn management techniques needed to effectively plan, organize, control and get the most out of your limited facilities resources.

Learn how to develop budgets, reduce expenditures and check productivity. With the knowledge gained in this course, you'll be better prepared to successfully sell accurate project budgets, timing and manpower needs to senior management . . . plus understand how to evaluate the impact of today's facility decisions on tomorrow's budget.

Call 1-800-448-8182 for more information

Seminars

For more information
visit Means Web Site
at www.rsmeans.com

2001 Means Seminar Schedule

Location	Dates
Las Vegas, NV	March 12 - 15
Washington, DC	April 23 - 26
Denver, CO	May 21-24
San Francisco, CA	June 11 - 14
Cape Cod, MA	September TBD
Washington, DC	October 1 - 4
San Diego, CA	October TBD
Atlantic City, NJ	November TBD
Orlando, FL	November 5-8

Note: Call for exact dates and deta

Registration Information

Register Early... Save up to $150! Register 30 days before the start date of a seminar and save $150 off your total fee. *Note: This discount can be applied only once per order.*

How to Register Register by phone today! Means toll-free number for making reservations is: **1-800-448-8182.**

Individual Seminar Registration Fee $875 To register by mail, complete the registration form and return with your full fee to: Seminar Division, R.S. Means Company, Inc., 63 Smiths Lane, Kingston, MA 02364.

Federal Government Pricing All Federal Government employees save 25% off regular seminar price. Other promotional discounts cannot be combined with Federal Government discount.

Team Discount Program Two to four seminar registrations: $760 per person—Five or more seminar registrations: $710 per person—Ten or more seminar registrations: Call for pricing.

Consecutive Seminar Offer One individual signing up for two separate courses at the same location during the designated time period pays only $1,400. You get the second course for only $525 (**a 40% discount**). Payment must be received at least ten days prior to seminar dates to confirm attendance.

Refunds Cancellations will be accepted up to ten days prior to the seminar start. There are no refunds for cancellations postmarked later than ten working days prior to the first day of the seminar. A $150 processing fee will be charged for all cancellations. Written notice or telegram is required for all cancellations. Substitutions can be made at any time before the session starts. **No-shows are subject to the full seminar fee.**

AACE Approved Courses The R.S. Means Construction Estimating and Management Seminars described and offered to you here have each been approved for 14 hours (1.4 recertification credits) of credit by the AACE International Certification Board toward meeting the continuing education requirements for re-certification as a Certified Cost Engineer/Certified Cost Consultant.

AIA Continuing Education R.S. Means is registered with the AIA Continuing Education System (AIA/CES) and is committed to developing quality learning activities in accordance with the CES criteria. R.S. Means seminars meet the AIA/CES criteria for Quality Level 2. AIA members will receive (28) learning units (LUs) for each two day R.S. Means Course.

Daily Course Schedule The first day of each seminar session begins at 8:30 A.M. and ends at 4:30 P.M. The second day is 8:00 A.M.–4:00 P.M. Participants are urged to bring a hand-held calculator since many actual problems will be worked out in each session.

Continental Breakfast Your registration includes the cost of a continental breakfast, a morning coffee break, and an afternoon break. These informal segments will allow you to discuss topics of mutual interest with other members of the seminar. (You are free to make your own lunch and dinner arrangements.)

Hotel/Transportation Arrangements R.S. Means has arranged to hold a block of rooms at each hotel hosting a seminar. To take advantage of special group rates when making your reservation be sure to mention that you are attending the Means Seminar. You are of course free to stay at the lodging place of your choice. (**Hotel reservations and transportation arrangements should be made directly by seminar attendees.**)

Important Class sizes are limited, so please register as soon as possible.

Registration Form

Call 1-800-448-8182 x5115/to register or FAX 1-800-632-6732. Visit our web site www.rsmeans.com

Please register the following people for the Means Construction Seminars as shown here. Full payment or deposit is enclosed, and we understand that we must make our own hotel reservations if overnight stays are necessary.

☐ Full payment of $ _____ enclosed.

☐ Bill me

Name of Registrant(s)
(To appear on certificate of completion)

_____

_____

_____

P.O. #: _____
GOVERNMENT AGENCIES MUST SUPPLY PURCHASE ORDER NUMBER

Firm Name _____

Address _____

City/State/Zip _____

Telephone No. _____ Fax No. _____

E-Mail Address _____

Charge our registration(s) to: ☐ MasterCard ☐ VISA ☐ American Express ☐ Discover

Account No. _____ Exp. Date _____

Cardholder's Signature _____

Seminar Name	City	Dates

Please mail check to: R.S. MEANS COMPANY, INC., 63 Smiths Lane, P.O. Box 800, Kingston, MA 02364 USA

Consulting Services Group

Solutions For Your Construction and Facilities Cost Management Problems

We are leaders in the cost engineering field, supporting the unique construction and facilities management costing challenges of clients from the Federal Government, Fortune 1000 Corporations, Building Product Manufacturers, and some of the World's Largest Design and Construction Firms.

Developers of the Dept. of Defense Tri-Services Estimating Database

Recipient of SEARS 1997 Chairman's Award for Innovation

Research...

- **Custom Database Development**—Means expertise in construction cost engineering and database management can be put to work creating customized cost databases and applications.
- **Data Licensing & Integration**—To enhance applications dealing with construction, any segment of Means vast database can be licensed for use, and harnessed in a format compatible with a previously developed proprietary system.
- **Cost Modeling**—Pre-built custom cost models provide organizations that expend countless hours estimating repetitive work with a systematic time-saving estimating solution.
- **Database Auditing & Maintenance**—For clients with in-house data, Means can help organize it, and by linking it with Means database, fill in any gaps that exist and provide necessary updates to maintain current and relevant proprietary cost data.

Estimating...

- **Estimating Service**—Means expertise is available to perform construction cost estimates, as well as to develop baseline schedules and establish management plans for projects of all sizes and types. Conceptual, budget and detailed estimates are available.
- **Benchmarking**—Means can run baseline estimates on existing project estimates. Gauging estimating accuracy and identifying inefficiencies improves the success ratio, precision and productivity of estimates.
- **Project Feasibility Studies**—The Consulting Services Group can assist in the review and clarification of the most sound and practical construction approach in terms of time, cost and use.
- **Litigation Support**—Means is available to provide opinions of value and to supply expert interpretations or testimony in the resolution of construction cost claims, litigation and mediation.

Training...

- **Core Curriculum**—Means educational programs, delivered on-site, are designed to sharpen professional skills and to maximize effective use of cost estimating and management tools. On-site training cuts down on travel expenses and time away from the office.
- **Custom Curriculum**—Means can custom-tailor courses to meet the specific needs and requirements of clients. The goal is to simultaneously boost skills and broaden cost estimating and management knowledge while focusing on applications that bring immediate benefits to unique operations, challenges, or markets.
- **Staff Assessments and Development Programs**—In addition to custom curricula, Means can work with a client's Human Resources Department or with individual operating units to create programs consistent with long-term employee development objectives.

For more information and a copy of our capabilities brochure, please call
1-800-448-8182 and ask for the Consulting Services Group, or reach us at www.rsmeans.com

MeansData™

For more information
visit Means Web Site
at www.rsmeans.com

New Titles

Means Illustrated Construction Dictionary, 3rd Edition
New Updated Edition with interactive CD-ROM

Long regarded as the Industry's finest, the *Means Illustrated Construction Dictionary* is now even better. With the addition of over 1,000 new terms and hundreds of new illustrations, it is the clear choice for the most comprehensive and current information.

The companion CD-ROM that comes with this new edition adds many extra features: larger graphics, expanded definitions, and links to both CSI MasterFormat numbers and product information.

- 19,000 construction words, terms, phrases, symbols, weights, measures, and equivalents
- 1,000 new entries
- 1,200 helpful illustrations
- Contemporary coverage of professional & trade terms
- Easy-to-use format, with thumbtabs

$99.95 per copy
Over 790 pages, illustrated, Hardcover
Catalog No. 67292A

Historic Preservation: Project Planning & Estimating

- *Managing Historic Restoration, Rehabilitation and Preservation Building Projects and*
- *Determining and Controlling Their Costs*

By Swanke Hayden Connell Architects

- Applicable standards and financing
- Site survey and documentation methods
- Protecting finishes and features
- Hazardous materials
- Identifying and qualifying specialty contractors
- Machanical/Electrical systems upgrades
- Restoring old building materials
- How to assemble a reliable, detailed estimate and budget for future maintenance

$99.95 per copy
Over 450 pages, Hardcover
Catalog No. 67323

Facilities Operations & Engineering Reference
An all-in-one technical reference for planning & managing facility projects & solving day-to-day operations problems

Ten major sections address:

- **Management Skills**
- **Economics** (budgeting/cost control, financial analysis, VE, etc.)
- **Civil Engineering & Construction Practices**
- **Maintenance** (detailed staffing guidance and job descriptions, CMMS, planning/scheduling, training, work orders, preventive/predictive maintenance)
- **HVAC & Energy Efficiencies** (optimizing energy use: heating, cooling, lighting, water)
- **Mechanical and Electrical Engineering**
- **Instrumentation & Controls**
- **Environment, Health & Safety**

Produced jointly by R.S. Means and
the Association for Facilities Engineering.

$99.95 per copy
Over 700 pages, illustrated, Hardcover
Catalog No. 67318

Qty.	Book No.	COST ESTIMATING BOOKS	Unit Price	Total
	60061	Assemblies Cost Data 2001	$149.95	
	60011	Building Construction Cost Data 2001	89.95	
	61011	Building Const. Cost Data–Looseleaf Ed. 2001	116.95	
	63011	Building Const. Cost Data–Metric Version 2001	89.95	
	60221	Building Const. Cost Data–Western Ed. 2001	89.95	
	60111	Concrete & Masonry Cost Data 2001	83.95	
	50141	Construction Cost Indexes 2001	198.00	
	60141A	Construction Cost Index–January 2001	49.50	
	60141B	Construction Cost Index–April 2001	49.50	
	60141C	Construction Cost Index–July 2001	49.50	
	60141D	Construction Cost Index–October 2001	49.50	
	60311	Contr. Pricing Guide: Framing/Carpentry 2001	36.95	
	60331	Contr. Pricing Guide: Resid. Detailed 2001	36.95	
	60321	Contr. Pricing Guide: Resid. Sq. Ft. 2001	39.95	
	64021	ECHOS Assemblies Cost Book 2001	149.95	
	64011	ECHOS Unit Cost Book 2001	99.95	
	54001	ECHOS (Combo set of both books)	214.95	
	60231	Electrical Change Order Cost Data 2001	89.95	
	60031	Electrical Cost Data 2001	89.95	
	60201	Facilities Construction Cost Data 2001	219.95	
	60301	Facilities Maintenance & Repair Cost Data 2001	199.95	
	60161	Heavy Construction Cost Data 2001	89.95	
	63161	Heavy Const. Cost Data–Metric Version 2001	89.95	
	60091	Interior Cost Data 2001	89.95	
	60121	Labor Rates for the Const. Industry 2001	199.95	
	60181	Light Commercial Cost Data 2001	79.95	
	60021	Mechanical Cost Data 2001	89.95	
	60151	Open Shop Building Const. Cost Data 2001	89.95	
	60211	Plumbing Cost Data 2001	89.95	
	60041	Repair and Remodeling Cost Data 2001	79.95	
	60171	Residential Cost Data 2001	79.95	
	60281	Site Work & Landscape Cost Data 2001	89.95	
	60051	Square Foot Costs 2001	99.95	
		REFERENCE BOOKS		
	67147A	ADA in Practice	72.95	
	67310	ADA Pricing Guide	72.95	
	67298	Basics for Builders: Framing & Rough Carpentry	24.95	
	67273	Basics for Builders: How to Survive and Prosper	34.95	
	67307	Basics for Builders: Plan Reading & Takeoff	35.95	
	67261	Bldg. Prof. Guide to Contract Documents–3rd Ed.	64.95	
	67312	Building Spec Homes Profitably	29.95	
	67250	Business Management for Contractors	17.98	
	67146	Concrete Repair & Maintenance Illustrated	69.95	
	67278	Construction Delays	59.95	
	67255	Contractor's Business Handbook	21.48	
	67314	Cost Planning & Est. for Facil. Maint.	82.95	
	67317A	Cyberplaces: The Internet Guide–2nd Ed.	59.95	
	67230A	Electrical Estimating Methods–2nd Ed.	64.95	
	64777	Environmental Remediation Est. Methods	99.95	
	67160	Estimating for Contractors	35.95	
	67276	Estimating Handbook	99.95	
	67249	Facilities Maintenance Management	86.95	

Qty.	Book No.	REFERENCE BOOKS (Cont.)	Unit Price	Total
	67246	Facilities Maintenance Standards	$159.95	
	67264	Facilities Manager's Reference	86.95	
	67318	Facilities Operations & Engineering Reference	99.95	
	67301	Facilities Planning & Relocation	109.95	
	67231	Forms for Building Const. Professional	94.95	
	67288	Forms for Contractors	79.95	
	67260	Fundamentals of the Construction Process	34.98	
	67258	Hazardous Material & Hazardous Waste	44.98	
	67148	Heavy Construction Handbook	74.95	
	67323	Historic Preservation: Proj. Planning & Est.	99.95	
	67308C	Home Improvement Costs–Interior Projects	19.95	
	67309C	Home Improvement Costs–Exterior Projects	19.95	
	67304	How to Estimate with Metric Units	24.98	
	67306	HVAC: Design Criteria, Options, Select.–2nd Ed.	84.95	
	67281	HVAC Systems Evaluation	84.95	
	67282	Illustrated Construction Dictionary, Condensed	59.95	
	67292A	Illustrated Construction Dictionary, w/CD-ROM	99.95	
	67295A	Landscape Estimating–3rd Ed.	62.95	
	67266	Legal Reference for Design & Construction	54.98	
	67299	Maintenance Management Audit	32.48	
	67302	Managing Construction Purchasing	31.48	
	67294	Mechanical Estimating–2nd Ed.	64.95	
	67245A	Planning and Managing Interior Projects–2nd Ed.	69.95	
	67283A	Plumbing Estimating Methods–2nd Ed.	59.95	
	67326	Preventive Maint. Guidelines for School Facil.	149.95	
	67236A	Productivity Standards for Constr.–3rd Ed.	159.95	
	67247A	Project Scheduling & Management for Constr.	64.95	
	67262	Quantity Takeoff for Contractors	17.98	
	67265A	Repair & Remodeling Estimating–3rd Ed.	69.95	
	67322	Residential & Light Commercial Const. Stds.	59.95	
	67254	Risk Management for Building Professionals	29.98	
	67291	Scheduling Manual–3rd Ed.	64.95	
	67145A	Square Foot Estimating Methods–2nd Ed.	69.95	
	67287	Successful Estimating Methods	64.95	
	67313	Successful Interior Projects	34.98	
	67233	Superintending for Contractors	35.95	
	67321	Total Productive Facilities Management	79.95	
	67284	Understanding Building Automation Systems	39.98	
	67259	Understanding Legal Aspects of Design/Build	79.95	
	67303	Unit Price Estimating Methods–2nd Ed.	59.95	
	67319	Value Engineering: Practical Applications	79.95	

MA residents add 5% state sales tax	
Shipping & Handling**	
Total (U.S. Funds)*	

Prices are subject to change and are for U.S. delivery only. *Canadian customers may call for current prices. **Shipping & handling charges: Add 7% of total order for check and credit card payments. Add 9% of total order for invoiced orders.

Send Order To: ADDV-1001

Name (Please Print) _____

Company _____

☐ **Company**

☐ **Home**   Address _____

_____

City/State/Zip _____

Phone # _____ P.O. # _____